Art and Identity in Oceania

Art and Identity in Oceania

Edited by
ALLAN HANSON and LOUISE HANSON

University of Hawaii Press
Honolulu

A CHP Book

First published in the United States of America 1990 by
University of Hawaii Press
2840 Kolowalu Street, Honolulu, Hawaii 96822
in affiliation with Pacific Arts Association
Published in Australia by Crawford House Press 1990

Designed & produced by
Crawford House Press
Panorama Avenue, Bathurst NSW 2795 Australia

Library of Congress Cataloging-in-Publication Data

Art and Identity in Oceania / by Allan Hanson and Louise Hanson, editors.
p. cm.
Selected papers of the Third International Symposium on the Art of Oceania, held in Sept. 1984 in New York; sponsored by the Pacific Art Association.
Includes bibliographical references.
ISBN 0-8248-1304-9 : $39.00
1. Art, Primitive – Oceania – Congresses. 2. Art – Oceania – Congresses. 3. Art and society – Oceania – Congresses. I. Hanson, Allan, 1939- . II. Hanson, Louise, 1940- .III. International Symposium on the Art of Oceania (3rd : 1984 : New York, N.Y.) IV. Pacific Art Association.
N7399.7.A78 1990
700'.995 – dc20 90-32710
CIP

Printed in Hong Kong by Colorcraft Ltd

10 9 8 7 6 5 4 3 2 1

Contents

Foreword

The Metropolitan Museum of Art has a long history of promoting scholarly symposia, often in connection with the great exhibitions it has organized, and of hosting independently organized events: It is not only one of the world's greatest repositories of arts, but also has a staff devoted to the accumulation and dissemination of knowledge. The museum's personnel are more than curators in the traditional sense; they publish and teach in order to bring a consciousness of the visual arts — and music as well — to millions of visitors. The institution's expressed aim is to be highly ecumenical, and a great stride to that end was taken in 1982 with the opening of the Michael C. Rockefeller wing, which was built to house the art of sub-Saharan Africa, the Pacific Islands, and native Americas. It was, then, especially appropriate that the Pacific Arts Association gathered at the Metropolitan Museum in 1984 for the Third International Symposium on the Arts of Oceania.

August and September 1984 were notable months for Pacific studies. The Wenner-Gren Foundation's symposium on "Sepik Research Today: The Study of Sepik Cultures in and for Modern Papua New Guinea" was held at the Museum für Völkerkunde, Basel, on August 19-26, followed by a week's tour of German museums. Some, again, joined numerous other Pacific scholars in New York for the Pacific Arts Association symposium on September 3-8. This was followed on September 10 by a moving ceremonial opening at dawn of the exhibition Te Maori: *Maori Art from New Zealand Collections* at the Metropolitan Museum. The sequence of these events was not by any means fortuitous, but was orchestrated by the organizers and institutions involved.

The Pacific Arts Association symposium was funded by a generous grant to the Metropolitan Museum of Art from the Evelyn A. J. Hall Foundation, obtained through the offices of Mr. John A. Friede. Among other purposes, the grant enabled a number of scholars from Pacific nations to come to New York in order to deliver papers and participate in the symposium.

Our gratitude is due, in the first place, to Philippe de Montebello, Director of the Metropolitan Museum, and to Meribell Parsons, then Vice Director for Education, for their enthusiastic support of the symposium and for allowing the Pacific Arts Association to use the Uris Center for Education, with its excellent auditorium and other working areas. The smooth running of services for the participants was due to the efforts of many museum staff, whose efficiency was so unobtrusive as to be barely noticeable. Most notable among these were Barbara Bridgers, then Manager of the Uris Center; Associate Museum Educator

Thomas Newman, who handled audio-visual arrangements; and Raymond Cusie, Technician. Margaret Sheridan, Controller, skillfully looked after the symposium's financial affairs.

Philip Dark, at short notice, took over the complex job of organizing the symposium, its contributors and program. He was assisted by Trudy Thomas. Barbara Lewis and Susan Ebersole, staff members of the museum's Department of Primitive Art, managed the mass of paperwork.

In the long run, of course, it was the members of the Pacific Arts Association, its council, officers, committee members, and, above all, those who presented papers who made this intensely active gathering a success. Louise and Allan Hanson took on the monumental task of putting together the ingredients of the pudding and here it is at last in permanent form. May it prove as stimulating in print as it was in the Uris Center Auditorium.

Douglas Newton
Evelyn A. J. Hall and John A. Friede Chairman
Department of Primitive Art
Metropolitan Museum of Art

1

Introduction: Art, Identity, and Self–Consciousness in Oceania

ALLAN HANSON AND LOUISE HANSON

In September 1984, the Pacific Art Association assembled at the Metropolitan Museum of Art in New York for the Third International Symposium on the Art of Oceania. The reason for this venue was, a few days after the symposium, the stunning exhibition "Te Maori: Maori Art from New Zealand Collections" opened at the Metropolitan Museum for the first of its visits to four American cities.

Artists and students of Pacific art converged on New York from many Pacific countries, North America, and Europe to present and discuss more than forty papers at the symposium. Nineteen of these papers — submitted by their authors, scrutinized by referees, and refined for publication — are collected here.

The topic of the symposium was art and identity. Those who write about Oceanic art, however, are as independent and varied in their interests and expressions as is Oceanic art itself. Neither the papers presented at the symposium nor the subset of them represented here can be construed as orbiting closely around any central theme. Each was written for its own purpose and may stand alone.

At the same time, taken together the essays demonstrate a variety of ways in which individual and cultural identity may be expressed in art. These range from the relatively unself-conscious expression of cultural themes and preoccupations in the art of traditional societies, through artistic reflections of rapidly changing values and lifestyles, to the self-conscious deployment of art as a tool — even a weapon — in the political struggle of colonized peoples to retain their cultural integrity and to achieve a more just economic and social position.

The first of the papers, by Eric Schwimmer, raises the question of how scholars may come to grips with aesthetic meaning and ascertain its relation to personal and cultural identity. Schwimmer's examples primarily concern the relation between visual art and ritual in Papua New Guinea, but the discussion is also relevant to art of other forms and provenances. His essay may be taken as a theoretical orientation to the collection as a whole.

About half of the papers are concerned with societies at a time when they had experienced no, or relatively little, contact with the West. Art here is concerned with traditional subject matter, is produced for traditional purposes, and expresses identity unself-consciously, as an articulation and dramatization of values and forms of organization significant in the traditional culture. This is definitely not meant to give an impression of unchanging art in unchanging societies. Every culture is constantly in a state of flux, and that includes its art. Steel tools, for example, quickly replaced stone ones upon European contact. The initial effect of such a replacement, however, was often to enhance the capacity of carvers to produce works dealing with traditional subject matter and for traditional purposes rather than immediately introducing new subject matter and purposes.

Kominimung art is a good example of this type. Dirk Smidt's essay is another in his series on the art of this Papua New Guinea society, this time focussing on carved and painted one-legged figures. Smidt demonstrates how these figures are concrete expressions of traditional Kominimung cultural themes such as moiety and clan social organization, themes in male initiation, and symbolic attitudes connected with the sexes.

The paper by Tobias Schneebaum contributes to our general understanding of the artistically rich Asmat region of Irian Jaya by distinguishing four style areas within it.

Oceania has been long enough influenced by outside contacts that the study of art traditions of the unself-conscious/traditional sort in most areas of the Pacific is largely a historical enterprise which necessarily relies more upon documentary evidence and museum research than on fieldwork. One example is Deborah Waite's study of the graceful *mon* canoes of the Western Solomons. Rather like Smidt, she analyzes the artistic form of the canoes and their relations to ritual and other parts of the culture, but in her case the task is largely one of historical reconstruction.

Working at a historical distance somewhat greater than half a century, George Corbin was able to combine fieldwork that probed the memories of older informants with documentary/museum research in his explorations of the fantastic masks and other art objects collected from the Sulka of East New Britain between 1900 and 1930. Another historical approach is John McKesson's study of how the form and mythological and ritual associations of traditional New Caledonian masks may be interpreted in an effort to ascertain their origin.

The Santa Cruz Islands are especially well represented in this volume, being the subject of three essays. Lawrence Foanaota sets the stage with an archaeological reconstruction of prehistoric cultural sequences on Santa Cruz Island, and William Davenport follows with an analysis of the carved figures produced on the same island during the pre-Christian period. (It is interesting to compare Davenport's paper with McKesson's on the question of the origin of art styles and arguments for possible routes of diffusion.) Roger Rose discusses the costumes and ceremonial significance of the masked Tamate dancers of Vanikoro, in the southern Santa Cruz Islands.

It is possible to detect in Rose's paper some elements of social change in art. While discussing the origin and traditional significance of Tamate dancers, Rose also notes that they have performed in modern contexts such as a visit of the British High Commissioner, and have represented Vanikoro in a Festival of Traditional Music and Dance and at the Solomon Islands independence celebrations. Moreover, the costumes have recently been sold to collectors and museums following their ceremonial appearances rather than adhering to the traditional practice of burning them. Attention to both traditional and more modern uses of art is also evident in the paper by Edward Ruhe. He scours documentary material for evidence of bark painting among Tasmanian aborigines in an effort to determine both what bark painting existed at first contact and how it developed after European presence on the island had been established.

Phillip Lewis is also concerned with historical changes in art, comparing artistic developments in the Sepik region of New Guinea and New Ireland over the past few decades. Interestingly, he found that style has changed less and quality of contemporary art is higher in the Sepik, with its heavy tourist market, than in New Ireland, where the tourist market is very small.

The history of social change in New Zealand is well enough documented that it is possible to identify any number of intervening steps between Maori art of the pre-European period and that of the present. Roger Neich takes advantage of this wealth of sources in his study of a shift from carved to painted figures in some Maori meeting houses. He demonstrates how the lack of traditional constraints on painting, as compared with carving, enabled painted houses to be more sensitive indicators of changes in Maori life and identity in the late nineteenth and early twentieth centuries. Allan and Louise Hanson are also concerned with Maori art, although the specific grist for their mill is what has been said about Maori art rather than the art itself. Their effort is to articulate the major questions that have been asked about Maori art over the last century or so, and to ascertain the historical shifts in those questions. Therefore, although the art in question is Maori, the identity explored in their paper is that of the scholarly field of Maori ethnology, and anthropology more generally.

The remaining papers in this volume are concerned with the contemporary art of the Pacific, and with demonstrating how contemporary issues are embodied in art. Artistic expression of social change is particularly clear in the relic displays of the Mountain-Ok of Papua New Guinea, studied by Barry Craig. The displays contain, among many other things, traditional objects such as skulls from marsupials and humans. However, as the circumstances of Mountain Ok life change toward a cash economy based largely on gold and copper mining, these relics are joined or replaced in displays of distinctly modern objects such as broken cassette-radios and empty food tins. Another art form that reflects both traditional and modern considerations is Tongan dance. Stephanie Reynolds' analysis of the relation between gender and dance indicates that female styles are conservative or traditional, while male styles are much more open to change in response to outside influences and new demands such as tourism.

The artistic component of change in Tonga is particularly clear in Jehanne Teilhet-Fisk's study of grave decorations. Non-traditional materials such as concrete, painted "bill boards," and even beer bottles figure prominently in this exuberant art form. Novel materials, subject matter, and purposes for art production are found in abundance in Philip Dark's essay. In the widest-ranging paper in this volume, Dark surveys what is happening in the art world today on a variety of Melanesian, Polynesian, and Micronesian islands.

The sort of relation between art and identity which we have termed self-conscious is most apparent in the final two papers. Artists and other members of society recognize art as something that expresses their own cultural values, and one of their reasons for producing and supporting the art is to promote those values. Hirini Mead discusses the role of art in defining and maintaining the identity of the Maori people. His paper is part of his effort to explain to American audiences the significance of the objects they viewed in the "Te Maori" exhibition. Vincent Megaw also addresses the relationship between art and ethnic identity in his exploration of the role of art in the aborigines' demands for more respect and influence in Australian society.

Self-conscious identity in art seems to occur especially among those who feel that their cultural values and identity as a distinct people are threatened. These circumstances have been well described by Lafi A. Sanerivi, General Secretary of the YMCA of Western Samoa:

> We were victims of the Western "dare sport" of exploration and domination of the then called "dark and uncivilized lands." In school we studied of the "mighty ships" that braved the unknown seas that came back to England with riches and tales of vast stretches of lands. . . . They came with their education and we got educated. Their way. We learnt their language, but they did not learn ours. If we did have a history, we were told to forget it because it is a history of savages. Their manners and ways of living became a model. . .. Suddenly, we open our eyes and see. . . . And ironically enough, we realize that we have actually learnt of how our countries were exploited, our ancestors murdered and enslaved, our values discarded, our cultures vanishing. . . . We open our eyes and come to our senses and find ourselves in the Third World. . . . We are the poor. We are the underdeveloped. We are the "have nots". . . . Now we try and sift through the mess to identify what is really ours and what isn't. . . . Our present awareness attempts to build a people from non-entities, build a nation from a colony.[1]

Mead's and Megaw's essays pertain to peoples of the Fourth World rather than the Third, but Sanerivi's observations apply equally well. In their own ways and in response to their particular circumstances, New Zealand Maoris and Australian Aborigines are concerned to reconstruct their ethnic identity and pride. In each case, art plays an important role in the endeavor.

Although only two essays in this collection address it directly, the self-conscious expression of identity in art was "in the air" more than any other topic at the symposium. A particularly interesting moment came on the afternoon of the penultimate day. A certain uneasiness had developed among the participants concerning what can only be termed the politics of the study of Pacific art, and we held an open forum in order to express opinions. The issue had to do with who owns Pacific art and who should appropriately study it. A degree of resentment was expressed by some of the Pacific islanders present that scholars of non-Pacific heritage living in Europe or North America would presume to identify the meanings and importance of art in Pacific cultures. They seemed to hold that members of the cultures that produced the art should also have exclusive rights to comment authoritatively on it. The art is theirs, the identity it expresses is theirs, the struggle to establish that identity and to achieve their rightful place in society is theirs, and they do not welcome outsiders meddling in what is a deeply meaningful and politically important part of their lives.

Those from non-Pacific nations took a considerably more detached view. While nearly all of them strongly support the Pacific people in their political endeavor, they hold that Pacific art is part of the general human heritage and should be available for study by anyone who wishes to devote the necessary time and effort to it. These scholars find a variety of things to interest them about Pacific art, only one of which is its identity-strengthening role in a political struggle.

The reality, of course, is that non-Pacific people are among those who study Pacific art, and that is not likely to change. What will change, it is hoped, is the overwhelming dominance of scholars of non-Pacific ethnic heritage in the field. In this book, as also in the volumes resulting from the first two international symposia on the arts of Oceania, only a few papers have been contributed by scholars of Pacific ethnic heritage. They did, however, present several other papers at the New York symposium which were not submitted for publication. It is to be hoped that their contributions will constitute a much larger proportion of future symposia and publications. This seems entirely likely, because many individuals native to the Pacific belong to and hold offices in the Pacific Art Association. As their voices are more widely heard, the tenor of our meetings and publications will certainly change. That is an inevitable part of increasing pluralization, and a development which can only enrich the association and all of its members.

We must close this introduction on a sad note by reporting the death of one of the contributors, Edward Ruhe, in June 1989. Ed was a devoted scholar and collector of Australian Aboriginal bark paintings. As our colleague for many years at the University of Kansas, he was our close personal friend. He will be missed by all students of Aboriginal art.

Note

1. From a 1985 mimeographed report on leadership training in 'Upolu and Savai'i, quoted by Eleanor Leacock in her "Postscript" to Lowell D. Holmes *Quest for the Real Samoa: The Mead/Freeman Controversy & Beyond* (South Hadley, Mass.: Bergin & Garvey, 1987:180-81).

2

The Anthropology of the Ritual Arts

Eric Schwimmer

In a brilliant paper read at a colloquim at The Museum of Primitive Art in New York, Robert Redfield (1959) compared comments by ethnographers and art critics who had interpreted the same African sculptures from their particular points of view. His paper soon fastened on the image of a lady visiting The Museum of Primitive Art and judging these particular sculptures to be "horrid." What could he tell this lady? He could tell her that she needed more semantic information (on world view, etc.) if she wished to *understand* the sculptures; perhaps she had better go to The Museum of Natural History . . . . Yet, Redfield recognized that if the lady should follow this advice she had many years of study ahead of her. In the end, she would still have no clue about the *aesthetic* message of the sculptures. Perhaps, then, she had better go backwards and forwards between the two museums and see whether this would clear things up for her. In that case, Redfield could promise her "a mixed experience." But will acquisition of knowledge of the meanings and values in the native life be helpful to her when she turns to consider the aesthetic meanings? "This is the part of her uncertainty which I share; I find that I cannot fully solve it."

Even today, we have not fully solved that problem. Certainly, aestheticians have greatly improved our insight into the relation between cognition and perception and into the nature of aesthetic information. Moreover, much progress has been made by anthropologists in developing theories and methods for analyzing the aesthetics of messages conveyed in paintings, sculptures, music, poetry, and other "art" genres. At the same time, the main effect of these anthropological explorations of aesthetics[1] has been to show how beneficial aesthetic analysis can be for our understanding of cognitive systems. They never aim to show how it happens that (for instance) very many Papua New Guineans find in their own arts an evident source of overwhelming aesthetic experience. How do these arts cast their spell? By what powers of mimesis, by what artistic schemata, do they present the manifestation of spirit powers as a perceptible reality?

As Clifford Geertz (1983:120), remarked this is a new kind of question for anthropology. Before trying to answer it, we need to pose two preliminary issues: Would the answer be of any importance in anthropology? Are there known methods by which such an answer could be obtained?

The question of the possible utility of developing an aesthetic anthropology certainly needs asking, for not only would such perception studies in Papua New Guinea cost much money and effort, but also we need to avoid burdening Papua New Guineans with inquiries of remote and dubious interest. On this point of utility, it suffices probably to insist that the traditional arts of Oceania constitute one of the greatest contributions made by that region to world civilization. Nonetheless, neither aestheticians nor anthropologists have ever grasped what were their rules of perceptual balance, order, and expression and what were the schemata by which Oceanic artists created their representations. The scientific interest of the answers to such questions is evident.

Moreover, there is reason to think that such studies might also provoke much interest in Papua New Guinea itself. That country has shown its determination to preserve its arts and to adapt them to today's conditions by establishing some notable national and regional institutions to that end. The aesthetic aspect of these arts is prominent in the image that is being developed of Papua New Guinea national identity.[2] Organizations such as the National Cultural Council, the Institute of Papua New Guinea Studies, the National Theatre Company, and the National Arts School would probably be interested in such a field of study, in which their own part could be a highly creative one.

Papua New Guinea would be a highly appropriate venue for such studies because the popular arts there, in the view of their creators as well as the public, are almost totally identified with initiation and with other ceremonies in which the relationship between man and spirit is represented. It is for these occasions that the greatest work in dance, song, theatre, sculpture, painting, architecture, body decoration, instrumental music, ceramics, and so forth is destined. Those who foster these popular arts today, whether professionally or in the government, are deeply aware that they are sacred arts.

An interesting example of this orientation is found in the *Papua New Guinea Post-Courier*'s "special independence anniversary issue" of 1979 which is devoted to a preview of the South Pacific Arts Festival of the following year, and to a survey of Papua New Guinea activities in the arts. In his introductory message to this hundred-page tabloid, the Prime Minister, then the Rt. Honorable Michael Somare, dwelt on only one aspect: He had been unable to complete his own initiation cycle before becoming chief minister in 1973. Shortly after assuming this post, however, he returned to his birthplace at Murik Lakes for his last ceremony. He writes: "It was important that I establish my identity at home and receive the wisdom and strength that my elders were willing to pass on to me from my forefathers. . . . I ask you all to preserve the cultures of your forefathers for you will be persons without identity if you depart from them" (1979a:2).

By prefacing a publication about Papua New Guinea aesthetic traditions with this message, Somare shows that for him these traditions derive their deep significance wholly from their association with initiation or similar ceremonies. His message also implies, however, that he is deeply conscious of the aesthetic spell which lies at the core of the ceremonies. Most ethnographers are probably equally conscious of this but the fashionable aim of initiation studies is still to analyze the cognitive system.

Yet even if anthropologists are truly enthusiastic about including aesthetic meanings in their field of study, they still could not do so if valid methods of study are lacking. It must indeed be admitted that no valid methods are at hand if we are to seek them exclusively in the discipline of aesthetics. Anthropologists usually lack training (even though some would not lack talent) to study perception and artistic schemata, while aestheticians normally lack training in the subtleties of Papua New Guinea village settings. However, even if we could find people trained in both fields, the problem arises whether Redfield's problem is solvable in the context of particular art forms such as sculpture, painting, dance, or oral literature.

This is because one obvious difference between arts in Papua New Guinea and in Europe, for instance, is that the highest manifestations of the various art forms in Papua New Guinea are multi-media while in Europe they tend to be in one genre only. Assuredly, Europeans combine numerous genres in opera, ballet, and theatre (not to mention cinema and television), but then the degree of complexity in each individual genre tends to be less than in the highest manifestations of single genre. For example the verse found in operas is not necessarily the highest poetry likewise, the music used in the theatre is normally less complex than what one hears at a classical concert. In the art traditions of Papua New Guinea, however, the highest forms of expression occur at the great ceremonies when they are all massed together.

Abraham Moles has made a study of multiple aesthetic messages from the viewpoint of information theory.[3] He found that there is an apperception limit to the amount of aesthetic information a human being can absorb. When multiple messages are being sent — as in ballet where three partial messages (musical, kinesic, visual) are combined — each partial message is simpler, less rich in information, more redundant than if they were isolated, and the sole object of attention. Moreover, they tend to bear an extremely social aspect, both in their creation and in the audience addressed. The spell cast by a Papua New Guinea ceremony is therefore not to be explained by the impact of any of the partial messages (none of which can be said to dominate the others) but by their aesthetic or perceptual synthesis. The aesthetic anthropologist working in Papua New Guinea must therefore be interested, first of all, in multiple message systems and their perceptual synthesis, secondly in the constituent message systems (such as dance, sculpture, painting, and so on), and thirdly in modes of articulation of the partial messages.

Now the totality that thus becomes our object of study — that is, the total ceremony — is a very familiar object for anthropologists, but it is usually studied from the ritual aspect. We agree with Lévi-Strauss' distinction between ritual (and myth) on the one hand and art (and play) on the other. Ritual claims to have as its end result a kind of preordained equilibrium corresponding to certain conditions of life that are fixed and unalterable. This fixity of outcomes is absent from both art and play, where there must exist a plurality of possibilities and an unpredictable course of events (Lévi-Strauss 1962:38-44).

This view of ritual agrees essentially with that of Victor Turner, who regards its study as the "standard hermeneutics" of a culture, for the purpose of explaining the "stylized gestures" and "cryptic songs of ritual performances" (Turner 1969:9) and of discovering the ideological meanings of its ritual symbols as perceived by informants. Turner notes "wide variation from performance to performance" but this is chiefly to show that "the same principle or idea can be expressed in different symbols" (pp. 23, 25). Rituals are to him a kind of drama arising in conflict situations, but he perceives them primarily as directed to social outcomes: "The final phase consists either of the *reintegration* of the disturbed social group or of the social recognition and legitimation of irreparable schism between the contesting parties" (Turner 1974:41).

Most students of "ritual drama" aim at "processual analysis," that is, explaining social processes by semantic analysis of ritual. In Turner's later writings, emphasis shifted to the study of "communitas" and "liminality," meaning that of a "sacred condition" of the group such as undoubtedly arises during Papua New Guinea spirit impersonation ceremonies. The chief concern of these later studies was to show the "genuine cathartic effects" (p. 56) of which ritual is capable. Though this term is ambiguous, it is clear from the context that, unlike Aristotle, Turner regards and explains catharsis as a religious experience only.

Aesthetic anthropology is equally concerned with catharsis, but from the viewpoint of the human actor whose art brings it about. We are not debating whether initiation ceremonies *are* ritual or art. Our point is that these ceremonies have an aesthetic as well as ritual aspect. Those who attend the ceremonies do not necessarily distinguish these two aspects. Many ethnographers have collected statements from informants who had experienced catharsis during these ceremonies. Now there is no doubt that an audience derives this catharsis from "communitas" coupled with a revelation of the spirit world. On the other hand, it is equally certain that this revelation is induced by multiple aesthetic messages emitted by human actors, and furthermore that it is the function of initiatory ceremonies to teach novices how to emit these messages. It is with this second aspect that aesthetic anthropology is concerned. Before dealing with methods, we need to summarize briefly some of the chief characteristics of these aesthetic messages.

The most convenient starting point might be the problem of how to explain magic. A rain-maker burns water weeds in order to produce clouds. If the procedure is efficacious, this is explained by the rain-maker's *mana*. But what is *mana*? As Mauss (1950:120) pointed out, *mana* is the copula by which /smoke from water-weeds/ is linked to /cloud-production/.

If so, then the semantic value of *mana* must be zero. It appears to be used in a great variety of contexts but always when there is a problem of fitting a signifier into a semantic scheme (Lévi-Strauss 1950:il-l).

In the equation, /cloud production/ = /smoke from water-weeds/ + *mana*, the expression on the right-hand side is the "retrieved significatum" made up of a cunningly chosen second signifier and an "extra ration" of sense that has to be added if the equation is to hold. Obviously a notion like *mana* may be used to bolster up an almost infinite number of equations of this kind. For that reason, Lévi-Strauss calls it a "floating signifier". He calls it an entailment of all closed systems of thought, but also the guarantee of all art, all poetry, all mythic and aesthetic invention.[4]

Lévi-Strauss thus appears to draw a neat dividing line between semantic and aesthetic analysis. Semantic analysis has to do with the relations between signs like /cloud production/ and /smoke from water-weeds/, which are percepts to which a particular culture may give symbolic value. Aesthetic analysis, on the other hand, is concerned with what we called, above, an extra ration of sense whose semantic value is zero. Now such a formulation is tenable only, of course, if we use the term "semantic value" here as referring to "translatability." We suggest that the primary characteristic of what Lévi-Strauss has called the floating signifier is its untranslatability. It is a necessary part of an equation that makes sense but it has no sense by itself.

In the analysis of ritual, Victor Turner's "hermeneutics" is a most pertinent analytical tool, especially where informants are willing and able to discuss the ideological meaning of ritual symbols, that is to say what ritual objects "stand for." There remains, however, a residue of ritual actions where such translations are impossible to obtain. Anthropologists such as Forge (1966), the Stratherns (1971), and Gell (1975), who studied sculpture, painting, masks, dances, and body decoration in a Papua New Guinea ceremonial context, found their "translatability" to be very low indeed. One might therefore say that these anthropologists were impelled by this obstacle to study not only the ritual aspect of these ceremonials (a traditional concern of our discipline) but also the aesthetic aspect (on which anthropological discourse is much less developed).

If we wish to study the ritual aspect of a ceremony it is crucial to discover its purpose, for by any definition ritual is purposive action. Thus, by Turner's theory, rituals serve the purpose of reintegrating social groups. In Papua New Guinea ceremonials, this effect may occur but more importance is often attached to other social purposes such as the pursuit of status rivalry,[5] that is demonstrating the greatness of the hosts. This demonstration requires not only a certain quantity of gifts and exchanges, but also a public performance during which a great many channels of communication are used — including visual, auditory, gustatory, and even olfactory genres. All these expressive genres combine in order symbolically to overwhelm the guests. The political and aesthetic ends of the feast are thus wholly convergent. It is therefore only by aesthetic analysis that we can explain adequately how status rivalry is conducted. Thus it is only by studying the *untranslatable* message system of Melpa body decorations (Strathern and Strathern 1971) that the *moka* exchange institution of that tribe becomes intelligible. The body decorations constitute that "extra ration of sense," the "floating signifier" by which the semantic equation of *moka* exchange is made to hold.

Moreover, it is only in a very limited sense that Papua New Guinea's great ceremonies can be said to have a fixed and unalterable outcome. Thus, Gell intended to study the ritual aspect of Umeda ceremonials and, in particular, the *ida* performances whose intended outcome was said to be the increase of sago; it was supposedly a "fertility ritual." In the course of his admirable analysis of that institution he became less and less sure of the link between *ida* and the increase of sago. The performances he saw conveyed to him many meanings that went altogether beyond that theme. How important was it really in the minds of the performers? Did they think their performance could really benefit sago fertility at all? Here is one reply he received to that question from a key informant: "Typically Auyai imputed the efficacy of *ida* as a ritual to increase sago, not to the dancing, public ritual and so forth, but to the subsidiary magical operations of the old men, magic of which both he and I were largely ignorant" (Gell 1975:219).

This information shows that there was indeed a ritual aspect to *ida* but that for performers such as Auyai the dancing, masks, and body paintings were not "translatable" into the theme of sago increase. Gell was even assured that there was no shortage of sago, nor had there ever been in the informants' memories. Both to Gell and his informants, the performance was untranslatable semantically; the only kind of analysis to which it could respond — and did respond, in Gell's hands — was aesthetic.

Because of their essential untranslatability, these message systems may convey quite a variety of meanings to different observers, to different members of an audience, or they may convey many meanings simultaneously. This is implied in their status as "floating signifiers." Papua New Guinea people tend to be aware of such meanings but prefer not to speak of them for if they talked about one meaning, the others might be lost to consciousness. When Forge (1973b) tried to elicit the "meaning" of Abelam paintings, the younger men objected to the ethnographer's glosses but the older men just nodded their heads. One does not quite discover why the older men nodded. Forge thinks it was because they agreed with him, but it might be safer to say that Forge had learned correctly some Abelam ideological discourse and their assent applied to the discourse, but that they themselves were not inclined to reduce the paintings to discourse. In this respect, they were like artists everywhere. Roland Barthes (1970:12) has convincingly argued that the ideal artistic "text" is a galaxy of signifiers rathers than a structure of significata; it has several entries of which none is the principal one; it lends itself to an indefinite number of readings.

By the same token, we may distinguish between the ritual aspect and the aesthetic aspect of a performance by the degree of freedom allowed to performers. We shall illustrate this by the example of orchestral music as Moles has researched it, and we know of no examples in ethnology. We believe that the relation of ritual to a "standard hermeneutic" is rather similar to the relation between a musical score and an orchestral performance. In both cases there is a schema that remains unchanged and experts who produce each time a new performance based on that schema.

The degree of artisticity in performance depends on the degree of freedom afforded by the ritual scheme or musical score. Moles distinguishes between semantic information (logical, structured, enunciable, translatable, setting up actions) and aesthetic information (untranslatable, setting up states). These are, then, the same distinctions as between the ritual and aesthetic aspects of Papua New Guinea ceremonial performances. In music the semantic, translatable component is the score to which we need to add some structuring principles. Now Moles shows that this component is weak, giving little real information. There is, of course, a plethora of very complex, rigid, dogmatic rules about solfeggio, melody, harmony, counterpoint, orchestration, and so forth, but this, according to Moles (1972:207), forms a sort of folk system lacking solid experimental foundation. The deep structural rules by which musicians are guided in real practice are few in number and little known. The markings on the score refer to a far richer symbol system on which the musician in fact relies but which cannot be recorded by standard notation. The chief degrees of freedom of a musician using a normal score are: imperfections in the score, variations in orchestration, variations in the construction of instruments and music halls, and differences and latitudes of interpretation. The full scope of all these dimensions became obvious only when concerts began to be recorded and comparison became possible.

Moles (1972:204-10) compares these degrees to the amount of aesthetic information in the system. Quantitatively, it is possible to express the combinatory of these degrees of freedom as a proportion of the total number of dynamic intervals that are differentiated in a musical code. He publishes a diagram from which it appears as though this proportion varies from 50 percent to 90 percent for different kinds of European music.[6]

Gell's masterly analysis of *ida* ceremonies of the Umeda provides a good idea of the constraints of the code as well as the degree of freedom available in the system. In certain elements, the redundancy is very great and the degree of freedom and of aesthetic information is very low. Examples are the text of the chants, the drum beats, the set of ritual roles, the set of pigments used for body decoration, and the set of colors allocated to each role. Gell also discovered some deep structural rules of *ida* that remain constant from one performance to another and that determine the sequence of episodes, the core attributes of masks, costumes, and painting, the differentials between dance styles, mask types, and mask fringes, and a multitude of other coded differentials.

For some other elements, redundancy is less but still very considerable. Examples are the overall construction of the masks, the time during which each character is on stage, the time allocated to preparation and training, the number and the real ages of actors, the composition of the audience, certain "representational" body paintings showing fish species, tree species, and so on.

All this still leaves a great degree of freedom. With regard to body-paint designs "there is considerable flexibility in the execution, some designs I recorded containing a large element of free 'improvisation' by the painters on the motif provided by a particular standard form" (Gell 1975:190-91).

Our information on the choreography of *ida* is sketchy. We are told what the dancing characters "represent." On the contrasts between them, data are much fuller. There are descriptive images of characters' styles, for example, "the tight-reined loping of the *ipele*," and of some actions, "the fish also frequently turn about, facing each other in pairs, seeming to threaten each other with drawn bows" (p. 272). Yet such directions leave actors with great freedom of improvisation during the long period that each is on stage. The constraints described by Gell resemble what Gombrich would call style or schemata guiding performers in expressing their own conceptual and perceptual experience. This is brought out in the following description of a fish-dancer: "His identity was merged with the 'fish' only at the level of formal symbolism; as an individual dancer he was, in a very important sense, playing himself. . . . Each dancer's style was a revelation when considered in conjunction with his character in daily life" (Gell 1975:276).

This comes very close to "theatrical" rather than "ritual" analysis. So does Gell's excellent general appraisal of *ida* when he calls it "a dramatic performance which runs in parallel to the performance mounted by nature itself" (p. 223).

We have now probably established sufficiently that aesthetic anthropology could, in principle, provide knowledge about culture that is not a double or a reflection of findings already available. Our next task is to outline methods such a science can use to explain aesthetic communication at Papua New Guinea's major traditional ceremonies. We need to show also that these methods are not limited to description and iconography but are extendable to the "iconological" level[7] and have a contribution to make to broader contemporary cultural issues.

The success of aesthetic anthropology, however, will primarily depend on the quality of its fine-grained iconographic analyses. These will in principle bear on all artistic genres, but it must be kept in mind that the genres uppermost in European arts — such as painting, sculpture, music, poetry — are in Papua New Guinea largely ancillary to multi-channel communication at the great ceremonies. Though many objects are created outside that immediate context, even those carry numerous and constant allusions to themes whose primary expression is found at the ceremonies. Even ornamental lime gourds, trading canoes, and cooking pots depend for their aesthetic appeal on such allusions. We believe, therefore, that the study of complex theatrical productions should have high priority for studies of Papua New Guinea aesthetics.

Iconographic studies of such performances should attend to two aspects which — following some recent French research[8] — we might term aesthetic and poietic. *Aesthetic*, in this connection, refers to an audience's perception of artistic productions, while *poietic* refers to processes of artistic construction. The participants in the performance, whether initiatory or otherwise, have learned schemata for representing spirits. Although the perceptual artifices used by performers serve in their own view and in that of the audience to reconstitute a spiritual reality, the aesthetic anthropologist would study them by the methods set out in Gombrich's *Art and Illusion*, and by the French *poiesis* research team.

Such impersonation is effective (and thinkable) only if there is a second category of persons, namely the viewers, who do not know the fine points of the *poiesis* and who believe in the reality of the spirits. It is made up of children, invited guests, and — in many Papua New Guinea cultures — women excluded from initiation. It would be rash to suppose that these viewers experience their role of audience as humiliating and unjust. Kept rigorously uninformed about how the illusion is produced, they experience it in its purest form, free from all awareness of stage business and technical trickery. They see the dancers only when they wear their masks. It is irrelevant whether they really believe them to be spirits. What matters is whether they judge them to be theatrically convincing representations and whether they believe in them in that sense. Also, it is important that they should not kill the performance by signifying their disbelief. This is what the French research team still calls "aesthetics" and what Panofsky (1955) and others studied as iconography.

We agree with Gell that these performances "run in parallel with those mounted by nature itself." This excellent phrase implies that we should not entirely regard them as what Gombrich calls "conceptual art." Papua New Guinea art often stands in a mimetic relation to nature, not only when it imitates movements, colors, and habits perceived in nature, but also when it seeks, by its constructed images, to reveal hidden truths about nature. For whenever New Guineans speak of the "catharsis" of initiation or of *ida* performances, they do so in terms of perceptual revelation. The Orokaiva term for initiation is *embahi kiari* — seeing the spirits. One of Gell's informants likewise spoke of a feeling of heightened perception while dancing, which he expressed in the pidgin English phrase "hai bilong yu klia ologeta" ("your eye entirely clear" 1975:192). Such experiences should not, as Arnheim (1954) rightly argues, be treated as subjective states independent of what is put on stage; but on the other hand these untranslatable multi-channel messages are not presented to the audience as "closed texts" but rather as what Eco (1962) called *opera aperta*. We mean by this that no initiatory performance could be wholly successful unless it was aided by the audience's "inferential walks" and constructs of "possible worlds."

Allowing for some mimetic elements whose importance is still to be tested in field study, Papua New Guinea art is grounded on learned *a priori* knowledge, on "conceptual images" that the artist imposes upon nature. Furthermore, New Guineans often say (as Somare said) that the experience of initiation — of seeing spirits in action — is an important part of education. Some anthropologists, such as Iteanu (1983), have doubted this, rightly pointing out that very little verbal instruction is given and that very little learning of facts and rules takes place. However, initiation educates by non-verbal signs: visual, auditory, tactile, gustatory, olfactory. It arouses new perceptual awareness in the form of schemata that can hardly be verbalized. What the schemata teach is the theatrical representation of spirits.

This cognitive function is at the heart of what aesthetic anthropology needs to explore. Merquior (1977:39-40) suggests that art is a form of knowledge operating by means of signs. When the initiated artist "shows the spirits," he therefore acts as a pedagogue. His artistry consists of the skill to construct an object capable of transmitting knowledge of spirits, and his audience must have the skill to receive that knowledge. The success of this construction depends not only on the order and pattern of the signifiers used but more particularly on an "extra ration" of sense, a "floating signifier," that is, the expression of the work of art — the quality that makes it "untranslatable" and capable of inducing catharsis.

Art in which this cognitive or pedagogic function predominates is of necessity operating on mimesis and conceptual images simultaneously: it represents, it constructs, it expresses. As modern Western art normally relegates the pedagogic function to a secondary position, Western aesthetic theory has often neglected it. On the other hand, aestheticians whose primary interest did not lie in the Western tradition have been much concerned with these pedagogic syntheses of the mimetic and the conceptual. Lévi-Strauss (1962; 1975; 1983:chs. XVIII, XIX) suggests that art is a miniature or reduction of nature on the ground that reduction implies abstraction, hence conceptualization. Most anthropologists will find such a view closer to their experience than the prevalent Western tendency to treat cognition as a kind of derivation from perception. After all, one has to have an idea of spirits before a rustling of leaves and a vague shape in the distance can suggest the presence of spirits, and before the initiatory artist can simulate by such means the impending arrival of spirits.

In the case that mostly concerns us here, however, the human body itself is used as principal artistic medium. Admittedly, spirits are often referred to in Papua New Guinea as larger than men, but masks are likewise often larger. One might say that masked figures are as large as actors can conveniently handle, but the spirits represented may be conceptualized as larger still. People like the Orokaiva who use no masks but only decorated human bodies probably do think of these figures as miniatures of spirits. Nothing in spirit impersonation therefore appears to go counter to Lévi-Strauss' theory that the art object is essentially a miniature.

If we wish to develop a methodology on this kind of basis, a good starting point would be the programmatic statements of Antonin Artaud who, fifty years ago, opened the way to fundamental renewal of the theatre in France and elsewhere.[10] Those who would wish to do aesthetic analysis of Papua New Guinea spirit impersonation ought not only to read *Le théâtre et son double* but almost know it by heart, for to Artaud true theatre was never anything else but spirit impersonation. His theatre is emphatically multi-channel communication. We find in each channel the same special care to deflect the audience from everyday perception, to make gestures express ideas and mental attitudes as well as aspects of nature, but also to suffuse the scene with danger, to let a "puff of that great metaphysical fear" blow on it. What Artaud can explain to us better than any other source we know are the unspoken motivations of countless details of spirit impersonation stage production.

His more general point is that everything in theatre has its shadowy "double." To every actor, then, there corresponds an "analogous affective organism" whose radiating force he should capture. Artaud writes: "pour se servir de son affectivité comme le lutteur utilise sa musculature, il faut voir l'être humain comme un double, comme le Kha des Embaumés de l'Egypte, comme un spectre perpétuel où rayonnent les forces de l'affectivité" (Artaud 1964:201).[11] The "analogous affective organism," then, is two things at once: a spectre and a spectrum, as Artaud suggests in his untranslatable pun. It is a spectre because its power is in some way derived from the dead; it is a spectrum because it contains within itself the totality of all perceptible messages. The actor's gestures and words are mimetic because they should but imitate what the spectral dictates. Moreover they are all "untranslatable" for, as Artaud says, the actor "invents a language of gestures designed to evolve in a given space outside of which they cannot have meaning" (p. 94). Finally, this language cannot help being structured conceptually because, as Artaud also says, the actor's interpretation of a theme, even if his text may be improvised, must be "coded from beginning to end" (p. 152). As we have seen above, *ida* was performed by the same principles: It was an improvisation by actors who were consistently obeying some spectral spectrum, some analogous affective organism, and who remained true to their theme even though they were improvising the details of their performance.

The above remarks will have shown that anthropologists can find inspiration in the work of many aestheticians who have developed methods of description and analysis. In this very general approach to the aesthetics of spirit impersonation, two chief objectives emerge. The first is to lay bare the processes of poiesis as they operate among New Guinea artists, both traditional and modern. These general processes of poiesis can be derived only from detailed studies of particular ceremonies.[12] It is not only as an anchor to the Papua New Guinea sense of national identity that such a reconstruction would be timely, but also because the question of poiesis has general relevance for contemporary civilization. In New Guinea, it is a practice of every initiated person; everyone has the possibility of becoming a creator in his own right. This does not mean, as we have seen, that he is repeating some ritual, but that he is "playing himself," as Gell put it (1975:276). For every man has his own analogical affective organism. Artaud was trying to restore a creativity that Europe had lost. But we have rich evidence to indicate that it is still alive in Papua New Guinea. This is surely another good reason why we should study and describe the operation of poiesis in Papua New Guinea.

All this analysis would revolve in a void unless we intended, true to the principle of Panofsky's "iconology," to return in the end to determine the content of the performance as a whole. Even if particular messages are untranslatable, the variations within a series of messages may create a pattern that is comparable to the patterns of other more general aspects of culture. If we study a multiple channel message, each series of partial messages will have its own pattern and these patterns are normally not uniform. Much room therefore exists for syntactic analysis within a multi-channel message system, and also for relating the results of aesthetic analysis to general problems of the culture.

The arts are never products of pure imagination. Their imagined worlds seek to overstep contradictions whose existence in the social world is real enough. Thus Gell demonstrated, for instance, that the masks and dancers of *ida* set up contradictions between red and black colors and between old and young, corresponding to inter-generational contradictions that are very real in the Umeda social world. In *ida*'s imaginary world, this opposition was mediated by roles that were neither black (old) nor red (young) but intermediate in color and in dancing and acting style (Gell 1975:265-69). It thus showed in a weakened and more acceptable form the trauma of the passage of the generations and established a balance between the anguish of the young (who are troubled by their dependent position) and of the old (who must accept the young as successors).

Anthony Forge performed a similar "iconological"

analysis, though on a smaller scale, in his analysis of Abelam paintings referred to above. He showed contradictions (1979:286) in the relationship between male and female creativity to be the real underlying theme of these paintings, although particular designs taken by themselves may "lack obvious symbolic reference" (1973b:188-89).

This interest in the total cultural conditions in which the arts are created is essential to all the methods we have discussed. The study of poiesis is never confined to artistic activity in isolation, but always includes the reaction of the artist to his real conditions of existence as part of the poietic activity. To the extent that performance is individual, the artist can express himself as a person, but where the poiesis involves the participation of many artists, a remarkable accommodation occurs between individual and collective concerns. The articulation of individual and collective messages is highly complex and little understood. Yet such articulation, observable on a small scale between the members of a performing troupe, provides a model not only for aesthetic anthropology but for the study of social groups in general.

Notes

1. Several major anthropologists showed keen aesthetic sensibility but most preferred to write about how tribal peoples "conceived" the world rather than about how they actually "perceived" it directly. One point on which most agree is that there is a strong mimetic element in what traditionally goes by the name of "primitive art." (See Lévi-Strauss 1958:chs. XIII, XIV; 1962:ch. I; 1975; 1983:chs. XVIII, XIX; Leach 1954b, 1973; Bateson 1973; Forge 1973a.) We find discussions of double representation, of the aesthetics of scale reduction, of the pleasure of plural readings and polysemy, of style, or works where the elements are mimetic but the composition surrealist, and so on. We also find discussions of order and complexity of design (e.g., Bateson, Lévi-Strauss) stressing the same kind of considerations as Arnheim (1954, 1966:123-35). While they are thus all interested in order, balance, pattern, and expression, their greatest contribution has been to show how art teaches people to "see" the ultimate contradictions in their cultural system. Thus "the object . . . contains a confusion of visual themes and . . . led the artist to express the inexpressible with outstanding vigour" (Leach 1973:234).

2. Somare's two statements (1979a, 1979b) both express that these works of art are ancestral spirits and souls; that they must be judged by aesthetic criteria and that New Guineans regard them as "a genuine expression of the personality of the artist and his cosmos" (1979b:xiv).

3. Moles' analysis of multiple messages is too complex to be reproduced here. A table in his book (1972) shows the nature of the complexity: Each partial message is subject to its own laws and constraints, which are different for each channel. Coordination is limited. Moles assumed, incidentally, that the whole production (of a ballet, opera, etc.) would be controlled by a single person responsible for all its aspects. This is never true for folk art where formal coordination of the channels is minimal. This makes it almost incomprehensible how the audience at such performances can believe that all the partial messages are fully orchestrated together, that there is harmony among them. For evidence of absence of coordination and harmony achieved in spite of this, see Dorothy Leadbeater on the Sicilian cart (Smith 1961:36-47, 51-52, 55-56). For a discussion of all the channels involved in Papua New Guinea ceremonies, see Schwimmer (1979).

4. Although Lévi-Strauss made a considerable number of extended statements about aesthetics, he was careful never to construct what might look like a coherent structuralist aesthetic theory. Merquior carefully analyzed the various structuralist texts and set out (1977) what such a coherent theory might have looked like. We feel he correctly stresses the importance of the "cognitive function" in structuralist aesthetics. It is only towards the end of his book that he raises the issue that aesthetic messages are, perhaps by definition, "untranslatable," that is, not susceptible to semantic analysis. Merquior argues that, in Peircian terminology, this merely implies that such messages are not "symbolic." But if they are iconic or indexical, Merquior continues, they could be "aesthetic," not directly translatable but still subject to semiotic analysis. This view is supported by Mukarovsky (1977), who speaks of the porosity of aesthetic signs, and by Barthes (1970), who speaks of "lecture plurielle"—manifold reading. Eco is much less hopeful, arguing that an iconic text sets up a code but does not follow one (1978:164) and that it is not a semiotic phenomenon (p. 182). In a text not available to Merquior, Lévi-Strauss (1983:327-31) comments on Max Ernst's paintings, saying that they speak "innumerable languages" and quoting Goethe to say that they are a chorus guiding us to a hidden law. According to Lévi-Strauss the artist does not create but meditates and encounters. Such a view denies that there is an opposition between what is "translatable" and what is "untranslatable." We accept that view, but have used the term "untranslatable" in this paper to designate a system whose elements cannot be easily transposed one by one into a linguistic code.

5. Andrew Strathern (1971:216) writes: "One of the most striking features of the *moka* is the basic rule that to make *moka* one must give more than one has received. It is strictly the increment that entitles a man to say he has made *moka*". Where this condition obtains, we may take it that status rivalry is a major motivation of the ceremony.

6. Although Moles (1972:194) makes a clearcut distinction between semantic and aesthetic information, he does not fail to point out that any text is susceptible to manifold readings, some of which are more aesthetic than others. Moles wishes to reduce these manifold readings artificially to two types (semantic, aesthetic): two kinds of stocks, of organization rules, of structure, and therefore of originality (p. 195). For the difficulties in this scheme, see note 4 above. The concept of "degrees of freedom," as used by Moles and by myself, is operational and quantifiable. As for translatability, it may be useful also to consider the nature of "style" in the sense of Gombrich (1960) and Lévi-Strauss (1975:ii, 117-24). Style contains rules that are translatable by comparative and other analysis, but these rules describe only the "translatable" part of the styles. Arnheim (1966:136-50) confirms that translatability is a function of the

aesthetic education of the perceiver. Thus "really seeing" may be a cathartic state, as in initiation and spirit impersonation.

7. Anthropologists have rightly tended to conceive of the arts as serving the purpose of mediating social contradictions. Gell (1975) follows in this tradition. Their fault has been that they attempted to practice what Panofsky (1955) called "iconology" without ever carrying out a systematic "iconography." The Panofsky method has been adopted not only by Lévi-Strauss (cf. Merquior 1977:119-23; Lévi-Strauss 1983:337) but also by Francastel (1965), Duvignaud (1972) and, of course, Gombrich and Mukarovsky. Our own analysis of Orokolo bull-roarer designs (Schwimmer 1981b) is another example. One may wonder why iconology has so long been neglected by social scientists. The answer may lie in the dominance of Durkeimian theory in the social sciences while the humanities have long had a tradition closer to the sociological theory of Gabriel Tarde (1890; for a review see Joseph 1984). Perception and aesthetics play a key part in Tarde's explanatory framework for social processes.

8. Inspired by the work of Defrenne, many younger French aestheticians are exploring the basis of human creativity. They form a team of the Conseil National de Recherches Scientifiques, Paris. In writing this paper, we have been especially struck by a series of papers by Chabert, Geblesco, Tamba, Villiers, and Prudhomme (all 1976), that appear to follow in Artaud's tradition in reconstructing a model of artistic creation which is very similar to what is found in Papua New Guinea spirit impersonations. The social theory on which such work is based appears to be close to Tarde's (see note 7 above). It is a microsociology analyzing degrees of freedom open to the individual artist. In this, they confirm Gell's analysis, as does also Leach's interesting commentary on New Ireland art (in Smith 1961:81-85, 107-8, 120-23) and Herdt's analysis of culture in terms of "personal scripts" provided by its members (1981:284).

9. Eco's (1979) classification of text as open or closed is helpful if we consider the difference between public masked performances and secret initiations, in both of which Papua New Guinea often uses spirit impersonations. It would appear that the former are open texts and the latter closed. The public is induced to imagine; the initiate must "know." On these aspects Gombrich's (1960) discussion of "illusion" is of crucial importance, as it treats the perceptual aspects of creating and of succumbing to various forms of theatrical trickery. Yet, as Arnheim (1966:151-61) rightly points out, Gombrich's use of the term "illusion" is troubling in its ambiguity. While the masks are recognized as symbols by the initiated who know how they are made, the initiated still believe that these objects carry within them a very real spiritual power investing wearer, costume, and mask (Sieber 1962:8-9). See also my own discussion of secret and public channels of communication (Schwimmer 1981a).

10. In distinguishing between semantic and aesthetic information, Moles points out that certain artistic genres contain a far higher proportion of aesthetic information (as compared to semantic) than others. Thus music contains, in general, a higher proportion of aesthetic information than discourse. Artaud was greatly concerned about this fact; it was important for him to develop a theatrical language in which semantic information would be at a minimum and aesthetic information at a maximum (1964). Le Marinel (1981) showed how the "new theatre" in France (best known internationally through Beckett, Genet, and Ionesco) developed a theatrical language of that precise type.

11. "In order to use our affectivity as a wrestler uses his muscles, we must look upon the human being as a double, as the Ka of Egyptian mummies, as a perpetual spectre (/spectrum) from which the forces of affectivity shine forth."

12. For anthropological works that can be usefully studied to show the aestheic use of degrees of freedom of symbolic expression by individual members of the society, see Fortune (1935), Read (1965), and Herdt (1981).

3

Kominimung One–Legged Figures: Creative Process and Function

Dirk Smidt

Under the aegis of the National Museum and Art Gallery of Papua New Guinea about eight months of fieldwork were undertaken among the Kominimung between 1976 and 1980. Research among the Kominimung formed part of a larger study: the so-called Ramu Project, which focused on the Middle Ramu River area. Six linguistic groups were surveyed (Akrukay, Banaro, Breri, Rao, Romkun, and Igana), and more intensive work was undertaken among the Kominimung (see figs. 3.1 and 3.2).

The main aims of the Ramu Project were: (1) to identify tribal art styles in the area and to link them to specific linguistic groups, as well as delimit other styles either beyond or within the tribal art style boundaries (Bascom 1969); (2) to establish the provenance and collect further information about undocumented artifacts which were acquired from dealers and are now in the collection of the National Museum; (3) to assemble a comprehensive and documented collection of the material culture and art from the area; and (4) to collect data on the communicative aspects of art in its cultural context and the role of the artist in society (Gerbrands 1967).

During initial survey work I developed a notion of the cultural differences between the various groups in the domain of the Middle Ramu, particularly in terms of their art styles. In this period the choice was made to settle among the Kominimung, as their culture appeared to have undergone less change than the other groups surveyed. Data on the cultures of the Middle Ramu are scant. It is sufficient to look at a recently published map which presents an overview of intensive anthropological fieldwork in Papua New Guinea to realize that this area has been neglected by anthropologists (Gordon, Waiko and Heaney, ca. 1982). Published work amounts to only two books (Moyne 1936, Kasprus 1973), a few articles, and some illustrations of objects in catalogues of collections, exhibitions, and auctions. In these publications, hardly any reference is made to the Kominimung.

The Kominimung

The Kominimung form a small group of about 330 people, who speak a non-Austronesian language which has been classified under the Tamolan family of the Goam stock of the Sepik-Ramu Phylum (Z'graggen 1975:35). Situated on the middle course of the Goam River, a tributary of the Ramu River, they engage in subsistence agriculture, fish-

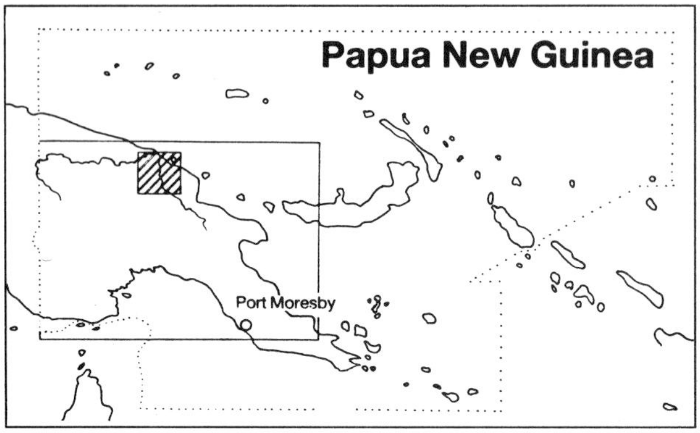

FIGURE 3.1.

ing, and hunting. Their staple foods are taro and sago. The diet is supplemented with yams, coconuts, bananas, fish, small game, birds, pigs, and, occasionally, crocodiles. Their nearest neighbors are the Romkun, downstream on the Goam River; the Igana, upstream on the Goam River; and the Breri on the Ramu River. These groups are related by linguistic affinities (Z'graggen 1975:35) and other cultural similarities. However, by and large, their art styles are quite distinct, particularly with regard to woodcarving.

The relative geographical isolation of the Kominimung and their small number (which made them of less interest than larger groups in the area to foreign agencies such as missions) must have contributed to the fact that outside influences have disrupted them much less than the societies on the Ramu River.[1]

One-Legged Figures

Kominimung shields and masks have been discussed elsewhere (Smidt 1983; Smidt forthcoming b). In this paper I intend to present information pertaining to the one-legged figures (*ase*) of the Kominimung. One-legged figures constitute a rather rare phenomenon in Papua New

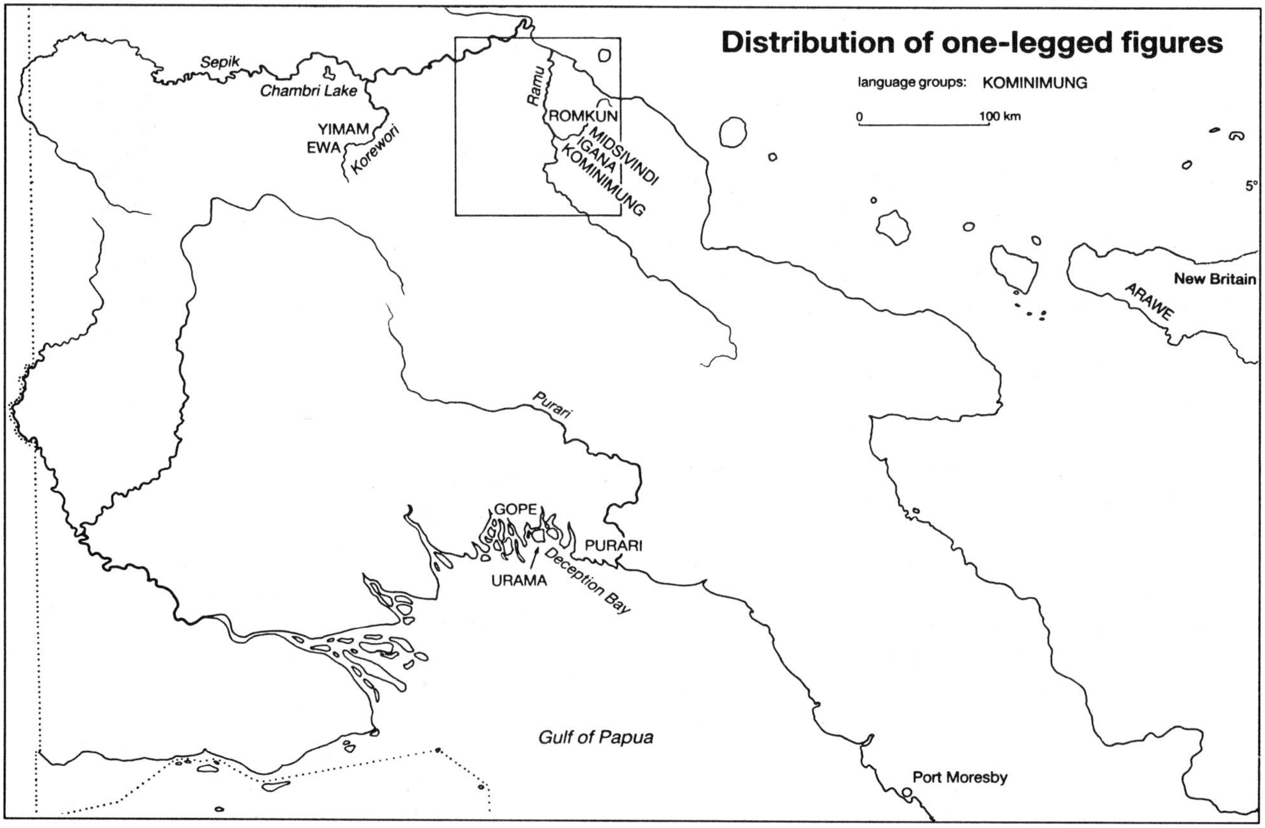

FIGURE 3.2.

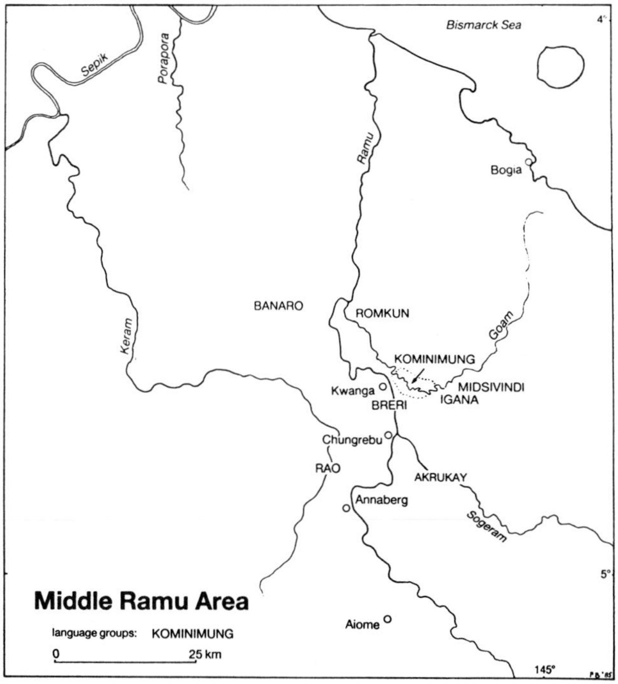

FIGURE 3.3.

Guinea art (that is, as far as we know Papua New Guinea art from the published sources). Although I have not yet made a thorough survey, I have gained the impression that one-legged figures have been reported only from the Arawe area, South New Britain (Damm 1962); the Gulf of Papua[2] (Smidt 1975); and, in the region of the Korewori[3] River, the Yimam[4] (Forge 1960; Haberland 1968; Haberland and Seyfarth 1974), and the Ewa[5] (Kaufmann 1974). As far as the Middle Ramu River and its tributaries are concerned, my own observations indicate that one-legged figures occur among the Breri, the Romkun, and the Igana, but apparently not among the Rao. According to Kominimung informants, they are also to be found at Isarikan, a Midsivindi village (see fig. 3.3). A one-legged figure from the Ramu River region is published in Batkin (1981:35).

The one-legged figures of the Kominimung are more or less cylindrical and rather slender (fig. 3.4). These figures represent powerful mythical ancestors who play an important role with regard to male initiation and marriage. Women are not allowed to see the figures; men, on the other hand, must see them before they are allowed to marry. The limitation in shape, to one leg only, seems to be determined by the function of the figures in the context of initiation ceremonies. During certain phases of initiation, particularly when the boys are rounded up, male dancers manipulate the figures in such a way that the boys are "kicked" by them.

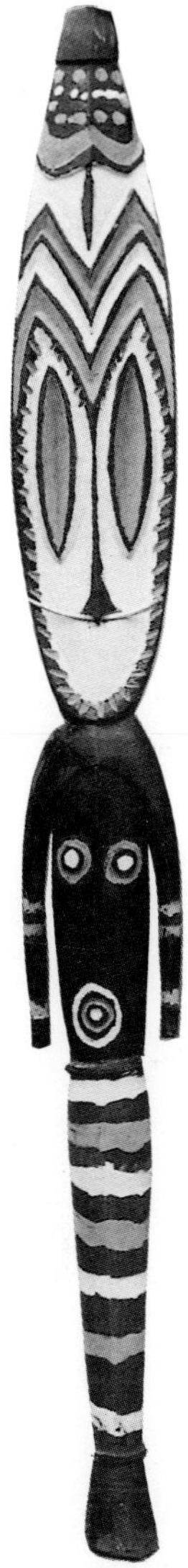

FIGURE 3.4. A Kominimung one-legged figure. H. 121.5 cm. National Museum and Art Gallery, Port Moresby, 79.62.140.

I will not present here a thorough comparison of the form and function of Kominimung one-legged figures with those of other areas. Suffice it to note that the Kominimung figures are not so two-dimensional and silhouette-like as the Yimam and Ewa figures (figs. 3.5 and

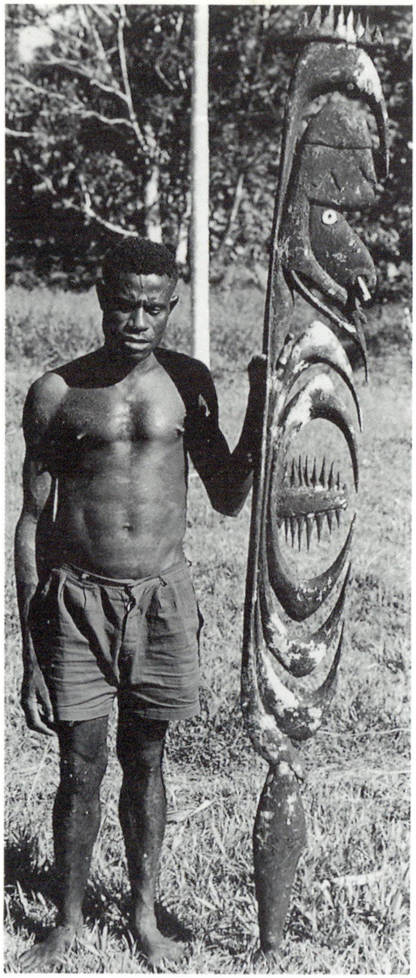

FIGURE 3.5. A Yimam one-legged figure. H. 237 cm. National Museum and Art Gallery, Port Moresby, E 10428.

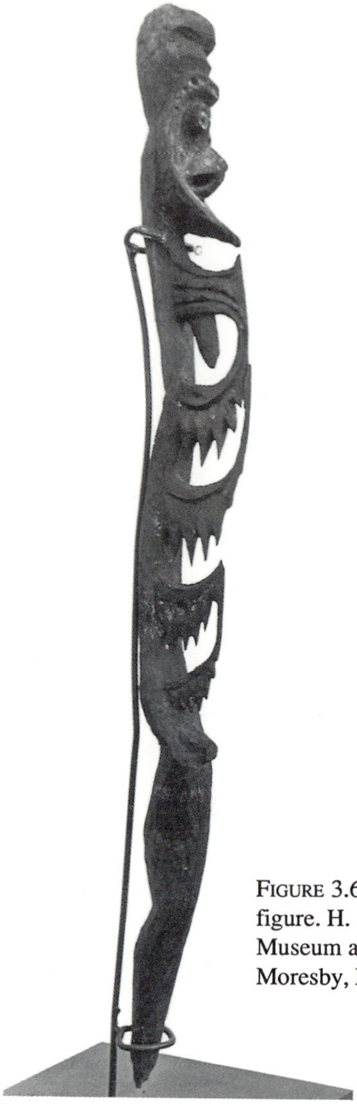

FIGURE 3.6. An Ewa one-legged figure. H. 104 cm. National Museum and Art Gallery, Port Moresby, E 16429.

3.6), but are rendered in a more compact and cylindrical form. Divided from each other only by a ridge, the torso and leg are nearly indistinguishable. Arms are usually visible, either carved straight and parallel to the torso or forming a semi-oval curve that connects the shoulder directly to the waist (fig. 3.7). The elongated head is dominant, both in size and coloring. Usually the head accounts for nearly half the length of the entire figure. Nipples and navel are carved, and knee and ankle joints are indicated by ridges carved along the circumference of the leg. A vertical row of chevrons is often carved and/or painted on the back of the head, indicating the backbone and rib cage (figs. 3.29 and 3.33). Sometimes a vertical row of oval-shaped or diamond-shaped motifs are carved and/or painted on the back of the head (figs. 3.8 and 3.9). These motifs, called *ovongku*, are more difficult to interpret. They may represent the backbone proper, without the rib-cage. The average height of the one-legged figures that I collected is approximately 130 cm. The smallest figure measured

112.5 cm.; the largest 146 cm.

Process of Manufacture

The one-legged figures of the Kominimung are made in secluded spots, out of sight of women, children, and uninitiated adolescent males. A woodcarver may work by himself for a while, or he may be joined by one or two other men who are working on their own figures. More often than not, however, woodcarving is done by a larger group of men working together.

To make a one-legged figure a suitable tree must first be selected in the bush near the hamlet of the woodcarver. Occasionally this is not necessary because a section of a previously felled tree may be used. Such, indeed, was the case for the figure whose carving is described here. Analysis of the one-legged figures collected for the National Museum and Art Gallery at Port Moresby revealed that several types of wood were used; *Sloanea, Macaranga,*

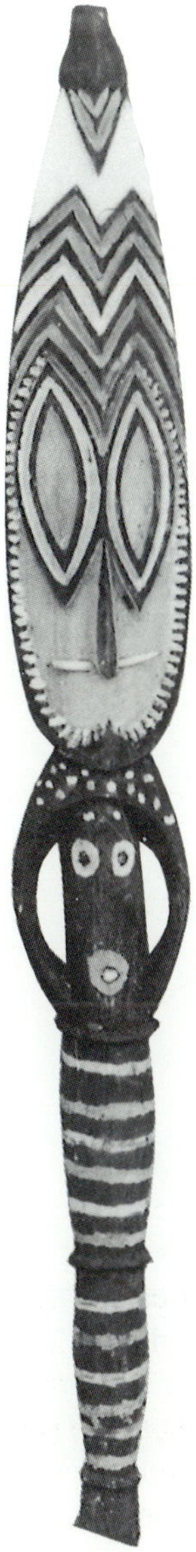

FIGURE 3.7. A Kominimung one-legged figure with curved arms. H. 117.5 cm. National Museum and Art Gallery, Port Moresby, 79.62.130.

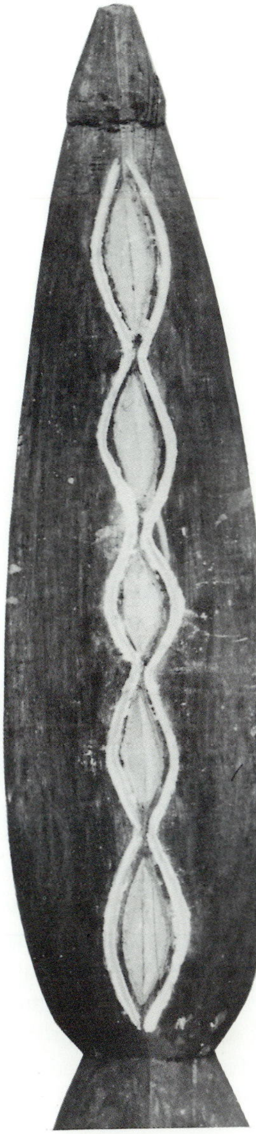

FIGURE 3.8. Oval-shaped motifs on the back of the head of a one-legged figure, possibly representing a backbone. Detail of the figure depicted in fig. 3.7.

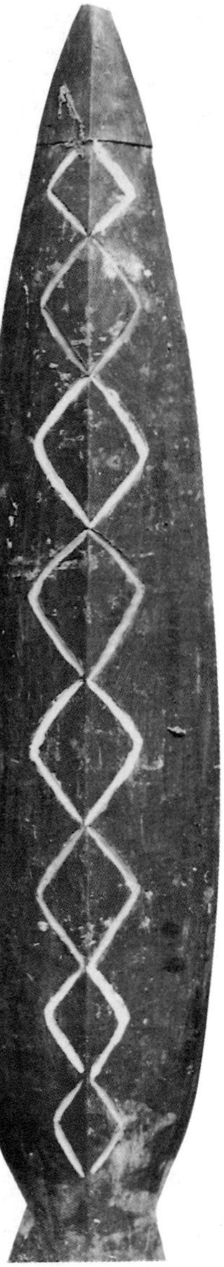

FIGURE 3.9. Diamond-shaped motifs on the back of the head of a one-legged figure, possibly representing a backbone. Detail of the figure depicted in fig. 3.37.

Nauclea, Campnosperma, Thespesia, and *Cryptocarya,*[6] are types which occurred more than once in the collection. This applies to carvings of recent manufacture (made at the time of my fieldwork). Of the four somewhat older and used one-legged figures in the collection, three were made of *Thespesia*, and one of *Vitex*. The one-legged figure whose manufacture is described and illustrated in this paper was said by the carver, Mangal, to be made of *nambawan garamut* (Melanesian Pidgin, meaning "excellent quality *Vitex*"). However, at Port Moresby it was analyzed as *Cryptocarya*. For another one-legged figure the same woodcarver used the wood of a tree of which canoes are also made. Because of a lack of early, well-documented Kominimung one-legged figures in museum collections,[7] it is impossible to know whether in the past the Kominimung were more selective in the choice of wood for their figures. One wonders, for example, whether a shift from the use of hardwoods to a wider range of softwoods has occurred.

The following is a description of the various phases in the process of manufacture of a one-legged figure, made by the woodcarver Mangal.[8] Initially, Mangal worked by himself in the bush near his hamlet. Later on, he was joined by two other woodcarvers who also started to carve one-legged figures.

First, a block of wood is cut out of a tree which has been felled.[9] To that end, the bark is removed from a section near the base of the tree. This is done with an axe. Then the axe is used to make two horizontal incisions approximately 115 cm. apart. These mark the upper and lower end of the block of wood. Next, while standing over the log, the

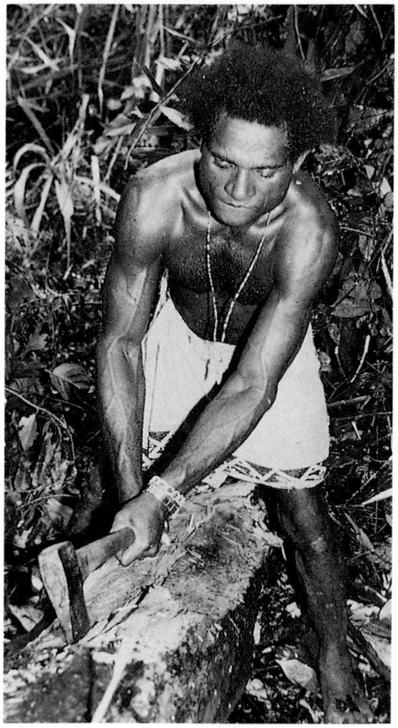

FIGURE 3.10. Making longitudinal incisions with an axe.

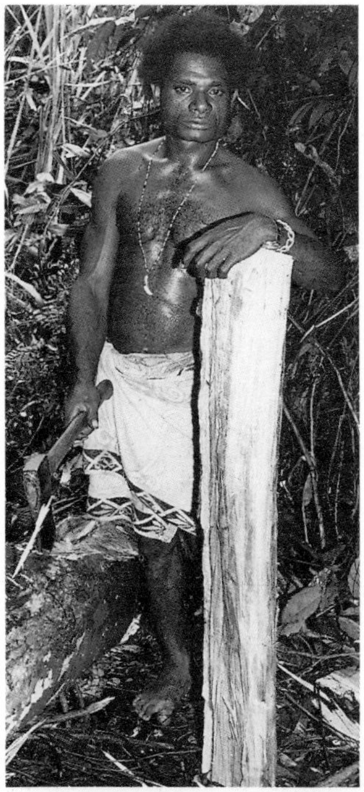

FIGURE 3.11. Mangal shows the block of wood which he has cut from the tree trunk.

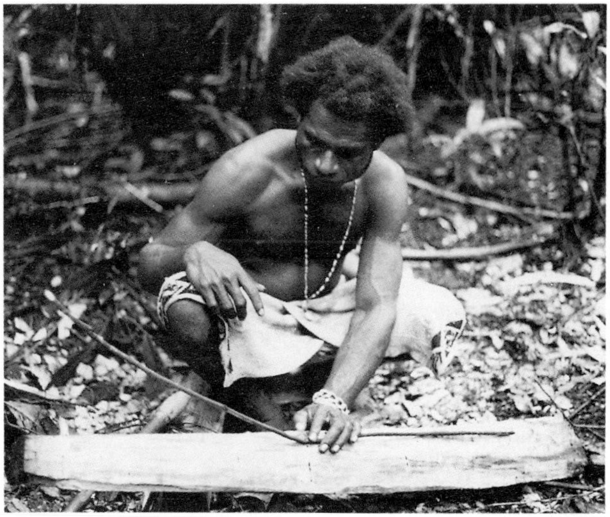

FIGURE 3.13. Determining the length of the head in relation to the body.

carver makes a longitudinal incision between the two horizontal incisions (fig. 3.10). Sometimes the axe is used as a kind of wedge, to make the incisions wider and deeper. A block of wood defined by these incisions is removed from the tree trunk (fig. 3.11). This takes about thirty minutes of strenuous work. Another thirty minutes is

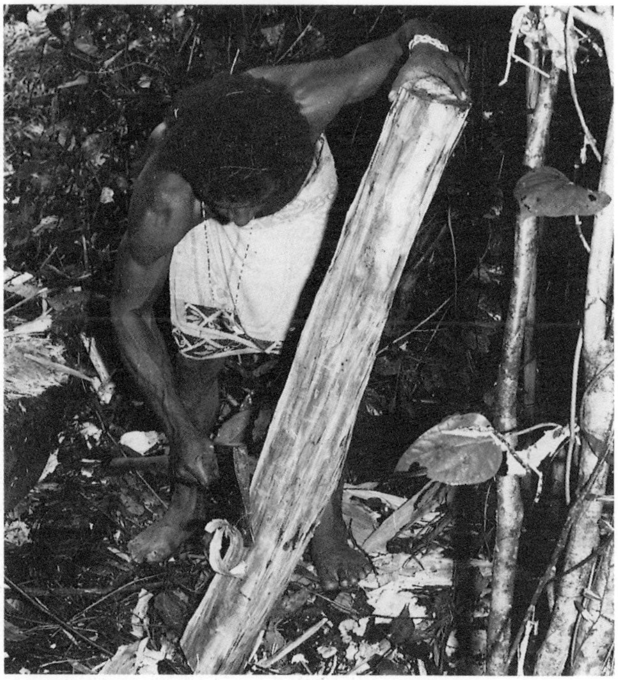

FIGURE 3.12. Cutting away superfluous wood.

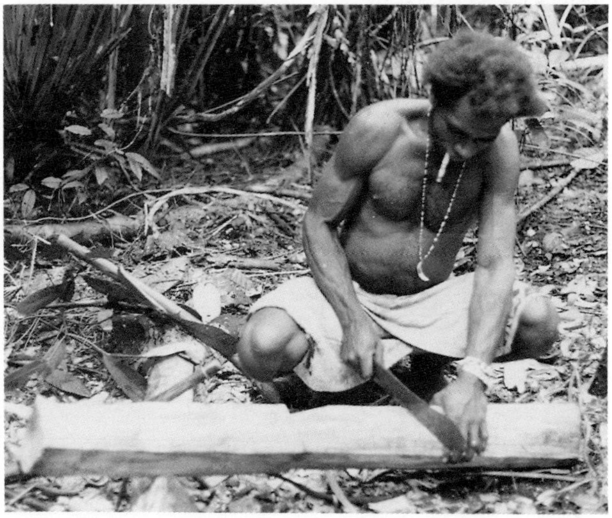

FIGURE 3.14. An incision is made to mark the length of an arm. Incisions to mark the position of the neck have already been made.

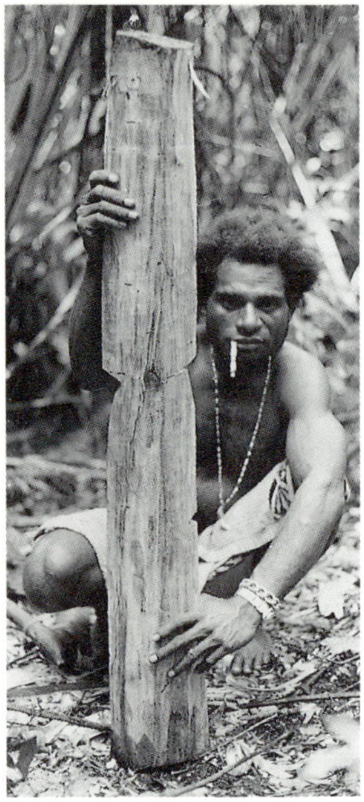

FIGURE 3.15. Mangal shows the block of wood with its incisions marking the neck and length of an arm.

required to trim the piece further with the axe (fig. 3.12). Only then are adzes, of various sizes, used to continue the work of roughly shaping the sculpture.

After about fifteen minutes of adzing, a section of a liana

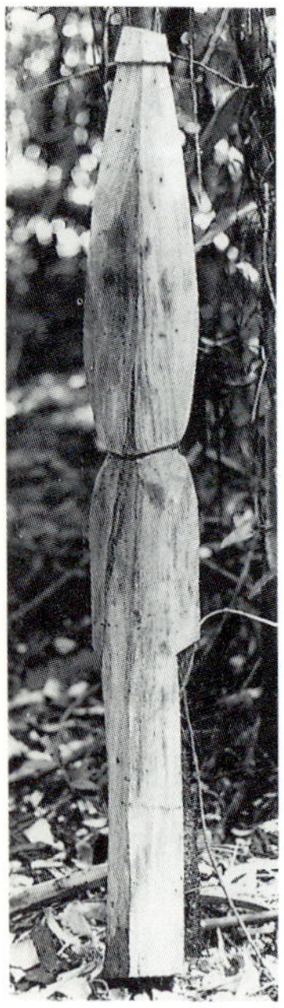

FIGURE 3.16. The shape of the head, including the hairline, is almost completed; arms and leg have been roughly indicated but require further treatment.

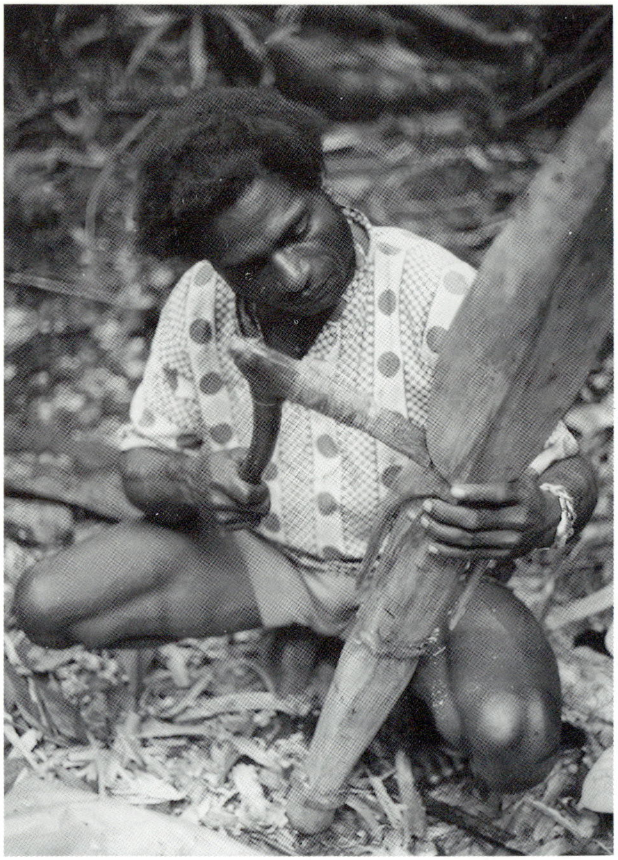

FIGURE 3.17. The neck is worked to perfection with an adze. Note the arms, which have been "freed" from the trunk.

is used as a measuring device to ensure that the nascent sculpture will be well-proportioned (fig. 3.13). In this way the correct position of the neck is established. Cuts are made with a knife (fig. 3.14), then deepened with an adze, to demarcate the neck and the hands (fig. 3.15). More adzing is done to shape the head, and then gradually the lower section is made into a leg. During work the piece of wood is turned frequently and held in many positions, including upside down. When the sculpture is in a lying position, a cylindrical piece of wood is often used as a support base.

In the next stage, a ridge is carved on the head to mark the top knot or hairline. From the moment of marking the position of the neck until this phase, two and one-half hours have elapsed (fig. 3.16). For the first time, the

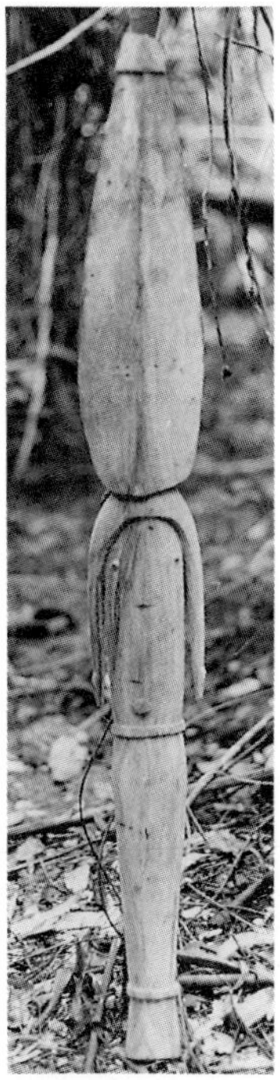

FIGURE 3.18. Apart from the face, the sculpture is completed. Note the fine nipples and the navel.

smallest adze is used to carve the arms and to pierce the area between arms and trunk. This area is subsequently also worked by knife. It takes more than one hour to complete an arm.

The carver continues with the shoulders and makes the bottom of the foot flat. By positioning his thumbs on the trunk, the carver determines the correct position for the nipples. He subsequently carves a nipple, using the smallest adze. With a thin woodchip he measures the distance between the nipple and the neck, to ensure that the other nipple is carved at the same height. After further shaping the breastbone with a large adze, the carver uses a small adze and a knife to form the navel. Further shaping of trunk and leg is done before the carver stops working in the late afternoon. On this day he has worked without interruption from 11:00 to 17:00. The unfinished sculpture is hidden in the bush, just behind the tree from which the wood was taken.

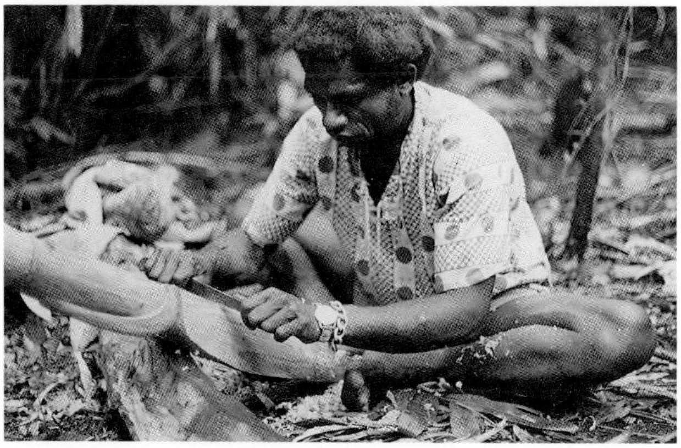

FIGURE 3.19. The head is scraped smooth.

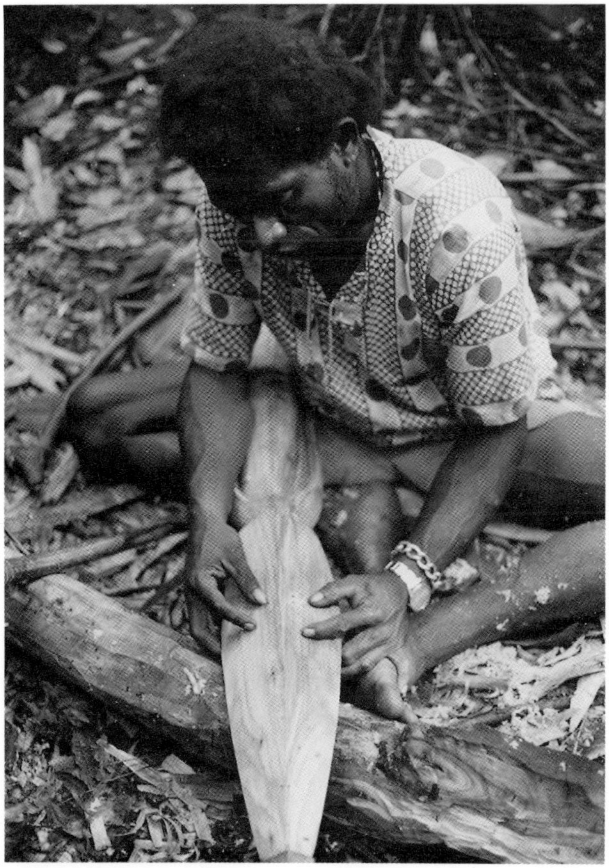

FIGURE 3.20. The position of the eyes is carefully considered.

The next day, beginning at 11:30, the carver works for about an hour adzing the breast and back. At 12:25 he carves a wrist. Measurements are taken with a woodchip to ensure that the other wrist is carved at a similar level. The leg is shaped further, and at 13:20 the ridge around the waist is clearly marked, using an adze initially and then a

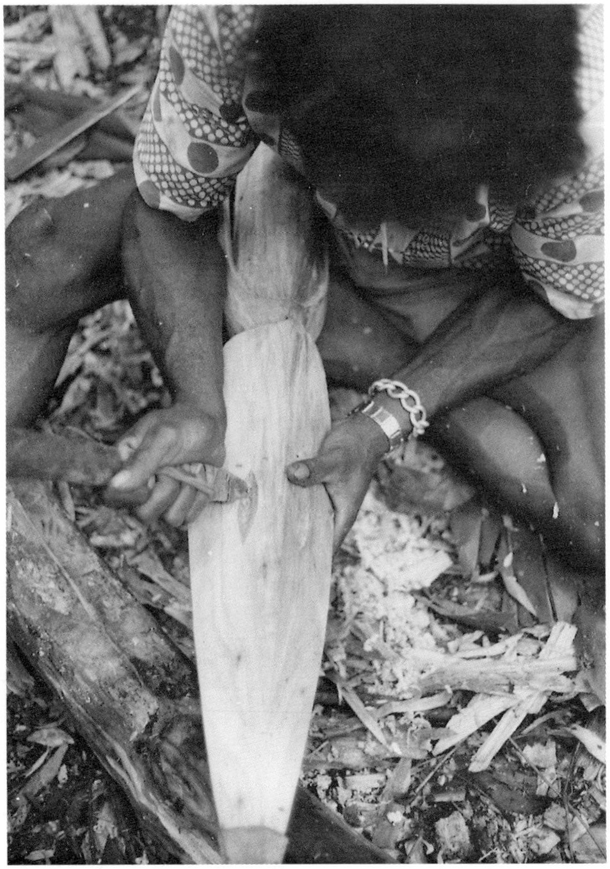

FIGURE 3.21. Hollowing out the eye sockets.

knife for the proper finish. The ridge above the foot (which indicates the ankle) is carved in a similar fashion, and other parts, such as the neck, are adzed to perfection (fig. 3.17). At 14:35 the sculptural work is completed (fig. 3.18). Now it is a matter of scraping the surface of the wood with a knife to make it smooth enough for the paint to stick (fig. 3.19), and to carve the facial features.

The correct position of the eyes is a crucial matter which requires careful consideration. A woodcarver who is not completely confident will first draw the outlines of the eyes with charcoal. Even an experienced woodcarver may first ascertain the position of the eyes by holding index finger and thumb of both hands at the appropriate places (fig. 3.20) before driving the adze into the wood. At 14:55 the outline of one eye is marked with an adze. A measuring device is used to ensure precise symmetrical rendering

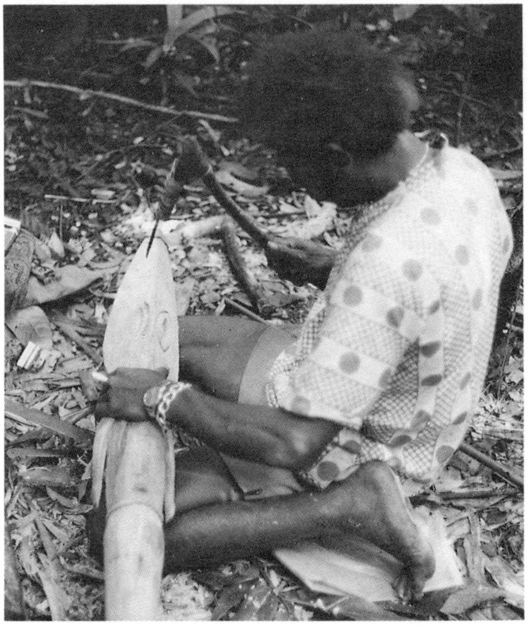

FIGURE 3.22. Cutting the grooves around the eyes.

and equal height of both eyes. The eye sockets are hollowed out with a knife (fig. 3.21). Three grooves are carved around the eyes, during which adze and knife are

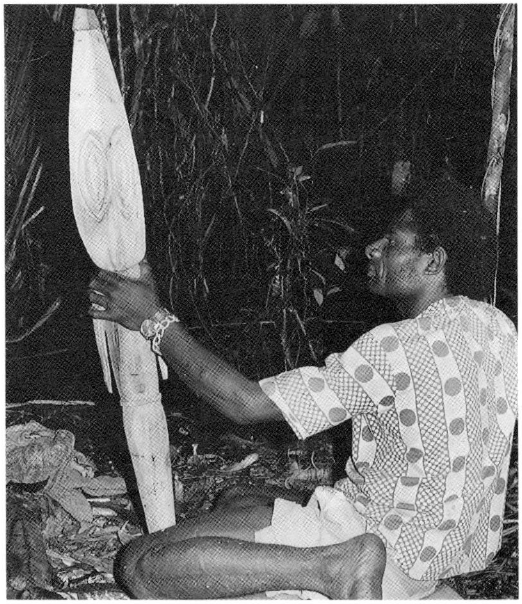

FIGURE 3.23. The carver pauses to consider his work.

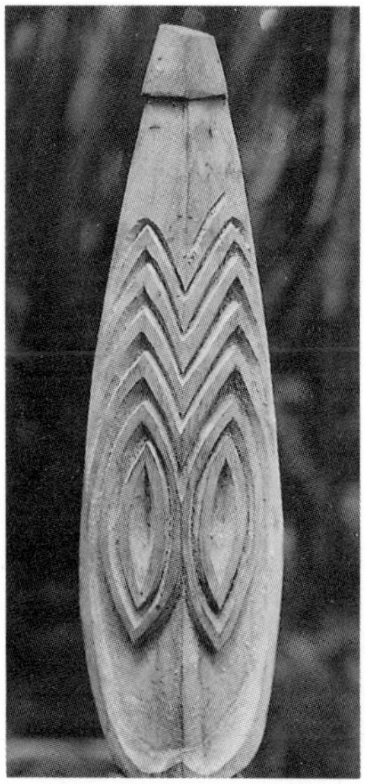

FIGURE 3.24. The head after eyebrow grooves and facial rim have been added. Motifs on the forehead and nostrils remain to be done.

used alternately (fig. 3.22). Mangal pauses occasionally to scrutinize the carving, and to ponder his next move (fig. 3.23). The work with the knife, in particular, is time consuming. It is not until 17:15 that the eyes are completed. Subsequently, the facial frame is accentuated and the area below the eyes deepened a bit. At 17:55 the carver leaves his work, with the sculpture still unfinished.

On the third day work is resumed at 10:50. Now, the eyebrow grooves are carved, six of them altogether (fig. 3.24). That task requires slightly over two and one-half hours. Finally, after some deliberation, the upper part of the head is filled in with a few motifs: a pair of triangular designs at the top and a circular one below them. As will be discussed, these are very important. It is not by chance that the artist has reserved them for the final phase in the carving process. By 14:15 these motifs have been completed. Some further adzing is done on the facial plane below the eyes and at 14:20 the nostrils are carved. The "septum" is pierced and later a piece of wood or pig's bone may be inserted in the opening. The carving is finished by 14:45, and it is ready to be painted.

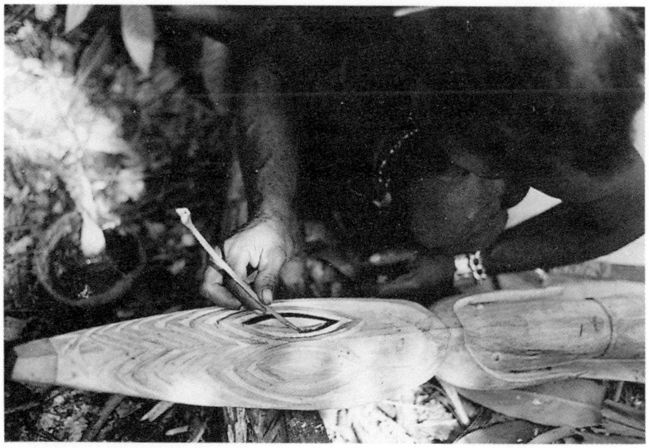

FIGURE 3.25. Raised parts of the face are painted black.

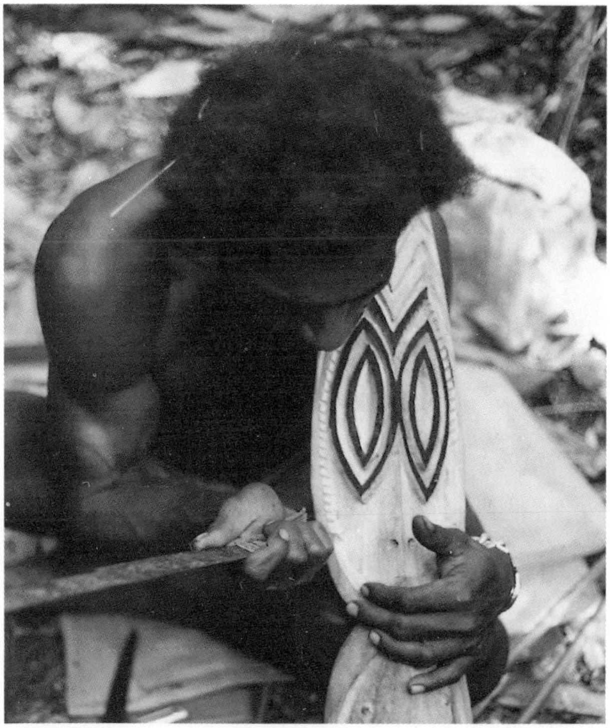

FIGURE 3.26. Cutting incisions in the facial rim.

Between 14:45 and 15:00 preparations are made to paint the figure. A rough brush is cut from coconut fiber and four fine-tipped brushes, of varying degrees of thickness, are made from leaf-stems (probably the victory leaf). Black paint, made from charcoal mixed with water, is prepared in a coconut shell. With a fine-tipped brush, the raised areas of the face are painted black. Just as the eyes were the first facial feature to be carved, they are the first to be painted (fig. 3.25).

At 15:35 Mangal discovers that he has forgotten to carve

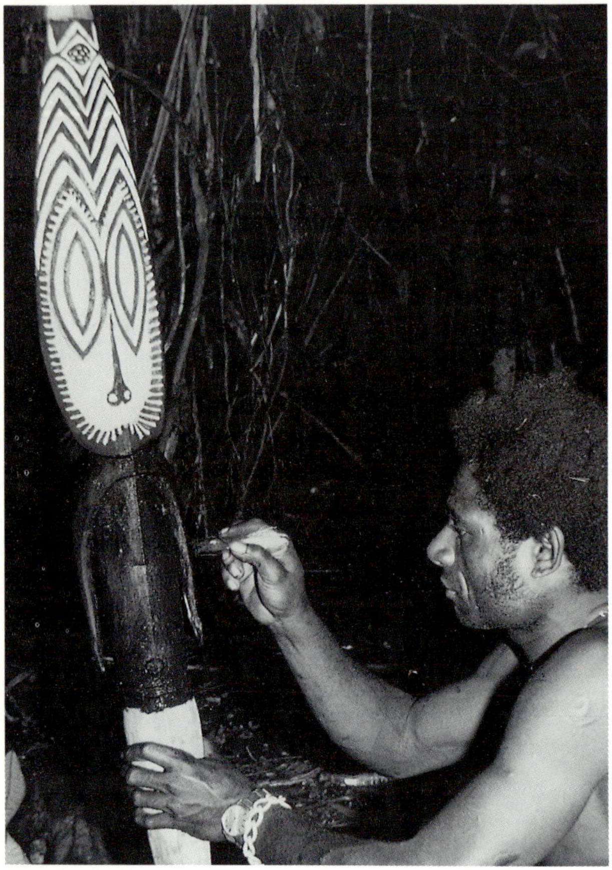

FIGURE 3.27. Painting the trunk, arms, and leg.

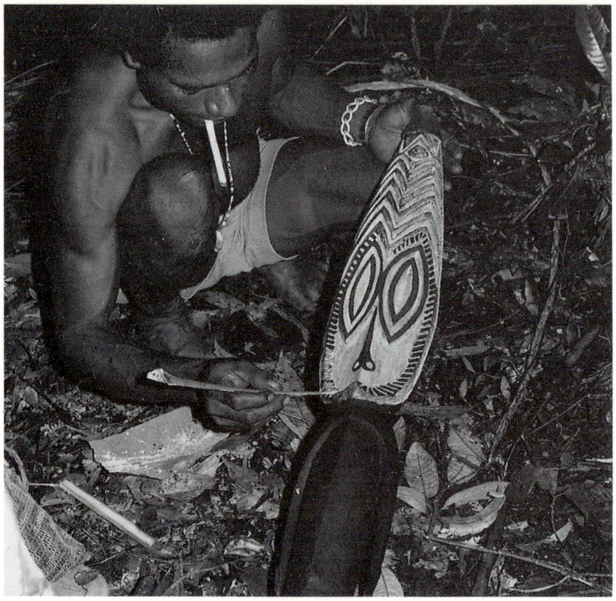

FIGURE 3.28. Applying the varnish.

the many incisions, called *pempe*, which should decorate the facial rim. He interrupts the painting process to carve these incisions with a knife (fig. 3.26). At 16:05 he carves the last incision and continues painting the figure. It takes until 17:00 to paint black the raised parts of the face. After having painted the circular motif on the forehead, a few incisions (like dots) are carved in this motif. With the rough brush of coconut fiber the larger planes are now painted black. First the back of the head, then the back of the torso, then the front of the torso, and finally the arms (fig. 3.27). The leg is painted last.

At 17:25 the figure is laid aside temporarily while the carver goes to collect some white tree sap (latex). He mixes this with the juice of wild sugar cane and saliva (he has chewed the sugar cane for that purpose). This mixture is brushed over the black paint, in the same sequence as the carving and painting processes: first the face (fig. 3.28), then the remainder of the figure. The milky fluid loses its color and becomes glossy when dry. It serves as a type of varnish to prevent the black paint from smudging when touched. At 18:30 this part of the work is completed and the carver returns home.

In the next few days other things happened to come up which caused Mangal to set aside the figure temporarily. The work is resumed five days later, at 15:00. Mangal cuts

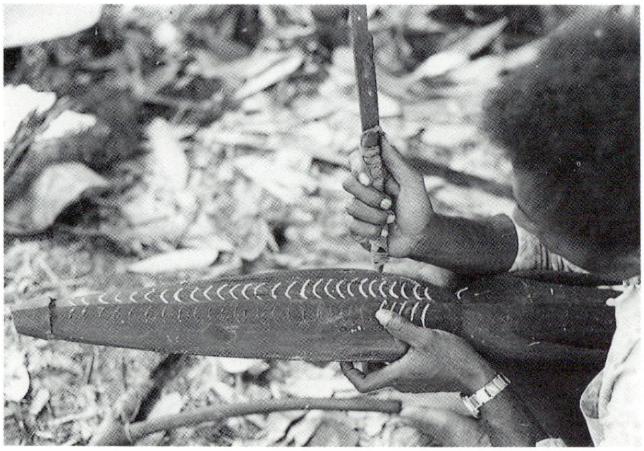

FIGURE 3.29. Carving the back of the head.

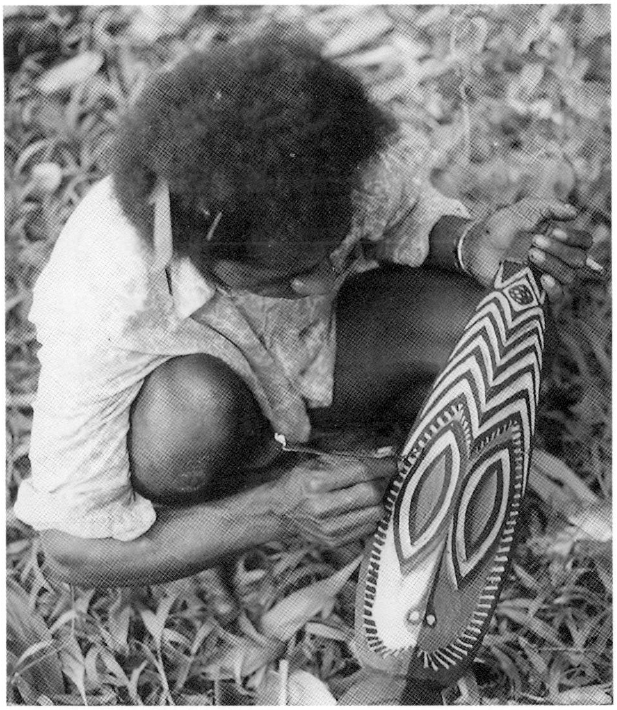

FIGURE 3.30. Painting the face.

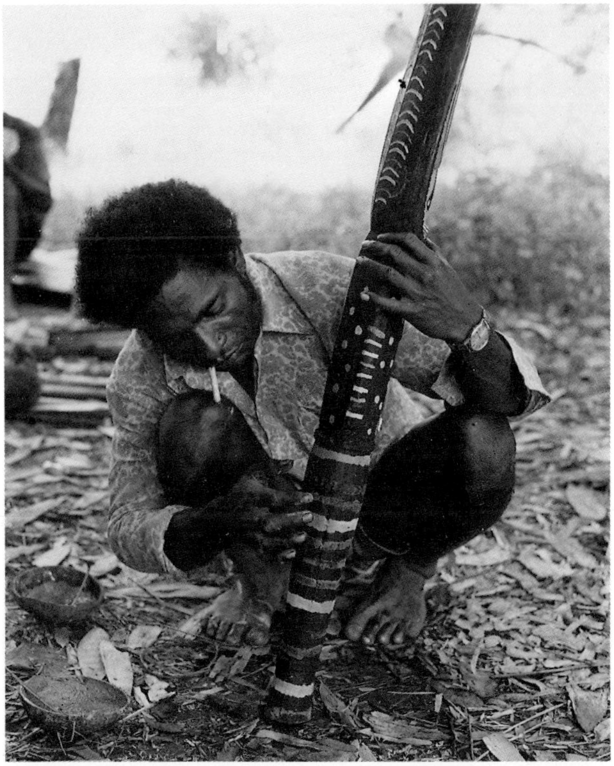

FIGURE 3.31. Painting colored bands on the leg.

a long row of chevrons running down the back of the head (fig. 3.29). These represent the backbone and rib cage (*asanta*). He then prepares the paints: white, made of white clay mixed with water; yellow, made of the inner bark of the mango tree which has been chewed and mixed with lime; and red, made of the seeds of the *Bixa orellana* mixed with water and saliva. At 16:30 Mangal starts to paint his figure. The eyes are done first. These are painted red, and then the facial area below and around the eyes is also painted red (fig. 3.30). Next the grooves around the eyes are painted yellow. After this the many eyebrow grooves are painted one by one with alternating colors. One of the Kominimung aesthetic rules is that colors should be arranged so as to contrast with each other. Accordingly, adjoining grooves should not be filled with the same color. After the area above the eyes has been painted, the small incisions of the facial fringe are painted in the same manner, color by color. At 18:00 the work comes to a halt, but the figure is not yet completely painted.

The next day the brush is taken up again at 10:30. Mangal first paints coloured rings around the arms and small concentric circles around the navel. Then he paints the chevrons on the back of the head. This time his method is different: Rather than painting groove after groove, whereby the colors (and the respective brushes) alternate, he now fills in all the grooves requiring white paint first, followed by all the yellow grooves and, finally, all the red grooves. Then he paints white bands around the leg, white dots on the torso and the shoulders, red bands around the leg, yellow bands around the leg, yellow dots on the torso and the shoulders, and, finally, red dots on the torso and the shoulders. No brush is used to paint these bands and dots; the paint is applied by finger. The bands around the leg are painted by finger while the figure is rotated slowly with the other hand (fig. 3.31).

At 12:30 the entire job is completed (figs. 3.32 and 3.33). In all, twenty-five hours and fifteen minutes were required to make this one-legged figure: eighteen hours and thirty minutes to carve the figure and the motifs, and

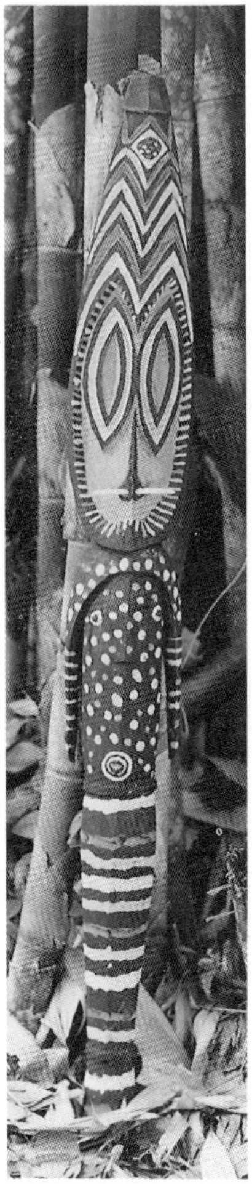

FIGURE 3.32. Mangal's finished figure, which represents a mythical ancestor or *tambaran* associated with Mangal's catfish clan. Note the clan emblems on the forehead (see also fig. 3.38), the nose ornament, and the dotted motifs on the shoulders and trunk, representing the juice of the breadfruit tree. National Museum and Art Gallery, Port Moresby, field number FN 1360.

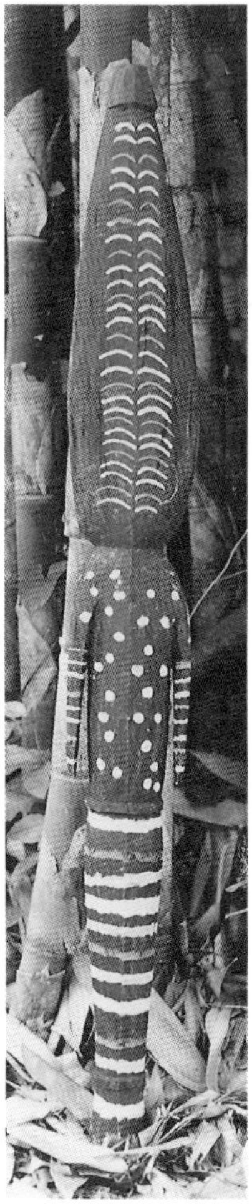

FIGURE 3.33. The back of Mangal's figure. The motifs on the back of the head, called *asanta*, represent the backbone and rib cage.

six hours and forty-five minutes for the painting. Work on this particular piece was done on five different days, occurring between April 18-26, 1977.

Social Structure and Religious Background

To understand the art forms of the Kominimung in their cultural context it is necessary to have some knowledge of their religious beliefs and their social structure. For the Kominimung, the cosmic world, nature, and society are classified into a dual structure. A large number of totemic clans are organized in two exogamous moieties. These are called black-eye and red-eye, and are considered respectively male and female. Of crucial importance for every Kominimung man and woman, and for Kominimung society as a whole, are the mythical ancestors or ancestral spirits. Their generic name is *bwongogo* (or *tambaran* in Melanesian Pidgin). There are many individual *tambaran*, both male and female. Each *tambaran* is associated with a particular clan, and within that clan with a particular male and female guardian.

An individual *tambaran* does not permeate all areas of life. Its sphere of influence seems to be restricted to particular important types of activities such as gardening, hunting, fishing, warfare, and initiation. *Tambaran* are clearly associated with the promotion of these activities or, if they are provoked, with the obstruction of success in them. Apart from its main function, a *tambaran* may have additional or secondary functions related to the well-being of its guardians, such as preventing sickness. However, I will not deal with these secondary functions in this paper.

At ceremonial occasions the *tambaran*, who belong to the spirit world, are brought into the realm of human beings by means of theatrical performances which are prepared in the men's house. The *tambaran* are made tangible and visible through the woodcarvings and additional paraphernalia worn or manipulated by initiated male performers. Many such paraphernalia may symbolically refer to the mythical and social context of the particular *tambaran*. For example, parts of plants and animals (such as croton leaves, pig's tusks, hornbill feathers, cuscus skins, betel nuts, and so on) may indicate the totemic clan with which a *tambaran* is associated. It would appear, however, that these are to be considered as supporting elements to the woodcarving, a man-made object which can be regarded as the most distinctive and central visual element of the *tambaran.* I suggest that the multitude of *tambaran* can be classified into a few categories according to their main function. Likewise, each *tambaran* category is visualized by a particular type of woodcarving. Thus, each type of woodcarving refers to a particular function.

When the *tambaran* perform, the category to which they belong and the function they fulfill is not only indicated by visual symbols but also by audible symbols. A certain type of music is associated with each category of *tambaran,* in all cases representing the voice of the *tambaran.* Various combinations of musical instruments and singing are possible, depending on the type of *tambaran* and the nature of the occasion. These include: hand drum only, hand drum and singing, slit gong and singing, traverse flutes only, and slit gong only.

The one-legged figures not only constitute one particular type of woodcarving or art form, but when imbued with power they represent a particular type of *tambaran.* In Melanesian Pidgin my Kominimung informants invariably referred to this type of *tambaran* as *strongpela* (powerful) *tambaran.* In their value system it appeared to be of a higher order and more awe-inspiring than the other types of *tambaran.* This type of *tambaran* plays an essential role during the crucial phases of male initiation. Only after having gone through this initiation phase and after having seen the *strongpela tambaran* will the young men be allowed to marry.

Art in Its Context: One-Legged Figures and Initiation

No initiation ceremony was held during my stay among the Kominimung. According to my informants, the most recent initiation ceremony took place in 1976, shortly before my arrival. The following description is based entirely on data obtained from informants. The one-legged figures are apparently used in two phases of male initiation. The first phase occurs when the boys are about fourteen to fifteen years old.

A number of *strongpela tambaran* appear in the village and chase the women and children away. This apparently happens at night. The *tambaran* do not seem to appear as fully masked figures, but rather as men whose bodies are painted and decorated with leaves and flowers. They also wear particular items of dress: a skirt of sago leaf fibers, a traditional waistband of plaited vine strips in which leaves are inserted, and plaited armbands also bristling with leaves. A net bag is worn on the breast, decorated with *melo* shells and tubular projections. These represent female breasts, and are covered with *nassa* and cowrie shells. In front of the genital parts, apart from the skirt, a woven loincloth or penis cover is worn. This is a band woven from the fibers inside the aerial roots of the pandanus palm in the same manner as the netbags are made. Such a penis cover may be more than 100 cm. long and about 10 to 15 cm. wide. One end covers the penis, and the rest of the band passes over the waistband, then downwards to form a loop suspended between the legs and finally upwards again so that the dancer clenches the end of the band in his teeth. This description is based on a spontaneous mock-up by one of my informants who, without my asking for it, dressed up to demonstrate (fig. 3.34).

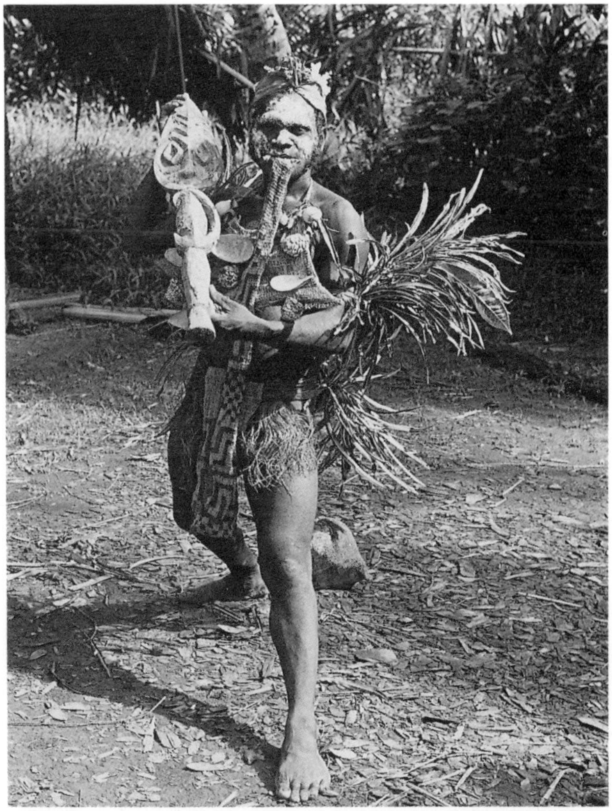

FIGURE 3.34. An initiation dancer with a one-legged figure.

The performers wear facial paint, the color (and perhaps also design) of which some informants say indicates the moiety with which the particular *tambaran* is associated. The yellow color seems to be linked with the black-eye moiety, and the red color with the red-eye moiety. This color symbolism operates in other art forms of the Kominimung as well, particularly in woodcarvings that represent mythical ancestors and that have clan emblems carved in them. It applies, for example, to shields (Smidt 1983:157), masks (Smidt, forthcoming b), and figures — both two-legged and one-legged. When the *tambaran* perform, each of them holds a one-legged figure. The figure is held in a diagonal position, the head of it is supported by the raised hand of the right arm while the foot is supported by the left hand. The head of the figure is held at the same level as the head of the performer while the foot is held at breast height (fig. 3.34).

After the women and children have been chased away, the boys who are to be initiated are rounded up. In the course of this action the initiates are prodded or beaten on the chest or back with the feet of the one-legged figures (fig. 3.35). After the initiates have been herded to the men's house, the one-legged figures are placed in a room of the men's house where only fully initiated men are allowed to see them, while the initiates sleep in another room. During this first phase of initiation the boys are circumcized and some bloodletting is done on their glans to remove the female blood with which they are still contaminated. The glans may be scraped with a snake's tooth, a sharp spine from a catfish fin, or an eagle claw.

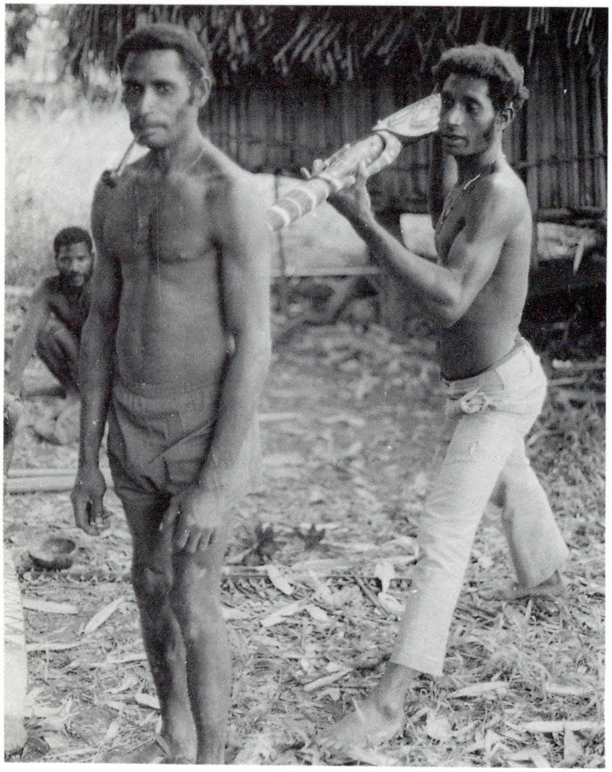

FIGURE 3.35. An informal demonstration of how one-legged figures are used to prod initiates on the back.

Some years later, when the boys are ready to marry, they are rounded up again in the same manner as described above, to undergo the last phase in their initiation. They are brought to the men's house, where they are now allowed to see the one-legged figures. They are given the approval of the *tambaran* to marry. They are told in which clan they should marry, and further details on marriage arrangements are possibly also transmitted to them. During the time that the *tambaran* are present in the men's house they are given food which has been prepared by the men themselves. While the women were allowed to prepare food for the other types of *tambaran*, it was said that only men were allowed to prepare food for the *strongpela tambaran*.

In addition to their function in the context of initiation ceremonies, the *tambaran* represented by one-legged figures seem also to be beneficial in other ways. After the initiation ceremony is over, some one-legged figures remain in the men's house, while others are taken to the family houses. When kept at a family house they protect the house (*was long haus* in Melanesian Pidgin) and the people who live there. They also ensure successful hunts, particularly of pigs, and they seem to ensure a sufficient supply of food in general. They are apparently displayed in standing position while leaning against a wall. They may be put on a platform of black palm with a semicircular fence of sago palm leaves in order to hide them from the eyes of women, children, and uninitiated males. If women and children were to see the one-legged figures, they would not only get sick, but the gardens would be destroyed by roaming wild pigs and pig and crocodile hunts would be unsuccessful.

Symbolic Connotations of the One-Legged Figures

It is in keeping with the sacred nature of the *strongpela*

tambaran and the decisive power they wield in Kominimung society that the one-legged figures which represent them are not to be seen by women and uninitiated males. Likewise, women are not allowed to see the figures being made, and only fully initiated men are allowed to make them. Consequently, they are made in a secluded spot, either in the bush not far away from the hamlet, or on the grounds of the men's house, usually within a fence. On such occasions the carvers, who are associated with the particular men's house, do not sit far apart when working on their one-legged figures. This allows for easy social interaction, and instruction on the part of the more experienced woodcarvers.

Notwithstanding the sacred nature of the carvings, the atmosphere at such a workshop is usually quite relaxed and the carvers often joke and poke fun at each other. For example, someone may pretend to prod a fellow carver with the one-legged figure he is making, in the same manner as the figures are used while rounding up the boys at the beginning of an initiation ceremony (fig. 3.36). Once, a man who was "threatened" in such a manner made a remark which clearly illustrated the important function of the one-legged figures in relation to marriage. He said: "If you touch my back with that figure, you should give me another woman; I will then be married to two wives" (in Melanesian Pidgin, "*Yupela sutim baksait bilong mi, bai yupela givim wanpela meri moa, bai mi marit long tupela meri*").[10] Sometimes, the figures' connotation of male growth and fertility is humorously reversed when one carver threatens to crush the testicles of another with the foot of a figure. The second man may wittily reciprocate in kind by vowing to cut off the first fellow's testicles with his adze!

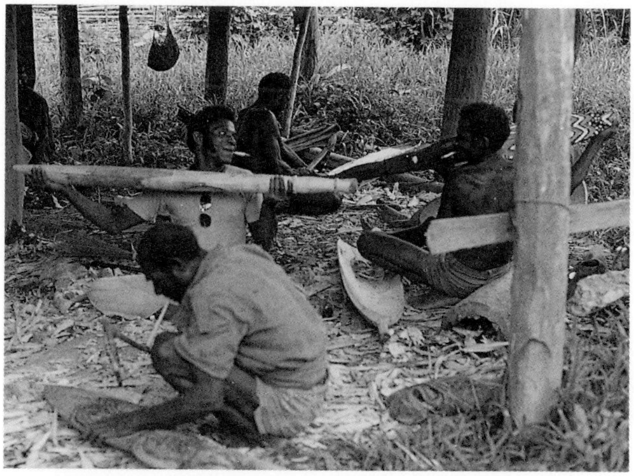

FIGURE 3.36. Two wood carvers playfully threatening to strike each other with the one-legged figures they are making.

Elsewhere I have discussed the relationship between Kominimung masks and the social structure (Smidt, forthcoming b). What has been said there is for the most part also applicable to the one-legged figures. The relationship between one-legged figures and social structure may be considered at two levels: the level of social action and the level of iconographical interpretation. On the first level we observe in what social context and by whom the one-legged figures are manipulated. On the other level, we look at the figures themselves and try to decipher the meaning of the motifs carved on them.

On the level of social action, as with the masks, four key people are particularly associated with each figure. In Melanesian Pidgin they are called *papa*, *mama*, *pren*, and *pikinini*, which may be translated as "father" or male guardian, "mother" or female guardian, "friend," and "child." I have already described the functions of these four categories, their place in the social structure, and how their functions are inherited (Smidt, forthcoming b). Here I will only remark that the "child" manipulates the one-legged figure during the ceremony and performs as the *strongpela tambaran* of which the "father" and the "mother" are the guardians. It is noteworthy that the "father," "mother," and "friend" belong to one moiety while the "child" belongs to the other. One might think that, during an initiation ceremony, the *strongpela tambaran* would seek out and prod a boy from the clan with which he is associated. However, informants stated that the boys were rounded up and pushed with the one-legged figures quite indiscriminately. At the conclusion of the ceremony, however, the boys appear in a transformed state. They are painted and decorated in the same fashion as the one-legged figures and the *tambaran* performers. As such, they may be considered as a reincarnation of the *tambaran* with whom they are associated.

Clan Emblems

A major conclusion to be drawn from an iconographic analysis of Kominimung one-legged figures is that certain carved motifs can be considered as clan emblems. Such clan emblems are also present in other types of woodcarvings, such as masks and male or female two-legged figures. The clan emblems are always rendered on the forehead. However, the available space on the forehead of one-legged figures is much more restricted than on masks. Therefore the relevant totemic being may be rendered in full on masks (catfish and flying fox, for example), although occasionally it is given in part (such as a spine representing a catfish).[11] On one-legged figures, however, part for whole rendering is more common. Examples are a pair of pig's tusks representing the pig as symbol of the pig clan (fig. 3.37); a pair of (poisonous) spines standing for a catfish[12] (fig. 3.38); and a hornbill represented by a hornbill beak (fig. 3.39). Only very seldom is a complete totemic animal rendered on the forehead of a one-legged figure. An exception is the praying mantis, symbol of the praying mantis clan and associated clans of the red-eye moiety (fig. 3.40).

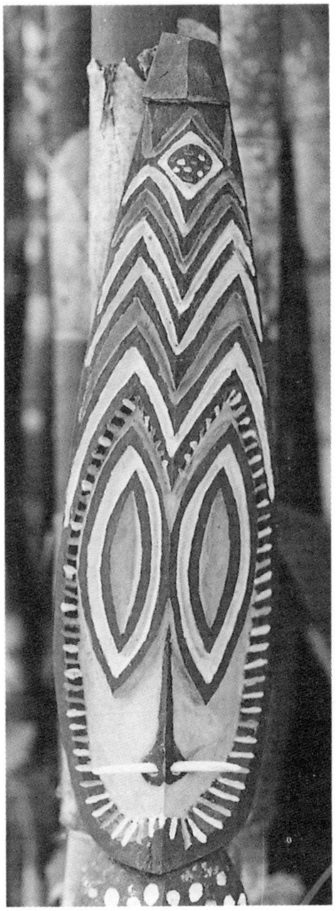

FIGURE 3.38. Head of Mangal's figure (see also figs. 3.32 and 3.33). The two black triangles immediately below the hair ridge represent the poisonous spines of the catfish (*agmandaga*; in Melanesian Pidgin, *nil bilong kondong*), emblems of the catfish clan. The circular, dotted motif below the spines represents a nest of insects, probably bees, a motif frequently but not exclusively associated with the catfish clan. The red color, found particularly in the face and eye sockets, indicates the red-eye moiety, to which the catfish clan belongs.

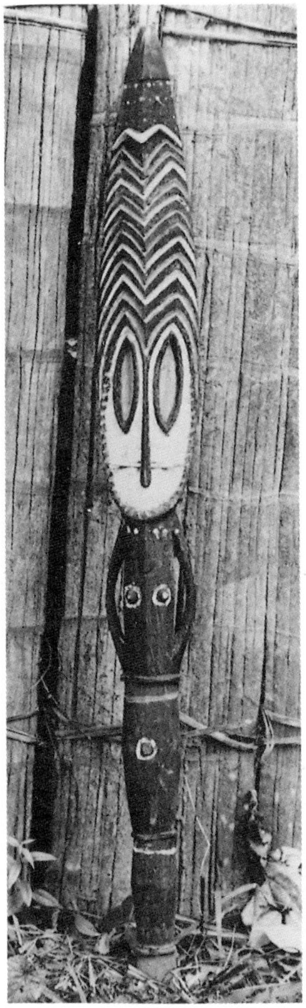

FIGURE 3.37. One-legged figure made by Esbhi in 1977, representing a mythical ancestor associated with the pig clan. The zig-zag motif on the forehead and pig's bone piercing the nose septum are symbols of the pig clan. Apart from the neutral colors white and black, the dominant color is red (particularly the eyes). This indicates the red-eye moiety, to which the pig clan belongs. H. 130.5 cm. National Museum and Art Gallery, Port Moresby, 79.62.121.

My informants have repeatedly and emphatically stressed that these and other motifs which are rendered on the forehead of one-legged figures[13] are indeed clan emblems. As they said in Melanesian Pidgin, "*Em mak bilong bisnis.*" Moreover, the interpretation of the specific clan emblems by local informants was remarkably consistent, even unanimous. As most clan emblems occurred more than once on various types of woodcarvings I collected, I was able to check the interpretation of similar motifs with different woodcarvers.[14] In the course of these investigations I encountered no disagreement as to the interpretation of the clan emblems as a whole or their association with specific clans. However, informants were sometimes uncertain as to the meaning of certain details of the clan emblems, and of secondary motifs.

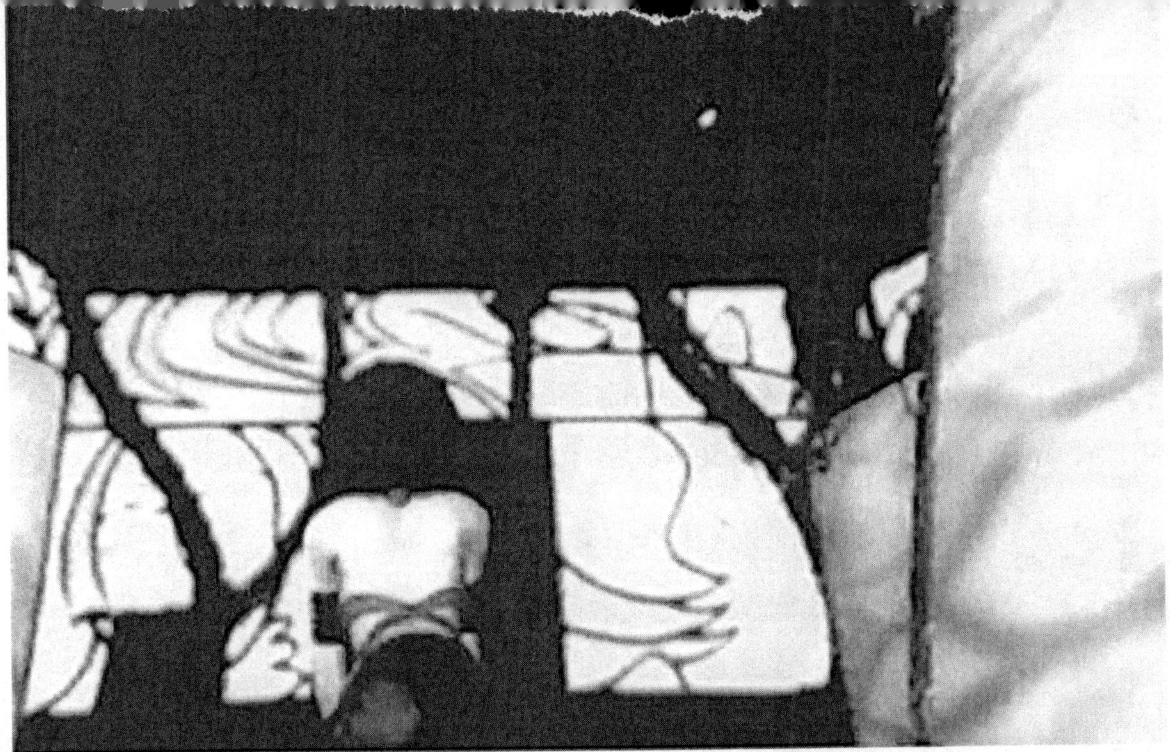

FIGURE 2 and 3. Mirrors flanking Malice's bed.

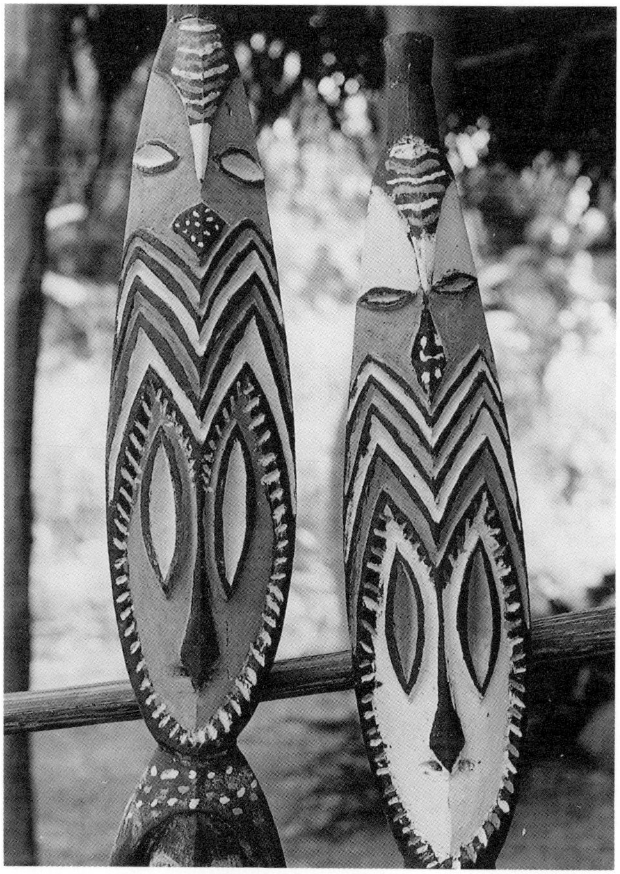

FIGURE 3.39. Heads of two one-legged figures carved by Evinya in 1979. They represent mythical ancestors associated with the hornbill clan, and the carved hornbill beak on the forehead of each figure is the emblem of that clan. The pairs of white oval-shaped motifs beside the hornbill beak represent shell ornaments that are worn by masqueraders on ceremonial occasions. These are general motifs, not linked to specific clans. The dotted, diamond-shaped motifs between the eyebrows are interpreted as a rooster for the figure on the left and, for the other figure, as a nest of insects, possibly bees. The dominance of red indicates the red-eye moiety, to which the hornbill clan belongs. H. 141 cm. and 128 cm. National Museum and Art Gallery, Port Moresby: right figure 79.62.137; left figure 79.62.138.

Of the forty-eight one-legged figures that I collected, forty-one bear the emblems of the maker's own clan. This is not surprising because in this matrilineal society instruction by the mother's brother seems to be the preferred mode of passing the skill of woodcarving from one generation to the next. However, a man may also learn to carve the emblems of his wife's and/or his father's clan. Four of the one-legged figures that I collected carry the emblems of the maker's wife's clan, while on two the carver chose to render the emblems of his father's clan. The remaining figure has a mixture of clan motifs.

The decorations added to a one-legged figure at ceremonial occasions also refer to particular totemic clans — either the same clan represented by the carved motif or closely associated clans from the same moiety. The top of a one-legged figure does not carry carved motifs because this spot is reserved for additional decorations such as feathers and/or a cuscus skin. Moreover, the color pattern indicates the moiety with which a figure is associated

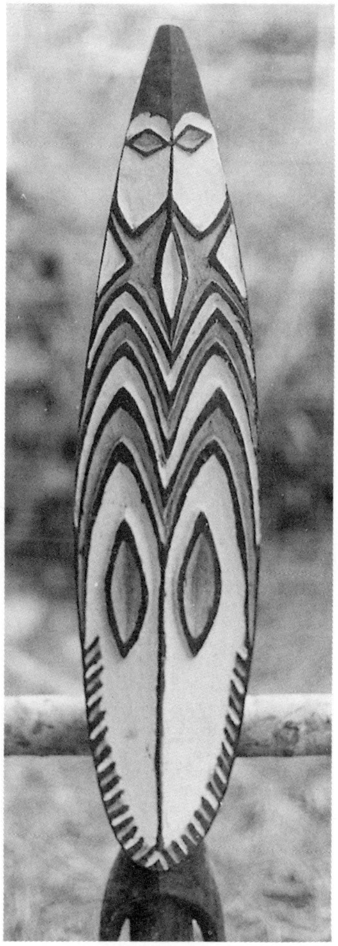

FIGURE 3.40. Head of a one-legged figure made by Gupu in 1979. The praying mantis motif on the forehead is associated with the praying mantis clan and also the cassowary clan, to which the maker belongs. The dominance of red indicates the red-eye moiety, to which the cassowary clan belongs. This figure was not acquired.

because red is predominantly linked with the red-eye moiety and yellow with the black-eye moiety.

Conclusion

The Kominimung produce various types of woodcarvings: masks, shields, male and female figures, and one-legged figures, among others. In this paper the one-legged figures have been discussed in some detail. One-legged figures represent mythical characters or ancestral spirits (called *tambaran* in Melanesian Pidgin) which appear to be of a somewhat higher order than the *tambaran* which are associated with other types of carvings. Their special importance is indicated by the Pidgin phrase *strongpela tambaran*; the adjective *strongpela* is not used with regard to the other types of *tambaran*. They play a paramount role in the context of male initiation and the subsequent rite of passage from bachelor to married man. It would be impossible for men to marry without having undergone initiation by the *strongpela tambaran*.

Adult male performers disguised as *tambaran* beat and prod the initiates with the feet of one-legged figures. While the one-legged figures are male, the performers show in their dress both male and female elements. This may be indicative of the ambiguous state of the initiates who are on the threshold between the female world in which they have been reared, and the male world they are about to enter. When the initiates re-enter the village after a period of seclusion they are painted and decorated in the same manner as the *strongpela tambaran*. As with the one-legged figures, colored rings are painted around their legs and dotted patterns on their bodies. From their facial paint their moiety association can be inferred.

The initiates are either reincarnations of the various *strongpela tambaran*, or perhaps one could say that a mutual permeation has occurred between them and the *strongpela tambaran*. Not only is the outward appearance of one-legged figures and initiates similar, but I contend that a similarity also exists in internal structure. An equation may be postulated between the light-colored wood (after the bark has been removed) used for one-legged figures and human bone. Likewise, the charcoal with which the figure is painted may be symbolically related to the black skin of the human being. This interpretation becomes more convincing when one considers an alternative method, used by various Kominimung woodcarvers, of painting one-legged figures and other types of woodcarvings. By this method, a red tree sap is painted on the wood as an undercoating and a layer of mud is smeared over it.[15] In my view, the red sap signifies human blood, while the mud represents the black skin of a human being.[16] Finally, the colors white, red, and yellow, which are applied to initiates as well as to one-legged figures, bring about the transformation from human beings, respectively carvings, to *tambaran*.

Motifs which the Kominimung identify as clan emblems are carved and painted on the foreheads of one-legged figures. While specific motifs refer to particular clans, the colors give added meaning by referring to other aspects of the social structure. Black and white are neutral or general colors which may be used indiscriminately by all clans of both moieties. Red, on the other hand, is restricted to the red-eye moiety and the clans thereof, while yellow refers to the black-eye moiety and its clans. Motifs and colors reinforce each other. Motifs make the message of the colors more specific; colors affirm the message of the motifs. In a way, motifs and colors of a one-legged figure underline aspects of the dual organization outlined above. Many one-legged figures performing together, in the context of an initiation ceremony, portray the social structure of the Kominimung. Even more, they refer to the world of the totemic beings and their supernatural order, and also to the world of the living and their society. They represent both the mythic past and the present. As such, one-legged figures project a cogent visual statement about Kominimung world view and social organization.

Notes

The maps appearing with this essay were drawn by Mr. Paul Bijvoet, Leiden. I wish to thank the organizers of the symposium, in particular Douglas Newton, for inviting me. I am grateful to the Director of the Rijksmuseum voor Volkenkunde, Leiden, Dr. Willem R. van Gulik, and the Dutch Ministry for Welfare, Public Health and Culture (Ministerie van Welzijn, Volksgezondheid en Cultuur) for supporting and sponsoring my trip to New York. The fieldwork on which this paper is based was sponsored by the Trustees of the National Museum and Art Gallery of Papua New Guinea. I am also grateful to the former Director of the National Museum, Mr. Geoffrey Mosuwadoga, for his encouragement. At various times during fieldwork I was accompanied by Mr. Resonga Kaiku and Mr. Soroi M. Eoe, at that time both staff members in the Anthropology Department of the National Museum. They have contributed to the results of this research. Without the practical assistance of the Australian Churches of Christ mission at Chungrebu, transport in the

Middle Ramu area would have been impossible. The Catholic mission at Annaberg was helpful in many ways. I owe a great debt to the Kominimung people for the hospitality, kindness, and friendship they have extended to me, my wife, Inez and son Joris. My special thanks are due to Pita Mangal, who acted as brother and teacher, and good-humoredly allowed me to observe and photograph him during the process of artistic creation. Finally, I wish to record my indebtedness to Professor Dr. Adrian A. Gerbrands for starting me on the path of studying art in its cultural context.

1. In other publications I have made comparisons between the present situation of the Rao and the Kominimung, and stressed the contrasts in acculturation (Smidt 1983:139-40; forthcoming a).

2. Including the following language groups (see Wurm and Hattori 1981): Purari (Koriki or Namau), North-Eastern Kiwai (Urama and Gope).

3. The spelling is after Kaufmann (1974). Other spellings used are: Korowori (Haberland and Seyfarth 1974) or Karawari (Haberland 1964; Laycock 1973:34).

4. After Haberland and Seyfarth (1974). They use the word Yimar, but according to Les Bruce *yima-r* is the singular form of "man," while *yima-m* is the correct plural (Kaufmann 1974:712n). In other publications these people were called Arambak (Forge 1960:6), Arambrak (Haberland 1964:54), or Alamblak (Laycock 1973:29). These names apparently come from their northern neighbors (Haberland 1964:54), while Yimam is derived from their own language. The name Yimam has not been entered in Wurm and Hattori (1981) nor in Bruce (1984); their designation is still Alamblak.

5. After Kaufmann (1974:713). The name Ewa has not been entered in Wurm and Hattori (1981), who use Enga (Iniai).

6. Wood identification is by Maru Kumul, Forest Products Research Centre, Port Moresby. With regard to these and other botanical names used in this paper, Paijmans (1976) was also consulted.

7. Apart from the National Museum and Art Gallery at Port Moresby, I do not know of any other museum in the world having one or more Kominimung one-legged figures.

8. Co-author of *The Kominimung* (1980). For more information on Mangal, see Smidt (1983).

9. The tree had been felled by Mangalabout a year before. Apparently it was supposed to be used as a house post but, for reasons unknown to me, it was not used for that purpose after all.

10. The spelling of Melanesian Pidgin words throughout this paper is based on Mihalic (1971).

11. See Smidt (forthcoming b).

12. These represent the poisonous serrated spines on each side of the forktailed catfish. The catfish has a third, larger, poisonous serrated spine on the back (see Cochrane 1974:15-16). Sometimes the three poisonous spines are rendered together on Kominimung woodcarvings, with the larger spine in the middle and the smaller ones flanking it; see, for example, Smidt (forthcoming b).

13. With the exception of one one-legged figure that I saw and collected, and which had clan motifs carved both on the forehead and on the back of the head, clan motifs are always carved on the forehead.

14. In making these investigations I was careful not to ask leading questions or to show that I knew the interpretation of the particular motif beforehand. The Kominimung must have thought me a very slow learner, I am afraid!

15. For a more detailed description and a visual impression of this method, as used in the process of manufacturing shields, see Smidt (1983), particularly figures. 6, 7, and 8.

16. The equations suggested here between raw materials, used for woodcarvings, and substances of the human body, only occurred to me after I had left the field. They need to be verified during follow-up research among the Kominimung. A point which needs clarification is whether human flesh is connected with the red tree sap (together with blood) or with the wood (together with bone).

4

The Areas of Asmat Artifacts

TOBIAS SCHNEEBAUM

All carvings in Asmat, Irian Jaya, can be said to be of ceremonial use to the extent that each carving is named for a recently dead relative. This naming process acts as a constant reminder to the living that all death must be avenged. Only in this way can the living exist without the vexatious interference from the spirit world, for the spirit of the dead person will not rest until vengeance has taken place. This pattern of revenge, in the past, led to the never-ending cycle of warfare, giving impetus to headhunting in coastal Asmat, where it became necessary to initiation rites. It was only through death that life could be renewed, only through the death of an enemy that an initiate could pass into the life of adulthood. Initiation rites did not demand headhunting in all regions of Asmat, but the taking of heads was part of vengeance and warfare everywhere.

To placate ancestral spirits and to force them on to Safan, Land of the Dead, it was, and in certain areas still is, necessary to hold feasts that use carvings and other artifacts as focal points in their rituals. Although all artifacts — from body ornaments to carvings, fireplaces, and houseposts in men's houses — may be named for the dead, this paper is limited to objects produced by respected carvers either for their own use or for those who requested them, those ritual objects and artifacts in daily use that are intricately carved with headhunting symbols. The more simply carved objects made by the ordinary man without designs, such as paddles, food bowls, and sago pounders, will not concern us here.

Asmat may be divided into four distinct artistic regions, each with its own category of ritual objects and other carvings and its own recognizable style. The four basic areas are:

A. Coastal and Central Asmat, from Flamingo Bay down through the Casuarina Coast.

B. Northwest Asmat.

C. The Tjitak of Eastern Asmat.

D. The Brazza River area and the people near the foothills in the northeast.

All four of these areas produce shields, spears, digging sticks, canoes, and bows and arrows, but only Areas A and B have the great variety of figurative carvings that are known throughout museums in Europe and the United States.[1] In Areas C and D, three-dimensional works do not appear or are more simply made. Within each region, it is often possible to determine the river and sometimes the particular village from which a carving comes. Styles may overlap in borderline villages. In some villages distant from one another it is also possible to find identical designs, but this appears only where people have fought within a village and separated — one section remaining at the original site, the other moving far upstream to sago grounds or to forestland not occupied by any particular group.

Ritual Carvings

Only Areas A and B have the elaborate feasts demanded by ancestral spirits; only in these two areas are the great ritual carvings made. The most famous of these, the ancestor pole or *bis*, was made for a feast celebrated when the men decided the time had come to avenge the deaths of those killed in battle or through magic, a feast that combined a headhunting raid with initiation ceremonies.

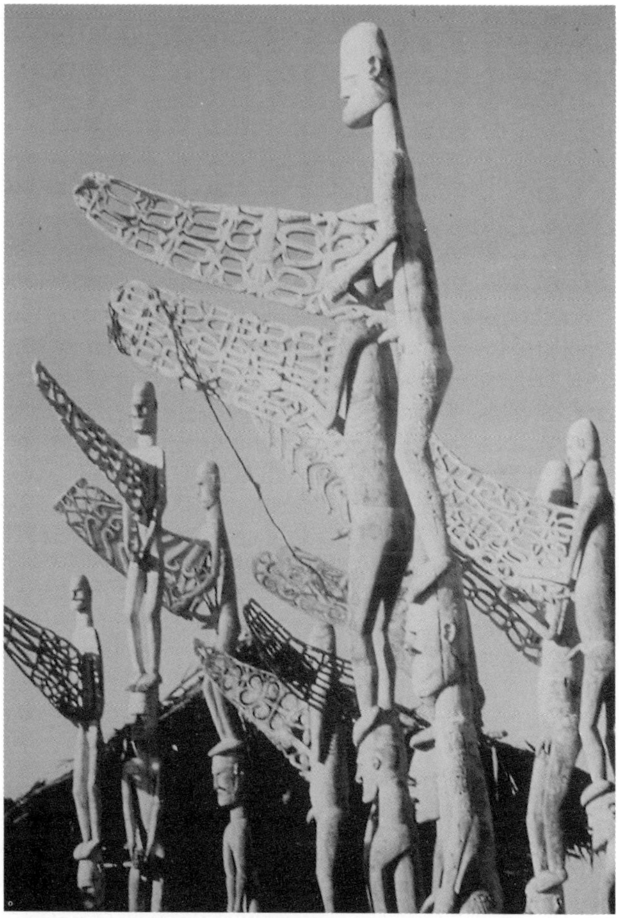

FIGURE 4.1. Ancestor poles at Bajun, Area A.

It is sometimes thought that these great poles were made throughout Asmat, but they were, in fact, limited to a region of the coast in Area A that includes the Bisman area and part of the Casuarina Coast, more or less from the village or Ewer in Flamingo Bay down to Otsjanep on the Ewta River. Although there is no longer any headhunting in this area, the *mbis* feast continues as part of ritual life in many villages. Recent outside influence has induced villages on the Fajit River and the villages of Japtambor, Santambor, and Bajun to begin to carve these ancestor poles, partly with the hope of selling them and partly as a showpiece for the rare group of tourists that might appear. However, even when poles are carved for sale, each carved figure is properly named and some kind of accompanying feast takes place.

Along the middle Siretsj or Eilanden River of Area A, the villages of Jaosakor, Awok, Kaimo, Damen, and Biwar Sor make a completely different type of ritual carving, the *basu suangkus*. This is sometimes called the cylinder log because of its shape: a section of tree trunk with its bark removed and with a carved head at each end. The words *basu suangkus* literally translate into "visible killed head" or, in my interpretation, the making visible of the heads of men who have been killed in battle. These carvings, like the ancestor poles, were made when the men felt prompted by feelings of revenge; a headhunting raid would occur not long after the carvings were finished. Two carved cylinder logs are put together with two uncarved logs to form a square into which sago worms are poured. These larvae are later distributed among the men according to their rank in the village, including those who will go on the raid into enemy territory and who may not eat of the worms until their return. The village of Betjew, not far from the villages given above, has a similar feast with a carving much the same as the *basu suangkus*, but quickly recognizable as coming only from Betjew.

Farther down the Casuarina Coast, still in Area A, where neither the *mbis* nor the *basu suangkus* is seen, long crocodile poles are carved as memorials to those killed by crocodiles. Nothing is known of the original rituals. Celebrations of this feast within the past several years give no

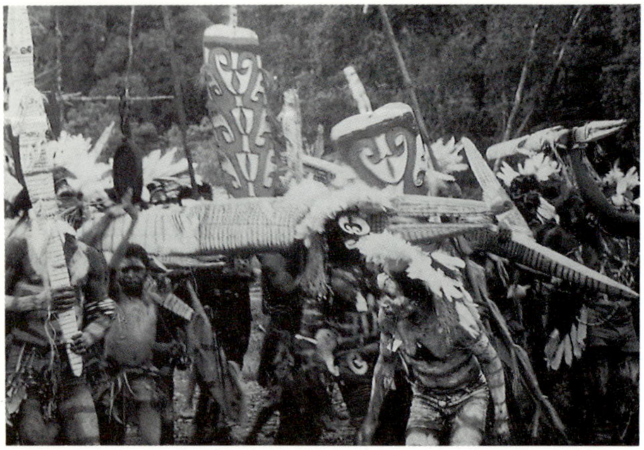

FIGURE 4.2. Crocodile pole feast, Santanbor, Area A.

hint as to what they had been like before contact.

Another kind of carving, the sago worm container, is made still farther down the coast, in the village of Semendoro. Present information insists that only four of these carvings exist today, all made at the same time in Semendoro around 1972. Each container represents a dead person. All were carved from a single piece of wood and have shoulder straps in back and a headband.

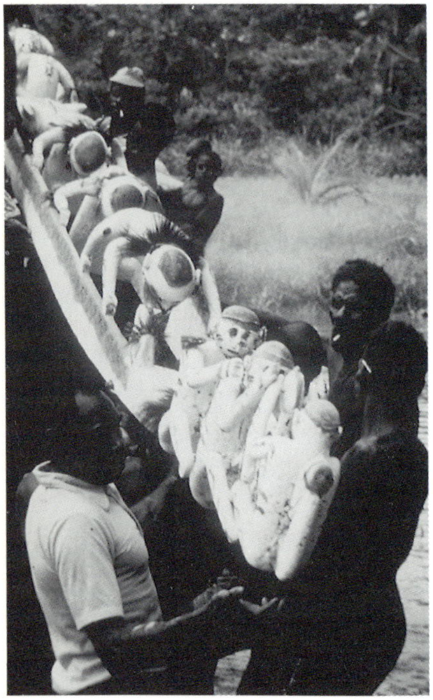

FIGURE 4.3. Soulship being loaded onto mission boat in Kapi, Area B.

Area B, in the northwest, has two known types of large ritual carvings: the soulship, or *wuramon*, and the *omu*, a word which has not been satisfactorily translated. The soulship is part of an initiation ceremony called the *emak cem* or bone house feast and is celebrated in the villages of Jamasj, Kapi, Ao, and As-Atat. The *emak cem* is the isolation house in which the initiates live for a period of two or three months. The house has a central beam that slants down to the floor and ends in the carved head of a crocodile. The soulship itself has various carved figures: *etsjo*, a human-like figure; *ambirak*, a crab-like animal that lives at the bottom of streams; *okom*, a z-shaped creature that lives in the same waters as the *ambirak*; and the *mbu*, a turtle, symbol of fertility. When the initiate leaves the isolation house, he crawls over the turtle or the *okom*, depending upon the village, and is then scarified.

The *omu* is a mysterious carving exclusive to three or four villages: Irogo, Pupis, and Momogo, and probably Weo. The *omu* are carved in pairs and tied onto the central beam of the men's house. In Momogu, it is said that the men dance on top of the beam; in Pupis a bride and groom dance along it, the groom coming from one end, the bride from the other. Sexual activity appears to be part of the ritual, taking place either on the beam itself or below it.

Farther upstream in Area C, among the Tjitak of the upper Eilanden, the Becking, the lower Wildeman, and the many inter-connecting rivers, carving is limited to shields, spears, digging sticks, bows and arrows, and pipes decorated with scratched or burned designs. The great feasts celebrated downstream are not seen here. The few drums of this area have little or no decoration, though the people of the villages of Senggo, Vakam, Daykot, and others say that their drums were taken from them by outsiders and destroyed.

Much of what has been said of the Tjitak is also true of the people of the Brazza River in Area D. Nothing yet is known of their ritual life.

Shields

The clearest way to show the distinction between the styles of the four areas may be through the shapes of the war shields.[2] Those of Area A are rectangular, narrowing slightly from top to bottom. A cylindrical form called the *cemen*, or penis, projects from the top. This may be a carved phallus, human figure, or human head. The shields of Area B are oval, wider near the bottom than the top and more curved than those of Area A. A clearly separated head section shows incised carving on a face which is sometimes called the head of a rayfish, *visi*, sometimes the head of a turtle, *mbu*, and sometimes the head of a cassowary, *pi*. Occasionally, a complete ancestor figure is carved within the outline of this head. The entire shape of the shield is phallic. Most of the shields of Area C are taller than those of other areas and have a wide surface; the point at the top is slightly rounded and the bottom is flattened. Area D shields of the Brazza River are carved like those of Area C in shape, but with the bottom rounder and the top often coming to a sharp point. All shields of Areas A and B use lime for white paint; lime can also be found on some shields of Area C but many villagers use kaolinite mud, the white normally found on shields of Area D.

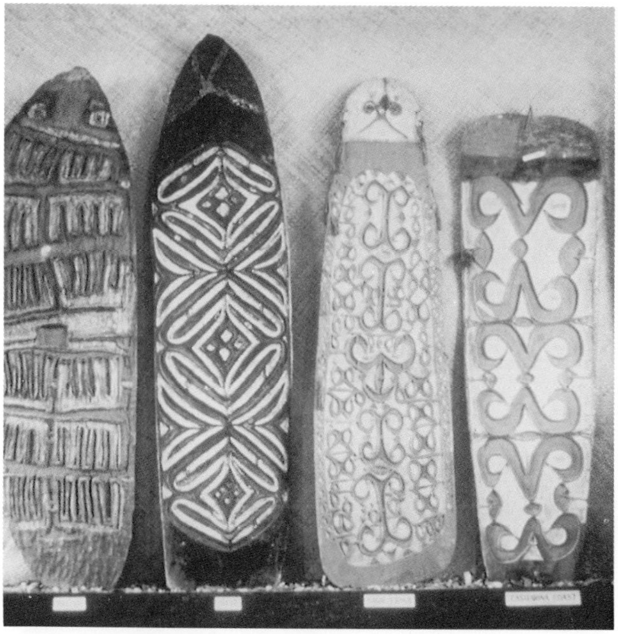

FIGURE 4.4. The four styles of Asmat shields.

In Area A, the bold designs may be put one above the other or side by side. The most common large designs are the shell nose-piece, the *ainor*, the cuscus tail, the ancestral figure, and the praying mantis in human form. Of particular interest is the *ainor* motif which appears only in Area A. No translation has yet been accepted for the design, but it is intended to frighten the enemy. When seen, the *ainor* so terrifies the enemy that he is immobilized, drops his weapons, and is then easily captured. There is also a series of smaller designs: the heads of hornbills and black king cockatoos, bone designs, navels, canoes, bowls, crocodile vaginas, flying fox feet, and the very common "S" design, *was wow*. The latter has been described in several villages as a clearing in the jungle; it is sometimes used as a place where men meet to talk about warfare and sometimes as a meeting place for sexual activity. The backs of Area A shields are painted white, with two vertical red zigzags edged with black. The handle is usually double-grip, though carried in one hand. A ridge runs from the handle to the top and to the bottom of the shield, often ending in a carved hand.

The body of shields of Area B most often contain the image of a flying fox, a motif repeated several times one above the other, down the center of the shield. Motifs of wading birds are also seen. These large designs are surrounded by smaller motifs explained as cuscus tails, whirlpools, larva tracks, wiggling snakes or worms, elbows and spirit hands, flying fox feet, and frog's legs. The back of the shields is vertically divided in half and painted white on one side, red on the other. The head is left white, though it may be incised with the features of the rayfish head on the front. The handles are single-grip, except for those of the upper Unir River area where they are double-grip.

Most of the shields of Area C have an abstracted human head at the top, a vertical hour-glass shape painted white or black that represents the forehead while the red sides are called cheeks or ears. The most commonly carved design is that of swirling water, *amos tabi* or *epmak mbi*, the symbol for water swirling down the sago trough. Other designs are fish stomach, rat teeth, bends in the river, and whirlpools. All handles of both Areas C and D are single-grip; the backs are not painted.

Shields of Area D have a human face at the top, with incised eyes, nose, and sometimes a mouth as well. The eyes and nose are painted white, with black around them. Designs are similar to those of Area C but little information has been gathered about them to date.

By narrowing down design information we can sometimes identify specific rivers and villages, as well as areas. Remaining with shields for a moment we find that it is difficult to identify the villages of Area A, partly because

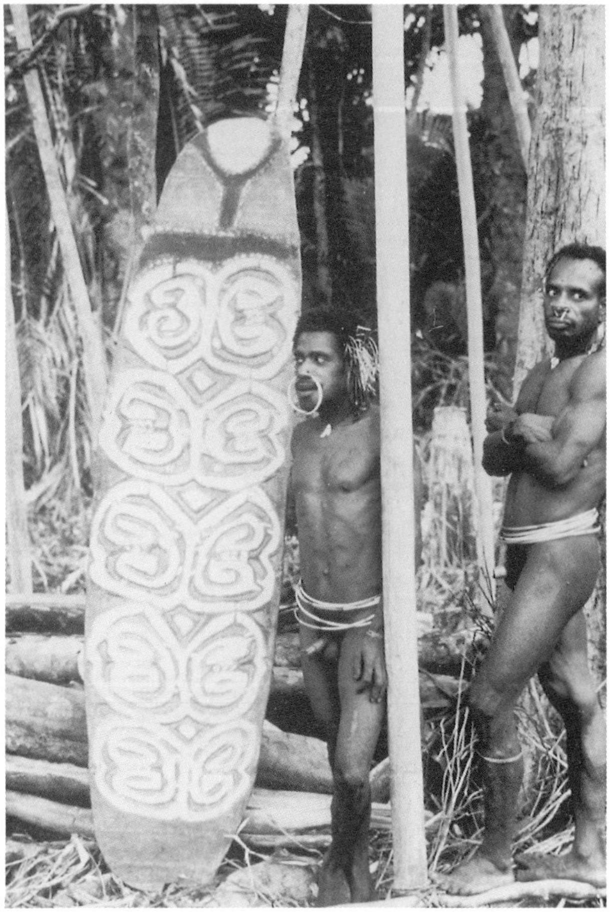

FIGURE 4.5. Shield in Area C with swirling water design.

the men in several villages south of the Ewta River did not carve shields in the not-so-distant past but traded for them with dog's tooth necklaces, stone axes, pandanus leaf mats, cuscus skins, and shells from the sandy beaches of the South Casuarina Coast. Shields were often captured in warfare and designs stolen in this way. There are certain groupings that do occur, however, in Area B. The village of Avemu is the only one to carve perforated diamond-shaped heads at the top of their shields. Cuscus tail and tree worm designs are carved in a regular vertical pattern unknown elsewhere except for the nearby village of Sagapu, which has a similarly regulated pattern of these same motifs. In Sagapu, however, the designs are more disorganized. The great painted mouth designs of the turtle and/or cassowary head appears only on shields from Pupis, Weo, and Momogu. In the village of Karmbis, originally on the Brazza River, now on the upper Siretsj at the junction of Areas A, C, and D, a new motif is being incised on the top of the shields that has double spiral eyes; the rest of the shield continues to conform with the designs of other villages of the Brazza.

Horns

The difference between Asmat horns of Area A and those of Area B is immediately apparent. Horns are made from a section of bamboo, with one end open, the other end with a pierced hole. In Area A, the end with the blowing hole is smoothly rounded and the general effect is clearly phallic. In Area B, the blowing hole end is cut off sharply and the open end frequently has two legs extending from it. Area C probably had simple undecorated horns in the past, if this assumption can be made from the two new horns found in Tamenim, a small village that recently combined with Senggo. No horns have been found in Area D.

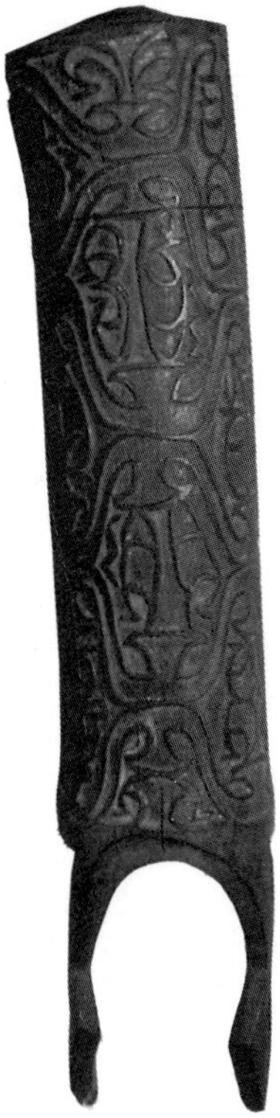

FIGURE 4.6. Bamboo horn with legs from Jamasj, Area B.

Tobacco Pipes

Smoking pipes are made in Areas A, C, and D. Area B may have had them in the past, but today all smokers there wrap tobacco in nipah leaves. All pipes consist of two sections, one made of bamboo which is permanent, the other of reed which burns down as the pipe is smoked. We are concerned here only with the bamboo section, usually elegantly carved and incised. In Area A, the older men usually use the pipes. In this area, the pipes are the smallest in Asmat, probably because the brackish waters of the swamp and tidal forest are not conducive to the growth of bamboo. The bamboo in which water is stored is traded from far upstream. The pipes used today in Area A are found only in villages along the Casuarina Coast — from Biwar Lait, near the Siretsj River, down to the Mappi region. The pipes of Area C are made of a heavy bamboo, with the smoking end rounded. In Area D, the bamboo is thinner and lighter, with both ends squarely cut off. The designs of all three areas are completely different from one another.

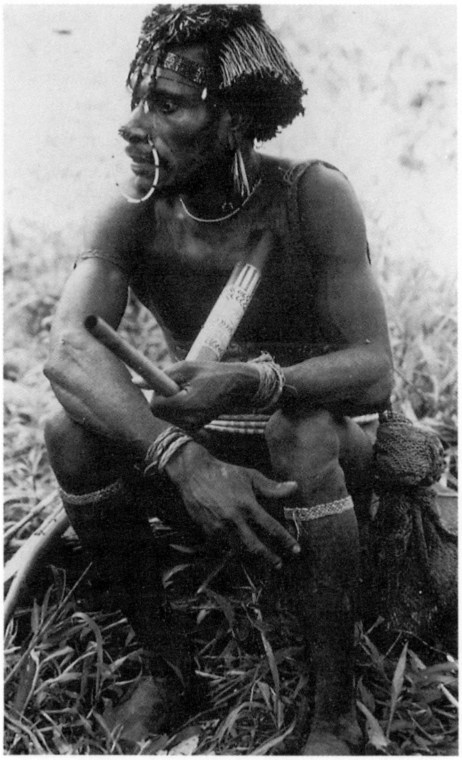

FIGURE 4.7. Area C pipe in Tajan.

Drums

Drums from the four areas are easily distinguished, though they are rare in Areas C and D. Drums have virtually disappeared in Area C, primarily due to contact with certain missionaries. In Area D, where there still has been little contact with outsiders, drums seem not to play as great a part in ritual life as in coastal and northwest Asmat. The basic difference between drums of Areas A and B is size, those of the south in Area A being much longer. It is not unusual to find drums there as long as 160 cm., while in Area B 60 cm. would be normal. There are also differences in design. Only in Area A, and primarily in the village of Atsj, is the *utsju* or banyan tree root design found. In the far south of the South Casuarina Coast, drums are influenced in motif and shape by those made by the Sawi people who live in enclaves surrounded by the Asmat.

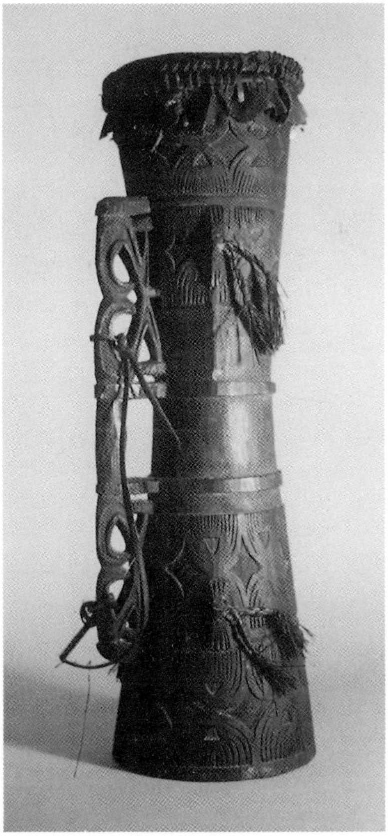

FIGURE 4.8. Drum from Jufri, with frog feet design, Area B.

Ndaise of Basim, on the Fajit River, carves figures on drums that are distinguished by humped shoulders and angular noses, chins, and hairline. At least two villages, Naneu and Buepis, carve a design as an overall pattern which is found only in one other village throughout Asmat, and that village — Jufri — is in Area B. In Jufri, what is referred to as a frog design is carved in a highly symmetrical manner, whereas the carvers on the Fajit River work more haphazardly. Unique to the village of As-Atat is a motif of rows of wiggling snakes. It originated with a carver who was jailed in Agats for taking revenge for the death of a relative. To pass the time in jail, he began carving drums and developed this zigzag motif, which was later copied by most carvers in As-Atat.

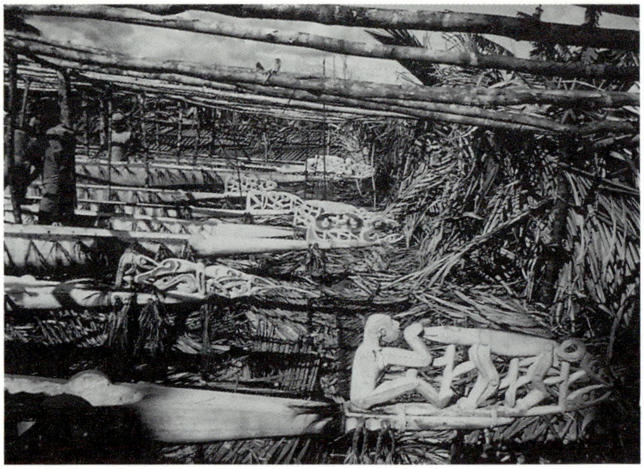

FIGURE 4.10. Display of new canoes in Jamasj, Area B.

Canoes

Canoes in Areas A and B may have elaborately decorated prowheads and edging incised with symbols. Those in Areas C and D are more simply carved, without embellishment of any kind.

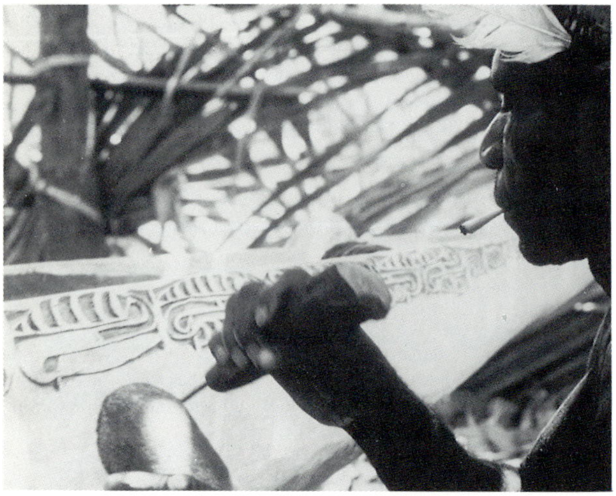

FIGURE 4.9. Edge of canoe being carved with praying mantis and hornbill designs.

Individual Styles

Some carvers have a readily recognizable style. Warsekomen, war chief of Sjuru and one of Zegwaard's most important informants, elaborately incised ironwood handles for stone axes in so refined a way that others could not duplicate them. It may even be that certain carvers

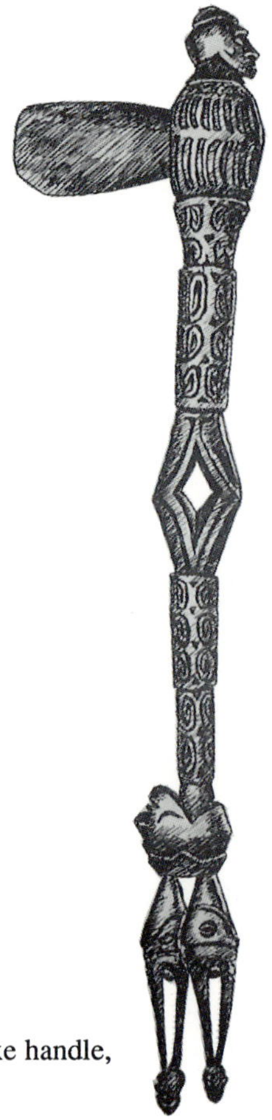

FIGURE 4.11. Beautifully decorated axe handle, made for sale, Area A.

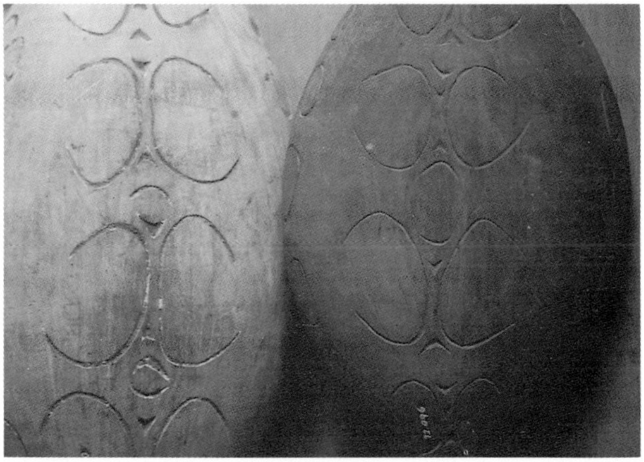

FIGURE 4.12. Wooden bowls incised on bottom with what may be the carver's signature, both made by Sesak in Esmapano, Area B.

"sign" their work with specific designs, such as a particular set of curlicues that no one else may use. This is apparent at present only for carvers of bowls in the northwest in Area B. Unfortunately, detailed information is scarce because of a lack of documentation in bowls collected early,as well as the decline in the making of wooden bowls. However, some carvers in the village of Komor and Esmapano have confirmed that only they use the whirls and curves on particular bowls; an examination of the undersides shows the obvious variations and similarlities.

Conclusion

Biwar Laut has figure carvings with elongated bodies, and faces with long noses and a projecting mouth. The cluster of villages between the Asewetsj and Siretsj Rivers may be grouped together as having a related style that often makes it impossible to distinguish those made in one village from those of another, although the village of Per tends to have carvings with the larger noses and smaller chins.

This paper does not consider all the differences in Asmat carving and design, nor all the types of carvings. Paddles, for instance, may often be identified as having been made by particular carvers. Spears, on the other hand, rarely can be recognized as the work of a specific carver or village, although the blades on spears common to Areas A and B are much smaller in Area C, and completely disappear in Area D. Carved wooden bowls, neckrests, and carrying bags of sago frond have been found only in Areas A and B, but further research is necessary before these and other artifacts can be properly categorized.

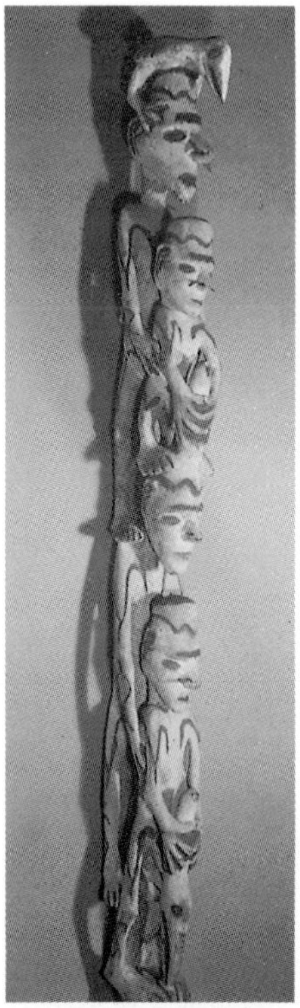

FIGURE 4.13. Ancestor figures from Biwar Laut, Area A.

Notes

My fieldwork in Asmat took place between 1975 and 1983, during which time I spent a total of four years in the area, cataloging the collection of well over a thousand artifacts at the Asmat Museum of Culture and Progress in Agats.

1. It has been known since the early days of missionaries in Asmat that the carving of ancestor poles, soulships, crocodile poles, and so on was limited to certain regions, but few exact locations were specified. With the help of several Catholic missionaries, I was able to travel throughout Asmat, including completely untouched areas. In this way, I learned the limits of most types of carvings. In working on the museum's catalog, I drew some 380 artifacts in detail and was thereby able to categorize most of the objects.

2. Konrad, Böhning, and Sowada (1975) divided Asmat shields into two types, with Type A in the south and east and Type B in the north, northwest, and northeast. In 1975 I subdivided Type B shields into two categories, B and C. Later Gunter Konrad further subdivided category C into Types C and D.

5

Mon Canoes of the Western Solomon Islands

DEBORAH B. WAITE

Canoes repeatedly evoked admiring comments among early visitors to the Solomon Islands. Alvaro de Mendaña recorded in 1568 that they were "Very well-made and very light; they are shaped like a crescent, the largest holding about thirty persons. . . . Their speed in rowing is marvelous" (Amherst and Thomson 1901 1:109).

In 1767 the French explorer Philip Carteret mentioned canoe construction and decoration. A canoe seized by his ship off the northwestern tip of Malaita was "Large enough to carry eight or ten men and . . . was very neatly built with planks well jointed; it was adorned with shell-work and figures rudely painted; and the seams were covered with a substance somewhat like our black putty, but it appeared to be of a better consistence" (Fleurieu 1791:68).

Just two years later another Frenchman, Jean François de Surville, described canoes which he saw at Port Praselin on the north coast of Santa Isabel Island as

> constructed with good sense and finished with much skill, they are not formed of a trunk of a tree made hollow by stone implements or fire . . . but are made of pieces put together. In the small canoes, the planks are not more than a third of an inch in thickness and in working them they form on the inside a kind of loop which at intervals [is] tied strongly with rattan to ribs of wood bent in the shape of the boat and serving as its frame; nor are the planks held together by any other means; the joints are stopped with a black mastic, tolerably hard, which renders these frail vessels impenetrable to the water. The prow and stern are raised very high, apparently for the purpose of defending the warriors in them from arrows, by presenting either end to the enemy; and, in general, they are ornamented with pieces of mother-of-pearl forming different designs and applied with mastic . . . . One was seen fifty-six feet long by three and one half feet broad. (Fleurieu 1791:134)

C. M. Woodford, First Resident Commissioner of the Solomon Islands, and A. C. Haddon, anthropologist, have provided detailed information regarding the different types of canoes in the Solomons as well as their construction (1909, 1937). This paper does not repeat their analysis, nor does it attempt to examine types other than the mon, the crescent-shaped canoe with upraised prow and stern that is referred to in the earliest writings. The selective focus has been determined largely by available literature, in particular, the detailed field data of A. M. Hocart for Simbo Island in the New Georgia island group.

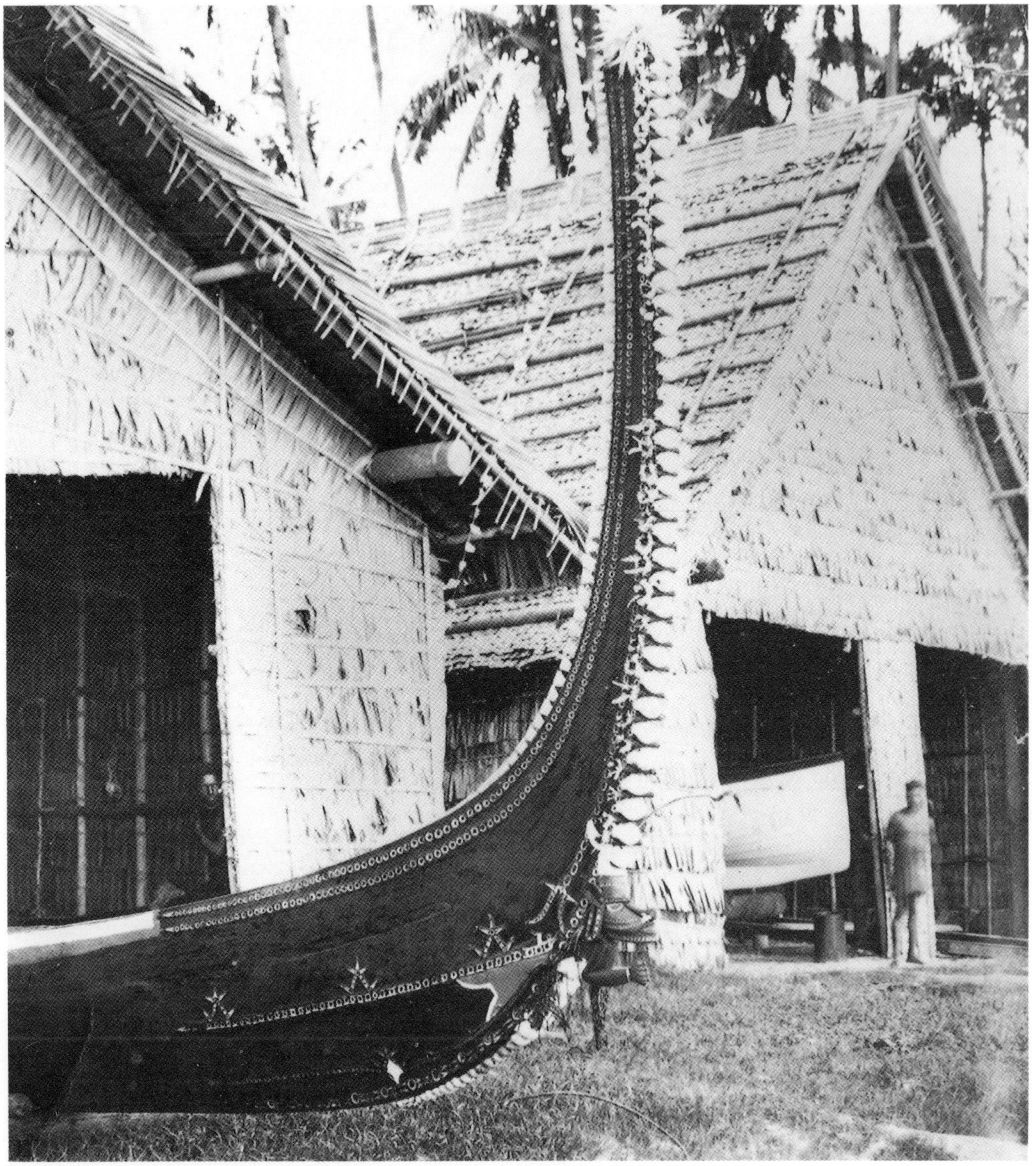

FIGURE 5.1. Canoe and canoe houses. Vella La Vella. British Museum, Photo Archive No. LXXII/13. Photograph courtesy of the British Museum.

Although numerous early recorded descriptions of canoes exist, photographs and drawings of *mon* canoes from the Central and Western districts come largely from a twenty-three year period, 1887 to 1910. This was a time of dramatic social change in the islands, marked particularly by the cessation of headhunting brought about by order of the British colonial government as well as missionary influence and native initiative (Zelenietz 1983, White 1983).[1] Many *mon* canoes had served as war canoes, and large numbers were burned or otherwise destroyed. Some survived, and periodically others were built according to traditional specifications; this occurred as late as 1967 in one instance (figs. 5.3 and 5.4).

Canoes of the *mon* type were employed on Alu and Faisi islands in the Bougainville Straits, Choiseul, the north-west coast of Santa Isabel, the New Georgia Islands, and

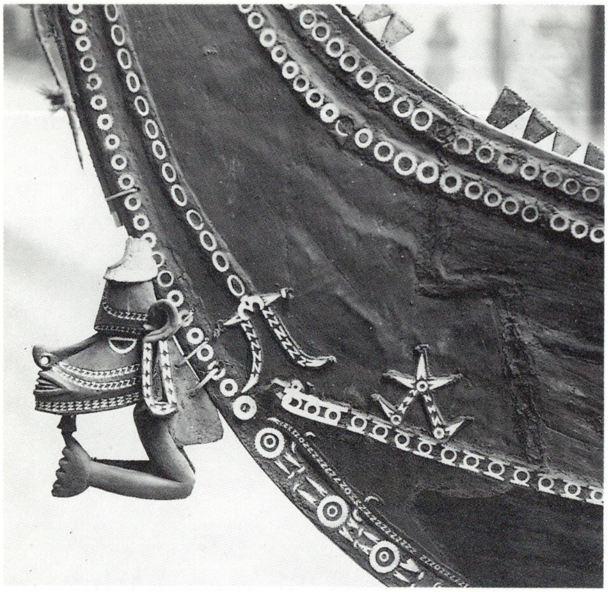

FIGURE 5.2. Detail of canoe shown in figure 5.1 Vella La Vella. British Museum 1927.10-22.1. Photograph courtesy of the British Museum.

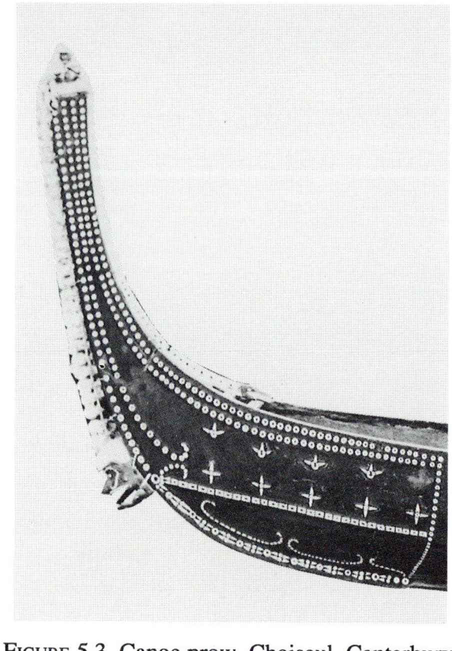

FIGURE 5.3. Canoe prow. Choiseul. Canterbury Museum, Christchurch, New Zealand, 5935. Photograph courtesy of the Centerbury Museum.

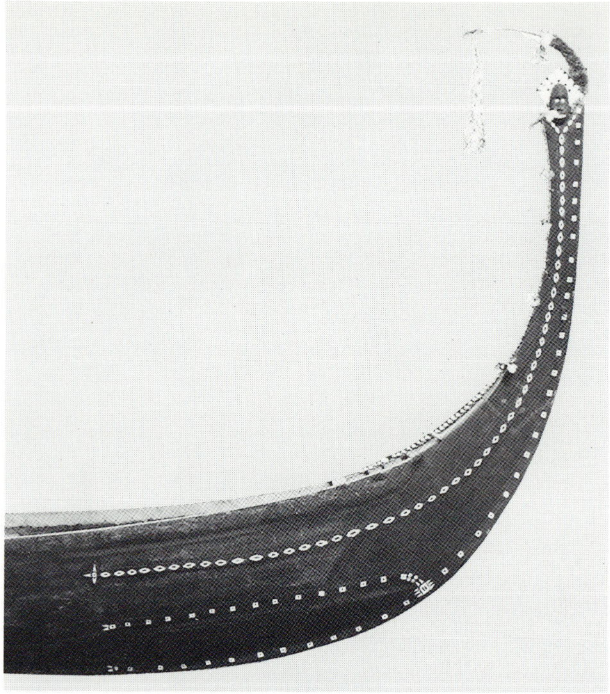

FIGURE 5.4. Canoe stern. Choiseul. Canterbury Museum, Christchurch, New Zealand, 5935. Photograph courtesy of the Canterbury Museum.

Florida Island. Reports of their construction and decoration indicate a certain degree of regional specialization. Penny, for example, indicated that the best builders of the Florida Island *peko* (*mon*) canoe lived on Santa Isabel, although canoes of other types apparently were built locally (Penny 1888:79-80). Hocart recorded one case of prepared canoe boards which were brought from Roviana to be assembled on Simbo (Hocart 1931:308; 1935:102). Reports of local *mon* canoe construction also come from Alu, the Marovo Lagoon (New Georgia Island), the Kómbakotta district on the east coast of Renongo (Ganongga) Islands, Simbo, and Vella La Vella (Ribbe 1895:238; Somerville 1897:369; Woodford 1909:509-10; Hocart MS).

Canoe Decoration

SHELL INLAY

Decorated *mon* canoes constituted works of art (fig. 5.1). Wooden carvings were attached to the bow as well as to prow and stern peaks. Rows of ovulum shells and triangu-

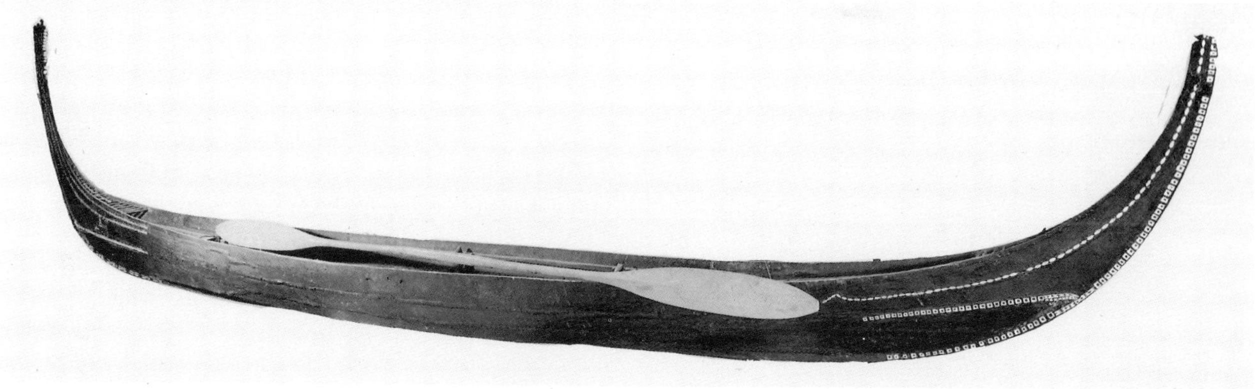

FIGURE 5.5. Canoe. Merseyside County Council Museums, Liverpool, 55-144. Photograph courtesy of the Merseyside County Council Museums.

lar pieces of tridacna gigas clam shell known as *barava* (cf. note 3) were fastened along the upraised prow. Sides of canoes from Choiseul, Santa Isabel, and the New Georgia and Florida islands were richly ornamented with designs produced by inlaying thousands of small pieces of pearl shell into parinarium nut paste.

> This inlaying process is a tedious job, as each piece of mother-of-pearl has to be rubbed into shape on a stone or filed and then stuck into the cement while it is plastic. The rubbers and filers — files are in great request for this purpose — . . . need not be skilled workmen. When a chief has a canoe built, he requisitions his dependants for these prepared pieces — 1,000 or 2,000 per village — which the artist fashions into devices and patterns on the sides of the canoe. I have heard of 50,000 of those pieces being used to inlay one canoe. This entails considerable expense in food and native money. (Penny 1888:79-80)

The type of canoe which Penny wrote about was probably a *mon*, but this is not specified; nor did Penny state whether he was discussing the practice as it occurred on Florida, where he resided, or on Isabel, where the best *mon* canoes allegedly were built. Hocart acknowledged that, on Simbo, decoration of the raised prow and stern required skill demanding the work of experts in the case of "finer canoes." Half a dozen men were mentioned to him as being experts. They reputedly acquired their skills by watching and learning, not through a formal apprenticeship system (Hocart 1935:97).

Traditionally, pieces of shell were inlaid in rows that repeated the upswept curve of prow and stern, while

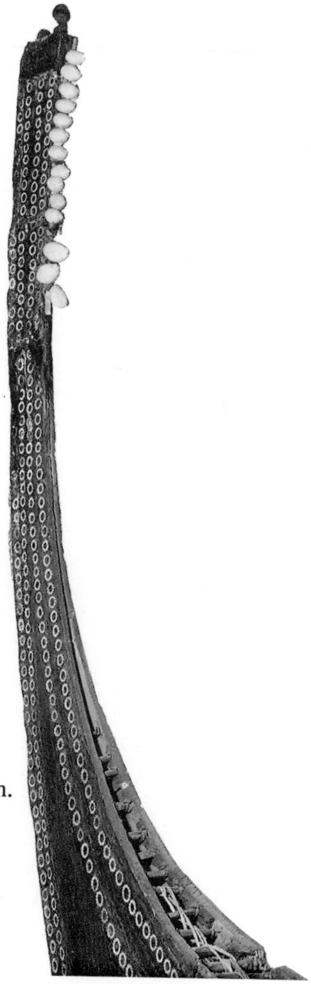

FIGURE 5.6. Canoe stern. Merseyside County Council Museums, Liverpool, 55-144. Photograph courtesy of the Merseyside County Council Museums.

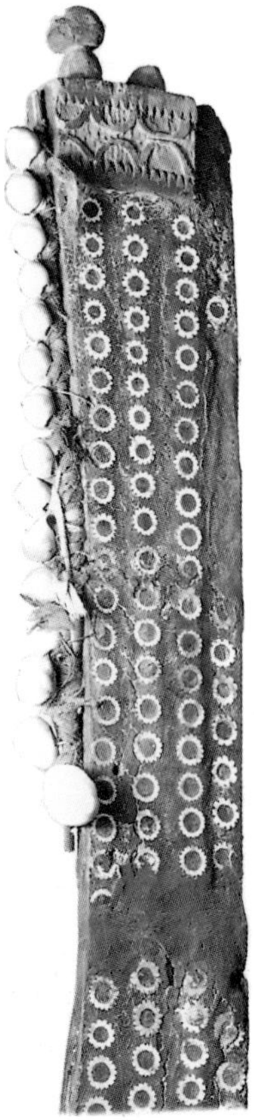

FIGURE 5.7. Detail of canoe stern. Merseyside County Council Museums, Liverpool, 55-144. Photograph courtesy of the Merseyside County Council Museums.

intervening spaces could be occupied by smaller design units. Shell pieces were cut in circular, triangular, rectangular, Z, and X shapes. Recorded evidence reveals specific names for the differently shaped pieces.[2]

The admittedly limited recorded information indicates that the pieces of inlay fall into three categories: those named according to their shape, those which reproduce personal ornaments (*lanono* or *hokata, hinuili* and *barava*),[3] and those with natural prototypes such as fish, birds, seeds, stars, and clouds. There are discrepancies: A Z-shaped design was given a name, *asepaleo*, that referred to its shape according to a Roviana informant and, on Choiseul, *nöle paleo*, signifying the jawbone of the *paleo* fish. The fish referent, *paleo*, is common to both. Pieces of the same shape, that is, Zs, Xs, and rings were more restricted (e.g., *kela, kuru*, and other shapes from Choiseul). Variations among the periods of manufacturing and conditions under which the information was acquired should not be overlooked and probably account in part for discrepancies.

Woodford provided terms for the parts of the *mon* canoe on New Georgia and Vella La Vella including the inlay, but named patterns created by the inlay work rather than specific pieces of inlay. *Kanda* (New Georgia) and *kerava* (Vella La Vella) were apparently general terms for shell inlay work (cf. *kada* in the Waterhouse dictionary). The "inlaid ornament on the stern representing [a] rainbow" was called *busambigombigo* (New Georgia) or *goai* (Vella La Vella). *Busagamutu* was a "triangular white patch on [the] lower part of stem and stern" (New Georgia). Woodford also mentioned an arm painted in white on the side of the canoe after a successful headhunting expedition: *limabovo* (New Georgia) or *kurukuru* (Vella La Vella). Supposedly, if rendered on the prow end, the painted arm indicated that male heads had been obtained in a hunt; if on the stern, the heads were female (Woodford 1909:512-13, pl. XLI; cf. Hocart 1931:313).

The patterns in which pieces of inlay were arranged appear to reflect regional variations. Generally, the inlaid section extended from the tip of the prow or stern down along the sides for from one-fifth to one-third the total length of the canoe. Shell pieces were inlaid in single or double rows following the curving outer and inner contours of prow and stern. Circular pieces were most commonly used for these rows, but rectangular, triangular (*barava*, or lozenge-shaped pieces could be utilized (figs. 5.4 and 5.5). Other patterns were inlaid between these rows, such as the short semicircular and stepped lines seen on canoes from Roviana (Woodford 1909:pl. XLII; Brown 1908:plate opposite p. 412; Thorpe 1923:289). Widely-spaced *kela* and *kuru* designs were inlaid along the sides of canoes from Choiseul at the prow end (figs. 5.3, 5.5, 5.8; cf. Ribbe 1895:plates 14 a-c; Festetics de Tolna 1903:353).[4] Designs comprised of a *kuru* element to which an inverted V is appended adorn canoes from Vella La Vella (figs. 5.1 and 5.2; cf. Elkington 1907:plate opposite p. 100).[5] A Florida Island canoe has wide U-shaped patterns at the prow end which alternate with designs resembling *kela* near the bottom of the canoe (fig. 5.9).

Shell-inlaid patterns of two canoes are marked by the absence of radial motifs such as the *kela* and *kuru*. The two middle rows of shell which lead down from the prow peak terminate in a pattern resembling the head of a crocodile, an image found in the same position on canoes of the

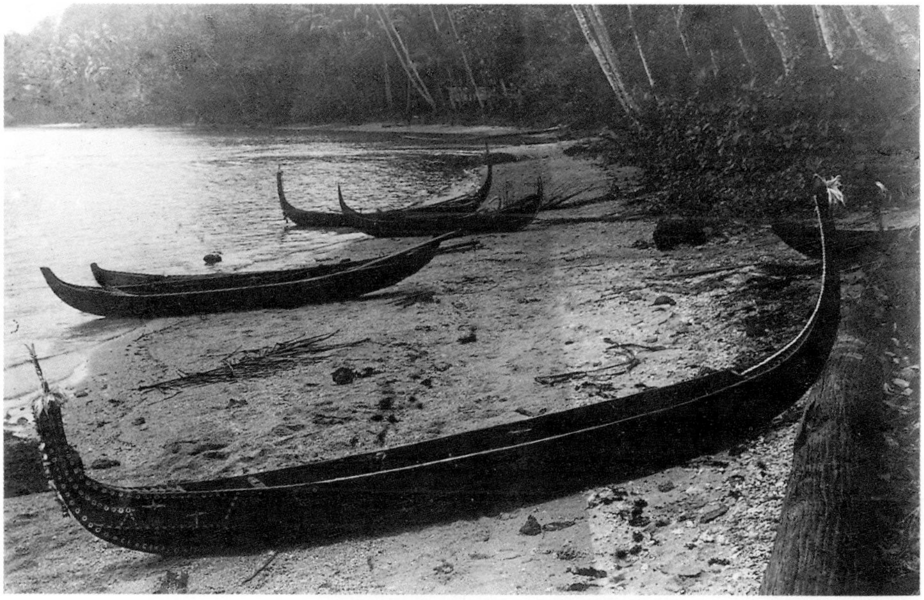

FIGURE 5.8. Canoes of Choiseul. Museum für Völkerkunde, Staatliche Museum Preussisches Kulturbesitz, West Berlin. Photo Archive No. VIIIc 1464. Photograph courtesy of the Museum für Völkerkunde.

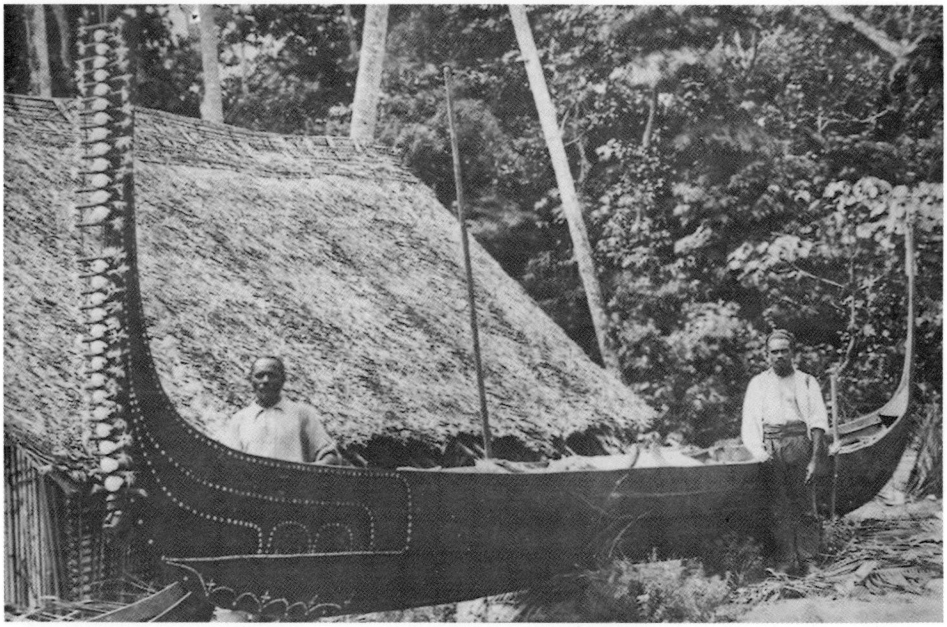

FIGURE 5.9. Canoe. Florida. Beattie photograph. Auckland Institute and Museum. Photo Archive No. 35039. Photograph courtesy of the Auckland Institute and Museum.

biabina type from Santa Isabel[6] and rendered as a small carved three-dimensional head positioned at the end of a row of clam shell carvings on the rim of a canoe from Choiseul (fig. 5.3). One canoe displaying an inlaid crocodile head has no geographical attribution (fig. 5.10; British Museum Q72.Oc.85). The other, presented to the Ulster Museum, Belfast, in 1898, may have originated from Gavutu (Florida) or Gatukai (Nggatokai) Island (fig. 5.11).[7]

A canoe with prow decoration that departs radically from the traditional shell inlay was photographed on Vella

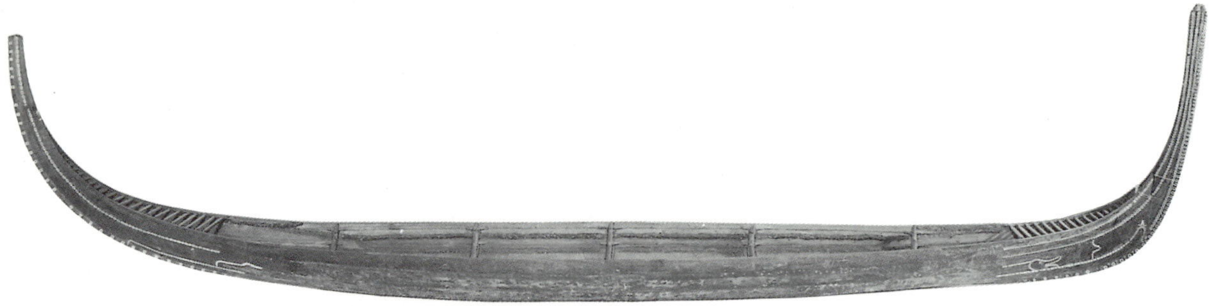

FIGURE 5.10. Canoe. British Museum 072.Oc.85. Photograph courtesy of the British Museum.

La Vella by Edward A. Salisbury (1922). It was one of a group of war canoes said to have been brought out of hiding to take part in a staged headhunting expedition which Salisbury filmed. On the upraised prow superimposed panels of anthropomorphic figures and designs resembling canoe prows alternate with narrow bands of geometric motifs (fig. 5.12). This imagery, particularly the two lowermost sections of paired curving "canoe" designs, has close parallels in the decorated facades of two small huts built to contain skulls of the deceased as well as a monument built on Roviana for the trophy skulls of the big-man Ingova (Festetics de Tolna 1903:331; Brown

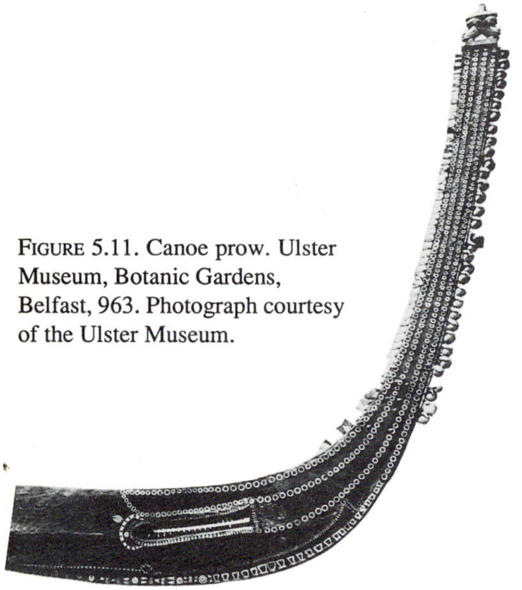

FIGURE 5.11. Canoe prow. Ulster Museum, Botanic Gardens, Belfast, 963. Photograph courtesy of the Ulster Museum.

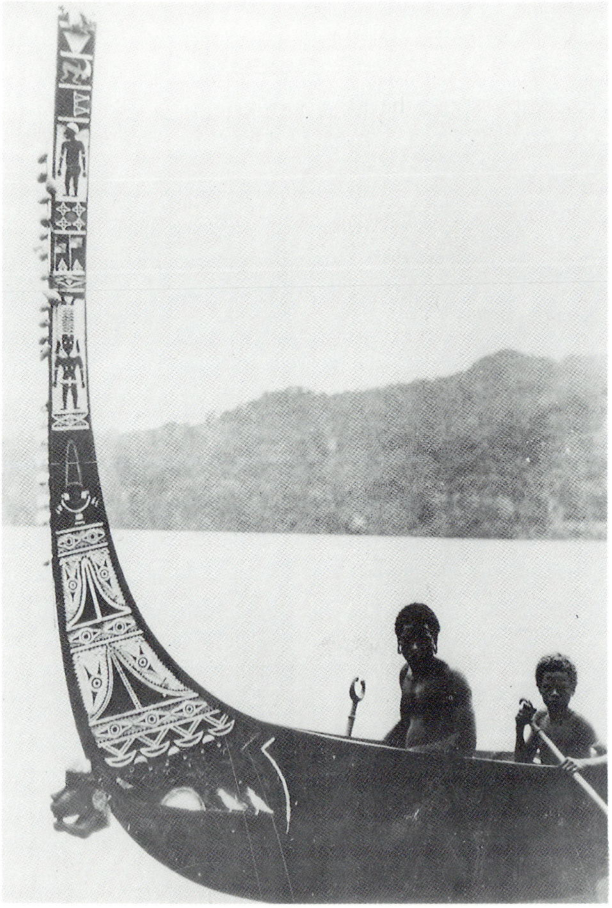

FIGURE 5.12. Canoe photographed on Vella La Vella. Edward A. Salisbury photograph. Smithsonian Institution Photo Archive No. 85-3854. Photograph courtesy of the Smithsonian Institution.

1908:opposite page 516; Stöhr 1972:180, illus. 427). The similarities suggest that this canoe might have been captured from Roviana.

CANOE CARVINGS

Carved prow and stern ornaments completed the decorative assemblage of a *mon*. An anthropomorphic figurehead was lashed to the bows of *mon* canoes from Choiseul, Santa Isabel, the New Georgia Islands, and Florida. Most consisted of an anthropomorphic head with arms raised to the chin (figs. 5.2, 5.13), but a few were seated figures with arms raised to the chin and elbows on the knees (fig. 5.14). They were termed *njununjunu* (Simbo), *musumusu* (New Georgia), or *totoishu* (Marovo Lagoon, New Georgia). According to Somerville's informants in the Marovo Lagoon, their function was largely protective: "Low down on the prow above the waterline the head and shoulders of a 'debbledebbleum' called Totoishu is suspended.... The

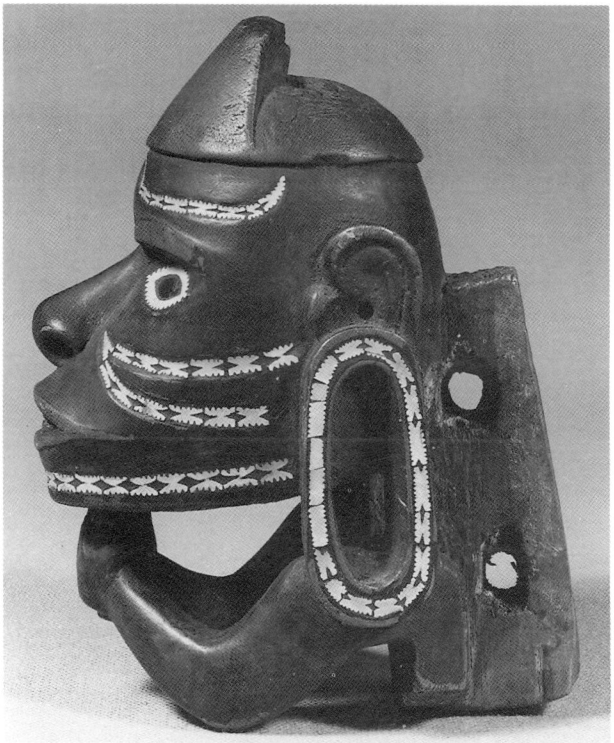

FIGURE 5.13. Canoe prow figurehead. National Museum, Copenhagen, Iall. H. 21.5 cm. Photograph courtesy of the National Museum.

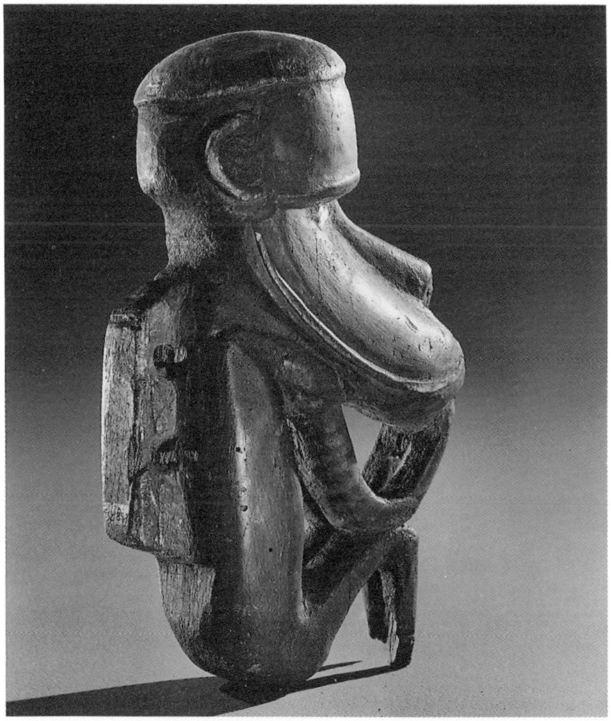

FIGURE 5.14. Canoe prow figurehead. Field Museum of Natural History, Chicago, Fuller Collection, 1895.22.162. H. 55.3 cm. Photograph courtesy of the Pitt-Rivers Museum.

function of this Totoishu is to keep off the Kesoko, or water fiends, which might otherwise cause the winds and waves to overset the canoe, so that they might fall on and devour its crew" (1897:271).

A board surmounted by a pair of carved anthropomorphic or frigate bird heads might be lashed to the bow just below the figurehead (cf. Codrington 1891:296; Edge-Partington and Heape 1890 I:204, no. 5).

Three types of images might be carved at the tip of the canoe prow. One was a seated anthropomorph with a frigate bird replacing the head; this was identified as a being named Kesoko (fig. 5.15; cf. Elkington 1907:opposite page 98; Somerville 1897:384; Hocart 1937:35, 38). Six examples of this image have been collected on New Georgia Island in the vicinity of Ramada Island in the Nggerasi Lagoon and the Marovo Lagoon. Five additional canoe carvings closely comparable in imagery and style include a seated image with prognathic head (fig. 5.16); a

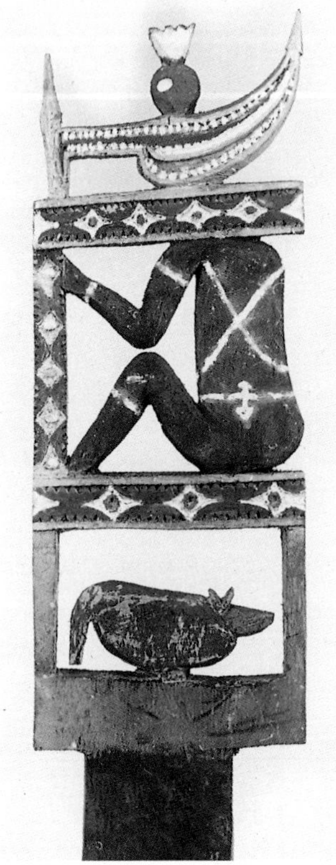

FIGURE 5.15. Canoe carving. Hoava District, Ramada Island, New Georgia. Pitt-Rivers Museum, Oxford University, Summerville Collection, 1895.22.162. H. 55.3 cm. Photograph courtesy of the Pitt-Rivers Museum.

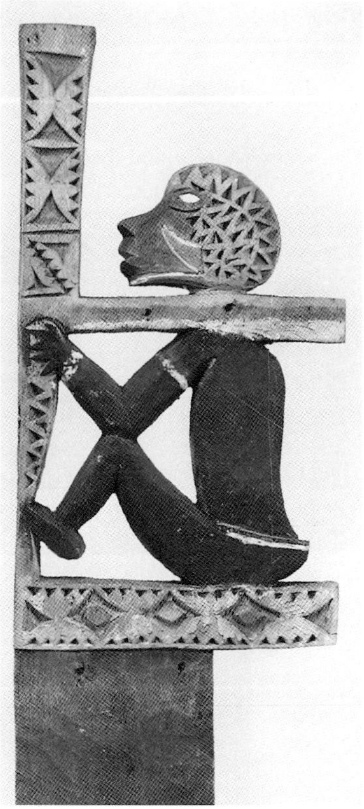

FIGURE 5.16. Canoe carving. Pitt Rivers Museum, Oxford University, Monro Collection, 1926.23.55. H. 47.6 cm. Photograph courtesy of the Pitt-Rivers Museum.

pair of seated headless anthropomorphs, their heads replaced by frigate birds (Australian Museum, Sydney, E35025); a bird with prognathic anthropomorphic face (Auckland Museum and Institute, no number); a frigate bird depicted on top of a spiral form (fig. 5.17); and a profile anthropomorphic head (Waite 1979:250, fig. 13-8). Only the first of the five, the anthropomorphic figure, was referred to as Kesoko (Hocart 1937:35, 38; Somerville 1897:384). These carvings, together with two prow/stern carvings representing crocodiles (Pitt-Rivers Museum 1894.26.47.1-2; Gathercole, Kaeppler, and Newton 1979:231, fig. 15.12) were painted in blue, white, and yellow instead of the ubiquitous black paint with shell inlay. All were embellished with low-relief carved images of *barava*, the triangular tridacna clam shell charms fastened to the inner edge of the canoe prow.

Traditions from Simbo and the Marovo Lagoon, New Georgia, described Kesoko as a spirit associated with net fishing and, like the other net spirits, with the crane. He

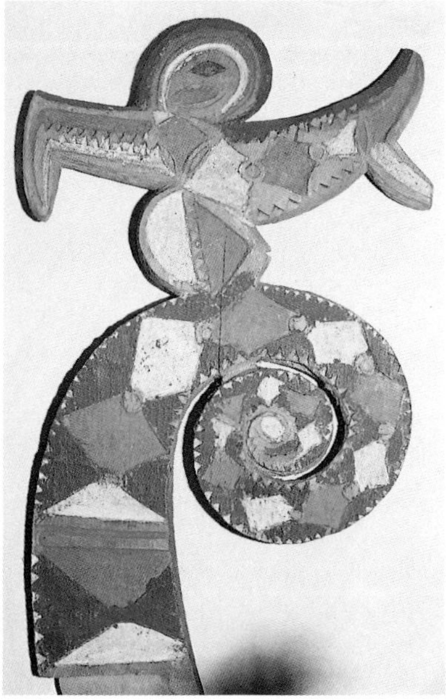

FIGURE 5.17. Canoe prow carving, New Georgia. Pitt-Rivers Museum, Oxford University, Monro Collection, 1926.23.57, 1924. Photograph by Deborah Waite.

was said to have only one leg, a feature evident in the seated profile figures — especially since these figures are not, strictly speaking, completely in profile; their backs are rendered in full, as revealed by the crossed bandoliers which appear in figure 5.15. A three-dimensional seated figure with prognathic face clearly reveals the single leg and arm said to be features of Kesoko (fig. 5.19; cf. Cambridge Museum for Archaeology and Ethnology Z219). "[He] is said to live in the sea and to be able to command the wind and waves, to capsize canoes; and when this is accomplished it falls upon the occupants and devours them. . . . His power is combatted by the Totoishu" (Somerville 1897:384).

Hocart hypothesized that there may have been a belief in two Kesokos, as suggested in a myth about One-Leg and Three-Legs (Hocart 1937:35, 38). He was also told that Kesoko was "man old time," a belief perhaps echoing the recorded former existence on Simbo of a *mbangara*, or district manager, named Kesoko (Hocart MS 3.5).

A more recently collected tradition from Roviana identified Kesoko with the prow figurehead and described him as

> man-like in form but physically invisible. Kesoko was believed to have functioned as a pilot of the great *tomako* (canoe) through unknown waters, passages, reefs, and . . . to [have] look[ed] out for enemies to see that none escaped. . . . The feet of Kesoko were short and his mouth was like that of a frigate bird or a seagull. . . . Kesoko was an expert fisherman and . . . in the past [he] was the patron of fishing for the Vuraghare *mbutambutu* [clan] of Roviana. (Beti 1977:40-47)

According to Roviana myth, Kesoko was a headhunter who joined forces with two boys from Mburaghusu Island in taking heads near Wagina Island south of Choiseul. In the myth, he showed the boys how to take heads as well as how to dry and preserve them (pp. 40-47). Kesoko was, thus, associated with net fishing, headhunting, and bonito fishing. The last association was legitimized by the presence of images of frigate birds on Kesoko carvings (cf. the Roviana tradition recorded by Beti). The sight of frigate birds and white *elekai* birds in the distance traditionally inaugurated the bonito fishing season on Simbo; the birds fed upon smaller fish that swam with the bonito (Hocart 1935:102).

Paired anthropomorphic heads depicted back-to-back

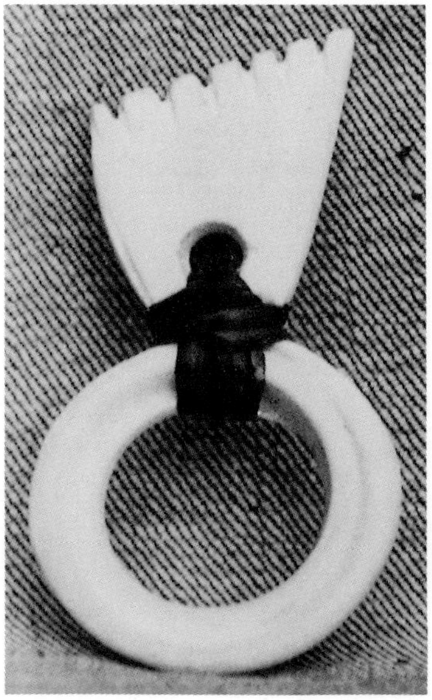

FIGURE 5.18. *Serebulu* charm. Rukuru village, N. Vanguru, Marovo Lagoon, New Georgia. Solomon Islands Museum, 72.160. H. 8.7 cm. Photograph by Deborah Waite.

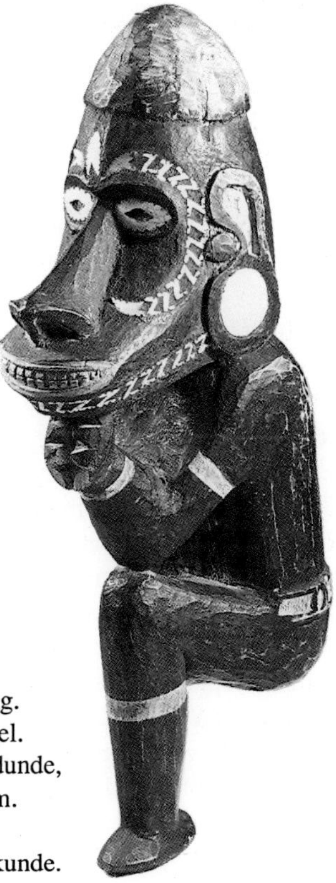

FIGURE 5.19. *Kesoko* carving. Wulegar village, Santa Isabel. Rijksmuseum voor Volkendunde, Leiden, 1134-87. H. 31.5 cm. Photograph courtesy of the Rijksmuseum voor Volkenkunde.

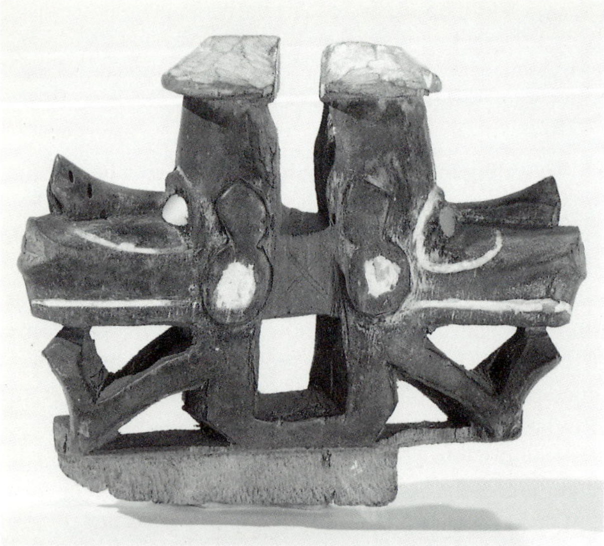

FIGURE 5.20. Canoe prow peak carving. Museum for Archaeology and Ethnology, Cambridge University, Rivers Collection, Z225. H. 9 cm. Photograph courtesy of the the Museum for Archaeology and Ethnology.

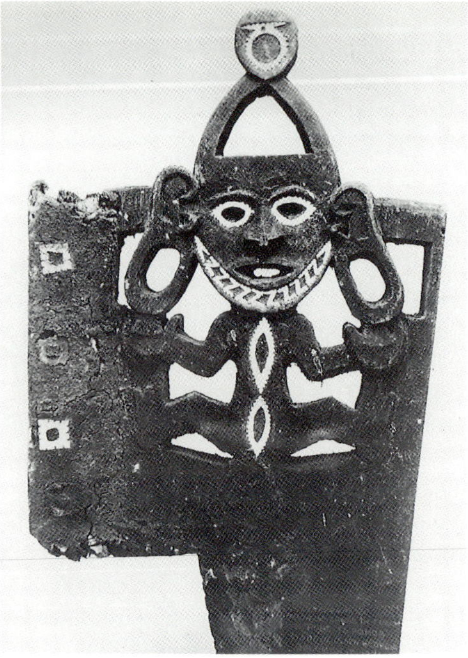

FIGURE 5.21. Canoe carving, *Hope ta Ponda.* Marovo Lagoon, New Georgia. Pitt-Rivers Museum, Oxford University, Somerville, 1895.22.204. H. 47.7 cm. Photograph courtesy of the Pitt-Rivers Museum.

adorned prow and stern tips on canoes from the New Georgia island group and Choiseul (figs. 5.11, 5.20). The prow peak heads were called *beku* on New Georgia or *gelana* on Vella La Vella (Woodford 1909:512, pl. XLII). On Simbo, *beku* apparently signified an image but not necessarily a spirit (Lanyon-Orgill 1969:68).[8] Stern peak heads were called *batungela* on New Georgia, or, again, *gelana* on Vella La Vella (Woodford 1909:513, pl. XLIV). These were flat Janus heads that faced starboard and port, whereas the three-dimensional heads on the prow faced fore and aft (fig. 5.4; Barraud 1972:fig. 8; Woodford 1909:513, pl. XLIV).

Two carvings from the Marovo Lagoon, New Georgia, were collected by Somerville and identified as *hope ta ponda*. Both are frontal images whose upraised hands support their huge earrings (e.g., fig. 5.21; cf. fig. 5.3). One is a displayed figure[9] and the other is standing.[10] A circular *hinuili* pearl shell ornament is inlaid at the top of the head of each image. *Hope*, according to Somerville, were "good spirits" who lived in the sun, moon, and stars. *Ponda*, "their special friend," lived in the shooting stars. *Ponda* or *pondo*, apparently also rendered as *sondo*, referred in addition to the "abiding place of souls" (cf. Hocart 1922:95). Somerville referred to *hope* as "human emanations" as opposed to *manggota* spirits of land and sea among whom he included Kesoko (Somerville 1897:383-84). On New Georgia, these two images may, thus, have been looked upon as ancestral images in contrast to Kesoko and *totoishu* (prow figurehead). Hocart, however, classified Kesoko as a *tomate*, spirit of the dead, along with the cranes and *elekai* birds which allegedly were also *tomate* (Hocart 1937:40).

Canoes from Faisi and Alu lack shell inlay decoration and prow figureheads. Anthropomorphs and anthropomorphic heads rendered three-dimensionally (*beku*) and as flat carvings painted identically on both sides (*bosara*) adorned prow and stern peaks (Woodford 1909:509 and pl. XL). Stylistically, they differed completely from their New Georgia counterparts despite similarities in nomenclature (figs. 5.22 and 5.23).

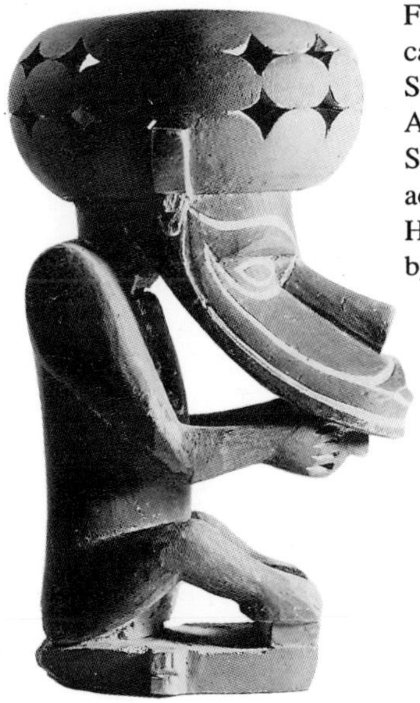

FIGURE 5.22. Canoe carving. Bougainville Straits Islands. Australian Museum, Sydney, E 43957, acquired 1937. H. 27.4 cm. Photograph by Deborah Waite.

The Ritual Context

Hocart recorded an account of canoe construction by Sanu, an expert canoe builder on Simbo Island:

> I cut the canoe. When the canoe is finished, the sacred areca bunch. After hanging up the bunch when the canoe is finished, I lauch it in the sea, paint it, put the line on the rod, go down to embark in the canoe, go out to fish in the deep sea, follow the bonito, turn round, scoop the water. It jumps up, the bonito follows. . . . After catching bonito I go back to land blowing the conch, come ashore, cook the bonito, make pudding for the return, fish, come ashore, go fishing again, come ashore, make puddings, each man gets a ring. (Hocart 1935:109)

The account reveals that canoe building, fishing, and ritual were inextricably mixed; the construction and decoration of a bonito canoe were not considered isolated processes. The same was true of war canoes,[11] and comparative examination of Hocart's material on the two types, obtained on Simbo in 1908, reveals striking parallels. This is shown in Appendix II, which contains field data taken from Hocart's articles.

Within traditional contexts, separate canoes were employed for bonito fishing and for headhunting expeditions,

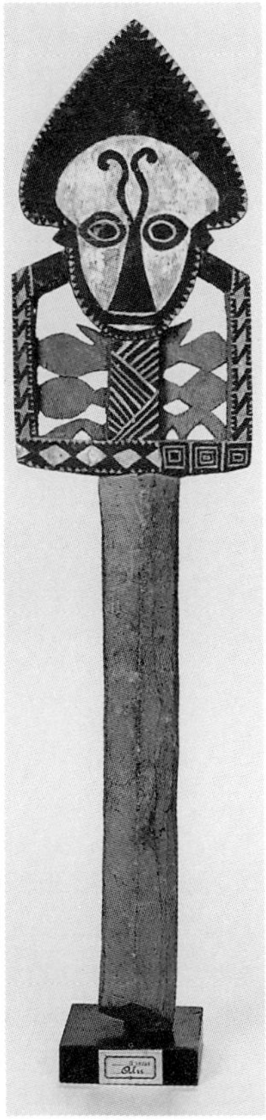

FIGURE 5.23. Canoe carving. Bougainville Straits Islands. Institute für Völkerkunde der Universität Göttingen, Oz1945. Photograph courtesy of the Institute für Völkerkunde.

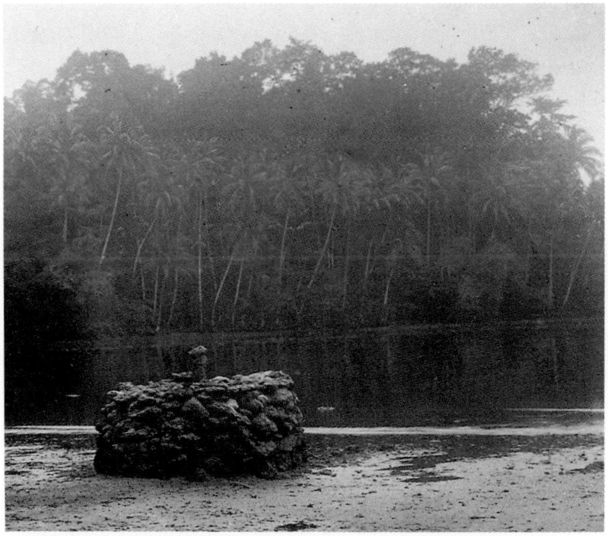

FIGURE 5.24. Fishing(?) shrine, Solomon Islands. Museum für Völkerkunde Staatliche Museum Preussischer Kulturbesitz, West Berlin. Photo Archive No. VIII c 1465. Photograph courtesy of the Museum für Völkerkunde.

but the ritual systems involving bonito and headhunting canoes displayed common features. A stone on the beach — either a fishing shrine (*inaru*) or a war canoe shrine (*inatunu*) — was the focus of offerings or chants made to spirits prior to departure in order to guarantee safety and the efficacy of the expedition (e.g., fig. 5.24). Protection and effectiveness were also insured by the presence of plants placed between the boards of a fishing canoe, around the wrists or waists of crewmen, or eaten by crew members. Taro puddings were presented as offerings to the spirits and consumed in both contexts.

Certain specific charms were repeated in the case of each canoe type. *Tita vagarata* ("caulking to make bite"), which consists of placing insects on the canoe, was employed during the construction process for a bonito canoe, the initiation for a fisherman, and prior to the departure of a war canoe to ensure the preservation and strength of the craft or fisherman. *Ngula*, or stroking, in which the canoe or its lead crew member was stroked four times with leaves to ward off potential harm or disaster and to guarantee effectiveness of the expedition, was also performed in both contexts.

The stroking ritual occurred in other instances. Upon the return of one war canoe to Simbo, a female slave captured on Choiseul was stroked in order to remove from her the *inatunu*[12] of men from Vella La Vella who had "made *inatunu* on her" (Hocart 1931:313; cf. Hocart 1922:107). The same practice was employed to cure sickness[13] and was performed on the body of a priest or caretaker of the skull house at his ceremony of consecration (Hocart 1922:106-7).

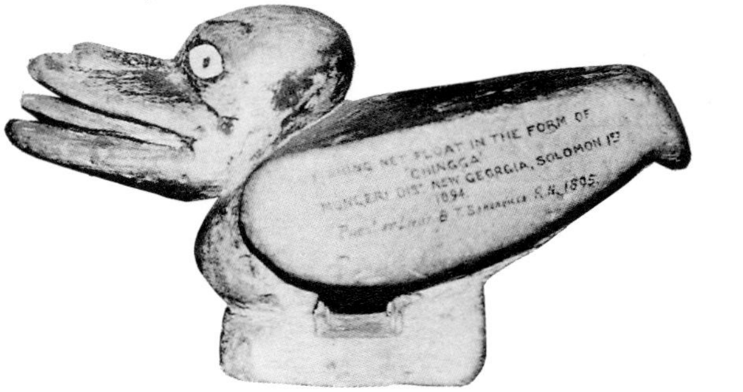

FIGURE 5.25. Fish net float. Mungeri district, New Georgia Island. Pitt-Rivers Museum, Oxford University, Somerville Collection, 1895.22.169, 1895. H. 9.5 cm. Photograph by Deborah Waite.

The rituals were directed by district leaders or *mbangara*.[14] On Simbo and New Georgia, the *mbangara* had exclusive rights over headhunts or fleets of fishing canoes. "He also commands the canoe throughout and with his colleagues directs the ceremonials at landing, the presentation of rings to the successful warrior, the festivities in honor of the canoe" (Hocart MS. 6.14-15).

Rituals performed in connection with net fishing and pig hunting resemble canoe rituals in certain respects. Chants propitiating spirits were made at a fishing shrine prior to net fishing. The wooden net floats (figs. 5.25, 5.30) were stroked (*ngula*) "with the rind of *eru* and of *niniru*, two sea plants, to make plenty of fish run into the net." Shell rings were given by "all the men concerned" to the owner of the net, who placed them on the shrine for the net spirits. As in bonito fishing, the leader or owner of the net could put no lime on his face and wore only undyed white barkcloth. He was referred to as the "widow of the net" (Hocart 1937:35). Before pig hunting, in which a net was once used, chants were uttered to spirits at a special shrine, and the net was stroked with *piro* leaves to the following accompaniment: "Let me stroke the pig net, let it catch on the outside, let it catch on the inside." Offerings of yams were made at the shrine, and yams and puddings were carried by the hunting party into the bush (Hocart MS. 19.3).

The transactional nature of the four processes of bonito fishing, headhunting, net fishing, and pig hunting is manifest in the presentation of food offerings and shell rings to the shrine owner for the spirits of the shrines, and to members of a headhunting or fishing canoe upon the return of an expedition. Big-men, or *mbangara*, also gave shell rings to the fathers of ritually desirable women prior to the *vavolo* ceremony.

METAPHORS

The use of metaphor punctuates references to the canoes, canoe carvings, and pertinent spirits. *Tita vagarata*, "caulking to make bite," apparently implied making the bonito bite in the case of a bonito canoe (Hocart 1935:97-99), but when recited before a war canoe set out on a headhunting expedition, the phrase seems also to have referred to making the canoe bite and to be strong enough to do so. To bite an animal is not specified but implied.

Specific allusions to animals in relation to the canoe

appeared in the name Eavo, crocodile, given to one ancient canoe (Hocart 1931:308) and in the crocodile heads inlaid or carved at the prow ends of others. The presence of the image, even if not referred to verbally, may have served as a visual metaphor for the canoe and an invocation that guaranteed safety and effectiveness.

Spirits invoked at the shrines and in other situations were often conceived of as being like birds in appearance or behavior. *Kesoko*, associated with fishing nets and canoe ornaments, was crane-like in appearance and was depicted in carved form as an anthropomorph with a frigate bird replacing the head. Other spirits of the nets were depicted on wooden net floats as birds with prognathic anthropomorphic heads (fig. 5.25). Similar images were also carved and painted on canoe paddles allegedly from Santa Isabel (cf. Waite 1979:261, figs. 13-15). Hocart recorded the existence of five upright stones called the "Five Frigate Birds"; stones which allegedly had once been men, not birds (Hocart 1922:264). Other spirits included *mbelama meka*, a "frigate bird of storms because it flies about when a storm is impending" (p. 293). Mbanara pu tatava, "the chief that flies," was a spirit known on Simbo; Ave, an evil spirit from Santa Isabel that made people ill, allegedly resembled a man but flew like a bird (pp. 267, 280). Rokoveo, an invisible spirit, "lives at sea and can sit on it just like an *elekai* bird or a frigate bird. He eats small fry such as the *inambuku*; he walks on top of the water and catches them with his hand" (Hocart 1935:105).

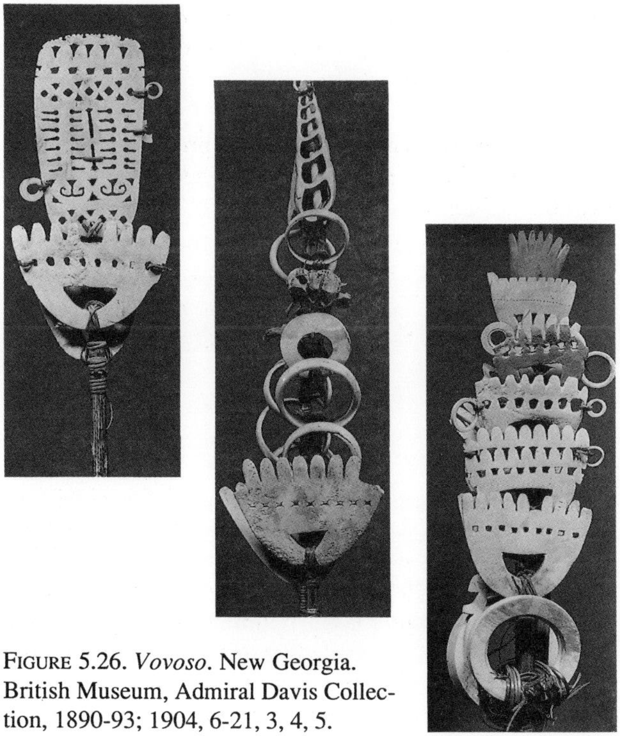

FIGURE 5.26. *Vovoso*. New Georgia. British Museum, Admiral Davis Collection, 1890-93; 1904, 6-21, 3, 4, 5.

The *vovoso* (Simbo) or *serenbule* (New Georgia), a stick of wood to which clam shell rings and triangular charms (*barava*) were attached (fig. 5.26), was fastened inside a headhunting canoe before a raid, and upon return of the expedition was taken to the miniature huts where the skulls were ultimately placed (see Appendix II). On Simbo, the *vovoso* was "tambu belong kill him man." One from Karivara district was reputedly named Crocodile and belonged to a canoe given the same name. "It used to be kept in the skull house at Vepa. When fighting was stopped, the mortuary priest broke it and hung the fragments on the rafters of the skull house. The canoe was allowed to rot" (Hocart 1931:310).

Before putting the *vovoso* in a canoe, the following took place:

> For the *vovoso* they kill a pig and make puddings . . . Kunda makes a burnt offering saying, "This is the pudding for you the departed chiefs, be propitious to this canoe, and let us go out to sea and let us club the men, put them on board this canoe. This is the pig for you, the spirits of departed chiefs, the *vovoso*, and be efficacious for this canoe, and may we put on board the men." (p. 310)

The charm was then fastened in the canoe and presented with a shell ring.

A portion of a chant recorded for a *vovoso* from Simbo evokes types of hunting other than headhunting:

> At the end let us go out to sea, let us go together, even we; lie in wait, let us . . . be efficacious in the meeting at sea, thou, be efficacious in the attack, be efficacious in the going up, be efficacious in the catching crabs . . . in the turtling canoe . . . in the fishing canoe . . . in the fish trap raft (i.e. grant that we may overtake a victim on his raft when he is looking at his traps), be efficacious in the bonito-fishing (i.e. may we fall in with men out bonito fishing). (Hocart 1931:310)

The *vovoso* served, thus, as one of the major charms for the canoe but, unlike other charms, it was the focus of rituals and offerings similar to those performed for the canoe itself. (For example, the *vovoso* was destroyed when the canoe was allowed to rot after the cessation of headhunting, as described in a passage from Hocart quoted above.) Moreover, both *vovoso* and canoes were decorated with shell charms (*barava*) and rings, the rings being attached to the *vovoso* and inlaid on the canoe. Hence the *vovoso* may be said to have served both as canoe charm and canoe metaphor. It seems to have functioned as a vehicle through which the spirits of departed chiefs were addressed in order to achieve success: "This is the pig for you, the spirits of departed chiefs, the *vovoso*, and be efficacious for this canoe" (p. 310).

The *ragomo*, another charm made of shell rings, was similarly used and addressed on Simbo to cure wounds and bites. The charm allegedly originated from Santa Isabel and consisted of

> superimposed rings of decreasing diameter with a large ring as the base. They are tied together with *asama*. Four vertical rows of small rings called *hinuili* were tied to the sides of the pile in a plane with two diameters of horizontal rings at right angles to one another. (Hocart MS. 38.10)

Riambule, the owner of this charm on Simbo when Hocart was there, hung it above the bed of a person with a spear wound. Every day for eight days (four plus four) Riabule chanted the following: "I stroke thou Ragomo, cure this man, make him well. Let the spear come out." Apparently, if the *ragomo* told Riabule to take the spear out after three days, he did so, but the patient could not wash for eight days. When he did so, his relatives made a pudding, some of which was placed in the house thatch. As in the case of the *vovoso*, the *ragomo* served not only as a means through which to communicate and secure ancestral power to cure the spear wound, but was also addressed as though it were the spirit. When the pudding was deposited in the house thatch, Riabule would intone: "Here is for you the *tomate*, thou Ragomo, cause him to live, ease this man whom I have bathed this day." Brothers of the patient then presented gifts of shell rings, calico, and tobacco to Riabule (Hocart MS. 38.10).

PARALLELS IN STONE AND CLAM SHELL CARVINGS

Shell rings and stone carvings of prognathic anthropomorphic heads and crouching anthropomorphic figures similar to the canoe carvings were to be found on other sacred sites, usually the graves of big-men. This was true not only for coastal peoples, but also for inland dwellers such as the Kusaghe of New Georgia Island, where the images were called *mbeku patu* (Tedder 1976:73, 85). Two stone carvings from the Marovo Lagoon, recorded as "stone turtle net weights" despite that they were found on graves, depict a prognathic head with a facsimile of a shell ring replacing the upper torso and a crouching anthropomorphic figure clasping a large turtle (Solomon Islands Museum 74.100 and British Museum 1959, Oc.6.24).[15] A variant of the stone head on top of a ring occurs in at least one canoe carving of a prognathic head in which the ear has been replaced by a perforated ring (Waite 1979:fig. 13-8).

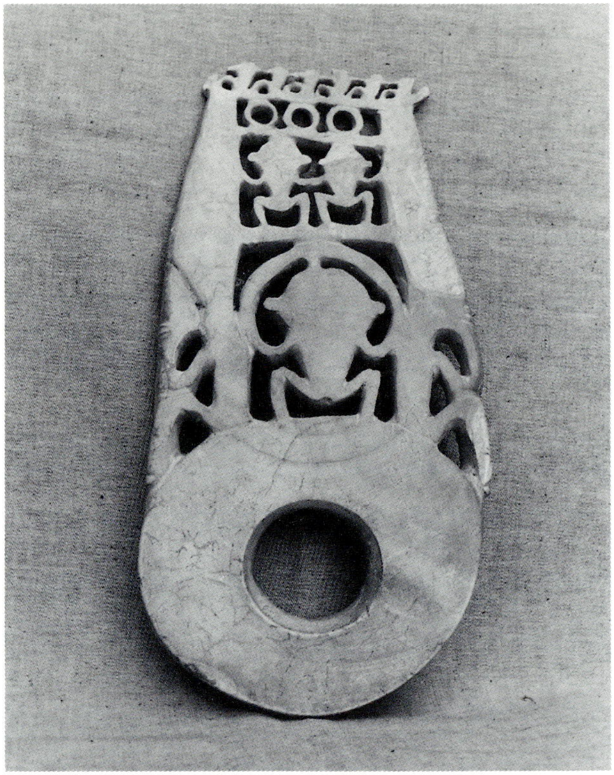

FIGURE 5.27. Tridacna plaque. Wagina Island, Choiseul. Solomon Islands Museum, L75.36. H. 42.3 cm. Photographed by Deborah Waite.

Crouching profile anthropomorphic figures with prognathic heads as well as frontal displayed figures (similar to the *hope ta ponda* figures) formed part of the ornamentation of tridacna clam shell plaques placed on or near memorial skull huts of big-men (Waite 1983:61-62; fig. 5.27). The plaques comprised images of frigate birds, an occasional canoe, and always large and small rings like the shell rings that were exchanged and offered to the spirit in each of the ritual contexts mentioned above. Canoes, grave sites, shrines, and skull huts therefore employed similar imagery, always in conjunction with shell currency or replicas of it. The images may be viewed as visual spirit metaphors, one of whose functions was to demonstrate the connection between these contexts. There was, however, one difference: Composite anthropomorphic/bird images appeared only in relation to water — on canoes, canoe paddles, and net floats — and never in association with land.

Canoe carvings may be said to have served two functions: as charms and as signiers. Allusions to headhunting, even on bonito canoes, were evoked by the presence of carved heads on bow, prow, and stern peaks. Kesoko images may also have functioned as headhunting signs, just as the human arm painted in white on bow or stern indicated a successful raid. The duplication of heads may have constituted simply one more version of the repetition that was so much a part of chanting, stroking, and other rituals. The appearance of four heads, one pair on the bow and another on the stern, reiterated the standard unit for numerical repetition in ritual. The carvings may in this manner have evoked the presence of spirits whose protection and guarantee of efficacy was sought through ritual offerings and chants.

FUNERAL RITUALS

The full nature of the signification process becomes evident in parallels between canoe rituals and rituals for the deceased on Simbo. Analogies between treatment of a corpse and the canoe occurred in the initial stages of funeral and canoe rituals. One of the first things done to a corpse, be it that of a commoner or a big-man, was to make a line with lime "across the face of the dead from one side of the forehead to the opposite cheek over the top of the nose" (Hocart 1922:81-82). A similar though invisible "line" was made across the bonito canoe when pieces of *lava* creeper were inserted between boards on the forward right and aft left sides of the canoe during the construction process (Hocart 1935:97-99; Barraud 1972:70).

Crew members of a bonito canoe were designated as widowers of the canoe, *namboko pa na mola. Namboko* referred to the widow who survived her husband and remained unmarried, a mandatory custom for widows of commoners but optional for widows of big-men, who could also choose to die and follow their husbands into the afterlife. The widow removed all ornaments, put no lime on her face or hair, and wore only brown bark cloth. Bonito canoe crew members also had to remove white lime from their faces. They wore white barkcloth from the time of departure until the fourth day, *Mande-Mola* (cf. Appendix II).

The seated posture with updrawn knees characteristic of Kesoko and canoe figurehead carvings reproduced the posture adopted by a widow who sat in this position within a special enclosure (*kuipi*) for the duration of the funeral festival (Hocart 1922:81, 84, 89). The corpses of big-men and commoners were displayed in the same posture. On the day of death or the day immediately following, the body was taken to a remote spot in the bush or to the shore, where it was placed in a special rectangular enclosure. Hocart recorded one instance of depositing a body in a wooden framework called *era*, the term usually given to stone enclosures for the bodies of big-men. The head was propped up with sticks so that it would be visible above the wall or frame (p. 82). It is perhaps not without coincidence that each of the Kesoko canoe images is rendered seated within a framework, one bar of which separates the head (or the bird replacing the head) from the body.

On the fourth day of a funeral, a feast called *vamande* ("to make four") was held. Pigs were killed and eaten and yam puddings were made. "Two puddings are made of four times four sweet yams," one for the elderly men and the other for the elderly women. A bit of pudding put on the end of a stick was rubbed on a tree for the *tomate*, or spirits. The "Prayer of the Sacred Pudding," recited by the officient at the feast, exhorted the spirit of the dead person to leave the village and travel to a remote place, apparently a temporary abode until the final journey to Sonto, the land of departed spirits. If the bereaved family was too poor to provide a pig for sacrifice, the deceased was urged to put a basket on her head or to shoulder his club and depart on its journey. For big-men, aquatic metaphors were employed which involved the setting out of a canoe:

> Set out you people of Gele, you people of Lavalava, you people of Vonjavonja, you people of Elusana. Go up to Aku,

> launch four chiefly sticks (a periphrasis for canoe); go down to None, launch four eel boards, launch four embracing nights; cast out four hawsers (Large ropes for mooring ships); shout people of Gele, shout people of Lavalava, shout people of Vonjavonja, shout people of Elosgana; let him come down sounding the conch, come down casting . . . go off to Mala Kinda, scoop the water four times (see note 7); go off to Keulala, scoop the water four times; go to Kokorai, scoop the water four times; go off to Puta Lavata, cast four hawsers; go to Kusni, scoop four times. (Hocart 1922:88-89)

The chant continued in this fashion until the spirits anchored the canoe in its final resting place. Bonito fishing referents supplied the major metaphors in this version of the chant, but in others specific reference was made to canoes (Hocart 1922). Not only was the voyage of the spirit of a big-man likened to a canoe voyage, but the number four was directly associated with this particular transitional passage.

From the moment of death, shell rings of large and small denominations representing the personal wealth of the deceased played a critical role in the funerary rituals.

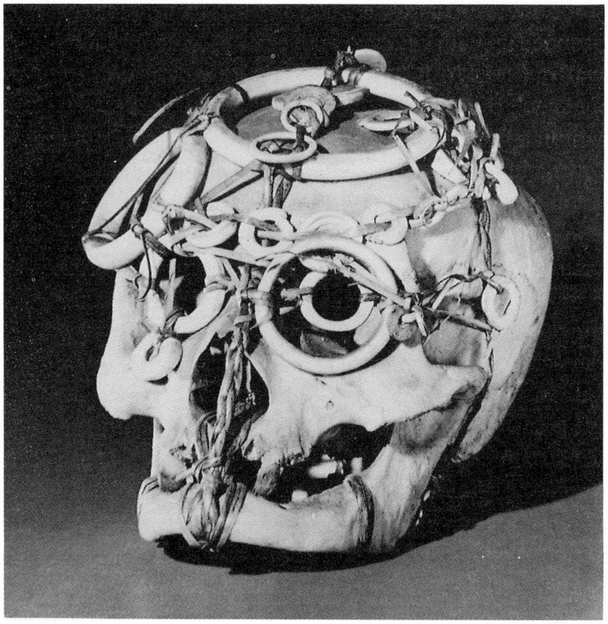

FIGURE 5.28. Skull with shell rings. Field Museum of Natural History, Chicago, 276646. Photograph courtesy of the Field Museum of Natural History.

Rings, along with other possessions of the deceased, were broken at death and placed near the body (Hocart 1922:82, 86). On the third day after death, the soul, which had allegedly emerged from the mouth of the deceased, was called into a dracaena leaf threaded through an *ovala* ring. The *ovala*, one of the rings of lesser denomination, was then wrapped in the leaf and placed in the gable thatch until the eighteenth day of the funeral (pp. 83, 84). On that day the skull was removed from the corpse, which had been preserved in a sitting position since death, and was placed in a skull house. This process was called *vatome tomate*, "putting in the dead." If the skull belonged to a big-man, a pig was killed and sacrificed. Then the jawbone and cheekbone of the skull were tied together with *lave*, the same creeper that was placed between boards of the canoe. *Ovala* rings were put in the eye sockets and ears and, in some cases, a string of *ovala* was draped across the head (fig. 5.28). The soul ring was removed from the house roof and placed near or on the skull, which was then deposited inside the skull house on top of a large orange-stained tridacna clam shell ring of highest value, *mbakhia*. People then presented *ovala* rings to the priest, who put them in the skull house. On the same day, the widow paid armrings to her husband's relatives and was set free. The next major event was *londu* ("to sink or set"), the final journey of the soul to Sonto. This land of departed spirits apparently was thought to be located on Bougainville. Spirits who came from Sonto to fetch the soul travelled in a canoe (pp. 91-95).

The *vavolo* was the last ceremony performed at the funeral of a big-man or other person of distinction. Since a head was taken in honor of a deceased big-man, the headhunting and funeral *vavolo* were often one and the same (cf. Appendix II). Within the funeral context, a living big-man sponsored the *vavolo* in commemoration of a deceased one. Puddings were offered to the spirits, and much food was consumed. At this time the hair of the widow was shaved, after which she paid for the hair with two orange-stained rings. This ritual apparently made it possible for her to re-marry. "Brothers" (*tamatasi*) of the host contributed shell rings for expenses which included payment to musicians and all visiting big-men (Hocart 1922:97-98).

Since the funeral of a big-man was always concluded with a headhunting raid, the placement of the *vovoso* stick with shell rings into the headhunting canoe and its return to the skull hut (cf. Appendix II) can be seen as culminating ritual acts of the funeral process. This reaffirms the identifications among a *vovoso*, the deceased big-man or his spirit, his skull, and the canoe.

Canoe imagery incorporated other elements of funeral ritual in addition to the seated posture of death and the rectangular enclosure for the corpse. Repeated use of the number four occurred in both contexts and apparently served as a canoe metaphor. A pig, whose sacrifice accompanied funeral rituals for big-men, appears silhouetted in relief within its own enclosure beneath the Kesoko in one canoe carving, perhaps serving as a visual reminder indicating the big-man status of the canoe owner (fig. 5.15). The presence of detached heads singly (figurehead) or in pairs (prow and stern carvings) may have been more than just a sign of the importance of headhunting in view of the ritual detachment of the heads of deceased tribesmen, their decoration, and their final resting place admidst trophy skulls in the skull hut. One canoe carving of an anthropomorphic head displays a ring placed within the ear socket, a reiteration of the placement of *ovala* rings in the ear sockets of big-man skulls (Waite 1979:250, fig. 13-8).

Shell inlay on the body of canoes acquires a significance beyond mere ornamentation in view of the frequent offerings and exchanges of shell rings in bonito fishing, headhunting, and funerary contexts. Certain shell inlay pieces were specifically named after personal ornaments, such as *hinuili* and *barava*. Moreover, the overriding presence of rows of shell-inlaid rings with or without names testifies to their importance as surrogates for the shell rings used in offerings (figs. 5.6, 5.7). The triangular clam shell *barava* fastened to the inner rim of the upraised prow and to the *vovoso* sticks also occurred in low relief on many of the canoe carvings (figs. 5.16-5.18, 5.22). In one instance, single *barava*, each attached to a shell ring, are carved in low relief on the body of a frigate bird canoe carving (fig. 5.17). A shell ring with attached *barava* (or *rano* — cf. note 3) from the Marovo Lagoon, now in the Solomon Islands Museum, has been described as a "magic charm used for asking for good weather, for burial sites, to prevent sickness, and for good fortune in headhunting" (Solomon Islands Museum 72.160; fig. 5.18).

Other *barava* as well as *hinuili* had alleged protective powers when worn as personal charms (Somerville 1897:393). Application of the term *barava* to the clam shell openwork plaques that were placed in or on skull huts (fig. 5.27) suggests that the word had an additional layer of significance relating to the afterlife and ancestral spirits (Waite 1983:58).

The occurrence of visual signs and rituals associated with death in connection with canoes used for bonito fishing and headhunting has been suggested as evidence that the canoe represented the deceased chief (Barraud 1972:75). Certain elements and metaphors were indeed exclusive to funerals for big-men, such as the canoe voyage of the deceased spirit, the pig sacrifice, the *vavolo* ceremony, and the *vovoso* sticks. But other elements — the seated corpse position, induction of soul into an *ovala* ring, and dress of widows — were not limited to big-man funerals.

LIMINAL RITUALS

Death-related imagery is characteristic of liminal rituals, which mark periods of transition from one state of life to the next and result in new or enhanced status. Initiation, marriage, and funeral rites constitute primary liminal periods, but so may sickness; social rituals which have analogous structural principles and goals may incorporate similar symbolism. Becoming structurally dead to a former state such as childhood may be symbolized in rituals that involve treating the initiate like a corpse (Turner 1964:5-6). Accordingly, the first ritual treatment given to a newly constructed bonito canoe on the threshold of its first voyage was to apply *lave* leaves to form an invisible diagonal line across the length of the canoe comparable to the line drawn across the face of a dead person. For the same reason, references to widows as well as widows' garments and lack of face paint occurred in the initial stages of bonito and net fishing.[16] The crossed bandoliers visible on several canoe images representing Kesoko were worn by bonito fishermen and also by priests during ceremonies performed for the renovation of skull huts (Hocart 1935:104; 1922:108). Belts from various vines and creepers were donned in all of the above mentioned contexts mentioned above. The presence of the protective *barava* charm, *vovoso* sticks, and canoe carvings was a particularly suitable form of protection — for an individual as well as a canoe — during a potentially polluting unstructured liminal period. The offerings of puddings and shell rings before, during, and after a canoe voyage or net hunt may also have offset any dangers to crewmen or fishermen who, at the outset, were "uninitiated."

Ambiguity and ambivalence are characteristic of liminal periods during which people are, in effect, neither here nor there (Turner 1964:7). Thus, spirit images are depicted on canoes, paddles, and net floats as part-bird part-anthropomorph and are described in myth accordingly as they flew through liminal space. One canoe carving combines paired bird heads, a frontal displayed anthropomorph, and vertically oriented crocodile jaws into a composite creature that embodies the essence of ambiguity (fig. 5.29). A net float depicts a seated anthropomorph whose prognathic jaw extends downward in the process of becoming a bird beak — another visual example of liminal transformation (fig. 5.30).

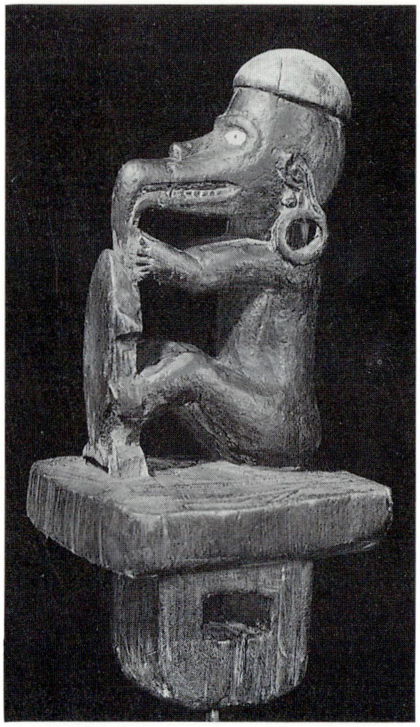

FIGURE 5.30. Net float. Barbier-Müller Museum, Geneva, 4501/A. H. 14 cm. Ex-Lord Glasgow Collection; collected pre-1855. Photograph courtesy of the Barbier-Müller Museum.

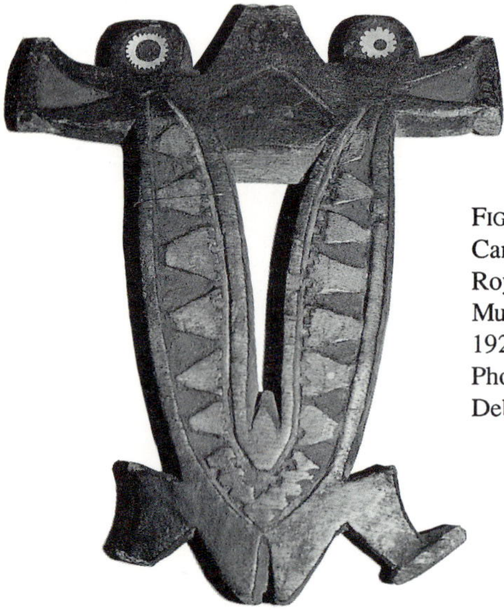

FIGURE 5.29. Canoe carving. Royal Scottish Museum, Edinburgh, 1924-448. Photograph by Deborah Waite.

Liminal ambiguity is reflected in a mythical account of still another *vavolo* ceremony, associated in this case with marriage. The myth, called Tuna Mbelama, "The Son of the Frigate Bird," was recorded on Simbo and Vella La Vella. In it, the *vavolo* was held to celebrate the marriage of a *mbangara*'s daughter with a handsome man, "the man of the air," who originated from the sky. The mythical dancing ground was encircled by posts, and the dancers played bamboo flutes at the conclusion of the dance just as in the headhunting *vavolo* (Appendix II). After the marriage ceremony, all the women of the area requested the bridegroom to sleep with them, which he did to the consternation of his new bride who would not be appeased by his offering of shell rings. Realizing that she would not forgive him, he transformed himself into a bird and flew up into the air, whereupon she hanged herself in despair (Hocart 1931:320-21).

The myth has both direct and inverted relations with traditional customs, as is typical for liminal subject matter. Customarily in Simboese society, the bridegroom approached the bride and her family to ask for marriage, not the reverse as in the myth. The passage in which women sought sexual union with the bridegroom after his marriage may be seen as an inversion of the rite of *manjaka*. This was the ritual procurement of young women, daughters of big-men from other islands, by sponsors of a headhunting raid before the final headhunting *vavolo*. In myth, the departure of the bird-man occurred after the *vavolo* took place; in reality, departure of a big-man from this life preceded the *vavolo*. Transformation of man into bird represents another ambiguous process which constitutes quintessential liminal behavior (cf. figs. 5.16, 5.26, 5.28).

Liminal symbols are particularly fitting for headhunting canoes, since headhunting expeditions were ordered for essentially liminal occasions such as funerals of big-men or the inauguration of new canoes, communal houses, and skull houses (cf. note 9). Bonito fishing, too, was a cyclical event which, like net fishing and pig hunting, could be viewed as an activity that periodically renewed and enhanced the welfare of the community as well as the status of the big-man who inaugurated and sponsored it. Thus, all four qualify as liminal rites. The instrumental artifacts in each situation — bonito canoe, headhunting canoe, fish net, and pig net — functioned as instruments of procurement and transition: procurement of desired commodities and transition to renewed or enhanced status. This context fully elucidates the significance of the *mon* canoe and canoe carvings and justifies their close resemblance to funerary and other spirit carvings in the Western Solomon Islands.

Appendix I

Names of shell-inlay pieces on canoes from the Western Solomon Islands (See note 2)

Choisel

Lanono (Hokata): shell bracelet (Ca.)

Toe Paja: ear wig (Ca.)

Nöle Paleo: jawbone of *paleo* fish (Ca.)

Pöti Boboe: *boboe* seed (Ca.)

Kela: white cloud, star on evening horizon (Ca.)

Kuru: bird in flight (Ca.)

Motif (unnamed): borrowed from Roviana (Ca.)

Roviana (New Georgia Island)

bobolokuhai: round, circular; *kada bobolokuhai*: "a certain design used in inlay work" (W.3)

pikupikutu: "to show part of its tail out of water, a fish-tail design" (W.81)

asepaleo: reversed Z-shaped design (W.3) (cf. Ribbe 1895:300, fig. 78b, where the design is unnamed)

gelegele: (W.36)

gunai: "a pattern in inlay work" (W.20)

barabarava: "design in inlay work" (W.5) (cf. Ribbe 1895:301, fig. 79)

reqereqete: "vandyked, serrated" (W.93)

viqala: "to split, as a block of wood" (W.129)

moku: "to break" (W.65)

Marovo Lagoon (New Georgia Island)

"Wheeled Circle" (S.379)

hinili (S.343)

barava (S.379)

Appendix II

Bonito and war canoe rituals in the Western Solomon Islands

A. Construction of bonito canoes[17]

1. The placement of four *lave*[18] creepers into the joints of the planks on the bow and stern of the canoe.
2. Painting of the canoe.
3. Insertion of ribs in the interior of the canoe.
4. Attachment of an anthropomorphic figurehead to the bow of the canoe.
5. Placement of the *lanolano* charm. Leaves and creepers were tied to the canoe to make it light and to serve as a curse on competing canoes.
6. *Gusara* charm. Spider-like insects were put on the canoe, twelve on the bow and twelve on the stern (cf. *tita vagarata* below).
7. The canoe was smoked for four days.
8. *Tita vagarata* ("caulking to make bite") charm. Twelve black ants (*kandiki*) and twelve fruits of *lavalava* were stuck with *tita* (*parinarium* nut) paste in the bow on the inner surface of the junction of the two forward second strakes (planks) to the accompaniment of the following chant: "Caulk for biting, thou the canoe, thou Itutanambae, thou the bonito shrine in Pendere, thou the bonito shrine in Ngema, make effective this canoe and may it catch bonito" (Hocart 1935:97-99).

B. Initiation of fishermen[19]

1. Fishermen had to be initiated by the owner of the bonito shrine before being allowed to fish.
2. A new canoe was inaugurated.
3. A new fishing altar was set up.
4. The *Tita vagarata* ("caulking to make bite") was performed over the canoe.
5. The first fishing trip then took place (Hocart 1935:104).

C. Rites connected with the first fishing expedition of the bonito fishing season

1. An offering of sacred taro pudding was made to spirits of the fishing shrine by the owners of the shrine; more of the same pudding was given to members of the fishing crew.
2. Crew members donned personal ornaments, i.e., shell neck ornaments and bandolers. Special girdles of *elove* and *njorutu* plants were tied around the waist of the coxwain to the accompaniment of the following chant: "here is a man, let him catch bonito; be effective you spirits."
3. The performance of *ngula*. This was a ritual in which someone stroked the body of the coxwain downwards on both sides with leaves of *nyou*.
4. *Ngoro keala*, white barkcloth, was donned by members of the fishing crew. They were termed "widowers for the canoe." They also removed from their faces any traces of the white lime paint that they would otherwise have worn for social occasions.
5. *Manda-mola* ("fourth of the canoe"). This was the fourth day of the bonito fishing expedition. A sago pudding was eaten by the crew to mark this day; afterwards, pudding was eaten every day. After this day, the coxwain could remove his girdles. Crew members no longer had to wear white barkcloth, and face paint was permitted.
6. *Ovaka*. This was a feast held after about one month of fishing. The crew received shell rings at this time. On return to shore, some of these shell rings were handed over to the owner of the fishing shrine (Hocart 1935:100-101).

D. Rites connected with war canoes

1. *Votu manja* ("bring out the clubs"). This ritual was performed before the departure of war canoes at a war canoe shrine on the beach. The crew, led by the owner of the shrine, walked in procession to the shrine, each man bearing a club and one shell ring (*ovala*). The shrine owner put all the rings on the shrine. The men then put their clubs on the shrine saying, "This is the club, thou the *inatunu*. Grant me an enemy to slay and let me club." Flowers of the *vonjamboe* were wrapped in betel pepper leaf and eaten while the following prayer was chanted: "Give to eat to my men here. Let them club a man, let them surprise him in the house, surprise him on the shore, club him my men." After eating the betel, a special girdle was donned.
2. *Tita vagarata*. Before the departure of a war canoe, this charm was performed. Twelve spider-like insects were placed at the bow and twelve beneath the stern boards. The following was chanted: "Caulk to bite [four times] thou the war canoe here and do not rot, be the boards like stone, be you like stone, ye boards, be strong, ye boards, and be efficacious, thou."
3. On the day of departure, the t*ita vagarata* charm was performed over each war canoe. Eight spider-like in-

sects were put on board on the right-hand side of the canoe at the bow and the left-hand side at the stern. The following chant accompanied this ritual: "I make *tita vagarata* on this canoe, be efficacious *vovoso* charm. You that come down to embark, be efficaious, spirits; make *tita vagarata* on this canoe here. Let it depart, this canoe; let the men embark in it, go to Isabel; let them shed blood in the pursuit, at the coming down" (i.e., when the enemy came down to the beach).

4. *Ngula* ("stroking"). Before departure and when the canoe was in the water, it was stroked up and down four times on the right side of the bow with leaves: "Stroke [four times] away the smell, the evil spell, stroke away the murdered man; stroke away the witchcraft, stroke away the spirits, and let this canoe depart. Be efficacious, let it depart and let it kill men."

5. Return of war canoes from a successful headhunting expedition: *kuvili paro* ("blowing the conch shoreward"), the triumphal return of the boats to shore. As the canoes approached the shore, shell rings were thrown into the water by a greeting party and were picked up by the canoe. *Lipa vovoso* ("bail *vovoso*"). Water was put into the canoe four times, then was bailed out four times, once after each time the following was chanted: "Come down, come down, the *vovoso* (stick with shell rings and shell *barava* carvings attached); come down, sit on the land; come down and sit in the skull house; abide. When we depart, we shall put thee on board." The *vovoso* stick was taken from the canoe, placed near a shrine for three days, then taken up to the skull house: "Go up and sit. Go up, be angry. Go up, be incensed. Go up, kill. Go up, be true. When chief says, 'let us go,' come down, embark."

6. *Vavolo* festival in honor of a successful canoe. An abundance of taro was cooked. The institution of Manjaka occurred. The resident big-man sought one or more young girls from another island and paid shell rings to their fathers for loan of them. The girls were at the disposal of any man on payment of one arm ring to the big-man for three to four months. The girls were paid with the head of a pig, a pudding, and two orange-stained rings at the final feast.

A dancing ground (*kakambare*) was prepared and defined by posts set up in an outer and an inner circle. The posts were hung with coconuts and were connected two by two by a horizontal pole. Another pole joined the center of each inner post with the center of the corresponding outer one. Puddings were set up on the poles.

The dance was called *votu minate* ("the people come forth"). The big-man entered the circle bearing the head of a newly slain enemy. Other men followed, dancing with spears and shields (Hocart 1931:308-9, 314, 317-18).

Notes

1. "Heads were not caught at random but for the definite purpose of inauguration, *vapenja*. . . . The occasions of *vapenja* are new canoes, new communal houses, new skull houses (for skulls of deceased leaders), the death of a chief, and the release from confinement of a widow" (Hocart 1931:303).

2. The list of inlay pieces and corresponding names in Appendix I was compiled from four sources. Three of these are accession files from the Canterbury Museum, Christchurch, New Zealand, Somerville (1897), and Waterhouse (1928), and these are abbreviated in the list as Ca., S., and W., respectively. The canoe in the Canterbury Museum is a traditional *tomako* (*mon*) from Choiseul built on commission for the museum between 1967 and 1968. I am grateful to Joan Woodward, Curator of Pictorial History, for supplying this information. Somerville and Waterhouse recorded terms without accompanying illustrations. The fourth source is Ribbe (1895). He illustrated a number of the inlay pieces without associated terms; references to his illustrations have been inserted in the appendix where they correspond.

3. *Hokata* were thin rings of tridacna clam shell worn as armlets and widely traded. The *hinuili* was a small ring made from trochus or conus shell and used primarily as a votive offering or part of a charm (Woodford 1905:39; Miller 1978:292). The triangular-shaped *barava*, made from clam shell, was worn suspended around the neck as a protective (Somerville 1897:379; Lanyon-Orgill 1969:67). The flat end of the triangle was notched; the suspension hole at the narrow end varied considerably in size from one *barava* to the next, though, like the *barava* itself, the hole was triangular in shape. Barraud (1972:81, illus. 16) labelled the *barava* lashed to *vovoso* sticks as *pangosia*, but *pangosia*, according to Lanyon-Orgill, was the name of a nautilus shell ornament (1906:109). The discrepancy is resolved by an artifact in the Somerville Collection at the Pitt-Rivers Museum; it consists of one large triangular tridacna pendant to which six small nautilus shell triangular pendants are attached with fiber. This would suggest that there was a difference in size as well as material between the two. Two triangular *barava* in the Solomon Islands Museum are labelled *rano* (69.24, 70.108); both come from Choiseul. Application of the term *rano* for these ornaments apparently reflects New Georgia usage. Conversely, on Choiseul *barava* referred to the tridacna shell plaques placed in or near skull huts (Waite 1983:61).

4. The canoe in the Merseyside County Council Museums, Liverpool, 55-144, (figs. 5.5-5.7) was thought to have come from San Cristobal (personal communication, Jill Sweetnam, Keeper of Maritime History, 2/21/85). However, it displays canoe ornaments and inlay patterns characteristic of canoes from the Western Solomon Islands. Triangular and oval-shaped pieces of shell inlay predominate, and these have been

recorded for Vella La Vella and Roviana canoes (cf. Ribbe 1895:247, 300). *Kela* and *kuru* designs are absent. There is not enough available information to assign a more precise location for the canoe.

5. This canoe, now in the British Museum (1927.10-22.1), came from Guava, Gizo District, Vella La Vella Island. It was built around 1910 for a Captain R. Broadhurst-Hill who subsequently sold it to Lord Leverhume, donor of the canoe to the museum. Islanders apparently built the canoe thinking that with Broadhurst-Hill's approval and presence, they could use it in a raid like the headhunting raids of the past. Broadhurst-Hill paid the islanders with trade goods during the process of construction to ensure completion of the canoe but then managed to stop the expedition from taking place (British Museum, Ethnography Document 986).

6. Cf. Ribbe (1895:314, fig. 82).

7. The canoe was presented to the Ulster Museum by Rear Admiral John Casement in 1898 (personal communication, Winifred Glover, Senior Research Assistant, Department of Antiquities, Ulster Museum 5/13/83). In 1895 Casement was appointed commanding officer of HMS. *Rapid*, a screw corvette in the Royal Navy. The *Rapid* was in the Solomons from April through August, 1897. The ship's log for the period indicated that it called at Gavutu, Vella La Vella, the Marovo Lagoon, New Georgia, Rendova, and Gatukai (Nggatokai) islands. An entry for Tuesday, 10 August, Gavutu to Gatukai, noted that after an expedition was landed on one island (unspecified), the small boats returned to the *Rapid* and were hoisted aboard, and then a canoe was hoisted in. This is the only instance in the log where the term canoe was employed, and it may possibly refer to the acquisition of the canoe from the Solomons given by Casement to the museum (*Log of H. M. S. "Rapid" 1897*).

8. The same name was employed for seated images on the islands of the Bougainville Straits and in the southern part of Bougainville Island for seated spirit images with hands beneath chins carved on posts or as canoe ornaments (Thurnwald 1910:131).

9. A cylindrical bamboo scoop from the Mungeri district, north coast, New Georgia Island bears images of the frontal displayed anthropomorph carved in low relief together with images of frigate birds and *barava* (Somerville Collection, Pitt-Rivers Museum). The scoops were used in bonito fishing; the noise that they made when scooping water supposedly attacted the bonito (Somerville, recorded notes for scoop, Pitt-Rivers Museum).

10. The standing image (Pitt-Rivers Museum 1895.22.205) resembles stylistically the seated displayed image in every way except for the posture (cf. Barraud 1972:illus. 7). Somerville's notes attached to the carving in the Pitt-Rivers Museum state: "I could never get an actual name for this figure, and he is best expressed as I have done, signifying 'sacred thing belonging to Ponda,' Ponda being the presiding good spirit over all."

11. By 1908, the date of Hocart's field research on Simbo, there were reportedly no longer any real war canoes on the island; at one time there had been several in each district, and each canoe was named. *Mbangara*, or district leaders, allegedly were not the exclusive owners of canoes on Simbo: "Man he savvy make *ngeto* (canoe), that's why he got *ngeto*" (Hocart 1931:308). On Roviana, war canoes appeared to be limited to big-men (Hocart MS, 6.15).

12. *Inatunu* is a term used by Hocart to refer to objects and to a process. It has appeared earlier in this essay with reference to a war canoe shrine, its usage with reference to a war club is found in Appendix II, and in the present case it refers to people. According to Waterhouse (1928:34), *inatunu* were "charms carried or worn during a raid or fighting." Apparently, it also could imply charming or otherwise affecting a person.

13. The process was termed *salanga ikerenga*, treatment for a condition caused by Ave, a sickness-causing spirit: "Njiruvidi held a leaf of *piro* by its stalk over the head of the patient and made four sweeping passes with it from the head over the chest and then with a sweeping action three it out of the door, and then repeated this with threw other *piro* leaves. 'I stroke and throw away the sickness, the heat, the sweat, let it finish.' Successive rituals involved additional rubbing with leaves" (Hocart MS, 19.3).

14. The *mbangara* was manager ("chief") of the social group known as *butubutu*, comprised of "kinsmen of common cognatic connection" who functioned as a corporate group in the areas of subsistence, warfare, and religion and selected activities (Scheffler 1962:137). There were, at the time of Hocart's field research, two or more *mbangara* in a district with variable degrees of influence (Hocart MS 6.3).

15. The stone carving from the Solomon Islands Museum is illustrated in *A Short Guide to the Material Culture of the Solomon Islands*, p. 75. The stone turtle-holding figure is illustrated in Waite (1969:fig. 171).

16. Every stage of canoe building in the Eastern Solomon Islands also involved rituals. The crew of a bonito fishing canoe was regarded as being in a sacred state, and ritual accompanied each stage of the fishing process. The rituals signified the sacred contract between the canoe owner and the supernatural deity in whose honor the canoe was built (Davenport 1985).

17. All details of canoe construction are not cited; those that are have mainly to do with the decorative process.

18. *Lave* was also the term for war shield. According to Lanyon-Orgill (1969:93), the word signified "shield, protection, an amulet, 'a kind of cushion made of wickerwork with a handle on which was strung a small ring'" (cf. Hocart 1931:312; Waterhouse 1928:53).

19. Hocart's information about the initiation of fisherman is summary in nature. He wrote that he had not been able to obtain the complete ritual as performed at any one fishing shrine (1935:104).

6

Salvage Art History Among the Sulka of Wide Bay, East New Britain, Papua New Guinea

George A. Corbin

In an article entitled "The Central Baining Revisited: 'Salvage' Art History Among the Kairak and Uramot Baining of East New Britain, Papua New Guinea" (Corbin 1984), I reported results obtained by using photographs of early twentieth century Baining art in interviews with Baining artists in the field. During my field study in East New Britain in 1982 and 1983, I carried out similar research among the non-Austronesian speaking Sulka of Wide Bay. This research was conducted under the sponsorship of the National Museum and Art Gallery in Boroko, Papua New Guinea, and funded by a Faculty Research Award of the City University of New York.

To prepare for my work among the Sulka, I photographed major collections and copied archival photographs of Sulka art at the Field Museum of Natural History in Chicago, at the Museum of Archaeology and Anthropology in Cambridge, and at the Museums für Völkerkunde in Basel, Berlin, and Hamburg. My photographic survey consisted of several hundred examples of masks, shields, war clubs, dance wands, and canoe arts, all collected between 1900 and 1930. From these I selected a representative sample of fifty pieces to be used in the field. Each photograph was given a code number from one to fifty, then randomized and later presented in the same order to each informant in the field.

During January 1983, Mr. Chris Isaac (my Sulka assistant from the National Museum and Art Gallery) and I interviewed twenty-eight Sulka big-men in eight Sulka villages (from Millim in the north to Kalampan in the south) and an additional seven Sulkanized Mengen big-men at Setwi, Tagul, and Sampun villages.[1] The majority of our informants were over sixty years of age and all had made traditional Sulka art. Six of the Sulka informants — Paul Anis (Kilalum village), Kapi and Renwai (Iwai village), Magil and Guma (Millim village), and Gabriel Lengmark (Guma village) — were considered by all Sulka interviewed to be the most "expert" on traditional Sulka art and we spent many days interviewing them about the photographs and other art-related matters.[2]

The literature on the Sulka tends to fall into two broad categories. One deals with exploration, religion, and general ethnography.[3] A second category focuses on Sulka art.[4] In the following pages I shall try to fill in some of the gaps in our knowledge about early contact period Sulka art.[5] My "salvage art history" technique of using photographs to elicit information about early contact period Sulka art

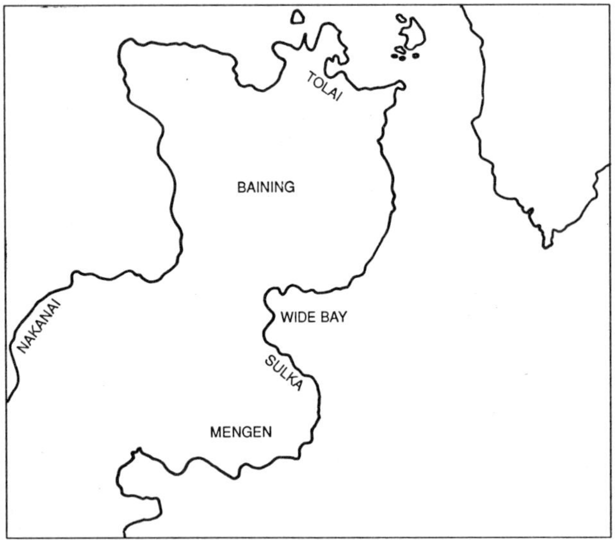

FIGURE 6.1. Map of East New Britain and Southern New Ireland, Papua New Guinea, including the Sulka and neighboring language groups. After Chowning (1976) and Wurm (1975).

revealed a high degree of agreement among informants as to the iconographical, technical, and contextual interpretations of the objects depicted in twenty-seven of the fifty photographs. These are the illustrations I have selected for this paper. The investigation suggests that there were at least five distinct types of *hemlaut* masks, seven types of *susu* masks, two types of decorated dance wands, two types of war shields, eight types of war clubs, two types of men's house carving, and two types of decorated plank-built canoes in existence from the late 1890s through the late 1920s.

A *hemlaut* mask in the Field Museum of Natural History in Chicago (figs. 6.3 and 6.4) consists of a pith cone-shaped lower form (*mnekiet*) on top of a large pith praying mantis (*kovio*) beneath a large pith umbrella-like form (*elpek*). The cut-off cone shape was identified as representing a species of wild taro known as *kakal*. On either side of the mantis are large claw-like shapes representing the pincers of the mantis. Pincers are also created as painted patterns on the underside of the umbrella along with painted geometric patterns. Patterns were generally called *mla* or sometimes *riteak*, "writing". The costume beneath the mask consists of two parts, both made from

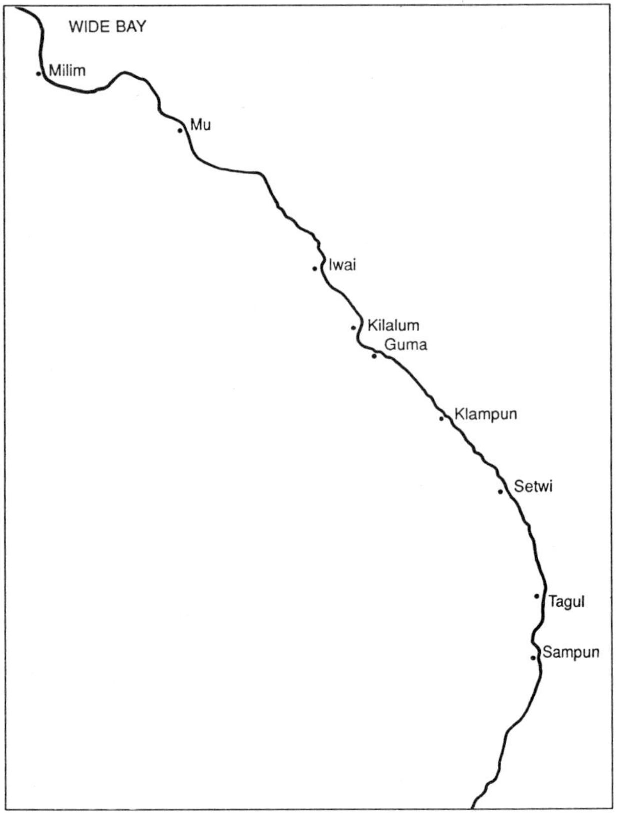

FIGURE 6.2. Map of Sulka village on Wide Bay in East New Britain. After Papua New Guinea, Topographic Survey Maps: *Kol* (Sheet 9387 [Edition 1] Series T601).

leaves. The upper skirt (*powan*) is made from *wuvrik* and *patelei* leaves, while the lower leaves (*ningel*) of a palm comprise the lower skirt (*wok*). The top and bottom areas of the cone have bulbous curved rings protruding from the surface (called *pur*) which represent welts formed by cutting a surface. The parrot feather decorations (*plang-pupu*) are decorative elements added to the outer edge of the umbrella. Figure 6.4 shows the same mask with the umbrella pushed backward to reveal the patterns on its underside. These patterns contain representations of the wings of the praying mantis in addition to the pincers noted previously.

These two illustrations actually reveal two important dance movements common to *hemlaut* presentations. The first (with the mask on the horizontal plane) involves the dancer jumping up and down with the mask held in place.

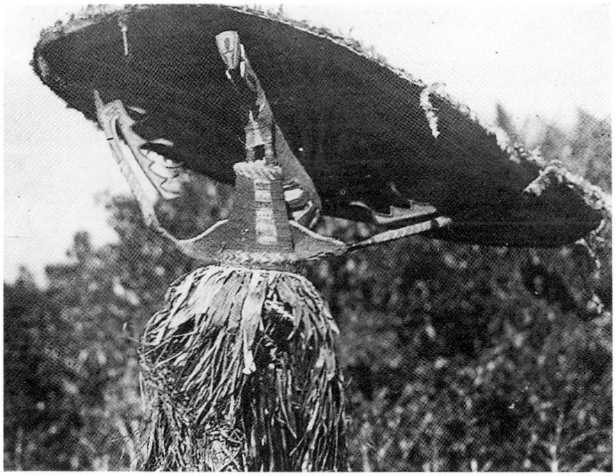

FIGURE 6.3. Sulka *hemlaut* mask with praying mantis form. Field Museum of Natural History, Chicago, negative No. 33604 (A. B. Lewis, 1909). Photograph courtesy of the Museum.

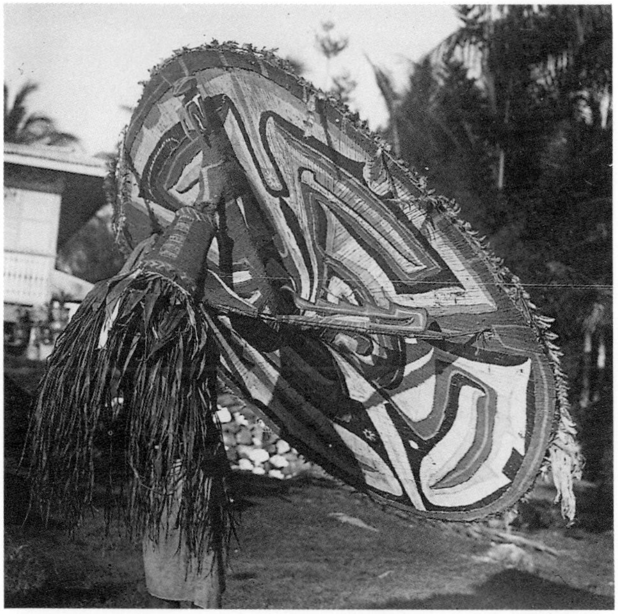

FIGURE 6.4. Same *hemlaut* mask as in figure 6.3 with the umbrella shape thrown back to reveal the painting on the underside. Field Museum of Natural History, Chicago, negative No. 33584 (A. B. Lewis, 1909). Photograph courtesy of the Museum.

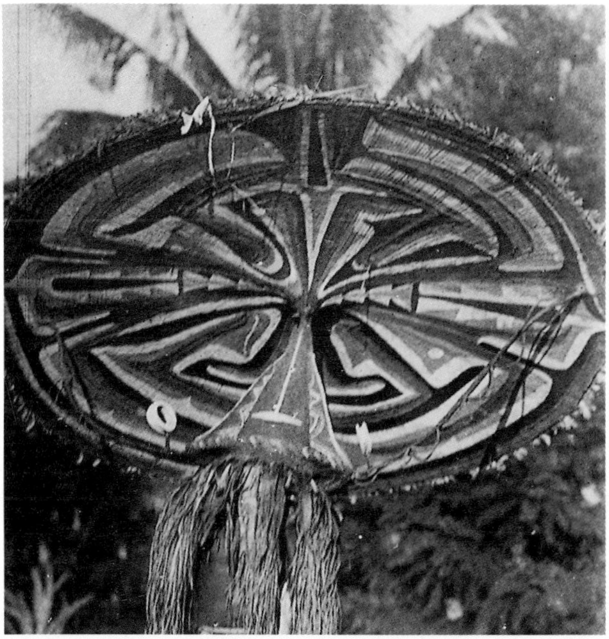

FIGURE 6.5. Sulka *hemlaut* mask with shell rings and shell money strung beneath elaborately painted umbrella shape. Field Museum of Natural History, Chicago, negative No. 33581 (A. B. Lewis, 1908). Photograph courtesy of the Museum.

The second (with the mask thrown back on a diagonal plane) involves the dancer showing off the painting on the underside of the umbrella to the audience. The upright dance position is called *kneng a kapun*, and the second position *kneng a kakhai*. Both are accompanied by special songs. The diplay of the patterns beneath the umbrella is called *tkhinem a riteak*, that is, showing the writing. Virtually all Sulka informants agreed that this mask came from the Sulka. At Iwai village, leaders from the Porgwan clan claimed authorship for this mask type, saying that they had seen their clan ancestors dance with a similar mask before World War II in an inland village called Worlorum (now defunct).

A second type of *hemlaut* mask (fig. 6.5) consists of a cone-shaped lower area, an umbrella above, and long branch-like extensions wrapped with shell money and holding up two large shell rings on either side of the cone. The shell rings are known as *pek* (singular) or *alopek* (dual) and are still considered an important form of gift exchange. They were said to have been brought over from Southern New Ireland by trade sometime in the nineteenth century, and have never been made locally. The smaller strands of shell money were also said to have been brought into the Sulka area through trade with neighboring groups such as the Tomuip, Mengen, and Nakanai. These displays of shell-money wealth were often associated with special ceremonies, such as one which mourns the dead (known as *nek*), as well as at initiations and marriages. The painted underside of the umbrella contains an irregular pattern, repeated in four quadrants, which is derived from a wild palm leaf (the palm is called *vrek*). The circular umbrella shape is bisected by a band of geometrical patterns (called *krien*) which is said to be an eye-catching device to attract the attention of the audience. The red and black wild palm-leaf patterns are set against a white ground so that they will stand out visually. Likewise, most of the geometric patterns are painted in white, creating an arresting visual stimulus. The alternating triangular patterns within this area contrast with the undulating, swelling, and constricting shapes depicting the wild palm-leaf patterns. Sulka informants from the Guma village area claimed to have seen a similarly painted *hemlaut* mask in the past at Mankis, an abandoned village in the hills behind Guma.

The most universally recognized *hemlaut* mask from these early period collections was that in the Museum für

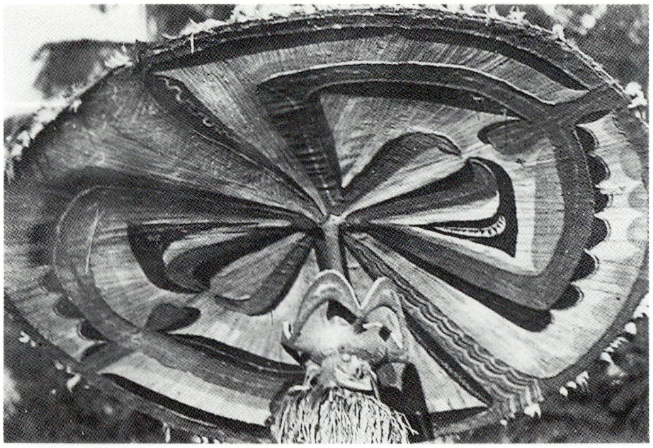

FIGURE 6.7. Sulka *hemlaut* mask with anthropomorphic form beneath the painted umbrella. Field Museum of Natural History, Chicago, negative No. 33582 (A. B. Lewis, 1909). Photograph courtesy of the Museum.

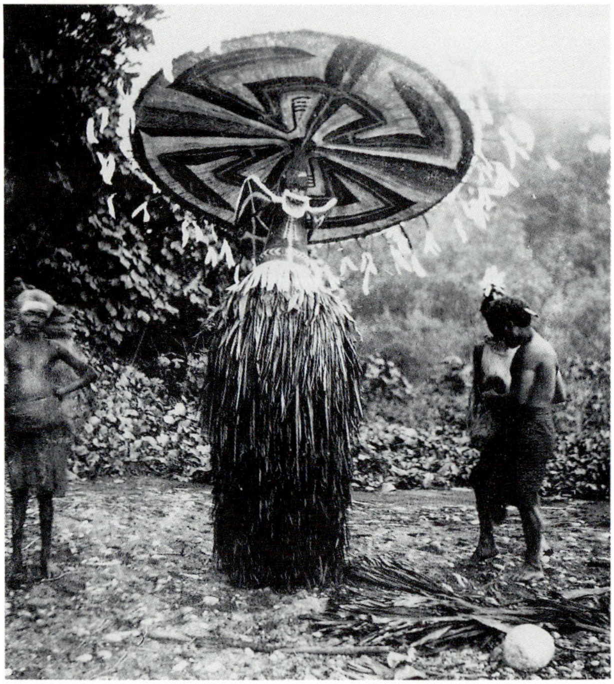

FIGURE 6.8. Sulka *hemlaut* mask with monstrous anthropomorphic/serpent form beneath the umbrella. A 1928 field photograph by Gregory Bateson. American Museum of Natural History photograph. By permission of Gregory Bateson.

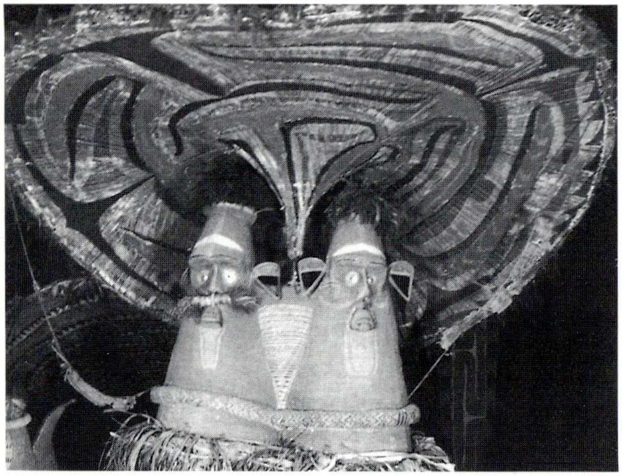

FIGURE 6.6. Sulka *hemlaut* mask called "Lopela" from the Museum für Völkerkunde, Hamburg, Museum No. 6425, collected 1908-10. Corbin negative No. 1982.6.7A.

Völkerkunde, Hamburg (fig. 6.6). This two-headed mask was called "Lopela" in every village where I interviewed Sulka and Sulkanized Mengen informants, suggesting a widespread distribution and knowledge of this mask type. Informants at Kilalum and Klampun villages claimed to have seen such a double-headed mask in their villages in the 1930s, while men from Millim and Iwai villages had seen such a mask after World War II. A man from Iwai named Matpar (now deceased) had made them after World War II and several Iwai village men claimed still to be able to make such a mask today.

The cassowary hair on top of each head is called *msasin*. The essentially human-like shape and details of the double cone shapes were called *nunu* (human-like), acknowledging the anthropomorphic source for the sculptural forms. The pierced ears and nose depict traditional Sulka body deformation practices. The shell ornament for the ears is called *suslang*, while the nose ornament is known as *arrgon*. The bulge near the bottom of the two bodies is called *pur*. As noted earlier, it represents a raised welt from cutting. The patterns (*mla*) painted on this bulge may be derived from the crest pattern on top of a hornbill's beak (*porgong-ka-rirr*, "hornbill-its-beak"). The two skirts beneath the woven pith sculpture are the *powan* (top) and *wok* (lower) noted earlier. The umbrella (*elpek*) is held up by a central strut (*sluk*), while the painted lower surface (*riteak*, "writing") is bordered by attached parrot feathers (*plang-pupu*). This *hemlaut* type is unusual in that it danced with a pair of dancers beneath it rather than the more common single dancer. Several informants at Guma, Kilalum, Iwai, and Klampun villages related having seen such a double mask dance shortly before World War II. On that occasion one of the dancers jumped up at the wrong time, thereby thrusting his head through the top of one of the two heads. All informants related this event with great relish, even though there are strict taboos against the masked dancer revealing his identity to the audience.

A second *hemlaut* mask with a human-like lower sculptural form is illustrated in figure 6.7. This piece and others in Chicago's Field Museum were collected for the museum between 1909 and 1913 by A. B. Lewis. The high-arching curved shapes (*pra*) over the eyes were said to represent prominent eyebrows (*pieng*). The painted patterns on the umbrella were identified as representing the claws (giu, singular; *galugio*, dual) of a crayfish (*hiwortick*) which appear to be reaching for some type of fruit hanging from a vine.

Another *hemlaut* mask (fig. 6.8) was photographed by the late Gregory Bateson during his fieldwork among the Sulka in 1928.[6] Sulka informants identified the four-part pattern on the bottom of the umbrella shape as representing the leaf of a species of wild palm, as was the case for the mask depicted in figure 6.5. The decorative band which divides the circular form into four parts can clearly be seen, as can the parrot feather decorations along the outer edge of the umbrella. In 1980 Monique Ballini, a French anthropologist, photographed a *hemlaut* mask made by Magil of Millim village which had a very similar

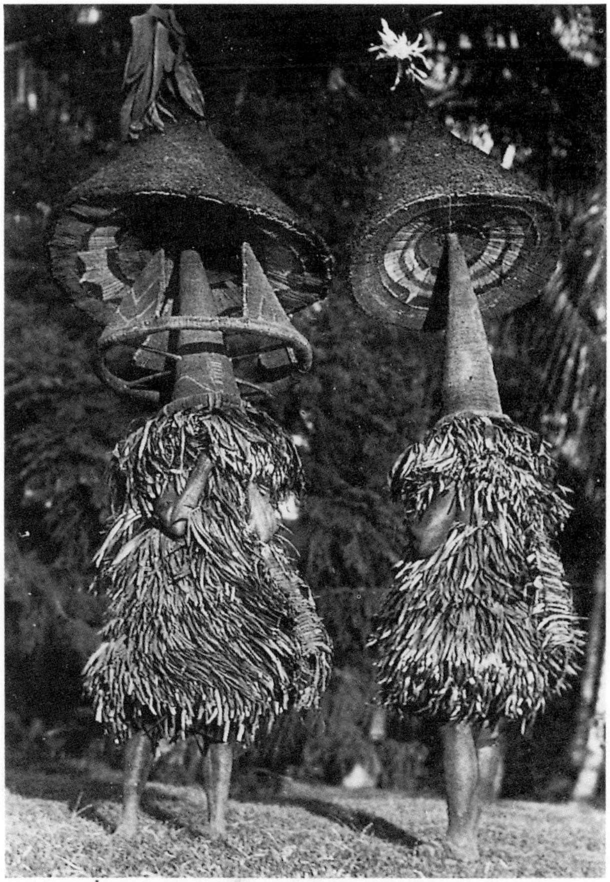

FIGURE 6.9. Two *susu* masks of the *tokati* type. Field Museum of Natural History, Chicago, negative No. 33579 (A. B. Lewis, 1909). Photograph courtesy of the Museum.

pattern painted on the lower side of the umbrella. During my discussions with Magil in 1983 he said he would call the pattern beneath the *hemlaut* in figure 6.8 a wild palm leaf (*vreck*). Several informants identified the open-mouthed lower face on the body of the pith cone as representing a serpent spirit called Kot. Among the Sulkanized Mengen to the south this face was identified as belonging to a female cannibal spirit called Pagansae, who lives in caves like snakes.

A second type of Sulka mask known generically as *susu* was more varied in form than the *hemlaut* types. My field study identified at least seven distinct types in the early period collections. Figures 6.9 and 6.10 show similarly shaped *susu* masks. The simple cone shape on top of each was identified as representing the cut tip of a taro tuber (called *tokati*, "to cut the taro tip") which was then planted in the garden. This style *susu* mask was, therefore, called a *tokati susu*.

The men in both photographs are wearing costumes consisting of *wuvrik* and *patelei* leaves on the whole upper part (*porwan*), and *ningel* (betel palm) leaves on the lower part of the skirt (*wok* or *grea*). The photographs also show a tail-like construction (*wurstein*) hanging down over the lower skirts. It consists of aromatic lemon grass and Alpina species leaves (called *tiptip* and *seren*, respectively). Sulka men believe that the tail will attract women to them. The protruding superstructure on the mask to the left in figure 6.9, and on both in figure 6.10, was called *pra*, and appeared to have no special meaning beyond something surrounding the cone part of the *susu* masks. The geometric patterns painted beneath the *susu* masks in both photographs were called *mla*, and were said to be put there

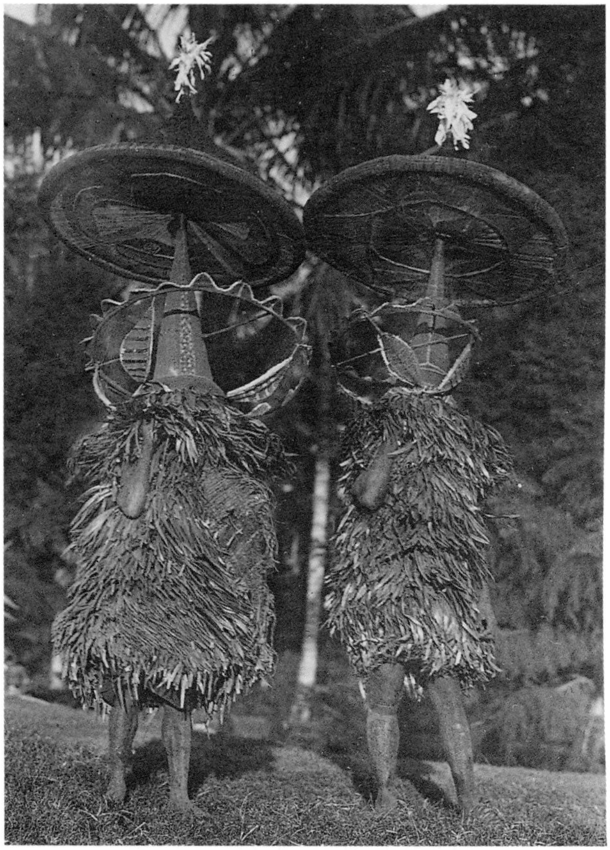

FIGURE 6.10. Two *susu* masks of the *tokati* type. Field Museum of Natural History, Chicago, negative No. 33578 (A. B. Lewis photograph, 1909). Photograph courtesy of the Museum.

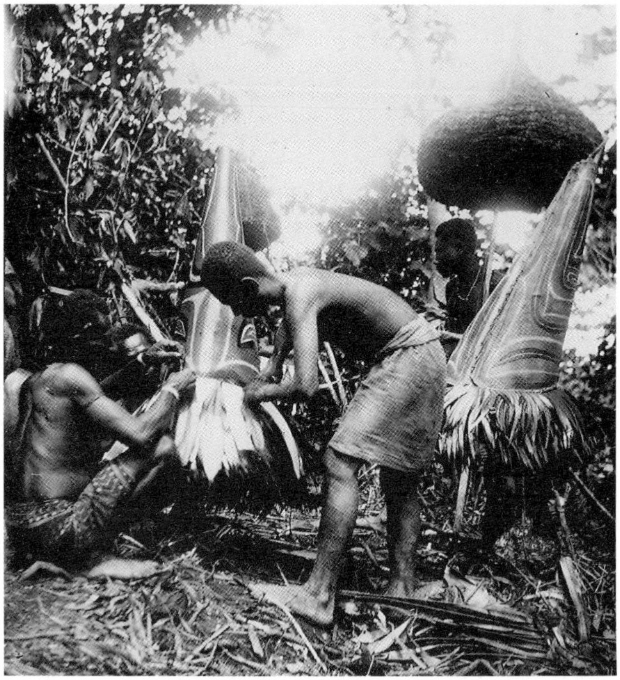

FIGURE 6.11. Sulka men making *susu* masks of the *kulkan* type. A 1928 field photograph by Gregory Bateson. American Museum of Natural History photograph. By permission of Gregory Bateson.

to attract the attention of the audience to the masks. The same was true of the small geometric patterns (again called *mla*) found on the sides of the supporting cones in both illustations. The two *susu* masks in figure 6.10 also have an additional roll along the bottom of their upper cones. This decorated roll was called *litarga*, and some informants called these *tokati susu* by the name *litarga susu* as well.

The masks under construction (fig. 6.11, an unpublished field photo taken by Bateson in 1928) were called *kulkan susu* by most Sulka informants. They named them thus due to the large shape seen on the right side of the photograph, which was said to represent a species of wild taro called *kulkan*. The wild taro form is carried on top of these painted, wrapped-bark *susu* masks, as is the case with the *tokati susu* masks discussed above. The bark of a tree (called *inglis*) was shaped into a cone-like form, tied along its edge, then painted with patterns identified by most informants as *matpil* (these patterns are found on many varied art forms). Most Sulka and Sulkanized Mengen agreed that this style *susu* mask probably originated among the Sulkanized Mengen, where it is called a *kurkas sisi* mask. The leaves on the bottom of both masks are similar to the ones discussed previously for other *susu*-type masks. This wrapped-style bark *susu* mask is very common today.

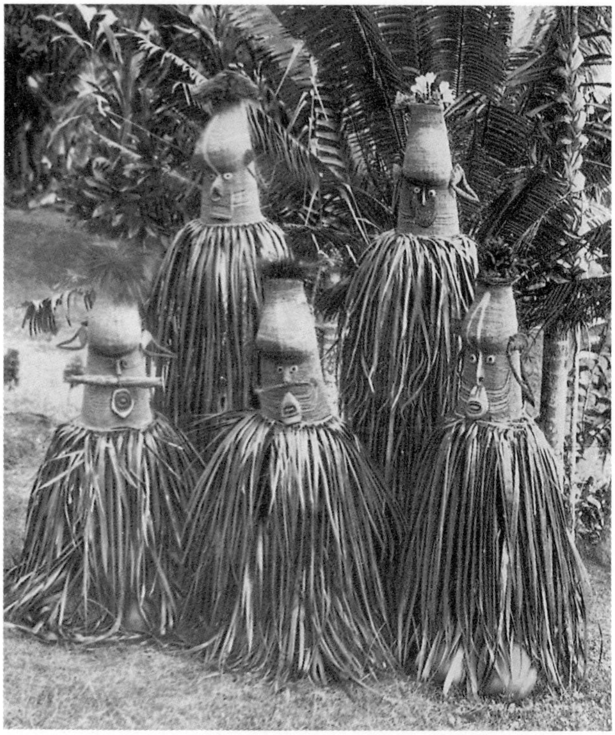

FIGURE 6.12. Five *susu* masks of the *wowoi* (also *gitvung*) type. After Parkinson (1907:plate 46, opposite p. 720).

A third type of *susu* mask is represented in figures 6.12 and 6.13. Figure 6.12 (from Parkinson 1907) shows five *susu* masks that were identified as *wowoi susu* or *gitvung susu* by the Sulka. *Wowoi* apparently refers to a locally found shellfish which has a similar shape to the head of this *susu* mask. The *wowoi*'s flesh is also eaten by the Sulka. The long skirt covering the maskers is called *wok* and consists of shredded betel palm leaves. The top-knot of hair consists of cassowary feathers (*msasain*). The blackening around the painted teeth on the attached wooden mouths was identified as representing teeth-blackening (*nunkir*), a cosmetic practice associated with male initiation. During initiation the initiates were called *gitvung*, the same term used for the mask. The nose plugs and elongated earlobes reflect earlier Sulka cosmetic practices which are no longer in fashion today. The human-like countenance of this *susu* type was usually referred to as *nunu*, that is, reflection. It seems justified to assume that this type of *susu* mask was traditionally tied to the initia-

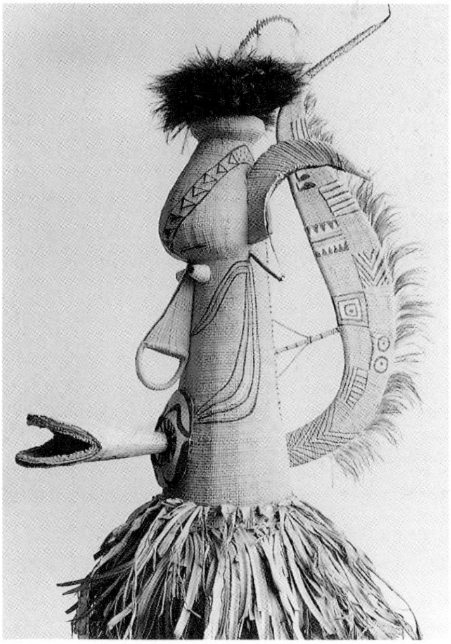

FIGURE 6.13. A *susu* mask of the *gitvung* type from the Übersee Museum, Bremen. Photograph courtesy of the Museum.

tion of youth. In fact, A. B. Lewis calls this type of Sulka mask a *gitvung* in his unpublished field diary from 1909 to 1913, supporting the association of this *susu* mask with initiation and teeth blackening.

The *susu* mask in figure 6.13 was also called *nunu* (human-like) or *gitvung* by many Sulka informants. There was also general agreement that the artist had seen this spirit in a dream (*tmick*) and that the serpent form coming out of the mouth and entwined around the rest of the mask represented a dangerous spirit called Kot. Kot was said to manifest itself near reefs as a sea snake (*vulung*) or in caves as a python (*ragrlaut*). The top and back of the mask are covered with cassowary feathers and the lower section

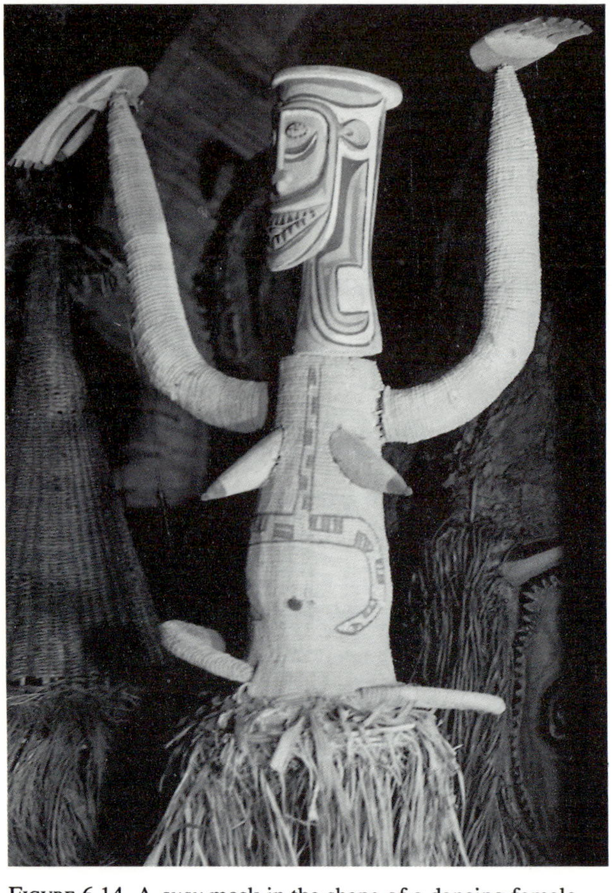

FIGURE 6.14. A *susu* mask in the shape of a dancing female. Museum für Völkerkunde, Hamburg. Museum No. 12.135.252 (collected by Thiel). Corbin negative No. 1982.6.23).

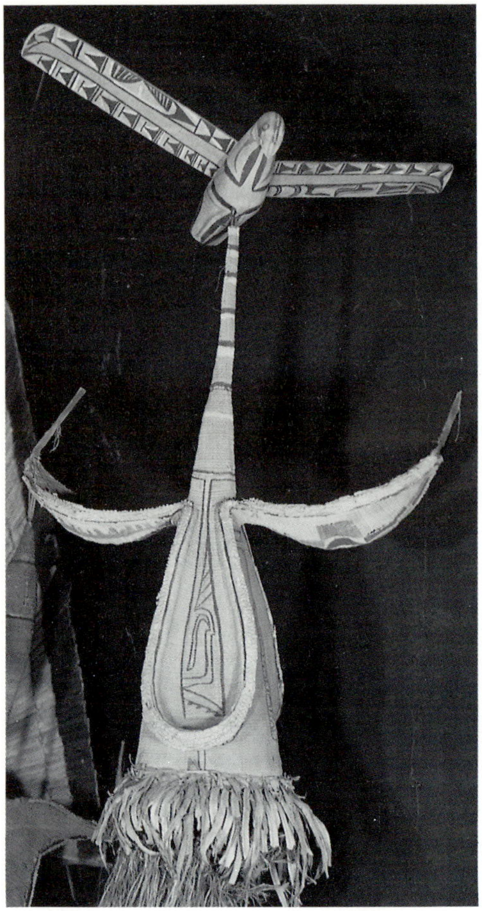

FIGURE 6.15. A *susu* mask surmounted by a carved and painted bird with outstretched wings. Museum für Völkerkunde, Hamburg. Museum No. 12.135.255 (collected by Thiel). Corbin negative No. 1982.6.15.

consists of shredded betel palm leaves (*wok*), as noted for the masks in figure 6.12. The geometric patterns painted on the forehead and the serpent's body are called *kair*, and were said to be placed there to attract the attention of the viewer. Some of the patterns on the serpent's body were also said to be derived from markings found on a snake, although highly abstracted and formalized rather than mimetic. Some informants related that when a man dreamt of such a powerful spirit he would feel compelled to model (*kaunun*) a likeness of the dream image from beeswax and clay, to guide him later in the construction of a mask for ceremony.

A highly anthropomorphic female *susu* mask, one of a male and female pair from the Museum für Völkerkunde in Hamburg, is illustrated in figure 6.14. The pith has been formed to create sagging pointed breats, upraised tubular arms, and a sloping torso with a pair of semi-circular shapes (*praga*) extending outward from the lower torso. The hands and head (*kalpek*) are carved in wood and attached to the pith arms and torso, respectively. The head is carved in low relief shapes articulating the eyes, nose, ears, hair, and mouth, while elaborately painted patterns (*krain*) cover the entire head. There are also eye-catching decorative patterns (*mla*) painted on the chest and stomach. Since this mask is anthropomorphic in form it too was called a *nunu susu* by most Sulka informants. Several informants had seen similar masks dance in inland villages before World War II and suggested that the raised arms represented dance gestures similar to ones used by men and women when dancing with palm leaves held high in their hands in various ceremonies.

An unusual *susu* mask, also from Hamburg (fig. 6.15), is topped by a painted wooden bird with outstretched wings. It was consistently identified by Sulka informants as having come from their tradition, even though none of them had seen one like it dance during their lifetime. The cone-shaped pith part of the mask terminates in a pointed stick surmounted by the bird image. Many Sulka men considered the bird to represent a species associated with the Sulka totem group called *aninenglaut* (big-bird). Some thought that it represented a large coastal bird called *kaeng* (zoological identification unknown to me). Some informants suggested that the protruding *praga* shapes may represent taro tubers that the bird is about to eat. The painted patterns (*mia*) on the body of the mask and the geometric patterns on the bird's wings, the upper stick, and the protruding shapes were identified as *krien*. They served to catch the viewer's attention.

The last two mask types identified by the Sulka as being *susu* masks (figs. 6.16 and 6.17) were generally thought to have originated among the Southern Sulka, or possibly among the Sulkanized Mengen near Jacquinot Bay. Figure 6.16, from Hamburg, represents a male figure fashioned in pith standing with his arms upraised upon a nearly cylindrical-shaped pith base. The male figure is wearing a

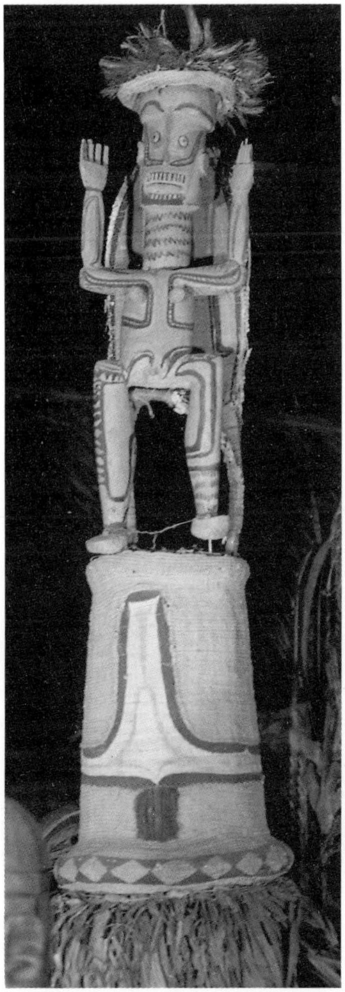

FIGURE 6.16. A *susu* mask surmounted by a carved and painted male figure with a shield on his back. Museum für Völkerkunde, Hamburg. Museum No. 12.135.274 (collected by Thiel). Corbin negative No. 1982.6.25.

shield-like form on his back. The head is carved of wood and painted similarly to the *susu* mask depicted in figure 6.14. The Sulka called this a *nunu susu* because of its anthropomorphic form. The assertion that this mask type may be from the Southern Sulka or Sulkanized Mengen is supported by informants at Setwi, a Sulkanized Mengen village, who claimed that they had seen a similar mask made by a man named Kolol (now deceased) in the now defunct inland village of Navio during the 1920s. They further identified the mask as representing a male spirit who lives around a pond near the village, and called the spirit Talpupukes after the name of the pond.

The carved wood heads on top of long betel palm frond

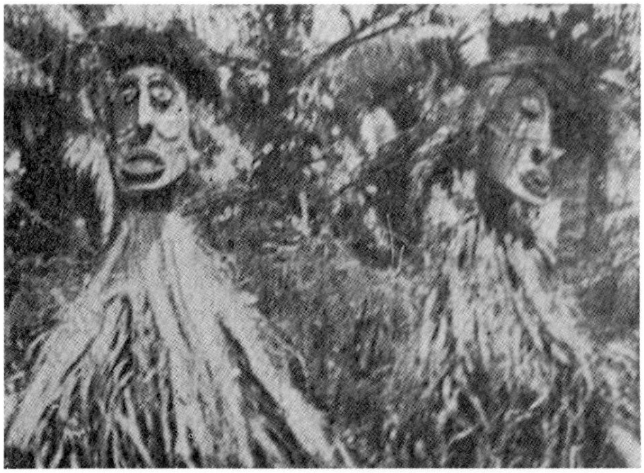

FIGURE 6.17. Two carved and painted headdress masks called *Kepong* or *Alorr* from the southern Sulka/Sulkanized Mengen areas. After a Museum für Völkerkunde, Hamburg, b/w photograph from *Der Erdball*, Heft 8, 1920, p. 3111. (Box 55, No. 45). Corbin negative no. 1982.20.14.

costumes (fig. 6.17) were identified by most Sulka informants as *alor* or *kepong* spirits. These are names generally associated with masks of the Papatar-Tolai speaking peoples of the Gazelle Peninsula, the Duke of York Islands, and Southern New Ireland, as well as the Malanggan art traditions in Northern New Ireland. Most Sulka informants said that they had seen similar masks among the Sulkanized Mengen and the Mengen, although informants at the central Sulka village of Iwai called the masks *sungrum* and claimed to have seen them in an inland Sulka village named Mannmen between the world wars. Sulkanized Mengen informants claimed that the mask had been derived from contact with people of Southern New Ireland. Stylistically these masks are consistent with wooden *alor* masks from Southern New Ireland and other Papatar-Tolai areas. One must remember that Southern New Ireland is directly opposite the Sulka and Sulkanized Mengen and that there is a tradition of their shell-ring money (*pek*, singular; *alopek*, dual) being brought to New Britain from Southern New Ireland, probably through some form of inter-island trade by outrigger canoe.

A 1928 field photograph by Gregory Bateson (fig. 6.18) shows a group of Sulka at a commemorative mortuary ceremony known as *a nek*. The young man standing near the front of the crowd wearing a criss-cross necklace

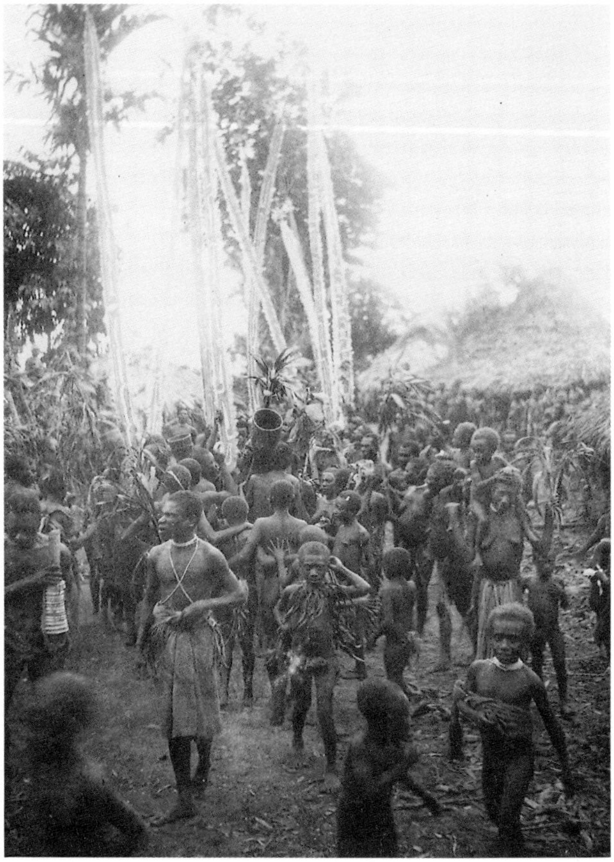

FIGURE 6.18. Sulka people at a mourning ceremony with shell rings, drums, and dance wands. A 1928 field photograph by Gregory Bateson. An American Museum of Natural History photograph. By permission of Gregory Bateson.

(*agoven*) of shell money was identified by several Sulka informants as a Klampum village man named Pleletiep (now deceased) from the Letun clan. The necklace signifies his high status in the clan. On the left side of the photo a man holds a cone-shape display (called *a gul*) of shell rings, highly prized by the Sulka as a form of currency and as heirlooms. Virtually all Sulka informants agreed that these shell rings had been made in Southern New Ireland and had been brought to New Britain a long time ago. Several men in the photograph are carrying inverted hourglass-shaped drums over their shoulders in a manner common to the Sulka. The drums (*okamup*) are made today by Sulkanized Mengen at Tagul village and then

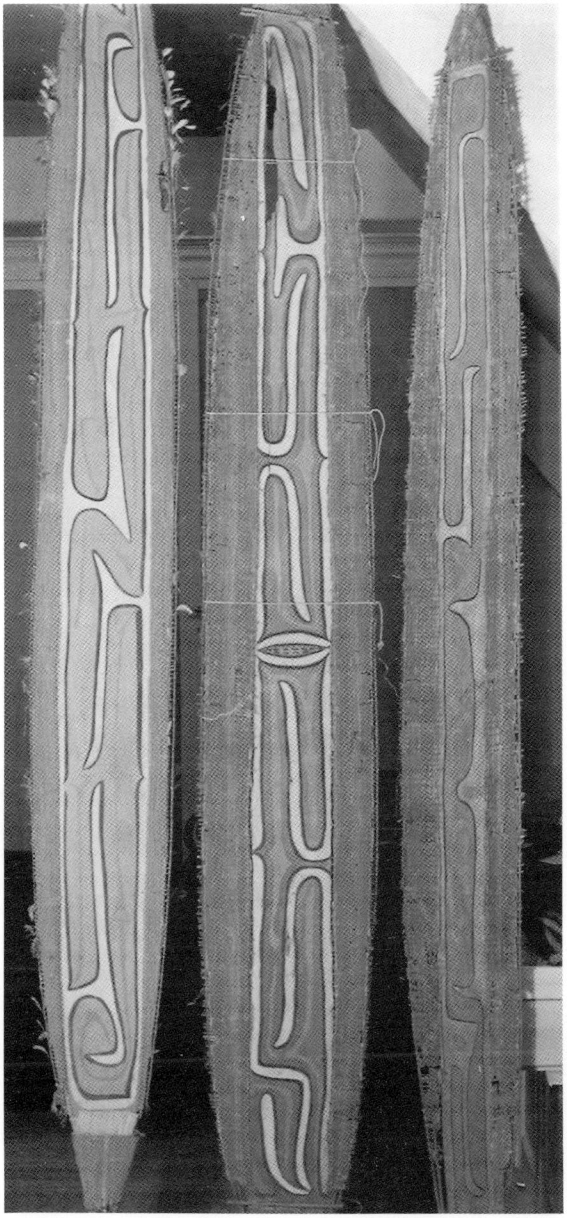

FIGURE 6.19. Three decorated dance wands of the long type used by Sulka males. Museum für Völkerkunde, Basel, Museum Nos. (left to right) Vb 4966, Vb 28165, Vb 28164. Corbin negative No. 1982.24.11A.

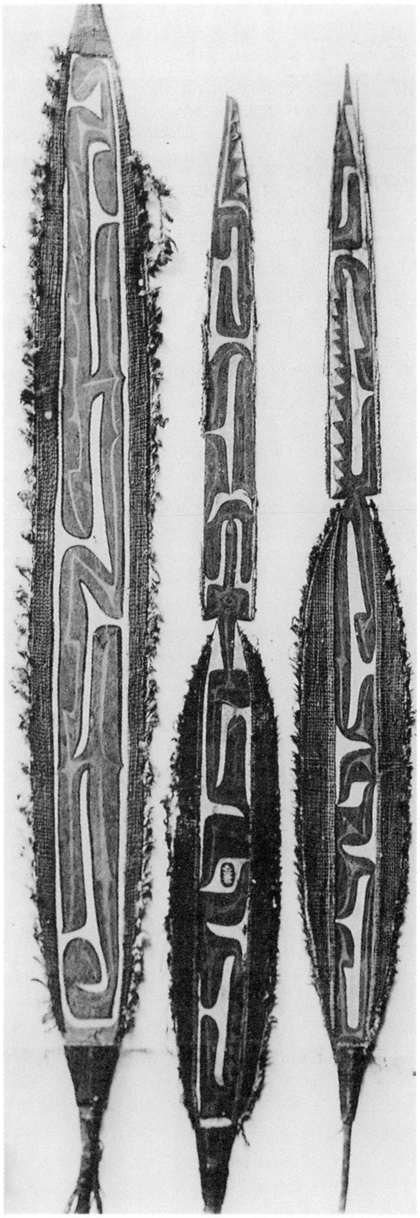

FIGURE 6.20. Three decorated dance wands. Center and right, the short wands used by Sulka women; the left wand, the long type used by Sulka men. After a Museum für Völkerkunde, Basel, archive photograph No. 4311, Vb h2, E117. Corbin negative No. 1982.25.31.

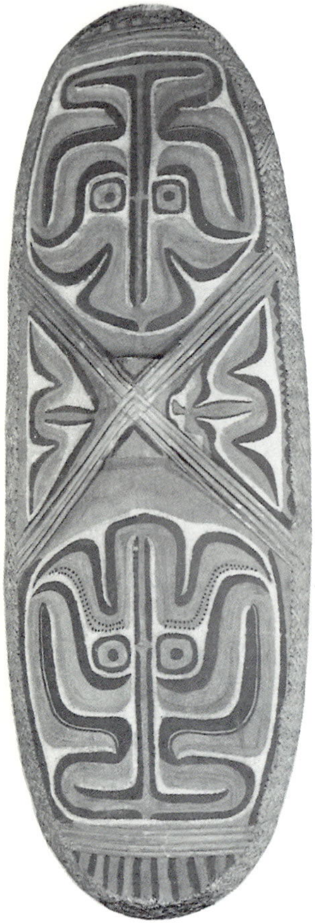

FIGURE 6.21. Front view of a Sulka war shield (*agaile*) from the Museum für Völkerkunde, Hamburg. Museum No. 14.91.1 (collected by Thiel). Corbin negative No. 1982.10.23A.

FIGURE 6.23. Front view of a Sulka war shield (*agaile*) from the Museum für Völkerkunde, Hamburg. Museum No. 6341 (collected by Thiel.) Corbin negative No. 1982.10.26A.

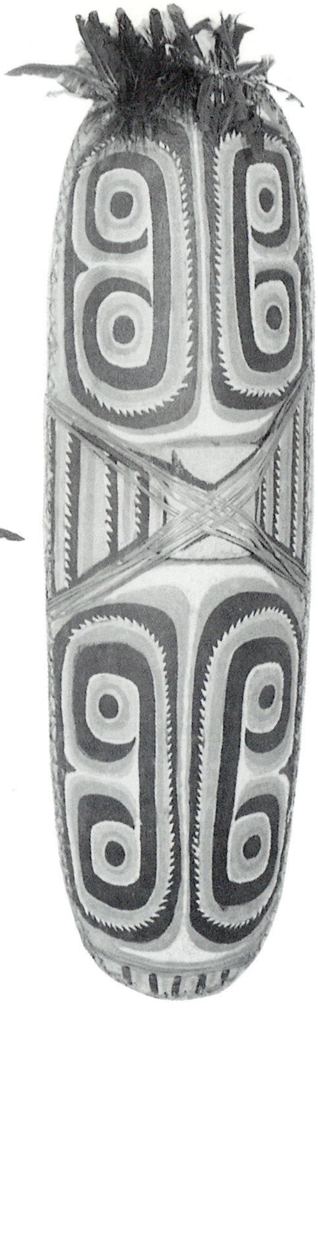

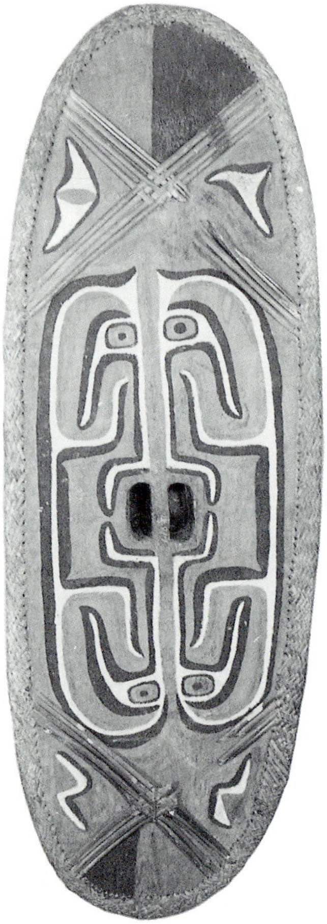

FIGURE 6.22. Back view of figure 6.21 above. Corbin negative No. 1982.10.24A.

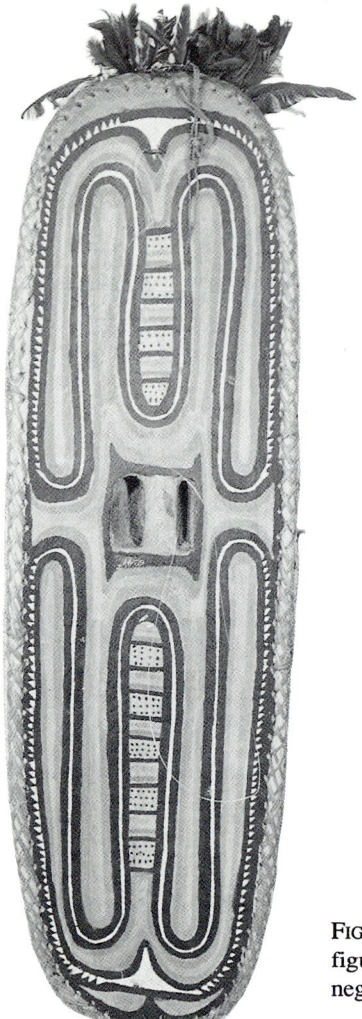

FIGURE 6.24. Back view of figure 6.23 above. Corbin negative No. 1982.10.27A.

sold to the Sulka.

Several decorated long dance wands (*rei*, singular; *orei*, plural) are displayed near the center of the group. These long dance wands are used in the *a nek* mortuary ceremony and are accompanied by two lines of dances, an outside group carrying the *rei* and an inside line of men without dance wands. The mourning ceremony involving the long dance wands consists of six songs beginning with an entrance song (*kavres*) sung as the participants enter the dance ground. Then, a mourning feast song (*kamit*) is sung followed by a third song (*papammum*) during which time the lines of participants criss-cross in pairs. During the fourth song (*mokalu*) two participants run back and forth along the lines of celebrants. The fifth song (*kangarup*) is a purification song and the sixth is a ghost chasing song (*kangursin*) during which the spirit of the deceased is lured into chasing one of the participants, who grabs the ghost's hand and leads him out of the line of dancers. By so doing, the spirit of the dead is properly separated from the world of the living. After these last two events the *nek* feast is concluded.

The six *rei* dance wands depicted in figures 6.19 and 6.20 are identified by Sulka informants a having been made by the Sulka. Four of the dance wands are very long, at least eight or nine feet in length, while the two shorter wands in figure 6.20 (center and right side) are only about seven feet long. The longer ones were identified as being used by males and are called *hal*, while the shorter ones (*kapek*), are used by women. Many Sulka informants identified the white figures on the two outer wands (fig. 6.19) as representing sea gulls (*anandu*) standing on the sand. The shapes resemble an abstracted bird stretched out horizontally against the darker reddish background. The center wand has U-shaped curved white forms which constrict at some places, creating a repetitive balance of shapes within the entire elongated oval composition. These white forms were identified as the intestines of a pig (*avra ka vrick*).

Most informants thought that all three wands in figure 6.20 represent variations on the sea-gull motif, although some identified the patterns on the wand at the right as a cut-up vine called *sprang ka mnas*. The serrated designs on the center and right pieces were called *krien*, and served as "eye-catching" visual devices. All informants agreed that the dance wands consist of four distinct sections: a bottom handle or cone-shaped headdress (*kapurei*), the framework which holds up the entire piece (*kawanwan*), the painted center section (*ramsai*), and the top or "head" of the wand (*a rei kalpek*, "the head-of-the-*rei*").

The front and back view of a pre-World War I Sulka war shield (*a gaile*, figs. 6.21 and 6.22) show good examples of traditional patterns of shield design from the time shortly after sustained contact with Europeans. The shield is in the Museum für Völkerkunde in Hamburg, and like most Sulka shields, it has a plaited outer edge (*a gukaptak*), a plaited criss-cross pattern (*a palvio*) over a raised central boss (*kwie*), and painted patterns over low-relief sculpture on the front (*ktar*) and back (*kevok*) of the shield. The symmetrical face-like patterns on the front were called *nunu* (meaning reflection or face) and were said to be protective in nature. The abstracted bird-like images on either side of the raised center boss were called *salmunu*. A *salmunu* motif or profile bird heads with circular eyes was also used on the back of the shield above and below the grip (*grom*). These motifs were said to be based on the *salmunu* bird whose cries alerted Sulka warriors of the approach of an enemy party. The shield was painted black (*kwai*, derived from burnt galip nuts mixed with a paint called *rum*), red (*kam*, made from the bark of a tree scraped and mixed with water), and white (*kuvio*, derived from a white clay found in local streams).

A second shield from Hamburg (figs. 6.23 and 6.24) was also identified by the Sulka as one made by their ancestors. Informants from the central Sulka village of Guma recalled seeing similarly painted shields at an inland village called Mankir (now abandoned) before World War II. The colorful symmetrical serrated patterns on the top and bottom of the shield were called *ralgien*. Sulka informants were unable, however, to identify the source of the designs. The Sulkanized Mengen from south of the Sulka called the patterns *railegigen* and claimed that they represented the eyes and tear patterns seen around the eye of a snake and that they too were protective in nature. The similarity in terms for the patterns from the two language groups suggests a common origin. Perhaps the snake eyes and tears motif should also be attributed to the Sulka as well. The two long bulbous shapes on the back of the shield were frequently identified as the thorax of the praying mantis (*ra-kovoi-ka-ngntick*, "mantis-its-belly").

Another war-related art form used by the Sulka con-

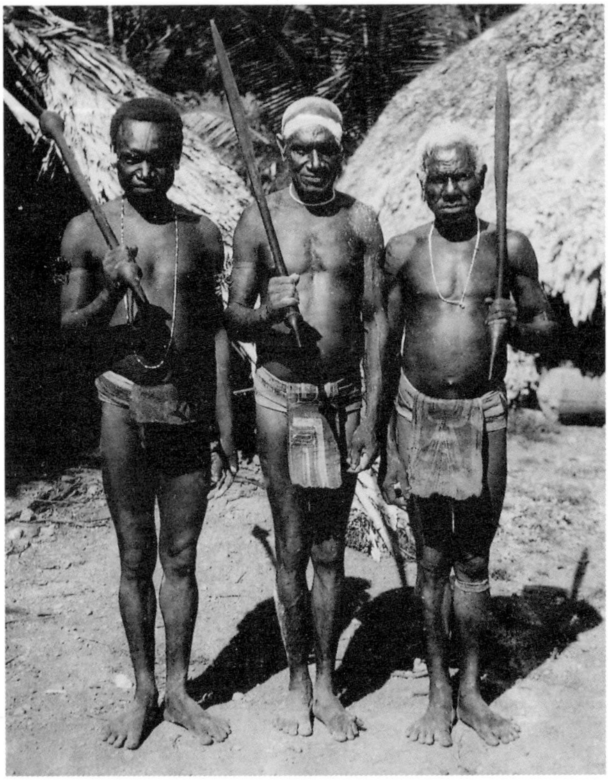

FIGURE 6.25. Three Sulka men wearing traditional painted barkcloth clothing (*katan*) and carrying carved war clubs. A 1928 field photograph by Gregory Bateson. An American Museum of Natural History photograph. By permission of Gregory Bateson.

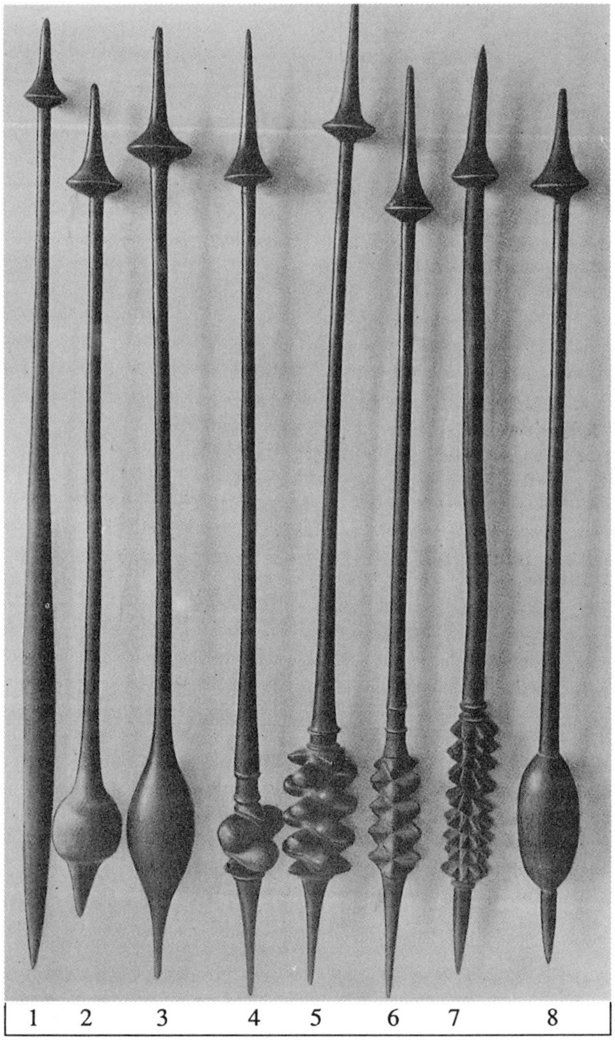

FIGURE 6.26. Eight carved Sulka war clubs. After Parkinson (1907:fig. 32, p. 229).

sisted of carved wooden war clubs with distinctly shaped heads. Figure 6.25, a 1928 photograph by Gregory Bateson, shows three men holding two different types of war clubs over their shoulders. Sulka clubs terminate at the proximal end (*kavogul*) in a sharpened cone-shaped point. The men in the center and right of the photograph hold a club called *rek* (*alurek*, plural). The long flat shape of this club head was said to represent the inside of the *pit-pit* plant. The man on the left is holding a club type called *mye* (also *meae*), the head of which was said to resemble a type of fruit which contains seeds that are used as dance ornaments on *susu* masks. All three men in the illustration are wearing traditional barkcloth pubic coverings called *katan* after the breadfruit tree from which the barkcloth was made. The patterns painted on the barkcloth were called *tlepoin* and may represent the fruit of a local plant used in house construction. These painted barkcloth pieces were also used as brideprice (*kainlol*) by the Sulka.

Mr. Paul Anis of Kilalum village is one of the very few Sulka men alive today who is capable of making war clubs in traditional styles. He identified the war clubs in figure 6.26 as representing (from left to right) a *rek* (no. 1), a *krier* (no. 2, based on a round stone attached to a rope and thrown as a weapon), a *sal* (no. 3, a flat broad shaped

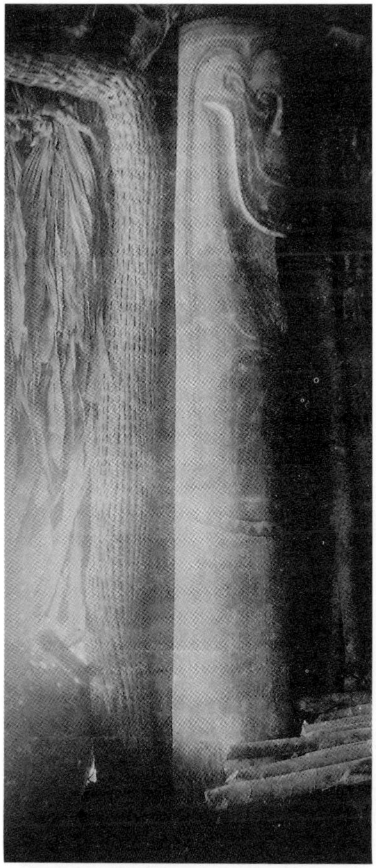

FIGURE 6.27. Commemorative house post carving inside a Sulka men's house (*aggulu*). This male post was flanked on the opposite side of the doorway by a similar female post. A 1928 field photograph by Gregory Bateson. An American Museum of Natural History photograph. By permission of Gregory Bateson.

paddle with two cutting edges), a *karingring* (no. 4, the bulges represent the breast [*vlomsei*] of a young girl), a second *karingring* (no. 5, the bulges in this case represent a pandanus nut), a third *karingring* type (no. 6, the small pointed shapes represent the fruit of a tree [*tieux*], the leaves of which are used in making ceremonial dresses), a *gokon* club (no. 7, the fruit of a wild banana called *lom*), and the *mye* type (no. 8) as discussed above. Today some of these war club types are made in slightly larger sizes for use as dance ornaments in ceremonies, although knowledge of their manufacture seems to be restricted to only a few elder Sulka men such as Paul Anis at Kilalum village.

Large-scale wood carvings were made for use in the Sulka men's house (*aggulu*). Most Sulka informants identified the anthropomorphic post in figure 6.27 as a male commemorative figure (called Mormingudor) which was paired with a female counterpart (also Mormingudor) at the end of a mortuary celebration (*nek*). Typically there were two carved anthropomorphic commemorative posts, seven or eight feet high, placed on either side of the inside of the rolled doorframe (*avuk* or *apur*) of the men's house. The face in figure 6.27 is clearly defined, whereas the torso is carved in low relief with painted patterns. Some informants also called this type of carving a *matpil*, a name usually reserved for the low-relief carved and painted type of post seen in figure 6.28. This *matpil*-type post and the anthropomorphic type seen in figure 6.27 were erected at the conclusion of the *a nek* mourning feast. These feasts were usually held to honor big-men or women of great social standing in the community. The circular pattern near the center of the *matpil* post was identified as the "eye" of the spirit, and a similar stylistic trait can be found on both figural and post-like carvings which are still being

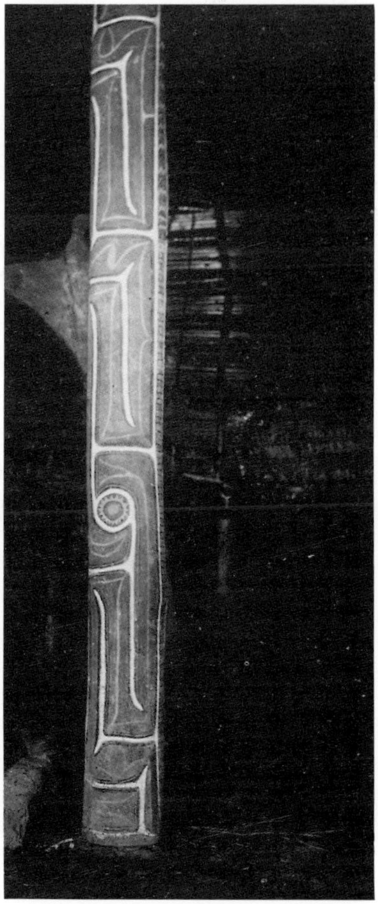

FIGURE 6.28. Commemorative center post carving within a Sulka men's house (*aggulu*). This type of post and the patterns carved and painted on it were identified by the Sulka as *Matpil*. A 1928 field photograph by Gregory Bateson. An American Museum of Natural History photograph. By permission of Gregory Bateson.

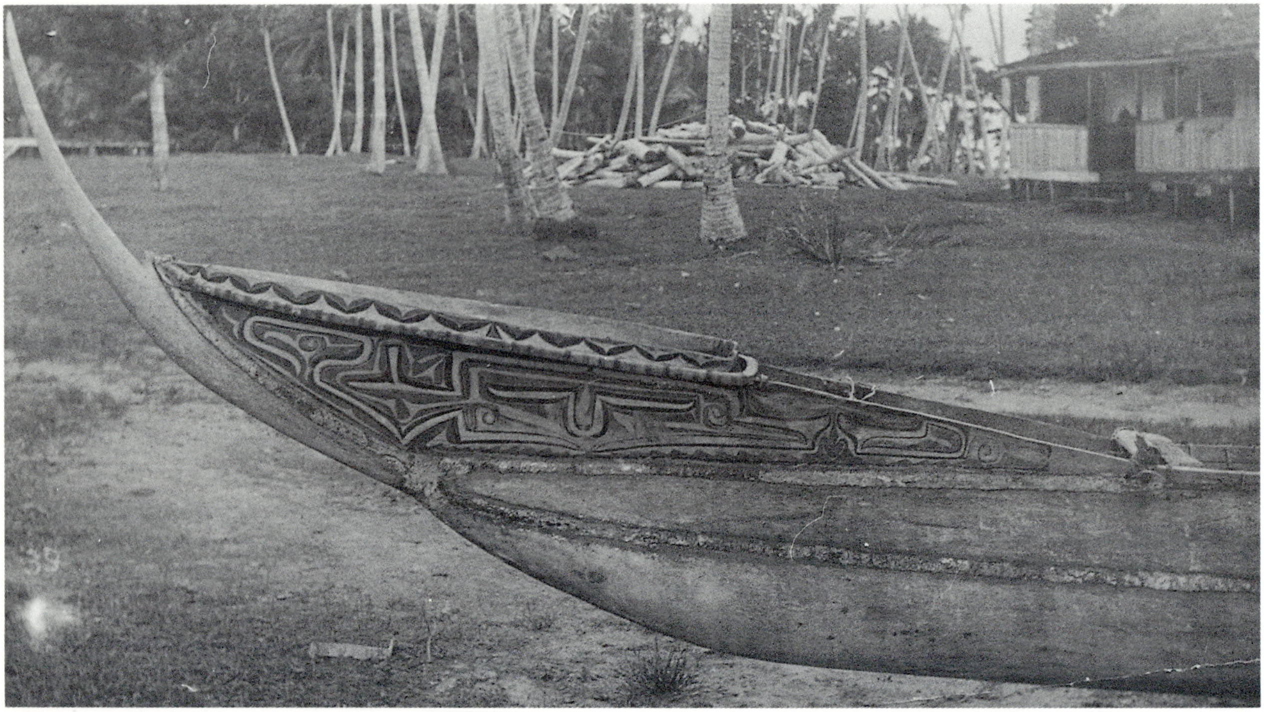

FIGURE 6.29. Detail of one end of a Sulka (attribution) plank-built canoe beached on Mioko Island in 1895. The Sulka called this type *Lepun* and distinquished it from the *mon* type (see figure 6.30) more commonly seen in the twentieth century. After a Museum für Völkerkunde, Hamburg, archive photograph (Box No. 52, Plate No. 38). Corbin negative No. 1984.20.25.

made by the Sulka. Bateson was told that the thin white patterns carved and painted along the vertical axis of the post represented the fat which shows through a pig's skin when he is being cut up for food.

A detail of a late nineteenth century photograph from the Museum für Völkerunde in Hamburg (fig. 6.29), depicts a painted plank canoe identified by the Sulka as having originated in their area, although they did not recognize the patterns painted on the prow and stern. They usually called this type of plank-built canoe a *lepun*, not *mon*, which they said was a later variation patterned after Solomon Island canoes. This old-type canoe consisted of prow and stern projections (*totmai*) painted with patterns called *lepun*. The lower dugout part was called *nan* (mother), while the first attached side board was called *kaukai* (singular) or *kalukai* (plural). The cross-pieces used to sit on were known as *trank*. The edges were sealed with a liquid called *alee* made from breadfruit juice mixed with crushed fruit from a *mallos* tree. The planks were sewn together with a tough vine known as *akaca*.

While the Sulka informants claimed that this *lepun*-type decorated canoe had originated in their area, they had not seen one like it during their lifetime. Sulkanized Mengen also recognized this canoe type and called it *laipun*, a variant of the Sulka *lepun*. The canoe types that most resemble this Sulka form may be found in late nineteenth century Papatar/Tolai areas of Southern New Ireland, the Duke of York group, and East New Britain. There is a great deal of evidence in Sulka oral traditions that there was contact with Southern New Ireland, whence the Sulka claim they derived their large shell money and some masks. Perhaps there were some shared canoe building traditions between early coastal Sulka and Papatar/Tolai speaking peoples in nearby Southern New Ireland. This *lepun*-style decorated canoe appears to have been displaced by the Solomon Islands *mon* canoe with its small

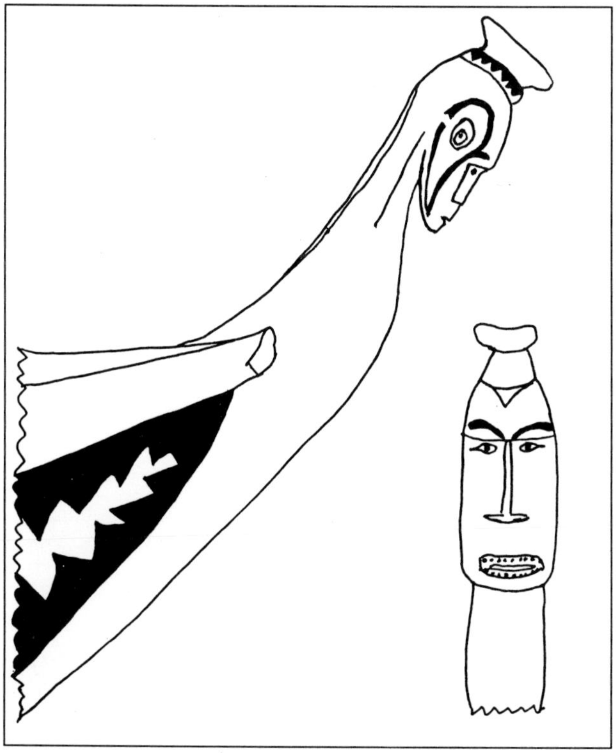

FIGURE 6.30. Prow and stern carvings and decorations on a Sulka plank-built canoe of the *Mon* type. After a field drawing by Gregory Bateson (1928). Line drawing by the author.

prow carvings, a type seen by Bateson in the late 1920s (see fig. 6.30) and one which many Sulka men claim they are still able to make today.

The results of this "salvage art history" technique — using photographs of early period Sulka art to gather information from knowledgable contemporary art makers — suggest that a great deal of data can be obtained from these elder men, helping to reconstruct the history and meanings of their traditional arts over the last eighty or more years.

Notes

Special thanks are due Mr. Geoffrey Mosuwadoga, Mr. Soroi Eoe, and Mr. Barry Craig of the National Museum and Art Gallery for suggesting and later sponsoring my research among the Sulka. Thanks also to the Office of the Premier, Mr. Ronald ToVue, East New Britain Province, for granting me a three month visa in 1982-83 to carry out fieldwork among the Baining and Sulka. My three months in the field were supported by a City University of New York Faculty Research Award, for which I am grateful.

My work in the museums was greatly aided by the professional curatorial and support staff. Special thanks are extended to Dr. Phillip Lewis of Chicago, Dr. Christian Kaufmann of Basel, Dr. Gerd Koch and Dr. Klaus Helfrich of Berlin, and Dr. Clara Wilpert of Hamburg.

1. The use of Sulkanized Mengen follows the local custom for identifying their neighbors to the south. The people interviewed at Setwi, Tagul, and Sampun villages would be identified by Ann Chowning as speaking the Orford dialect of the Austronesian Mengen language family (Chowning 1976).

2. Father Kellerher of the Guma Catholic Mission was kind enough to offer me a guest room at the mission during my stay in Wide Bay. Many thanks go to him for our conversations about his twenty-eight years among the Sulka, allowing me to use mission records for background information about people and places, lending the mission truck and driver to take us to distant villages, and for his general good humor and support of my work among the Sulka. Guma Mission is centrally located along the Sulka territory.

3. See especially Bateson 1928; Eichhorn 1916; Laufer 1952, 1955, 1962; Lewis 1909-13, 1934; Luschan 1900; Meier 1911, 1914; M!uller 1915/1916; Nevermann 1933; Parkinson 1907; Powell 1883; Rascher 1904; Schmidt 1904; Schneider 1954; Speiser 1932; and Wurm 1975.

4. See especially Bühler, Barrow and Mountford. 1962; Bodrogi 1959; Corbin 1983; Fraser 1962; Linton, Wingert, and d'Harnoncourt 1946; Schmitz 1971; Tischner and Hewicker 1954; and Wingert 1946, 1953, 1962.

5. While in the field I photographed various *susu* and *hemlaut* masks as well as carved figure posts and war clubs as we came across them. I also followed up on Barry Craig's and Roewina Hill's 1982 visits to the Sulka by showing my informants photographs of various pieces they had seen and/or collected for the National Museum and Art Gallery in order to gather further documentation (see Craig 1982; Hill 1982). Chris Isaac and I collected several *susu* masks and war clubs for the National Museum and Art Gallery. In addition, we commissioned the making of a *matpil* post for the National Museum and Art Gallery. I photographed the entire artistic process from original laying out of design, the carving of the pole, and its final painting by Paul Anis of Kilalum village.

6. In 1974, after my return from East New Britain, Margaret Mead retrieved from storage a metal box containing Gregory Bateson's field notes on the Baining and Sulka and made them available to me for my research. Later, I met with Dr. Bateson and he gave me permission to use his Baining and Sulka notes and photographs in my continuing research. I have used many of his unpublished photographs from the Baining and Sulka in my "salvage art history" research. Today they are housed in the Library of Congress in Washington, D. C., and in the Museum of Archaeology and Anthropology in Cambridge, England.

7

In Search of the Origins of the New Calendonian Mask

JOHN A. MCKESSON

The New Caledonian mask is among the best known and least understood objects in Oceanic art. With its large curved nose, dark coloring, and strange accoutrement of hair and feathers, the mask is familiar to any neophyte in Melanesian art. It was also among the earliest objects collected. Where these masks came from and what function they originally served, however, remains shrouded in mystery. As Maurice Leenhardt lamented in 1933: "The tradition concerning them was not gathered; it is lost today" (1933:3; all translations here are by the author).

Early missionary accounts, New Caledonian legends which have come down to us, other forms of art on the island, and the very characteristics of the masks themselves all provide, however, partial clues to these enigmas. Considerable research on the mythology and function of the masks has, moreover, been undertaken by Leenhardt and Jean Guiart. The present paper will review the known facts, assess the various opinions advanced and suggest an overall interpretation of the available evidence.

The central question is whether these masks are indigenous to the island or were introduced by migrants. Some scholars have suggested the possibility of a foreign origin of the masks, but none has attempted to present any detailed argumentation in support of this proposition. Others hold firmly to the belief in an autochthonous origin. It will be the contention of this paper that the many known elements (mythological, historical, morphological, and iconographic) render a foreign origin more plausible, and it will further be suggested that a migration from Vanuatu would seem to be a strong possiblity.

No pretense will be made here to close the debate and a definitive conclusion in the matter may, indeed, never be attainable. What this study hopes to do is to bring together various factors into a coherent pattern which strongly suggests a given interpretation. The paper will review briefly the characteristics of the masks, and the historical facts and theories concerning their function. An attempt will then be made to show how all these elements, when taken together, appear to render more likely a foreign origin.

New Caledonian mythology is highly complex and known to us only in a fragmentary and confusing pattern. Like all Oceanic peoples, the New Caledonians had numerous gods and spirits. Many of the same gods had different names in different parts of the island and the matter is further complicated by the fact that "the word

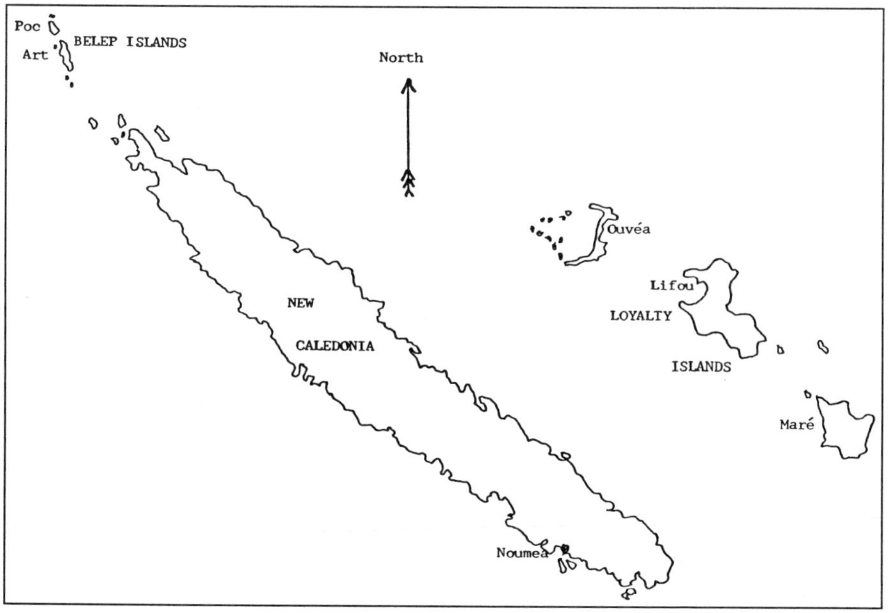

FIGURE 7.1. Map of New Caledonia.

dianua, which in the Caledonian language had very broad meaning, could equally well, according to circumstances, apply to a supreme being, evil geniuses or even the souls of the dead" (Guiart 1966:3, quoting a 1905 statement of the missionary Gangnère). Various spirits engaged in a variety of playful and at times malefic activities and the tales told by missionaries, such as Lambert, Beziat, Gangnère, and Roussel, parallel those recorded in Vanuatu, the Solomons, and even parts of Polynesia. Spirits perched on trees, for instance, would play tricks on passers-by. Others, located in cemeteries or at the entrances to villages, were helpful to members of their own clan and harmful to others.

In addition to and quite aside from these beliefs, the New Caledonians developed a very strong ancestor worship or "cult of the dead." According to Father Roussel, "in Caledonia the temple is the private home and offerings as well as invocations are addressed by a member of the family only to the ancestors and protective spirits of that family" (Guiart 1966:5). The powers of ancestors were frequently transmitted from generation to generation through amulets known as *iarig* made up of strands of hair and various herbs. Father Gagnère related accounts of these *iarigs* being carried into battle for protection against enemies.

The land of the dead is described in various legends. It was an island off the northwest coast beyond the small island of Poc. The land of the dead keeps expanding as new souls arrive. Things there are basically the same as in the land of the living, except that no one has to work and crops grow without cultivation.

One myth particularly relevant to this study is the legend of Azyu. This very involved tale relates the marriage of Dea, of the island of Belep, to Tea Pulivac, ruler of the island of Poc, and the adventures and trials of their son Azyu. Motivated largely by jealousy, Azyu's enemies decide to kill him. After several unsuccessful attempts, they manage to trick him and murder him. Then they tear off his nose and tongue. His mother Dea wants to bring him back to life, but he refuses because of what has happened to his face. Later Azyu journeys to the land of the dead and fashions a mask which he sends to the mainland from the island of Poc. The prominence of the nose on the mask is symbolic of the nose which Azyu has lost (Leenhardt 1954:9-20).

Leaving New Caledonian mythology for a moment, let us turn briefly to the art of the island. Except for the masks, this art is almost entirely centered on the decoration of men's houses. Not surprisingly, this decoration is related to ancestor worship. New Caledonian houses are unique in

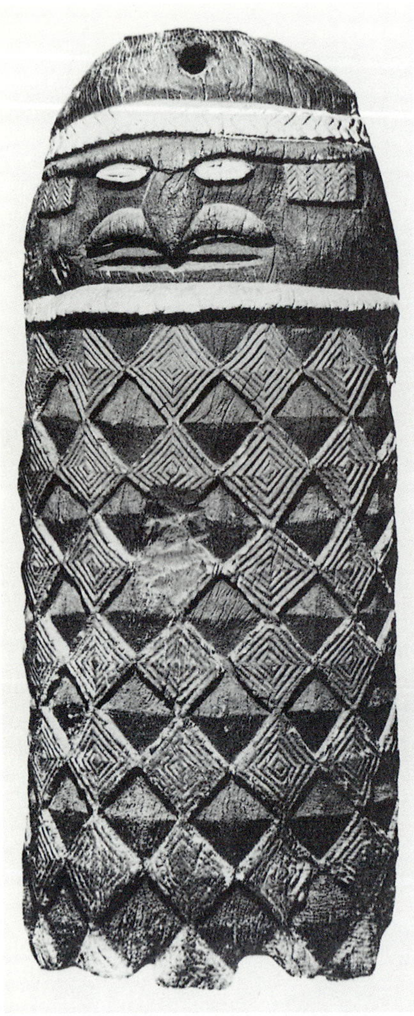

FIGURE 7.2. New Caledonia door jamb. Josefowitz Collection.

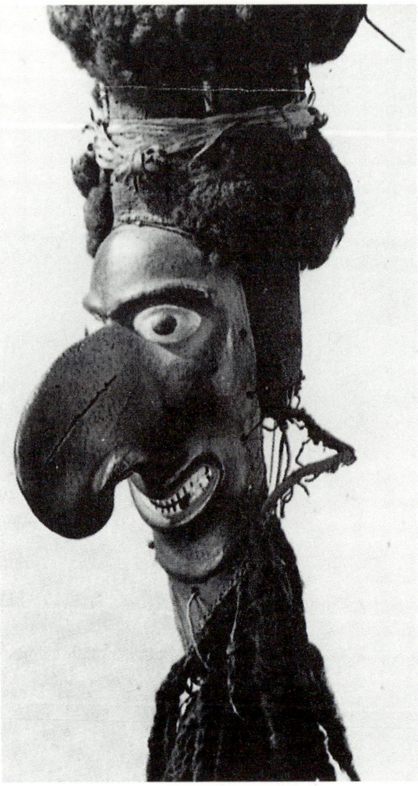

FIGURE 7.3. New Caledonian beak-style mask. Musée de l'Homme, Paris.

Melanesia in being cylindrical with conical roofs. They are built around a large central post and the outer rim of the roof rests on a number of smaller posts. The roof is thatched and surmounted by a spire; a single doorway constitutes the only opening. The decorated elements are the roof spires and the doors. The finials consist of superimposed geometric designs and more or less abstract figures. The entrance consists of an opening flanked by two door jambs in the form of large wood panels. Doorsteps, lintels, and side-posts are also carved. The famous door jambs invariably depict a large flat face on the upper portion of the jamb and a geometric design of lozenges beneath (fig. 7.2). All of the faces in these decorations represent ancestors (male or female).

What is important to note with regard to this art is that all the faces on the door jambs and sills are relatively flat, carved in low to moderate relief, showing the face frontally with a very broad, flat nose. The mouth is a horizontal opening without teeth and the eyes are almond-shaped and closed. Virtually all New Caledonian sculpture, aside from the masks, is essentially two-dimensional. Even the decorated ceremonial jade maces show the same flat faces. The relatively rare three-dimensional statues of finials seem to be of recent vintage (Leenhardt 1937:104). It seems reasonable to assume that this art style, which is found throughout the entire island, represents the original ancestor-based New Caledonian style which goes back to a very distant time. One might be tempted to suggest that it represents a two-dimensional view of the universe.

With the beak-style masks, we come to another, three-dimensional, world. What is most characteristic about

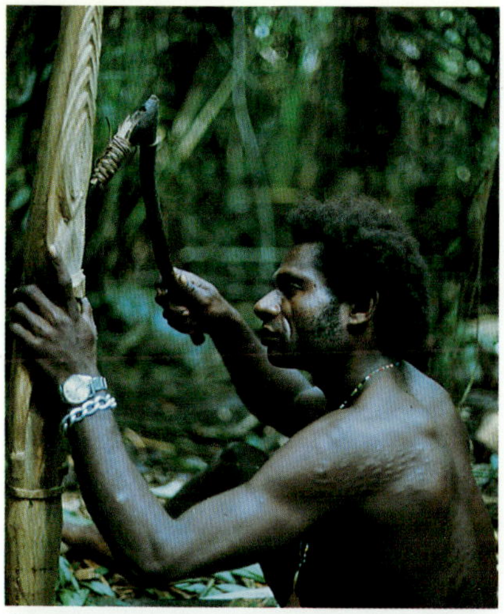

1

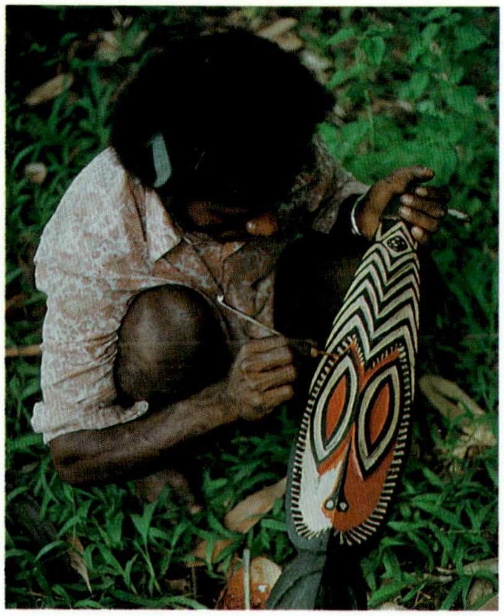

2

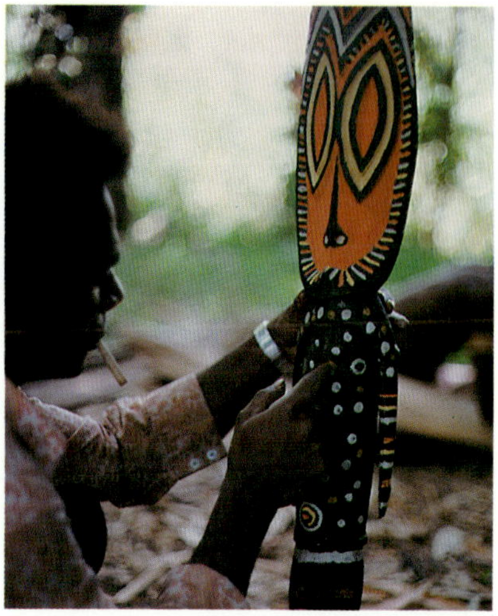

3

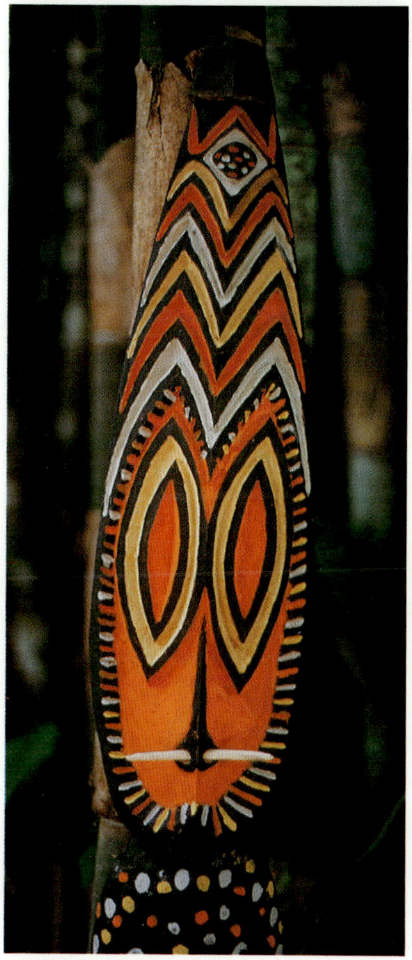

4

KOMINIMUNG ONE-LEGGED FIGURES: CREATIVE PROCESS AND SYMBOLIC FUNCTION

Chapter 3

PLATE 1. The area around the eyes of the figure is adzed.

PLATE 2. Red paint made of the seeds of the *Bixa orellana* mixed with water, is applied to the face of the figure with a leaf-stem.

PLATE 3. The trunk of the figure is dotted. At first white dots are applied, then yellow ones, and finally red ones. These dots represent juice of the bread-fruit tree (*emingnyié*).

PLATE 4. The head of the finished figure carved by Pita Mangal. Note the emblems of the catfish clan carved on the forehead immediately below the hair-ridge: a pair of inverted triangles in black representing the poisonous spines on the sides of the catfish (*agmandaga*; in Melanesian Pidgin: *nil bilong kondong*). The dotted circular motif below the catfish spines represents a nest of insects, possibly bees. This motif is frequently but not exclusively associated with the catfish clan. The dominant color of the face is red, indicating the red-eye moiety to which the catfish clan belongs. The wooden nose-ornament represents a pig's bone. This might refer to a particular association between the catfish and pig clans which both belong to the red-eye moiety.

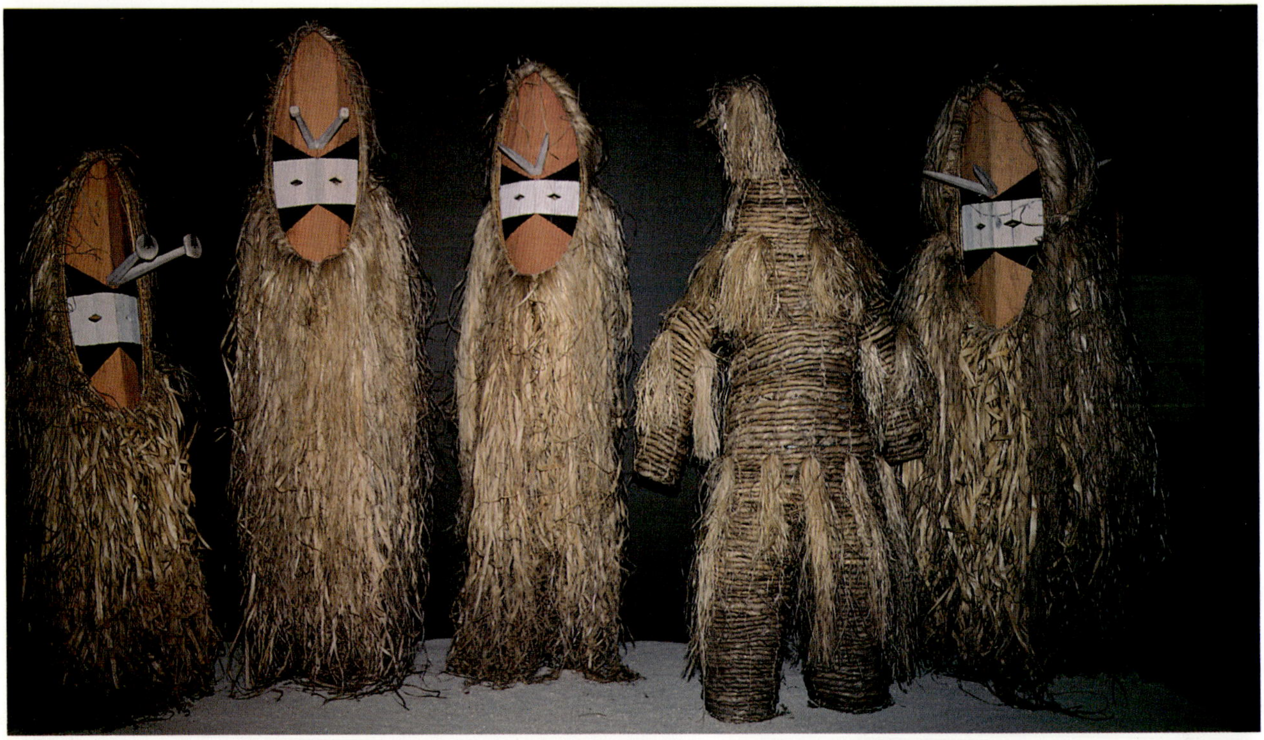

5

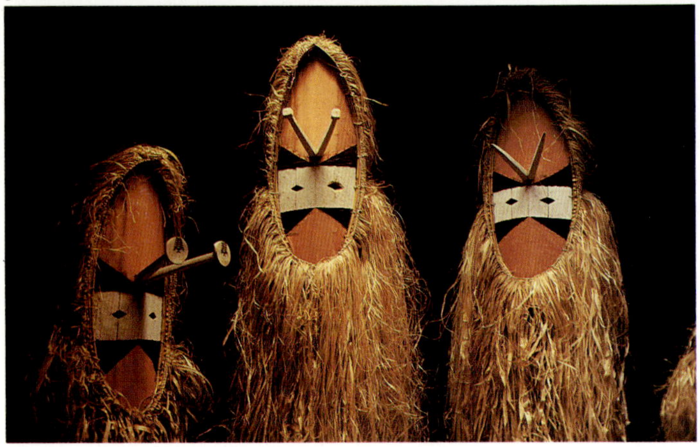

6

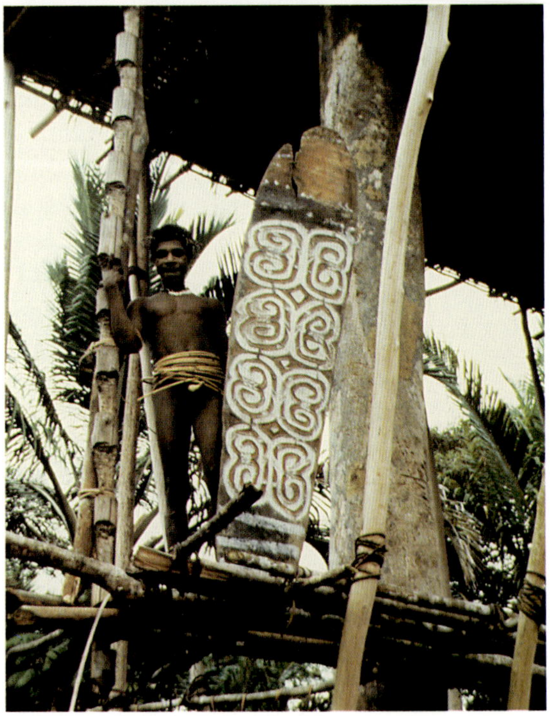

7

PLATE 5. Tamate mother flanked by her four sons (see chp. 10).

PLATE 6. Kolokolo, Aeleteulungo, and Matatilu, from the oldest surviving set of Tamate costumes (Bishop Museum 1964. 60.05, 03, 06) (see chp. 10).

PLATE 7. Asmat man with shield, Amarou Village, Area C (see chp. 4).

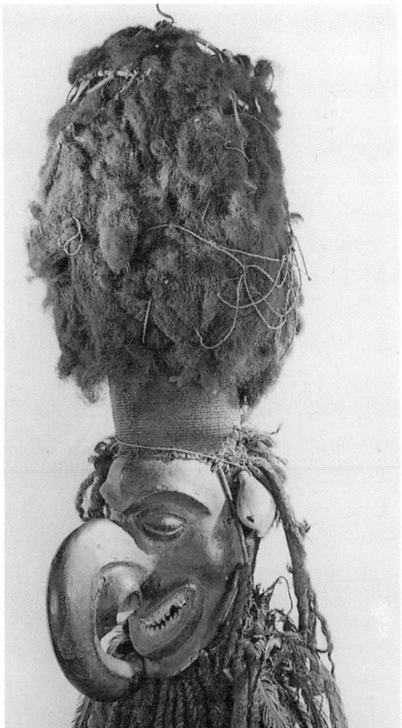

FIGURE 7.4. New Caledonian beak-style mask. Musée de l'Homme, Paris.

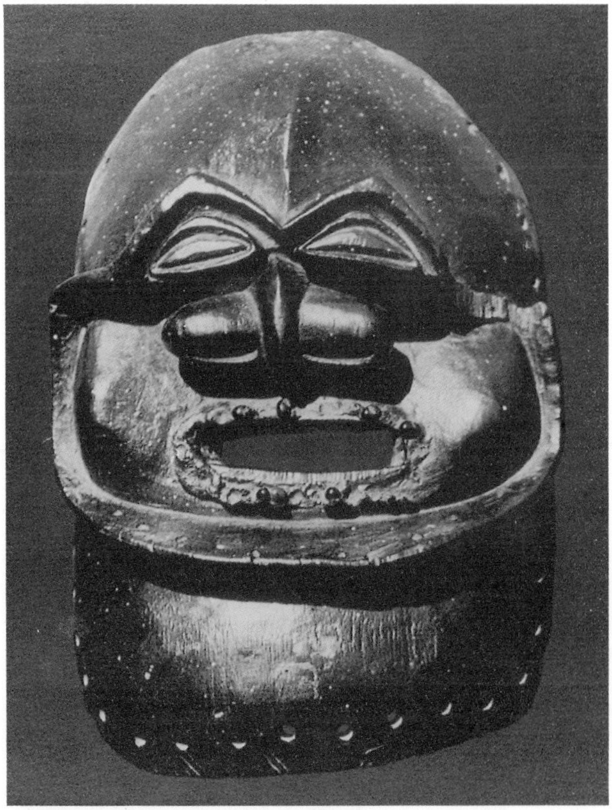

FIGURE 7.5. New Caledonian door-jamb style mask. Musée de l'Homme, Paris.

these masks is, indeed, the very protruding nose and the fact that the entire face is sculptured in the round. The mouth and eyes also differ markedly from those on the door-jamb faces. Along with the large curved nose, we find a curved smiling mouth with small teeth and wide open eyes with pupils. With the mouths themselves three-dimensional, the cheeks are almost non-existent in the slender faces. The wood from which the masks are carved is different from that used for other New Caledonian sculpture.

The masks consist of three parts: the face itself, to which we will return, the headgear, and the clothing. The headgear is made of a wicker basket, which corresponds to the *tidi* or native hat worn by high-ranking elders, surmounted by a large mass of human hair. The lower portion consists of a beard made of hair and fibers, a bat skin tied around the lower part of the mask holding a large fiber net, and a cloak of feathers attached to the net. This cloak entirely covers the body of the mask wearer and comes down to his thighs.

An examination of the faces of the masks reveals that

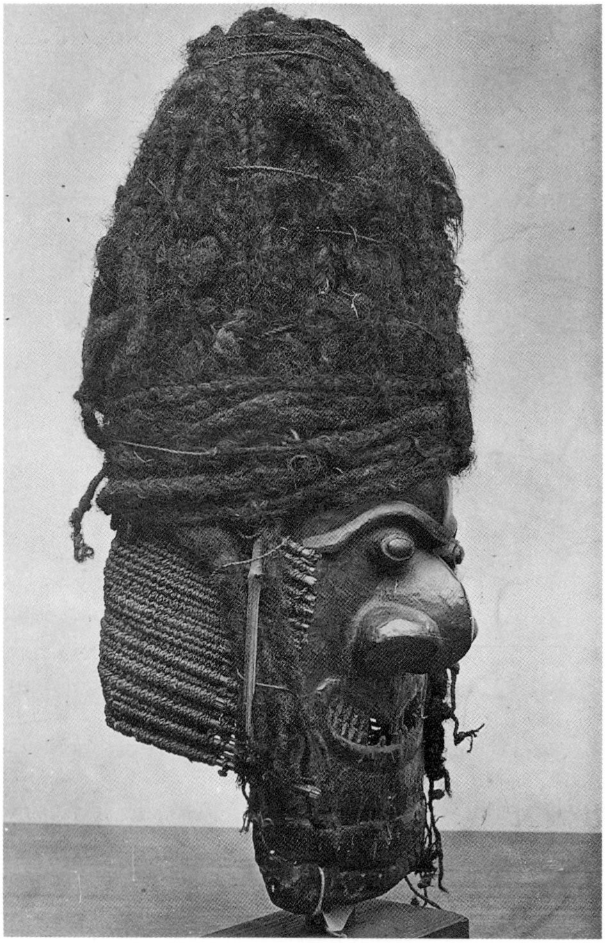

FIGURE 7.6. New Caledonian intermediate-style mask. Musée de l'Homme, Paris.

there are two clearly identifiable types: (1) large protruding curved nose, slender cheeks, upward curved mouth showing small teeth and eyes which frequently show the pupils (figs. 7.3 and 7.4); (2) much flatter broad nose, wide puffy cheeks, a straight open mouth without teeth, and invariably closed almond-shaped eyes (fig. 7.5). It will immediately be noted that this second type closely resembles the faces on the door jambs. A number of masks of an intermediary style have features somewhat between those of the first two types (fig. 7.6). The beak-style masks are found only on the northern end of the island, while the door-jamb style masks are spread over most of the remainder of the island. As one moves away from the northwest, however, masks become more scarce and none at all are found in the southeast.

Let us now turn to the question of the function of the masks. As they have long ceased being used, our search must take us back in time, beginning with the latest recorded function of these objects. The last appearance of the mask in an indigenous environment goes back to the latter part of the nineteenth century. We have a number of accounts, mostly from missionaries, of the usage of these masks during this final period before their disappearance. All of these accounts concur in attributing to the masks a theatrical role on festive occasions. "This horrible object," writes Father Lambert, "only leaves the smoke-filled hut in order to serve as an ornament to a festivity" (1900:147). Fritz Sarasin states, "the use of the masks is confined to festive occasions" (1929:239) and goes on to quote a number of authors who wrote at the end of the last century:

> Garnier saw during a pilou [festive occasion] a masked man coming from the sea shore being received by cries of joy and dancing before his comrades who accompanied him with howls and movements of their spears and clubs. Lemire speaks of a masked sorcerer participating in a pilou. Opigez says that the masks serve as an amusement at pilous, and Legrand relates that a masked warrior, standing in front of the others, waves his weapons to give the beat to his men lined up behind him . . . Delaplanche speaks of a pantomine with masks.

Sarasin goes on to say that the wearer of the mask enjoys certain privileges. He may ignore customs, violate taboos, and insult and savage bystanders (1929:239).

There are many reasons for believing, however, that the masks performed a more meaningful role in earlier times. This earlier function has been lost today and must be reconstructed from bits of evidence from various sources. After listing briefly the most important known elements, we will summarize the conclusions of earlier writers.

As opposed to the house decorations, the mask is not associated with the ancestor cult. Nor does it appear to have been connected with any secret societies, as was the case in other parts of Melanesia. Many early writers describe it as a "war mask." Sarasin, who rejects this interpretation, nevertheless cites no less than seven different observers of the nineteenth century who independently related warlike attributes of the mask. Curiously, neither

Leenhardt nor Guiart seem to attach any importance to this possible connection. The role of the mask as an agent of social control seems unclear. According to Leenhardt, the New Caledonian mask is not used to enforce any code of behavior (1933:19). Guiart, on the other hand, quotes a legend which states that "the mask remains in the house and sees everything which goes on (violations of taboos); it inflicts punishments" (1966:35).

Of particular importance is the fact that the masks are linked by myths to gods and spirits. If the word ancestor is never used for masks, the various words for spirits are often applied. The mask is most often associated with Gomawe, a powerful god who wears a cloak of feathers (Leenhardt 1933:19). The reference to the masks as "water spirits" derives from this association with certain gods, although it may be too restrictive. The name of the New Caledonian masks at the Musée de l'Homme in Paris is Apouema, and this is the same as Pouemoin, the name of the masks given to Sarasin which, according to Leenhardt, is the name of a god who lives near the water. According to Sarasin, this evil spirit can change into two different personalities, each with a different name. As Pouemoin, he lives in the water in the mangrove swamps by the coast. When irritated, he rises out of the water in the form of a mask and chases the fishermen who have disturbed him. When he is in the mountains he is invisible and causes those who have accidentally disturbed him to be buried up to their necks (Sarasin 1929:241). Leenhardt reports that this legend of Pouemoin is widespread in the north of the island, where it is told of gods bearing different names, but is unknown as one moves farther south, where the mask is known as Punumuru, which means only bird feathers (1933:12). Various legends tell of men using masks to invest themselves with the power to do things (including murder) normally beyond their capacities.

Finally, Guiart identified elaborate connections linking villages, clans, and gods with their respective totemic animals and plants, as well as demonstrating how village chiefs associated the masks with myths (1966:127-50).

Faced with this array of factual elements, most earlier writers, like Sarasin, did not attempt to draw any final conclusions concerning the original function of the masks. Leenhardt and Guiart, on the other hand, offered two somewhat divergent interpretations. Leenhardt concluded that the mask in New Caledonia has undergone an evolution during which it has appeared successively under three different aspects. At first it represented a mythical being, a free-wheeling and powerful spirit. It then became the means for a man to invest himself with another personality, enabling him to do more powerful things. Finally, from the notion that the mask enabled the wearer to assume another role, the mask degenerated into a theatrical disguise. With regard to the mask's original function, Leenhardt adds the further suggestion that "the mask may have represented Gomawe, Kavereu, Puemoa in the north a long time ago and a secret society may have existed under their patronage. But the vestiges of this remain to be discovered" (1933:20).

Guiart stresses the association of the masks with various clan chieftaincies and argues that many of the gods, including the one represented by the mask, constituted a category of virtually interchangeable spirits. Guiart sees an evolution of this relationship between the multi-faceted gods and the chieftaincies which sought to use the mask for their own purpose. In the end, Guiart suggests, the masks became little more than "plastic symbols" which served to "proclaim the existence of the chieftaincies." Guiart adds that this historical evolution leads one to "suspect for the mask an ancient existence rather than a foreign origin" (1966:147-50). In point of fact, Guiart's evolutionary theory would merely suggest that if the mask had a foreign origin it was a fairly distant one in time.

We have now assembled the essential elements on which to base any speculation regarding the origin of the masks. A non-New Caledonian origin was suggested as early as 1909 by Fritz Graebner (1909:740), although he merely alluded to the possiblity. Sarasin raised the issue again some twenty year later, referring to Graebner's suggestion and commenting that this would explain the legends of the mask coming out of the water and the fact that it bore no relationship to the ubiquitous ancestor worship on the island (1929:241). Leenhardt, according to Guiart, "drew the conclusion of a foreign origin of the mask" (1966:32), based on the myth of Azyu. Guiart himself rejects this possibility and affirms that "the mask appears as autochthonous in New Caledonia as elsewhere in Melanesia" (1966:149).

Six factors, in particular, might shed light on the origin of the masks and these will be examined successively. All of them tend to favor a foreign origin. None is conclusive in itself and, even taken together, they do not lead to any absolute certainty in the matter. They do, however, fit together and reinforce each other in what appears to be a more plausible hypothesis than any alternative interpretation. The last of these factors, moreover, introduces a new and particularly persuasive element not presented in any previous study.

The Legends. In addition to the myth of Azyu, which recounts how the mask was brought from the land of the dead in the northwest via the island of Poc, there are countless other references to the mask coming out of the sea, or from somewhere in the north beyond the seas. Guiart attempts to explain away these legends by the following rather curious argument.

> The origin [of the masks] by Poc and Belep does not signify in any way, in our view, as one might think, an origin foreign to the archipelago, but an itinerary along the east coast of the Grande Terre, which reached Art and Poc before coming back down along the west coast. (1966:33)

In the absence of any firm evidence of such an itinerary, the legends, in themselves, would certainly seem to weigh somewhat in favor of a foreign origin.

The Beak-Nose Style. The highly accentuated three-dimensional style of the beak-nose masks is so different from the rest of the art on the island (nose, mouth, eyes, cheeks) that a foreign import assumption has considerable plausibility. There are, of course, many cultures which have masks or other objects in radically varying styles. But the different styles invariably correspond to other differences explainable by myths or functions (e.g., the beauty/beast dichotomy in African art). But in New Caledonia, we have no recorded differences in any legends between the beak-style mask and the door-jamb style. We have no explanation for the unusual features of the beak style other than the Azyu legend relating to its appearance from overseas. Here again, the evidence leans toward a foreign origin.

The Northern Location of the Beak-Nose Style Masks. The fact that the beak-nose style masks are found only on the northern end of the island, while the door-jamb style masks are found farther south, is easily explainable if one assumes that a beak-nose style mask arrived at the northern end of an island where a door-jamb style flourished. As the masks penetrated deeper into the island they would, quite understandably, acquire more and more the characteristics of the art style of the island. There are, of course, many other conceivable scenarios, but none seems to be as plausible. Among the more likely, one could assume that a beak-nose style mask originated autochthonously in the north and either did or did not spread throughout the entire island. Either way we run into difficulty. If we assume that it did not spread, and since we know that there were door-jamb style masks on other parts of the island, we must posit that two entirely different style masks (and one in-between style), fulfilling the same functions and heir to the same myths (the legends make no differentiations), sprang up independently in different parts of the island. If we assume that the autochthonous beak-style mask did spread from the north thoughout the island, we are faced with the question of why a culture with a pervading art style would spontaneously produce an object in a radically different style only to modify it gradually back to the style of its original artistic production. One would normally assume that if the beak style mask were indigenously created there would be reasons for giving it features radically different from the art norms of the society and it would seem somewhat odd that the mask would later shed all those features. It should be stressed that these scenarios, and still others which present even greater difficulties, are by no means impossible. There could be factors involved which have left no trace. Once again, it is merely suggested that the foreign origin interpretation offers a somewhat more plausible explanation of the known facts.

War Association of Masks. The war attributes of the mask, some even associated with the mask coming out of the water, are hard to dismiss and yet they vanish so completely that they do not figure in either Leenhardt's or Guiart's interpretation of the function of the masks. If the mask had been originally introduced by invading forces, its initial interpretation as a war mask would be quite natural and we would also normally expect this association eventually to vanish. It would, of course, be easy to generate scenarios in which war significance was associated with a locally developed mask form. The difficulty would come in explaining why, in the latter case, the association disappeared so completely. Guiart makes abundantly clear the way in which the various clan chiefs used the mask to affirm their authority. Nowhere does he suggest that the masks were connected with inter-tribal

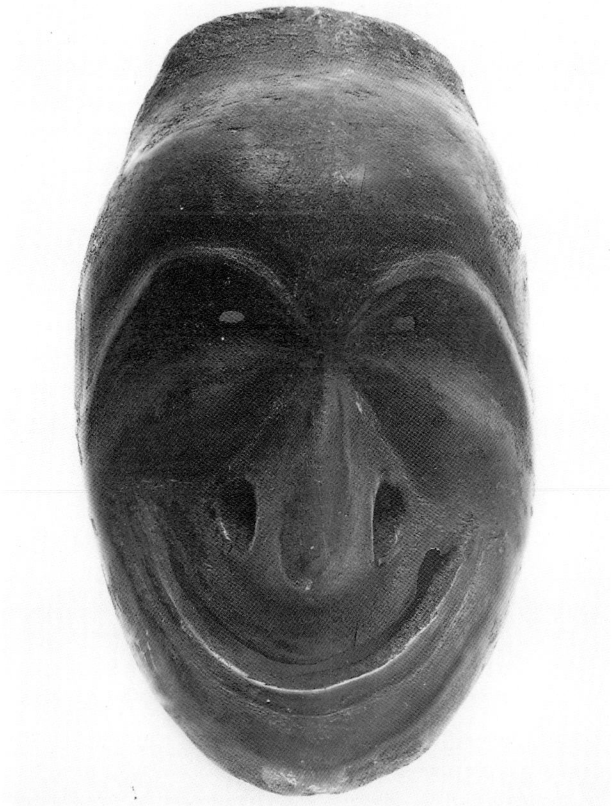

FIGURE 7.7. Vanuatu mask (South Pentecost). Museum für Völkerkunde, Basel.

warfare.

Unclear Early Function of Masks. We have seen that Leenhardt and Guiart give rational and documented accounts of the late use of the masks, as theatrical objects and as symbols of the chieftaincies. Both also refer to an earlier association of the masks with gods and spirits but leave unclear, for lack of evidence, the nature of that association. None of the other earlier writers have sought to elucidate that mystery. We are left with the thought that the masks might have been connected with secret societies which disappeared, might or might not have had a role in behavior control, represented gods or perhaps water spirits, and may have had a war association. The reason why the many missionaries and later scholars who studied the question were never able to generate a satisfactory explanation of the original function of the masks may well be that it was simply not to be found on the island. It should be stressed that neither the mystery of the early function of the masks nor the preceding question of the war association of the masks are presented here as arguments in favor of a foreign origin of the objects, but rather as enigmas which a foreign origin would explain. There could, of course, be other explanations of which we are simply not aware.

Possible Vanuatu Origin. If the New Caledonian mask did have a foreign origin, it should be possible to find some traces of it outside the Grande Ile. It will be recalled that Felix Speiser suggested many years ago a general west-east migration of the beak-style sculpture. Tracing its possible origin to India, Speiser suggested that a wave of Hindu immigrants might, perhaps, have brought the style to New Guinea and that "from New Guinea, the beak-style was then brought to the Solomons, the New Hebrides and

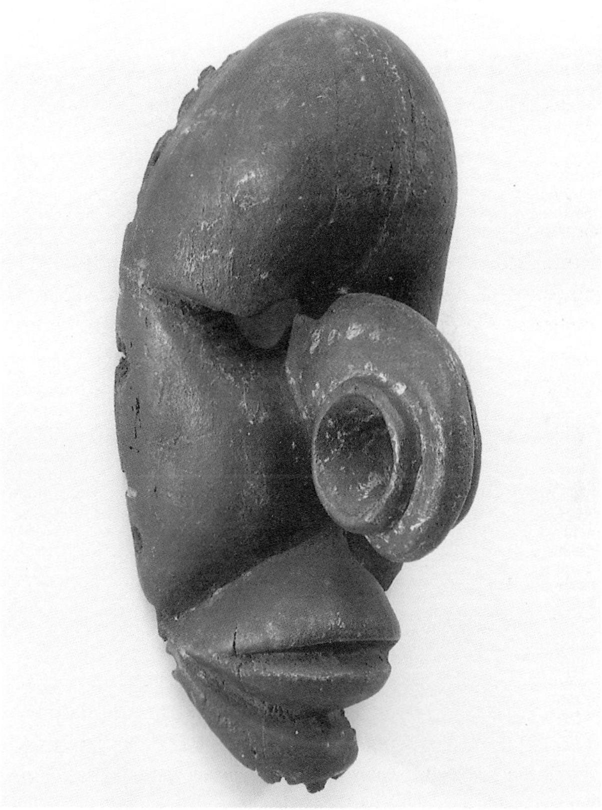

FIGURE 7.8. Vanuatu mask (Ambrym). Museum für Völkerkunde, Basel.

New Caledonia" (cited in Fraser 1966:151). Without going into the validity of Speiser's suggested migration of the beak style sculpture, Vanuatu (New Hebrides) would certainly seem to be a logical geographic origin for any migration of the style to New Caledonia. An examination of the art styles on Vanuatu reveals striking resemblances between certain masks from Ambrym and South Pentecost and the beak-style masks of New Caledonia (figs. 7.7 and 7.8). It would be hard to dismiss these similarities as purely fortuitous. They involve not only the beak-style nose, but also the circular nostrils, the curved smiling mouth, the overall shape of the face and the dark coloring.

It might be objected that, even if a link would clearly seem to exist, the mask could have traveled the other way, from New Caledonia to Vanuatu. While this is theoretically possible, the known general direction of migration in Melanesia, along with the other reasons for suspecting a foreign origin of the New Caledonian mask, would seem to render a movement from Vanuatu south more probable.

Clearly, it would be helpful if further research were to provide additional linguistic, archaeological, mythological, and other evidence relevant to the hypotheses suggested by the morphology of the masks. What can now be said is that the various considerations discussed above, when taken together, build a pattern of probability for a foreign origin of the New Caledonian mask, which the apparent link with Vanuatu sculpture substantially strengthens.

8

Prehistoric Sequence of Nendö Island, Santa Cruz, Southeast Solomon Islands

LAWRENCE FOANAOTA

In the Solomon Islands, the prehistoric period for the large islands is currently unknown except for the island of Guadalcanal. The archaeology is still in its exploratory stage with the exception of the intensive work that has been done in the Southeast Solomons region, which provides dates for those islands of over three thousand years before the present (Green and Cresswell 1976:265).

This paper will cover only the prehistoric sequence for Nendö (Santa Cruz) Island in this region. It is an example which clearly shows how a pottery tradition emerged and then through time changed until it disappeared completely from the present inhabitants' knowledge.

The limited archaeological evidence now available for this island currently allows the prehistoric sequence to be divided into an early, a middle, and a late period. These different periods are characterized by the existence of decorated pottery, undecorated pottery, and, finally, the absence of pottery from this region. This evidence was uncovered through archaeological investigations carried out between 1970 and 1978 on the island of Nendö by various archaeologists attached to the Southeast Solomon Islands Project. The following discussion is based mainly on the kind of archaeological work undertaken and the evidence available from each of the sites. It will describe the nature and duration of the time spans and the artifactual remains which mark these periods as well as indicating the gaps which fall between the known sites.

Europeans first set foot on the shores of Nendö, the main island in the Santa Cruz group, in the late sixteenth century. After Alvaro de Mendana y Neyra discovered the main chain of the Solomon Islands during his first voyage between 1567 and 1568, he returned in 1594 with the aim of establishing a colony there. He never accomplished it but in 1595 stopped instead at Graciosa Bay on Nendö Island, which he named "Santa Cruz." His effort to establish a permanent colony there failed because of hostility encountered from the indigenous inhabitants of the island, disputes that broke out among members of the expedition, and ill health which claimed the lives of several expedition members, including Mendana. The survivors of the expedition abandoned the site and left for Manila in 1596 (Green and Cresswell 1976:19-29).

After this initial contact, two centuries elapsed before traders, recruiters, missionaries, and colonial administrators arrived. Marking another era in the history of the island, these contacts with the outside world have contin-

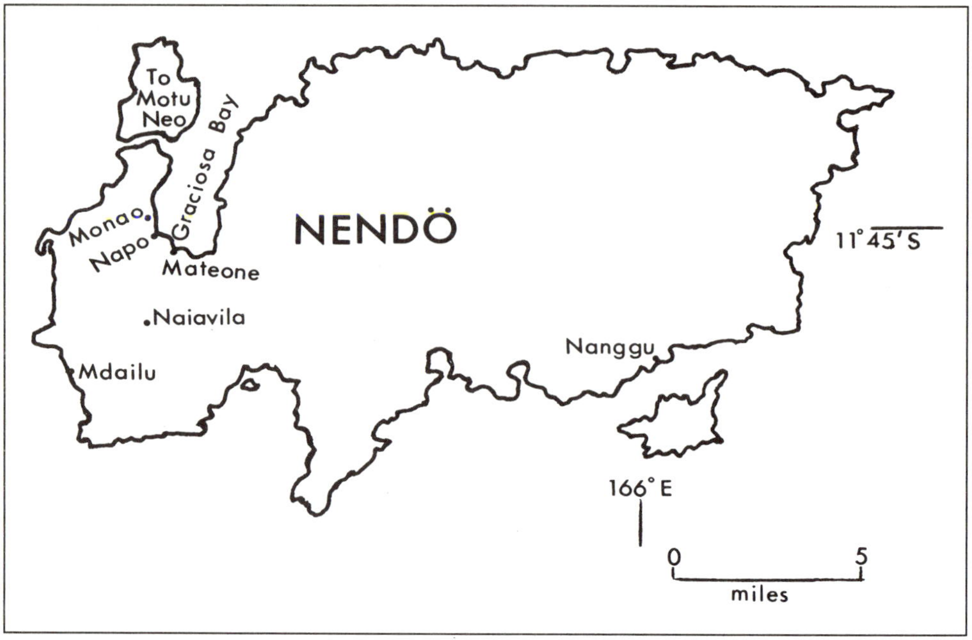

FIGURE 8.1. Map of Nendö.

ued throughout the nineteenth and twentieth centuries (Green and Cresswell 1976:31-46).

According to the records available from the early explorers' accounts, Nendö Island was inhabited at the time of first European contact. However these accounts are limited in their descriptions of the indigenous people of the island and their way of life. Little was known or described for the periods prior to contact. The first Europeans who went to the island were mainly interested in achieving personal goals and did not inquire into issues such as when the local people first settled the island, where they came from, and how long they had been there. It was not until the 1970s that these problems were investigated. The Southeast Solomon Islands Cultural History Program, established by Roger Green and Douglas Yen, brought together experts from various scientific fields who worked on these problems at various times between 1970 and 1978.

The first phase of the program involved archaeological investigations of a probable site of the settlement period. This site was located by Green at Nanggu on the southeast coast of Nendö, where he found Lapita potsherds. It proved to be the earliest site of the local prehistoric sequence. The site was located 518 meters inland in flat garden land, about five to six meters above the present day sea level (Green and Cresswell 1976:250). The natural environment and the high rainfall in the area made the location favorable for settlement. The high rainfall is particularly important, for in areas of low rainfall streams that supply fresh water for drinking and fish for food might dry up. The archaeological excavation of the site revealed evidence of both plain and decorated potsherds. Their distribution over the site indicated a settlement area of fourteen thousand square meters.

Apart from the recovery of pottery, evidence of cooking activity was indicated by the midden remains of shellfish and bone concentrated mainly around ovens and pits. Other cultural items found on the site included pieces of pottery vessels, both shell and stone adze blades, shell scrapers, and tools similar to those found in other prehistoric Oceanic sites. The discovery of Lapita potsherds established the existence of early Western Lapita style ceramics in this part of Melanesia.

The archaeological evidence obtained from analyzing obsidian and chert flakes found on the Nanggu site suggested some form of long distance trade because these materials were not available locally. Most of the obsidian was brought from the Talasea source in New Britain

(Green and Cresswell 1976:259).

The Nanggu site appears to represent the period of first settlement on Nendö. Shell samples were dated and the results suggest that the site was occupied prior to the fourteenth century B.C.

The middle period of the prehistoric sequence is best represented by archaeological evidence from Mdailu site at Manoputi on the west coast of Nendö Island. Set two hundred meters from the coast in an abandoned garden area which was also occasionally used for keeping pigs, this is a pottery site with evidence of plain potsherds. The first surface collection of sherds was made by Roger Green. In 1977 and 1978, during the second phase of the Southeast Solomon Islands Culture History Program, the site was excavated by P. C. McCoy.

The excavation at Mdailu was carried out in order to determine the chronological relationship of the plain pottery to the Lapita cultural complex. At the time of excavation, seven natural and cultural layers were uncovered. The earliest cultural layer contained a small number of incised and dentate-stamped Lapita potsherds. Above it were two occupation layers with pottery that had limited decoration restricted to incised and V-shaped cut-outs on the rims (McCoy and Cleghorn 1978:17). Other artifactual material associated with the plain pottery sherds include: simple one-piece fishhooks, "compound-shank" trolling hooks, shell adzes of various forms, chert flakes, and various other items. There was also evidence of round shaped houses and earth ovens marked by outlines of coral cobbles and clusters of coral on the surface of the occupation layer. The interpretation of the archaeological evidence obtained from Mdailu suggested that the plainware pottery was of a later Lapitoid type dating from around 700 B.C. (McCoy and Cleghorn 1978).

Further archaeological work was carried out at the Minanualomia site, on a terrace at the back of Monao village on the west side of Graciosa Bay. This confirmed the existence of the plain pottery tradition in more than one site and that it was late Lapita tradition. Unfortunately, no structural remains or middens were found in the test excavations. The artifactual material was limited to twenty-two plain potsherds, four chert flakes, and one ground stone adze fragment. This site was not dated due to lack of organic material. However, comparison of the small collection of artifactual material remains and the plain potsherds with those found at the Mdailu site suggests a probable date of about 600-700 B.C. for the site. A possible explanation for the limited number of artifacts and the absence of structural remains and midden is that the area was not an occupation site. Rather the artifacts were probably introduced at the time the area was under cultivation by the present population's ancestors. This is indicated by the fact that there was no other evidence of either manufacturing activities or raw materials available at the site. Doubtless the artifacts were abandoned there because they were broken or replaced with metal tools.

A cave site on the small adjacent islet at the head of Graciosa Bay, To Motu Neo, revealed some twenty-one layers. It was called Novlao. Plain pottery was encountered from layer twenty-one, dated at 1300 B.C., to layer eight, dated around 100 B.C.

From the archaeological investigations of these sites much light has been thrown on the existence of a "plainware" period which followed the typical early Lapita period. The evidence suggests that this middle period lasted until about 100 B.C. The end of this plainware period is marked by the absence of pottery and the two forms of fishhooks.

The best archaeological evidence for the later period of Nendö Island's prehistoric sequence comes from Mateone Dance Circle site. This was excavated in 1977 by McCoy and Cleghorn. The lowest level in the stratigraphical sequence was dated to about A.D. 1325. The site had evidence of six cultural layers. The lowest layer, which was above the fossil beach sand, contained two superimposed habitation units with structural remains. There was also evidence of a wide range of artifacts including shell arm rings of trochus and shell adzes of tridacna and terebra. Bone artifacts were rare except for some arrow points. A small number of obsidian flakes, cryptocrystalline flakes, several grinding slabs and abrading stones were also recovered (McCoy and Cleghorn 1978).

In the uppermost layer, the material remains were mainly metal, glass, and plastic items of European origin. The main activity in the area was trochus shell arm ring manufacturing, which has continued up to the present day. This was studied by ethnographic investigations carried out after the excavation in 1978. The lowest layers of the site represented the beginning of the late period, marked by the absence of pottery and its associated artifactual types as well as the presence of new types of cultural material remains and activities.

Excavation of a midden site at Napo by P. V. Kirch in 1978 recovered only limited information, but he was able to suggest that the site was of the late period as well (Kirch 1978).

The archaeological investigations carried out by Allen and Yen in 1971 were aimed at filling in the gap in the prehistoric sequence for Nendö at the time of the Spanish contact and after. The Spanish settlement site had already been located and confirmed by the work of Green. The settlement proved to have been located on the west bank of a stream fed by a major spring at the end of Graciosa Bay. It was excavated and dated by Allen. Carbonized wood from a posthole gave C14 results which suggested that the site was occupied sometime between A.D. 1490 and 1660 (Green and Cresswell 1976:23). This, together with the Spanish pottery recovered, confirm the early records of the Spanish explorer Mendana who landed at Graciosa Bay in A.D. 1595 and tried unsuccessfully to establish a colony there.

In his search for archaeological evidence about the local inhabitants at the contact period, Yen excavated an inland settlement site at Naiavila (Green and Cresswell 1976:204). The site was located on the western limestone plateau of Nendö. The archaeological remains he uncovered included various structures with stone alignments, ovens, fireplaces, and a sparse collection of nineteenth and twentieth century European materials. Animal remains, which included pigs, were few but sufficiently varied and spatially distributed to suggest a continuity of exploitation of both the forest and gardens. Marine resources were probably obtained through trade with people on the coast.

From the archaeological evidence available, this site appears to represent both the last part of the prehistoric sequence just before European contact and the contact period up to the twentieth century. For example, dates from the site using charcoal samples obtained from the ovens and fireplaces suggested that the site initially was occupied between A.D. 1410 and 1760, which places the earliest occupation layer of the site at about the time of Spanish discovery of the island in 1595. The late European items unearthed at the site, together with oral historical accounts, indicate that it was abandoned at some point in the twentieth century when the people moved to settle near the coast.

In summary, it can be stated that the prehistoric sequence of Nendö (Santa Cruz) Island consists of three main periods.

The early period is represented at Nanggu and other sites with decorated Lapita pottery, along with various types of plain pottery. The evidence suggests that it was the dominating tradition and was the earliest in the prehistoric sequence. In Santa Cruz this tradition continued for perhaps four hundred years, but began to be replaced after 1000 B.C.

The middle period is represented at Mdailu and Novlao. These sites yield evidence of pottery dominated mainly by "plainwares." They are suggested as part of a later Lapitoid phase. The presence of plainwares in the Minanaulomia site on a raised marine terrace confirms its placement as a later tradition. This phase continued for about one thousand years.

The late period in the prehistoric sequence is characterized by the absence of pottery and its associated artifactual types, the presence of rectangular as well as round shaped houses, dance circles, and, finally, European materials. This period is well represented by archaeological data obtained from sites such as Mateone, Napo, and Naiavila, as well as the Mendana settlement site at Graciosa Bay. This period began as much as seven hundred years ago and continued until the present historic sequence began on the island.

The nature and duration of the time gaps which fall between these known sites were probably marked by gradual changes in the material culture. For example, the Lapita tradition of highly specialized and decorated ceramic ware was slowly phased out. This might have been because the expert potters were becoming fewer in number or were not passing on their skills to the next generation, or because the decorated ceramics no longer served an important function. This process continued for some centuries before the appearance of a well-developed "plainware" pottery phase which represented the middle period in the prehistoric sequence. Further development of new technology and skill based on adequate knowledge of the environment indicates a localized pattern of varied activities. This process continued for a millennium and perhaps longer. There is a gap here of some centuries. Then new forms of artifactual types made from locally available raw materials and new types of structures emerged, followed by the introduction of European items. These demarcate the beginning of the late prehistoric periods on the island and the type of culture encountered by Europeans in the late sixteenth, nineteenth, and twentieth centuries.

Finally, the separation of these different periods from each another is not clearly defined. But the archaeological evidence already available from the excavated sites suggests that the changes were gradual, implying a basic continuity of activities and population. However, each period is determined by the presence or absence of certain types of cultural remains, or tool types. These are used as markers to separate the three periods in the prehistoric sequence of Nendö Island in the Santa Cruz group in the southeastern Solomon region.

9

The Figurative Sculpture of Santa Cruz Island

William Davenport

The first illustration of a piece of sculpture from Santa Cruz Island (fig. 9.1) was published in 1890 (Edge-Partington 1890:pl. 163). Another piece (fig. 9.2) was published in 1909 (Graebner 1909), but only with the publication of an article by Gillett (1939) about the Beasley collection, then at the Cranmore Museum, was it established, among those concerned with Melanesian art, that a distinctive, yet minor, tradition of figure sculpture was located in Santa Cruz Islands.

Human figure sculpture is restricted to the main island, called Nendö (Ndeni, Nitende, Nidu), and its off-lying islet of Temotu or Trevanion Island (fig. 9.3). Elsewhere in the Santa Cruz Islands, all sculpture — such as it is — consists of low relief carving in geometric patterns, which is also found on the main island along with the representations of human forms that are the subject of this chapter. On Nendö there was also some carving of naturalistic animal forms, usually pigs and fowl, but these will not be considered here.

A recent search has revealed that a total of only fifty-three pieces of figure sculpture seem to have been removed from the island between 1885 and 1978 and are now in museum and private collections in the United Kingdom, New Zealand, Australia, the Solomon Islands, Berlin, West Germany, Austria, Switzerland, France and the United States.[1] Most of the hundreds that once existed were destroyed by the people of Nendö during the 1920s and 1930s in the course of British colonial pacification and conversion to Christianity. The majority of those that are preserved were collected and removed from the island by missionaries of the Melanesian Mission (Anglican); a few were collected by anthropologists, and the remainder were obtained by travelers, government administrators, and European residents. Recently, several pieces were carved and given to Europeans, one of whom managed a timber extraction operation, as mementos of their brief residence there.

Even though much of the religious ideology and some of the public ritual is still alive, the use of sculpture in ritual is finished. If there are any more religious figures dating from before World War II still on the island, they are securely hidden and there is slim chance of their coming to light. The last of such pieces to be collected (fig. 9.4), in 1959, had been seized by a deacon and turned over to the bishop of the Melanesian Mission who removed it from the island. Five pieces of sculpture made since 1959 and

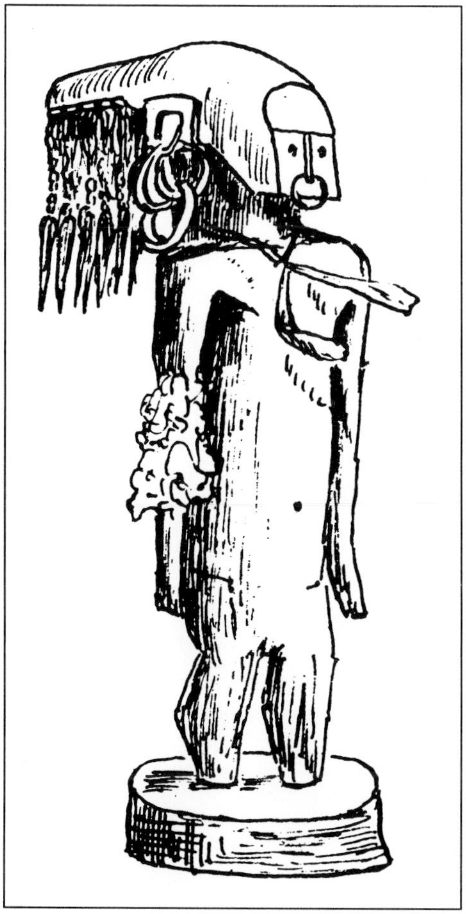

FIGURE 9.1. The Lister-Kaye figure, H. 30.5 cm., location unknown. Collected about 1885, the first human sculpture from Nendö to be published. From Edge-Partington (1890: 163, no. 1).

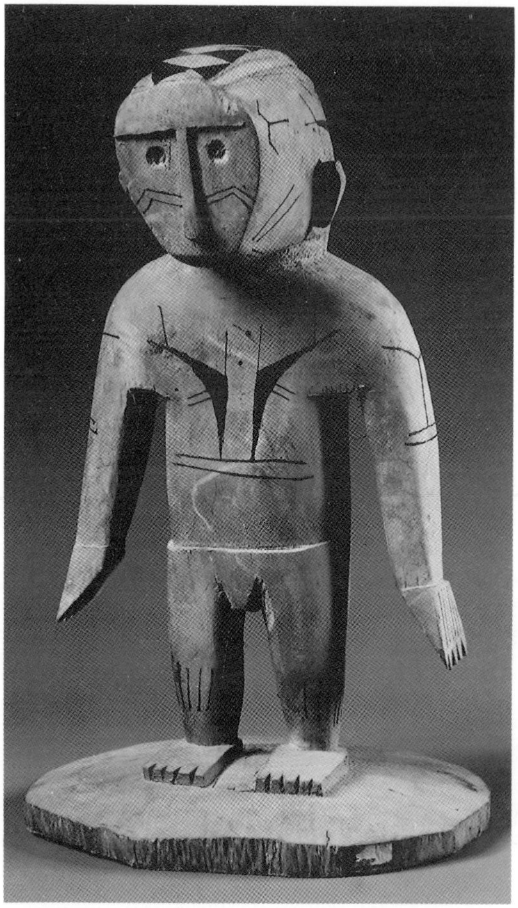

FIGURE 9.2. Male figure, H. 26.5 cm., Museum für Völkerkunde, Berlin No. VI-15-990. Details: headdress curves downward behind the head; geometric designs painted on crest of headdress; linear motifs on face, side of head, and chest represent face and body painting; motifs on upper arms represent arm bands with a spray of leaves; lines on shins represent knee rattles with leaf decorations. Collected by Wilhelm Joest at Lue Sialeba, north coast of Nendö, 1897. No signs of ritual use. Photograph published with permission of the Museum für Völkerkunde, Berlin.

now in museum collections clearly reveal that there are still persons with carving skills living on Santa Cruz Island. Four of these figures show that the carvers did know what older figures looked like (but in the case of the sculpture in fig. 9.5, this familiarity may have come from seeing published pictures of them), while the fifth figure bore little resemblance to the traditional figurative style.

This figurative sculptural tradition consists of statuettes, usually a single standing male, but occasionally a figure seated on a stool (fig. 9.6), or a female figure (fig. 9.8) or two standing figures (fig. 9.7). All have an integrally carved base, and on most of the male figures a prominent form projects backward from the head. This projection represents a type of headdress, called *abe* (cf. fig. 9.14 and figs. 9.1, 9.5, 9.9, 9.10, and 9.11), and it is

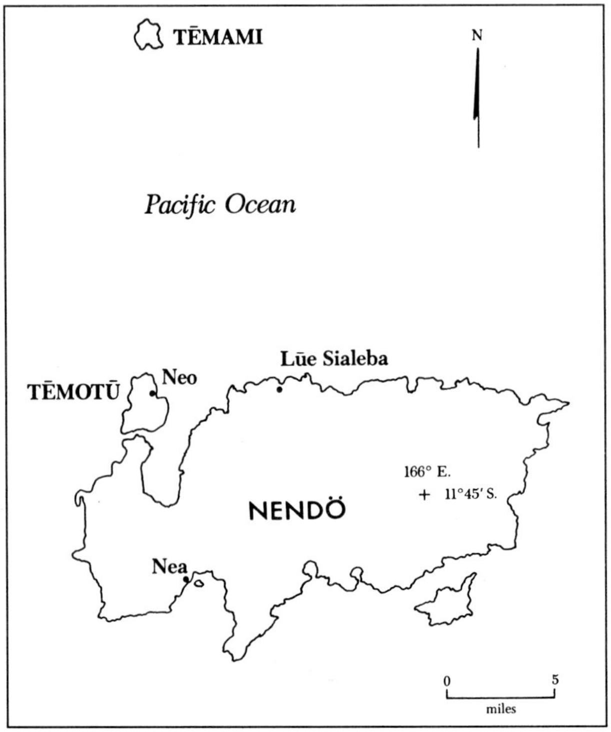

FIGURE 9.3. Santa Cruz Island (Nendö).

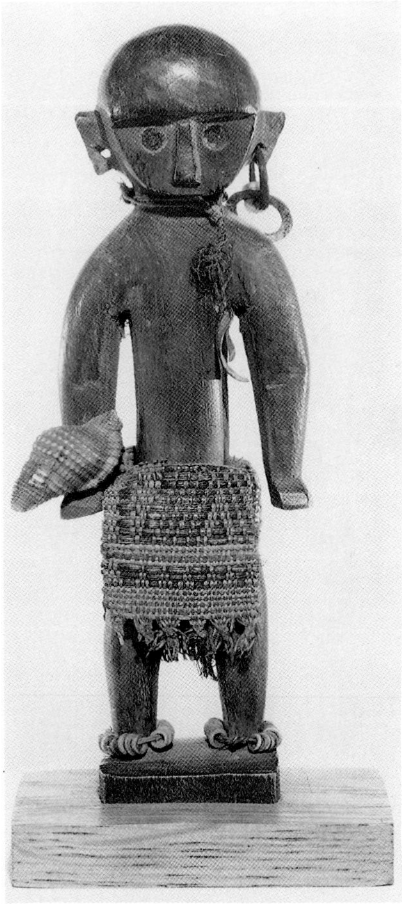

FIGURE 9.4. Male figure, H. 13.2 cm., from a private collection. Portable image. Details: no headdress, human fingernail hanging from neck, loom-woven fabric for breechcloth; traces of turmeric on body. Figure from Nea village; collected by William Davenport, 1959; the last known figure to have been used ritually.

usually ornamented with fiber fringes (figs. 9.1, 9.5, 9.6). Because ornamentations of the headdresses have been lost from some pieces (fig. 9.11) or the entire form has been wrapped with a fan palm covering in order to protect the fringes (fig. 9.10), a culturally naive viewer cannot always discern the meaning of the form. By 1958 the *abe* headdress, although still admired by older men, was out of fashion and no longer worn at any time.

An important aspect of the figures is that they were fully dressed in ritual or cermonial regalia. The *abe* was formerly an essential part of such men's costumes, but was restricted to men with some standing in the community. Other ornamental items of dress consist of nose pendants, earrings, breast ornaments, arm bands, fragrant leaves tucked under the arm bands, shell ornaments attached to wrists and knees, shell bead necklaces, seed rattles attached at the calf, fiber belts, and breechcloths. Some of the breechcloths were even specially woven for the images. Together, these items of clothing and adornment constitute the costume that is worn only for religious rituals, although some of the items might be worn singly for secular ceremonies.[2]

Each figure represents a tutelary diety and is called a *munge-dukna*, "image of a deity." All deities have personal names and many have idiosyncratic personalities, habits, or bodily characteristics. These are sometimes depicted in the sculpture, which may therefore be thought of as a kind of portraiture. For example, figure 9.5 portrays a deity named Melake who is always described as sitting under a great tree. Here, however, he sits on a stool shaped like a neckrest. Details about a deity were often known only to the clients of the tutelary, and this information was considered to be private knowledge, so most of the existing images cannot be positively identified with particular deities by even the most knowledgeable informant.

The supernatural powers and miraculous deeds of each deity — and there were/are hundreds of them — are described in myths. Only mature men venerated tutelary deities, and the relationship between a client and his tutelary deity amounted, on the one hand, to a quest for personal power and control over life, and, on the other hand, to protection against the hostile supernatural powers of other deities. In order to maintain his tutelary relationship, a client honored his deity regularly in the context of his household or men's house, on occasion at great public religious celebrations, and privately during personal crises. For each of these uses there is a corresponding type of image. While all are called *munge-dunka*, I shall refer to them as household images and portable images.

With few exceptions, household images are anthropomorphic carvings in the form of statuettes. Public images are mostly batons or large staffs on which are carved abstract or semi-abstract forms in geometric motifs. They represent either the supernatural power of the deity or some facet of how, according to myth, the deity received its power. Portable images are the most varied. They may take the form of miniature statuettes; utilitarian objects on

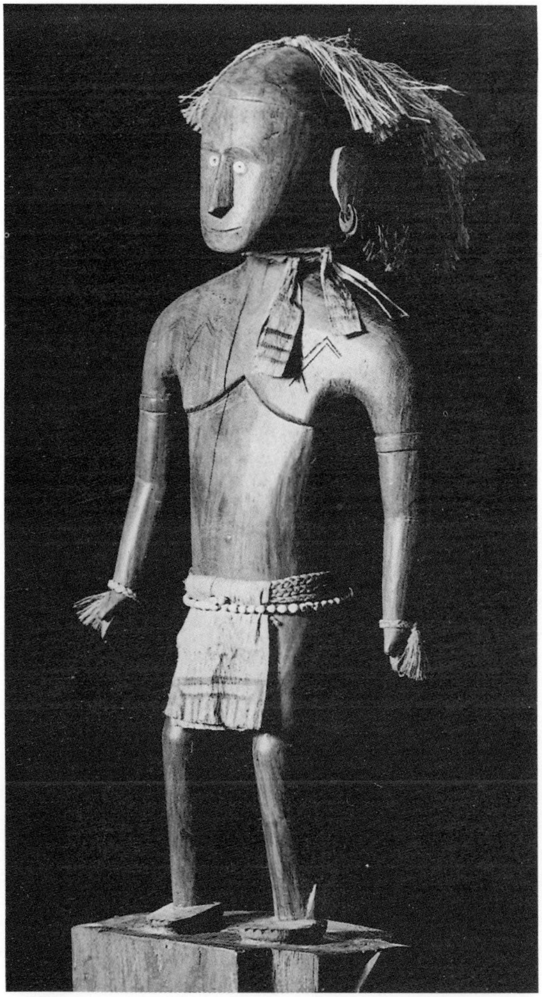

FIGURE 9.5. Male figure, H. 69 cm., Australian Museum No. E77577. Details: decorated headdress (*abe*); spurs at ankles. Carved as a gift to Mr. and Mrs. McCleary, July 1978, the most recent *munga dukna* known. Photographed by Adrian Pitman, published with permission of the trustees, Australian Museum.

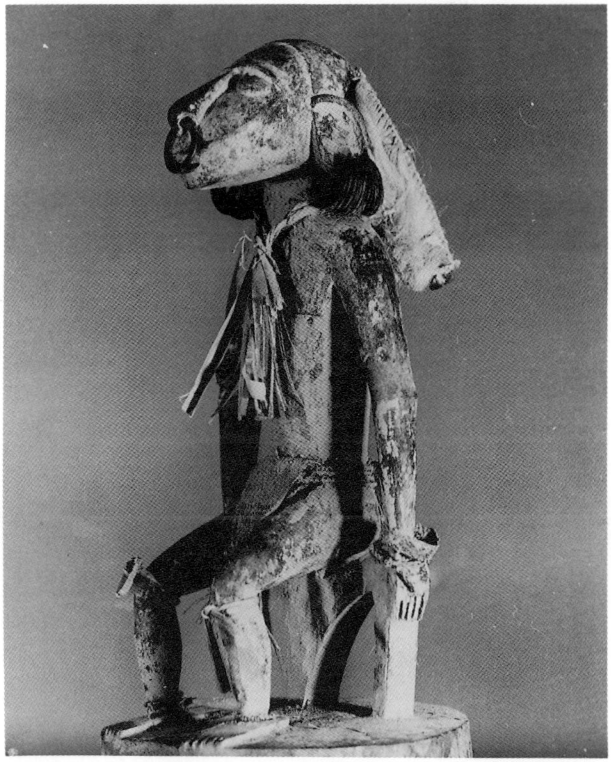

FIGURE 9.6. Seated male figure, H. 39 cm., Otago Museum No. 029.131. Details: complete ritual dress; body covered with turneric. Collected about 1928 by the Rev. George West on Temotu islet. Photograph published with permission of the Otago Museum, Dunedin, New Zealand.

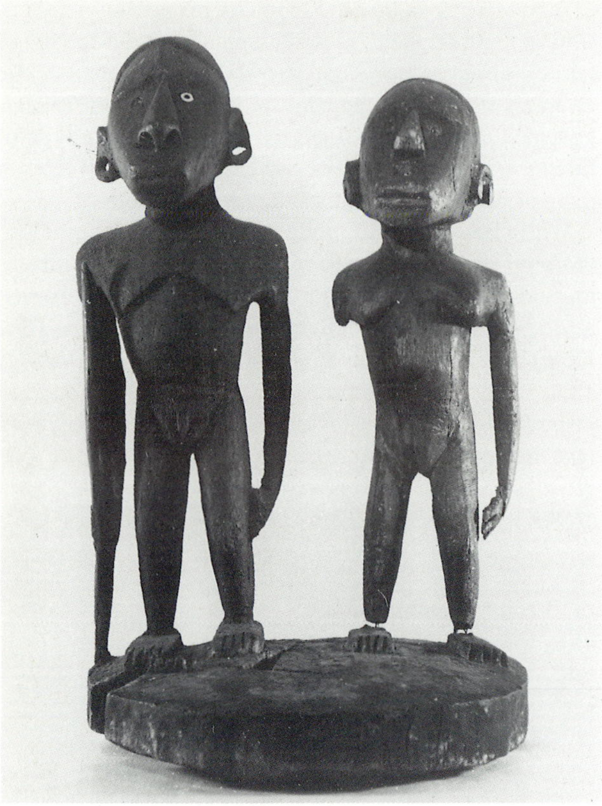

FIGURE 9.7. Paired figures, male and female, H. 37 cm., Otago Museum No. 031.94. Details: male figure has headdress and carries a ritual baton; clothing and other adornments missing. Collected about 1930 by the Rev. George West on Temotu islet. Photograph published with permission of the Otago Museum, Dunedin, New Zealand.

which a geometric or animal representation of the deity is painted or carved; miniature replicas of utilitarian objects that the deity commonly uses; objects that have been in close physical association with the deity; or prepared charms into which powers of the deity have been injected by ritual. However, all of them have one common feature: They are small enough to be carried about in a shoulder bag, concealed in clothing, used in canoes, or wrapped up with valuable objects in order to protect them. Hence, I have called them portable images, but they could just as easily be called personal charms. The variation in portable images is due to their many uses; household and public images, on the other hand, are used in relatively fixed contexts, and therefore are not so variable in size and shape.

Most of the surviving representations of deities are of the household type. As few as they are, their number is greater than all the other types combined. One of the reasons for this skewing is that many of the public images were destroyed in the 1920s by the police as they established government control over Nendö. Those public images that were not destroyed by police actions were destroyed by their owners in order to avoid trouble with government authorities. Few portable images and charms have been collected, because mission and government authorities did not know about them, and they could be hidden. Household images, however, were displayed in nearly every dwelling and in many men's houses, and, as Christianity was accepted, they were collected by missionaries. Usually the images turned over to the missionaries were destroyed, but some of them eventually got to museums and into private collections.

Household images were usually installed on an altar located in one corner of the men's side of the dwelling (*mabau*). The men's part has a doorway opening toward the closest men's house (*madai*), the nearest canoe passage or the main path leading to the next village. Opposite is the wife's or woman's part, where the cooking hearth is located and another door opens toward paths leading to the gardens. However, some men who were leaders of men's house groups maintained altars in their men's houses. In either case, the image of the tutelary deity was the centerpiece of the altar, even though one or more skulls and some rolls of old red-feather money[3] might be placed alongside the statuette. The feather money placed on the shrine was worn by use, had little red color left, and had no monetary value. It was placed there, not as an offering, but as a symbol of wealth and prosperity. The skulls were those of former clients of the deity, from whom the current client had received his relationship to the deity. The feather money was a kind of token offering to the tutelary, but more significantly it was a symbol of the achievement and economic prosperity that the client sought but could not obtain without supernatural help. At each mealtime, the male head of the household spoke a few words to his tutelary, as represented by the image of the altar, inviting him to eat. Sometimes a morsel of pork or fish was placed on the altar for the deity. Even though women and children

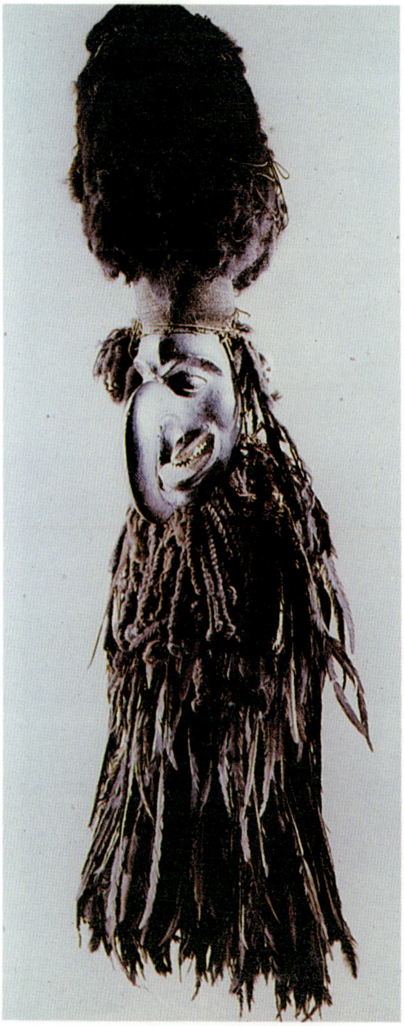

8

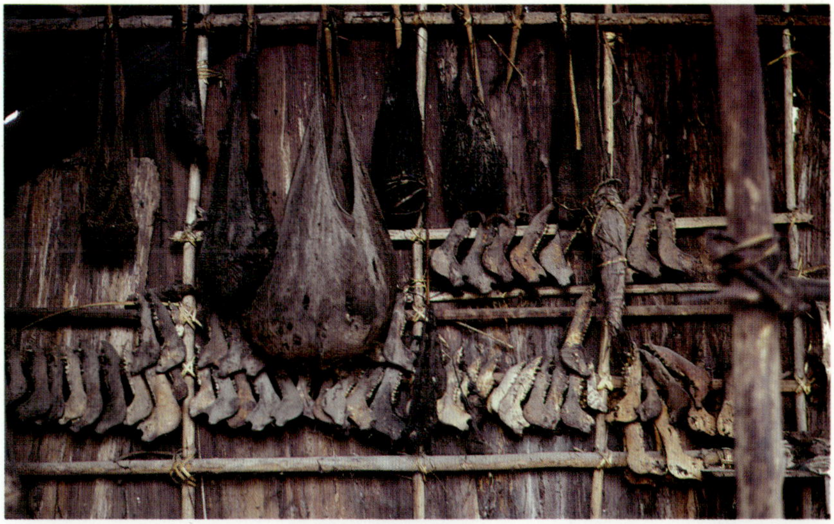

9

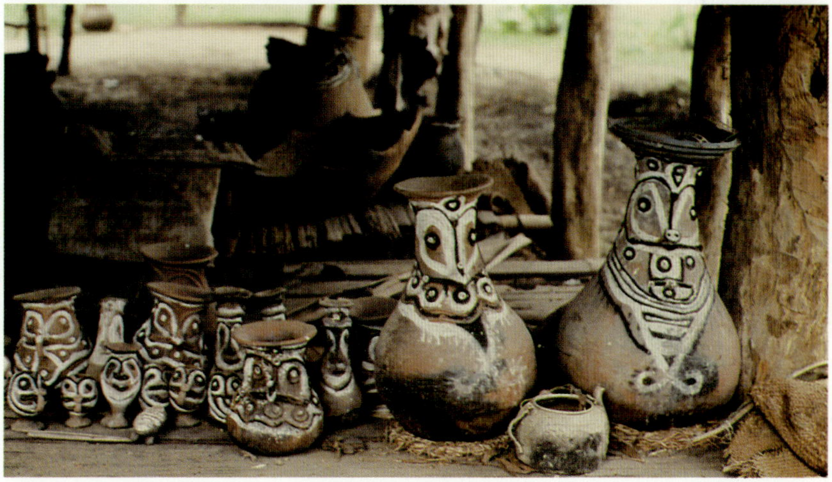

10

PLATE 8. New Caledonia mask. Musee de l'Homme, Paris (see chp. 7).

PLATE 9. Relic array in 'woman-house', Bogalminavip village, Ifitaman, Telefolmin (see chp. 15).

PLATE 10. Effigy pots, Aibom village, Chambri Lakes, Sepik. Photograph by P. H. Lewis (see chp. 12).

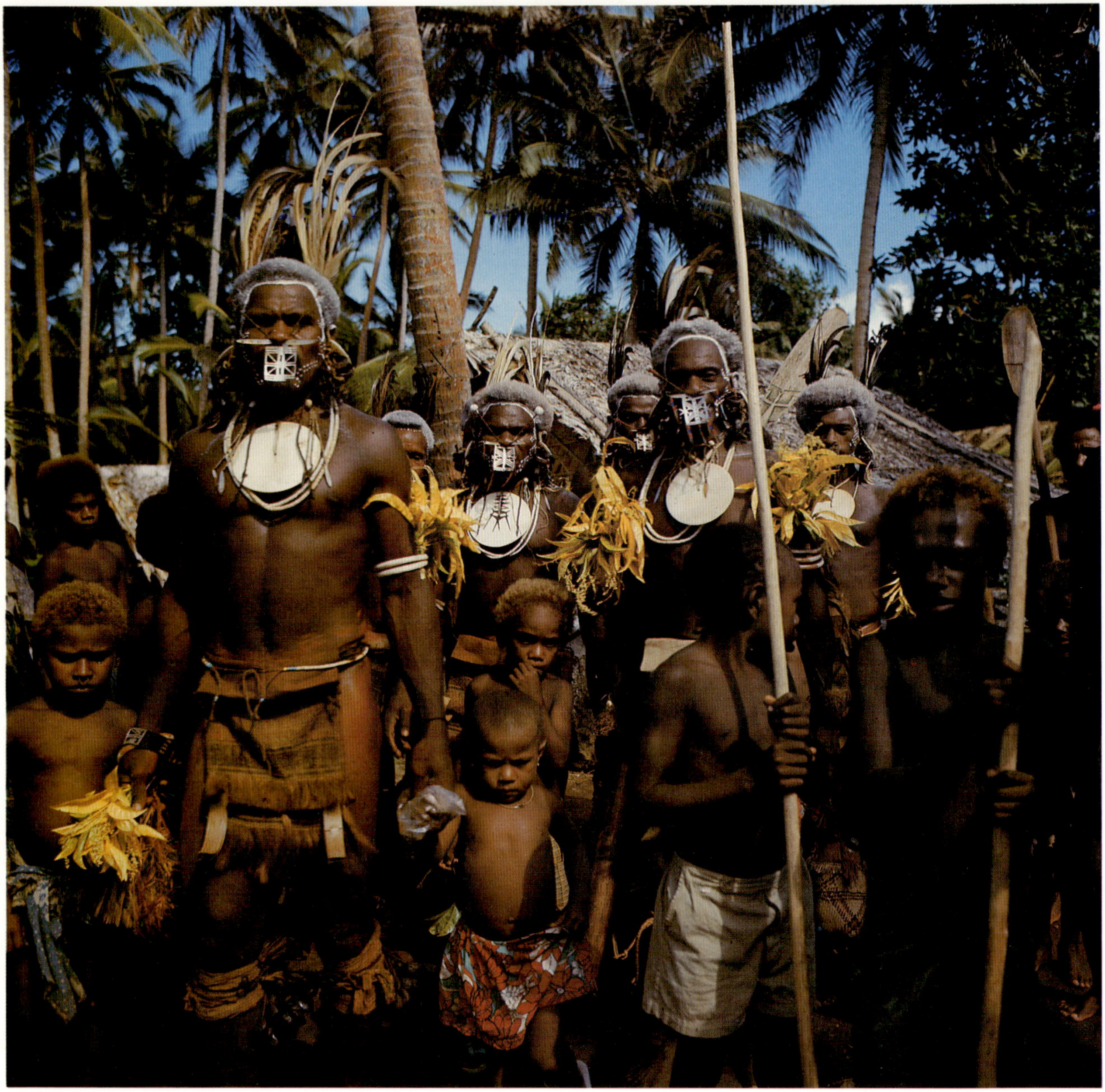

PLATE 11. Ritual dancers, Nendö, 1974 (see chp. 9).

of the household avoided the immediate vicinity of the altar, the assignment of a small but conspicuous space in the dwelling for the altar suggests that the tutelary deity was considered to be a permanent — albeit immaterial — member of the domestic group.

As mentioned above, men who were heads of men's houses might locate their only shrines, or second shrines to the same tutelary, in their men's house. This alternative placement of the domestic altar is related to the fact that the dwelling was thought of as primarily the domain of women and children, which, however, contained an area assigned to the husband and other grown males. The men's house, on the other hand, was the main residential locality of males, the place where all unmarried men slept, and where most males took their daily meals men worked at their special crafts. On the other hand, men never kept their feather money in their men's houses. That, for safety's and privacy's sake, was kept in the dwelling, and the resident women of the dwelling were charged with protecting it, and especially with carrying it to safety if a fire or hostilities threatened the village. A man might wish to locate his altar close to his hoard of money, hoping that his deity would offer some additional protection, or he might wish to locate his altar in the milieu of the men's house where he spent most of his time, or he might have an altar in both localities.

An altar in a men's house could be located against the wall where the client spread his mat at night to sleep, or it could be integrated into a massive rack that was constructed over the central, communal hearth, and on which were kept all valued items that had to be protected against rats, mold, and mildew. In the latter case, an image of the deity might be carved into the supporting posts of the rack. The ritual in the men's house was the same as in the dwelling: an invitation at mealtimes to share the food.

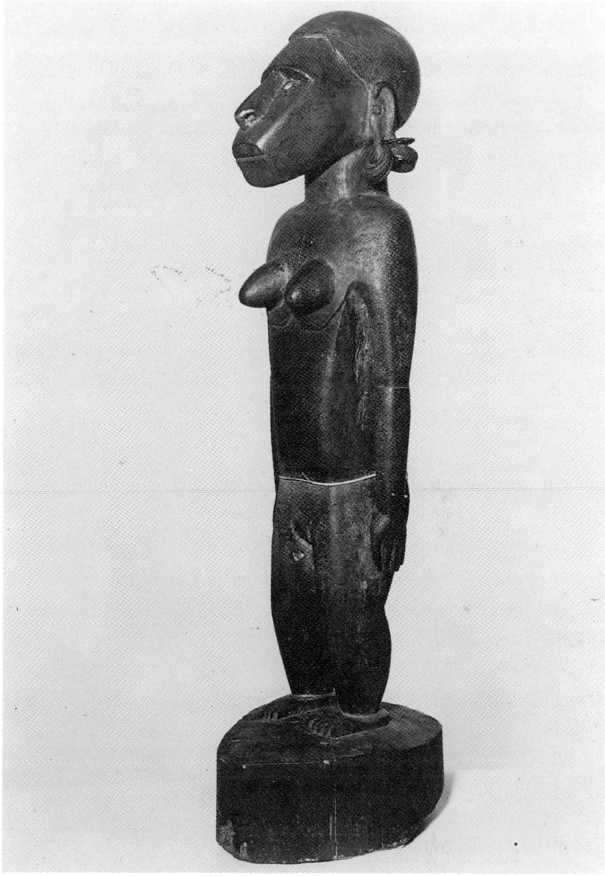

FIGURE 9.8. Female figure, H. 48 cm., Museum of Mankind, British Museum No. 1944 Oc. 2, 1178. Beasley collection, collected with others on Temotu islet prior to 1928 by a missionary of the Melanesian Mission who sold the collection to Capt. Fred Jones, a trader, who resold the collection to Mr. Beasley. Photograph published with permission of the British Museum.

Each men's house contained another object and area that was considered to be sacred to all the tutlelary deities venerated by all the senior residents of the house. The object was a decorated length of bamboo suspended from the rafters on which red-feather money was draped for inspection, evaluation, and exchange. The floor area beneath the bamboo pole was sacred. At certain times the leader of the men's house group might sleep on this area as part of a ritual of thanks to his tutelary; otherwise the area was set aside as if it were a sleeping area reserved for the deities. Nevertheless, some men's house leaders set up images in those areas reserved for the deities, and at mealtimes food bowls were placed there, as if the deities were actually in residence.

The direct association of feather money with tutelary deities is not an obscure one. As already mentioned, economic success came from powers granted by tutelary deities. Seen in another way, supernatural power exerts a great influence over people's minds and behavior, and feather money also has the "power" to influence people's

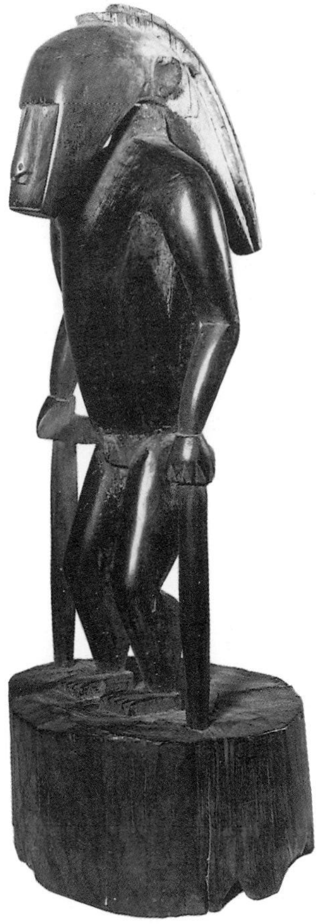

FIGURE 9.9. Male figure, H. 30 cm., Museum of Mankind, British Museum No. 1944 Oc. 2, 1177. Beasley collection (as above). Details: two stanchions connecting hands with the base, as well as a transverse bar connecting hands to hips, are structural reinforcements for the pendant arms and represent nothing. Photograph published with permission of the British Museum.

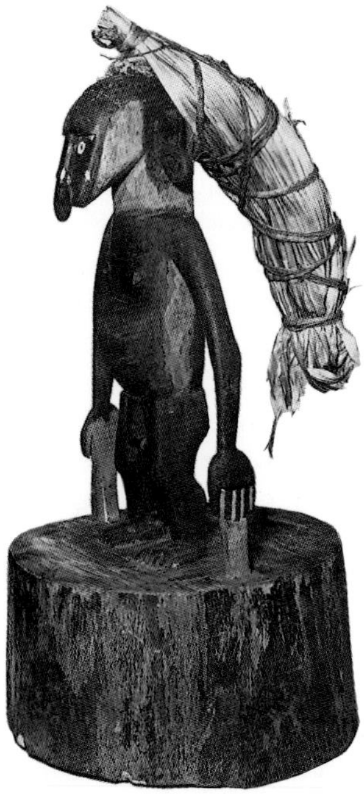

FIGURE 9.10. Male figure, H. 30 cm., Museum of Mankind, British Museum No. 1944 Oc. 2, 1176. Beasley collection (as above). Details: the wrapping on the headdress is not a decoration; the headdress was wrapped with fan palm, probably on Nendö, in order to keep attached fringes clean (as in figs. 9.4 and 9.5). Photograph published with permission of the British Museum.

feelings and actions. So, in the logic of Nendö beliefs, there is an equation between the two forms of power, and from a symbolic point of view, feather currency can be regarded as another material representation of supernatural power.

The main use of what I have called the public images was in parades that opened and closed extended dance cycles. These cycles were, and still are, organized to entertain, honor, or appease deities. Formerly, between their uses in these public ceremonies, all the public images of a village were kept in a special house (*madukna*, "place of deities") that was somewhat removed from the dwelling areas.[4] Women and children were not allowed in the vicinity of these houses. Occasionally, a man or a small group of men might go to the *madukna* to eat a ritual meal in communion with their tutelaries. Here, too, some figures of dieties might be carved on the racks against which the public images were leaned, and damaged or worn out rolls of feather currency might be placed next to the images just as on household altars. Many of these *madukna* were burned to the ground during the repressive phase of government pacification mentioned before. Today, churches have been built on some of the former sites of *madukna*.

Of the many kinds of portable images, two are of concern here because they involve figure sculpture. One is a carved stopper for betel lime containers, and the other is a diminutive statuette, similar to household images. Some stoppers are carved with figures representing deities, and functioned both as plugs for the lime containers and as altars, especially in canoes. Fishermen always take the ingredients for betel to sea with them, so when an altar image is combined with a lime container stopper, a worshipper can conveniently offer betel to his tutelary as he dips lime for his own. This is the equivalent of inviting a deity to share a meal. However, it was (and is) not ordinary subsistence fishing that is involved here. Rather, it was fishing for sharks, turtles, and billfishes which was done by specialists in order to earn money. In former times, too, specialized traders who plied the seas of the Santa Cruz Group in the large cargo canoes called *tepuki* also carried portable images of their tutelaries in this and other shapes.

Miniature statuettes (fig. 9.4), small enough to be carried in a man's shoulder bag, were used for setting up the equivalent of a household altar when away from home. In former days some men took them when they went off island on labor contracts. Most men seem to have carried portable charms of other kinds, and this is still the case.

As already mentioned, the deities are always depicted in full attire. While this style of dress is considered to be normal dress for deities, who invented it, for humans it is special ritual regalia and to wear it imitates the deities. Humans wear it, in full, only at the ritual dances which are held in honor of deities. These are also the most important social occasions of Nendö life. Each dance event is a part of a series that lasts for several years. A series of dances is initiated when misfortune has befallen a community. It is sponsored collectively by a group of senior men and is dedicated to the deities of all the sponsors. These cycles are still maintained, albeit in simplified forms. For example, nowadays there are no salutatory parades and stunts to the deities at the opening and closing events of the cycles. Formerly, the public images were paraded and displayed at these points. At all the dance events between the opening and closing celebrations a chorus of young men dressed in imitation of the deities (figs. 9.12-9.13) is the central feature. This chorus leads all the singing and dancing, while invited guests join in. The sponsors or hosts are also conspicuous as masters of ceremonies. As long as the dancing lasts, which is at least one full day, the men of the chorus are under severe ritual restrictions, for they are living (as opposed to material) representations of supernatural beings.

A part of the propitiatory rituals in which figure sculptures were used was the occasional refurbishing of the images. Articles of clothing and adornment would be replaced, and perishable materials, such as leaves and fibers, were renewed. The bodies of household sculpture were coated with turmeric, a substance that is considered to have magical properties and supernatural affinities. Thus, any image which today has traces of orange (i.e., turmeric) is likely to have been used ritually.

An anatomical detail on some of the images, which is not always obvious, is small spurs or barbs at the ankles, the wrists, or at the groin (figs. 9.5 and 9.11). Only one group of deities have spurs on their bodies, and they are an example of the special characteristics that are attributed to deities. The deities who have these appendages use them to snag fish, sharks, even humans. Iconographically, the spur or barb, called *nula*, has several associations. The obvious one is with fishooks. Another is the stinger of a sting ray, and a third is the rooster's spurs and the way cocks use them to fight. Still further associations are with the barbs on the special arrows that were used for feuding and warfare. The spurs of the deities signify both their supreme skills in fishing and their powers to harm humans. Reciprocally, however, the power to harm humans by

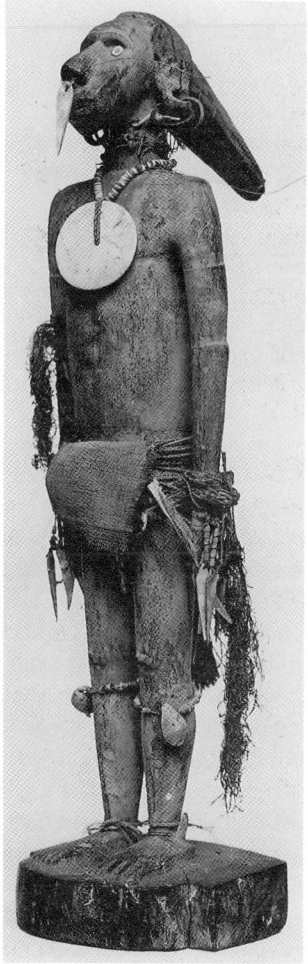

FIGURE 9.11. Male figure, H. 47 cm., Museum of Mankind, British Museum No. 1944 Oc. 2, 1169. Beasley collection (as above). Details: the fiber bands at the left wrist have slipped down from the upper arm; the dried leaves are an aromatic plant which are worn by men as part of their dance costumes; fiber fringes are missing from the headdress; spurs at the ankles. Photograph published with permission of the British Museum.

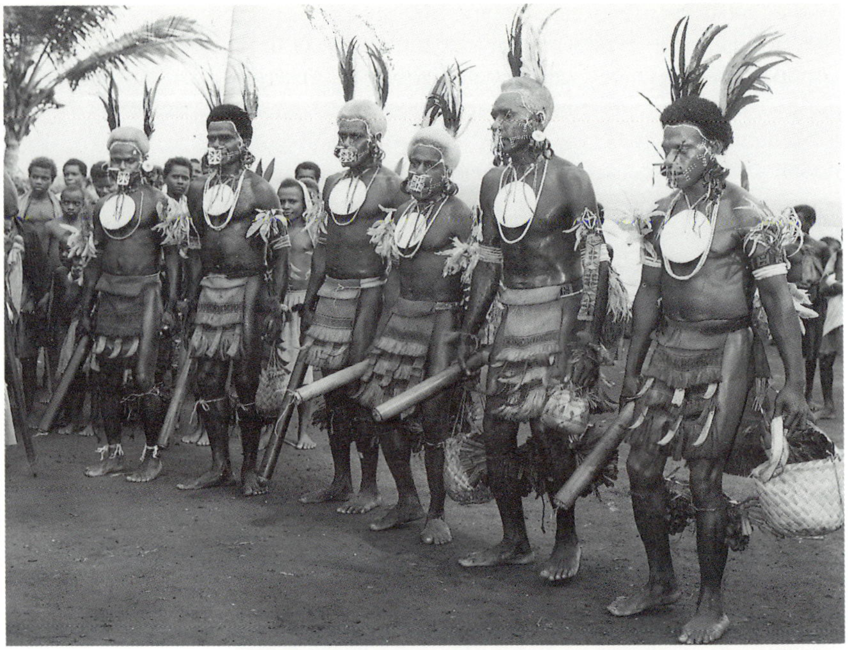

FIGURE 9.12. Ritual dancers, Nendö, 1958. Except for the head decorations, the costumes depicted on most of the male stauettes are like the costumes of ritual dancers. Just before the turban headdress (*abe*) went completely out of fashion, it was worn by the older men who were the sponsors and leaders of the ritual dances, not by the costumed dancers. Three of these leaders are in the foreground.

inflicting disease or disaster is also a protective power, for the best protection against a threat of harm is an equally potent retaliatory threat. Thus, the spurs represent a superb skill, a power to inflict harm, and a defense against attacks from others. These are the powers that men seek from their tutelaries.

Turning now to aspects of sculptural style, the Santa Cruz Island figures are like many other Melanesian traditions of figurative sculpture in that more emphasis is placed on heads than on bodies and limbs. Bodies are subordinated by the added adornments; hands and feet are merely sketched in, and on some pieces even ignored. Aside from some of the elements that represent specific cultural traits (such as the headdress) the most diagnostic aspects of Nendö sculptural style are the forms and composition used to represent the face. Brow ridges are represented by a continuous horizontal line, at right angles to which is a nose form, which varies from linear to triangular. The face does not taper to a chin, but is shaped to resemble the muzzle of an animal. No information given by informants suggested that this squared, muzzle-like treatment of the face had any specific iconic value, other than it was ugly. It is possible that this emotional response was intended by carvers, but I am far from certain.

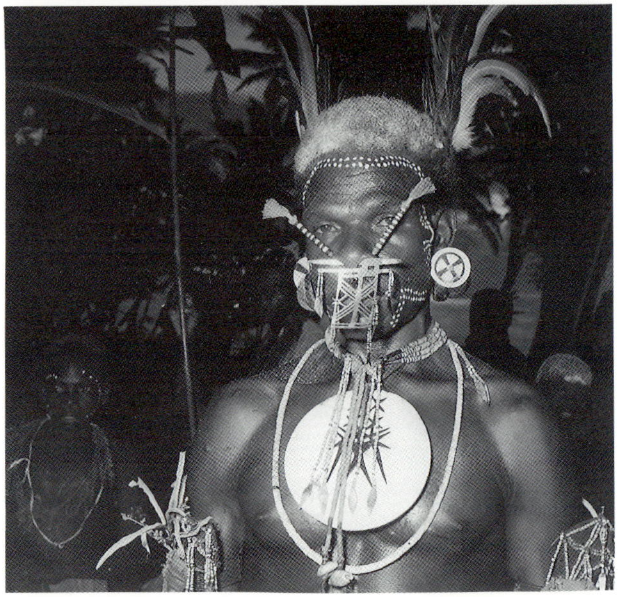

FIGURE 9.13. Nendö dancer, 1958. At some point the turban headdress was replaced in the dancers' costumes by black and white powdered hair and bird feathers. However, the turban headdress was retained as part of the costume of male statuettes.

The relationship between the opposed volumes of the headdress and the muzzle is one that some carvers have creatively manipulated. On some figures the two forms are opposed along a horizontal axis, on some they form an inverted V shape (figs. 9.6, 9.11), and on others they are joined along an arcuate or elliptical axis (figs. 9.1, 9.9, 9.10). Between the two forms there can be either a measure of balance or severe imbalance (cf. figs. 9.9 and 9.10).

The eyes are usually, but not always, circular and often accented by the use of inset shell discs. The forehead area is often bounded by a raised surface indicating hair. Upper halves of the ears are sometimes greatly enlarged and carved with anatomical accuracy, but the lower halves are shaped more for the purpose of attaching turtle shell earrings than for appearance. Incised and painted designs on faces, bodies, and arms variously represent scarification, body painting, and features of clothing and adornment. On some figures (not illustrated here) fish and sharks are carved in high relief on the chest or on the back.

Within these general features of style, there is notable variation in overall sculptural quality. For example, compare the objects depicted in figures 9.1 to 9.5 with those in figures 9.6 to 9.11. The latter set are more elaborately conceived and executed than the former set. For convenience I shall refer to the more elaborately carved objects as representing a developed style and the others as belonging to a generalized style. As can be seen from just the few examples illustrated here this style difference is not hard and fast, but it is a trend that is easily seen when one compares extremes, such as the carvings of figures 9.1 and 9.2 with those of figures 9.6 to 9.8 and 9.11. I now turn to some of the factors that might explain this trend.

The earliest piece to be collected, about 1885, is in the generalized style (fig. 9.1). Another collected by an anthropologist in 1897 (fig. 9.2), one collected by myself in 1958 (fig. 9.4), and the last piece known to have been obtained on Nendö in 1978 (fig. 9.5), are in this style. This spread of dates attests to the age and persistence of the simpler carvings. Furthermore, specimens in this style are known to have been carved, as well as collected, at locations on both the northern and southern coasts of Nendö. In other words, the generalized style cannot be attributed to any period of time or local area.

All but one of the specimens belonging to the developed style that can be located precisely were collected on Temotu, which is an islet lying off the northwest corner of Nendö. Moreover, most of these came from a single village, now called Neo. The exception (not illustrated) came from a community on the south coast of Nendö, the same location at which the sculpture in figure 9.4 was collected. Nearly all of the carvings from Temotu were obtained by missionaries attached to the Melanesian Mission which initially concentrated its efforts in that area. It would seem, then, that the developed style was, in the main, a regional phenomenon.

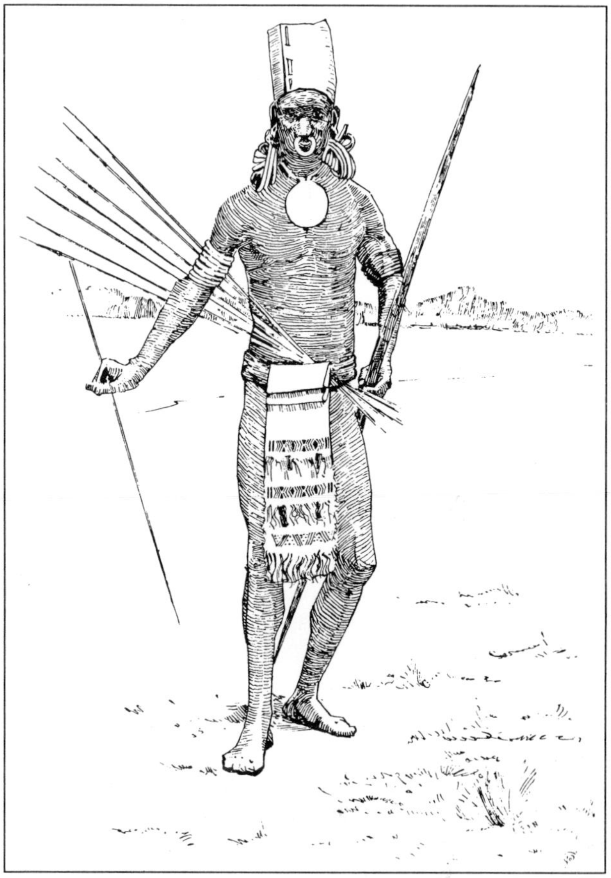

FIGURE 9.14. Drawing of a Nendö man in formal dress, including turban headdress (*abe*). From Edge-Partington (1890:154.)

I was partially aware of this distribution of style types when I did field research in the Santa Cruz Islands from

1958 until 1960, and I had with me photographs of most of the objects now located in the British Museum, Cambridge University Museum, and the Museum für Völkerkunde, Berlin. These included objects in both the generalized and developed styles. The people of Nendö were very interested in those pictures, because it had been many years since religious figures of this kind had been in common use, much less carved. Women, however, were often uncomfortable looking at the photographs, and some were overtly frightened of them. Some mothers would not allow their young children to look at the pictures. It was explained that the fear and avoidance that the photographs elicited were the same as women's reactions to actual figures in former times, when every household displayed a statuette on its altar.

In the course of showing the photographs, the last owner of the carving in figure 9.11 emerged. He lived in Neo village, Temotu, and from him I obtained valuable data about his figure and information on how the largest assemblage of images, the Beasley collection, had been obtained (see note accompanying fig. 9.8). He did not know when or by whom his carving had been made. He had inherited it from a classificatory maternal uncle who had become his surrogate father. After inheriting the image, he replaced all the ornaments and the loom-woven breechcloth and carried on the role of client until he converted to Christianity. The special powers of the deity represented pertained to catching sharks, an economic specialty of that part of Temotu.

I was also able to commission the carving of three pieces by men who were only nominal converts to Christianity. Coming from both the north and south coasts of the main island, the three carvings are very similar to the one depicted in figure 9.2; that is, they are easily classed in the generalized style. From informants all over Nendö it was confirmed that the statuettes used on Temotu, generally speaking, were slightly different from those used elsewhere. It was agreed everywhere, however, that there never had been specialized carvers of religious images, and that while some figures had probably been carved by specialists in carpentry — men who made canoe paddles, food bowls, mortars, and other implements — most of the statuettes had not been. Not one person could recall a carver who in the past had earned a reputation for making fine religious objects, even though the names of many other kinds of specialists were well remembered.

This information suggests that the developed style that seems to be closely associated with Temotu was due to local taste alone, and was neither associated with the presence of specialists in carving nor the inclusion of the carving of images into the rituals of propitiation. Since no one I encountered could offer any specific explanation for why there seems to have been more aesthetic interest and concern about figure sculpture on Temotu than elsewhere, I offer the following culture historical hypothesis.

The people of Temotu, and especially those from the community now called Neo, claim to have had, from antiquity, a very special relationship with the peoples of the easternmost portions of the Solomon Islands, which lie about two hundred miles due west. This claim is expressed in both myths and stories about recent involuntary drift voyages to Temotu-ni-Olra ("The Islands of Women") as they call Santa Ana and Santa Catalina islands. There was no deliberate voyaging between the eastern Solomons and Nendö, at least not in recent history. At Santa Ana and Santa Catalina drift voyagers from Nendö always received gracious hospitality (including the companionship of females, hence the Nendö name for the islands) and were helped to refurbish their sailing canoes so they could return when winds were favorable. This was not always the case farther to the west on San Cristobal Island, and not the situation at all on Malaita Island. This special relationship between Temotu and Santa Ana and Santa Catalina islands is confirmed by the latter peoples, where I have also done extensive field research. It is also mentioned in reports of two missionaries of the Melanesian Mission. Therefore, there is reliable evidence of occasional canoe trips from Temotu to Santa Ana/Santa Catalina and return in recent times.

In the eastern Solomon Islands, sculpture is a much more significant and highly developed tradition than it is anywhere in the Santa Cruz Islands.[5] Figurative sculpture is an integral part of ritual and the architecture of the sacred canoe houses, which also function as men's houses, where male visitors from other islands are usually housed. Thus, it is possible that ideas about figurative sculpture could have been brought back to Temotu by the survivors of drift voyages that ended up on Santa Ana and Santa Catalina islands or any of the friendly communities on nearby San Cristobal.

Evidence also exists for the diffusion of other aspects of culture between the eastern Solomons and Nendö. One item is a variety of yam that bears the name of The Islands of Women. Another is an entire initiation ritual that seems to have been borrowed from the eastern Solomons. This rite did not diffuse entirely across the island of Nendö and it died out in the early 1900s, but memories of it persist. It is unlikely that the initiation rite diffused in the other direction, because the male initiation rites are among the most prominent celebrations throughout the eastern Solomons, and they persist, in some communities, despite vigorous opposition by all the Christian denominations.[6] On Santa Ana Island is a deity whose home is a fiery volcano in the Santa Cruz Islands. This deity corresponds to a tutelary, well-known on Nendö, who haunts Temami (Tenakula) — an active volcano located not far off the northwestern corner of Nendö. Hence it is possible that ideas about figurative sculpture might have diffused from the eastern Solomons to Santa Cruz Island, and the area of entry could have been Temotu.

Assuming that this account has some validity, it is also reasonable to assume that selection and modification of sculptural ideas took place as they were transferred from the eastern Solomons to Temotu, and this resulted in what I have designated the developed style. The most notable of these modifications is the substitution of Nendö forms of ornamentation, namely the articles of clothing and adornment, for those used in the eastern Solomons. In other words, the people of Nendö changed the dress of the sculpture to conform to their own ritual attire. The most prominent feature here is the addition of the male headdress, which does not occur in the eastern Solomon Islands.

It is also possible to assume that further modifications in style occurred as the sculpture rediffused from Temotu to the main island. This was a simplification of both conception and execution of the anthropomorphic forms, and this resulted in what I have called the generalized style. In brief, this hypothesis suggests that the stylistic trend from developed to generalized is due to an attenuation of the sculptural concepts as they spread away from the area of initial introduction.

Finally, I point to some formal sculptural features that corroborate this diffusionist hypothesis. The greatest support is provided by the muzzle-like treatment of the lower facial features. A similar treatment of facial features does exist in Solomon Islands sculpture, not only in the eastern Solomon Islands but in the western islands as well, and has been often described as snout-like and prognathous. In fact, the best known pieces of Solomon Island sculpture — the stem figures of the so-called headhunting canoes of the western islands — are in this snout-like style. In the

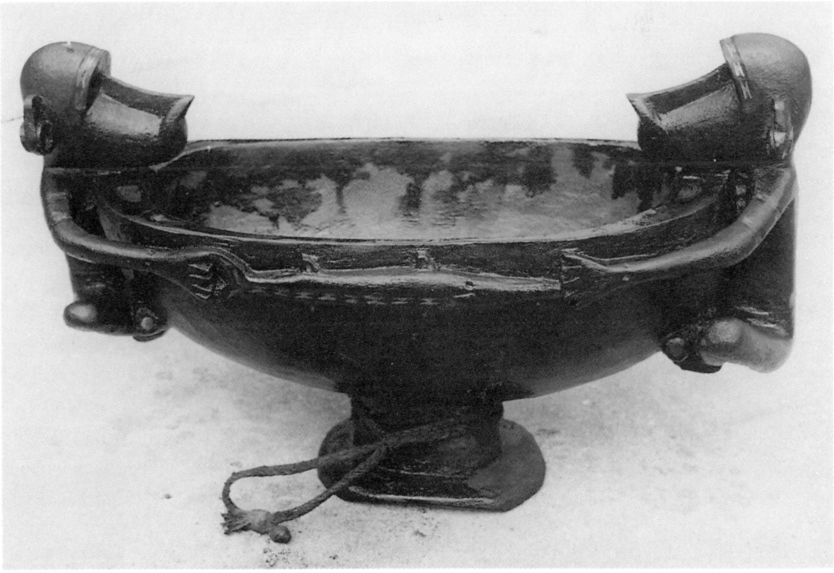

FIGURE 9.15 Ritual food bowl (*apira*) photographed at Santa Catalina Islands, 1966.

eastern Solomon Islands anthropomorphic figures with dog-like muzzles are also carved to depict deities. Small ones are occasionally placed on the bows of some canoes, and in the sacred canoe houses there is usually at least one sculptured post which has such a figure prominently carved on it. It must be pointed out, however, that this is not the only way in which deities are represented in the eastern Solomons. In recent times at least, another, more naturalistic, style has also been utilized by carvers to represent the deities.[7] In other words, two ways of depicting anthropomorphic faces exist side by side: naturalistic and prognathous or muzzle-like. Apparently, only the latter diffused to Santa Cruz Island.

The traditional religion of Santa Ana and Santa Catalina islands also includes a cult of tutelary deities, even though the details of belief and ritual are quite different from the veneration of tutelaries on Santa Cruz Island. The principal ritual object in the tutelary cult is a carved food bowl, not a statuette. Most of these ritual bowls are decorated with carvings of fish and birds, but some have anthropomorphic figures or heads. All of the latter type that I have seen have heads and faces that are carved with animal-like muzzle (fig. 9.15). Thus, I suggest that Santa Cruz figurative sculpture was borrowed, most likely from the vicinity of Santa Ana and Santa Catalina islands, and for this reason it should be considered the easternmost extension of the better known Solomon Islands sculpture tradition.

Notes

1. The locations of the known pieces are as follows:

Museum of Mankind, British Museum, London	14
Art Gallery and Museums, Brighton	1
Cambridge University Museum, Cambridge	4
Sainsbury Centre, University of East Anglia	1
Royal Scottish Museum, Edinburgh	2
Otago Museum, Dunedin	4
Auckland Institute and Museum	3
Melanesian Museum, Auckland	1
Southland Museum and Art Gallery, Invercargill	1
National Museum, Wellington	1
Australian Museum, Sydney	2
Solomon Islands National Museum, Honiara	1
Museum für Völkerkunde, Berlin	1
Linden-Museum, Stuttgart	1
Rautenstrauch-Joest-Museum, Köln	1
Museum für Völkerkunde, Basel	1
Barbier-Müller Museum, Geneva	1
Musée de l'Homme, Paris	1
Bernice P. Bishop Museum, Honolulu	4
Field Museum, Chicago	1
Faith and Martin Wright, New York City	2
Raymond J. Wielgus, Tucson	1
Private collection	1
Allan Frumkin, New York City	1
Alan Lister-Kaye Collection, location unknown	1
Total	52

2. A complete description of men's ceremonial dress is presented in Koch (1977:108).

3. This currency is described more fully in Davenport (1962).

4. A photograph of a house with public images is reproduced in plate XIII of Rivers (1914). While this picture was taken on Matema Island in the Reef Islands, it is the same as those on Santa Cruz Island.

5. A brief survey of this sculptural tradition is in Davenport (1965).

6. This initiation is briefly described in Davenport (1981).

7. Cf. figures 15 and 31 with 17 and 19 in Waite (1983).

10

The Masked Tamate of Vanikoro

ROGER G. ROSE

Vanikoro (or Vanikolo), southernmost of the Santa Cruz Islands, is home to a song/dance performance remarkable for its elaborate masked costumes. In it four Tamate brothers dance wearing skirts that completely conceal the performers. They are accompanied by a comic mother-figure dressed in a fitted suit of fiber ropes that also covers the entire body, and by one other character only vaguely associated with this family. Tradition states the Tamate cycle was introduced from an unidentified island named Veluko somewhere to the south of Vanikoro. The songs are in a language no longer understood by Vanikoroans and are only recently tentatively identified.

The Tamate is undoubtedly related in some manner to the secret societies of the same name in the Banks and Torres islands, the nearest neighbors south of Vanikoro beyond Tikopia. Recent archaeological investigations have unearthed Mangaasi-style ceramics on Vanikoro, suggesting contact with these islands and/or others of northern Vanuatu beginning in the first millennium a.d. but ceasing before European contact.

Consideration of the Vanikoro Tamate cycle may one day help to pinpoint these relationships more closely. This paper brings together: historical background; anthropological data collected by William Davenport in 1958-60, including the oldest surviving set of Tamate costumes; notes, songs, and drawings from *Our Custom Way Vanikoro* by Ben Tua, who inherited rights to the Tamate from his father; and my observations and analysis based on field studies on Vanikoro in 1978.

The Background

The Santa Cruz Islands lie about two hundred miles east of the Solomons and one hundred miles north of the Torres and Banks islands, which are the northernmost extensions of Vanuatu. Centered around the main island of Nendö, the group occupies a roughly triangular area about ninety miles on a side with Vanikoro and it's sister island Utupua forming the southernmost apex. Out of sight about sixty miles distant, Vanikoro consists of two high volcanic islands — Banie, the central massif, and, separated by a narrow passage to the northeast a smaller island called Teanu (or Tevai) — historic home of the Tamate. About thirteen by eight miles the heavily forested landmass is surrounded by a fringing coral reef, the first encountered moving northward from New Caledonia and Vanuatu.

Before severe depopulation and other late nineteenth

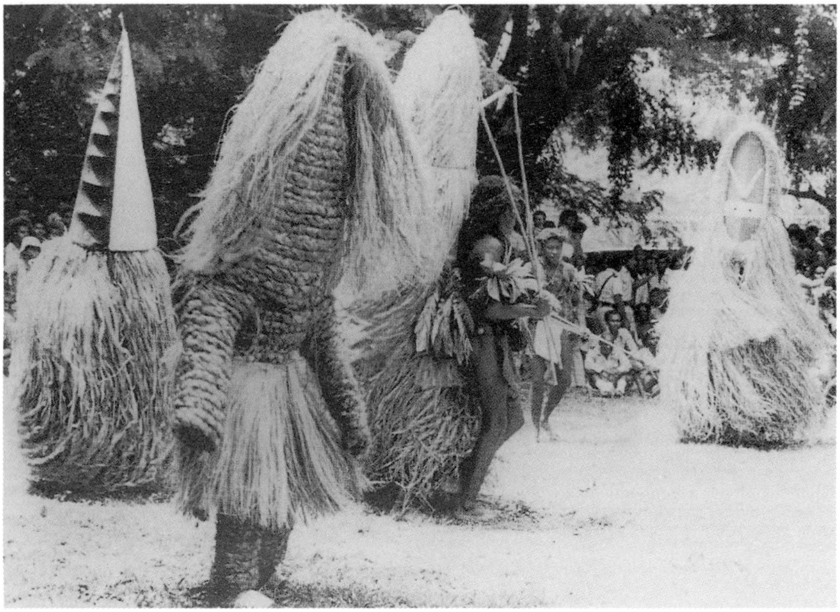

FIGURE 10.1. Scene from the Festival of Traditional Music and Dance, Honiara, Solomon Islands, December 1976. Tamate costumes, not in the Solomon Islands Museum, include (from left) Basamuo, with conical headdress; Takulalevioe, the mother in fitted rope suit; and two of four Tamate brothers. After Foanaota (1977).

century disruptions Vanikoro was culturally and linguistically quite complex. Despite limited size and a relatively small population it boasted three distinct languages: Vano (also spelled Vana, Vanou, or Fano) on the north and west sides of the main island; Tanema (Tanima or Tetau) on the south; and Teanu, the language of present-day Buma Village on Teanu Island and the adjacent coast of the main island. Unequivocally Austronesian although not yet fully classified, they share many features with the three languages of Utopua, in plain view some thirty miles to the northwest. Formerly in regular contact by *te puke* sailing canoe, both islands are culturally quite similar, as William Davenport (1968:213) concluded after fieldwork throughout the Santa Cruz group in 1958-60: "Together they differ sufficiently from the rest of the Santa Cruz to be thought of as a separate cultural sub-province."

Vanikoro and Utupua were first sighted by Europeans during the mid eighteenth century but contact was minimal until the closing decades of the nineteenth century. It is likely that Vanikoro's first European visitors were survivors of one of the Pacific's most celebrated shipwrecks, the loss of La Pérouse's *L'Astrolabe* and *La Boussole* on the treacherous reefs during a storm sometime in 1788. Solving the mystery nearly forty years later, Peter Dillon in 1827 collected one of the earliest accounts of a Melanesian society while gathering eye-witness reports of the disaster (Dillon 1829). Rushing to the scene, Dumont d'Urville (1833) spent a month in 1828 gathering more information and erecting a monument to France's lost navigator.

Thereafter Vanikoro was inexorably drawn into contact with the outside world. From the 1830s on Vanikoroans experienced sporadic and largely undocumented exchanges with the growing number of whalers and traders working the area. Partly because of the fierce reputation Santa Cruz Islanders enjoyed, contact was minimal and blackbirders seeking recruits for the Fiji and Queensland sugar plantations tended to avoid the area. Even the Melanesian Mission was conspicuously slow to establish a presence on Vanikoro, nearly fifty years elapsing between first tentative contacts in 1856 and the arrival of Reef Islander missionaries in 1904.

The British Solomon Islands Protectorate was established at Tulagi in 1893 and was formally extended to the Santa Cruz group in 1898. Rarely felt until an Eastern District office was opened at Kirakira on San Cristobal in 1918, government presence reached Vanikoro in 1923 in the form of a subdistrict station that remained an official port of entry until World War II. Opening of this station at Peu marked the beginning of sustained European contact, for it coincided with the commercial exploitation of Vanikoro's extensive forests of "kauri pine" and other valuable woods. Logging, begun in 1924 by the Australian firm of San Cristobal Estates, Ltd., had little direct effect on the Vanikoroans, however, since most of the laborers hired out from the Solomons or Santa Cruz Islands on contract and lived in relative isolation near Peu. Marginally profitable at best, operations ceased in 1965 following several company reorganizations and a brief interruption during World War II.

In common with many other parts of Melanesia, Vanikoro suffered a drastic population decline after Western contact. The first estimates by Peter Dillon in 1828 put the figure at one thousand; Dumont d'Urville's calculations a few months later ranged from twelve hundred to fifteen hundred. By 1875 the number had fallen to not more than six hundred, prompting Commander James Goodenough (1876:345) to wonder: "Where are they?" When the Melanesian Mission finally established regular contact in 1903, church officials numbered them at three or four hundred — too few to justify a European missionary.[1] Although introduced diseases were undoubtedly a major cause of depopulation, one German trader in the area about 1912 commented: "The natives of this island were very warlike and in fact this fighting has been the main cause of the great fall of the population, only now eighty in all told on this island."[2]

That number had fallen even lower by the time the first national census was compiled in 1931, plunging the survivors into such total cultural collapse that survival of the Tamate is remarkable in itself. To facilitate supervision government officials in 1927-28 concentrated the last remnants from scores of deserted villages into two settlements, the only ones recorded in 1930: Tanema, population seventeen; and Buma, thirty-nine — for a total of fifty-six persons.[3] Reviewing the situation in 1937, when their number had risen to sixty-five, District Officer Dr. N. Crichlow attributed the abandonment of "nearly fifty villages" to disease, especially dysentery and virulent epidemics of influenza and poliomyelitis.[4] Census figures for 1944 show an increase to eighty-five, all nominally Christian,[5] and this upward trend has continued: one hundred persons in 1955, and 120 in 1959.[6] During fieldwork in 1960 Davenport (1968:264) recorded 138 persons in five scattered settlements; latest official figures for 1970 place the number at 163 (Solomon Islands Annual Report 1976:169).

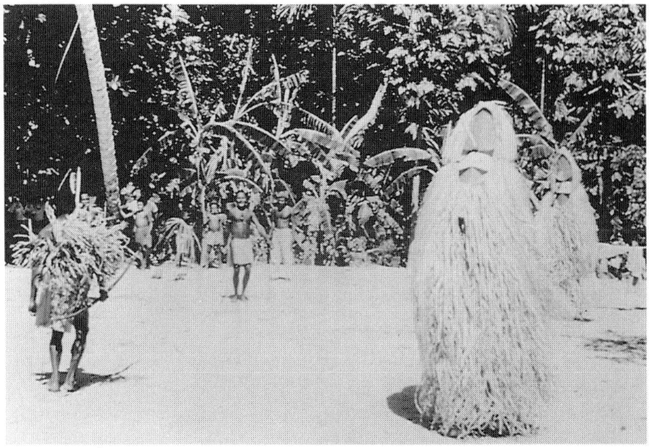

FIGURE 10.2. Tamate performance celebrating visit of retiring High Commissioner Sir John Gutch, Buma Village, Vanikoro, July 1960. Photograph by Jim Leggett.

Today there are seven small settlements boasting a slowly growing population. Given the cultural vicissitudes and drastic population upheavals that have affected Vanikoro since Western contact, survival of the Tamate into the present generation is surely a testimony to its cultural leaders, as well as an encouraging prognosis for the future.

The Tamate

Ben Tua of Buma Village, the current possessor of exclusive rights to the Tamate, grew up during the period of intense cultural turmoil. Well acquainted with the last elders of Vanikoro, he recorded some very important facts in two composition notebooks sometime after he returned home following a number of years attending school and working in the Central Solomons. Ben Tua's account of the Tamate — translated by Peter Lincoln from his native Teanu language — is reproduced from *Our Custom Way Vanikoro* (Tua 1979). The cave referred to in the text, Bonge ma Takole, or Bonge ma Tamate, near the old village of Vetele on the exposed windward tip of Nomianu Islet off Teanu, is still significant to the Teanu people as the traditional residence of the first Tamate. Veluko Island has not been identified.

> Tamate are now here because they came from Veluko Island (between Vanikoro and Tikopia). A man and his wife

brought them back from Veluko. The couple went past Teanu (on a return voyage from Utupua) and went ashore on Veluko Island. They stayed until there was favorable wind. When they left, they tried to take three (Tamate creatures) with them but the creatures flew back along the way. The couple went back to Veluko. This time the wife wrapped the Tamate creatures in her menstrual skirt. Then the couple brought the Tamate all the way to Teanu. The couple put them in Takolo [sic] cave on east side of Nomianu. Then they went to the village and gave orders to grow taro for a feast. When it was ready, they gave a feast. The man himself led, and the Tamate danced toward the village. Finally the people all came (out of hiding for fear of Tamate) and joined in. (Tua 1979:10)

Noting that abbreviated versions were heard from several other informants, William Davenport obtained from Ben Tua a more detailed version of the Tamate myth during fieldwork on Vanikoro in December 1959 and January 1960:

A man from Teano (near Buma), Tevai Islet, named Bulawawu and his wife went to Utupua for a visit. They stayed for several months and when the wind was right they started back to Tevai. On the way the wind shifted and they missed Vanikoro altogether. Eventually they landed at a small island far to the east called Feloko (Feluko). Coming ashore there they heard singing and dancing, and they crept up cautiously to the edge of the dance ground to watch. There they saw the Tamate dancing, and they were very frightened. The Tamate saw Bulawawu and his wife and in a friendly manner invited them to join them. Bulawawu and his wife stayed at Feloko for a month or so, dancing, singing, and feasting with the friendly Tamate.

When the wind came up from the right direction Bulawawu made ready to return to Tevai Islet. The head Tamate asked him if he would like to take some Tamate with him as a present. Bulawawu assented and he was given five whose names were Matesilu, Ilitolong, Kolokolo, Masiatefa, and Takolefia. But Bulawawu was instructed to burn the five Tamate after they had danced so that they could return to Feloko.

Bulawawu arrived back at Tevai, but he landed on the opposite side of the islet from his village. There he hid the five Tamate in a cave before he went on to the village. After two days, Bulawawu, who was a very important man, told all of his people to make new gardens and to fatten one hundred pigs for a large feast, for he wanted to hold a big dance and celebration.

After many months the gardens and pigs were ready and the celebration was held. On the fourth day Bulawawu told everyone to wait on the beach while he walked up to a point with long joint of giant bamboo. At the point Bulawawu began to beat the bamboo on the ground and sing the Tamate songs he had learned on Feloko. This summoned the five Tamate, who were in the cave, and they came down the beach dancing. Seeing them for the first time the people were frightened, just as Bulawawu and his wife had been, but when they saw how gay the dances were they joined in. After a while the Tamate retired to the men's house to rest. And so it went for about a month; the Tamate danced and then rested in the men's house. Then Bulawawu built a big fire, and when no one was looking, the Tamate all came out of the men's house and entered it. When the fire burned down the people placed staples on it to roast, and they mourned the loss of the Tamate. (Davenport 1968:267-69)

From then on, according to Davenport (1968:269), this myth is reenacted whenever the Tamate is performed. As in the myth the costumes are made across the island out of sight of everyone, and the dances are rehearsed in secret under the direction of a descendant of Bulawawu, who possesses exclusive rights to the cycle. In 1960 this was Ben Tua, who had inherited the knowledge and rights from his father.

Little else is recorded concerning traditional Tamate activities. Noting only that the Tamate was most frequently performed as entertainment at maturation rites, Davenport (1968:271) reported: "It has even been performed for maturation feasts on Utupua by Tua and his family, who will not produce the Tamate unless paid well." Traditionally such festivals could be held at any one of the following occasions (Davenport 1968:240-41):

(1) When the wife's abdomen becomes noticeably distended at pregnancy and she dons a special belt to hasten and ease the birth.

(2) A few weeks after the birth when restrictions are lifted and the father is permitted to touch and carry the infant.

(3) When the child's earlobes are pierced, sometime before it is a year and one-half old.

(4) When the child's nasal septum is pierced a short time later, although this practice has always been very rare.

(5) When the child is trained in genital modesty and dons its first clothing, sometime between the ages of five and nine.

(6) When a boy has nearly mastered kinship etiquette and makes a formal entry into the men's house association, about age ten or twelve;

(7) When a boy goes through a special five-day isolation and is ceremonially reintroduced to the village through his men's house association.

(8) When a girl observed her first menstruation.

During Davenport's fieldwork the Tamate was still a favorite. In the intervening years it has emerged as a local symbol of cultural identity within the Solomon Islands, although now produced more frequently to celebrate visits from government officials or foreign dignitaries. So distinctive have the performances become, in fact, that in 1976 Ben Tua was invited to Honiara, the nation's capital, to present the Tamate as part of a UNESCO-sponsored workshop and Festival of Traditional Music and Dance held for three weeks from November 28 to December 20 (Foanaota 1977). During my visit some fifteen months later, plans were underway for another performance at Graciosa Bay, Nendö, as part of Vanikoro's celebration of coming Solomon Islands Independence, July 7, 1978.

The Tamate Makers

The Tamate, as mentioned before, is performed under the direction of a descendant of Bulawawu of the origin myth, who possesses exclusive rights to the cycle. In 1960, as well as in 1978, this was Ben Tua, who had inherited the knowledge and rights from his father, Benjamin Ramoli. Born about 1921 in Buma Village, Ben Tua recalled that his father had moved to Buma before marrying his mother, Rachel Nobema, who came from Ngama, near Lale, on the western coast of Vanikoro. He also remembered seeing white men for the first time at about age eight or ten, a Mr. Selkar and a Mr. Johnson who were evidently connected with the newly established timber company.

Benjamin Ramoli was born in the closing years of the last century at Vetele, a village on Nomianu Islet that in his generation was associated with the Tamate. In the opening years of the twentieth century Ramoli went to Norfolk Island to study at the Melanesian Mission school, very possibly being one of the first three boys taken from Vanikoro to the school in 1903. With another Vanikoro student named Kopele, Ramoli was baptized there on April 5, 1908, and apparently returned to Vanikoro two days later via the *Southern Cross*.[7] His son, Ben Tua, recollected Ramoli returning from Norfolk Island "about 1907," bringing carpentry tools that Ben Tua and Ramoli's grandsons still use.

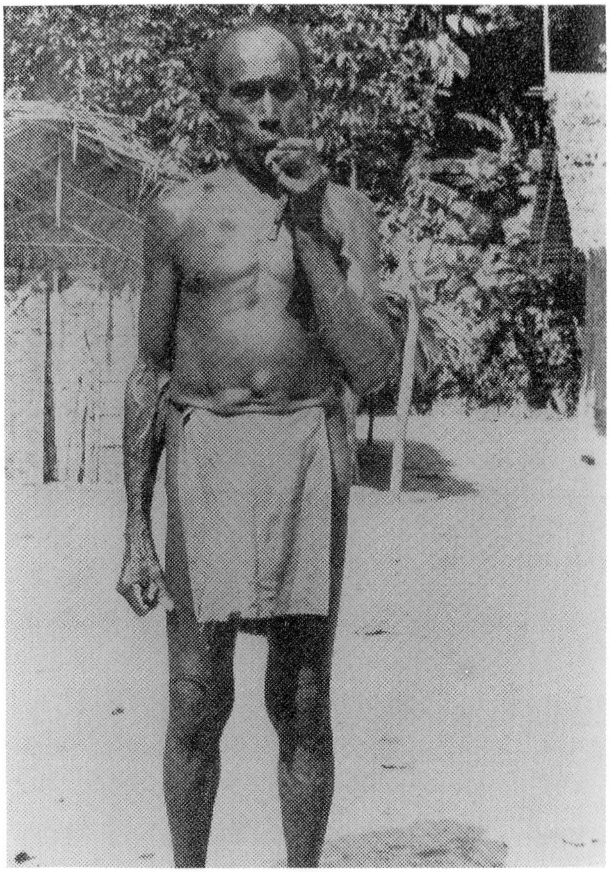

FIGURE 10.3. Tamate maker and former Headman of Vanikoro, Brown Wewo, ca. 1959. After Discombe and Anthonioz (1960).

Benjamin Ramoli was descended from a line of Tamate makers. His father, Pae Ngapuiae, anotherd Tamate maker, died when Ramoli was away on Norfolk Island.[8] According to family recollections in 1978, Ramoli's mother's brother, Tua, was also from the complex located on Nomianu Islet, either the village of Vetele, Aneve, or Epao. When Ramoli returned from Norfolk Island, Tua, a "heathen" chief of Tetau and Vana, was married to a Tetau woman named Nandoi. Ramoli's mother's father, Tanimalu, came from Manieve village, just across the bay on Vanikoro (Banie) Island where the Teanu language was spoken. Tanimalu is said to have moved into Vetele village, becoming a Tamate maker.

The name of one other recent Tamate maker is preserved. A "nephew" of Benjamin Ramoli, Brown Wewo was born either at Aneve on Nomianu Islet, or at Tanema. When interviewed in 1959 by a member of an expedition looking for remains of La Pérouse's ships, Brown Wewo was reported to be "an old man . . . aged between seventy and eighty years, the oldest man on the island" (Discombe and Anthonioz 1960:12). Surviving into the 1960s, this craftsman of considerable skills is still remembered for carving in his final years a pair of bird figures to decorate Buma's new courthouse, erected in 1962. Brown Wewo is said to be the maker of the oldest surviving set of Tamate costumes, discussed later in this paper.

Extant government records contain no information about the Tamate, but occasional District Office reports do provide some insights into the lives of these individuals, who were all big-men in the classic Melanesian sense. As was official policy, a number of headmen were appointed throughout the Santa Cruz area to help achieve administrative control soon after government presence was established in the 1920s. On Vanikoro one of these was Brown Wewo, who, as headman, prompted District Officer B. E. Crawford to complain in 1934:

> Headman Brown of Vanikoro is inclined only to visit me when his quarterly pay falls due. His appointment as Headman was, I feel sure, a mistake and in effect he is little more than the messenger of Ramoli, the Chief, who is the real power at Vanikoro. This dual control no doubt makes Brown's work difficult and certainly confuses his relations with the District Officer.[9]

Headman Brown came to official notice again in 1937 when he claimed his canoe was fired upon by a Japanese sampan, apparently shell poachers working the area.[10] Early in 1939 the "Headman of Buma," presumably Wewo, reported another Japanese fishing vessel believed to be poaching — or spying — off Palu Passage.[11] Convicted of a minor offense the following year, "District Headman Brown" was replaced on July 1, 1940, by Ben Ramoli, "Chief of Buma." Thereafter Headman Brown disappeared from official reports.[12]

One of the last truly influential men of Vanikoro, Ramoli served as headman until his death in December 1953. Appointed successor, his son Ben Tua has been the acknowledged leader of Vanikoro to the present day. Although he still exercises exclusive rights to the Tamate, with advancing age it appears that Ben Tua will in due course pass the rights to his eldest son, Christian Ramoli.

The Tamate Costumes

The Tamate are four similarly-costumed characters considered to be "brothers" — Matatilu, Aeleteulungo, Kolokolo, and Matateva — and one of completely different appearance claimed to be their "mother," Takulalevioe. Basamuo, a sixth character discussed later, is said to be related to the Tamate but the association is unclear. As the Tamate enter the village dancing, the four brothers

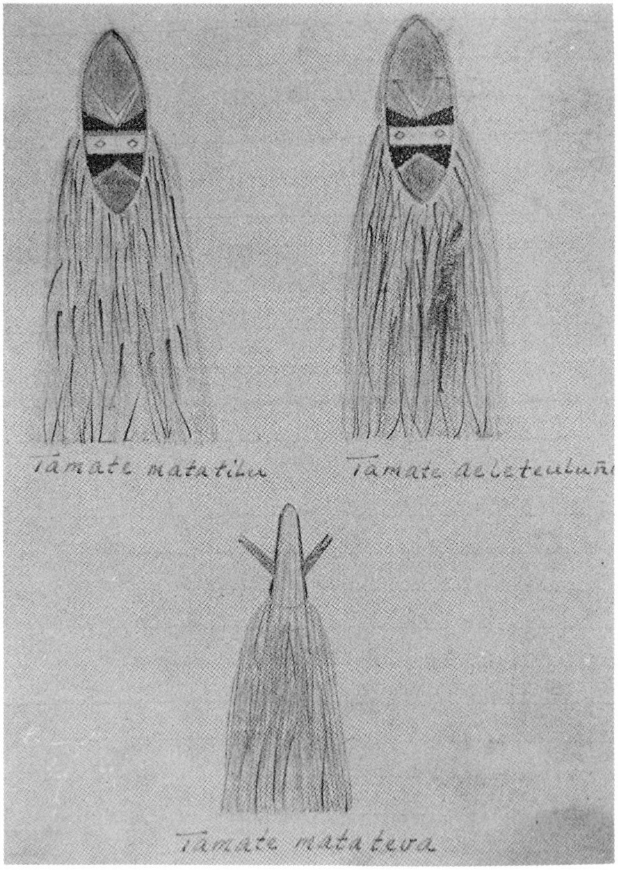

FIGURE 10.4. Original pencil drawings by Ben Tua of Tamate Matatilu, Tamate Aeleteulungo, and Tamate Matateva. After Tua (1979).

come first playing serious roles, followed by the mother who acts as comic imitator. In the origin myth the Tamate were supposed to frighten the women, and this behavior remains a part of contemporary performances. Coming down the beach and into the village from their place of concealment the Tamate first challenge and then chase away the girls and women, causing much merriment through their wild antics (Davenport 1968:269-70).

Ben Tua's description of the Tamate costumes records many details of materials and sequence of construction. Neatly executed in black, red, and blue pencil, his accompanying drawings name only three of the Tamate children, Tamate Matatilu, Tamate Aeleteulungo, and Tamate Matateva. There is neither mention nor drawing of Kolokolo, the fourth brother, who was recorded by Davenport and is represented by extant costumes.

> We cut three pieces of wild hibiscus wood. The first piece goes in the middle. We shape corners at the forehead. The other two pieces go on either side of the middle piece. The eyes of the Tamate are shaped like "V". We cut *gaiene* wood and strips of mangrove wood that are rolled into five rings of increasing diameter. Two straight strips are bent over forming the frame of the cone. The five rings are placed inside this frame; i.e., the two bent strips are on the outside of the rings. Then we attach the three pieces of wild hibiscus. These are attached to the side of the head. One goes inside the head to the flat surface of the Tamate forehead with the root of the *nuko* banana. When we have this securely tied, tie it again with *mibile* leaf going over the *nuko* banana root. Then we tie the pandanus root over this, and finally the wild hibiscus. Then we use the strings around the back of the head. Then from the inside the skirt of strips of broadleaf sago leaves are attached. Then the V-shaped eyes of *gaiene* wood are put on the front of the Tamate mask. (Tua 1979:29)

Davenport's account of the costumes provides details of how they are manipulated during performances, as well as further information about the brothers' appearance.

> The four brothers' costumes consist of similar wooden masks with fibre fringes that conceal the upper part of the body and a fibre skirt that hides the lower parts. The masks are carried, not worn, in both hands by a long handle that projects down from the bottom of the mask face, but which is concealed behind the fibre fringe. By tilting the mask in various ways, the masker achieves humorous effects. The mask face with its handle is carved from a single piece of wood. The face, which is about three feet long and about eleven inches wide, is oval in shape, convex from side to side, but slightly concave from top to bottom. On each mask is painted a stylized face consisting of a white band across the center, top and bottom areas colored red or reddish white. Two diamond perforations are cut through the white band for the masker to see through. The mask to Matesilu (Two Eyes) has no other features. Ilitolong (name of the stool-type coconut grater) has two cube-shaped "eyes" on its stalks that project forward. Kolokolo (name of the ground shell disc worn as a breast ornament) has two cone-shaped eyes on its stalks. Masiatefa (Double Face) has two spike-shaped stalks for eyes, and the costume consists of identical masks worn front and back. Takolefia (proper name), the mother, wears no mask. Her costume is a fitted suit of fibres rolled into pliable ropes that covers the entire body and is crowned with a topknot. (Davenport 1968:269-70)

Bulawawu, in the origin myth, was instructed by his teachers on the island of Feluko to burn the Tamate at the close of the performance. Davenport (1968:269) reported, "Today, too, at the end of the dance the masks and disguises are burned as they were in the origin myth." This has not always been the case in recent times, however. Since 1960 at least two full sets of Tamate costumes and parts of others have escaped burning and are now preserved in museums (see Appendix I). Another partial set, examined while in the possession of Ben Tua at Buma Village in 1978, was subsequently featured in Solomon Islands Independence celebrations and is presumed also to be still in existence. The effort required to make these costumes is considerable. It is apparent that original mythological instructions to burn these products of such effort are no longer considered binding — at least for performances held outside traditional Vanikoroan society.

The first set of Tamate costumes known to have escaped traditional burning was featured in celebrations held July 30 or 31, 1960, to honor the last official visit to Vanikoro of retiring High Commissioner Sir John Gutch. William Davenport, who was then on Nendö, obtained the costumes in October with the help of J. P. McNaught, then engineer at the Kauri Timber Company, and Jim Leggett, Forestry Officer on Vanikoro. Davenport subsequently transferred the costumes to Bishop Museum in Honolulu, one of the Tri-Institutional Pacific Program sponsors supporting his fieldwork in Santa Cruz.

Little is known about the origin of this set of Tamate except for information obtained in 1978 from Ben Tua and his eldest son Christian Ramoli. According to Ramoli, the costumes had been made possibly some time about 1954 by Brown Wewo, the former headman of Vanikoro, while Ben Tua looked on. They are undoubtedly the same Tamate that Ben Tua recollected having sold "about 1962" to a "John Macanito" from Scotland, a "manager" at the timber company — the same J. P. McNaught, incidentally, whom Davenport (1968:207) acknowledged "for checking and rechecking the information on Tamate." Ben Tua also recalled having received "fifty-two

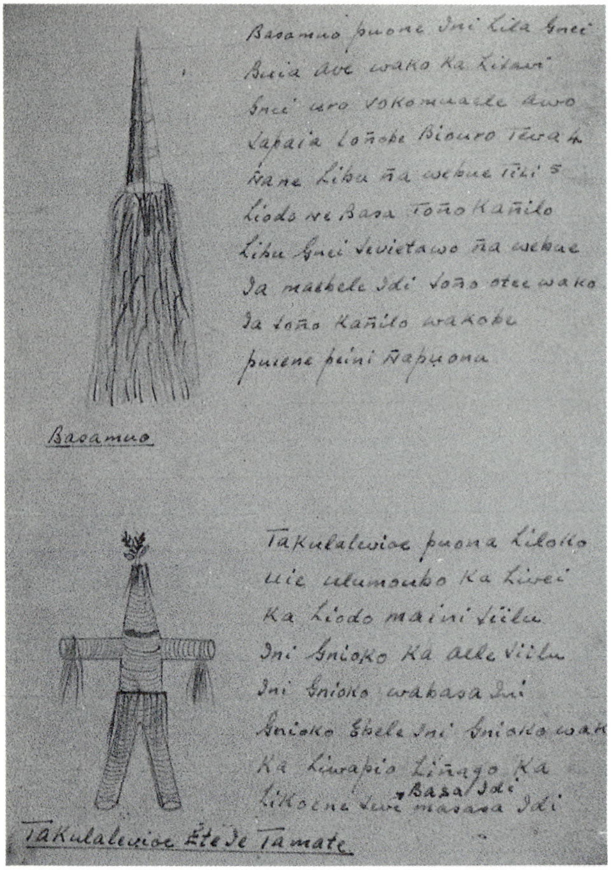

FIGURE 10.5. Original pencil drawings by Ben Tua of Basamuo and the Tamate mother, Takulalevioe. After Tua (1979).

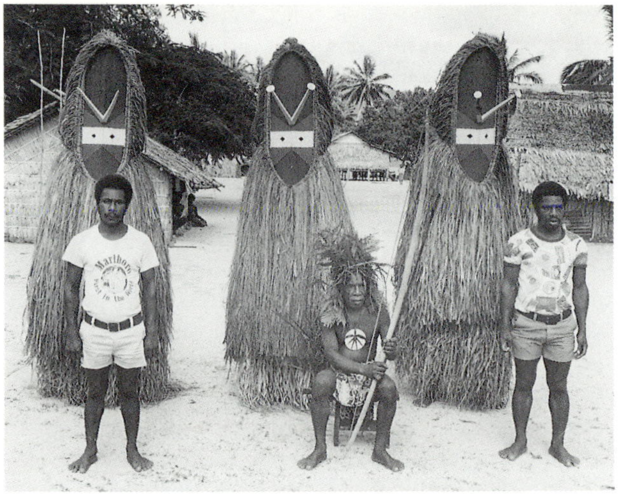

FIGURE 10.6. Ben Tua (center), with sons Christian Ramoli (left) and Timothy Bila (right), posing for author with three Tamate costumes named Matatilu, Kolokolo, and Aeleteulungo, at Buma Village, Vanikoro, April 1978.

dollars" (presumably fifty-two Australian pounds) for the double-faced Tamate, "twenty-six dollars" each for the single-faced variety, "twelve dollars" for the rope mother, and "twenty-four dollars" for Basamuo.

The following notes on the construction of these Tamate are supplemented by information kindly provided in 1978 by Ben Tua and his sons, Christian Ramoli and Timothy Bila. Additional information is based on the three Tamate then in Ben Tua's possession: Matatilu (with pointed eye stalks), Aeleteulungo (with disked eye stalks bearing red cloth streamers), and Kolokolo (with disked eye stalks and no cloth streamers). Further comparisons are based on the full set of costumes featured at the 1976 Festival of Traditional Music and Dance, which Ben Tua afterwards sold to the Solomon Islands Museum for essentially the same figures (but in Australian dollars) quoted above.

Nearly identical except for eye stalks, the basic Tamate costume consists of a wooden face mask attached to a conical framework headdress that provides support for a bulky fiber skirt. The face mask itself is formed from three shaped pieces of light-weight hibiscus wood, *wavoro*, fitted together along a vertical axis to form an elongated face averaging 70 cm. tall by 30 cm. wide. Two lateral panels flank a slightly ridged center piece that terminates in a rounded carrying handle that projects below the mask

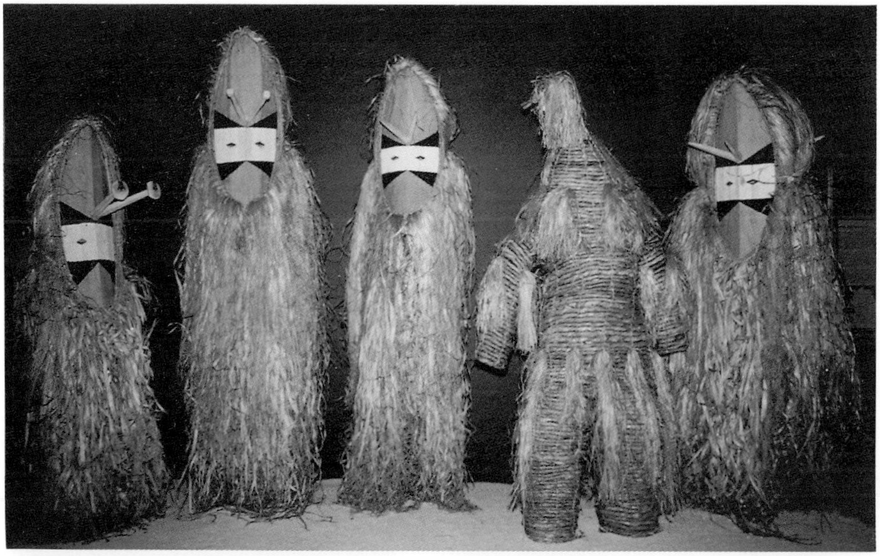

FIGURE 10.7. Oldest surviving set of Tamate costumes, collected by William Davenport after performance for High Commissioner Sir John Gutch in 1960, and now in Bishop Museum. From left: Kolokolo, Aeleteulungo, Matatilu, Takulaleveioe, and Matateva (underskirts not exhibited on mounts).

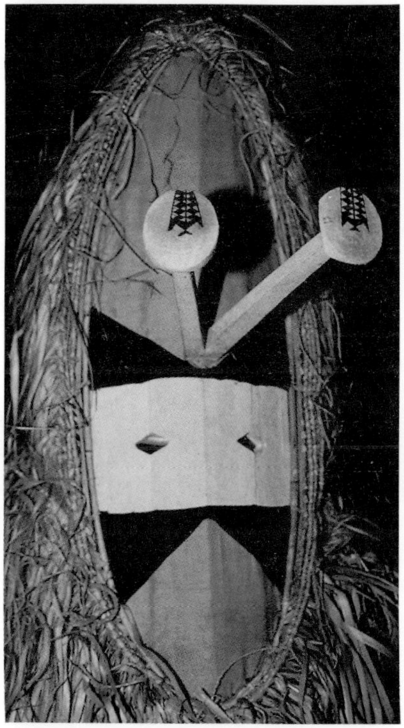

FIGURE 10.8. Tamate Kolokolo, with eye stalk terminals patterned after traditional breast ornament of same name. Bishop Museum 1964.60.05.

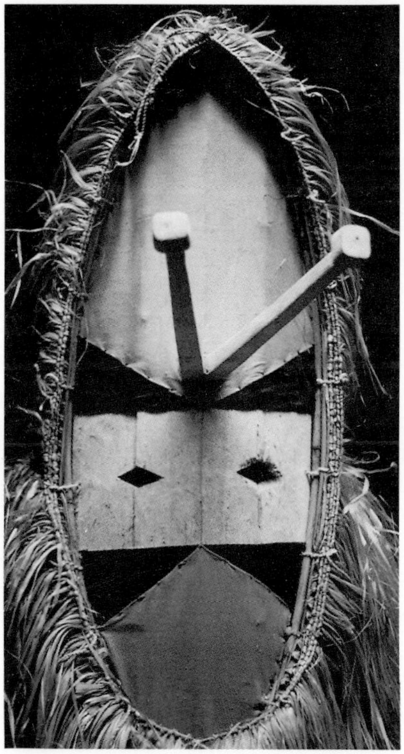

FIGURE 10.9. Tamate Aeleteulungo, with squared eye stalks. Bishop Museum 1964.60.03.

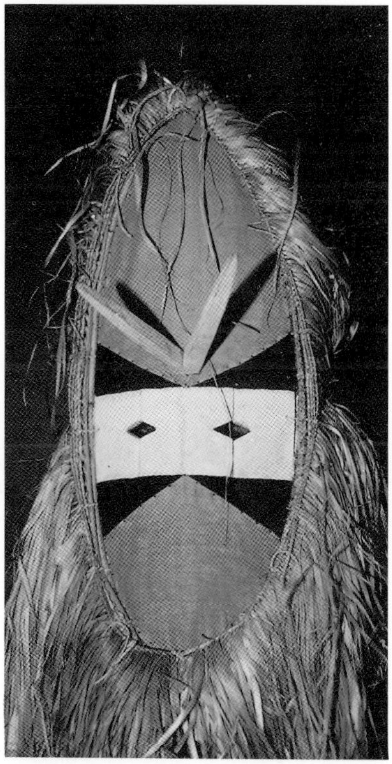

FIGURE 10.10. Tamate Matatilu, with pointed eye stalks. Bishop Museum 1964.60.06.

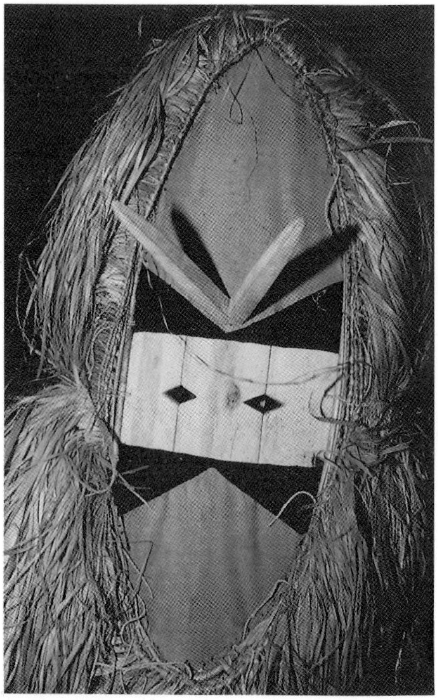

FIGURE 10.11. Tamate Matateva, showing one of two identical faces on opposite sides of mask. Bishop Museum 1964.60.04.

40 or 50 cm. into the interior of the costume. Two diamond-shaped eye-holes, about 5 cm. wide by 2.5 cm. high, are cut into the mask on either side of the seam where the three wooden pieces are joined. The eye stalks, nearly 50 cm. long and differing only in the carving of their tips, are fitted snuggly into squared holes near the center of the face.

This wooden face mask is attached to a conical frame support that fits over the head of the dancer. It is constructed of five or six circular rings of split rattan or cane, *momboro*, which are lashed horizontally to six vertical supports of the same material using hibiscus bark or bast, or other strong fibers such as *wie membile*, *wameloi*, or *ekuo*. The lowermost horizontal ring must be of a proper diameter to rest on the dancer's shoulders while the upper four or five decrease progressively in size to the tip of the cone. This interior framework is called *wembwe* because it is circular like the similarly named armrings of leaf or shell still worn on special occasions. Construction follows the same pattern for the double-faced character Matateva or Masiatefa, except that the rear face has only a vestigial carrying handle.

The face of the Tamate is decorated by a combination of traditional and innovative methods. First, the wooden surface is prepared by rubbing it with banyan tree sap, *tepulu peini boke*, and then white lime, *awo*, the latter coloring the center horizontal band where the diamond-shaped eye holes are cut. (White lime is made by burning branch coral, *olawo*, in a wood fire, then wrapping the burned coral in leaves and allowing it to disintegrate slowly into powder.) Next small, paired black triangles (or blue, on later costumes) are applied immediately above and below the white horizontal band, leaving broad expanses of red or reddish orange to fill in the remaining top and bottom of the face. Formerly both red and blue are said to have been produced from different parts of the same fruit, *watemo*, and smeared over the smooth wooden surface. Today the red and black (or blue) portions of the face are made of ordinary plain-weave cotton cloth carefully cut to the appropriate shapes. (On two of the Bishop Museum costumes the black cloth is applied over the red, while on the other two the red is fitted over the black.) The appliques are held in place with wooden pegs or small nails, both known as *lilikoe*, stuck directly into the cloth or through wooden battens, *kanoko*, framing the face. Finally a single reed, *via puene* (the same as used for arrow shafts), is tied around the perimeter of the mask, neatly outlining the face.

The fiber skirts of the Tamate are prepared from two or three different materials and attached to the mask in layers to build up the full skirt. The first layer, a single young sago palm frond with the leaflets turned into the mask interior, is almost totally concealed except for a narrow strip of glossy yellow stalk exposed to view where it is fastened around the face with two-ply twisted *ekuo* cordage. Tied over this is a full and heavy fringe of shiny yellow-brown palm leaves, *viro*, probably a species of fan palm. (Sometimes other leaves are used, such as swamp or sago palm, or big-leaf sago palm, *ote*, such as that used for *kotakote* thatch panels.) This fringe is made by knotting long thin leaves in two layers over a pair of sturdy cords of twisted *ekuo* or other fiber, then securing the assembled skirt through evenly spaced holes encircling the face.

The topmost skirt is made from shredded hibiscus bast, *wavoro*, which is made in a similar fashion into a long, delicate fringe. Supple yet strong, it is tied either to the outer edge of the mask or to the underlying coarser skirt, usually completely around the face. (The bast is prepared by heating roughly meter-long stalks of hibiscus wood over a fire of coconut leaves, removing the outer bark, and then peeling away and splitting the clean inner bark into very fine strands.) When assembled the various layers of skirts are combed out to make them appear neat and uniform, then kept in place by a pair of twisted two-ply *ekuo* cords stretched taut around the back of the mask.

It is said that on some costumes aerial roots of the edible pandanus, *karawombo* or *karamombo*, are used for the main skirt. These are preferred because the comparatively heavy fibers do not swing and sway so erratically as to distract from the dancing. To prepare this material the outer surfaces of selected root segments are scored and long thin strips pulled off slowly to prevent tearing. Washed in salt water and sun dried, the uniform strips are made into a fringe or skirt by knotting them over two sturdy foundation cords that are then attached to the mask.

The Tamate are normally worn over another separate skirt that rests snugly on the dancer's shoulders, keeping his lower body well hidden. Built up from a long fringe of *viro* or fan palm fibers similar to those attached directly to the mask, this underskirt is just large enough in diameter to slip over the dancer's head and long enough to rustle on the ground. It is made by coiling a length of prepared fringe four or five times around itself and then stitching the upper edge together with a half-dozen bands of twisted *ekuo* cordage or other bast fibers spaced 10 to 15 cm. apart, forming a tight coiling.

Heavy and quite cumbersome, the masks are controlled by a wooden handle projecting inside the costume, an extension of the central wooden panel of the face. In motion the dancer holds the mask high by this handle, pulling a few fibers of the skirt aside to provide visibility. Resting, he allows the conical frame to ride gently on his shoulders, peering out the eye-holes cut into the front of the mask.

Takulalevioe, the Tamate "mother," is constructed in an entirely different manner and from a material point of view she bears little discernible relationship to her Tamate "children." Ben Tua recorded the making of her costume as follows:

> For Takulale Elephantiasis, we gather the leaves of the edible pandanus. Then we weave the two arms separately, then the two legs separately, then the head separately, the body separately, then we tie it all together. The dancer enters through the chest. (Tua 1979:26)

The two extant costumes conform to Ben Tua's formula. They are made from dark brown pandanus leaves rolled tightly into thick ropes, which are then built up in coils to form a tubular body tapering to a barely differentiated head. On the Bishop Museum example the moderately flexible coils are laced securely into place with double rows of stout hibiscus bark running vertically up the torso in parallel bands about 10 to 15 cm. apart. The legs and arms are made in a similar fashion, only smaller, and attached to the torso in the appropriate places. Tufts of hibiscus bast are tied with twisted *ekuo* cordage in bunches around the waist, on the upper arms, at the level of the neck, and at the back and tip of the "head," perhaps imitating skirt, armbands, and the tufts of fragrant leaves

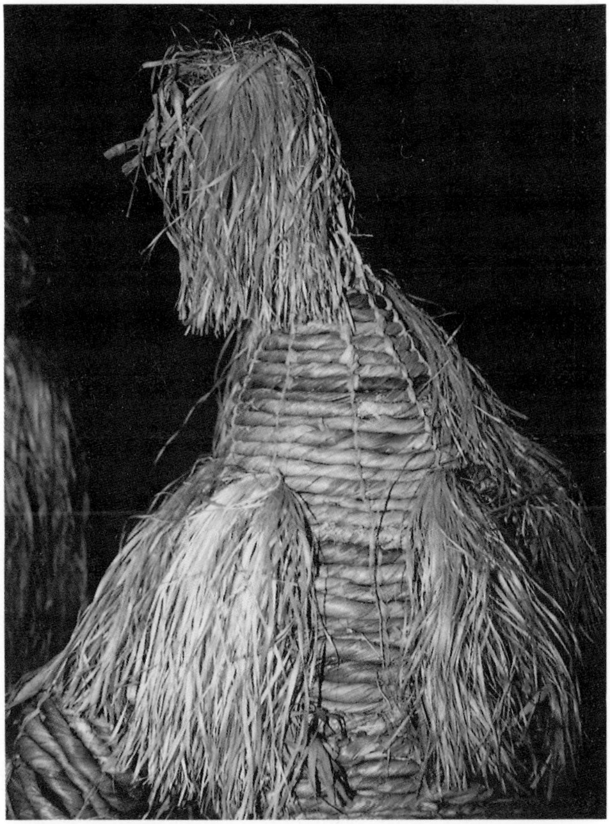

FIGURE 10.12. Detail showing construction of the Tamate mother, Takulalevioe, from coiled pandanus leaf ropes and hibiscus bast fringe. Bishop Museum 1964.60.01.

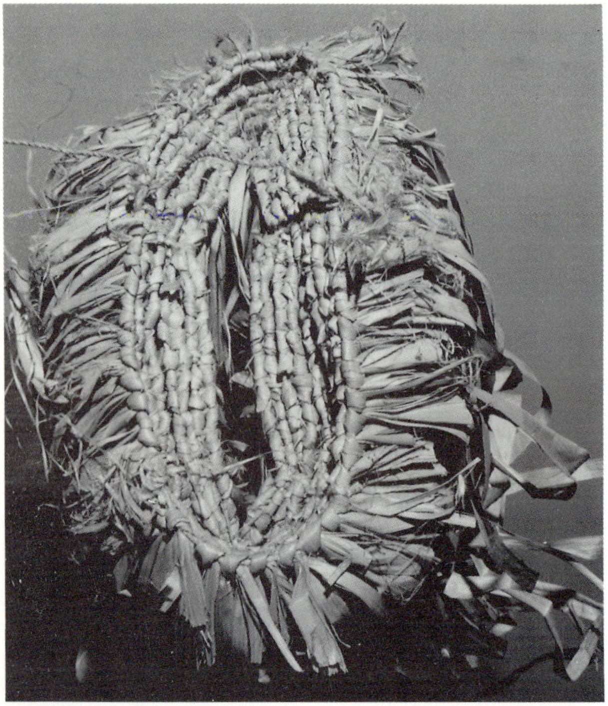

FIGURE 10.13. Detail (top view of collar) showing construction of Tamate underskirt worn around dancer's neck. Bishop Museum 1964.60.07.

worn as ornaments on festive occasions. The dancer enters the costume through a horizontal slit between the coils of the torso.

Basamuo

In addition to these five costumes, another traditionally associated with the Tamate is called Basomore or Basamuo. Davenport (1968:269) learned from Ben Tua that "Basomore was originally some sort of Tamate but not from Feloko. He, too, was burned to make him leave Tevai. No other details of the relationship between Basomore and the other five Tamate could be remembered." Basomore, according to Davenport,

> has a conical headdress of translucent spider webs that are colored red, white and black. Below this web headdress hangs a thick fringe of fibre, concealing the face of the wearer. A long, thick dress of leaves is also worn to hide the lower part of the wearer's body so that he is completely disguised. (Davenport 1968:267)

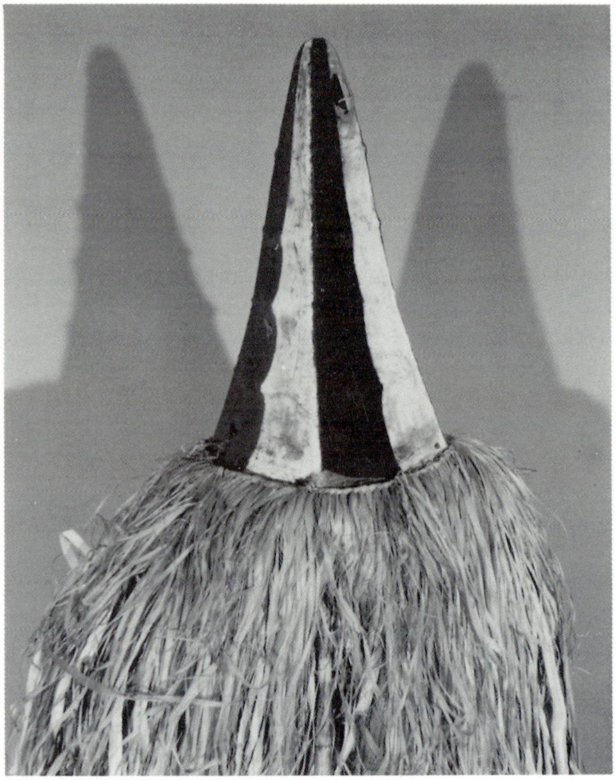

FIGURE 10.14. Detail of Basamuo costume, showing conical headdress made of painted spider webs and outer skirt of hibiscus bast. Bishop Museum 1964.60.02.

Accompanied by a realistic pencil sketch, Ben Tua's description of this costume states:

> For the Basamuo here, we use long spider webs. We decorate it with charcoal, ochre, and lime. We take four strips of mangrove wood and tie five rings around this cone. Then we gather the tops of the young narrow leaf sago shoots. These strips are then fastened to the bottom ring to clothe the body of the dancer. The shoots of the broad leaf sago may be used but the narrow leaf shoots are better. That is how Basamuo is made. (Tua 1979:26)

The framework of Basamuo is constructed substantially the same as the interior support for the Tamate headdress but without the wooden face mask. In the three extant costumes, the conical frame consists of five (or more, depending on size) circular rings of split rattan or cane, *momboro*, lashed horizontally to four upright supports of the same material, one extending below the bottom ring to form the handle. In the Bishop Museum example a small piece of coconut husk, *lambaro*, helps brace the apex of the cone, giving added support for the fragile covering.

Instead of wood and cloth the Basamuo headdress covering is a tightly stretched layer of spider web, *moe-iave*. Spread in thin sheets over the conical frame this paper-like material is collected from the bush by rotating forked sticks in the webs. On the Bishop Museum costume the four panels of the cone are each divided into two vertical halves and the right sections painted in alternating colors. The red and black, here ordinary oil-base paint, are separated by repeated sections of white, colored with lime (*awo*). (Traditionally, black was prepared from ordinary soot or ashes, *uro*; red, from an ocherous earth called *vokomaile* or *vokomaele* — or sometimes from chewed betel nut which yields a bright crimson that soon turns a dull reddish brown.) A palm leaf skirt, similar to those attached to the Tamate, is tied to the lowermost ring of the Basamuo headdress with two-ply twisted *ekuo* cordage. An outer skirt of golden brown hibiscus bast completes the headdress, which is worn over a separate neck skirt identical to those of the Tamate.

Cultural Affiliations of the Tamate

Davenport (1968:270), in summarizing his findings on the Tamate of Vanikoro, quite rightly observed: "These Tamate performances are obviously related in some way to the so-called secret society of the same name in the Torres and Banks Islands." Fortunately archaeological and linguistic advances in the years since Davenport's fieldwork, coupled with a fresh look at surviving historic accounts, can help clarify these relationships.

Several visitors to this part of Melanesia (among others, Coombe 1911:88, 103, 122 ff; Montgomery 1896:63-65; Wench 1961:55 ff; Yonge 1874, I:465) commented on the Tamate, and both R. H. Codrington (1891) and W. H. R. Rivers (1914) treated the phenomenon extensively. Describing some seventy-seven examples from Mota in the Banks Islands, Rivers pointed out: "One of the most extraordinary features of the *Tamate* societies is their large number. As has been seen, even in the island of Mota alone there are over seventy societies at least, while if the branches of the main societies are included, the number would probably reach a hundred" (1914, I:128, see also pp. 87, 110-19). Of differential prestige, depending partly on priority of establishment or status of the principal practitioners, the Tamate and other age-grade societies once permeated all levels of Banks and Torres islands society. Functioning as men's clubs and secret societies *par excellence* in the classic Melanesian sense, as well as foci for perhaps most spiritual and ceremonial activity, the Banks and Torres Tamate disappeared by the early twentieth century and have been generally overlooked in anthropological analysis.

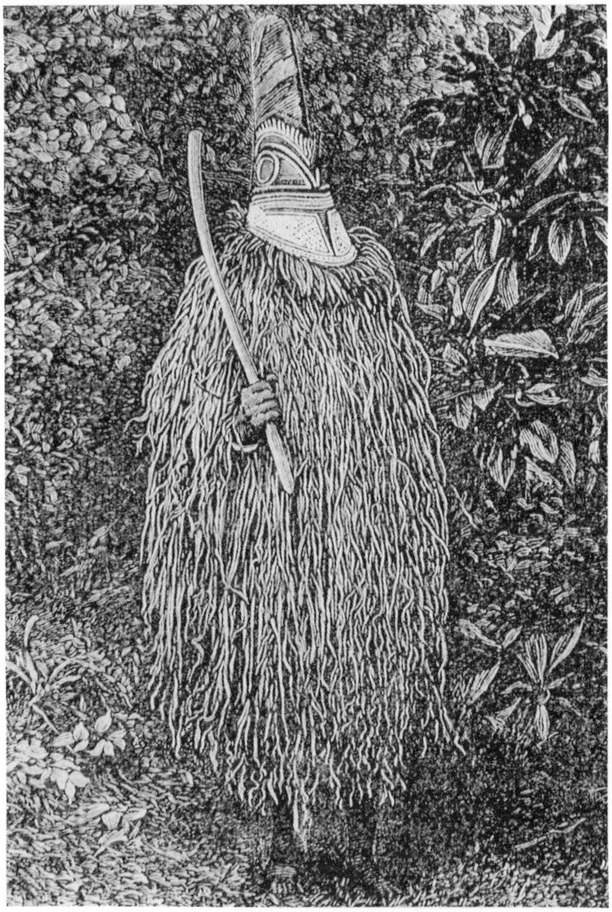

FIGURE 10.15. "Bank's Island Tamate." After Codrington (1891:73).

R. H. Codrington, a member of the Melanesian Mission from 1863 to 1887 who was thoroughly cognizant of the area, commented at length on the Banks and Torres islands Tamate — here, on their former prevalance and

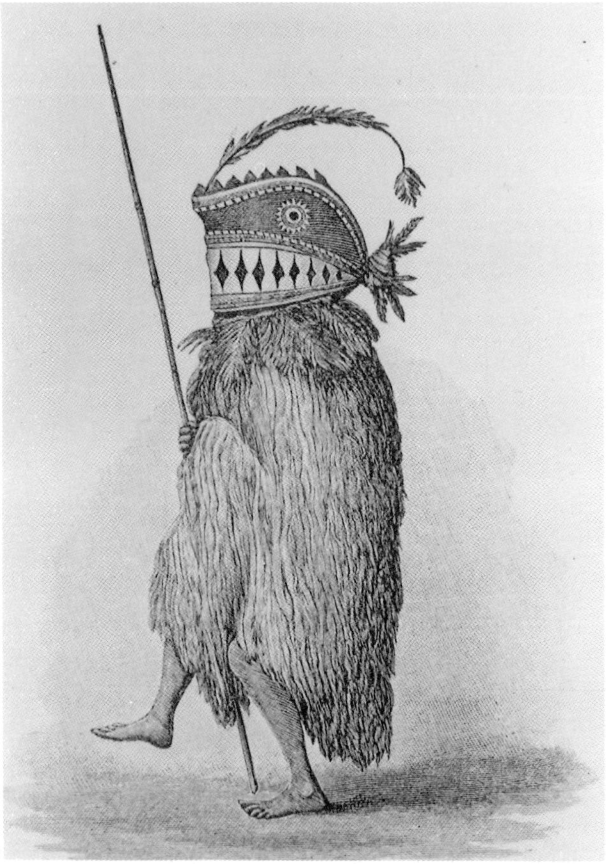

FIGURE 10.16. "Tamate, Valuwa, Banks' Islands." After Codrington (1891:78).

significance:

> In the Banks' Islands the *tamate* would very soon call for notice . . . . Very few days would pass without the appearance of some masked figures, or the sound of some strange noise or cry. In that group the number of these societies is surprising; some very insignificant, local, or recently started by individuals; some select and respected; one found everywhere, the principal and apparently original institution of the kind. In the Northern New Hebrides this Great *Tamate* of the Banks' Islands is not found, but others of the same character appear. . . .
>
> The Banks' Islands, with the neighbouring Torres group, are undoubtedly the chief seat of these societies, which are there universally called "The Ghosts," *o tamate, netmet*. In the Torres Islands alone there are a hundred of them, and every man belongs to four or five. The chief society, the *tamate liwoa* of Mota, is present everywhere, though in some places it is not so important as some more exclusive one of local origin. (Codrington 1891:72, 75)

Throughout the Banks and Torres Islands and extending into Northern Vanuatu, where related age-grade societies were also once prevalent, the Tamate exhibits certain common features. As Codrington indicated, in the Banks and Torres groups it is generally regarded as a ghost society or cult of ancestor worship, the name itself often being translated as "ghost." A long-time missionary in the area, Reverend W. G. Ivens (1931:157) explained: "The word *tamate* means 'dead person,' or 'disembodied human spirit,' 'ghost,' and the *tamate* who were worshipped on Mota were the disembodied spirits of dead ancestors or of the immediate dead." This division between the living and dead, according to Ivens (1931:159), "Appears on Mota in the use of the two words *ta-nun*, man, *ta-mate*, dead person, ghost. The *ta* in these two words=person, *nun*=real, *mate*=dead." On Vanikoro, however, there is no record of a similar etymology of the term, nor any clear association with a cult of the dead.

In the Banks and Torres islands the Tamate was also associated with men's houses, secret societies, and initiation rites. This was no longer the case on Vanikoro by the time Davenport first described the Tamate there:

> However, there is no tradition on Vanikoro that there was ever a club or society of men associated with the Tamate. Although Tamate dances are most frequently performed as entertainment at maturation rites and there is an element of concealment and secrecy about the costumery, there is no evidence that the introduction of boys to these "secrets" was ever part of a maturation celebration. (Davenport 1968:270-71)

When and from where the Tamate was introduced to Vanikoro remains an intriguing mystery that is still only partly explained. In the origin myth the Tamate are said to have come from an island called Veluko or Feluko, which, as has been pointed out, is of some interest because "in nearby Tikopia the name Varuka refers to Vanua Lava in the Banks" (Kirch 1983:70). Moreover, Vanikoro has other traditions of contact with the outside. In one, foreigners from a place called "Tonga" are said to have introduced a form of club dance called *telakau* (Davenport 1968:127). Among the songs Ben Tua (1979:33-34) re-

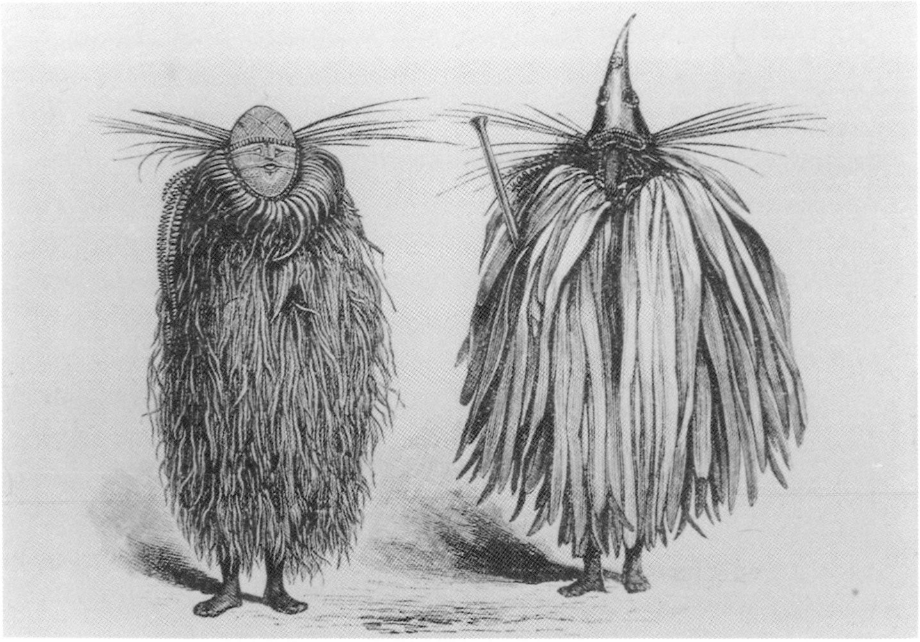

FIGURE 10.17. "Masked Dancers at Aurora." After Codrington (1891:91).

corded in an unknown and untranslatable language are also a number of so-called "Tonga Songs," *Tevie Dapa Tongo*. But, as Davenport (1964:137) noted elsewhere for the Polynesian-speaking atolls of the outer Reef Islands, "Tonga" is not really understood as a place name, but rather the name of a southerly wind.

Recent linguistic and ethnomusicological research also support derivation of the Vanikoro Tamate from islands directly to the south. According to Peter Crowe (1984:3), the Southeast Solomons, the Torres and Banks groups, and northern Vanuatu including Maewo, "is an area whose culture-history includes remarkable and attested contacts by canoe, of accidental and deliberate voyaging." Acknowledging that Feluko mentioned in the Tamate myth could have been somewhere in the Banks, Crowe (1984:5) thought he could make "poetic sense" of two of the six Tamate texts available for analysis. Cautioning that "as song texts frequently do not employ the syntax or logical narrative sequences of ordinary discourse, [and that] such 'poetic' verisimilitude was rather tenuous," Crowe reported:

> On consulting the *Mota Dictionary* published by Codrington and Palmer in 1896, with its near ten thousand entries, I found it possible to ascribe probable meanings to most of the Vanikoro *tamate* songs' words, which is a very tentative but suggestive result, full of dangers for the tyro. At the same time, I have not found a single element of the discernible music structures in these Vanikoro songs which is incompatible with song types existing on both the Banks and Maewo. (Crowe 1984:3)

The first archaeological investigations to be carried out on Vanikoro in 1977 and 1978 revealed physical evidence pointing to contact with islands to the south. From a prehistoric village site at Emo on the eastern side of Teanu Islet, Patrick Kirch unearthed sherds of classic Mangaasi-style pottery whose temper characteristics suggest importation rather than local manufacture, "quite possibly from Espiritu Santo" (Kirch 1983:107). Although radiocarbon dates are incomplete, the Emo Dune site suggested to Kirch (1983:108): "At least two phases of prehistoric occupation on Vanikoro, the first beginning early in the first millennium A.D. and probably extending to about A.D. 1200, characterized by the importation of Mangaasi pottery." Comparing this deposit with the Sinapupu Phase of Tikopia, "which corresponds in time quite closely with the tentative 'Emo Phase' of Vanikoro," Kirch (1983:108) concluded: "Both the Tikopia and Vanikoro materials appear to be evidence of a period during which there were contacts with the northern New Hebrides, perhaps indicative of a formerly more extensive exchange network" (Kirch 1982). Thus,

> It seems likely that the presence of Mangaasi pottery in these sites does not signal a cultural replacement but rather the initiation of exchange or trade relationships between Tikopia and Vanikoro with the Banks, Torres, and/or Espiritu Santo to the south. The exact nature of these relationships remains a significant problem for future investigations. (Kirch 1983:109)

At the time of European penetration into the Santa Cruz Islands, the people of Vanikoro professed to have no knowledge whatsoever of the Torres or Banks islands, even though Tikopia was in regular if infrequent contact. Instead Vanikoro (and Utupua) maintained regularized and well-documented (cf. Davenport 1964, 1968, and elsewhere) trade relationships by *te puke* sailing canoe with Nendö, exchanging red feathers of the *Myzomela* sp. honeyeater for shell disks and loomed fabrics of banana fiber. These were among commodities used as a medium of exchange in an extensive trading network of which Vanikoro and Utupua formed the southernmost nexus. Although Vanikoro (and Utupua) shared certain cultural similarities with islands to the south — for example, kava, which never penetrated into Northern Santa Cruz — the main cultural affiliations were clearly to the north.

The Tamate itself never moved northward beyond Vanikoro. With all its local variations, the culture of Vanikoro and Utupua formed a distinctive southern focus within the Santa Cruz group. Yet, as Kirch (1983:109) postulated on the basis of archaeological evidence: "A major realignment of exchange relationships obviously occurred some time in the second millennium A.D. . . . Determining when the focus of Vanikoro's external relations shifted from the northern New Hebrides to the Santa Cruz Islands remains a problem for future investigation."

In hopes that the Tamate may one day help shed more light on these complex relationships, Ben Tua's texts of the Tamate songs are reproduced here for whatever additional linguistic clues they may hold for a future investigator. As Peter Lincoln notes in preparing the transcriptions,

> Most of the songs are untranslatable. The meanings of the lyrics have been lost. The author [Ben Tua] cannot even say what languages they are in. In the present versions, the sound patterns and letter frequencies do not seem to be very different from those of the modern Vanikoro languages; Teanu . . . Vana . . . and Tetau. . . . But without the meanings of any of the lyrics, we have little hope of verifying any suggested origins for these songs. (Tua 1979:1-2)

With the exception of Peter Crowe's most recent but still tentative results, only the last song has been translated.

Buro Peini Pe Li-mede Tamate (Songs to Lead in the Tamate)

Mule mule Ia mula mula mateie
mule mule Ia mulamula mateie
mula mula mateie=...*woo Lilie woo Lilie*

Bula Tamate (The Tamate Songs)
Tuku mete mele luo Tukumete meleluo
Ka tuo Iao Ia-ka tuo Iao Ia katuo
Tokoliao Tikumete meleluo=...*woo Lilie woo Lilie*

Ie wabulape Iemalia Iwonue Ie
wabulape ie malia Iwonue Sole Silongo
mae nat vanuo-ka Ioa oa Ioa=...*woo Lilie woo Lilie*

Solovaka Solou e Solovale vale
Solovaka solou e Selo valevale eselo
vale vale eselo namo nionova solo
namo niovole solovale mule=...*woo Lilie woo Lilie*

Ie Tamate ie Tavilo Longowo ie
Ta vilolowo Ita vilo loiae=...*woo Lilie woo Lilie*

E! Wulute kopio elute kopiau
Ialo Se mowe kamanale kialo
Kialo Semowe Ieulute ko Ibowo Lae
Lae Kaipo Se naelo=...*woo Lilie woo Lilie*

Ningilosa Lomale ningilosa Lomale
Tabulu bulu mate ie Tabulubulu mate
ie Tabulubulu ma Silole=...*woo Lilie woo Lilie*

Wolua Tawolua ko manibe wolua
Tawolua ko Silita ewolua Tawolua ko
manibey kaia Lema Ibey Ka Iwalo Te
Kaliwo kaia Lema Ivilo Lilie ko Laie Laie
Belulie ko Laie=...*woo Lilie woo Lilie*

Ka Silio nebage bagi Longo Longo Ie
Silio bage bagi Longo Longo Ie Siling
Bage nat vanuo=...*woo Lilie woo Lilie*

E! Lam Susuliwo Lam Susuli wo
Eselovaka ne masekele woka
vivio. Kaio veve Lamuka no veve=...*woo Lilie woo Lilie*

Ie muale Bisuo ie muale muale
wowo aia muale muale Bisuo ie
wele plio pemase=...*woo Lilie woo Lilie*

Ie neule malo velade Ka Sava Sumuo
Sava uvana Sumuo Suna Golawe Taie mane.
Ka usua usua tabe nabile ngatobele=...*woo Lilie woo Lilie*

I wowo mure manuko Iwonue Ie Lae
manuko Iwonue Ie Lae manuko
Iwonue Bulalete netio Ie bulale
Bulalitolea avanoa=...*woo Lilie woo Lilie*

Woie ie kasi Longo Longo Ebebe Amae Kasi
Longo Longo woie Ie kasi Longo Longo He
matawe be ae kasi Longo Longo=...*woo Lilie woo Lilie*

Ka wa Logoba niniule Ila Ekoe
Laela ka neila Lao=ie mavala Tabe woie
neilade a nela velua ie piluo pemas woie=...*woo Lilie woo Lilie*

Puanomo nomae puanomo nomio puanomo
nomae puanomo nomio Ekovanolie
Kosavae nom nomio Sulina kovani
puolo kisuo ie nom nomio Sulino vio=...*woo Lilie woo Lilie*

Ie neule ielengi wonue Eiebulale
Temata Sisimole niatado Lae wa
Lumuka mukape wo io Tamulele Etae
no Lobelobe=...*woo Lilie woo Lilie*

Kaialema wie we aka ia lema Toto uwo
Akaialema Liteli beli mana Tolea
Pusia Leale mana Silele=...*woo Lilie woo Lilie*

Ka Besingale Besingale ilo kosa ngilolo
woo bosa ngilolovea ulele Lengi mata
ulolo Lovia Basa nilolo woo=...*woo Lilie woo Lilie*

Ko Temisi kolea kotemisi kolea Io pe
Io ko Temisi kolea kotemisi kolea
Hoa Hoa me Itoume kalako Hoa Hoa
me Toume Kalako Io=...*woo Lilie woo Lilie*

Uwoo awoie uwoo awoie woo woo
woie awo wo woie awoie=...*woo Lilie woo Lilie*

Ie veleta veleta Buele Ie veleta
veleta Buele nava Leilo veleta veleta
Buele ie natangia mailo Epeilo Eveleta
Buele nava Leilo=...*woo Lilie woo Lilie*

Kia menu menu kalele
Epe Lika Lume Tamate
Lume Epe Lika namolo
tae kia menumenu kalele...*woo Lilie woo Lilie*

You and I, children, we are going. Oh yes, for they will come to Lume, the Tamate. To Lume, oh yes, they will come without malo. We children are going. Oh lili eh, oh lili eh.

Appendix I:

RECORD OF EXTANT TAMATE COSTUME

Bernice P. Bishop Museum, Honolulu, Hawaii
(Costumes collected by William Davenport, 1960)

1964.60.01 Takulalevioe
Height, 194 cm. Maximum diameter at waist, 122 cm.

1964.60.02 Basamuo
Height, 199 cm. Height of mask, 51 cm. Diameter at base, 27 cm.

1964.60.03 Tamate Aeleteulungo (squared eye stalks)
Height, 220 cm. Mask, 71 by 29 cm. Height with carrying pole, 116 cm.

1964.60.04 Tamate Matateva (double face)
Height, 150 cm. Front mask, 71 by 28 cm. Rear mask, 70 by 28 cm. Height (front) with carrying pole, 119 cm. Height (rear) with carrying pole, 96 cm.

1964.60.05 Tamate Kolokolo (disked eye stalks)
Height, 160 cm. Mask, 73 by 27 cm. Height with carrying pole, 118 cm.

1964.60.06 Tamate Matatilu (pointed eye stalks)
Height, 220 cm. Mask, 72 by 28 cm. Height with carrying pole, 116 cm.

1964.60.07 Tamate Underskirt
Length, 170 cm.

1960.64.08 Tamate Underskirt
Length, 170 cm.

1960.64.09 Tamate Underskirt
Length, 153 cm.

Solomon Islands Museum, Honiara
(Information based on registration records)

74.291 Tamate Kolokolo
Purchased for Museum from Ben Tua by former District Commissioner J. Tedder for $26, June 8, 1974; sold to Mick Pendergrast in January 1977 for $26 and sent to Auckland Memorial Museum, New Zealand, for a tem-

porary exhibition. Replaced by a new set December 18, 1976 (see 1976.283)
Mask, 87 by 28 cm. Height with carrying pole, 149 cm.

76.1.1 Basamo
Collected by Dorota Starzecka, Museum of Mankind, London
Conical frame of eight cane rings and four vertical supports covered with spider web colored in alternating panels of tan, white, and black.
Height of headdress, 90 cm. Diameter at base, 43-44 cm. Height with carrying pole, 163 cm.

76.1.2 Skirt for Basamo
Same history as 76.1.1
Darkish-brown split leaves of swamp palm (similar to sago) tied in a "collar" of four rows.
Average length, 146 cm.

76.1.3 Skirt for Basamo
Brought to Museum by Ben Tua for Festival of Traditional Music and Dance because original skirt (76.1.2) was considered too "thin," December 18, 1976.
Pale brown, young sago palm leaves tied in a "collar" of eight rows.
Average length, 144 cm.

76.2 Tamate Takolefioe
Acquired from Ben Tua, December 1975/January 1976.
Arms, legs, trunk, and conical head composed of pandanus leaf "rope" bound together at intervals with sago palm leaves; swamp palm leaves and another fiber cascade from top of head like hair; attached skirt of pale fibers.
Height, 210 cm. Width at torso, 44 cm.

76.282 Tamate Matateva (double face, pointed eye stalks)
Acquired from Ben Tua for $50 after Festival of Traditional Music and Dance, December 18, 1976.
Wooden masks painted white with lime and partly covered with blue and red cloth above and below horizontal band containing two diamond-shaped eye holes; overskirt of *kanuko* (banyan tree root), *vie mimbile* leaf, *kanombe* (pandanus roots), and young *wavoro* (wild hibiscus) fibers; wooden handles attached to masks also covered with *wavoro* fiber.
Masks (including fringe border), 90 by 29 cm.
Height with carrying pole, 160 cm.

76.283 Tamate Kolokolo (disked eye stalks, painted design)
(replacement for 74.291)
Purchased for $26, as above. Similar to 76.282.
Mask (including fringe border), 94 by 37 cm.
Height with carrying pole, 161 cm.

76.284 Tamate Ailiteolungo (disked eye stalks with red cloth streamers)
Purchased for $26, as above. Similar to 76.282.
Mask (including fringe border), 98 by 36 cm.
Height with carrying pole, 161 cm.

76.285 Tamate Matatilu (pointed eye stalks)
Purchased for $26, as above. Similar to 76.282.
Mask (including fringe border), 94 by 36 cm.
Height with carrying pole, 164 cm.

Nb. Three additional Tamate costumes representing the characters Matatilu, Aeleteulungo, and Kolokolo are in the possession of Ben Tua, Buma Village, Vanikoro.

Notes

Information on the Tamate was gathered during fieldwork on Vanikoro between March 10 and April 13, 1978. Research was conducted as part of the second phase of the Southeast Solomon Islands Culture History Program, sponsored by Bishop Museum and funded by the National Science Foundation (Grant BNS 76-17672). I am particularly grateful to Ben Tua of Buma Village for his support and assistance, and to his two sons Christian Ramoli and Timothy Bila. I am also indebted to Anna Craven, then with the Solomon Islands Museum, and to Peter Lincoln, who accompanied me to Vanikoro for linguistic fieldwork. I wish to thank William Davenport for sharing additional insights on the Tamate, and Peter Gilpin for preparing the illustrations accompanying this article. Doug Yen, Roger Green, and Lawrence Foanaota receive my appreciation for stimulation and encouragement.

1. *The Southern Cross Log*, April 1904.
2. Accession Record 23-47, D.1796, Peabody Museum of Archaeology and Ethnology, Harvard University.
3. District Office Eastern, Santa Cruz, Quarterly Report, March 31, 1930. Central Archives of Fiji and the Western Pacific High Commission (Auckland Institute and Museum Microfilm Nos. 131-32).
4. *Ibid.* Quarterly Report, September 30, 1937.
5. *Ibid.* Annual Report, 1944.
6. *Ibid.* Annual Report, 1955; Bi-Annual Report, January-June 1961.
7. *The Southern Cross Log*, May 14, 1908.
8. Accession Record 74.318, Solomon Islands Museum.
9. *Op. Cit.*, District Office Eastern, Annual Report, 1934.
10. *Ibid.* Annual Report, 1937.
11. *Ibid.* Quarterly Report, March 31, 1939.
12. *Ibid.* Annual Report, 1940.

11

The Bark Art of Tasmania

Edward L. Ruhe

The almost unknown bark art of Tasmania was first noticed, sketched, described, and published early in the last century by several of the French scientific observers attached to the expedition of Nicolas Baudin, 1800-4 (Péron 1807:273 and *Atlas*:pl. XVI; Plomley 1983:60, 138, 140). Tasmanian art received attention in John West's *History of Tasmania* (1852 I:89), James Bonwick's *Daily Life and Origin of the Tasmanians* (1870:47, 94), and H. Ling Roth's *The Aborigines of Tasmania* (1890:137, 1899:137). Its important place in the history of Australian Aboriginal art in general was recognized by Charles P. Mountford (1956:1) and by several later students concerned with the history of the art (Ruhe 1966:8; Kupka 1972:99; and especially Groger-Wurm 1973:1).

The located Tasmanian references nearly all fall within the period 1827-32. They have become numerous since the publication in 1966 of the bush journals of George Augustus Robinson under the title *Friendly Mission*, an edition admirably annotated by N. J. B. Plomley. In 1983, Plomley also published English translations of abundant materials from archives in Paris and LeHavre supplementing published texts rich in Tasmanian materials by Captain Baudin and Francois Péron, the official historian of his expedition. This recent flood of fresh source material has invited a full examination of abundant information now available with a view to understanding the artistic productivity of a race always likely to be remembered in the stubborn folklore of Europe as the most culturally undeveloped of all the peoples of the world. The present study should be useful primarily for making available quantities of detail extracted from a variety of rare sources and inviting independent assessment and further research.

Early Observations

The history begins with promising precision on February 19, 1802. On that date Captain Baudin dispatched his scientists on various missions relating to the exploration of the dumbbell-shaped Maria Island, halfway up the east coast of Van Diemen's Land, as Tasmania was then called, and of the unmapped coastline north to Freycinet's Peninsula. The corvettes *Géographe* and *Naturaliste* were anchored between the island and the mainland a little to the south of the entrance to Oyster Bay, when the botanist Jean-Baptiste Leschenault and the surgeon François Collas made for the island in a boat with Midshipman Breton at the helm. They landed, Leschenault later wrote, "on the

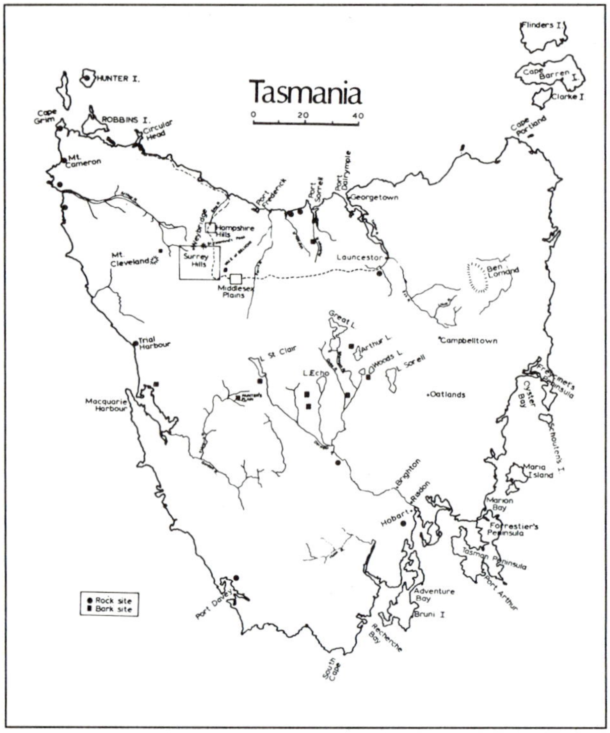

FIGURE 11.1. Tasmania. Approximate locations for reports of rock and bark art.

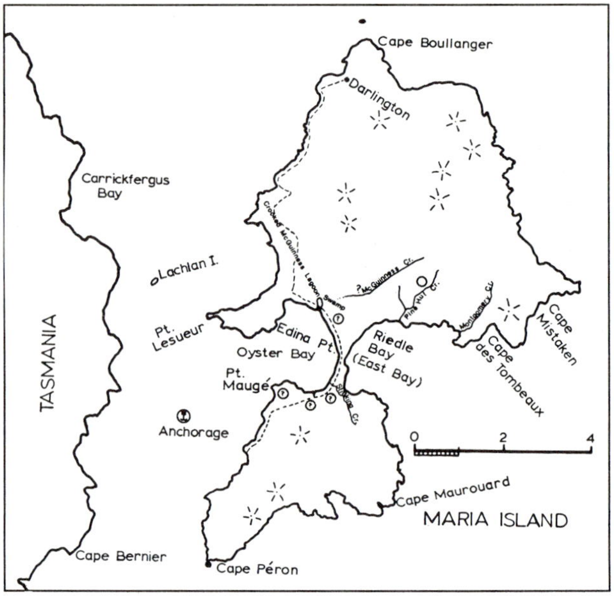

FIGURE 11.2. Maria Island. With conjectural locations for the East Bay and Oyster Bay burials.

western coast of the island" and soon, "at about 100 paces from the shore . . . came across two huts joined together" and unusually well made. The account continues:

> Fifteen paces from these shelters I saw another which appeared to have been knocked down. I was struck by the length and thickness of the bark and went nearer to examine it. I then realized that what I had taken for a shelter was a carefully arranged mass of bark covering a hemispherical mound. Turning over these pieces of bark, I noticed that they were covered with lines deliberately made, which resembled in form the tattooing of these people.

The structure, which "appeared to have been set up only a little time," sheltered a kind of burial pit "covered with a gramineous plant held in place by eight sticks curved like a bow, both ends of which were driven into the ground at equal distances apart." The pit proved to contain very fragile, calcined pieces of human bone among which Citizen Collas identified "a fragment of a femur and an astragalus" (Plomley 1983:138).

In a second report on the discovery Leschenault reported that the burial resembled one of the nearby bark shelters except that it "seemed to have been knocked down"; then, further repeating himself, he explained that what he "had taken for a shelter were some carefully arranged pieces of bark" (p. 140) bearing on their undersides markings as described in the other report (pp. 140-41). On departure, he wrote, "I restored as much of it as I was able in the same arrangement as I had found it" (p. 141). Citizen Breton's brief report mentioned "difficulty in removing" the "large pieces of bark" covering the mound (p. 111). As we read Leschenault, the discovery seems to have been made a very short time after the party went ashore (pp. 138, 140); Breton gives the impression that it took place at the end of the day's work: "We replaced everything as we found it, and returned on board" (p. 111). Minor problems created by this and many other inconsistencies in the available data are not quite worth putting before the reader of the present study. But we must note Leschenault's wonderfully misleading final remark: "Citizen Péron, the zoologist, studied another tomb on the same island, and it was very little different from the one I have just described" (p. 138). For if we visualize the solitary burial mound covered with heavy bark slabs 115 paces or so from the shores of Oyster Bay, as we were told by Leschenault, and seek a similar structure in the pictorial and verbal evidence cited in the opening sentence of the present essay, we will find Leschenault's account entirely bewildering. The burial discovered, described, and then depicted in the 1807 engraving (fig. 11.3) was indeed similar to the burial discussed above; but only sharp eyes and close study of the early texts can indicate how. The next few pages should accordingly be read with close attention to the accompanying illustrations.

François Péron, the "engineer-geographer" Charles Boullanger, and Midshipman Maurouard at the helm of the *Géographe*'s big dinghy, began a counter-clockwise circumnavigation of Maria Island in the early morning of that first day, February 19, 1802. Boullanger's sightings and soundings were to be responsible for the published maps of the island (Péron *Atlas*: map 5, and a different map, Plomley 1983, facing p. 161). Halfway around the island, near the north shore of the East (Riedlé) Bay, in mid afternoon, Péron came upon that other burial monument, or *tombeau*, mentioned by Leschenault. The many early pictures of it which survive make it look like a conical wigwam with sloping sides made of numerous narrow, overlapping bark slabs; and it stood, like the other burial, single and solitary on a small hill in an attractive, thinly wooded sort of parkland with a flowing spring at the foot of the rise. The structure proved to be a sort of pyramid made by planting four long poles in a square formation on the ground, lashing them together near their upper ends, and using them as supports for the sloping bark walls. Near the top, narrow loops of flexible bark supplied what we would call ornamentation. In its handsome natural setting it made a fine spectacle. Péron was moved to investigate further.

Removing several of the bark slabs, he discovered that the wigwam sheltered a round grassy mound about eighteen inches across, the bundles of grass held in place by eight "little twigs" (wands, saplings; *baguettes de bois* in Péron's original text) all anchored at each end by "a large flat granitic stone" (Plomley 1983:57). With growing curiosity he probed the mound with his hands, discovering that the "fine light grass . . . placed very carefully in concentric and very thick layers" covered a shallow circular pit containing the less-than-fully consumed scraps of bone and flesh of a recent cremation (p. 57). Here are those items — sticks, grass, bones — which establish the similarity of this burial to the other. All the same, Péron's discovery, with its four poles, its numerous bark slabs, its bark loops, and its granitic rocks seems quite different from and far more elaborate than Leschenault's. And we must now restate the evidence of the written record that the two burials stood separate and isolated, and at a considerable distance (perhaps several miles) from each other. A demon of didacticism led Péron and his artists to complicate every rendering of the burials but one with imaginary constructions and deconstructions of one or both of the wigwams, producing again and again a false impression of an exotic cemetery furnished with fresh and varied funeral monuments.

The single picture which most probably shows Péron's discovery just as he first saw it is a pencil drawing of a lone wigwam on a rounded hillock with several scrubby trees close by and an unidentifiable portion of ocean in the right background. This picture, never published, is no. 18.025 of the Lesueur collection in the LeHavre Museum of Natural History (Plomley 1983:233); a copy supplied by Jacqueline Bonnemains, curator of the collection, contains evidence that it is the work of the expedition artist Nicolas Petit, who was to join Péron three days later, February 22, when the latter revisited the two burials (Plomley 1983:62, 66, 75n.18). It thus appears to be a sketch made on the spot.

Meanwhile, early on February 20, Péron and Boullanger resumed their circumnavigation, sailing completely around the north lobe of the island, entering Oyster Bay toward dark, and landing for the night somewhere along the north shore. If we read Péron's account closely and trust him more strictly than he perhaps deserves (Plomley 1983:58, 62), we gather that he could have come upon the Leschenault burial well past sunset, possibly seeing it first by moonlight (full moon had been at 3:00 A.M. February 18, local time). Whether at this place and time, February 20, or later, Péron had an opportunity to examine it closely. He judged it to be older than the other and, as Leschenault had at first thought, in a state of collapse. Slabs from the wigwam lay across the mound, Péron noted; and the grass covering was "greatly altered by the damp air" (p. 60), while "the bones and ashes were disposed in almost [*à-peu-près*] the same way as in the

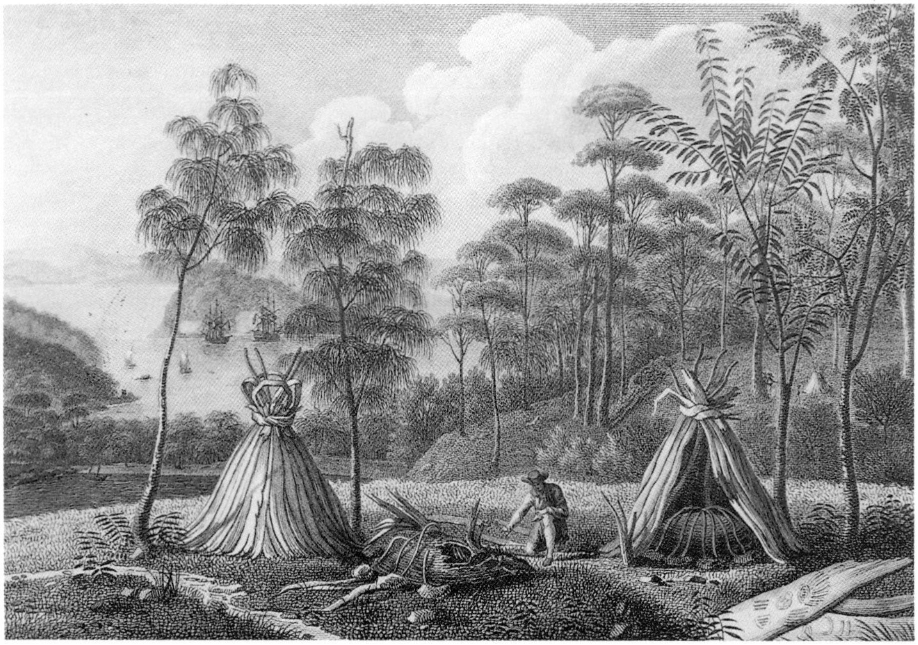

FIGURE 11.3. The Maria Island burials. An imaginary landscape devised by Charles-Alexandre Lesueur from on-site drawings made during a special visit to the two widely separated graves by Nicolas-Martin Petit, accompanying Péron, February 22, 1802. The structure found and described by Péron on February 19 is depicted at the left-hand side of the engraving. From Péron's Atlas, Plate XVI.

tomb at East Bay" (p. 60); but we hear nothing of poles, or bark loops, or anchoring granite stones at this site; and the probability that bark loops at least were indeed missing is supported by four of the early pictures which show reconstructions of the disarranged Leschenault wigwam and its mound (Péron *Atlas*pl.xvi; Bonwick 1870:94; Plomley 1983:pls. 11, 12). Péron's account tallies in one respect with Leschenault's:

> The only peculiarity which deserves special comment is that on the lower surface of some of the largest and finest pieces of bark, had been crudely drawn [*grossiêrement gravé*] some characters similar to those which the natives employ in tattooing their forearms. (Plomley 1983:60)

Péron elsewhere correctly identified the native practice as cicatricization (p. 91; Roth 1899:125-26) rather than tattooing, and shifted terms from "forearms" to "upper part of the arms" (Plomley 1983:92). The inscribed slabs, he continued, referring to the 1807 Lesueur engraving, "are shown in the drawing, the bark having been removed and placed in front of the tombs" (p. 60). Like the East Bay burial, this one, shown as reconstructed and resited in the 1807 engraving, stood on a slight "eminence" overlooking a flowing freshwater spring (Péron 1807:267, 268, 272; *couloit une source d'eau douce* is Péron's phrase), producing "the only [freshwater stream] to be found in this bay" (Plomley 1983:60), that is, Oyster Bay, west of the isthmus.

Our most attractive but most treacherous data appear in the pictures. The 1807 engraving (fig. 11.3), composed by the artist Charles-Alexandre Lesueur, was worked up from sketches made by Petit. During the Tasmanian explorations Lesueur had occupied himself with zoology; no known evidence connects him at that time to either of the burials. His engraving featured the burial on the hill above East Bay with its panoramic view of Oyster Bay and showed a good deal more of the island scenery, including the isthmus, many small boats, groups of Frenchmen here and there, and the two corvettes at anchor in shallow Oyster Bay (actually their anchorage was two or three miles southwest of the position shown in the picture). The recomposed landscape is far from faithful to Maria Island topography. The island behind the ships, for example, is imaginary. Péron appears front-and-center inspecting the fully exposed East Bay burial mound, with the intact Péron wigwam (as first seen) to his right, the Leschenault wigwam as conjecturally restored, with a flat three-pronged bark post beside it, to his left, and the running stream and inscribed slabs in the extreme foreground of the engraving. The barks were thus depicted perhaps miles from the Leschenault *tombeau*, where they were discovered and where they doubtless stayed. Another wigwam, wholly imaginary, appears on a hillside at some distance to the right, with tiny human figures close by. Lesueur worked closely with Péron during the years following the conclusion of the expedition and must have had his cooperation in concocting this rather festive conversation-piece of a picture.

The reports of the two discoveries discussed above are not the only sources of information on the burials. It appears that Baudin (1974:341, 349; Plomley 1983:109) and Captain Hamelin of the *Naturaliste* (Plomley 1983:127) took pains near the end of the Maria Island exploration, February 22, to visit the Leschenault site. The references in Baudin's journal show some confusion, for Baudin, like Leschenault, had no clear idea at the time of the wigwam shelter. But he may have noticed a detail that escaped the other observers. The burial pit, he said, contained "a heap of ashes"; and "at one end of the pile of ashes there was a small channel, which was probably where the natives placed the body for which they were performing the burial rites" (Baudin 1974:349).

Mr. Plomley has recently published three more depictions of the burials from the LeHavre collection (Plomley 1983:pls. 11-13). Those, and several additional unpublished pictures of the same subject, would all seem to derive from Petit's on-site drawings, although several are plainly copies varied in a number of ways in developing the composition of Lesueur's 1807 engraving (Plomley 1983:233, Le Havre nos. 18.020 through 18.023 and 18.025). The enigmatic designs so clearly to be seen on the bark slabs of Lesueur's engraving (fig. 11.4) seem substantially identical with those on the slabs in other pictures (nos. 18.017, 18.019, 18.020, 18.022, and 18.023); appreciable but to our eyes not radical variations occur in LeHavre 18.021 and 18.024, as Jacqueline Bonnemains has informally pointed out to me. That Péron, Petit, and Lesueur attached importance to correctness in the designs thus seems demonstrated over and over.

Studying all this evidence, we judge the bark slabs to be something like six feet long and perhaps eighteen inches wide, with straight sides and crudely chopped upper and lower edges. Baudin tells us of "slabs of eucalyptus bark that they lift off the trees" (Baudin 1974:345; Roth 1899:109n); and Breton's report of trouble lifting the funeral barks tells us that those used in the Leschenault burial were heavy — perhaps a botanical clue. Finally, we note that while Péron described the barks as *grossièrement gravé* — crudely engraved or scratched (Péron 1807:273) — Plomley plausibly uses the term "crudely drawn" (1983:60); and a glance at the reproduction of Petit's beautiful gouache of the scene (Plomley 1983:pl. 11) suggests that the drawings may have been black, in this way perhaps following the standard Tasmanian practice of drawing with charcoal against a light-colored bark surface.

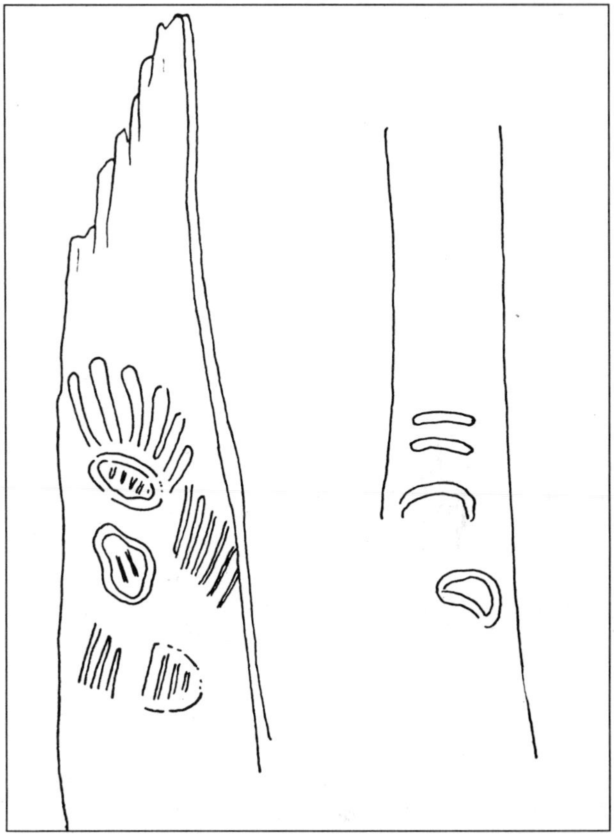

FIGURE 11.4. The Maria Island inscribed barks. Adapted from the preceding illustrations and numerous drawings and other graphics among the expedition records.

As for the resemblance of the figures to observed scar patterns, I have not discovered the portraits of natives

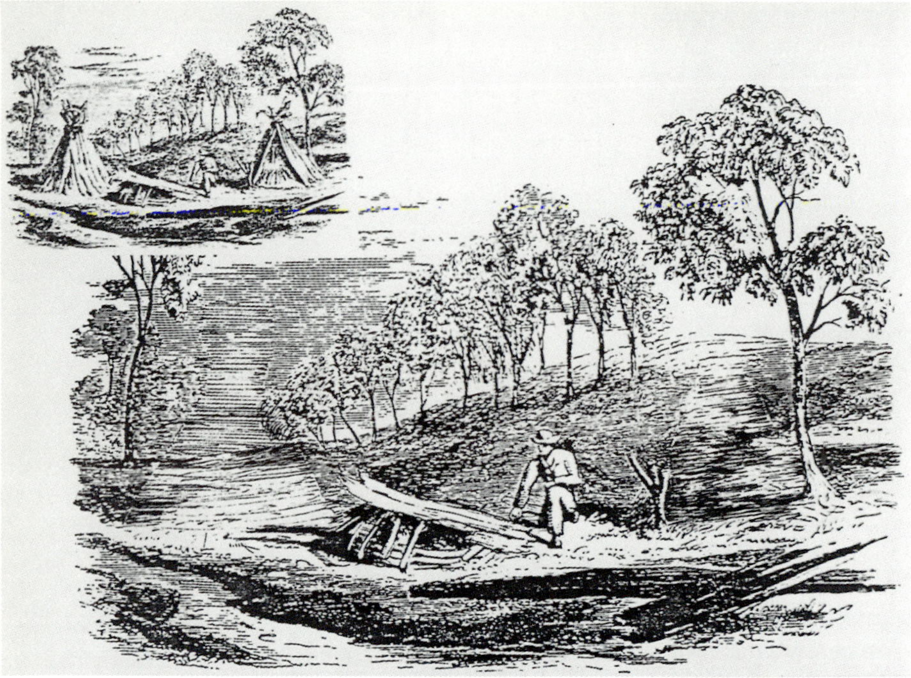

FIGURE 11.5. The Oyster Bay burial, adapted version. Modified depiction clarifying landscape features and showing the burial solitary, isolated, and something like a ruin, as noted by Leschenault and Péron upon first viewing. The original engraving appears in reduced form at upper left. If valid, the present doctored picture is closer than any known to the drawing Petit apparently made on February 22. From James Bonwick (1870:94).

which show cicatrices like the crescents, irregular circles, or other shapes we see in Lesueur's picture. But George Augustus Robinson has a journal item stating that women of the north coast were proud of circular cicatrices as large as three or four inches in diameter, with thick "margins" (=broad perimeters?), typically one on each side of the spine and sometimes on one or both hips. These could represent the sun and the moon and were thought to have therapeutic power. Plomley reports an illustrative drawing by Robinson of "a circle of about 1 1/2 inch diameter with a thick margin, its area covered with a number of short transverse lines" (Robinson 1966:581-82n.69) — rather like two of the figures on the larger of the Péron bark slabs. Elsewhere, "most of these eastern natives" according to Robinson "had the form of the moon cut in their flesh. This mark seems peculiar to them, and they count by the moon" (Robinson 1966:263).

This account of the Maria Island barks and their mysterious designs may seem excessively detailed. It happens that the available data, verbal and pictorial, are patently hard to explain; but it seems likely that in the history of bark art they are unsurpassed also for the information they convey, however enigmatically, about the ceremonial context in which they had their place.

The pictorial evidence has a further oddity. For while the Leschenault burial, with its inscribed bark slabs, might seem to have been the more important of the two, it cannot be identified in a single drawing, painting, or engraving mentioned so far. Is it likely that Péron and Petit failed to visit this burial? If so we would be hard put to explain the convincing pictures we have of these slabs. Or was the Petit on-site sketch lost or mislaid? It happens that a picture answering rather closely to Leschenault's description appears in the book by Bonwick already mentioned (1870:94) with the unexpected caption: "Tasmanian graves. (*By Péron*)" (fig. 11.5). Péron is not otherwise known to have been an artist, and the Bonwick picture shows some skill. We may remember also that while Leschenault deemed the bark slabs covering the burial mound to be "carefully arranged," Péron perceived the structure as a kind of ruin. We shall soon see how the artist, whoever he was, rendered it.

The evidence of the Bonwick engraving will gain clarity if we present it first in my edited form, for in the way of all but one of the other extant pictures known to us, it depicts a scene more like a cemetery than a solitary grave. We now

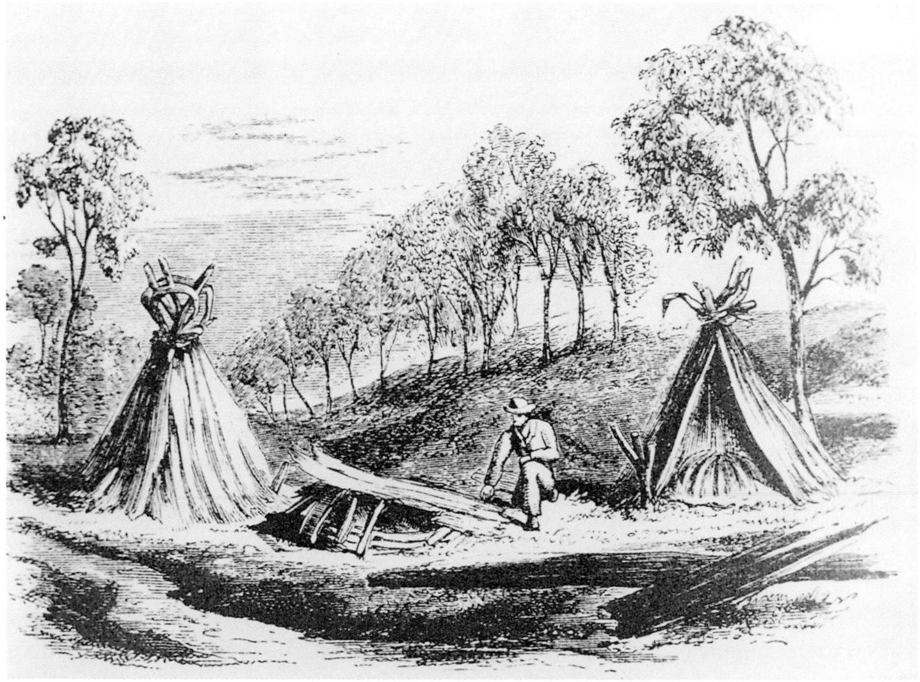

FIGURE 11.6. The Oyster Bay Burial. Another imaginary landscape, shown in reduced form in the preceding figure, and devised, like the 1807 engraving, by recomposing miscellaneous graphic materials from expedition records.

offer the picture in such a way as to show the burial standing single and alone in the moderately rolling countryside with occasional trees. The rivulet mentioned by Péron may be seen in the left foreground, the bark slabs to the right, and the three-pronged stake (a narrow trifurcate bark slab in the 1807 engraving) to the right of the mound. The pit reported by Captain Baudin is not exactly visible, if visible at all. The original, unedited engraving (inset, reduced in size) shows two wigwams which no witness reported at the Oyster Bay site. In the edited picture I have simply left them out, supplying rough fill-in material to suggest the appearance of the landscape without the imaginary *tombeaux*. It amounts to a conjecture and may accordingly invite a skeptical response. But if Petit in fact failed to make a sketch somewhat like this picture during that excursion of February 22 (Plomley 1983:62, 66), we might well feel surprised.

We need not worry excessively about how Bonwick might have come into possession of such a picture. For this Hobart schoolmaster was a research scholar of a certain energy and perhaps distinction, eventually securing an appointment as government archivist for New South Wales. He was in England in 1860-62 and 1869-71, permitting us to imagine fruitful contacts with archival officials in Paris, LeHavre, or other cities before 1870. That could explain his access to a valuable pictorial document perhaps lost or mislaid at a very early date, before Péron and Lesueur could incorporate its central figure in the series of sketches leading to the 1807 engraving.

We turn finally to the original version of the Bonwick engraving (fig. 11.6). On the right we see the putative Leschenault burial shelter in imaginary reconstruction; the East Bay wigwam is shown on the left. Leschenault noted that the barks lying across the burial mound were "carefully arranged," although resembling a structure in a state of collapse. On this theory, his was a burial quite different in form from, but using much the same materials as, the Péron. A third theory may now be proposed: Leschenault's was a ritual rearrangement of a complex burial similar to Péron's. The curious student may note the key details of the three most important pictures, the Bonwick, the Lesueur engraving, and the gouache (Plomley 1983:pl. 11): the bark loops and the "granitic stones" of the Péron wigwam; the lack of loops and stones in the Bonwick reconstruction of the Leschenault *tombeau*; and in the "collapsed" burial as the Bonwick picture shows it, a lack of stones, bark loops, supporting poles, and most of the bark slabs. On very close inspection of the Lesueur engraving we notice a stake emerging from the Péron wigwam, and (as noted before in the Lesueur and Bonwick engravings) a three-pronged post associated with the Leschenault. The pit noticed by Baudin may be dimly present in the Bonwick picture, while the flowing stream of water is shown in both. Most importantly, we see the inscribed bark slabs, although we cannot in the Bonwick version read their inscriptions.

The Tasmanians, always regarded as simple and backward, prove to have expended energy and elaborate invention in the funeral rituals of Maria Island, and, we may infer, in their ceremonial life in general — like Aborigines in all parts of Australia. We sense meaningfulness and perhaps spirit presence, as well as rather elegant craftsmanship in the details of both burials. We may be tempted to attribute the differences between the two burials and the enigmatic designs of the barks to differences in rank, sex, age, or clan affiliation of the deceased; to successive phases of a protracted funeral rite; to practices addressed to the active spirits, whether sad or dangerous or in need of guidance. As for the bark slabs, found face down across the Leschenault mound, we may note some of the ways in which they are characteristically Australian. First, provided we trust the European artist who sketched them, we note care and skill in the placing and inscribing of the figures. Those figures, we note, are perhaps fully cryptic, although they may invite us to speculate: A circle can always stand for the sun; an irregular closed figure may be a ceremonial ground; and so on. Concealed from human sight when discovered, the hieroglyphs seem not to have been addressed to human survivors after the manner of lapidary inscriptions; nor would we expect them to be doodles or mere decorations. It may be most important to note, and remember, that these earliest specimens of observed bark art were associated not with a human habitation but with a burial structure.

The foregoing speculations cannot substitute for reliable explanation. It must be enough to note that the mysterious shapes on the barks almost certainly put us in touch with the Tasmanian spirit world as perhaps no other Tasmanian evidence has done. Even if we discount for the pathos of the subject matter, we can not be indifferent to a mode of beauty which the *tombeaux* share with some of the early recorded native burials of temperate-zone Australia: the park-like landscapes seemingly favored for such rites; the fine workmanship of constructed objects as European observers reported and sketched them; the sense of strong traditionality (here in the similarity of the two burials and, as elsewhere in Tasmania, the practice of cremation); the prominent use of vegetable substances in sheltering the human remains (here saplings, grass, bark); and perhaps most significantly, the occurrence of enigmatic drawings in significant places. For the last, one would wish to call attention to the tendril-like figures appearing on barked trees close to the Oxley burial site on the Lachlan River, New South Wales, in 1817 (Oxley 1820:facing P. 139); the circles carved on nearby trees during funeral rites observed by George Grey at King George's Sound before 1831 (Grey 1841 II:334); and the "runic" figures which Péron thought he read in the white sands of a mysterious "Bosquet Religieux" — a ceremonial ground of a rare type seen along the River Vasse in June 1801 (Péron 1809:64; 1824:map 5). In none of these three cases do the hieroglyphs carry more than a vague resemblance to recognizable objects.

Further ranges of interest open when we notice that during the expedition's four days of constant activity on Maria Island, a band of natives was met and parleyed with repeatedly at various locations around Oyster Bay. They wholly vanished on the fourth day after what Péron misguidedly regarded as a dangerous encounter. Baudin (Plomley 1983:108) reported them as fearless but wholly free of hostility; and he saw them as the resident population. "The family then living on the island was not numerous. We never saw more than twenty-two persons together," he wrote. It is unaccountable that not a single French observer represented in the abundant published record suspected that they were the burial party. To be sure, Baudin noted that the women and children at the time of the very first meeting, February 19, were low-spirited (Baudin 1974:339). Twice the group were encountered walking along the north shore toward Point Lesueur, an obvious place of debarkation for a journey to the mainland, no doubt near the site where Baudin and Hamelin found native raft-canoes (Baudin 1974:342); but the inference that the group might have been a funeral party from the mainland; that their tracking skills would have permitted them to reconstruct the movements of the interlopers very closely; that their unknown system of beliefs quite probably led them to identify the white-skinned strangers as spirits, perhaps spirits of their own dead, even spirits of the recently deceased; that the native artist of the bark drawings would probably have been a member of the burial party—these and other possibilities which a further discussion of the burials might take up seem to have eluded the French observers.

Of course we have no way of testing for their likelihood. But it is clear enough that the French savants were wholly unprepared to make effective sense of their most interesting experiences. Péron disappoints us with a final assessment of the Tasmanians as perfectly ordinary stock savages of the kind imagined and reported by Europeans the world over, being (he wrote) ferocious, malevolent, capricious, ungrateful, deceitful, bold, and absurd (Plomley 1983:64-66). At one point, not without an overtone of grievance, he pronounces them "very intelligent" (p. 64). Because the Aborigines left no records of the encounter, we rightly feel cheated of a most interesting story, whether of the fearsome desecration of native graves and its consequences, or of consuming perplexity and curiosity about the mysterious invasion by white-skinned spirits who concealed their bodies, or about the intentions, whether deadly or merely mischievous, of those beings, or of possibilities inconceivable to culture-bound European imaginations. Thus we might wonder whether some powerful magic or the failure of such magic in the inscribed funeral barks could have been held responsible for attracting the strange beings to Maria Island and perhaps for materializing some of the recently dead. The present study has begun with a case involving very gross failures of European understanding. We are under some obligation, therefore, to pay the closest attention to the conditions of observation, so far as we can make them out, that underlie the reports of bark art still to be discussed.

Much of the data on Tasmanian bark art is remarkably circumstantial. For the second dated discovery, we know the observer, a surveyor named Henry Hellyer; the place, west of Middlesex Plains in the northwest of the island; and the date, February 18, 1827, just a day short of twenty-five years after Leschenault found the important burial on Maria Island. The quarter-century gap perhaps needs no special explanation. In early colonial days the project of reproducing the amenities of civilization in exotic settings was likely to absorb all of a European's time and interest. The Tasmanians, overwhelmed almost from the first day of the invasion, seemed to offer no resistance. At the time of his debarkation, January 1824, when the Hobart settlement was twenty years old, George Augustus Robinson found that they were considered "mild and inoffensive." This builder and lay churchman, who was to become their official "conciliator," saw them to be "poor and wretched," "with no one to look after them or watch over their interests" (Robinson 1966:52). The settlers plainly enough had little occasion to think about them.

Because the European population increased only slowly, there was at the start little sense of serious trouble on the frontiers. Unchallenged crimes against the natives there — frequent kidnapping of women, murder, mutilation, and other atrocities — were too numerous and frequent to be concealed (Bonwick 1884:19-49; Plomley, in Robinson, 1966:11, 571, etc.). But this persistent scandal was an evil the Europeans found it possible to live with. The sudden and unexpected resistance of the weak and ever-dwindling native population in the later 1820s is material for a historical epic. A sharply focussed kind of guerrilla warfare, usually directed against hostile farmers and stockmen and often pointedly accompanied by the appropriation of foodstuffs (Robson 1983 I:242), fed the Hobart press with a steady flow of horror stories and called down on the Aborigines intensified police action. "Roving bands" of vengeful settlers received government sanction; and martial law was declared late in 1828. All the while Governor Arthur and nearly everyone else understood that native resentment and outrage against the defects of colonial justice were more than sufficient cause for the hostilities.

If "extirpation" sentiment burgeoned and took permanent root in the folklore of the invaders, a fair-minded settler like James Ross, later Government Printer and leading journalist, could spend his first years in Tasmania, 1823-25, at the remote frontier sixty miles northwest from Hobart without ever finding reason to fear the Aborigines (Ross 1836:125, 146, 153-55). For as the remainder of the discussion will show, the Tasmanians at and beyond the outer limits of settlement were quite as inclined as the colonists to pursue their customary way of life whenever possible, even continuing some of their intertribal feuds. Ross's account of native art in the Big River district will bring the present discussion back on the track. Our source is again James Bonwick's *Daily Life of the Tasmanians*: "Dr. Ross relates his discovery of geometrical figures, as squares and circles, on the bark in the valley of the Ouse" (Bonwick 1870:47).

Bonwick tells us in the same passage that "marks or tokens [have] been detected on trees and rocks in Tasmania. Mr. John Batman described some he witnessed" (p. 47). Batman, later a founder of Melbourne, had arrived in Launceston in 1821 and settled in the Ben Lomond district (Plomley, in Robinson 1966:1022).

According to innumerable reports the Tasmanians always carried fire when they travelled and always had charcoal close at hand. They also cherished red ochre (Robinson 1966:582n.75, 600, 904). We know that they rubbed their bodies incessantly (it sometimes seemed) with powdered charcoal and with a greasy mixture of red ochre and animal fat; and the latter was also applied to their hair. In addition, as H. Ling Roth pointed out (1899:138), the Oyster Bay tribes had a term thought to mean "depict" reported in the early word lists: *macooloona* or *macoolana*. The Tasmanians, like tribal peoples the world over, used red ochre to leave "red hands" "on trees and rocks alike" (Bonwick 1870:191). A variant has also been noted: "impressions or drawings of hands, both right and left" had been "traced or drawn by using what appeared to us to be marl or limestone" against a red ochre ground "smeared" on the rock face of a cave on the Derwent near Ellendale (DeTeliga 1958:190). (These would be white hands.)

Of more importance in the present study are the ubiquitous circles. As noted earlier, Robinson described large circular cicatrices among women of the northern coast (1966:581n.69). He also came upon similar rock engravings — a circle surrounded by dots at Cape Grim (1966:233n.15, 183, 189); and at Green's Creek near the Thornton River on the west coast: "Large circles cut on the face of rocks done by natives. Some of them were a foot and eighteen inches in diameter, thus representing black and white men" (p. 790). It is hard to make sense of the interpretation Robinson elicited from his native informants. Sun and moon, men and women, black men and white men; but what about them? Red hands, stencilled hands, circles, served innumerable purposes and have had innumerable meanings across the world (Forge 1977:31; Moore 1977:322-24). For further information on the rare rock engravings of Tasmania, the reader may be referred to the survey by Peter C. Sims, published in 1977, and to the rich array of rock art motifs illustrated in Julia Clark's *The Aboriginal People of Tasmania* (1983:32; see also Flood 1983:125-26). We will have more gratifying matter to discuss in addition to circles as the discussion proceeds. Meanwhile, Plomley is surely right in his dictum: "The circle might be said to be the characteristic motif of Tasmanian aboriginal art. It is common in all their rock carvings and has been mentioned in [Robinson's] journals as decoration in the breakwinds and huts, and as a tribal symbol in some cicatrix inscribed on the body" (Robinson 1966:581n.65).

Now we may look to Bonwick for a reported remark on representational art:

> Mr. G. A. Robinson saw drawings of men and women, with some curious hieroglyphics, like the totems of tribes, when he was on the west coast, in 1831 [actually 1830 or 1833]. Inside the substantial huts of the Macquarie Harbour tribe were found a number of sketches of birds, beasts, and men, some of which were fairly executed. (Bonwick 1870:47)

From John West, the first historian of Tasmania, we have a more general account: "In several parts of the the colony rude drawings have been discovered. Cattle, kangaroo, and dogs, were traced in charcoal. These attempts were exceedingly rude, and sometimes the artist was wholly unintelligible" (1852 II:89).

Because West used the term "rude" twice in his account, we will recall Péron's explanation of the early barks as *grossiêrement gravé* (crudely drawn). We can do little with these particular judgmental terms beyond keeping the problem in view now and in reports on Australian art through the following century, and call attention to their frequency in the chronicles of Tasmanian art. They of course reflect subjective responses to the work of tribal peoples and the low opinion always entertained of the Tasmanians. Also, we must not forget the esteem for artistic realism entertained by ordinary citizens as well as by high-minded and sophisticated Europeans of the last two centuries (Forge 1977:29). Probably the best we can do in situations like the present ones is to match when possible our own sense of rudeness and crudeness in cases always complicated by the intervention of European copyists and engravers between ourselves and the native

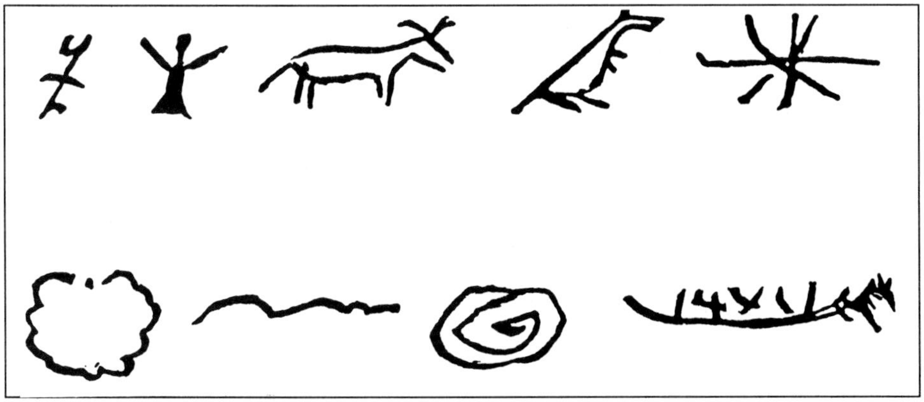

FIGURE 11.7. Tasmanian tree drawings. From James Bonwick (1870:47)

art. Bonwick offers an instructive exhibit supplied by the Commissary-General Joseph Stace Browne (Robinson 1966:83, 493): "I append some rude Tasmanian sketches of men and animals, with five drawings, as seen by Mr. Commissary Browne on a tree, representing the sun, the moon, some snakes, and five persons in a boat" (Bonwick 1870:47).

First we note the deficiency of Bonwick's description. We surmise that his sun, moon, snakes, and boat account for the moderately abstract bottom row of figures. Nothing is said of the five figures at the top, among which we can feel fairly sure only about a goat and a kangaroo. Now what guesses can we make about the perceived "rudeness" of these "rude sketches"? The European copyist appears to have been able to render smoothness and rudeness with equal ease. On reflection, only three at most show the irregularity we might ascribe to unskillfulness; otherwise, we would call the drawings schematized and fairly accomplished, rather than crude. But who could guess just what Bonwick had in mind? For us the interest is in the charm and quite adequate skill of the artist, especially as we sense that we are dealing with the kind of art which, like calligraphy, achieves its effects with sure single strokes and no second chances; and we know that on the whole the difficulties of a medium — of drawing with charcoal on a tree, for example — are not usually thought of by observers who are not themselves artists.

Later Observations

The remainder of the discussion will offer, with no more comment than necessary, fairly full source texts on all the Tasmanian bark drawing so far identified. All of it reports sightings of the art in the region south and east of Circular Head under exploration and development by the Van Diemen's Land Company after 1825, in the Great Lakes district of the center, and near the headwaters of the Franklin River.

The Van Diemen's Land Company, established in 1825 for the purpose of opening up settlement in the Northwest, employed the architect Henry Hellyer as its chief surveyor. James Fenton many years later reviewed the data on the Hellyer discovery mentioned at the beginning of the preceding section: "Mr. Hellyer discovered a large river (February 19th, 1827), which he named the Arthur, after the Governor. They found two native huts, in one of which was a drawing of the moon, done in charcoal, upon the inside of one of the sheets of bark which formed the hut" (Fenton 1891:14).

Hellyer's report was dated March 13, 1827. His dating of the find is precise enough but at odds with Fenton's. On February 18, Hellyer wrote, his party, moving northwest, came to the end of the Brown Forest (East of Mount Cleveland), then approached

> the high forest tier of woody mountains, near which we came upon a marshy country, and saw several snipes. We found here two native huts, and marks of many fireplaces in the neighbourhood, as if the spot had been lately occupied by a large body of natives. In one of the huts I saw a drawing of the moon, done with charcoal, upon the inside of one of the slabs of bark which formed the hut; and regarding it as an evidence of there being artists among them, I cut out the piece, and placed it carefully between two other pieces of bark in my knapsack. I sketched two figures of the moon with charcoal on the bark of the hut, and put the date of my

visit. I was now travelling northwest by north, towards the Dip Mountain. (Bischoff 1832:170-71)

The next day, February 19, Hellyer came upon the "rapid river, larger than the Don," which he christened the Arthur (pp. 171-72). The moon drawing on the wall of the hut should recall the cicatrices of the "eastern natives" (Robinson 1966:263). As for the graffiti which took its place, we may note that this Henry Hellyer was something of a wag.

The Surveyor-General, George Frankland, responded with excitement to a similar report many months later. In a letter he wrote February 4, 1829, to Governor Arthur, he spread some news and offered a proposal:

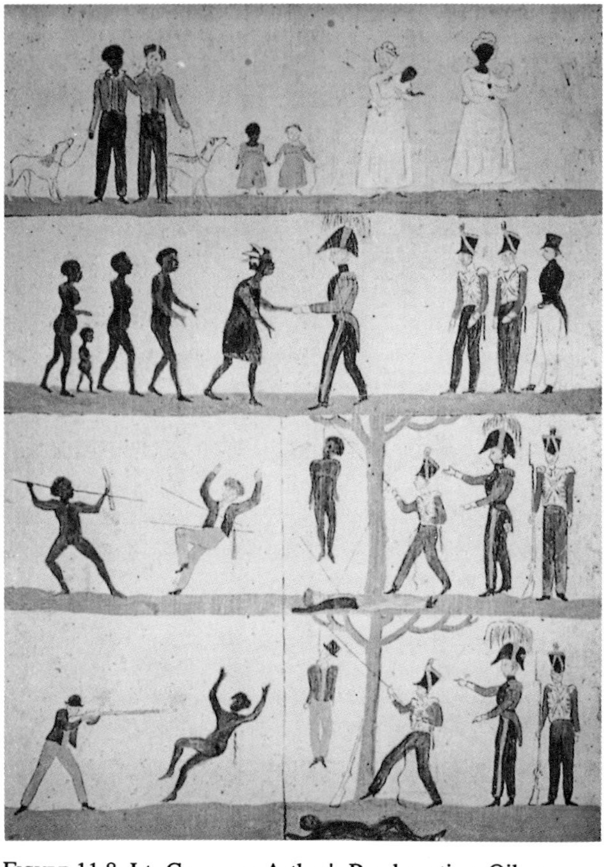

FIGURE 11.8. Lt.-Governor Arthur's Proclamation. Oil on wood, designed for posting on trees in areas where Aborignals remained at large. Reproduced from Dutton (1974: pl. XI).

I have lately had an opportunity of ascertaining that the aboriginal natives of Van Diemen's Land are in the habit of representing events by drawings on the bark of trees, and that the march of a certain party of Europeans over a country before unfrequented by us was found a short time afterwards drawn with charcoal on a piece of bark, by a tribe of natives who [had] been observed attentively watching their movements. The carts, the bullocks, the men, were distinctly represented, according to the exact number that really existed. (Robinson 1966:108)

The cart was owned by the Van Diemen's Land Company. At the outset Frankland, an amateur artist (Smith 1960:219), dreamed of seizing some advantage from the "newly discovered faculty" demonstrated by the bark drawings, "to impart to [the Aborigines] to a certain extent, the real wishes of the government towards them." With his letter he enclosed a sketch. The famous Proclamation of Governor Arthur to the Aborigines, 1830 (Dutton 1974:pls. xi, 33, pp. 154-55), was the outcome (fig. 11.8). Reproduced in various forms for posting on trees here and there in the bush, it showed Europeans and Tasmanians in blissful amity, but also killing each other and receiving justly equal punishments. Because rudeness and crudeness are such persistent motifs in the early reports on the native art, we should not lose the opportunity to produce specimens of amateur European art which might shed light on how those terms could be understood. The proclamation, whatever it owes to Frankland's sketch, appears to be an interesting specimen of English colonial naive or primitive art. It is not known whether work of this sort attracted artistic responses at all, nor should it have. The native production, on the other hand, seems to have brought out the spirit of art criticism in nearly every European observer.

The drawing of the bullock carts came to be rather widely known. It may have been a portable object rather than a part of a hut (we wish we could be sure), and we happen to have several accounts of it. The sighting of the carts probably took place in 1828, when Hellyer and Joseph Fossey were building a road from Launceston west to the Hampshire Hills, then north to Emu Bay. On February 2, 1828, Fossey, in charge of the east-to-west segment, had reached a point about two months short of the Hampshire Hills (Bischoff 1832:125-26), so that the discovery may be dated late March or early April 1828. In

1852 Reverend West reported the matter as follows: "At Belvoir Vale, the natives saw the Company's two carts, drawn by six oxen: they drew on bark the wheels, and the drivers with their whips. They were the first that ever passed that country" (West 1852 II:89).

Daniel Bunce, a botanist and pioneer settler who had traversed the area (he arrived in Tasmania in 1833), was able to offer a rich account of the landscape near Belvoir Vale, with Mount Cleveland in sight to the west and St. Valentine's Peak to the north.

> Some time previously, two carts, belonging to the Van Diemen's Land Company, had passed over this ridge, each drawn by six oxen, with their drivers. It appears that some natives had observed this: and, a short time afterwards, one of the company's servants passing that way, found in one of their rudely-constructed huts, a piece of the bark of a tree, with a rough drawing of the whole scene. The wheels of the carts, the bullocks drawing them, and the drivers with their whips over their shoulders, were all distinctly depicted in their rude but interesting manner. (Bunce 1857a:49-50)

In pronouncing the style of this apparently detached and portable bark as "rude but interesting" Bunce leaves the impression that he actually saw the picture, and perhaps he did. Bonwick, who had arrived in Tasmania in 1841, wrote as if he had seen both the bark and the site of its discovery; but for the latter he could have had every scenic detail from Bunce (pp. 48-49):

> In the lovely Vale of Belvoir, where the basaltic columns of May Hills tower over the limestone plain, a piece of bark was found, after the first two bullock-drays passed that way, bearing a really good copy of the drays, bullocks, and the men with their whips; it was better done than the markings of the cave-men of Périgord on the bones of the mammoth. (Bonwick 1870:47)

We may be jolted to learn that by 1870, well before the important discoveries of cave paintings at Altamira and in the Dordogne, a student of the Tasmanians was aware of important European prehistoric art. Thus Bonwick, no ordinary student, as we have seen, probably knew the engraved mammoth tusk from La Madeleine, discovered circa 1815 (Pfeiffer 1982:24). As for his artistic judgment, he must be the first student of "primitive" art who preferred an Australian to a European specimen.

In this most cheerful passage of the present study we may rejoice to see signs that the hunted Tasmanians were able to extract amusement from the clumsy machines of the grim invaders. Later, in July 1831, George Augustus Robinson witnessed a merry dance in which his Tasmanian friends reenacted the waylaying and pillaging of a supply cart drawn by bullocks and loaded with flour on the Port Dalrymple road (Robinson 1966:362-63, 463n.182).

Robinson had been reported as seeing well-done sketches of "birds, beasts, and men" in the huts of the Macquarie Harbour tribe (Bonwick 1870:47). The likely date for that event would have been April or May, 1830 (Robinson 1966:158-159). At that date he was travelling up the west coast with his "sable band," as it was called, making contact with the tribes along the way. By August he had reached the territory of the Van Diemen's Land Company. On August 11-12 at Weybridge, deep in the bush just west of Valentine's Peak, he met Henry Hellyer and learned something about the art of the area. "Rain during this day. Mr H informed me respecting drawing which the natives had done on their huts with charred wood. Mr H sketched on my map" (Robinson 1966:197).

For some time after that date Robinson was alert to empty native huts. On August 22 at Middlesex Plains he inspected "several huts in different directions...I looked for the drawing inside their huts, but discovered no signs of any" (p. 204); and he had the same luck with "a very large native hut" at the Vale of Belvoir the next day (p. 205). On the morning of September 20, along the Rubicon River some forty miles to the northeast, he heard the sound of native voices, passed "some peppermint trees recently barked" and immediately came upon some huts. "On arriving at them," he said, "I found the natives had gone. They had been preparing spears. The fires was still burning. From the marks of the feet, they had numerous dogs. The huts had been recently constructed, were two in number and very large, the best I had seen of this kind on this coast. Some rude drawing was on the inside of the bark of the huts" (p. 214).

We hear more about the camp but no more about the "rude drawing." The details are worth marking: the newly barked trees, the newly constructed huts, the owners lurking close by, the Europeans taking advantage of their absence to look for bark decoration.

The next year Robinson made five discoveries in native huts of the Big (Ouse) River tribe in the area where Dr.

Ross had seen "squares and circles, on the bark" (Bonwick 1870:47): near Arthur's Lake and Wood's Lake, and three west of Lake Echo, all rather close to the Ross homestead. The first entry, November 11, 1831, had him conjecturing about the native method of drawing circles:

> Observed in several of their huts several rude drawings, circles, broad arrows and other hieroglyphical figures representing men and women, and round circles which from their different diameters I judge to have been done by a pair of scissors. This is the country where the blacks have constantly domiciled and had remained undisturbed by their white enemies. (pp. 514-15)

The next day, "Saw numerous native huts, some newly erected, in one of which I found the back of a looking glass and some rude device of men" (p. 516); evidently, more "hieroglyphical figures" in charcoal.

On December 6, north of Arthur's Lake, he discovered the answer to his question about the circles:

> Before setting off this morning observed some rude devices on the inside of the natives hut which the aborigines had found, some resembling trees, men and women, also numerous circles of different diameter and similar to those I had observed on the inside of the bark huts of the LAIRMAIRRENER or Big River tribe and which I then supposed had been done by scissors, which I imagined the natives might have stolen from the whites, and those circles being of different sizes and a dot in the centre seemed to favour this opinion. Such was then my opinion, so little are we acquainted with the manners and habits of these people. It was not till this morning that I learnt how they made those circles. Hence it proves that time is necessary and that it is only by travelling and associating with those people that we can know their habits. On enquiry I found that those circles were made by means of a forked stick the same manner as we use a compass. I tried and made the same, with which they were much pleased. (pp. 542-543)

Plomley explains: "A marginal sketch in the MS...depicts the forked stick used in making the circles on the bark of the huts as having the shape of a capital Y" (Robinson 1966:581n.69). It appears then that the Tasmanians, if they did not invent the wheel, invented the compass, and Robinson had the wit to see the interest of the achievement. He went on to berate Henry Hellyer for the kind of frivolity noted earlier:

> Mr Hellyer, the Company's surveyor, happening to meet with circles done in charcoal, supposed that they were made to resemble the sun, and drew a face in the centre and sent it to his friends in England. How mistaken are such people; and it shows how fond those persons are to shew off with some story respecting the natives. Those circles are emblematical devices of men and women (p. 543).

The disgust with Hellyer is understandable but a little ironic. Robinson himself, as noted above, had also reported circles interpreted as the sun and the moon, and also as black men and white men.

Meanwhile he already knew far more and thought more intelligently about the Tasmanians than any other European. In the present context he proves interesting in ways he could not have foreseen. We turn to the journal entry for December 23, 1831. The conciliation party was relying upon a "woman of the Big River tribe" to lead them to the remnant of her group, which was still at large in the area. She was wife to Umarrah the storyteller, and her name was Woolaytopinneyer (p. 586n.97). "Proceeded on my route to the Lagoon of Islands. The woman of the Big River tribe had drawn some rude devices on the bark inside their hut, and which I had purposed to have brought away with me" (p. 563).

When Robinson uses the term "rude devices" for a second time, we see that again he perhaps means cryptic figures, like Dr. Ross's "geometrical figures, as squares and circles" (Bonwick 1870:47, noted earlier). Meanwhile, the ascription of a bark drawing to a named native artist, and a woman to boot, will prove to be of real interest in a comprehensive historical study of Australian bark art.

Robinson's Friendly Mission to the Big River tribe concluded with successful contact about thirty miles northwest of Mount Teneriffe, he tells us, on December 31, 1831. The location might thus have been a little to the south of Lake St. Clair, apparently undiscovered at that date (cf. Plomley, in Robinson 1966:572). The following day the group began its return to civilization: eighteen of Robinson's party accompanied by the sixteen men, nine women, and one child of the Big River tribe. On that day, January 1, 1832, the "chief" led Robinson to the top of a hill in order to surrender a cache of six loaded guns, all in good condition, concealed in a hollow tree. "On reaching this eminence I perceived a new erected native hut, the interior of which was decorated with an assemblage of rude sketches representing birds, beasts, human forms,

&c, and were for the most part tolerably well executed" (Robinson 1966:570-71).

It is reassuring to note the cases in which the native art escapes the European's condescension. The "tolerably well executed" pictures in a "newly erected" hut now can be recognized as paradigmatic, done as they were on newly peeled bark, and discovered through unlicensed search of a freshly vacated dwelling. Incidentally, the student can locate all the Robinson sightings with some exactness by consulting the route maps supplied by Plomley in his edition of the journals.

Robinson completed his mission in August 1834 while a small number of Tasmanians were still nominally unreconciled. By the following February he could declare that "the entire aboriginal population are removed" (pp. 925-26). The place of exile, Flinders Island, has been called straightforwardly a "concentration camp" by a recent historian (Robson 1983 I:220, 240). Perhaps nobody regarded the campaign as a Final Solution — but that is another story; and we must not forget that "extirpation" was in its regressive nineteenth century way a principled stand. Robinson became commandant at Flinders Island in October 1835 and retained the position until 1839, when he began ten years as Protector of the Aborigines at Port Phillip (Robinson 1966:925). On Flinders Island Robinson obliged us with one more interesting journal entry, dated December 26, 1835: "Visited the natives. In several huts are to be seen rude drawings on the wall of ships, others of letters and a variety of devices and hieroglyphics such as they had been accustomed to make in their own country" (Robinson 1966:917n.98).

It happened that the deportation of the Tasmanians was not quite complete. At least one small group remained at large, to be reported in 1836 and located later that year. They proved to be a family — a husband, a wife, and four children — who declined to accept official hospitality. One assumes that this was the same party — parents and five children — captured near the Arthur River in 1842 (Plomley, in Robinson 1966:926-27; Robson 1983 I:531); and they may possibly have been responsible for the last reported sighting of Tasmanian bark drawings.

In mid December 1840, the government surveyor James Erskine Calder (later surveyor-general, succeeding Frankland) was at work with a small party under official instructions to construct a horseback trail through the virgin wilderness of the upper Franklin watershed from Lake St. Clair to Macquarie Harbor. By mid December they had reached Painter's Plain, on the Surprise River within sight of Mount Arrowsmith. What a pity that we have so much precise information at every turn, and so little direct visual evidence! Here is what we do have.

Calder and his party came upon two abandoned "natives' huts." Some "half-decayed" kangaroo meat told them that the huts had been occupied recently. "On the bark that covered them," Calder wrote, "were some extraordinary charcoal drawings." When Calder returned to the place "some months after, [he] found the rude wigwams of these last of the aborigines of Tasmania were blown down, and the sketches obliterated" (Calder 1849:419). The account appeared in a paper read to the Tasmanian Society, August 4, 1847.

Calder had occasion to review the discovery twenty-five years later. The occasion at this time was the publication of a general essay on the Tasmanians under the title "Some Account of the Wars of Extirpation, and Habits of the Native Tribes of Tasmania" (1874). In this discussion he again described the four bark drawings, but only as examples of native art. The hut was rather well made, he wrote, and "adorned, according to their ideas of adornment, with several rude charcoal drawings." One hut of "several," he now reported (formerly there had been two), it "was, I suppose, the residence of a single gentleman, being the least of all" (Calder 1874:21; 1875:33), that is, the smallest. The inconsistency of the two reports, readily seen by comparing the following texts, is dismaying.

Text of 1847 (published 1849):
"extraordinary charcoal drawings"
1. "representing two men spearing an animal, which from its erect posture was, I presume, meant for a kangaroo; though the artist, by a strange oversight,had forgotten the animal's tail, and had made the fore legs about twice as long as the hinder ones"
2. "an outline of a dog and an
3. emu, really not badly done"
4. "some other designs, the exact meaning of which I was not able to make out."(Calder 1849:419)

Text of 1874 (occurring also in 1875):
"rude charcoal drawings"
1. "representing a kangaroo of unnatural appearance, that is, with its forelegs about twice as long as the hinder ones"

3. "Another was meant for an emu; a
2. third was also an animal that might have been either a dog, a horse, or a crocodile, according to the fancy of the connoisseur."
4. "but the *chef-d'oeuvre* was a battle-piece, a native fight-men dying and flying all over it."
(Calder 1874:21; 1875:33)

In the later of Calder's two texts, the first picture loses its two spearmen while the kangaroo tacitly gains a tail; but we wonder in both cases why the kangaroo identification was made at all. The picture of the dog seems to have gone out of focus in Calder's memory, for in the later account it looked also like a horse or a crocodile. The emu, "really not badly done" as of 1847, was made to sound rude and crude in the later text. Then the shadowy matter of the last 1847 picture comes into clarity as a violent battle scene. Had Calder recovered some lost memoranda or sketches — he was an amateur artist (Smith 1960:219) — in composing the later account? Had his memory done him tricks? It seems likely enough that by 1874 he had metamorphosed into a tiresome yarn-spinner who had told the story of the bark drawings perhaps over and over as old-timers will do. But we gather, also, that he knew George Augustus Robinson and had some sort of access to his papers. Some of Robinson's notes on Aboriginal star lore, unaccountably similar in both words and apocalyptic images to Calder's account of the fourth drawing, will be offered at the conclusion of the present study.

Meanwhile, the implications of large-scale inconsistency in Calder's two accounts of the 1840 drawings is unsettling in the extreme. We may feel full confidence in early documents when they first come to our attention, then find our trust badly misplaced when a second account of the same matter comes to light. Not only do witnesses differ. A single witness will appear to forget his initial testimony when he goes on record for a second time, as Calder did. The text François Péron composed for his published chronicle of the Baudin expedition is at odds again and again with his unpublished manuscripts of earlier date. Did he misremember? Or, surrounded by inconsistent reports, did he refine his narrative by weighing conflicting data from many sources? Elsewhere Plomley demonstrates how mistaken we were to trust Crozet's fascinating published account of the murder of a native at Frederick Henry Bay in 1772 by producing three little-known accounts of the incident from unpublished manuscripts (Plomley, in Robinson 1966:22, 37-39n.35). Plomley's recent publication of Tasmanian records left by many members of the Baudin expedition, far from resolving all problems, makes several important ones seem insoluble. Thus at the moment there may be as many as four likely locations for the Leschenault burial on Maria Island, and perhaps no decisive way to make a determination. We may wonder what good it is to know that *macoolana* according to Roth meant something like "draw with charcoal" in the Oyster Bay tribe. But having digested the datum, we find Bonwick offering the term as *macooloona*; and, hoping to settle matters, we discover that the appendixes in Ling Roth offer also *Macooboona* and *Makubuna* (Roth 1899:138, xxiii, lxii; Bonwick 1870:48). We may sometimes wonder whether ethnography of the kind pursued in the present study can be a serious subject.

And yet present findings seem reliable enough. Reported sightings of drawings in Tasmanian bark huts, all near or beyond the frontier, were numerous. Robinson saw such art at Macquarie Harbor, along the Rubicon River, and on five different occasions in the Great Lakes region, not to mention the drawings seen on Flinders Island after the natives had been resettled. The records credit Hellyer with at least two sightings in the Van Diemen's Land Company region of the Northwest — also the area of the bullock-cart picture. Calder found his four pictures in a hut southwest of Lake St. Clair. Geometric and representational pictures alike, the latter usually described as *rude* or *crude*, were reported in nearly equal numbers. The cryptic figures of the Maria Island bark slabs perhaps stand by themselves as shapes of peculiar sacredness and extraordinary power. A study like the present one which has the flat, rectangular, portable bark-slab art of Arnhem Land constantly in its background must take note of the fact that after 1802 one Tasmanian specimen only, the bullock-cart bark, might have been something other than a bark hut drawing. The lack of clarity in the contemporary descriptions creates this possibility, but is far from confirming it. On the other hand, the Maria Island barks were discovered in detached form and were roughly rectangular and certainly portable though heavy; and their function, lying across a funeral mound face down, seems to have been something other than protection of the human remains from the weather.

The general unawareness of the abundant evidence on bark art has been a fact of Tasmanian ethnography down to the present. The consequences of such neglect should not be overestimated, for the ignorance and apathy of Europeans in these matters will not be much changed by even the most favorable determinations as to the cultural achievements of subject peoples. At the end of the nineteenth century we find James Backhouse Walker ascribing the Calder barks to escaped English convicts, a proposal based on an ingenious misreading of the earlier source text (Calder 1849:418-19). He concluded as follows: "That the aborigines in their wild state had any skill in drawing seems therefore to hang on a very slender thread of evidence" (Walker 1900:6). This inference fell short of the remarkable finding of his friend Ling Roth at the conclusion of his discussion of Tasmanian native drawing, published the preceding year: "The whole question of the existence of drawings by aborigines before European advent is practically an open one, for as seen above the evidence is not satisfactory" (Roth 1899:138). We may neglect James Fenton's unimportant summary of Calder's 1875 text (Fenton 1884:94), as well as Walker's whole discussion, which added nothing to Roth's account aside from a mistaken reading of Calder. But what of Roth's negative findings?

The present essay rests in part upon a fresh examination of all the evidence to be gleaned from West, Bonwick, and Roth. Roth has always been the most useful of the ethnographers, with no substantial successors in the field since 1899. His treatment of the Tasmanian bark art may thus be indicative of the reliability of his compilation as a whole. Very simply: he was aware of (a) the Maria Island funeral barks; (b) West's brief account of the bullock-cart picture; (c) Bunce's extended account of the same picture, with a mistaken conjecture that he derived it from West; (d) Bonwick's account of the Robinson sightings at Macquarie Harbor; and (e) Calder's four drawings in the 1847 version (Roth 1899:137-38). Since West and Bunce treat the same case, Roth based his judgment on four sightings only. It hardly mattered: threatened by fairly solid evidence for creditable cultural achievement in a native population, an easy skepticism came to his rescue.

Conclusion

The simple and primary purpose of this paper has been to bring to light the data of an almost wholly unknown Tasmanian art and to present it in the form, in effect, of an amplified source-text and checklist for future investigation. The abundance of the evidence it offers suggests not that the data for study are all in hand, but that further search may prove unexpectedly rewarding. Meanwhile the richness of the record on Tasmanian art within the wider Australian context of indifference to the native population has been a riddle. It happens that the Australian capital cities seem remarkable to visitors from abroad as cultural centers. Hobart early achieved distinction of this kind. Its early colonial artists will be familiar names to many Australians: Thomas Bock, G. T. W. Boyes, W. B. Gould, Benjamin Duterrau, John Glover (sometimes called the "English Claude"). In addition, Henry Hellyer was an architect, while, as noted earlier, the Surveyor-General George Frankland and his successor, James Erskine Calder, were both amateur artists (Smith 1960:219). The highest government circles of Hobart included a substantial group of amateur and professional artists and art fanciers whom Calder (1875:42) loftily characterized as "the pseudo dilettante class (a class that flourishes very luxuriantly in Tasmanian soil)." The Baudin expedition included two skillful artists, Petit and Lesueur. Even George Augustus Robinson has a place in this picture because of the valuable, charmingly incompetent drawings frequently found in his journals. The solution to the puzzle thus seems obvious: We owe most of the Tasmanian art record to men who were themselves artists, who found the native production interesting, and then whose professional undertakings took them expressly to remote places in the bush where — most important — they observed much and kept records. We might attach importance also to Henry Hellyer, with his callow tricks, as perhaps a catalyser who unwittingly raised curiosity about the native art, helping to make it an object of observation, conversation, and thought. In seeking further information on the Tasmanian bark art the most promising source might be the papers and artistic remains of the members of the Hobart art circles.

In this light it is revelatory to learn that Baldwin Spencer, the ethnologist who commissioned fifty famous and important bark paintings at Oenpelli, N.T., in 1912, had been as a young man a prize-winning art student at the Royal Institution in Manchester (McCulloch 1968:516); that the leader of the American-Australian Expedition of

1948 which brought several hundred bark paintings into Australian museums — the ethnographer Charles P. Mountford — occupied himself with Aboriginal art continuously from 1929 to his death a few years ago, and was a superb photographer and cinematographer; that the Czech artist Karel Kupka, starting well before 1960, dedicated himself for a period of years to the publicization and exhibition of bark art, being responsible for superb collections in Paris, Basel, and Canberra; and that as Daniel Thomas has reminded us, the late eminent artist Tony Tuckson, Deputy Director of the Art Gallery of New South Wales, installed "the first regularly visible Aboriginal exhibits in an Australian art museum" (Thomas 1978:31), and probably knew the bark art of Arnhem Land more intimately than any figure in the wider world of Australian art down to the present. As Thomas observed, "artists can recognize each other, even across great cultural gaps" (p. 29) — a reminder of the decades early in the present century when the tribal arts of Africa and Oceania began to be collected, admired, and pondered over by then obscure painters like Picasso, Derain, Matisse, and Klee. Tribal and ethnic arts today after all owe most of their audience in Europe and America to effective sponsorship by a large number of our own artists of the first rank. It has been possible in the present essay to show that the European art community of Tasmania was at its height at just the time when several of its marginal members were displaying a decidedly un-English alertness toward the native art. This is not to credit the Tasmanian dilettanti with any tendency to anticipate the Post-Impressionists (Symbolists, Expressionists); nor was the discovery very imposing to amateurs like Frankland, Calder, and George Augustus Robinson, who doubtless found the native drawing more interesting for its surprising intimations of intelligence and cultural achievement than for impressive artistry.

Indeed the characteristic two-dimensional art of Australia does not strongly resemble the familiar tribal productions of Africa and Melanesia, known so well through their fascinating three-dimensional arts, especially wood sculpture, which Europeans have always happened to favor. The distinctive ambience is almost wholly benign, European preference for the relatively rare expressions of bizarre tribal fantasy and innocent sexuality notwithstanding, and the art is perhaps quite free of demonic overtones in its Tasmanian versions. Emerging at a very late date into European consciousness, the Australian art may well have as vital a message for the perturbed spirits of the Western world as the more familiar modes of tribal art; but the impression it makes on European minds is remarkably different in spiritual content — in fact, if we see much of the native production before white men pick it over for the specimens that seem beautiful or bizarre or powerful in some way, we may well marvel at the magnitude of the gap that exists between ourselves and the Australians. As for the art of the Tasmanians, our limited pictorial evidence may suggest that it was modest; but it can also suggest that at some period, perhaps even these undervalued people produced rock art and bark art of great power and beauty. Such speculations will not be idle if they supply encouragement for further Tasmanian culture studies.

Meanwhile, the value of the larger human treasure recklessly squandered in Tasmania is easier to understand now that we have George Augustus Robinson's rich journals to ponder. His entry for June 24, 1831, is one of many which confront us with the touching decency of his native friends and acquaintances, and with evidence for an unmistakable parity of white and black which a candid and warm-hearted European could elicit from time to time:

> One subject I omitted to mention when I was at the boat harbour opposite Swan Island, will tend to shew that the mind of an Aborigine is capable of the highest improvement. An aborigine who had been domesticated, asked me one night whilst gazing at the stormy firmament if I knew the planets Mars and Jupiter, and said if the sky had not been so obscured he would point it out to me. Gave him a piece of paper and a pen and he drew me a ship. (Robinson 1966:365)

Aboriginal art employing European media is one of the few tokens of happy relations remaining to us from the first century of European settlement in Australia. Robinson's pen-and-ink ship drawing, an early specimen of courtesy art created to please a European, will thus have importance in the study of native art down to the present.

Meanwhile, anticipating future studies in the visual culture of the Australians, the present case offers unexpected reasons for inquiring further into Aboriginal astronomy. A sequel, June 27, 1831, to the Robinson journal entry just quoted apparently has some connection to the dramatic bark drawing which, as noted above, Calder at first found impossible to decipher:

> In conversation with the natives respecting the stars. These people, like the ancients, have described constellations in the heavens as resembling men and women, men fighting, animals, and limbs of men; together with names for the stars. The aborigines pointed them out. (Robinson 1966:366)

Plomley quotes a similar passage from some of Robinson's stray notes: "all the stars and constellations near to Saturn and the planets are figurative of men: natives fighting, courting; husband and wife; men's legs, limbs" (p. 464n.188d). Can we now avoid recalling the conundrum posed by Calder's (1874:21) unaccountable memory lapse and recovery in the description of that fourth native drawing: the "battle-piece, a native fight, men dying and flying all over it"? Our detour into Tasmanian sky-lore has apparently brought us evidence for a convergence, not noted before, of native myth, native art, native astronomy, and perhaps native ritual as well. In trying to guess the reasons for Calder's seeming inconsistency, we might attach importance to the fact that he knew Robinson and had access to his papers; but we must still wonder about his earlier vagueness (1849:419). Did he have some dim memory of a partly intelligible picture which he preferred not to risk describing in the earlier account? or did Robinson's anecdote suddenly permit him to venture an interpretation of a baffling sketch preserved in his own notebooks? Whether or not a tenuous connection to native astronomy can shed light upon a lost bark drawing of uncertain content, the present study demonstrates a certain promising richness in the published record, especially as recently enhanced by Plomley's contributions.

It has also demonstrated a provocative cultural similarity between the Tasmanians and some of the better-known tribes of the Australian north coast, not to mention the bark hut artists reported in Gippsland, just across Bass Strait from Tasmania. The bark painters of Arnhem Land have seemed artistically hyper-productive (Spencer 1928 II:792; Mountford 1956:13), at least from the perspective of British civilization. And we may therefore recall that on the only encounter of the Baudin expedition with evidences for native ceremony during its coastal forays, bark slabs seemingly prepared for a funeral proceeding were discovered. Further, we may be tempted to extrapolate from the experience of George Augustus Robinson, who observed drawings in native bark huts rather often as soon as Henry Hellyer alerted him. Who knows how rich our record might be if the Tasmanians had been approached with intelligent curiosity during that twenty-five year gap between the Leschenault and the Hellyer discoveries, rather than abused, pursued, and slaughtered by shepherds, stockmen, sealers, hunters, whalers, soldiers, bushrangers, and "roving bands" (Plomley, in Robinson 1966:964-67)?

The Tasmanian art displays further resemblances to that of Arnhem Land: its prominent association with bark huts; its clear division into representational and cryptic (abstract, geometric, hieroglyphic) modes — the former unmixed in the case of the bullock-cart picture and the four drawings described by Calder, the latter unmixed in the Maria Island funeral barks and most of the reported rock engravings and hut drawings; and its demonstration of strong picture-making and symboling components in the native culture. The confluence of a bark-slab technology, a propensity to draw both representational and abstract figures on suitable surfaces, and the deployment of such uncanny two-dimensional creations upon sacred or secular artifacts (the Tasmanian record tells only of a funeral shelter and bark huts) with unknown religious or magical expectations, as we must suspect, would be sure to yield many forms of bark art in many tribes across the centuries. The apparently modest art of the present study can thus serve as a straightforwardly useful introduction to Australian bark art in general, suggesting far wider distribution in the far north during the first century of European settlement than the early known records have permitted us to imagine. This remark anticipates the curious and perhaps still disputed later history of bark art, especially ochre painting, and suggests reasons for the very late emergence of such art into the consciousness of white Australia.

Note

I am deeply indebted to Norman J. B. Plomley and Jacqueline Bonnemains for much assistance in coming to terms with the often bewildering records of the Baudin Expedition. For any errors I may have committed in assessing those materials I must take full responsibility. I wish also to thank Mary Ann Klotz for the maps and for the redrawings of the Maria Island bark slabs, work demonstrating extraordinary responsiveness to the requirements of the project. For strong and welcome support during several years I am most grateful to Louise and Allan Hanson of the University of Kansas.

12

Tourist Art, Traditional Art, and the Museum in Papua New Guinea

PHILLIP LEWIS

In 1981 I accompanied as a lecturer a tour group from the Field Museum in Chicago to Papua New Guinea. Also I was granted funds from the National Endowment for the Arts under their program of Fellowships for Museum Professionals, which enabled me to carry out research in New Ireland. As a foreign researcher, I was affiliated with the National Museum and Art Gallery of Papua New Guinea and agreed to survey and evaluate their New Ireland collection. Thus during the period May 1 through August 15, 1981, I spent two weeks on the tour with my group, about ten days at the National Museum, and the rest of the time in New Ireland. When it was over I had seen art from three different points of view in three different contexts: (1) a tourist setting, (2) a museum setting, and (3) an ongoing social context.

My control and expertise in these three differing settings varied, being weakest in the tourist setting, stronger in the museum setting, and strongest in the field setting. Prior to 1981, I had never been on a tour, had never visited the tour area (Madang, Sepik, Highlands), and knew practically nothing about the production and sale of tourist art — although I had, of course, met people at the Field Museum who brought in objects purchased in tourist settings to ask for curatorial opinion on their prizes. The museum setting was more familiar to me, as I have worked at the Field Museum since the early 1950s. The difference was experiencing the national museum of a new nation. (I had seen the National Museum's immediate forerunner, in 1970, when it was still located under the House of Assembly building in Port Moresby.) Finally, I have studied art in its indigenous context during several periods of field research in New Ireland, and have pursued studies of museum collections of New Ireland art in museums in Europe, the United States, and Australia. In this paper I will mention certain art activities seen in these three contexts in 1981, and then comment on some of the implications of and relationships between these art systems.

The Tour

The tour lasted from May 3, 1981, when we landed in Port Moresby, to May 15, when I said goodbye to the tour members in Jackson's Airport in Port Moresby as they returned to the United States. I served as lecturer and accompanied them everywhere they went. We flew from Port Moresby to Madang, then boarded the MV *Melanesian Explorer* on May 5 and set sail for the Sepik.

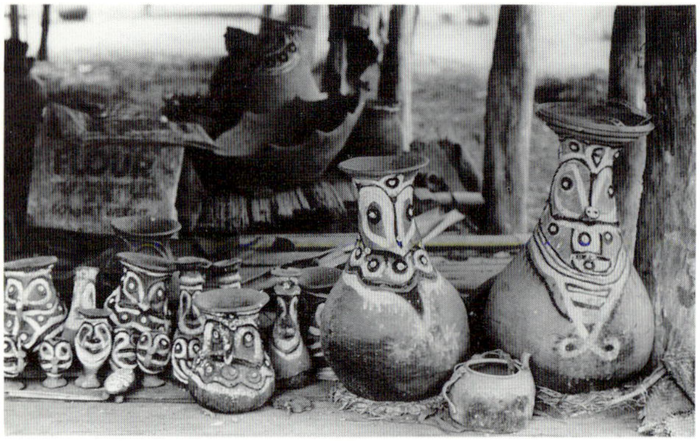

FIGURE 12.1. Effigy pots, Aibom village, Chambri Lakes, Sepik. Photograph by P. H. Lewis.

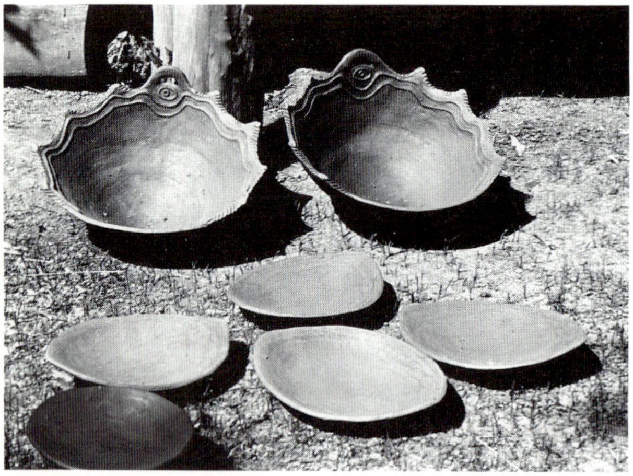

FIGURE 12.2. Pottery hearths, Aibom village, Chambri Lakes, Sepik. (Photograph by P. H. Lewis.)

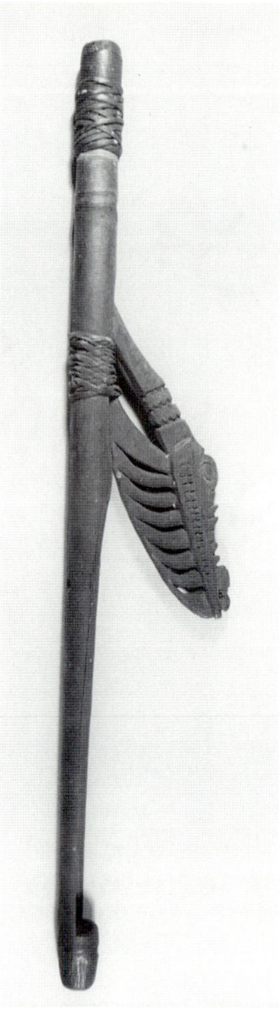

FIGURE 12.3. Spearthrower, bamboo, wood, collected in 1981 at Kambaramba village. Photograph by Field Museum of Natural History, Chicago, No. 259412.

The ship had two speedboats which took us ashore to visit Baliau village on Manam Island. In the Sepik we visited the villages of Kopar, Menam (in the Murik Lakes), and then Angoram, Agrumara (on the Yuat River), Tambanum, Kambarumba, Timbunke, and, in the Chambri Lakes, Wombun and Aibom. Returning to the Sepik, we visited Palimbei, Kanganamun, Yentchan, Korogo, and, finally, Ambunti. From there we flew to the Highlands, landing at Mt. Hagen. A bus took us to Minj, where we stayed a few days, making a few side trips from there to some Highlands tourist attractions. Then onward to spend a night in Goroka, and the next day to fly to Port Moresby. On the last day, May 15, we saw various points of interest in Moresby, including the National Museum. Just before midnight on May 15, the tour members left for Honolulu, and I remained in Moresby to carry out my survey of their New Ireland collection, and then to go on to New Ireland for a couple of months of fieldwork.

The Manam-Sepik part of the tour exposed our group to hundreds of artifacts offered for sale, presumably all made to be sold to tourists. The artifacts were mostly masks and a few figurines. At the Chambri Lake village of Aibom there were pottery bowls and hearths (figs. 12.1, 12.2). Most of these objects were done in recognizably traditional styles, and some of them looked quite good. Many trinkets were also for sale, such as necklaces, armlets. I bought a bamboo spearthrower at Kambarumba village

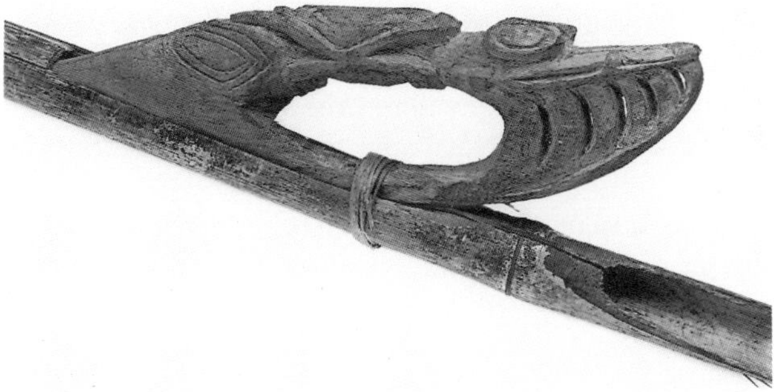

FIGURE 12.4. Spearthrower collected 1912-13 at Kumbragumbra (sic) village. Museum für Völkerkunde, Abteilung Südsee, West Berlin, No. VI 41491. Photograph by Fotoatelier Museum für Völkerkunde.

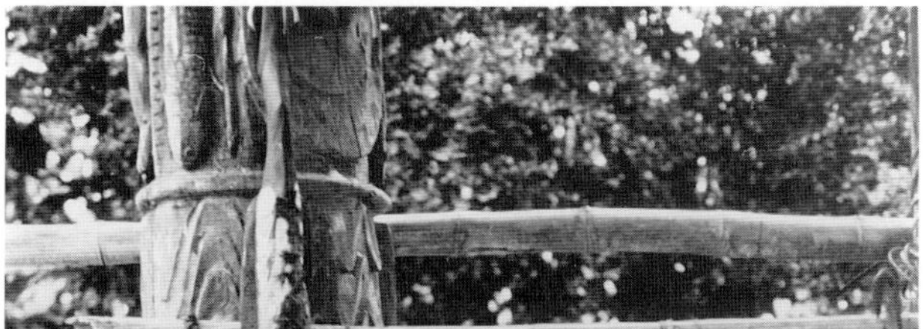

FIGURE 12.5. Carved house post of *haus tambaran* at Kanganamun, with a free standing sculptured figure in front of house post. Photograph by P. H. Lewis.

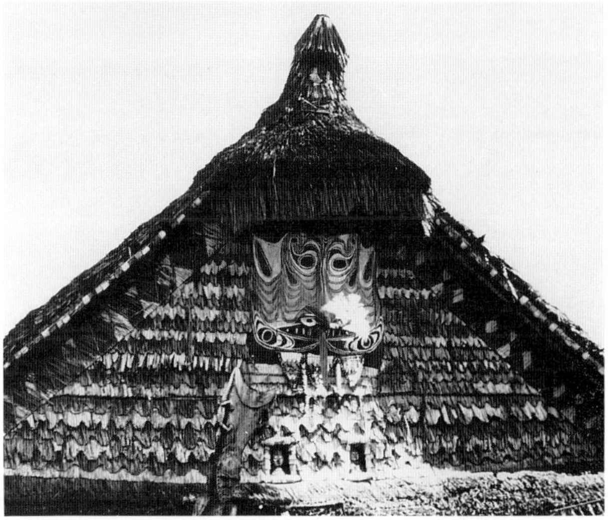

FIGURE 12.6. Gable mask on *haus tambaran* at Angoram. Photograph by P. H. Lewis.

(fig. 12.3) which, upon returning home, I found resembled ones collected during German times in 1912 (fig. 12.4) (Kelm 1968:pls. 423, 425). And there were out-and-out souvenirs, such as carved representations of the symbol of Papua New Guinea. Prices for all this ranged from one to seventy-five kina. Also to be seen were some excellent examples of traditional art, especially the *haus tambarans* and their constituent parts, such as house posts, gable masks, and roof-spire finials (figs. 12.5, 12.6). There were slit gongs to be seen, almost every *haus tambaran* having some. Thus a significant amount of traditional art was preserved in the Sepik *haus tambarans*.

The Museum

As a foreign researcher I was expected to carry out a project for the National Museum, with which I was affiliated. I agreed to examine their New Ireland collection and to write a report on it for the museum. On Monday, May 18, I saw part of their New Ireland holdings and, in the afternoon, I was invited to sit in on a conference of museum staff and a consulting architectural engineer from Australia to consider what could be done with the earthquake-damaged *haus tambaran* at Kanganamun. I found the meeting especially interesting because I had seen the house on the tour. The house was a National Cultural Monument, and it was the responsibility of the National

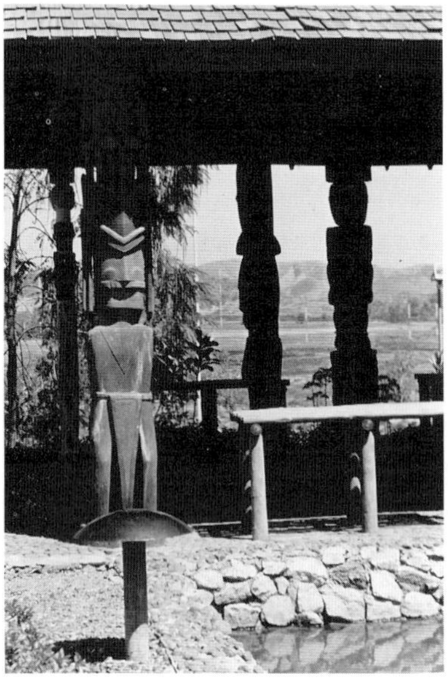

FIGURE 12.7. Carved post in form of Malanggatsak *malanggan*, outside the National Museum, Port Moresby. Photograph by P. H. Lewis.

Museum to preserve it. The task was immense because the house, a significant work of art, was in danger of collapse and had to be stabilized and, perhaps, restored. Various options were discussed in the meeting, each involving great monetary expenditures. The engineer favored using European technology, cranes brought in by barge, and Defense Force helicopters to lift house parts. The meeting ended on an all-too-familiar note in museum circles, namely, where would the necessary funds come from?

On the museum grounds there was a row of carved and painted wooden posts, each carved in various New Guinea art styles. I recognized two posts as being *malanggans* from New Ireland, and, moreover, as *malanggan* designs familiar to me (fig. 12.7). I discovered later that they had been made by a carver whom I knew, Lingi of Libba, and that he and another Notsi area artist, Lagiri of Langenia, had been brought to Port Moresby to carve the posts.

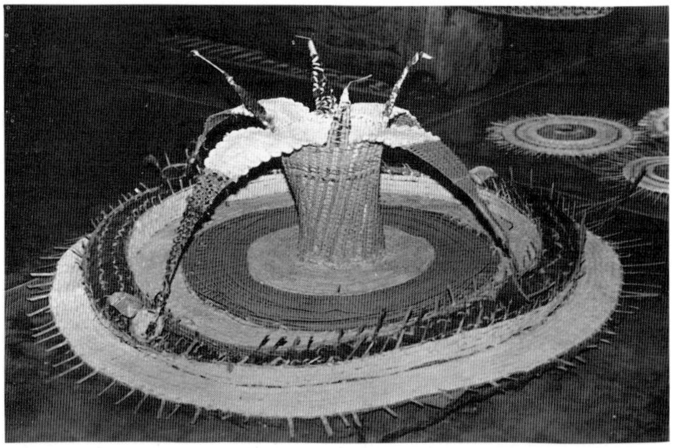

FIGURE 12.8. Wowara *malanggan* emblem in National Museum, Port Moresby. Photograph by P. H. Lewis.

In the museum was a considerable body of New Guinea art, the results of collecting, purchases, and gifts, a part of which was the New Ireland collection. After my fieldwork in New Ireland, which lasted from May 19 until August 8, I returned to Port Moresby for an additional week to complete the New Ireland survey.

THE NEW IRELAND COLLECTION OF THE NATIONAL MUSEUM AND ART GALLERY

In 1970 I had seen five New Ireland objects on exhibition in the old museum gallery, then located under the Parliament Building in Port Moresby, but I did not see any stored materials at that time.

In August 1981, the New Ireland collection numbered about forty objects, including four of those seen by me in 1970. The new National Museum building had suffered earthquake damage, followed by a leaking roof, which in turn made it necessary hurriedly to move much exhibited material to storerooms. All of this had resulted in a certain amount of confusion in the stored materials.

The Panemecho carvings number seven, and were found in a cave near Panemecho village on the west coast of New Ireland. They have been declared National Cultural Property, and their owners consented to sell them to the National Museum. The museum paid for the carvings, demonstrating its financial ability to purchase important works.

The best works in the collection are a great carved and painted fish, two fairly large and complex *wowara* disk *malanggans* (fig. 12.8) and the Panemecho carvings. The rest range from reasonable to poor quality. In no way could this small collection be considered as representative of the totality of the New Ireland art system as it can be seen in the older and larger overseas museum collections.

At least part of my reaction to the growing national collections was based on my knowledge of how little art I was used to seeing in the field, and how much more was to be seen in Western museums. Here in the museum was an already respectable quantity of art objects of uneven quality. A museum ambience was already established, the staff developing professionally — meeting crises and tasks as they came up. The Kanganamun *haus tambaran* project seemed very difficult. Indeed, the establishment of the National Museum as the agent which polices the National Cultural Property system seems to promise much difficulty for the museum.

The National Museum thus was filling several functions. It has obviously been building its national collections from Papua New Guinea and other parts of Melanesia, but it is also emerging as a patron of the arts (commissioning the avenue of posts), as a purchaser of older, better materials (the Panemecho finds), and as a repository for gifts. Also, as the responsible authority overseeing National Cultural Property, it finds itself engaged in projects to protect and preserve art works and monuments. In doing these various tasks it has become part of a specialized context of art in Papua New Guinea. The National Museum may emerge later as a major repository for art as it increases its collections and exhibitions, and thus it could furnish models for artists to follow.

Art in Context in New Ireland

This setting has been the most familiar to me, in that I have seen art being made and used in the context of *malanggan* memorial ceremonies in 1953-54, 1970, and again in 1981. In contrast to the tourist and museum contexts, the number of art objects involved is small. Indeed, at any given time in one of my fieldwork periods, a few pieces would be in process of manufacture, hidden from public view in the carver's shed located in the men's house yard. There are no "galleries" of New Ireland art in the villages, one simply does not see any objects on display or being saved for a future *malanggan.*

In traditional *malanggan* ceremonies, the art was made in secrecy, then was set up for a few hours of viewing, and ultimately destroyed, sold, or given away to expatriates. There is little or no tourism in New Ireland, inasmuch as there are few tourist facilities such as hotels or tour ships. Occasionally visitors come through on their own, sometimes in recent years going specifically to visit known carvers. However, visits from the outside are increasing and people are beginning to save some objects for possible sale to foreigners. The number of such objects is small. In contrast to seeing literally hundreds of masks for sale in or near one Sepik *haus tambaran*, there may be only ten to fifteen objects available for sale in one New Ireland language area. An exception to this seems to be Tabar, where recent reports show much carving activity. Obviously, the steady passage of tour boats and ships on the Sepik, and the exposure of art and artifact makers to hundreds of buyers per year makes the difference. The artisans there rise to the demands of the market, and produce what is wanted.

Basically, however, New Ireland art is still created and used in traditional social context. The nature and quantity of the several art objects produced are still determined by the demands of the socio-ceremonial system. In 1981, for example, ten *tatanua* masks were made at Libba. These were commissioned by a Libba big-man for use by Libba dancers at a *malanggan* at Amba. Each mask was made and tailored to fit a particular dancer.

My stay in New Ireland in 1981 lasted from May 19 to August 8. After a few days of shopping for supplies in Kavieng, I went to Lossu village, eighty-two miles southeast of Kavieng, where I resided for the remainder of the research period. *Malanggan* ceremonies were flourishing; the very day after arriving in Lossu, friends took me to attend a developing *malanggan* in Amba, a Notsi-language village about three miles southeast. By "*malanggan* ceremony" I mean the modern syncretic expression of memorial ceremonies for the dead, with cement tombstones being made instead of the carved and painted *malanggan* images of earlier times. As it turned out, in the two and one-half months I lived in the Notsi area in 1981, I saw parts of two *malanggan* ceremonies — one at Amba and the other at Lossu No. 2. I saw the climax ending at Amba, and the middle part of the Lossu ceremonies. In addition, I attended a funeral at Lossu which was the beginning of still another *malanggan* series.

An index of the size and scope of a *malanggan* ceremonial is the number of pigs consumed and distributed. The Amba *malanggan* had 109 pigs, including sixty-nine killed and distributed at the final ceremonies on the last day (fig. 12.9). Within a one month period in 1970, two different *malanggan* ceremonials (one at Kabil, a Kuot language village just south of Amba, the other at Libba), accounted for 140 pigs (seventy at each ceremony) being killed and consumed or distributed. Those were the only

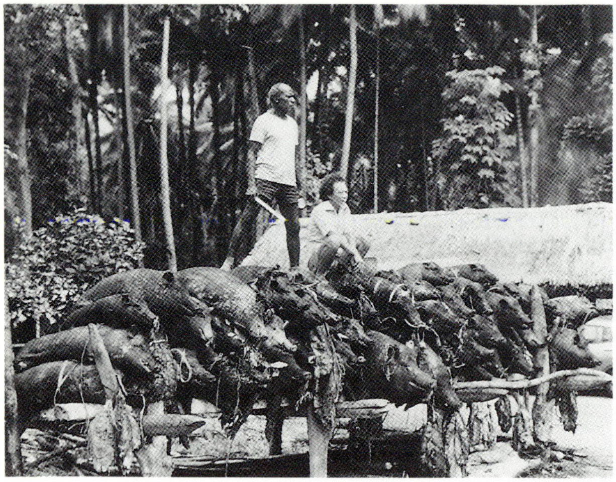

FIGURE 12.9. Pigs on trestle, Bota, Alan Chang on top, Amba, New Ireland. Photograph by P. H. Lewis.

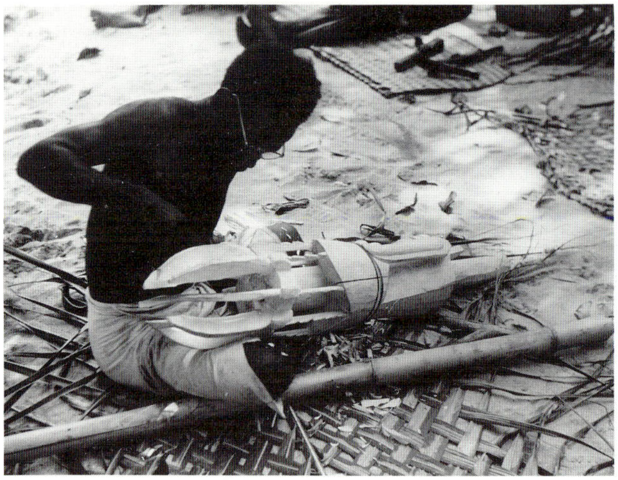

FIGURE 12.10. Eruel carving Malanggatsak *malanggan* at Nou, hamlet near Libba village, 1954. Photograph by P. H. Lewis.

malanggan occasions I saw in the Notsi language area for 1970. In 1954, at a *malanggan* at Nou, a hamlet near Libba, twenty-two pigs were killed and distributed at the climax, and perhaps some ten more during the stages prior to the climax. To compare consumption of pigs:

1954 Nou, near Libba, including 22 at climax	32
1970 Kabil, total for whole ceremonial	70
1970 Libba, total for whole ceremonial	70
1981 Amba, total, including 69 at climax	109
1981 Lossu No. 2, observed only a portion of ceremonials	?

Thus the pig consumption at the 1981 Amba *malanggan* ceremonial was greater than any other seen by me in 1954 and 1970. Little in the way of traditional *malanggan* carvings was produced, but the Amba ceremonies featured a presentation of the masked dance, Tatanua, in which ten masked dancers performed. I was able to see some of the making of the masks at Libba.

The glimpse I had of ceremonial activity in 1981 reinforced the view gained in 1970 that the social-ceremonial context was alive and well, but that the art was not. The Tatanua masks were of good quality, but other *malanggan* sculptures I saw were not. These latter consisted of several individual pieces in the possession of villagers in Lossu, perhaps being saved to be sold.

Clearly, the Sepik area is a much more prolific area for art. The world's museums hold more material from the Sepik than from New Ireland, and there is more available today as tourist art. Also, a fair amount of traditional art seems to be preserved for long periods of time in the Sepik region, in contrast to the ephemeral lives of New Ireland *malanggan* images.

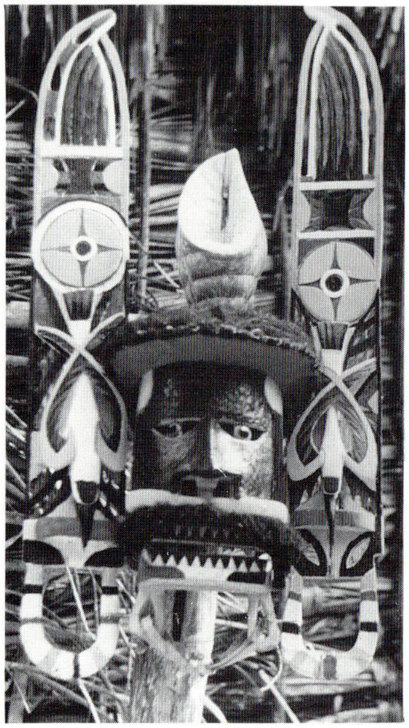

FIGURE 12.11. Completed Nit Kulegula mask, prior to use, in Nou, 1954. Photograph by P. H. Lewis.

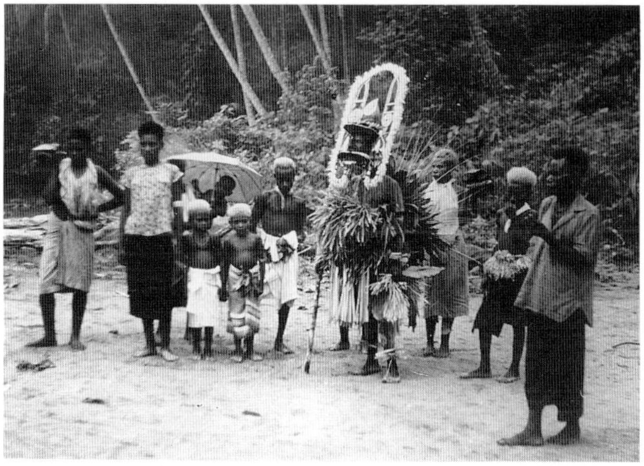

FIGURE 12.12. Nit Kulegula masker with four initiated boys and their female relatives at Nou, 1954. Photograph by P. H. Lewis.

Of the art objects that I desired to collect in 1954, only a mask carved by Eruel was refused to me. Eruel was a carver whom I observed in action in Libba, acting as both patron and carver (fig. 12.10). He carved and wore a Nit Kulegula mask in the 1954 *malanggan* ceremonies at Nou, in which he acted as escort for the initiated boys, one of whom was his son, Lingi (figs. 12.11-12.12). The initiates were led out of the enclosure where they had been sequestered for more than a month, and restored to their families. Eruel would not allow me to have the mask, preferring that it remain in the display house to weather away (see Lewis 1969:114-16).

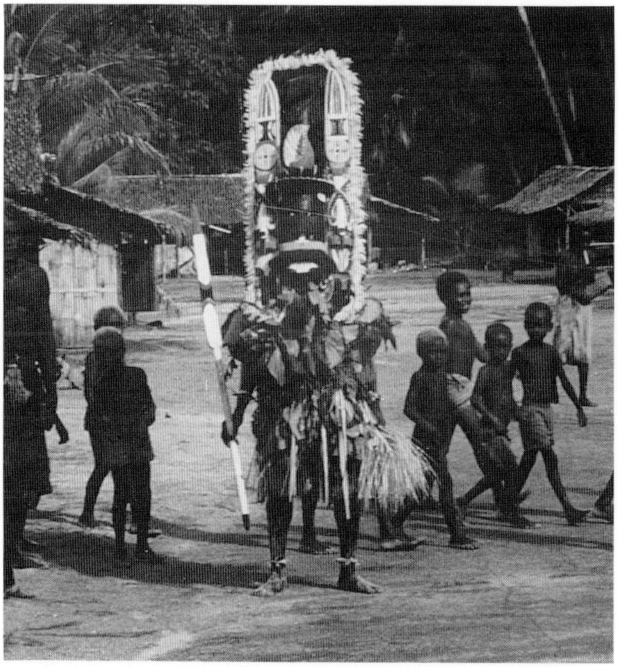

FIGURE 12.13. Nit Kulegula mask carved by Lingi, 1970. Photograph by P. H. Lewis.

By 1970, when I next visited New Ireland, Eruel had died, and he and his wife were being memorialized with a concrete tombstone made by Lingi, his son. Lingi is a carver who is partly traditional, but also is moving toward other modes of art production and sale. Lingi offered to reproduce for me the *nit kulegula* mask which Eruel had made in 1954 and had not allowed me to collect. Using photographs I gave him of the 1954 mask, Lingi did make it anew in 1970 and I bought it for the Field Museum (fig. 12.13). Lingi was trained in school to be a carpenter (house builder) and in 1970 had built a splendid European-style house for himself in Libba. The *smel* tombstone he made for his parents in 1970 was also very well done — a complex, massive concrete casting.

When I saw him again in 1981, Lingi was about forty years old. He told me that he had been approached several years earlier by a "Canadian business man" with a commission to make a copy of the nineteen-foot-long "soul boat" *malanggan*, illustrated as plate 174 in Carl Schmitz's *Oceanic Art*. The original was collected from Paruai village, on the northeast coast of New Ireland in 1903 by Boluminski, the German colonial governor of the island. Boluminski's *malanggan* is now in the Linden Museum, Stuttgart (fig. 12.14). The patron had given Lingi a copy of the Schmitz book to serve as a reference. Lingi completed the work, was paid handsomely for the job, and it was shipped at the patron's expense to Lae.

Lingi, with a fine New Ireland concern for legitimacy, told me that he had gone to Paruai to inquire about the *malanggan*. My guess is that he was scouting out possibilities of adverse reaction about his undertaking the commission. The object was reproduced full size, about nineteen feet long. I also saw, at Lingi's house in Libba, a five-foot-long version of a soul boat *malanggan* that had been commissioned by an expatriate but never actually purchased (fig. 12.15).

Thus, Lingi is known today in New Ireland as a tradi-

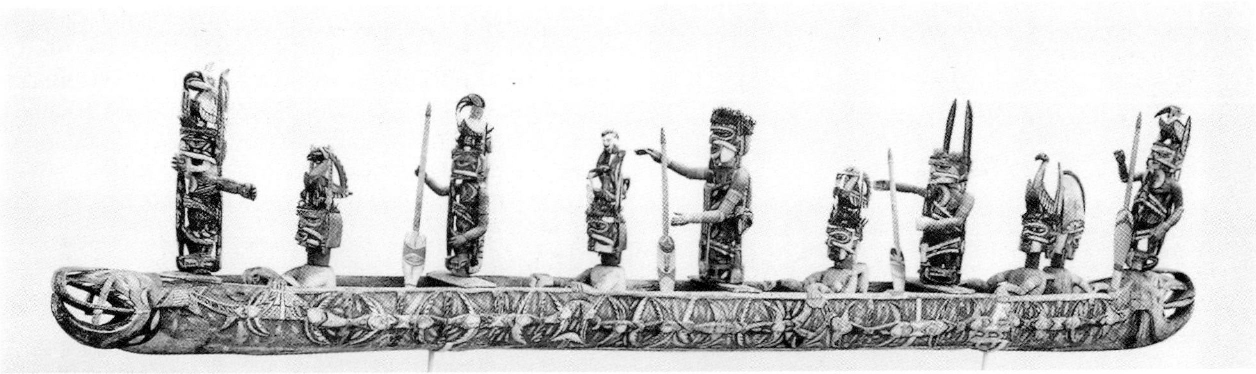

FIGURE 12.14. Soul boat *malanggan*, carved and painted wood, 5.89 meters long. Collected at Paruai village, northeast coast, New Ireland, by Boluminsky, 1903. Linden Museum, Stuttgart, No. 30158. Photograph by Ursula Didoni.

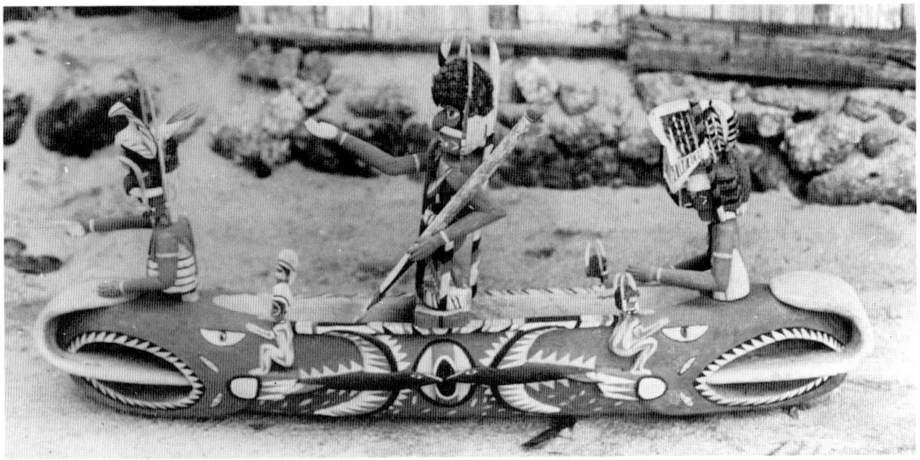

FIGURE 12.15. Lingi's five foot long soul boat *malanggan*, at Libba, 1981. Photograph by P. H. Lewis.

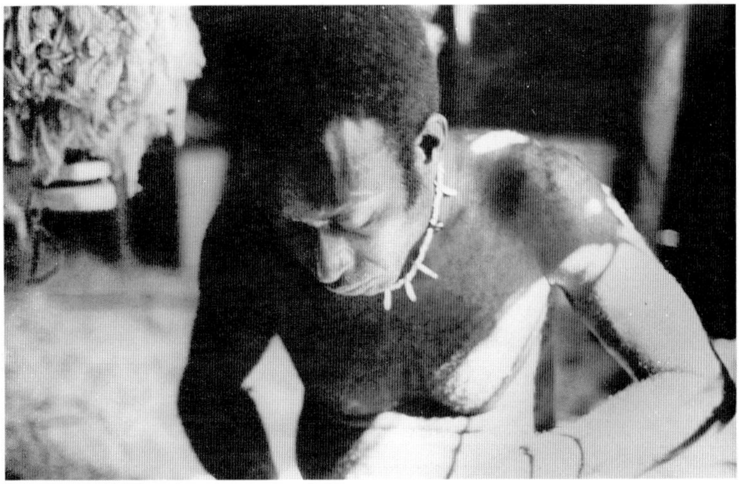

FIGURE 12.16. Lingi in carver's hut, Libba, 1981. Photograph by P. H. Lewis.

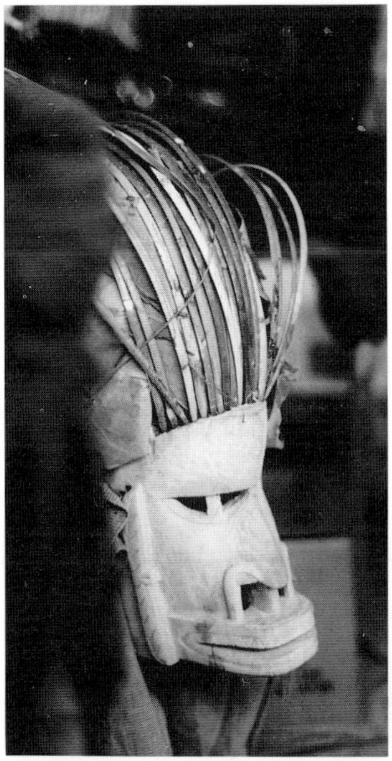

FIGURE 12.17. Detail of construction of Tatanua mask, Libba, 1981. Photograph by P. H. Lewis.

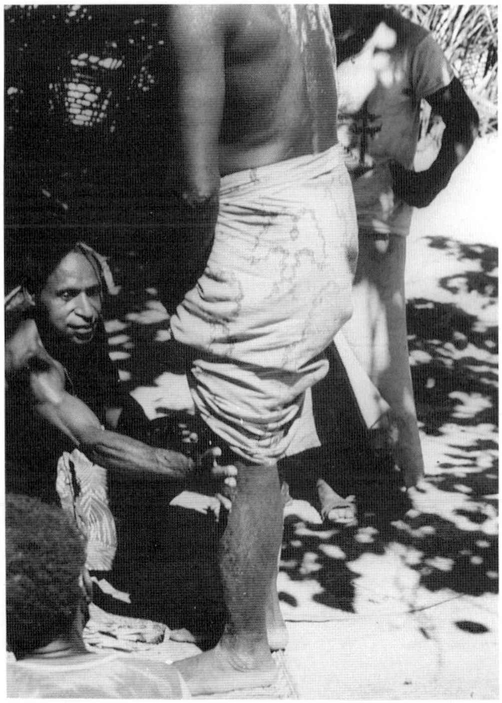

FIGURE 12.19. Applying dance magic to legs of Tatanua dancers, Libba, 1981. Photograph by P. H. Lewis.

tional carver who produces art in proper ceremonial context, but who also has been sought out by Europeans who have commissioned him to produce works for sale (in addition to his reproduction of the Nit Kulegula mask which he did for me of his own volition and sold for money). Lingi also was commissioned to go to Port

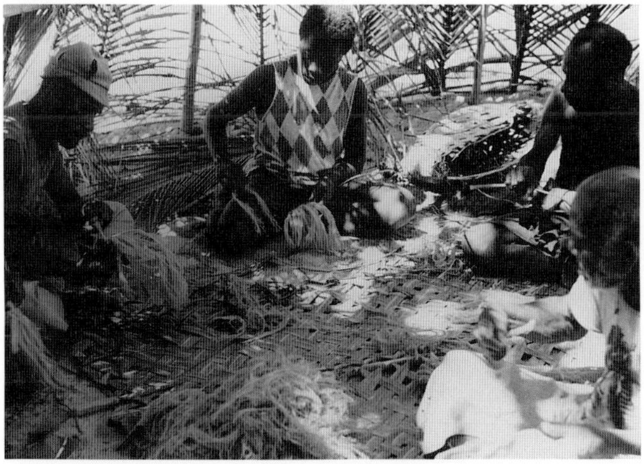

FIGURE 12.18. Libba men processing fiber for crests of Tatanua masks, 1981. Photograph by P. H. Lewis.

Moresby in order to carve two decorative posts for the "avenue of posts" at the National Museum. The two posts looked like Malanggatsak *malanggans*. Malanggatsak was the name given to an image made by Eruel for the Nou *malanggan* ceremonies in 1954 (see fig. 12.10 and Lewis 1969:78-84). Malanggatsak is a *malanggan* important to Lingi and his family.

In 1981 Lingi, working in traditional context, produced ten Tatanua masks for presentation by masked dancers from Libba at the Amba *malanggan* under the patronage of a Libba big-man. I saw Lingi and some Libba men finishing the masks in Libba — making and applying the yellow fiber crests to the carved and constructed face and headpieces (fig. 12.18). In order to protect the legs of the dancers and to insure their successful participation in the dance, magical potions were applied to their legs (fig. 12.19). The last rehearsal, called Agadip, took place in Libba a few days before the final presentation at Amba. This performance, in addition to fulfilling the obvious function of a dress rehearsal, was also to provide the aged

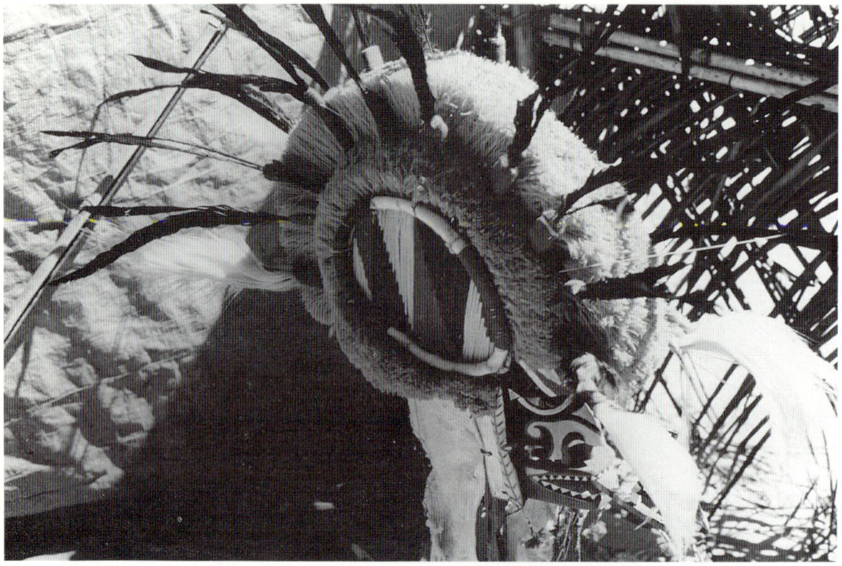

FIGURE 12.20. Completed Tatanua mask with feathers in hairdress. Amba, 1981. Photograph by P. H. Lewis.

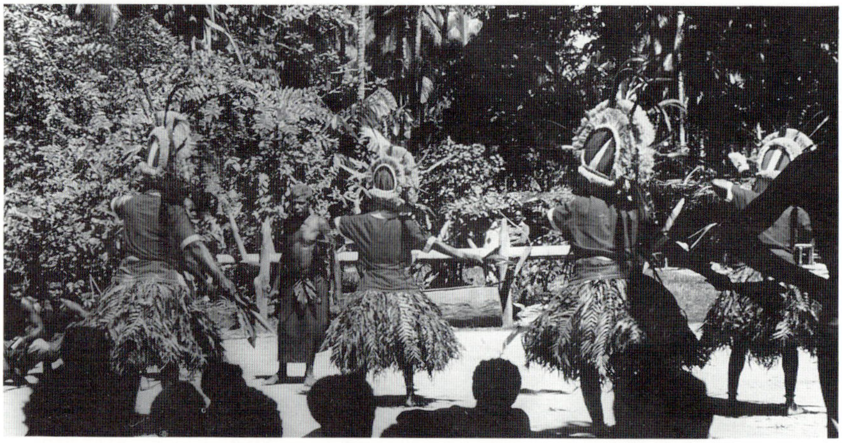

FIGURE 12.21. Tatanua maskers performing, Amba, 1981. Photograph by P. H. Lewis.

and infirm a chance to see the performance, because they would find it difficult to get to the actual *malanggan* in Amba.

The masks had been made in a carver's hut, inside the yard of a men's house in Libba. The yard was fenced with a coconut leaf screen, and the house had an inner closed and screened room and an outer open area. The carving of the faces, the construction of the headpiece, and the assembly of the masks was done by Lingi in the inner sanctum, but the processing of the fiber for the crests was done outside in the yard. Later, in the final performance at Amba, the dancers used the *malanggan* enclosure there, indeed costumed themselves while literally standing on the tombstone and graves.

Although he is considerably involved in production of art in the traditional context, Lingi also has displayed a tendency to produce art in new and different circumstances, one which can perhaps be called expatriate-commissioned art. Lingi is actually fulfilling the notion (Lewis 1979) that there could develop in New Ireland a two-tiered art system, one producing art for the traditional *malanggan* system, the other for sale to expatriates.

This is not tourist art, for Lingi does not produce works in anticipation of a stream of tourist buyers. So far he has worked on commission, in some ways not unlike the traditional patron-carver relationship, wherein he carves what is asked for, rather than anticipating what might sell. But as Lingi himself told me in 1981, he lacks a "road" to market his works, such as a local trans-shipment agency or an overseas dealer.

Comparisons

In 1981 I saw fragments of three art systems: tourist art markets of the Sepik, the traditional art and ceremonial system in New Ireland, and the growing corpus of art at the National Museum in Port Moresby. I started by thinking that these were distinct systems, each to be considered separately. They can, of course, be compared in terms of their differences, but I also found that they are interrelated rather than independent.

In form, style, and quality some startling points emerged. The traditional art of New Ireland, that is, *malanggan* objects and masks, made for and used in traditional ceremonies, were in formal quality much worse than many Sepik tourist art objects. Again, the resemblance between contemporary and earlier art (as seen in museums) is closer in the Sepik than in New Ireland. The art *forms* are similar in each case (same motifs, etc.), but the rendition of *style* of the New Ireland art had deteriorated badly while the style of the 1981 Sepik tourist objects closely resembled earlier, traditional Sepik art objects.

Of course, everyone concerned — the artists, the tourist buyers, the Museum staff, the patrons — held the traditional forms and styles of Sepik and New Ireland art as a desired standard. The main value of a Sepik tourist art object to a buyer is his belief that he is buying something which is more or less traditional in form and style. Of course, the expertise of the makers, buyers, and sellers of Sepik tourist art varies greatly, ranging from ignorance to considerable knowledge of what the commodity should be. In New Ireland, where there is little tourism, expectations of quality are held by the artists, patrons, the local public, and the staffs of museums, all of whom want quality of form and style and similarity to traditional art. Thus implicit in the thinking of everyone concerned with the contemporary art discussed here is the expectation that the style of objects look as much as possible like traditional art. Form, style, and quality of an artifact alone may not definitively show whether an object was made for traditional use or for sale. Graburn says that our ideas of "traditional" change. Yesterday's junk may become tomorrow's valuable art objects (Graburn 1976:14).

In a traditional system the art object's final disposition may be destruction, disintegration, or ritual preservation in a sacred repository such as a men's house. For objects made for sale, the expected final disposition is purchase by a tourist, to be carried back home for display as a souvenir. In some cases, the tourist may donate the object to a museum, which may thus become the last stop for many artifacts originating in a traditional *or* a tourist system.

From the museum's point of view, depending on the expertise of its staff, the size and quality of its collections, its needs, gaps in coverage, and whether or not it seeks to acquire examples of tourist as well as traditional art, the object may be accepted or declined. For the most part, museums aim to have examples of traditionally based art in their collections. But, because many museums accept donations of artifacts and because documentation may be less than perfect, inevitably some material is acquired which may actually have originated in a tourist system.

How does traditional art change into tourist art? Jerry Abramson has shown how traditional artists change their output to conform to a tourist context, and how others who had not previously been carvers get into the business as well. Iwam shields are now made by non-specialists. Abramson also reports how the new shields combine persistence and departures from old, traditional forms. With the decline of warfare the shields are no longer functional but are now made without ritual or mythological references; no longer as objects for use in warfare but as objects made to be sold (Abramson 1976:256-57).

When we see Sepik tourist arts of reasonable quality, it suggests that traditional artists of ability have taken up tourist art production. Anyone studying tourist art systems should deal with the crucial question of how and where the artists get their training. Must they come from traditional systems, or is it possible to learn carving and other art skills without such backgrounds?

The varying social contexts of art are most interesting to consider for these several kinds of art. In a traditional system, art is made and used in an indigenous context. In New Ireland, for example, the artists operate within a sacred milieu, working toward a specific goal and in a sacred locality. If they stray from these confines, they court accident, illness, or other misfortune for themselves and for others. The patrons also operate within these constraints and commission specific works of art for socio-ceremonial ends. The works themselves may be thought to be imbued with supernatural forces, and even to be dangerous.

The contrast with the tourist art system is obvious: The tourist works are presumably not thought to be dangerous, they are freely sold to buyers who do not have to be warned about any dangers from ownership and handling of the objects (although paying for the object may echo the kind of legitimization achieved by payments to patrons in viewing of ritual objects). The objects are very probably not made in a sacred context, and the maker may presumably make as many as he likes, subject only to his energy and market conditions.

In the museum context the public visits galleries in which art is displayed in a quasi-sacred atmosphere. Unlike a tourist context the displayed objects are not for sale, indeed may not be touched. But they may become part of a social context extending beyond the museum.

In the case of the National Museum of Papua New Guinea, art in the museum may accomplish useful ends. The artifacts remain in the country, and are thus more available as models to artists and budding craftsmen than if they went overseas. This is important because today many Papua New Guinea artists are not really familiar with the fine old, traditional material. In the revitalization of North American Northwest Coast art, native craftsmen have been known to frequent museums in order to see the fine old objects.

Another role museum-exhibited art can play is to imbue the art with social value. I was once asked by an elderly New Irelander, when I was showing photographs of old New Ireland art, "What do you people want with this stuff?" He knew the traditional New Ireland usage — set up the images, everyone comes in to have a look, pay the patron, honor the dead, and destroy the images — but he did not know what Westerners did with the images. In a museum setting, the spectacle of a public — expatriate as well as native — visiting the museum and respectfully viewing the exhibited art objects, which are guarded, set on pedestals, and explained, could lead to a perception that the objects are highly valued. That in turn could lead to greater respect and interest in making new art. Graburn says that changing art systems can attract craftsmen formerly not involved with the production of specialized arts. They enter into the new activity for the money, and do so in the spirit that income from art production may be valued more highly than manual labor or other commercial trade (Graburn 1976:31).

Patronage is a special aspect of the social context of art. The patron is a member of society who commissions an artist to produce something. In traditional Melanesian society — New Ireland, for instance — the patron owns the "copyright" to *malanggan* designs, he commissions a carver to do the work, and pays him for so doing. In New Ireland, it is *only* the patron who has the right (and the need) to have a *malanggan* carved. The artist is his tool and has little to say about what is to be carved, how it is to be used, or how disposed of.

In the tourist art context we may well ask, who is the patron? One kind of patron is the tourist buyer. He actually pays for the work, and carries the object away for his own use. It will be recalled that Lingi accepted a commission from an expatriate to reproduce the soul boat *malanggan*. Perhaps the traditional relationship with patrons predisposed Lingi's willingness to take on the job.

Much more commonly, however, tourist art sales are speculative. The works are not commissioned in advance by the buyer. The decisions as to what is to be carved, and in what form and style, are made by the artist, who completes the object and then offers it for sale in the marketplace. We may also speculate as to whether there may be traditional patrons involved in Sepik tourist art, that is, someone other than the artist who owns rights to given art objects. My ignorance of the Sepik art systems precludes answering this question, but I raise the possibility that a Sepik tourist art producer actually works with a patron's permission or blessing, and may actually have to share sales proceeds with him. It may also be possible that artists producing tourist art are traditional artists using the tourist art context to "escape" domination of their traditional patrons.

Finally, it should be noted that the National Museum has also acted somewhat like a traditional patron, in commissioning the avenue of posts.

Conclusions

Graburn's excellent discussion of the arts of the Fourth

World has broadened the field of discussion of primitive art, folk art, traditional, and tourist arts. Instead of treating these several entities as separate and significant, if we follow Graburn we see that the phenomenon to be studied is "the arts of the Fourth World," which subsumes all art found in Fourth World countries. Thus he points to the interdependence of societies formerly called primitive or folk, and the contexts called traditional and tourist. He says,

> The Fourth World is the collective name for all aboriginal or native peoples whose lands fall within the national boundaries and technobureaucratic administrations of the countries of the First, Second, and Third Worlds. As such, they are peoples without countries of their own, peoples who are usually in the minority and without the power to direct the course of their collective lives.
>
> Not only are they no longer isolated or autonomous peoples as they perhaps once were, but their arts are rarely produced for their own consumption or according to their own unmodified tastes. In many ways these peoples have become dependent part-societies .... whose very thought and culture reflect the differences from, and accommodation to, the realities of the majority peoples surrounding them. Thus, the study of the arts of the Fourth World is different from the study of "primitive" art, characteristic of most earlier anthropological writings, for it must take into account more than one symbolic and aesthetic system, and the fact that the arts may be produced by one group for consumption by another. The study of Fourth World arts, is par excellence, the study of *changing* arts — of emerging ethnicities, modifying identities, and commercial and colonial stimuli and repressive actions. . . .
>
> This volume, then, concerns one of the most neglected fields within the disciplines of anthropology and art history. It involves the study of what used to be called "primitive" art in the changing socio-cultural context of the modern world, a world in which small-scale nonindustrial societies are no longer isolated and in which holistic cultures with their inner-directed traditional arts have almost ceased to exist. (Graburn 1976:1-2)

In this paper I have considered the peoples of Papua New Guinea to be of the Fourth World. In two ways Papua New Guineans do not fit Graburn's criteria for Fourth Worlders, but in most other respects they do. First, Papua New Guinea has been an independent nation since 1975. Second, they never have been a minority surrounded by a majority culture, even during the colonial period of 1883-1975. They were a majority dominated and controlled by small, powerful, external, Western agencies.

However, in other ways the peoples and cultures of Papua New Guinea have behaved like the Fourth World cultures described by Graburn. In the last century, Papua New Guinean cultures have changed from their initial isolation as holistic societies to dependent parts of world industrial society. Another reason to classify New Guinean cultures as Fourth World is that changes have not taken place on one date, 1975, but have been changing since the late nineteenth century, and are still changing today. Various features of the pre-contact cultures have been suppressed or have dropped out, while other features still persist.

In my fieldwork in 1954 and 1970, I talked to older people who could still remember the past, such as skirmishes in warfare and isolation not only from the world outside Melanesia, but from other Melanesians. Now younger people sometimes travel to New York, London, Tokyo, and Sydney. They are concerned with trucks, bank accounts, Christianity, and cash crops. In other words, there has been a process of change from contact times to now, and during most of that time New Guineans have been more like Graburn's Fourth Worlders than like Third Worlders.

In the past, I have defended the term "primitive art" from critics who have opposed the term mostly because of its derogatory implications. Graburn (1976), however, has suggested that the best reason for not using the term "primitive art" is not merely terminological, but pertains to the nature of the phenomenon itself. One of the main difficulties with my "definition of primitive art" (Lewis 1961) is that there are few — perhaps no — societies in the world that are truly isolated and independent anymore. That was true in 1961, even more so in 1981 and since, and to some extent it was even true at the turn of the century, when many of the best artifact collections from Melanesia were formed. These societies, even though they were producing what looked like the finest, unchanged traditional art, which often provided the baseline against which we compare the newer contemporary and tourist art forms, were already changing. They often already had steel tools, their social systems and cultures were already experiencing the impact of western colonial regimes and they were beginning to be missionized. And, Western collectors were beginning to acquire art objects and other artifacts in large quantities.

Many thousands of artifacts in the New Ireland collections in American, European, and Australian museums were collected before 1914, some even before 1900. Although, on the whole, these objects were made for indigenous ceremonial use, the interest shown by Westerners, and the physical removal of the objects, could not but have had an effect on the peoples who made them.

In the early domination of Melanesian societies by Western colonial powers the demands for local labor in Western-inspired commercial, industrial, and church activities alienated large blocks of labor time from the indigenous ceremonial systems, to the detriment of the latter, thus interrupting the recruitment and training of native artists and craftsmen. The introduction of Western material culture actually displaced many objects of traditional design and manufacture. Who wanted to continue to make and use stone or shell-bladed adzes and axes, when steel bush knives, axes and adze blades were available? Who wanted to continue making and using pottery and basketry containers when chinaware, metal, and, later, plastic dishes and buckets were available? And, in New Ireland (and, I suspect, elsewhere in Melanesia), who wanted to continue to commission and produce the carved and painted wooden memorial figures, transitory and ephemeral, when solid, permanent cement tombstones could be made?

An important implication of Graburn's thesis is that there are no more isolated "primitives" anymore, and that the traditional arts have given way to new artistic entities, that the arts in the Fourth World have not died out but that they are changing into something different. Furthermore, he has directed us to pay serious attention to the "new arts" which include a gamut ranging from traditional to souvenir and commissioned arts. Most importantly, he urges us to look beyond the forms, to look at the multiple contexts of production, use, and meanings in which all the new arts are made — to look at Sepik carvers adapting their traditional arts to speculative tourist art production, and at Lingi eagerly and competently making a commissioned reproduction of one of the masterpieces of New Ireland art.

What does this portend for the future of Melanesian art? There will, of course, be produced a quantity of uninspired souvenirs, but there are some possibilities of something bigger and better emerging from a heightened awareness of quality production. Melanesian artists and craftsmen are beginning to produce their works for foreign buyers and, as Graburn has implied, producing and selling art, if one is reasonably remunerated, does not compare unfavorably with working on a road, or driving an earth moving truck at the Panguna copper mine.

Should we not try to preserve traditional art and culture? Surely we must try to do so, but Melanesians are not under Western control so that we may simply order them to do it. They are going to do what *they* want to do, for better or worse; their isolation has been broken, they have become part of the world industrial society, and they will participate in this new society as they wish. They are going to go to school, buy trucks, radios, and tape recorders, sell their timber to overseas interests, and use and appreciate Western medical services. They are going to do both wise and foolish things just as we Westerners do.

Their art is going to change — some of it is going to be good, some bad. Western contemporary artists, after all, do not all continue to work only in traditional styles and art forms. The modern Dutch painter Van Meegeren, who produced startlingly good works in the style of Vermeer, was not complimented for his efforts but arrested for fakery.

Where does the museum fit into all this, the National Museum of Papua New Guniea and our Western museums? We all have to broaden our views and concepts to deal realistically and holistically with the new output of Fourth World arts. We should collect and study them all, we should not turn up our noses at "tourist" arts and wait only for the chance to acquire traditional arts. As I have suggested above, the lines between these entities may not have been as tightly drawn as we have assumed in the past, and we may already have some non-traditional arts in our reserves. This might mean that Western collectors would respect the integrity of extant traditional arts in the Fourth World countries and seek to acquire examples of modern, contemporary, and even tourist arts.

Museums could mount exhibitions of these newer arts, give them more value in the world of art and, by so doing, stimulate production and provide a measure of quality control. Just as acceptance of illegally exported artifacts by collectors and museums stimulates looting, so would legal, ethical acceptance of the whole range of the newer arts stimulate their production. Western museums should also be sympathetic to and respond favorably to repatriation requests. Fourth World museums could then become focal points for revitalizing the arts of their countries.

In conclusion, I saw three contexts of art in 1981, Sepik tourist markets, New Ireland traditional ceremonies, and the new National Museum. At first I considered these three contexts as separate and independent of each other, and set out to compare their differences. I thought I would find that the "good" traditional art was being driven out by the "bad" tourist art; that is, that traditional art was dying out and all that would be left would be inferior tourist art. But there turned out to be surprising interrelationships between these several contexts.

Graburn suggests that the former "primitive" world no longer exists as a series of individual and separate, isolated entities, but that the various boundaries between the many tribes and other groups are broken and everyone is regrouping into larger units. Also, these new social entities still produce and use art, but differently from the former traditional societies. Thus, even if we can find and recognize traditional arts, they are no longer purely traditional, but have changed. Tourist arts have also changed, but some display forms and style of traditional art. We, as scholars of the phenomenon of art, have to adjust to these realities. This does not necessarily mean that we cannot specialize in subsets of total art systems. I believe we can do so, but with the knowledge that we must consider the interrelationships between the various kinds of art.

13

Maori Figurative Painting: Tradition and Innovation in the Search for Identity

ROGER NEICH

Beginning in the 1870s, a remarkable development of figurative painting occurred in New Zealand Maori art. Very quickly, several traditions of figurative painting had spread through the eastern areas of the North Island, lending a distinctive appearance to those Maori meeting houses in which paintings supplemented or replaced carvings. But within the short period of forty or fifty years, this painting art had almost ceased, downgraded in a government-sponsored revival of "traditional" Maori arts, painted over and obscured in many meeting houses, often completely forgotten by the people, even by the owners of houses bearing this art beneath layers of later paint.

Within the last fifteen years renovations of older meeting houses have started to reveal more of this art (fig. 13.1), but in many cases the only surviving records are fortuitous details in early photographs. From these varied sources a list has been compiled of about seventy-five meeting houses bearing examples of this art, demonstrating that figurative painting was much more widespread than previously realized. Even now, this art form is not represented in the museums or art galleries of New Zealand. It is all still in standing, functional meeting houses, owned and used by the local tribal and sub-tribal groups. Therefore, at the beginning, I want to pay a tribute to the owners and trustees of these meeting houses for looking after this unique art, for welcoming me and my camera to their *marae* (house compounds), and for giving me their permission and blessing to talk about the art in their meeting houses. I also pay a tribute to those modern Maori artists, especially Cliff Whiting and Para Matchitt but also many others, who have given so much of their own creative time to preserve this art and to foster its new appreciation.

The systematic study of the meaning and significance of Maori figurative painting has been hindered by the lacuna in people's experience of this art as a living tradition, along with other factors. The art of figurative painting did not require long training under the supervision of technical and ritual experts as did the traditional art of carving. Nor did figurative painting have a long-established body of conventional symbolism that the student leared and absorbed during his training, as was the case with carving. Consequently, figurative painting was a more individualistic art in which the artist had freedom to invent his personal symbolism. Some of this symbolism was leared and transmitted by the community but the more esoteric

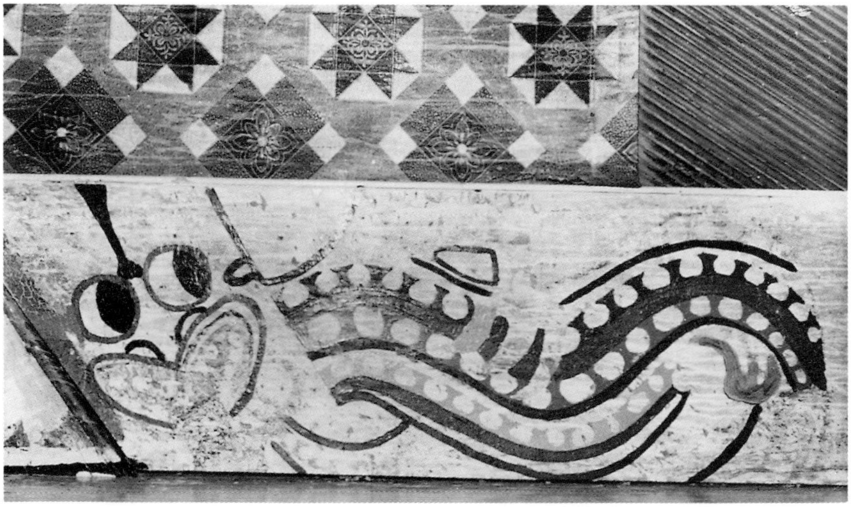

FIGURE 13.1. Painted figure in Hinetamatea house, Anaura Bay, East Coast. Uncovered in 1984 during renovations. Probably painted about 1900. Photograph by R. Neich.

details were soon forgotten.

Figurative painting developed in close relationship with the other arts of the meeting house, especially with *kowhaiwhai* (abstract scroll painting on rafters and other panels) and woodcarving of ancestral figures. A complicating factor for the study of figurative painting is that these other arts were themselves evolving at the same time, often in different directions and at different rates. One major painting tradition developed directly from *kowhaiwhai*, another tradition rendered woodcarving figures and motifs in paint, while a third borrowed from European naturalistic art. Some painted meeting houses used only one of these traditions, while others blended two or all three. Consquently, when all the arts of woodcarving, *tukutuku* (decorative latticework), traditional *kowhaiwhai*, and figurative painting were brought together in a particular meeting house, each discrete art form represented one stage in the development of that art. Only in rare circumstances would that same configuration of art stages be repeated in another house. Yet in order to interpret the meaning and significance of a particular meeting house, all the art forms realized in that house must be considered in concert as they all bring their contribution to the total message of the house.

In the early 1870s, as the Land Wars came to a close and the chase after the charismatic Maori leader, Te Kooti Rikirangi, was abandoned, the very concept of the meeting house was undergoing drastic changes. It was a period of intense political and religious realignment, as various tribal groupings sought to establish their historical identity and come to terms with indiscriminate land confiscations, the activities of the Maori Land Court, and the unpredictable actions of the European government. Spiritual leaders arose to guide their people through these perplexing times. Most prominent of these was Te Kooti himself, who was making the transition from a military leader to a man of peace and healing, and attracting many of his former opponents to his following.

Since the development of figurative painting is closely associated with Te Kooti and his Ringatu church, an understanding of Te Kooti's teachings and his wider influence is essential for a full understanding of this Maori art form. However, until very recently, Te Kooti and the Ringatu Church have been much misunderstood in European historical writings. Happily, a number of current studies (Binney 1984; Misur 1975; Ward 1980; and others still unpublished) have begun to correct this imbalance by interpreting Te Kooti's actions and teachings from a Maori point of view. These studies locate the Ringatu movement within a developing Maori historical consciousness and a theological interpretation of history. Te Kooti's teachings, with their strong millennial outlook, did not originate this theological interpretation but they certainly invested it with new vigor. He was perhaps one of the first of the Maori prophets to recognize that history had changed the Maori world once and for all. His movement was a dramatic realization that the stereotypic reproduction of original cosmological relationships transposed to the realm of man had at last ceased. His followers now had to locate themselves as individals and as a group as they moved through history toward redemption and fulfilment.

Through all these vicissitudes, the meeting house emerged as the preeminent symbolic vehicle for the expression of the people's view of themselves and their place in the new world. In many houses built at this time, figurative paintings gave a new flexibility and eloquence to this view which was not previously attainable in the more restrictive medium of woodcarving.

As modern Marxist and hermeneutic studies have revealed, the meaning and significance of a text is not something fixed for all time. Each reading of the text produces to some extent a new and different meaning, relevant to the time and viewpoint of the interpreter. As a consequence, we cannot assume that the figurative paintings in a meeting house built in 1880 had the same significance for the people of that time as they do for their descendants today. Modern informants' statements need to be assessed in this light. Of course, the modern interpretations are also valid and worthy of study, but if the aim is to understand the ethos that informed the execution of the paintings, then this distinction must be kept in mind.

Figurative Painting and Identity

As a basic generalization, the arts of the meeting house can be considered as an expression of an ideology of group identity through time. This would include the traditional *kowhaiwhai* painting, the carvings of ancestral figures, and the lattice-work *tukutuku* panels of a standard meeting house. It is not the personal identity of the artist that is being expressed but the identity of his group. In general terms, the traditional standard meeting house of the 1840s and later was expressing an ideology of group identity based on the idiom of descent. Then, in many later meeting houses built after the 1870s and especially in those with figurative paintings, there is a change to the expression of an ideology of group identity based more on history. This uses the specific history of the group to define their religious identity, their local and tribal identity, and their identity as Maori vis-à-vis the Pakeha Europeans. In some houses, this historically based identity replaced the expression of group identity based on descent. More often, however, these two bases of identity ran concurrently in the scheme of the house, with one or the other being dominant.

The development of this ideology of group identity based on particular local history arose out of special new circumstances: the effects of the Land Wars, the growth of literacy, the keeping of family records, differing new religious affiliations, and the activity of the Maori Land Court. Whereas previously, different group identities could be adequately expressed by selecting certain ancestor figures, now painted figures and symbols were used to express all these new and different types of identities. This was necessary to deal with increasingly fine distinctions among groups, distinctions that had not existed in the earlier Maori world. In recorded Maori speeches of this period the appeal to specific group histories as the basis of new identities becomes more common than the appeal to ancestral relationships.

This art was not just a means of expressing an already existing identity. Community leaders used the art to create and shape the new Maori identity of the post Land War years. Often, the community leaders were themselves the artists. Surrounded by the art in their meeting houses, the leaders could make constant reference to the events and personages represented. In this way Maori figurative art established and expressed ideology — a set of ideas systematically related to the people's actual and material conditions of existence, ideas which served a purpose in the society. The leaders used this art to teach, to exhort, to instill these ideas, to make the people conscious of their identity in a changing world. The art served to prove the historical continuity and cohesion of the defined groups through all the changes of colonial impact. Each *hapu* (sub-tribe group owning the meeting house) had a different history and the leaders could select the particular elements of that history that were needed to reinforce their people's sense of identity.

Because each group's identity was now so different, the basic scheme of the traditional meeting house was transformed in different ways by different groups to suit their special needs. The artists and designers of the meeting house could do this by choosing what was to be depicted, the style of dress of the figures, the placement of representations within the overall scheme of the house, and by variations in the relationships between ancestral and historical representations.

By interpreting its heritage historically as well as mythologically, and by elaborating this history as a living tradition, each group projected itself into the past as a separate entity, owning its lands and exploiting their resources. From this perspective, figurative painting can be regarded as a hermeneutic response as each group sought to interpret its own special historical experience.

This project of historical interpretation was stimulated by Maori acquaintance with the Biblical search for a meaning to history. It was an Augustinian theodicy applied to Maori history, charging history with religious significance. Hence the progress of history could be read as a clue to the design and direction of God's will, as it applied to the Maori people. This probably explains why figurative painting became so popular among the followers of the various Maori prophetic movements, especially the Ringatu church, with their strong religious interpretation of Maori contact history.

While art is permeated by ideology, it cannot be reduced to a direct statement of ideology. The artistic expression of ideology is always mediated by the aesthetic conventions and traditional codes of representation available to the artist (Wolff 1981). These determine to a great extent what can and cannot be said by the artist, although over time these codes and conventions are modified, enabling the artistic expression of new ideas. Figurative painting proved to be one of the most flexible and adaptable mediums available to the Maori for this expression. Nevertheless, for a better understanding of the message contained in this art, it is necessary to look at the origin and development of those aesthetic codes and conventions that governed figurative painting.

The Maori Cultural Evaluation of Painting

The art of Maori painting as a distinct art form has received very little attention in wider studies of the traditional Maori arts. Although it is often hazardous to separate one Maori art form from others, in this case it is advantageous to focus on painting in order to understand its particular conventions and course of development before trying to interpret its significance within the total scheme of a meeting house. This becomes especially important when it is realized that all the art forms of a meeting house have been actively evolving in different directions and at different rates. Therefore, in this paper I focus on painting, but without forgetting that understanding the meaning of any particular house requires consideration of all the art forms represented in it.

Maori figurative painting developed first out of *kowhaiwhai*, which is the traditional painted art form. However, *kowhaiwhai* itself has undergone some very rapid changes since European arrival and these need to be studied to see just where figurative painting had its beginnings. It is important to realize that painting was an art form of relatively low status in traditional Maori culture. This is clear from two parallel sets of myths about the origin of two more highly valued art forms: carving and tattooing.

The Rua and Tangaroa myth of the origin of woodcarving (Best 1925:775-77) is built around the possible ambiguities of the word *whakairo*, which is commonly used to denote carvings but means simply "design." It is usually qualified by another word to distinguish woodcarving from tattooing, painting, or weaving. When Tangaroa described the designs of his own house, he used the term "whakairo" unqualified, but his designs actually consisted of painted scrolls and painted human figures. Rua, the originator of carving in wood and hence of three dimensional art, was scornful of Tangaroa's two-dimensional designs. Later when Tangaroa visited Rua's house, Rua was delighted that he mistook the three dimensional carvings for living persons.

In a different version of the Rua and Tangaroa myth, recounted by Henare Potae and Mohi Ruatapu of the East Coast (Best 1928), their roles are reversed. Tangaroa had slain the daughter of Rua and fastened her body as a *tekoteko* (gable apex figure) on his carved house. Rua came in search of her, and in vengeance destroyed some of Tangaroa's children (the fish people), burned Tangaroa's house, and escaped back to this world with his daughter. Rua also carried away some of the carvings from Tangaroa's house, which became the model for Rua to teach carving to the people of this world. Thus, whether Rua or Tangaroa is responsible for originating woodcarving, adventures in the realm of Tangaroa the sea god are necessary before woodcarving can be established in this world.

At a later date, Best (1982:287-88, but written in 1929) published another myth of the origin of woodcarving which also explained the origin of painted designs and again assigned painting to a secondary rating. Unlike the Rua and Tangaroa myths, which derive these arts from the oceanic realm of Tangaroa, the present myth describes a celestial origin for the practice of adorning houses with carved or painted designs. When Whiro, Haepuru, and Haematua climbed up to the second heaven to obtain carvings for their house, they were informed by one of the gods that the art of decorating houses with woodcarvings had already been taken away by their younger brothers. Whiro and his two friends complained to the god that they could not go begging to their younger brothers for the art, so the god showed them how to embellish a house with painted designs, "painted it is said with red ochre, blue pigment, white clay and charcoal." Whiro and the others then descended and adorned their house with painted designs. Best obtained this origin myth from the teachings of Te Matorohanga, who in 1865 had promulgated a syncretistic doctrine combining Christian ideas of a supreme god and the battle between good and evil with Maori ideas of superimposed heavens and a host of Polynesian gods (Schwimmer 1966:114-16). In this cosmological scheme, Whiro was the god of the underworld and the personification of evil, darkness, and death. Hence the association of painting with Whiro and his companions can only reinforce the negative evaluation given to painting in more traditionalist accounts.

Myths that explain the origin of tattooing also refer to painting as a lesser art and hence reflect the same negative evaluation. In one account, Tama-nui-a-raki visited his ancestors in order to be tattooed with permanent facial designs, since his own were merely painted and washed away each time he went to bathe. After suffering acutely from the pain of the tattooing operation he returned home to his earthly family, happy with his new permanent facial decoration (Robley 1896:114-16). Best (1925:938) relates an episode pertaining to the demi-god Maui which reiterates the motif of painted facial designs washing off, this time by Maui's perspiration as he sat in a house by the fireplace. To remedy the problem, Maui sought out Mataora to have himself properly tattooed by the skin-puncture method. With this permanent tattoo Maui was able to win the affections of the woman who had previously spurned him when his paint began to run.

The name of Mataora is closely identified with tattooing, and the story of how he obtained knowledge of this art from Ue-tonga, his father-in-law who lived in the underworld, provides the prototype version of the tattoo-by-skin-puncture-replacing-facial-paint motif. This story was greatly elaborated in the 1865 teachings of Te Matorohanga (Best 1982:226-37; Smith 1913:186-87). After careful research into the extant manuscripts, Simmons (1976:386) has concluded that this material can be accepted as authentic tradition of the Hawkes Bay and Wairarapa tribal areas, current during the time of Te Matorohanga's teaching. In this story, Mataora descends into Rarohenga, the underworld, in search of his spirit wife who had fled there. He finds Ue-tonga engaged in tattooing using the skin puncture method. Ue-tonga explains that this is the real tattooing, just as carving by cutting into the wood is the real carving, both as opposed to painted designs on the skin or on wood which are "only painting." To prove his point Ue-tonga rubs away Mataora's painted facial designs. So Mataora has himself properly tattooed by Ue-tonga, finds his wife, and returns to the upper world where he becomes famous as the master practitioner of the new art of tattoo by skin puncture.

Judging from the dates of recording — that is, between 1865 and 1900 — all of these origin myths that relegate painting to a lesser status in comparison with tattooing and carving were current in the period when many meeting houses were being built with figurative paintings instead of carvings of ancestors. This was also the period when men's facial tattoos became obsolete, the last tattoo apparently having been done in the late 1860s (Simmons 1983:242). Tattoo and woodcarving were the two Maori arts most bound by the laws of *tapu*, which tended to lock those arts into conventionalized forms, suppressing any bold innovation or at least slowing acceptance of new ideas. Furthermore, the practitioners of carving and tattooing had been trained in strict schools and were very jealous of their status as experts. According to the myths of origin, both woodcarving and tattooing were not of this world, since the culture heroes either had to climb into heaven or descend to the underworld in order to learn them. On the contrary, painting — whether on the body or on houses — was essentially an art of this world which required no special spiritual intitiation. The only exception to these points is found in the myth of Whiro's search for the art of carving, where painting has a celestial origin. Here too, however, it is clearly a second-rate substitute for the preferred carving. This mythical situation reflected the actual historical circumstances of the latter half of the nineteenth century, when untrained people could practice the art of figurative painting, relatively free from the rules of *tapu*. Consequently, figurative painting was an art form much more flexible than the other formalized arts, and therefore more able to respond to new social and historical conditions.

The Beginnings of Figurative Kowhaiwhai

Most studies of traditional *kowhaiwhai* have relied upon one basic reference: the chapter by H. W. Williams published as part of Augustus Hamilton's book, *Maori Art* (1896-1901). But this reference gives only a very limited sample of the total range of *kowhaiwhai* designs then in use. Williams left out many patterns that he did not consider as "genuine traditional designs," especially those that incorporated new colors and European motifs. Williams' sample is also strongly biased regionally — out of his twenty-nine published designs, no less than twenty are from the Gisborne, Poverty Bay, and East Coast districts, while another three are from the nearby Tuhoe and Hawkes Bay areas, with four from the Arawa houses of Ohinemutu. Whole areas of the country are not represented in this sample. There is also a concealed temporal division in Williams' sample between his Poverty Bay designs, which date from 1849 until about 1860, and his Ngati Porou designs drawn by Riwai Pakerau and Tamati Ngakaho, which date from the 1890s.

To obtain a fuller representative sample of Poverty Bay *kowhaiwhai* from the 1840s-60s, two other sets of designs can be added. One set is the rafter designs in the house Te Hau-ki-Turanga, painted at Manutuke between October 1842 and March 1843 (Barrow 1965). The other set are the six surviving painted panels from the church commenced at Manutuke in 1849 (Phillipps 1944:90, pls. 36, 37), now in the National Museum, Wellington. Then, this large Poverty Bay sample of *kowhaiwhai* can be compared and contrasted to the contemporaneous 1840s Tainui and Tuwharetoa *kowhaiwhai* samples figured by Angas (1847, 1972).

Using a wide range of design features as criteria for differentiation, the three 1840s *kowhaiwhai* styles of Poverty Bay, Tainui and Tuwharetoa can be consistently distinguished. One major distinction suggested by Tovey (1961:43) is the division of traditional *kowhaiwhai* into three series according to the main motif of each design. In the *kape* series the main motif is an indented cresent shape, and in the *pitau* series it is a curved scroll with bulbed end. The third or *kape/pitau* series combines both of these motifs. The characteristic features of each of these styles may be summarized as follows:

Poverty Bay:
- all designs very complex using full range of *pitau*, *kape*, and *kape/pitau* combined
- minimal use of straight lines
- wide variety of large compositional forms, such as spirals and white sinuous shapes.
- no speckled lines but embattled infilling used infrequently in small areas of design
- all designs painted in three colors of red, white and black

Tainui:
- majority of designs simple, restricted to *pitau* series only
- some use of straight lines
- absence of larger compositional forms other than normal periodic repeating designs
- speckled lines of white painted dots outlining design elements in great majority of designs
- restricted to two colors, with red on black predominating

Tuwharetoa:
- designs moderately complex, restricted to *pitau* series only
- straight lines frequently used
- absence of larger compositional forms
- no use of speckled lines or embattled infilling
- restricted to two colors, either white on red or white on black

This analysis demonstrates that Poverty Bay style *kowhaiwhai* of the 1840s-60s is just one regional style among several others but even at this early date it was exceptional for the ornate complexity and range of its compositions. Hanson's (1983) symmetry analysis of *kowhaiwhai* has been the major recent advance in our understanding of *kowhaiwhai* design composition, but we can now see that he was dealing with one regional style from the 1840s-60s (Poverty Bay), another regional style from the 1890s (Ngati Porou) and scattered examples from other styles.

There is another set of *kowhaiwhai* designs which, as

Hanson (1983:213) recognized in Te Hau-ki-Turanga house, show bilateral symmetry not on single rafters but on pairs of rafters located on opposite sides of the ridgepole. It seems that all the designs with this "correspondence symmetry" come from the 1840s-60s period of Poverty Bay style and predate the later popularity of designs with repeating periodic bilateral symmetry. An analysis of the rare Maori paddles with painted *kowhaiwhai* designs on them shows that the Poverty Bay style featuring designs of the correspondence symmetry type was present as early as the time of Cook's voyages in the 1760s.

All of the painted paddles have their designs in two colors only, usually red ochre and the natural pale color of the wood. The earliest definite record of *kowhaiwhai* used as a house decoration, that in the first Christian church built on the East Coast in 1839, also used only the two colors of white and red (Clarke 1903:31). It can be hypothesized that these designs were transferred from paddles to houses at the time when larger fully decorated meeting houses were being elaborated, which probably was during the 1840s in this area. The technique of using translational symmetry then became a popular and efficient way to fill in the more extensive spaces of house rafters. It was probably also at this time that three-color *kowhaiwhai* patterns were introduced, since three colors allowed the production of systematic anti-symmetry which soon became the major technique for creating interesting variation within the overall unity of each extended rafter design. One could thus argue that bilateral symmetry is a period fashion rather than a universal and fundamental feature of *kowhaiwhai* design composition. From this perspective, the correspondence type designs would be not so much a break away from periodic repeating patterns as an independent line of development originating directly from non-symmetrical designs painted on paddles.

The beginnings of figurative painting are to be found within these correspondence symmetry type designs of Poverty Bay style *kowhaiwhai* in the period from 1849-63, in the pattern called *Te Pitau-a-Manaia*. This is the only design with correspondence symmetry in Williams' sample (fig. 13.2). Williams copied it from the frontal boards of the house Te Poho-o-Rawiri which had been built, carved, and decorated in 1849 at Kaiti (near present-day Gisborne, Poverty Bay) by Natanahira Te Keteiwi of Te Aitanga-a-Mahaki tribe. The only other surviving early examples of

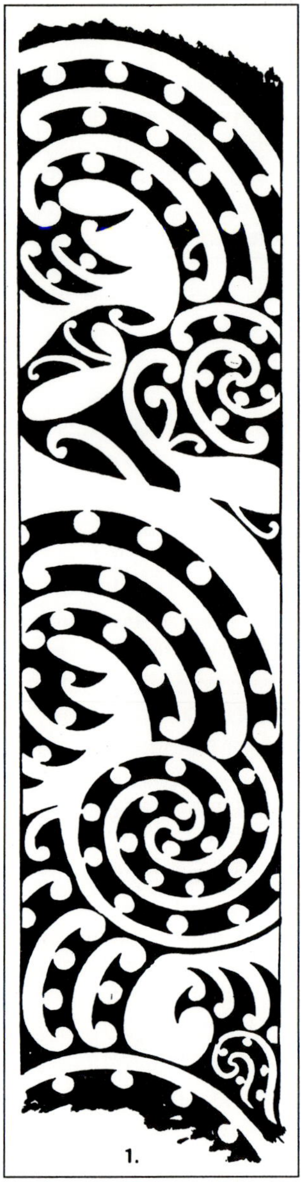

FIGURE 13.2. *Te Pitau-a-Manaia* design painted on Te Poho-o-Rawiri by Natanahira Te Keteiwi in 1849 (after Hamilton 1896-1901). Copied by H. W. Williams.

Te Pitau-a-Manaia design are those painted on the panels from the church commenced at Manutuke, Poverty Bay, in 1849 (fig. 13.3). Work on this church (fig. 13.4) lapsed in 1850 but was taken up again a decade later. Finally the church was opened, still unfinished, on April 19, 1863. The building was ninety feet long and forty-five feet wide with walls fifteen feet high and ridgepole supports twenty-

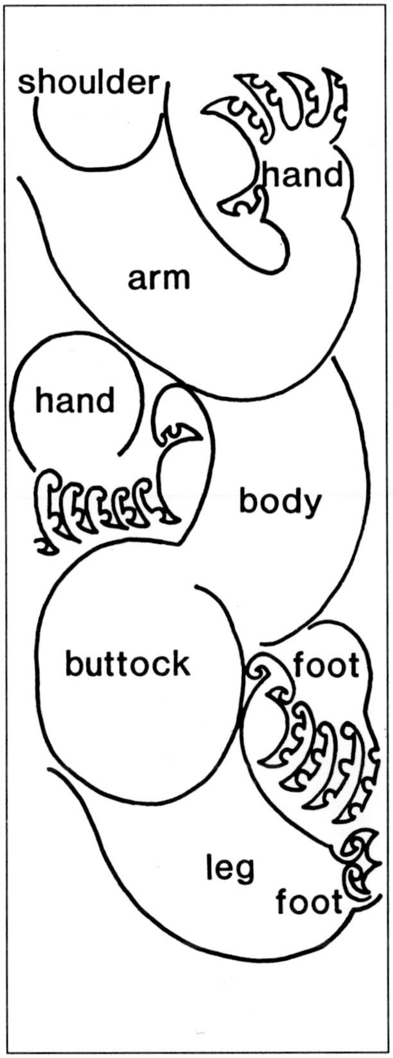

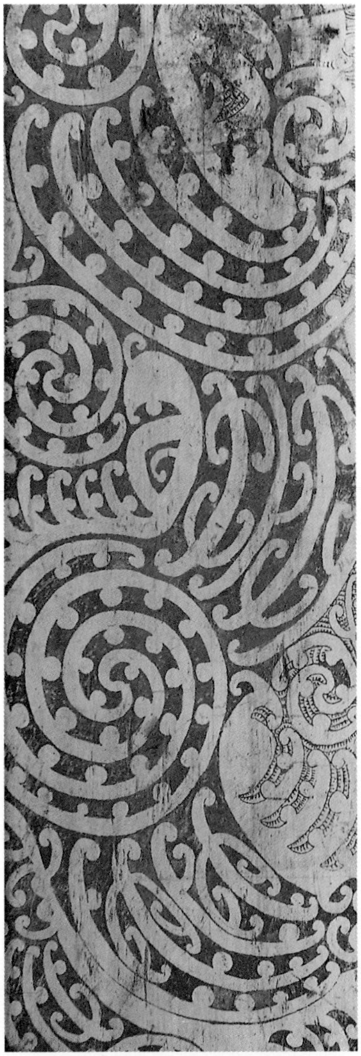

FIGURE 13.3. *Te Pitau-a-Manaia* designs from the Manutuke Church, Poverty Bay. Painted in 1849-50 or 1860-63. Photograph from the National Museum.

nine feet high. The *poupou* (side wall panels) were two feet wide and all these timbers were elaborately carved in Poverty Bay style. The *kowhaiwhai* paintings of the church probably date from the 1860-63 period, but they may have been planned in 1849-50, at the same time that Natanahira was painting the *Pitau-a-Manaia* design on the house Te Poho-o-Rawiri. Natanahira Te Keteiwi and Raharuhi Rukupo, the chief carver of Te Hau-ki-Turanga house seven years before, probably worked together on the Manutuke church, along with others of the famous community of Poverty Bay carvers and artists.

The ten-year delay in completing the church was partly caused by a dispute between the resident missionary, Rev. William Williams, and his Maori parishioners over the form of the carvings for the church. This disagreement, which arose in 1849, also provided the context for the first experiments with *Pitau-a-Manaia kowhaiwhai* design. The editor of the *Church Missionary Intelligencer* (1852:48) summarized the dispute in a footnote:

> The carving was commenced, during Archdeacon Williams' absence from the Station, in the old native style, in which grotesque and hideous figures are conspicuous, as in much

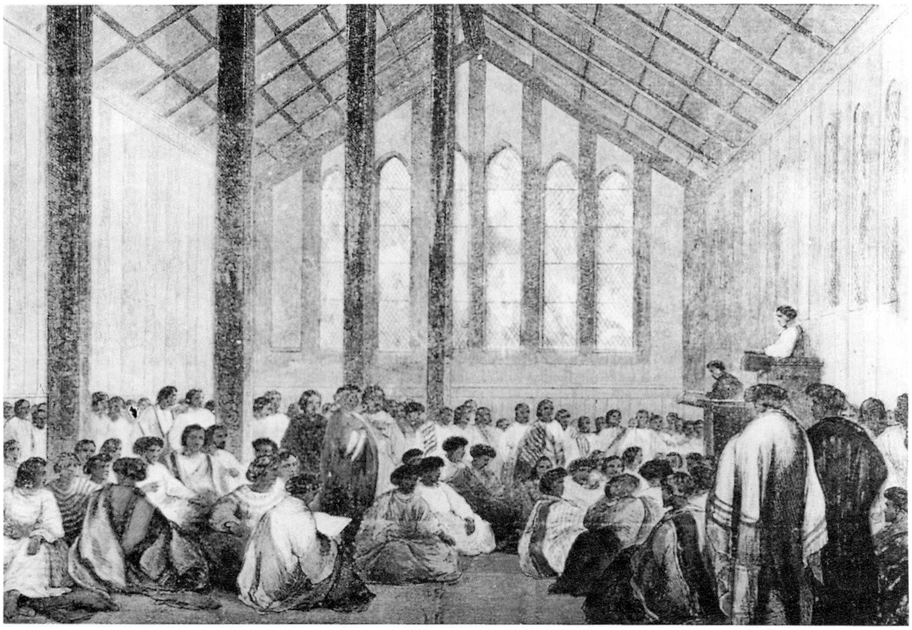

FIGURE 13.4. Interior view of the church commenced at Manutuke in 1849. Probably redrawn in England from a sketch by a Maori. Artist unknown. Alexander Turnbull Library.

> of the church architecture of our own country, executed during the usurpation of the Papal power. To this the Archdeacon strongly objected, as being improper for a Christian place of worship. Some of the Chiefs took offence, the carving of their tribe being famous throughout the island; but Archdeacon Williams remaining firm, and suggesting that they should adopt some other mode of carving, these disciples of the old school gave way. On going to the workshop, the Archdeacon found a man chalking out a new pattern upon a plain piece of timber, in which the character of native carving remained, without the devices to which he had objected.

The actual carvings produced under these conditions (fig. 13.5) were purely decorative, without any obvious human figures that would have represented ancestors. Instead, each panel was completely covered with a profusion of *manaia* figures that avoided any obvious representational reference. Probably the common use of the *kowhaiwhai* design of *Te Pitau-a-Manaia* on the rafters of this church was related to, and perhaps stimulated by, the carvers' compromise choice of *manaia* figures. This compromise produced a unique set of carvings, quite different from any previously seen in this area, yet purposely

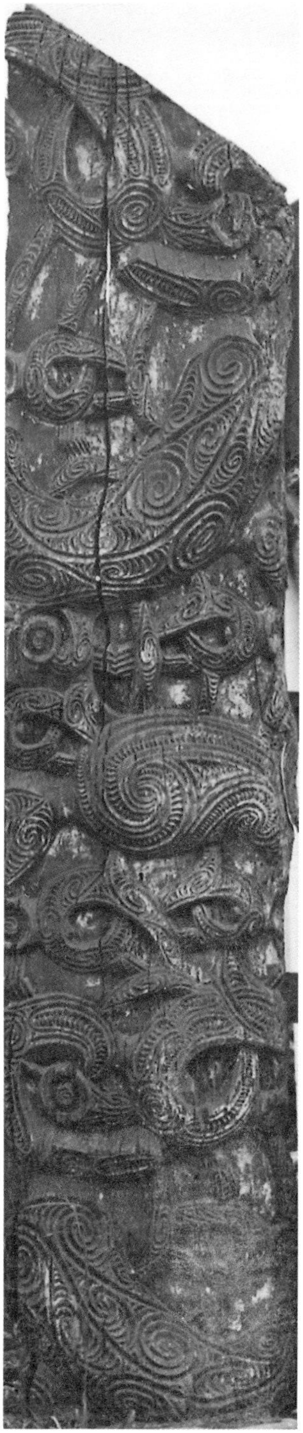

FIGURE 13.5. Carving of *manaia* figure from Manutuke Church, 1849-1863. Photograph from the National Museum.

calculated to display the virtuosity of the famed Rongowhakaata artists. Contrary to Williams' assertions about their conservatism making it "difficult to go out of the old track," once his interference had forced them to question their traditional assumptions about artistic form, the carvers demonstrated great innovative ability.

Although Williams had taken an interest in the carving of Te Hau-ki-Turanga by Raharuhi Rukupo (Lazarus) at Manutuke only seven years before, he made no attempt then to interfere with Raharuhi's use of traditional "heathen" images. But once Williams' criticisms broke the spell of the old assumptions and created a climate of artistic experimentation, subsequent carvings produced at Manutuke were among the most innovative in the country, especially those in the house Te Mana-o-Turanga which was built to replace Te Hau-ki-Turanga (Fowler 1974).

This climate of artistic experimentation engendered by Williams' strictures involved all the tribes of Poverty Bay and others farther afield, especially Ngati Porou and Ngati Kahungunu. Within these tribal areas, those most affected by the new attitude toward art were the carvers themselves, and presumably the painters also, who formed a working community of artists and woodworking experts drawn from several local tribes. This group had cooperated on several major projects during the 1840s, including the Manutuke church, in which they underwent the same experiences and shared the same attitudes towards art. Innovations pioneered by one member of the group would have been evaluated and adopted or rejected very quickly by the other members.

Out of this artistic ferment in 1849-50, the new *kowhaiwhai* design of *Te Pitau-a-Manaia* emerged, pioneered by Natanahira Te Keteiwi on the house Te Poho-o-Rawiri and appearing, as already discussed, either simultaneously or perhaps ten years later on the Manutuke church where the hands of Natanahira and Raharuhi were involved. The design was probably suggested by the experimentation with *manaia* forms in woodcarving, and that may be a better explanation of its name than any reference to mythological associations. As with the carved *manaia* forms, the *kowhaiwhai* design features curved profile limbs branching from large double spirals which mark shoulders or buttocks. Occasionally a strongly curved profile body appears. But unlike carved *manaia*, the *Pitau-a-Manaia* never includes a head or face form. The curve of each limb is repeated by white lines giving rise to branching *koru* (bulb) forms or by red and black positive crescents indented by negative white bulbs, always on the convex curve of the crescent. The hands and fingers are represented by red or black positive crescents indented by white bulbs, in some cases with embattled infilling. As on later figurative paintings developed from *Te Pitau-a-Manaia*, feet and toes are often represented in exactly the same way as hands and fingers. Natanahira Te Keteiwi painted his *Te Pitau-a-Manaia* on Te Poho-o-Rawiri in almost pure *kape* series, while those on the Manutuke church are painted in a very sophisticated *kape/pitau* combination. *Te Pitau-a-Manaia* was never rendered in pure *pitau* series *kowhaiwhai*, probably explaining the later preponderance of *kape* and *kape/pitau* series in figurative painting.

After laying dormant for about forty years, these early renderings of the *Pitau-a-Manaia* design dating from 1849 and 1860-63 determined to a considerable extent the way in which stylized figures were painted in later houses, such as Rongopai. *Te Pitau-a-Manaia* itself was only rarely used in later houses as a rafter design. However, beyond the particular design forms established by *Te Pitau-a-Manaia* and perpetuated in later figurative painting, the innovation of this design set a precedent for much of the later figurative painting deriving from other sources as well. The use of figurative *kowhaiwhai* spread into those tribal areas influenced by the disagreement over the decorations of the Manutuke church, especially throughout Poverty Bay, into the Wairoa area of Ngati Kahungunu, and north into the area of Ngati Porou.

Symbolism of *Kowhaiwhai*

As with all the other Maori arts, *kowhaiwhai* painting had a rich vocabulary of specific names for individual designs. At least thirty different *kowhaiwhai* names have been recorded, most of which designate forms from the natural world when translated literally. The connection lies in a perceived resemblance, often very fanciful, between a prominent characteristic of the plant or animal and a feature of the design. Students of *kowhaiwhai* designs have debated the priority of representationalism and conventionalism in their evolution. In the later development of figurative painting, there is a growing tendency to literalize cultural connotations and this may account for the popularity of detailed naturalistic renderings of red and yellow *kowhai* plants in later houses, since these were prominent *kowhaiwhai* design names. The early missionary-botanist William Colenso (1892:460) probably came closest to the truth when he stated that "the names derived from real or fancied resemblances — correlations as it were of the Maori mind. You should not expect the Maori name and its imitation to be exactly correct, it is the main outline as it were of the idea in the old Maori mind." Certainly, some of these names do set up deeper connotational associations, such as the connection between the tendrils of gourds, tattooing around the mouth of a gourd, and *kowhaiwhai* on gourds of high-ranking people.

However, from a consideration of the placement of *kowhaiwhai* within the total scheme of a meeting house, the chief connotation of *kowhaiwhai* seems to relate to ideas of genealogy and descent. *Kowhaiwhai* is regularly painted along the ridgepole (*tahu*) and down the rafters (*heke*). As an architectural component, the ridgepole runs the full length of the house, beginning at the front of the porch where the carved face of the eponymous ancestor is found at the apex of the bargeboards, and passing all the way to the rear of the house. In symbolic terms, the ridgepole or *tahu* is equated with the *tahu* of a tribal genealogy, which refers to the stock ancestors of the tribe listed in a single main descent line from the founding ancestor. As architectural features, the rafters branch at regular intervals from the ridgepole and run down to the top of sidewall posts, which are carved or painted to represent other ancestors. In symbolic terms, the rafters represent branching lines of descent and/or the historical migrations of ancestors, both of which are, together with the rafters themselves, meanings of the word "*heke*." Therefore, in the total symbolic scheme of the house, the eponymous ancestor at the front apex is linked by unbroken lines of descent to the subsidiary ancestors lining the walls, via the direct line of the ridgepole and the branching lines of the rafters, all painted with the continuously flowing curves of *kowhaiwhai*. Within the overall symbolism of the meeting house, Salmond (1978:9) has used the semantics of Maori words to identify a series of associations among topographical ridges and house ridges, lines and threads, which form a broad system of mediation and linking to express aspects of descent, authority, and communication.

Apart from decorated houses, the other major use of *kowhaiwhai* was on large tombs and monuments of important personages, as seen in the 1844 paintings by Angas (1847, 1972) from the Tainui area. All of the *kowhaiwhai* patterns in these paintings belong to the *pitau* series and here also the connotation is clearly to descent and inherited authority (genealogical *mana*), since these are the attributes which define the deceased as important.

Extending from these connotations of traditional *kowhaiwhai*, the later use of *kowhaiwhai* design elements to delineate actual figurative representations of important ancestors can be seen in Maori terms as a logical development, perhaps as part of the process of making traditional connotations more literal in modern times.

After the Manutuke church was opened in 1863, the idea of representing ancestors in *kowhaiwhai* lay dormant for about another twenty-five years, until the building of Rongopai and Te Poho-o-Rukupo houses in 1887-88 — but the precedent was already established in the church, still standing in the same immediate district.

Development of Naturalistic Painting

In the 1870s in widely separated parts of the country — on the East Coast, at Rotorua, and at Te Kuiti in the King Country — small naturalistic paintings borrowed from European models were incorporated into otherwise quite traditional meeting houses. These were the large houses built in the immediate post-war years, when the major tribal groups sought to establish their identities, both tribal and religious, in the rapidly changing political and religious situation. This was also the period when the Land Court was very active, forcing Maori groups to define themselves in European historical terms. Under this pressure to conform to a progressive linear view of history, each Maori group constructed its own modern history to serve its particular purposes, hence an ideological history.

Orbell (1968:xx) has noted a marked change in the style and content of Maori narrative after the 1870s. In reading the Land Court evidence, one gains the impression of a precontact situation of flux, with different groups ebbing and flowing across the landscape, merging to create new entities or splitting and regrouping to meet different situations. The process of giving evidence in the Land Court, however, forced tribal groups and tribal territories to become crystallized in a fixed configuration. One way

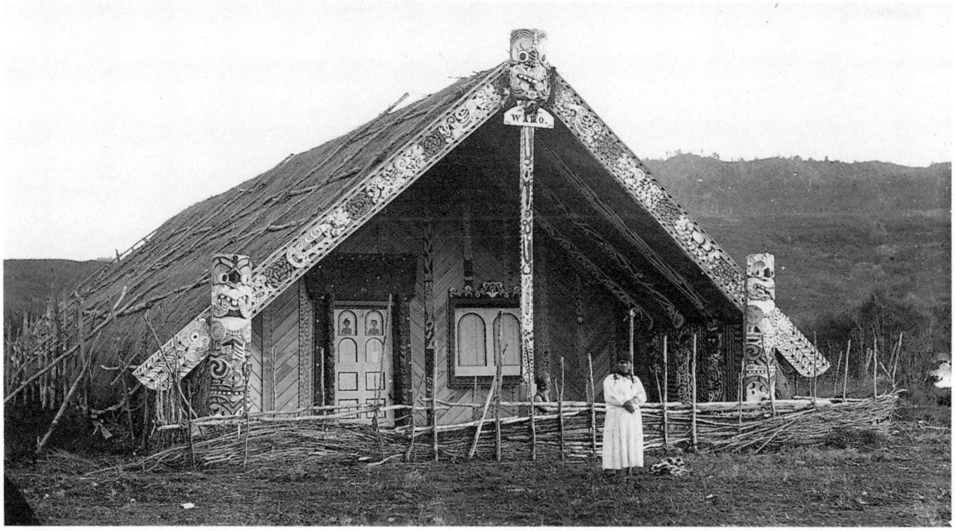

FIGURE 13.6. Te Tokanganui-a-Noho, Te Kuiti in 1885 showing the original design scheme on the porch and front. Photograph by Burton Brothers, National Museum.

for a group to define its identity through time was by tracing descent from one of the canoes which are held in Maori lore to have brought the original migrants to New Zealand. In the new historical interpretation of Maori traditions, the arrival of the migration canoes became a specific, dated event which provided a temporal focus for subsequent genealogies. Tama-te-Kapua house built at Rotorua in 1872 contained a naturalistic painting of the Arawa canoe, and it was the forerunner of many similar canoe paintings in later houses.

Also dating from 1872-73, the most innovative house of this period and the one that started many trends for later houses was Te Tokanganui-a-Noho, built at Te Kuiti in honor of King Tawhiao. It was built just after Te Kooti had taken refuge in the King Country among Ngati Maniapoto and under the protection of Tawhiao. Te Kooti is said to have supervised the carving of this house, and certainly the number of outstanding artistic innovations in Te Tokanganui-a-Noho bear the stamp of a bold planner. The carvings are in the style of the Mataatua canoe region and were probably executed by men from Ngati Awa, Whanau-a-Apanui, and Tuhoe who had come into the King Country with Te Kooti. Since its erection the house has been completely renovated and moved several times, but early photographs (fig. 13.6) allow the original decorative scheme of the house to be worked out. Looking at the house as a whole, integrated plan, some of its major innovations are:

- — painted naturalistic flowers and plants in the porch
- — painted *manaia* figures on the porch rear wall *heke tipi* (fascia board)
- — painted symbols of star within circle and circle surrounded by spots on porch panels and on interior rafters (religious symbols?)
- — painted *taniwha* (water monster) figures on porch panels
- — painted naturalistic portraits of historic personages on the door
- — painted naturalistic active figures on porch panels
- — carved ancestor figures on interior *poupou* (wall posts) with naturalistic elements and scenes illustrating and literalizing mythological events
- — most carvings painted in brilliant multi-hued color scheme
- — ancestor figure worked into *tukutuku* (latticework panel) of interior rear wall
- — some interior rafters painted with discrete symbolic elements (star in circle) instead of traditional *kowhaiwhai*

Many of these innovations were carried to other areas of the country, especially to the East Coast and the Eastern Bay of Plenty, by men who had worked on this house, by visitors to Te Kooti in the King Country, and by Te Kooti himself during his travels after his pardon in 1883.

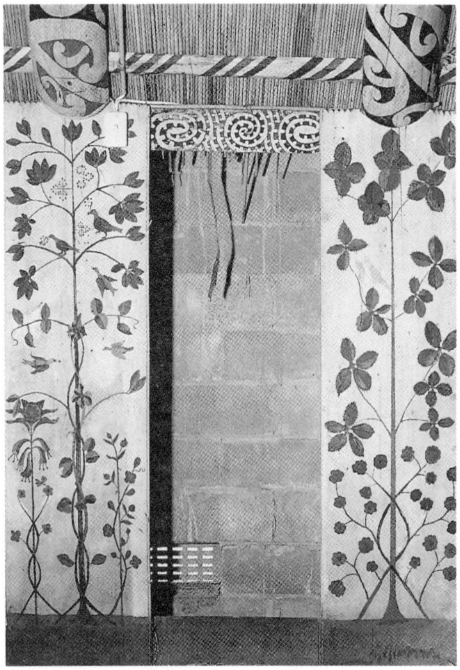

FIGURE 13.7. Interior *poupou* of Rongopai, Waituhi, Poverty Bay, 1887, painted with naturalistic plants and birds. Photograph by R. Neich.

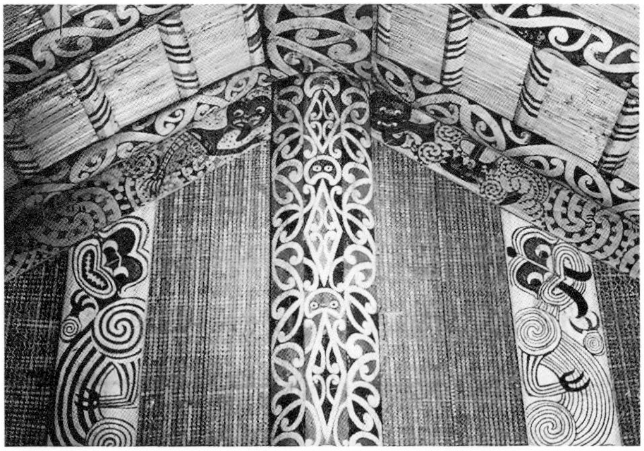

FIGURE 13.8. Upper portion of interior rear wall. Rongopai, 1887. Photograph by R. Neich.

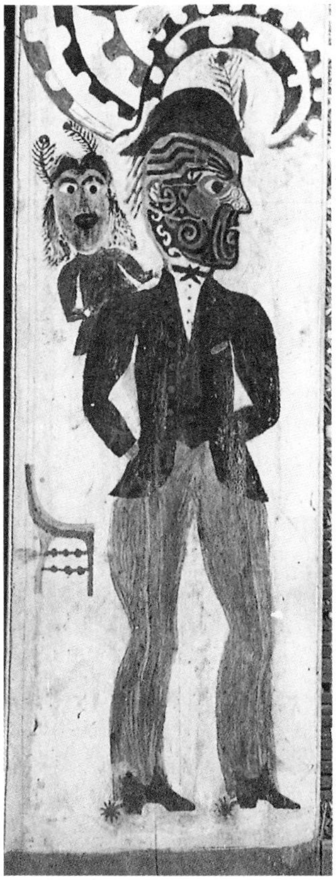

FIGURE 13.9. Portrait of Wi Pere and his mother, Riria Mauaranui. Rongopai, 1887. Photograph by R. Neich.

Rongopai: A New Synthesis

All of these influences were brought together in Rongopai house, built at Waituhi in 1887 by the Whanau-a-Kai *hapu* (sub-tribe) of Te Aitanga-a-Mahaki tribe as part of the preparations for the proposed visit of Te Kooti. Other groups of Te Aitanga-a-Mahaki also built houses in anticipation of this visit, but Rongopai is the most famous and most profusely decorated. Artistic ideas from Te Tokanganui-a-Noho in Te Kuiti, 250 kilometers away, were probably imported by Wi Pere, a prominent local tribal leader and national politician, and by his younger son Moanaroa. Wi Pere was a frequent visitor to Te Kooti in Te Kuiti and Moanaroa was a member of Te Kooti's staff (Ward 1980:32).

In fulfillment of one of Te Kooti's prophetic sayings, Wi Pere took responsibility for the erection of Rongopai and asked his son Moanaroa, assisted by Pa Ruru and others, to build the house. This could account for the painted naturalistic plants and flowers on many of the rafters and *poupou* (side wall posts) (fig. 13.7), the painted *manaia* and *taniwha* figures (fig. 13.8), the painted naturalistic portraits (fig. 13.9) and active figures (fig. 13.10), and the

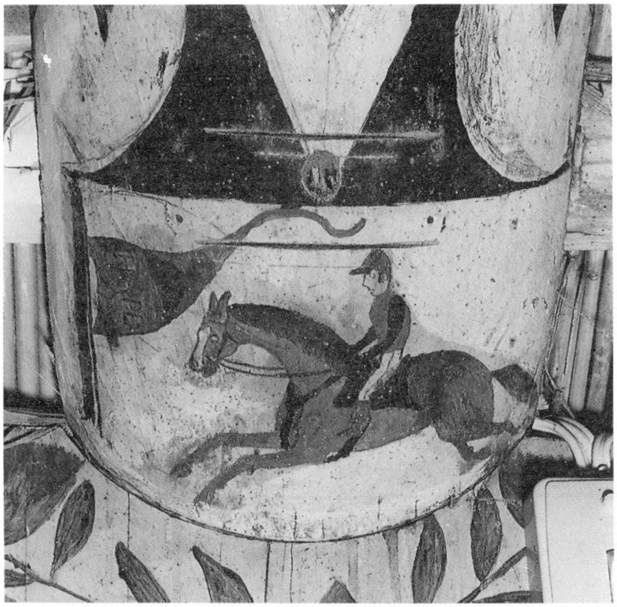

FIGURE 13.10. Racehorse painted on the lower end of an interior rafter. Rongopai, 1887. Photograph by R. Neich.

subtle indication of the faces of the ancestral twins Tarakitai and Tarakiuta worked into the *tukutuku* (lattice wall panels) (fig. 13.11).

In his teachings Te Kooti had taken a strong stand against selling Maori tribal lands. The naturalistic trees, plants, flowers, and fruit are probably symbolic of the land and all that it entailed in terms of produce, timber, prosperity, *mana* (prestige, potential power), and *turangawaewae* (a place to stand in dignity). The famous traditional story of Tarakitai and Tarakiuta, the twins killed by their relative Rakaihikuroa, identifies the locality of Rongopai as a critical dispersal point in the migration of famous tribal ancestors.

From the earlier Aitanga-a-Mahaki experiments with the *Pitau-a-Manaia* design come the ancestor and *manaia* figures of Rongopai rendered in *kowhaiwhai* elements with the addition of heads derived from carving designs (fig. 13.12). Most of these are painted in pure *kape* series *kowhaiwhai* elements with an occasional limb in *pitau* series. In some of the larger *manaia* figures, the lines of *kape* elements have been reduced to simple plain painted lines. Other ancestor figures of Rongopai, especially those on the *poupou* of the porch, display their more direct

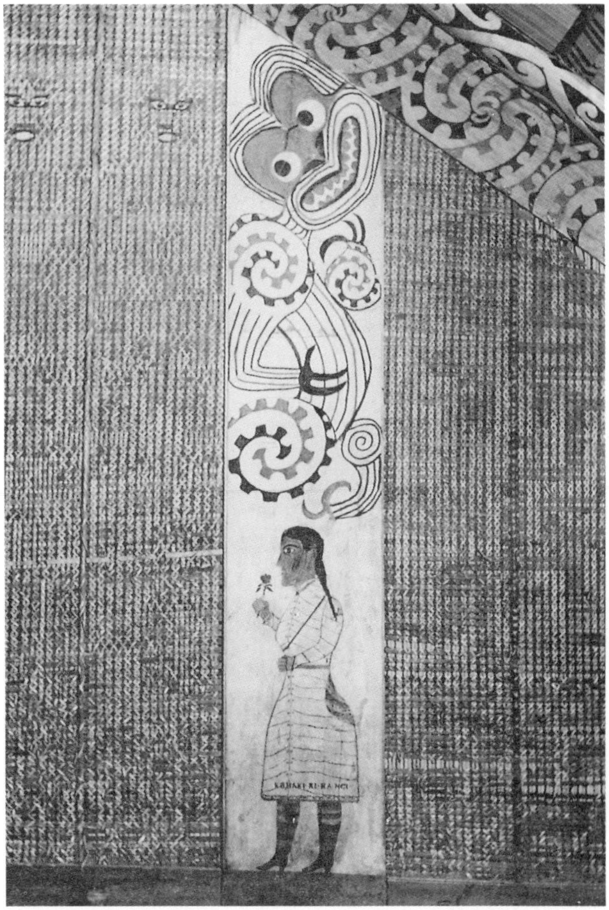

FIGURE 13.11. Painted portrait of ancestress named Hakirirangi, with faces of twins, Tarakitai and Tarakiuta, worked into *tukutuku* on left. Rongopai, 1887. Photograph by R. Neich.

derivation from the painted outlines of carved figure types. In yet other figures, influences from carving design, *kowhaiwhai* and naturalism were combined to produce a completely new type of composition (fig. 13.13).

Although the decorative work of Rongopai was a composite creation derived from various sources, the special genius of the house's designers melded these diverse influences into a magnificent statement of tribal identity and joyous optimism. While some accounts claim that the tribal elders were so shocked at this departure from tradition that they immediately declared Rongopai *tapu*, the house continued to function as a Ringatu church,

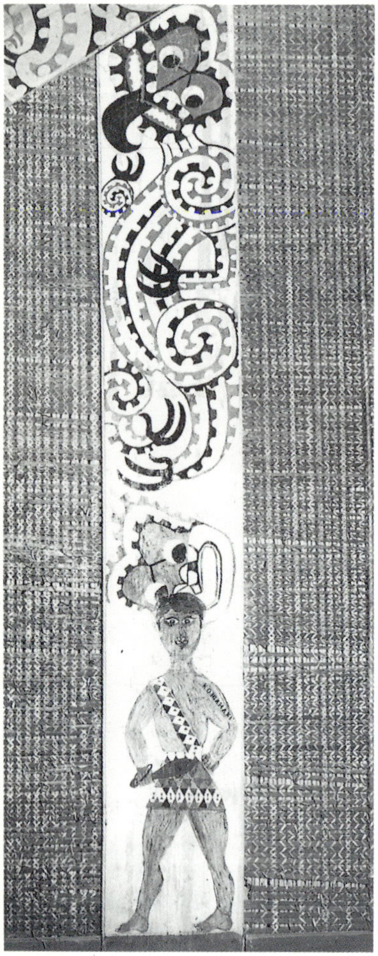

FIGURE 13.12. Upper painted figure showing relationship to earlier *Pitau-a-Manaia* design, above a naturalistic portrait of Mahaki, eponymous ancestor of Te Aitanga-a-Mahaki. Rongopai, 1887. Photograph by R. Neich.

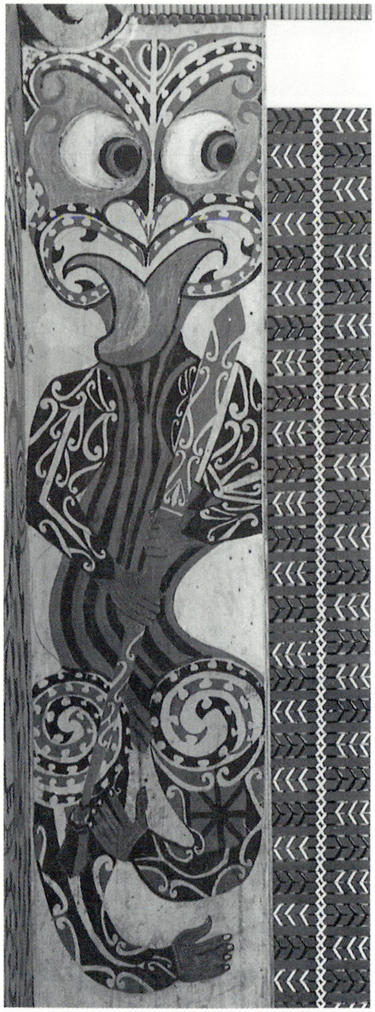

FIGURE 13.13. Painted figure combining carving design, *kowhaiwhai* elements and naturalism into a new synthesis. Rongopai, 1887. Photograph by R. Neich.

giving many people the opportunity to see and absorb the lessons of this new art. From Rongopai the new ideas spread north and south along the coast and inland, inspiring several later houses with similar paintings.

Changing Identities

Rongopai was unique in the wide range of its artistic expression. Later houses were more restrained and limited in the range of their artwork, often being restricted to one of the three major traditions of figurative painting. However, this restriction was frequently linked to a concentrated attempt to produce a more coherent communicative scheme in each house.

In the house Te Poho-o-Rukupo — built at Pakirikiri in Poverty Bay by the Ngati Kaipoho sub-tribe of Rongowhakaata probably at about the same time as Rongopai or perhaps even earlier — all the paintings are restricted to *kowhaiwhai* patterns of very unusual complexity and fine quality. On the interior *poupou* (sidewall posts), ridgepole, and rafters, the *kowhaiwhai* is almost all pure *pitau* series with some rare *kape* elements, in abstract patterns. On the interior end wall panels, on the porch *poupou*, and on the porch rafters there is figurative *kowhaiwhai* in finely detailed *kape* series on certain figures (fig. 13.14) and *pitau* series on others (fig. 13.15). The figurative *kowhaiwhai* of Te Poho-o-Rukupo represents a

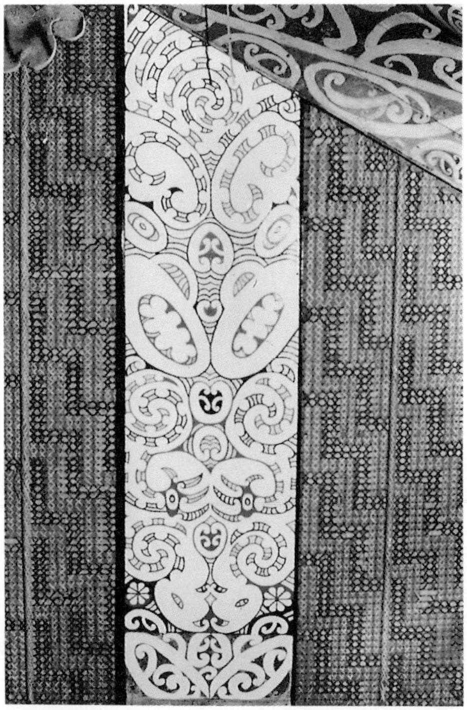

FIGURE 13.14. Figurative *kowhaiwhai* in *kape* series on end wall panel (*epa*) of Te Poho-o-Rukupo, 1887. Photograph by R. Neich.

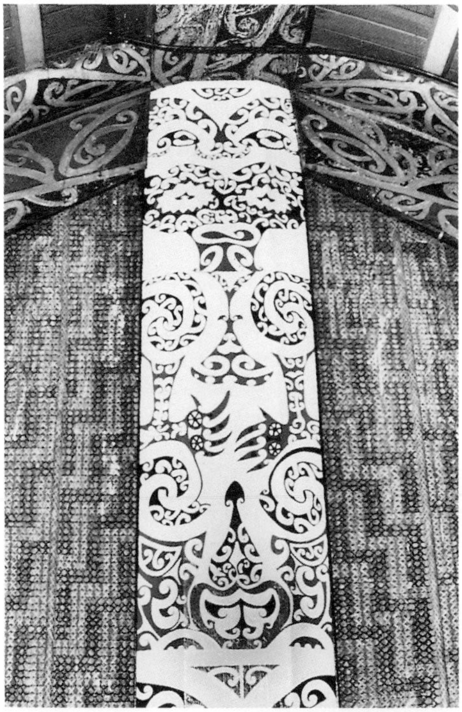

FIGURE 13.15. Figurative *kowhaiwhai* in *pitau* series on interior, front ridgepole support of Te Poho-o-Rukupo, 1887. Photograph by R. Neich.

development somewhat independent of that in Rongopai, owing more to the direct influence of carving figure design. Obviously painted according to a coherent master plan, almost all of these paintings were obliterated by overpainting at some later date and their existence was forgotten, along with the accompanying explanatory narrative.

No modern historical account is necessary to understand the overall plan of the house Te Poho-o-Hinekura, built at Te Kuha near Lake Waikaremoana by the Ngati Hinekura *hapu* (subtribe) of Tuhoe in 1912. Here, the complete scheme of a traditional fully carved meeting house has been transposed into painted figures and painted *tukutuku* (fig. 13.16). The painted figures preserve the surface decoration of carving design and the local Tuhoe style of carved figures. Name labels identify each painted ancestor figure and refer the viewer to well-known traditional stories concerning them. Identity by descent and ancestral interaction remains dominant, to the total exclusion of

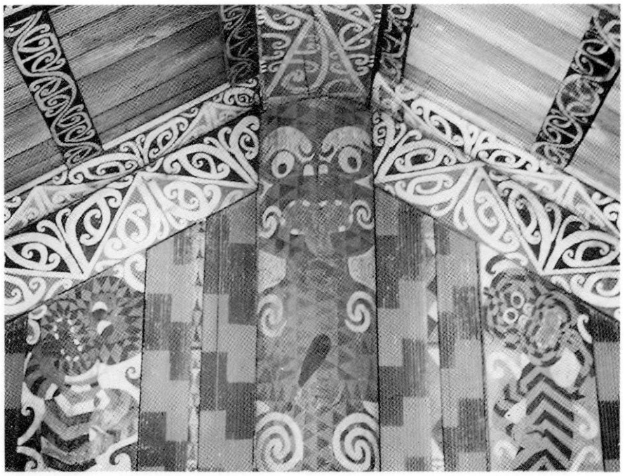

FIGURE 13.16. Interior rear wall showing painted figures and painted *tukutuku*. Te Poho-o-Hinekura, 1912.

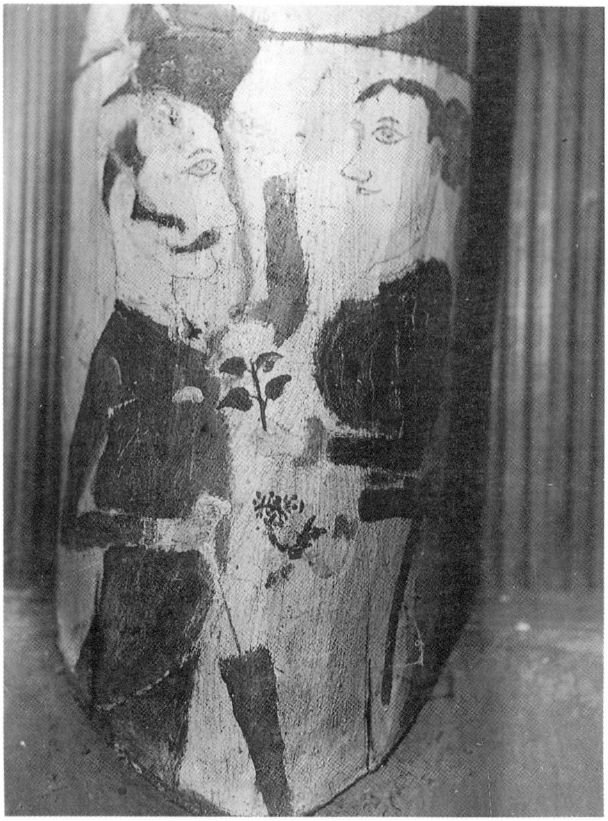

FIGURE 13.17. European settlers painted on lower end of rafter. Tutamure, 1901. Photograph by R. Neich.

modern history.

In contrast with Te Poho-o-Rukupo, with all its figures painted in *kowhaiwhai* elements, and Te Poho-o-Hinekura, with its painted figures reproducing carving types, the house called Tutamure at Omarumutu in the eastern Bay of Plenty contains only naturalistic figures and scenes, painted as small vignettes at the lower end of each rafter (figs. 13.17, 13.18). Built in 1901 by the Ngati Rua *hapu* of Te Whakatohea, this house seems to be basically a celebration of Ngati Rua's arrival in the modern world. Fortunately, Ngati Rua elders have retained a verbal narrative history of this house (Amoamo, Neich, and Tupene, 1984), which explains the paintings as they are viewed in order around the interior of the house. The carvings of the porch relate to the timeless, ever-present world of the ancestors. The doorway separates that world from modern linear history, which is depicted by paintings in the interior of the house. The lintel above the door bears the opening date of the house, the date when Ngati Rua celebrated their transition into modern history. Passing through this threshold, the ridgepole acts as a genealogical mediator linking the ancestors on the porch to their descendants of the modern period at the base of each branching descent line (*heke* or rafter). Hence in Tutamure, identity aboriginally defined by descent is modernized by the incorporation of recent history.

Houses such as Tutamure, for which a complementary verbal narrative has been retained, enable us to gain some understanding of the total communicative scheme of even those meeting houses for which the full verbal narrative is no longer known. In Te Waho-o-te-Rangi, a house at Whangara on the East Coast which dates from around the

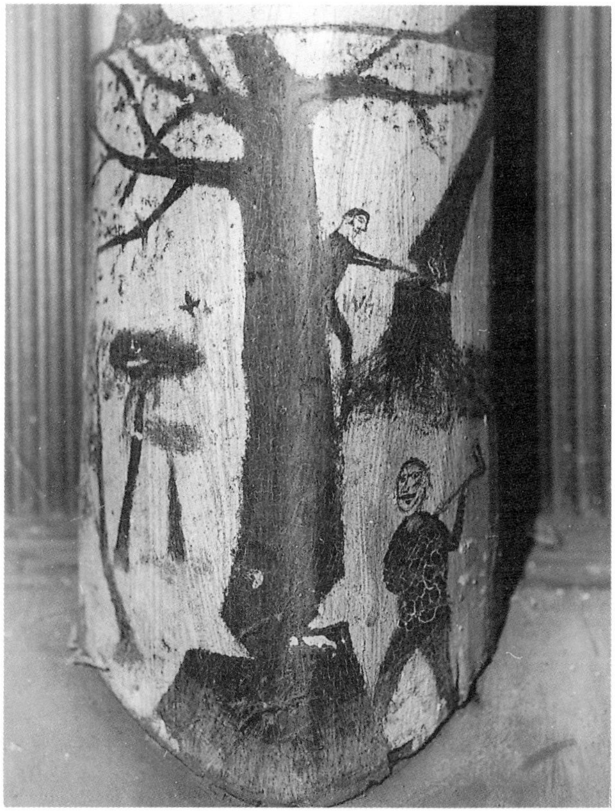

FIGURE 13.18. Tree-felling scene with elements of perspective. Painted on lower rafter end. Tutamure, 1901. Photograph by R. Neich.

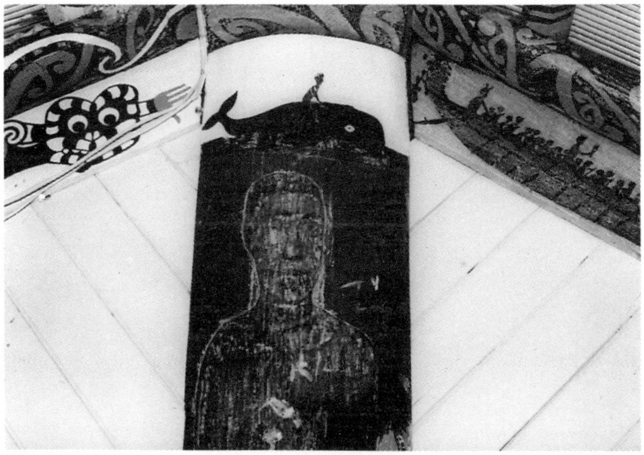

FIGURE 13.19. Interior front wall of Te Waho-o-Te-Rangi, Whangara. Freeze of Paikea and Ruatapu story running above a portrait of a Maori in traditional dress. Photograph by R. Neich.

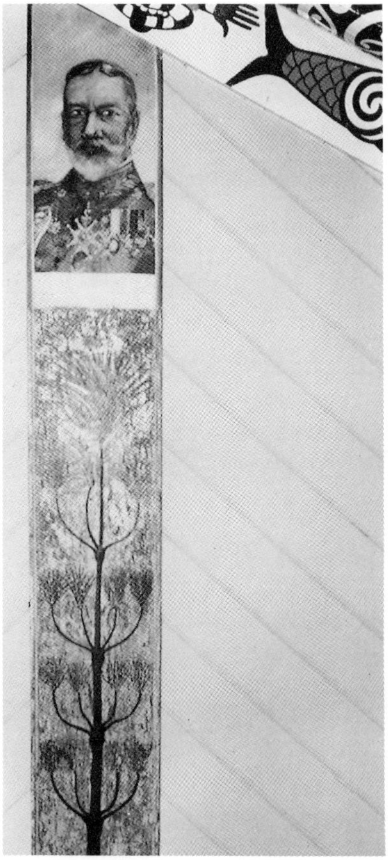

FIGURE 13.20. Portrait of King George of England on rear interior wall of Te Waho-o-Te-Rangi, Whangara. Photograph by R. Neich.

turn of the century, part of the verbal narrative has been lost but a very complex narrative structure is still preserved in the painting scheme. Running around the interior of the house above the *poupou* and up and down the *heke tipi* (fascia board), a continuous freize of naturalistic canoes, a figure riding a whale, and *taniwha* figures tells the famous traditional story of Ruatapu and Paikea (fig. 13.19). Ruatapu had tried to drown his seventy noble brothers by upsetting their canoe, but one named Paikea was saved by a whale and carried to the East Coast, where he eventually settled at Whangara and became the major ancestor of the people of this whole coast. The drowned chiefs are represented by the *taniwha* water monsters, distant derivatives of the *taniwha* painted on the front of the Te Kuiti house Te Tokanganui-a-Noho. Opposing *poupou* inside Te Waho-o-Te-Rangi bear matching pairs of painted trees which obviously refer to the trees painted in the Rongopai house. Then, in a third symbolic opposition, portraits of Maori personages in traditional dress painted on the vertical panels of the interior front wall (fig. 13.19) face portraits of British royalty and a missionary painted on the interior rear wall (fig. 13.20). These opposed paintings must be related to historical developments of significance for the modern identity of the Whangara people, but in the absence of more evidence the specific references cannot now be identified.

These brief analyses emphasize the importance of considering the figurative paintings as an integral element in the overall communicative scheme of each meeting house, instead of just as quaint "folk art" anomalies, as novelties or degraded copies of European art. For each painted house, it is necessary to study the relative positions of all the artwork, including the paintings, within the total scheme of the house in order to appreciate their meaning and significance (fig. 13.21). Each such house is different, with a unique message relating to the local people and their history. The message is more coherently expressed in some than in others, but it now becomes obvious that even a single painting in an otherwise orthodox house is an important element in the message of that house.

The basic communicative scheme of the meeting house may be transformed in many different ways. Apart from its artistic innovations, Te Tokanganui-a-Noho (fig. 13.21) followed essentially the standard traditional scheme of ancestors carved on the *poupou* facing each other across

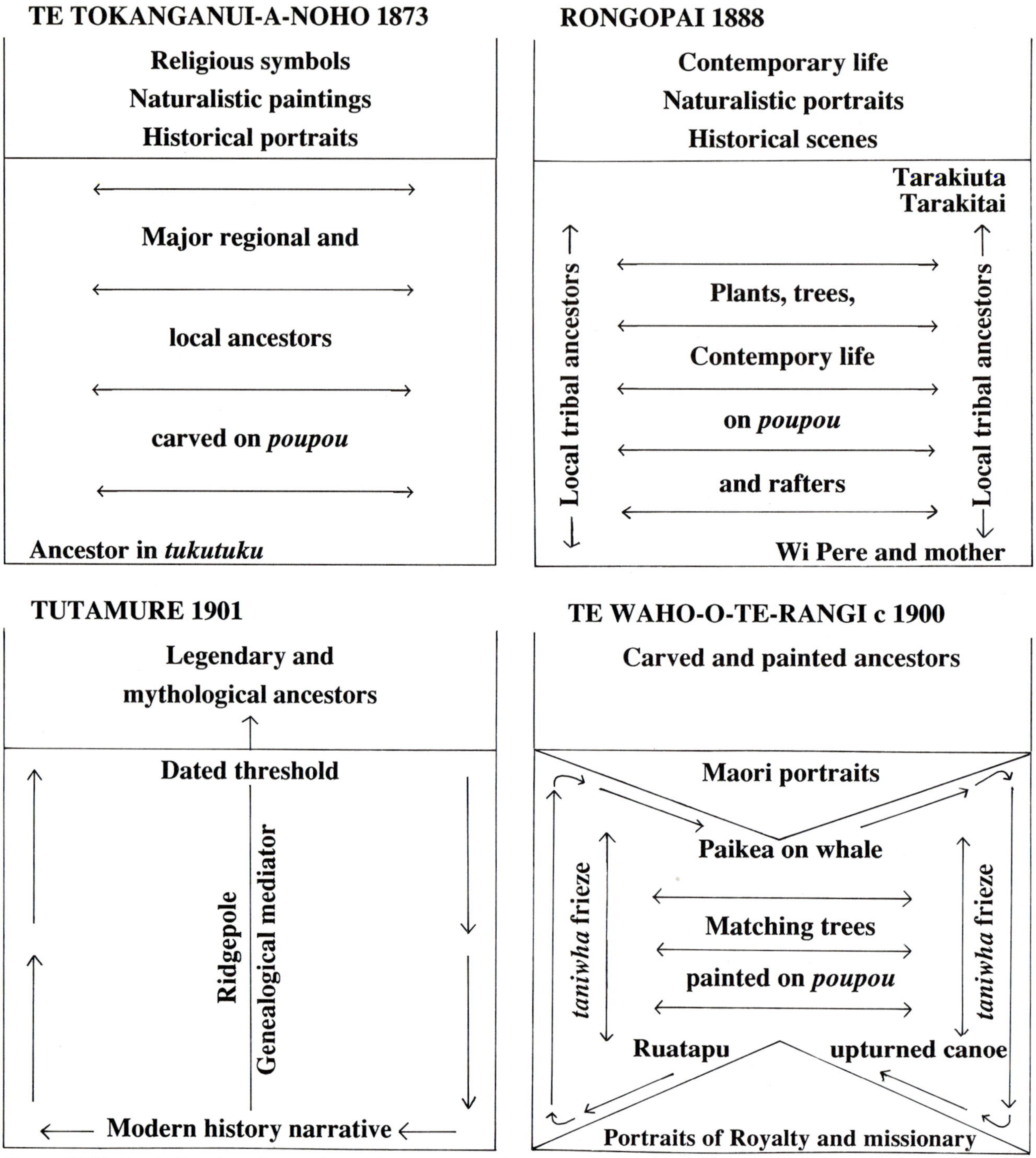

FIGURE 13.21. Symbolic orientations and narrative structure in four meeting houses.

the house, referring independently to their own mythology and legends but not producing a consecutive narrative around the house. The additional paintings on the front refer to the new historical and religious identity not previously indicated on meeting houses. In Rongopai, the opposing ancestors have been transferred to the end walls, facing each other along the length of the house. In their place on the *poupou*, as well as on the rafters of the interior and the porch, uncoordinated painted scenes, trees, and portraits refer to recent historical events and the concerns of tribal life in the 1880s. With the bolder transformations of the basic scheme in houses such as Tutamure and Te Waho-o-Te-Rangi, some of the basic oppositions are retained or transformed, but added to these is a consecutive visual narrative peculiar to each house. The development of a linear view of historical time is especially explicit in Tutamure, where each vignette around the house depicts a particular event or personage in recent tribal history which is also described in a complementary verbal narrative.

These few examples of the range of possible house plans enable some appreciation of the complex and rapidly changing architectural and pictorial language of oppositions and relative positions that was available to the meeting house designer. Each designer manipulated this language in order to communicate his particular message of identity relevant to his people in his time.

Notes

I wish to thank the following people for giving me permission to study their meeting houses and to illustrate them in this paper: Tiwai Amo amo, Ann Brown, Robert Emery, Peter Gibson, Mahanga Horsfall, Uenuku Ihimaera, Rangi Paenga, D'Arcy Ria, Heni Sunderland, Tuhi Tupene, and Bill Wahanui. Barbara Allum was most helpful with arrangements in the Gisborne district.

14

The Eye of the Beholder: A Short History of the Study of Maori Art

ALLAN HANSON AND LOUISE HANSON

This paper grows out of our bibliography of the arts of Oceania (Hanson and Hanson 1984). Having devoted a large part of the last few years to the tedious task of compiling the bibliography, we wanted to test it as a research tool for issues pertaining to Pacific art. Since New Zealand is our area of special interest, and since this volume was prepared in conjunction with the opening of the Maori Exhibition at the Metropolitan Museum of Art, it seems propitious to select Maori art as the focus of the exercise. Not so much Maori art itself as the attention that has been paid to it, for these remarks are intended to sketch a profile of what has been written about Maori art. We begin with a few basic statistics, and then pass to a discussion of trends in interpretation.

A Matter of Numbers

The bibliography contains 6,650 entries on Oceanic art, of which 816 deal exclusively or substantially with Maori art. These consist of books, articles in periodicals and anthologies, museum catalogs, pamphlets, and unpublished theses and dissertations. These 816 items do not exhaust what has been written about Maori art; not included are works that refer to Maori art only in passing, or catalogs and surveys that include Maori art as but one of a number of traditions treated.

Surely an outstanding bibliographic fact in the study of Polynesian art is the degree to which Maori material has dominated the field. The 816 Maori items constitute nearly half (47 percent) of all writings devoted exclusively to Polynesian art listed in the bibliography. The study of Maori art has been largely a New Zealand enterprise: Of the works dealing with Maori art 607, or 74 percent, were published in New Zealand. Two hundred items — nearly one-third of those published in New Zealand and one-quarter of the entire corpus — appeared in *The Journal of the Polynesian Society*, attesting to the difference that a single scholarly journal can make. Only forty-six items, less than 6 percent, were published in languages other than English: twenty-two in German, eleven in Italian, eight in French, four in Maori, and one in Russian.

For the most part, interest in Maori art as judged by number of publications has steadily increased over time. Except for set-backs in the decade between 1910 and 1920 and again in the 1930s and 1940s, a straight line rising at a forty-five degree angle charts the rate of increase in publications on Maori art from the beginnings through the

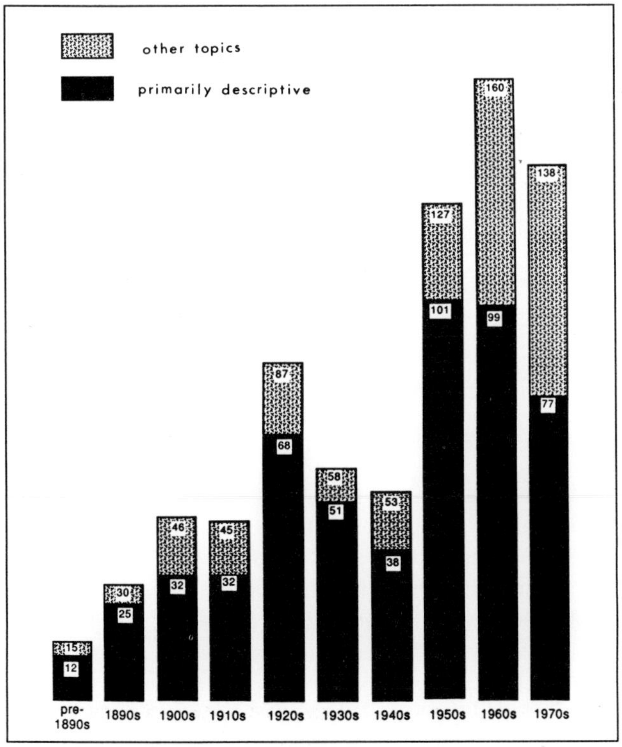

FIGURE 14.1. Publications on Maori art by decade.

1960s (fig. 14.1). Possibly the declines mentioned can be attributed to the diverting effects of the two world wars and the Great Depression. The drop in number of publications during the 1970s, however, demands another explanation.

The rate of publication on Maori art can of course be expected to level off eventually, and perhaps that process has begun in the last couple of decades. Another consideration, however, is in play. The publications for each decade are distinguished in figure 14.1 according to those which are primarily descriptive presentations of particular objects or art genres and those which attempt some sort of analysis beyond description. Through the 1950s the proportion of primarily descriptive works to the whole varied between 70 percent and 88 percent. In the 1960s, however, the total number of publications increased, but primarily descriptive works actually decreased slightly — now constituting just 62 percent of the whole. The same trend continued in the 1970s: The number of analytic works (sixty-one) was identical with that of the 1960s but the number of primarily descriptive works actually decreased so as to represent only 56 percent of the total output.

In other words, the primarily descriptive task of *presenting* Maori art dominated the literature until about 1960, after which increasing attention has been devoted to other topics. Although the total number of publications declined from the 1960s to the 1970s, the decline is entirely attributable to a decrease in primarily descriptive works. Analytic works also tend to be longer than primarily descriptive ones (many of which are a single page, or even a single paragraph), so that while the number of publications decreased in the 1970s it is entirely possible that the number of words or pages devoted to Maori art actually increased.

The shift from mainly descriptive studies of particular objects and art genres (woodcarving, stone pendants, etc.) to other topics in the 1960s and 1970s is the most important recent development in the study of Maori art. The magnitude and significance of that shift can be appreciated by specifying some of the topics that captured the attention of students of Maori art at various times. Before 1900 the very few publications that addressed subjects other than description were distributed among just three concerns: museum collections, motif analysis, and art as it relates to reconstructing Maori prehistory. In contrast, during the 1970s publications treated at least twenty distinct topics: descriptions of exhibitions, tourist art, legislation pertaining to Maori art, socio-economic contexts of art, and many others. The 1950s saw the beginning of instructional articles and manuals, published largely by the New Zealand Department of Education and the primarily-for-Maoris journal *Te Ao Hou*. These developments encouraged the revitalization of traditional art skills. The issue of repatriation of Maori artifacts to New Zealand did not enter the literature until 1975. Another subject of growing interest is the work of specific, named Maori artists. Only two items published before 1960 treated this topic, while thirteen publications focused on it in the 1960s, twelve in the 1970s, and eight in the 1980s up to 1984, when the bibliography was published.

A Matter of Interpretation

Our attention now shifts from statistics to an examination of the questions scholars have asked when they have

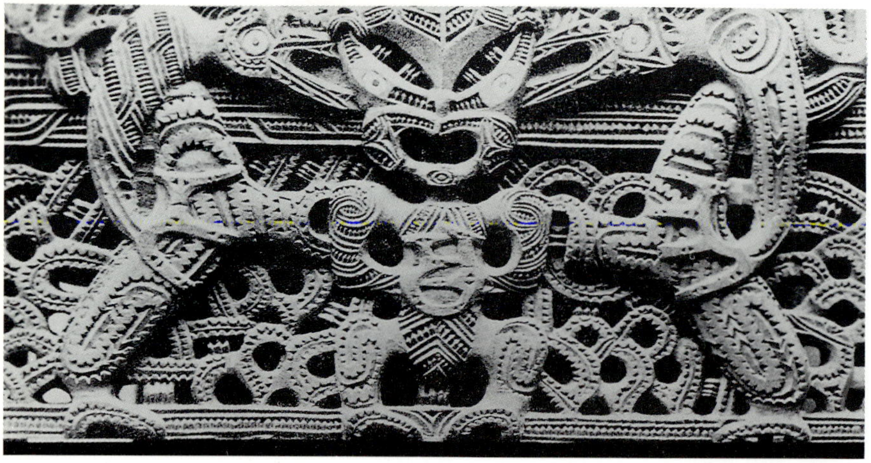

FIGURE 14.2. Threshold (paepae) from carved storehouse Te Oha. Courtesy of the Auckland Institute and Museum.

attempted to explain Maori art. Two basic issues have dominated this field. The larger one, measured by number of publications, is historical — analyses of the origins of art motifs and styles, and the nature of their development over time. The other issue concerns the symbolic meaning of Maori art forms, considered apart from their historical development.

Those concerned with the historical development of Maori art may be divided into the two familiar camps championing diffusion and local development: The one accounts for art forms according to influences originating outside of New Zealand, while the other constructs its analyses in terms of evolution within the country. The controversies between members of these camps are relevant not only to art but to the larger issues of Maori origins and New Zealand prehistory in general.

Authors favoring outside influences predominated during the earlier phase of the scholarly study of Maori art, while in recent years the balance has shifted toward those who look to local development. This, of course, is in line with the general loss of favor of diffusionism in anthropology as a whole, although that persuasion persisted longer in the study of Maori art than it did in the mainstream of British and American social anthropology.

Turn-of-the-century scholars allowed little to restrain their exuberance in locating the origins of Maori art. The common Maori motif of a *manaia* (beaked or profile figure) with its mouth touching the head of a human figure (see fig. 14.2) was linked by Percy Smith to an "idol" of the Queen of Sheba from Aden, in southern Arabia, which

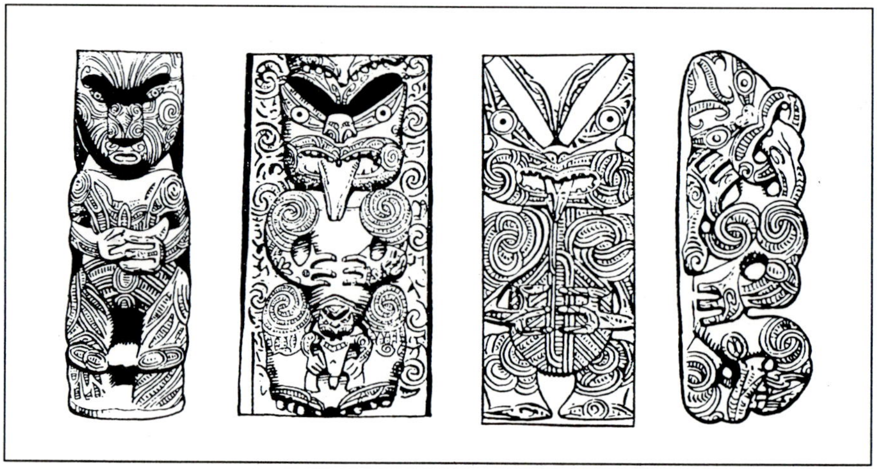

FIGURE 14.3. Carved figures with three-fingered hands. From Archey (1937:12).

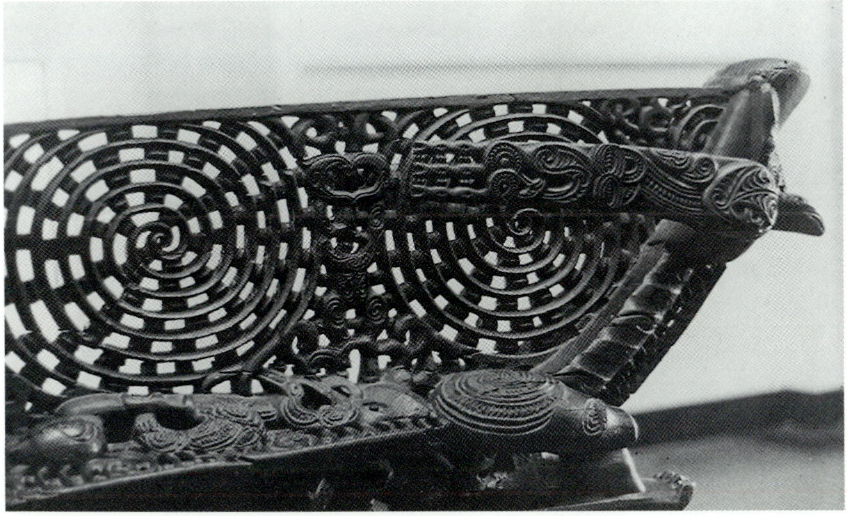

FIGURE 14.4. Canoe (Te Toki a Tapiri) prow. Courtesy of the Auckland Institute and Museum.

portrays a coiled snake with its head to the ear of a human figure (Smith 1917). James Edge-Partington related the same Maori compositional form to the Garden of Eden, claiming that it depicts an "ancient Maori legend of the temptation of woman by the *manaia*" (1900:35). In these matters perhaps no one surpassed Edward Tregear, whose explanation of the much-discussed fact that hands in Maori carvings often have just three fingers (fig. 14.3) spanned half the globe. Carved doors in Tunis feature a three-fingered hand, called "Fatima's Hand," which is supposed in that context to ward off the evil-eye, and he surmised that three-fingered hands in Maori carving were intended to accomplish the same end (Tregear 1920:224).

Again, the origin of the double spiral, so prevalent in Maori art (fig. 14.4), has occasioned a great deal of speculation among interpreters. For Tregear it is a version of the swastika. He imagined that since the swastika is throughout the world a symbol of the sun, the presence of the spiral in Maori art confirms that the Maoris were sun-worshippers. The spiral is also associated in Maori culture with the cobweb, linking up with an ancient Chinese propitious symbol of a cobweb formed around a swastika, and also with an association in Indo-European mythology between spiders and the sun. Add to all this the fact that ships in ancient India would carry the swastika as a sign of good luck, and for Tregear the meaning of the spiral on Maori war canoes was clear:

> If, then, two thousand four hundred years ago ships were afloat on the seas of Asia bearing the sign of the sun-god as an emblem of "good fortune," is it at all curious that a maritime people like the sun-worshipping Maoris should give their warships a benediction by carving on the bow-piece a symbol known in ancient times all over the world? (Tregear 1899:293)

It was not long, however, before the quest for outside influences on Maori art was disciplined by a few crucial issues. Paramount among these was the question of style in Maori art. Scholars were in agreement that the Maoris originally came to New Zealand from Polynesian islands to the north: the Societies, the Marquesas, or the Southern Cooks. Art in those islands is much more restricted than in New Zealand, figures tend to be small and intricate and the style is rectilinear. How, then, can the profuse and elaborate Maori art, with its bold, curvilinear style, be explained? Corollaries to this fundamental issue were questions about the origin of certain motifs, such as the spiral (the quintessential element of Maori curvilinear style) and the *manaia*.

One early strategy for dealing with these issues was to posit a pre-Maori population for New Zealand. This view, championed primarily by Percy Smith and Elsdon Best, has some support from Maori traditional history. The aboriginal inhabitants were Melanesian, they coexisted and intermarried with the Polynesian Maoris for a time (their traces are still visible in the Maori population), but eventually the Maoris rose up and exterminated them.

These inferior, dark-skinned, shifty-eyed Maruiwi, as Best called them, were responsible for the curvilinear style in Maori art, such a style being quite visible in their Melanesian homeland. Indeed, Best found the Maruiwi most convenient as an explanation for any element of Maori culture that was not readily attributable to Polynesian roots, and especially so for customs which in his eyes were beneath the dignity of the more nearly Caucasian Polynesians, such as large-scale cannibalism (Best 1915).

The notion of a pre-Maori, Melanesian population in New Zealand did not long survive, but the similarities between certain Maori art motifs and those in parts of Melanesia continued to demand explanation. H. D. Skinner was particularly intrigued by the fact that the spiral and curvilinear representations of the human form, so characteristic of Maori art, are also found in New Guinea, the Admiralties, and New Ireland (Skinner 1924:241). Together with Terrence Barrow, Skinner was also convinced that many *manaia* figures in Maori art represent birds, and this led them both to suspect connections between Maori culture and bird cults in Easter Island and the Solomons (Skinner 1974; Barrow 1956:317-19, 1967). The problem was to account for how Maori art could have so much in common with art in parts of the Pacific where historical connections with Maori culture are distant (New Guinea, other parts of Melanesia), while it has so little in common with the rectilinear style of the Polynesian islands with which historical connections are much closer.

Skinner's suggested explanation is that the Maori curvilinear style and resonances of a bird cult are actually older than the rectilinear styles of island Polynesia (Skinner 1924, 1951). When the Polynesians entered Oceania by way of Indonesia and the Philippines, they carried a curvilinear art style with its deepest roots apparently in China and India and shared by many Pacific peoples. This style, and a belief in the religious importance of birds, characterized the Polynesians as they settled Samoa and Tahiti and up to the time when various groups migrated from Tahiti to settle the Marquesas, Hawaii, Easter Island, and New Zealand in the eleventh to fourteenth centuries. To a greater or lesser degree (in the case of New Zealand, greater) these marginal areas of Polynesia retained elements of the original culture. "It may be," Skinner conjectures, "that Maori art stands very close to the art of the undivided Polynesian people when they had reached only the western borders of the Pacific" (1924:241). Hence the birdman cult of Easter Island, the appearance of birds in Maori rock art and the *manaia* motif are interpreted as remnants of the ancient bird cult, another vestige of which is the belief of the Solomon Islanders that the souls of warriors and chiefs become birds.

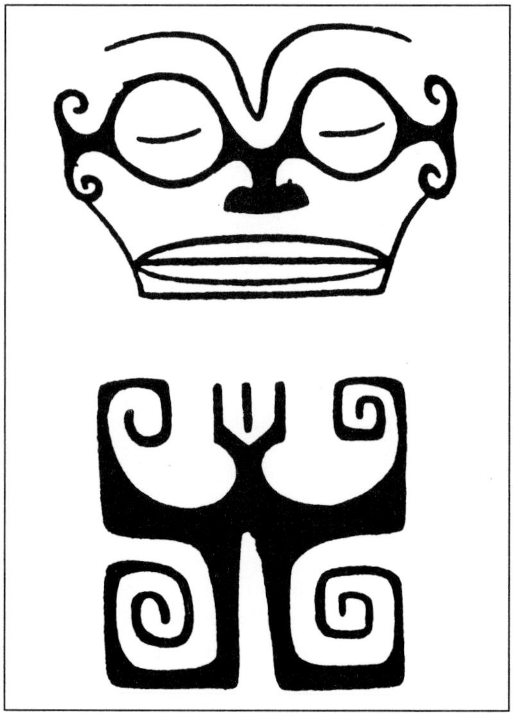

FIGURE 14.5. Curvilinear representation of the human figure in Polynesia. From Archey (1960:22).

This reasoning also accounts for the curvilinear style in Maori art, which shares, for example, the spiral (a motif so ancient that its roots can be traced back to India, Persia, and ultimately to Egypt) with the Sepik region of Papua New Guinea. Some remnants of the spiral and a curvilinear rendering of the human form may also be found in the Marquesas Islands, another part of Skinner's marginal Polynesia (fig. 14.5). But in Tahiti and other parts of central Polynesia, *after* the Maoris and other migrants had departed, art diminished and the original curvilinear style gave way to rectilinear forms. By this reasoning, Skinner is able to acknowledge a close historical connection of Maori society with the Polynesian islands to the north of New Zealand, but at the same time to maintain a still closer

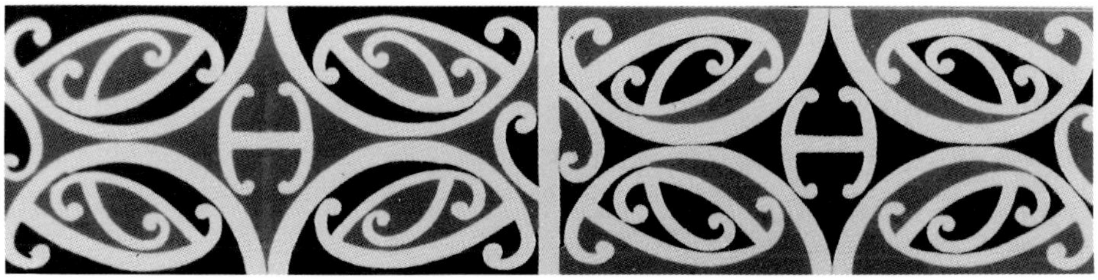

FIGURE 14.6. Rafter pattern (*kowhaiwhai*). From Hamilton (1901, rafter pattern design No.22.)

artistic affinity with certain parts of Melanesia.

Polynesian prehistory as reconstructed by Te Rangi Hiroa (Peter H. Buck) differs from Skinner's theory, and it generates a markedly different understanding of art. According to Hiroa, the Polynesian migration from Southeast Asia passed through Micronesia, bypassing Melanesia to the north. The sojourn of the Polynesians in Micronesia impoverished them culturally, leaving them with arts and crafts at the level of atoll dwellers when they arrived in the Society Islands. After the dispersal of Polynesians from the Societies, the various island cultures developed in diverse ways. In the Societies and nearby islands a rectilinear art style emerged, while in New Zealand art took curvilinear forms (Hiroa 1950:325-29).

With this theory we turn from the camp proposing outside influences as the outstanding factor in the history of Maori art to that advocating local development in New Zealand. Barrow (1956:314) finds explanations by local development unsatisfying because they obviously cannot meaningfully address the parallels between Maori art and that from other parts of the Pacific. Hiroa retorts that, so far as bird cults are concerned, beliefs in the Solomon Islands were concerned with the frigate bird, the Easter Island cult with the egg of the sooty tern, and that there is no evidence of a bird cult ever having existed in New Zealand. Therefore it is highly questionable to link any of these ethnographic facts together, to tie the *manaia* to any bird cult, or even to suggest that the figure represents a bird (Hiroa 1950:312-13). However one may react to these arguments, the bibliographic fact is that (the archaeological literature aside) publications tracing outside influences on Maori art have significantly diminished in recent years while those concerned with local development have been on the increase.

Studies of outside influences and local development pose significantly different problems. Those who are concerned with outside influences have the tasks of identifying similarities which exist between Maori and other art traditions and then developing plausible theories for how those similarities might have resulted from historical contacts. Advocates of local development face a different challenge. Basically, it is to demonstrate *how* the development might have occurred: to hypothesize the origins of styles and motifs and to reconstruct convincing developmental sequences. The first part of this research program was pursued in a more or less piecemeal fashion for some time. Herbert Williams suggested that the various *koru* patterns (bulbed stalks or scrolls) in rafter painting (fig. 14.6) are derived from natural forms such as fern fronds, other sorts of leaves, and the hammerhead shark (Hamilton 1901:118). The origin of the spiral has been of continuing interest to students of Maori art. Augustus Hamilton (1901:11) and Hiroa (1950:327-28) find it in the fern frond; Macmillan Brown postulated its source as the sailor's coiled rope (1907). William Phillipps, noting that the Maori spiral is normally double, locates its origin in another art motif: two interlocking *koru* (1955:19-22). But the first person to address the issue of local development in a systematic way, attempting to delineate evolutionary sequences of design as well as the origins of motifs, was Gilbert Archey.

About the only thing that Archey recognizes as shared between Maori art and that of the rest of Polynesia is style grounded in the representation of the human figure. But this common basis was developed and elaborated in a variety of ways in different parts of Polynesia, and Archey's dominant interest was to reconstruct the process in New Zealand. As he did so, Archey's orientation tended toward an "art for art" point of view. That is to say, he was not much concerned with relating Maori art to historical developments or other extra-artistic considerations of Maori culture. Instead, his explanations of development were largely internal to the artistic process itself, such as his argument that the human form became conventional-

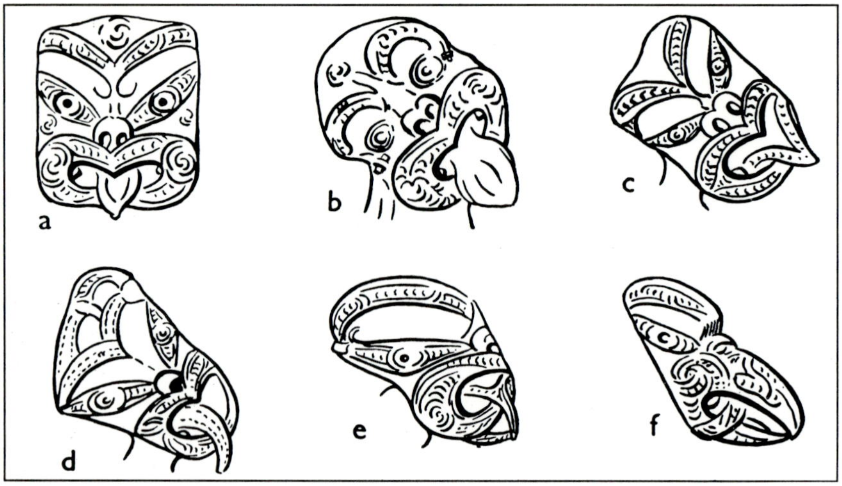

FIGURE 14.7. Facial compositions. From Archey (1960:10).

ized and elaborated in a curvilinear direction in Maori art because of the happy coincidence of soft woods and hard stone in New Zealand which liberated the carver, whereas it became conventionalized and simplified in a rectilinear direction in central Polynesia because the technical conditions were less propitious there (1933:186). Moreover, in Archey's work the aesthetic qualities of art and the creativity of the artist become much greater considerations than had been the case with previous students. His general view is that an art tradition begins with representations of familiar objects, but that as it develops artists become increasingly interested in exploring the aesthetic potentials of the forms they use. In the process, naturalistic representation gives way to increasingly conventionalized, abstract forms (Archey 1965:44-46).

Archey's main goal is to demonstrate how this process affected the presentation of the human figure in Maori art. His technique is to present several objects in an ordered series which depict each step of his postulated developmental sequence. Thus he traces representations of the human head and face from naturalistic depictions to the highly conventionalized *tiki* forms of rafter support posts, storehouse thresholds and side panels, and canoe wash-strakes (Archey 1967). Another such series has to do with the controversial *manaia* motif (fig. 14.7). His argument is that the *manaia* depicts neither a bird nor a reptile, but derives actually from the human form presented in profile (Archey 1933:172-73; 1936:49-54; 1960). He is supported in this by J. M. McEwen (1966), who demonstrates that each of the basic *tiki* or full-faced human forms in Maori art has its associated *manaia* form, which is simply half of the *tiki* face. Hence the *tiki* face can be understood as a form executed in split representation, composed of two profile *manaia* forms.

Fig. 14.8 about here

According to Archey, even the spiral is ultimately derived from the human form. He argues by means of another series (fig. 14.8) that the spiral may be understood as the result of progressive conventionalization of forms that depict interlocking *manaia* jaws (1933:179-82, 1936:59-62, 1960).

Archey has received less support for his interpretation of the spiral than for that of the *manaia*, and for a reason that is methodologically critical to his whole approach. McEwen claims that it is not possible to determine if the spiral results from interlocking *manaia* jaws or if their relationship is the reverse — Maori carvers exploring the motif of interlocking *manaia* jaws because of their prior familiarity with the spiral (1966). Page Rowe generalizes the point, suggesting that many of Archey's sequences "may just as reasonably start from the other end" (1935:121). In one place Archey does argue for the temporal development of his sequences (1936:59-61), but in a later publication he states that the progression is stylistic but not necessarily evolutionary (1967:229, see also 1962:273). Yet obviously the chronological aspect of the matter is crucial, because if Archey is going to claim that the local development in Maori art forms occurred in a

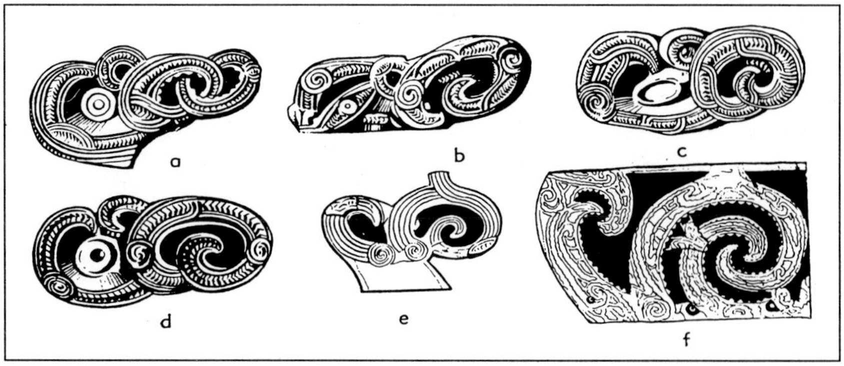

FIGURE 14.8. Archey's suggested sequence for the development of the double spiral. From Archey (1937:13).

certain way, he must be able to establish that the forms at the beginning of his sequences antedate those at the end of it.

This issue is of major concern to Sidney Mead in one of the most recent contributions to the debate about local development of the classical Maori art style (1975). Carefully surveying the available archaeological and historical information, Mead was able to deal impressively with the major problems in the development of Maori art. As with Archey, Mead presents progressions of forms — in combs, tattooing, textile decoration, and woodcarving — but unlike Archey, Mead's progressions are firmly linked to history. Therefore one has reason to believe that the initial forms actually do precede the later forms in the sequences. Mead's progressions reveal basic trends in the development of Maori art in New Zealand: From intricate, rectilinear patterns to bold, curvilinear ones. Most interestingly, Mead links these observations to an issue that Archey hardly mentions: Historical developments in Maori social and political life such as population movements and conquests within New Zealand that relate to the period of the legendary "Great Fleet" and the attendant reshuffling of priorities in genealogy and values relative to the past. Thus, for the first time, Mead interprets the local development of Maori art in a way that relates it to the history of Maori culture in general.

So far the discussion has been concerned with the development of classical Maori art: the art as it existed at the point of early European contact and settlement in the late eighteenth and early nineteenth centuries. Recently a new interest has surfaced, concerning the history of Maori art during the latter nineteenth and twentieth centuries. One early and gloomy precursor is a 1924 paper by George Pitt-Rivers. The art he observed during a visit to a small Maori village on the Wanganui River was in a state of decay. And little wonder, because art expresses the fundamental meaning and values of culture. When these are destroyed, as he thought was the case in Maori culture, then art must collapse as well (Pitt-Rivers 1924:64-65).

But, of course, Maori meanings and values have not been lost and Maori art persists. A growing literature addresses the revival of Maori art and culture inspired by Apirana Ngata and and other leaders, as well as the work of contemporary artists such as Para Matchitt and Cliff Whiting. Moreover, papers presented at the Second and Third International Symposia on the Arts of Oceania treated the influence of European patrons on woodcarving, changing relationships between tattooing and social status, and sociopolitical meanings of meeting house art, all in the period since the mid nineteenth century (Neich 1983 and this volume; Simmons 1983; Kernot 1983; Mead, this volume).

Although never as numerous as historical studies, inquiries into the symbolic meaning of Maori art have been published at a fairly regular rate throughout this century. They may be divided into three categories according to their perceptions of how Maori art conveys its meanings: iconographically, by means of more or less arbitrary signs, and by connotation and formal homology.

Most studies fall under the first category. The basic reasoning here is that an art object represents— is a picture of — something, and its meaning may be found in what it represents. From this perspective, of course, the researcher's mandate is to discover just what various art objects depict. We have already met some studies of this sort, such as Skinner's and Barrow's argument that the

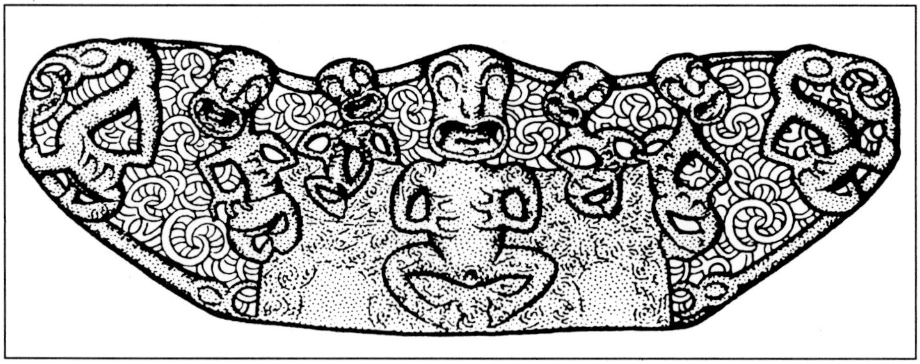

FIGURE 14.9. Hauraki lintel. From Archey (1960:16).

manaia form represents a bird or bird-man, and their further claims that this signified the presence of a bird cult, or at least important religious beliefs pertaining to birds, either in New Zealand or in the Maoris' pre-New Zealand cultural heritage.

Interpreting the *manaia* has always been one of the most engaging pastimes in the study of Maori art. Sidney Mead takes the form to have its origin in a "reptile-like monster" and suggests that Maori artists used it to depict land and sea monsters, guardian animals, and other spirit beings (1975:178, 204). Hamilton embraces both avian and saurian theses. Of the numerous sorts of *manaia*, "probably the snake form with the eagle's head is one of the most interesting, carrying us back to some of the older mythologies" (Hamilton 1901:6). William Phillipps was told that the flanking *manaia* figures on Taranaki door lintels represented the ghost of the lintel's central, human figure (Phillipps 1939). One of the most interesting interpretations of the meaning of the *manaia*, or rather, of door lintels in general, is that of Michael Jackson. Noting that some lintels have, in the spaces between the central human figure and the terminal *manaia*, what looks like disjointed heads, arms, and legs, he suggests that the lintels depict the decomposition of the central human figure and the recomposition of that same figure at the sides, but now in the *manaia* form. That in turn may be taken to represent the individual's dual roles in society: as a tribal, public figure and as a domestic, private figure. The transition between these roles occurs when he passes beneath the lintel (Jackson 1972).

Mythological allusions were most congenial to Percy Smith, who searched for iconography in Maori art as one might look for meaning in the stained glass windows of European churches, anticipating that they will depict some central event in a story or myth. He interprets the Hauraki lintel (fig. 14.9) as illustrating mythically based ideas about death: The obviously female central figure is Hine-nui-te-po, personification of death, and the small figures to either side of her are "human spirits in the process of being drawn into 'the-great-lady-of-night' as was the hero Maui when he attempted to destroy death on earth" (Smith 1919).

A remarkable iconographic interpretation of a Maori art form was contributed by a medical doctor, Charles O. Bechtol (1967). No Gilbert Archey, Bechtol is of the opinion that art forms are utterly faithful representations of natural objects. When he beheld Maori greenstone pendants (*hei-tiki*), he took them to be realistic depictions of human infants with as many as seven gross congenital deformities ranging from clubbed feet to cleft palates and severely misshapen heads (fig. 14.10). What effect, he muses, would the birth of such a being have on a superstitious people like the ancient Maoris? Granted that so multi-deformed a birth would be upsetting to almost anyone, Bechtol does not explain why the Maoris would want to start a tradition of making faithful representations of it and wearing them as ornaments.

A few interpreters of Maori art have understood it to be an esoteric language, each object being a combination of a great many information-packed signs not unlike hieroglyphics. The first student of Maori art, a missionary named Thomas Kendall who labored in New Zealand in the 1820s, falls into this category. He detected in Maori carving an expression of mythology and, beyond that, metaphysics. Carvings with three figures signified creation, that is, existence and imperfection. *Manaia* forms represented birds or, when they symbolized the passage of time, the sun and the moon. Lame figures might also

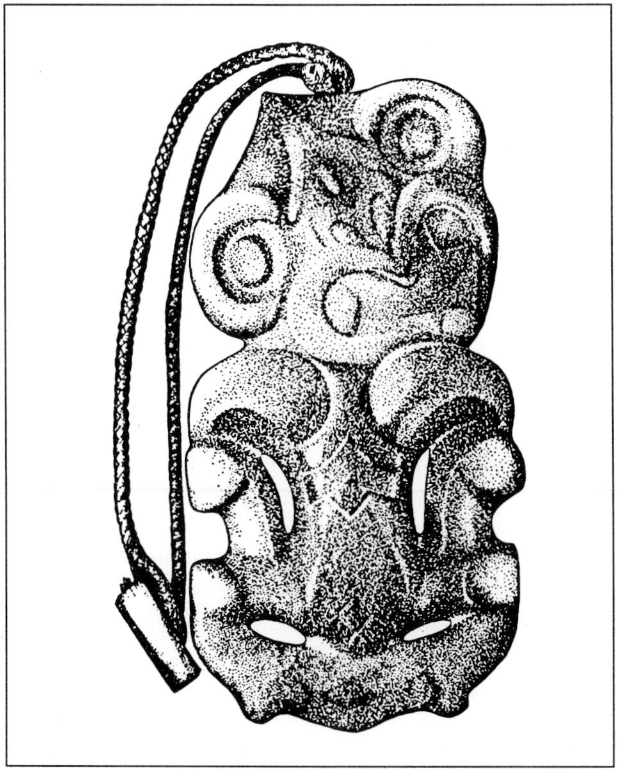

FIGURE 14.10. Greenstone pendant (*hei tiki*). From Archey (1937:15).

represent time, the crippled leg referring to the past and the sound leg to the present. A round knob carved between two fingers denoted man caught in the undifferentiated, prenatal First State of existence (Binney 1980:8, 11, 12, 20-21).

The other main example of this approach is the incredible book *Maori Symbolism*, recorded by the law court reporter Ettie Rout on the basis of information supplied by "an Arawa noble," Hohepa Te Rake. The claim here is that each example of woodcarving, tattooing, or other Maori art forms is a text. Its signs consist of every small groove, line, or curl in the entire composition. Its message may deal with any number of topics, such as exhorting the maintenance of Race Culture and Sacred Health Lore, glorifying the organs of reproduction as perpetrators of the Race, extolling the Maori intellectual aristocracy of Scientists, Doctors, Teachers, Lawyers, Architects, and Artists, or tracing the 6,630-year history during which the Maoris moved out of Assyria, through Europe and across the Atlantic to Mexico, Peru, and then across the Pacific to New Zealand.

David Simmons is currently engaged in a serious resurrection of the iconographic symbolism forwarded by Thomas Kendall. This knowledge was highly esoteric, according to Simmons, being imparted only in Maori schools (*whare wananga*) of the very highest level. Kendall was made privy to the sacred lore by two chiefs, Kiwikiwi and his half-brother Whareumu. Now that such Maori schools are becoming rare, restrictions shrouding the symbolism of carving have eased and the esoteric knowledge has been conveyed to Simmons by Te Riria and the Ahupiri Council, who have certified the accuracy of the text he published (Simmons 1985:19-24, see also Simmons 1986). Simmons' revelations have met with skepticism, however, on the basis of doubts about Kendall's knowledge, questions as to how such a complete system of iconography could have survived for nearly two centuries with so few people being aware of it, the probability of tribal variations in these matters, and the possible impact of Christian ideas. Moreover, few scholars other than Simmons seem to know of Te Riria and the Ahupiri Council of the United Tribes (Shirres 1987).

More recently efforts have been made to identify meaning in Maori art forms not so much by what they depict or denote as by more general relationships of formal composition or connotation. Working primarily with rafter paintings (*kowhaiwhai*), tattooing patterns, and woodcarving, Allan Hanson has suggested that compositional structures of dualism, symmetry, and near-symmetry in art convey messages about the Maori view of reality which are also conveyed by homologous forms in mythology and folklore, proverbs, and patterns of social and political relations (Hanson 1983a, 1983b, 1985). Roger Neich has noted that Maori carvers used an "aspective" style which represents their subjects (often ancestors) not as they would be seen from a particular viewpoint and at a particular moment in time (as is the case for much of Western art) but as ageless ideals. This mode of representation connotes the traditional Maori concept of time in general as organized around concrete events rather being an abstract continuum in its own right, and as containing "the timeless ever-present world of the ancestors" (Neich 1983:248-49; see also Neich, this volume).

All Things to All People

We will conclude with some remarks about one of the

most remarkable objects of Maori art: a woodcarving found around 1920 in a swamp near Kaitaia, in the northern part of the North Island, and now housed in the Auckland Institute and Museum (fig. 14.11). Beyond the fact that the Kaitaia carving is universally appreciated as aesthetically stunning, or more likely because of it, nearly every major scholar concerned with the interpretation of Maori art has seen in this carving evidence for his own pet theories. Percy Smith, who liked to think of art objects as illustrations of stories, suggested that the Kaitaia carving might represent the mythological Pou who, after travelling to Hawaiki in quest of sweet potato seed tubers, returned to New Zealand on the back of a great bird (1921:93).

H. D. Skinner was an early and frequent contributor to the literature on the Kaitaia carving. In a note appended to Smith's announcement of its discovery (1921:93-95), Skinner took the position that the terminal figures on the Kaitaia carving are *manaia* only slightly extended from the classic bird head and human body of that form. That constituted evidence of a connection between New Zealand and the Solomon Islands, where frigate birds were of religious significance and the bird-man figure appears in art. In later articles (1921, 1922) Skinner changed his identification of the terminal figures from bird-headed figures to reptiles. This led to a shift of long-distance connections from the Solomon Islands to Easter Island, because on Easter Island carved lizards would be put on either side of a door on ceremonial occasions and an object like the Kaitaia carving, as a door lintel, would associate lizards with the house on a permanent basis. However, the notion that the Kaitaia carving was a door lintel sat uneasily with Skinner when he realized that, unlike lintels, the Kaitaia carving was carved on both sides. His discovery of an object from Borneo with some forms somewhat like those of the Kaitaia carving, which was also carved on both sides and which served as the combing on the roof of a burial shrine, led him to assign the same function to the Kaitaia carving and to claim artistic and cultural links between Borneo and New Zealand (Skinner 1924). Human figures similar to that on the Kaitaia carving, carved on an object (fig. 14.12) from the Society Islands, Australs, or Cooks confirmed Skinner in the opinion that the art tradition stretching back as far as Borneo had its representatives in other parts of Polynesia as well as New Zealand (Skinner 1931). Further evidence for this position came from turtle-shell work from the Marquesas with chevrons that bear similarities both to the Kaitaia carving and to objects from central and northern Melanesia (1931, 1974). Despite his shifting interpretations of the terminal figures as birds or reptiles and the varying locales (always, however, outside of New Zealand) to which he links it, the Kaitaia carving constantly certifies Skinner's steady belief that Maori art and culture are part of an extensive tradition which may be plotted throughout the Pacific, back to Southeast Asia, and beyond.

Gilbert Archey finds in the Kaitaia carving still more evidence of the ubiquitousness of the human form as a basis for Maori carving designs, interpreting the sweeping chevrons as stylizations of bent arms or legs (1960:17-18). While most scholars consider the Kaitaia carving to be an ancient example of Maori art, Archey holds that it could as well be late as early. If it were late, its divergences from other Maori art would exemplify Archey's notions about particularly gifted artists pushing ahead in their own creative directions, perhaps in this case even to the point of surpassing the understanding and appreciative capacity of their audience (1960:18, 1962:281). We suspect that the terminal figures of the Kaitaia carving constitute another reason why Archey thinks that the carving may be recent

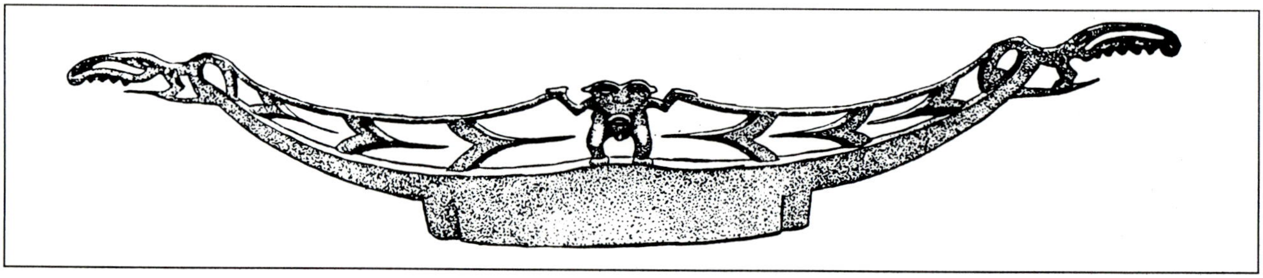

FIGURE 14.11. Kaitaia carving. From Archey (1937:11)

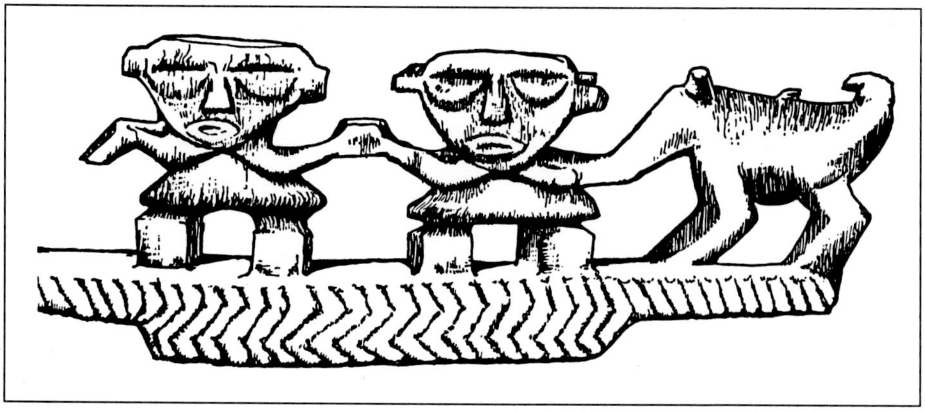

FIGURE 14.12. Society Islands wood carving. From Archey (1965:11).

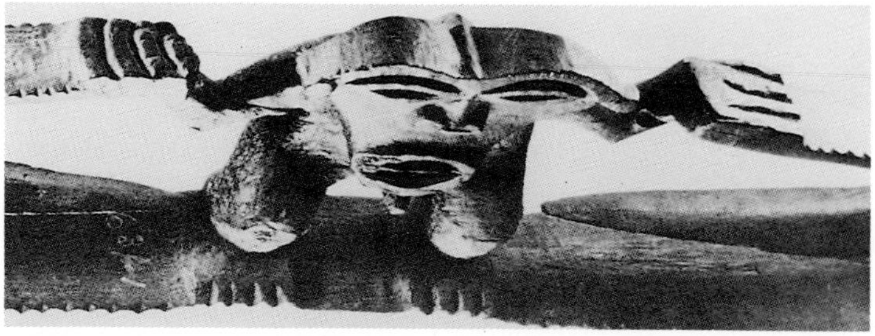

FIGURE 14.13. Detail of the Kaitaia carving. From Archey (1977:30)

rather than ancient. The figures would have to be classified as *manaia*, but they appear more animal and less human than almost any other *manaia* in the entire corpus of Maori art. On Archey's theory of the *manaia* having its roots in the human form, those of the Kaitaia carving would therefore have to be considered as extreme conventionalizations of the motif, and that would imply that the carving is a late product.

For Te Rangi Hiroa, on the other hand, the Kaitaia carving is very old — an example of the sort of art practiced by the Maoris not long after their arrival from the Polynesian islands to the north (1950:326). If this is true, then its rectilinear form (seen particularly in the treatment of the central human figure) would confirm Hiroa's theory that the distinctively curvilinear style of Maori art is a product of local development in New Zealand from the rectilinear style of the first migrants. Sidney Mead is in essential agreement with Hiroa (Mead 1975:199-206). The Kaitaia carving finds an early place in Mead's reconstruction of the shift from rectilinear to curvilinear styles in Maori art. The chevrons are especially interesting as a transitional form which has rectilinear origins as a straight-sided V shape but shows definite movement in a curvilinear direction. In later stages the chevron diminishes in importance relative to more purely curvilinear motifs such as the spiral, but chevrons still survive as notches in surface decoration. Mead's view of the terminal figures of the Kaitaia carving is also interesting. They are not really *manaia*, he argues, but early non-human forms in a progression of which the *manaia* was the end result. Mead recognizes that this turns Archey's line of development on its head, in that now the evolution of the *manaia* begins with an animal form and moves in a humanizing direction rather than having its genesis in the human form.

And finally, the Kaitaia carving satisfies Hanson's rage for symmetry and imaginative means of breaking symmetry in Maori art (fig. 14.13). The latter is accomplished in subtle ways in the positioning of the carving's terminal figures as well as in the rendition of the central figure's hands (Hanson 1983a:215). It would certainly appear that, as with other great works of art, the Kaitaia carving is truly inexhaustible.

15

Relic and Trophy Arrays as Art Among the Mountain-Ok, Central New Guinea

BARRY CRAIG

Once one's eyes have adjusted to the gloomy interiors of the small houses of the Mountain-Ok people of central New Guinea, it is possible to distinguish an accumulation of animal bones and soot-encrusted string bags on the back wall, facing the tiny doorway. These displays include rows of pig jaw bones, pig skulls, leg and pelvis bones of cassowaries, jawbones of many species of marsupials and rodents, an occasional crocodile skull or python skeleton or skull and, in the string bags, various human bones, including jawbones and skulls.

For a long while, I considered these arrays of ancestral human relics and animal trophies merely as materials connected with the cult of ancestors, and not conveyors of meaning in their own right. But then, in 1972, I saw a recently installed array of relics and trophies in a men's house of the Fegolmin and was struck by its symmetry and order. I asked about it and the information I was given prompted me to write in my notes: "The arrangement seems to be aesthetically pleasing and expresses the spatial relations of man, taro and the animals in his environment which are of particular concern to him as a food source."

Since then I have pondered this further, examined other arrays, and come to the conclusion that the arrays are models of the Mountain-Ok universe, often ecologically based models, and that they are, in their own right, works of art. This paper provides the evidence and reasoning that has led me to this conclusion.

The Mountain-Ok

The Mountain-Ok are people belonging to several tribes distinguished from their neighbors by their languages (Mountain-Ok sub-family, Trans-New Guinea phylum) and a common culture. They live in the highlands dividing the headwaters of the Fly and Sepik rivers, and on the slopes to the north and south, west of the Strickland Gorge as far as the Sibil Valley in Irian Jaya (fig. 15.1).

Their settlement and gardens are sparsely distributed through a chain of mid-montane highland valleys, along the ridgetops and valleys of the deeply-dissected northern slopes, and beneath the limestone escarpment of the Hindenburg Ranges in the south (fig. 15.2).

Considerable evidence suggests that expansion from at least one of the inter-montane highland valleys — Ifitaman — occurred to the north, south, and west. The prehistoric relationship of these people to the Sibil Valley

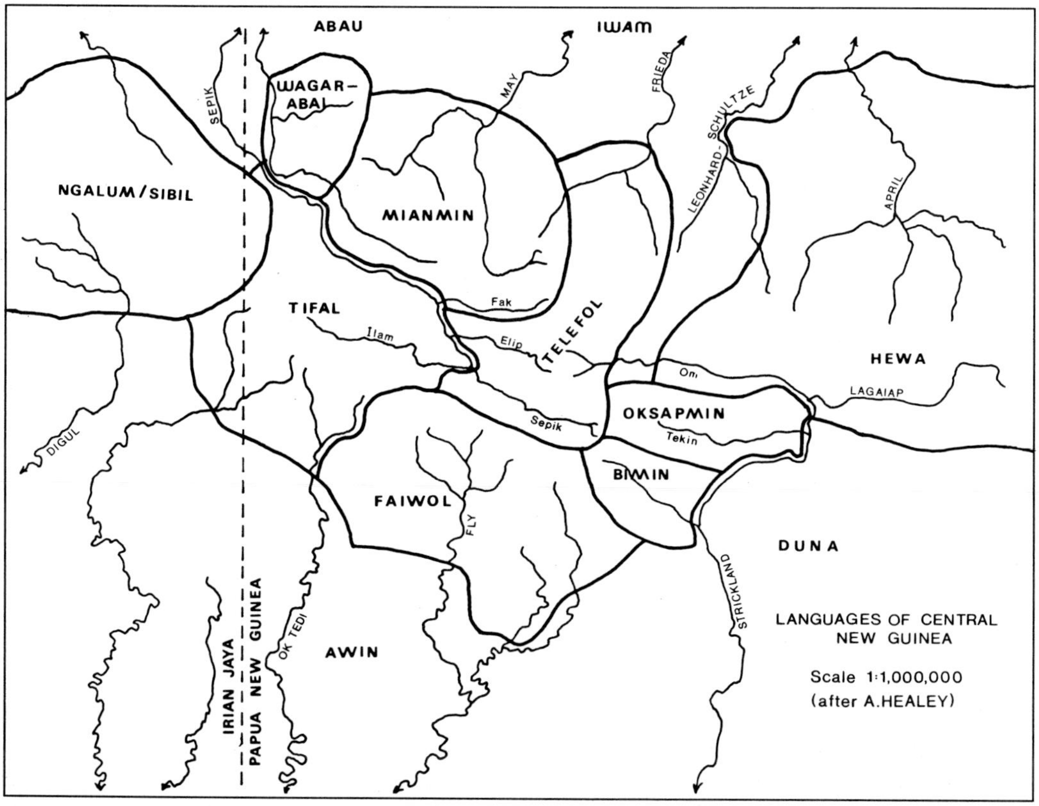

FIGURE 15.1. Language areas of Central New Guinea.

people far to the west is not at all clear. To the east the Oksapmin, living in the valleys on the western rim of the Strickland Gorge, speak a language not closely related to Mountain-Ok (Healey 1964:108) yet they share many aspects of Mountain-Ok culture.

Horticulture, Hunting, and Pig Husbandry

The favored garden staple is taro (*Colocasia esculenta*). However, with the introduction of sweet potato (*Ipomoea batatas*) no longer than three to four hundred years ago (Brookfield and Hart 1971:84), changes in exploitative strategies have taken place. Although sweet potato can be cultivated at elevations up to one thoudsand meters higher than taro, it is usual for the Mountain-Ok to plant taro higher than sweet potato. The main advantage of sweet potato is that it matures in half the time compared to taro, and can be fed to pigs without requiring cooking.

All Mountain-Ok people prefer taro to sweet potato even though several groups (e.g., Atbalmin, Oksapmin and, lately, Tifalmin) actually eat more sweet potato that taro. Other groups (e.g., Telefolmin), whilst growing large crops of sweet potato, use it for feeding their pigs.

The Mountain-Ok are primarily swidden horticulturalists, but they do spend considerable time hunting and gathering. Generally, the men do the hunting (since only they are permitted the use of bow and arrows) and women and children do the gathering. Hunted animals include many species of marsupials, rodents and birds at all altitudes; cassowaries and wild pigs are generally found in greater numbers at lower altitudes. Everywhere in the highlands, pigs are the most valuable property, provide the most favored protein source and are the largest animal eaten. The degree of domestication of pigs varies among Mountain-Ok tribes, depending upon the degree of environmental degradation brought about by human exploitation of the forest habitat of wild animals. This is illustrated by the feedback model in fig. 15.3.

Presumably this cycle operated at a low level of inten-

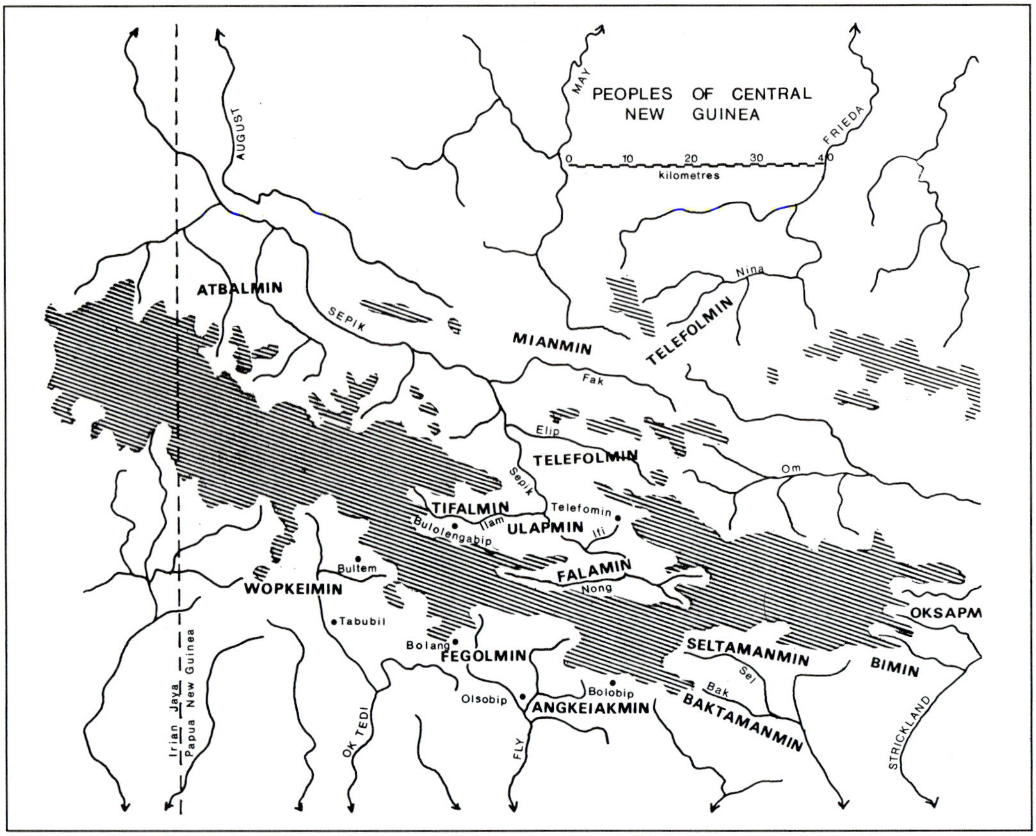

FIGURE 15.2. Tribal areas of Central New Guinea.

sity prior to the introduction of sweet potato, since taro must be cooked before being fed to pigs and this would operate as a limiting factor to the size of domestic pig herds, thus limiting population growth. With the arrival of the sweet potato, however, this limiting factor was removed and the cycle either began or, more probably, was accelerated (Morren 1977).

In the Mountain-Ok area, then, it is probable that the tribes inhabiting the inter-montane valleys were well advanced in the cycle of degradation of their environment when sweet potato arrived and immediately seized on the possibilities of the new crop to increase the sophistication of their pig husbandry. It may have been the urgency of their need that led to early success and a subsequent population "explosion" that has given the Telefolmin their reputation as an expansionist group. Ethno-historical accounts relate that, perhaps three hundred years ago, the Telefolmin drove out the Nukokmin from the southeastern

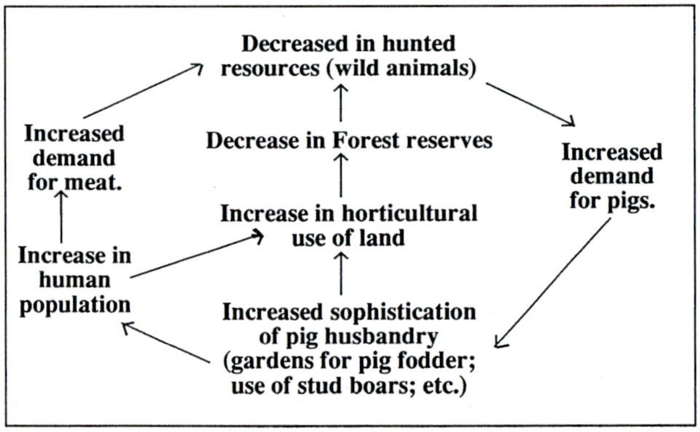

FIGURE 15.3. Feedback model of relationship among wild animal resources, horticultural use of land, and pig husbandry.

end of the valley and the colonizers came to be known as the Falamin. The Nukokmin were forced along the valley of the Nong westwards into the valley of the Ilam, to be

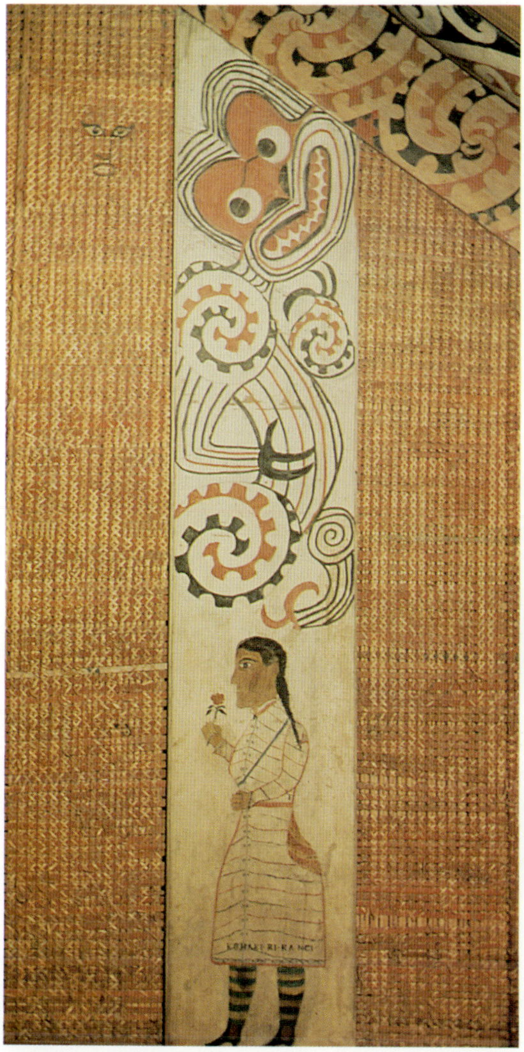

PLATE 12. Painted portrait of ancestress named Hakirirangi, with faces of twins, Tarakitai and Tarakiuta, worked into *tukutuku* on left. Rongopai, 1887. Photograph by R. Neich (see chp. 13).

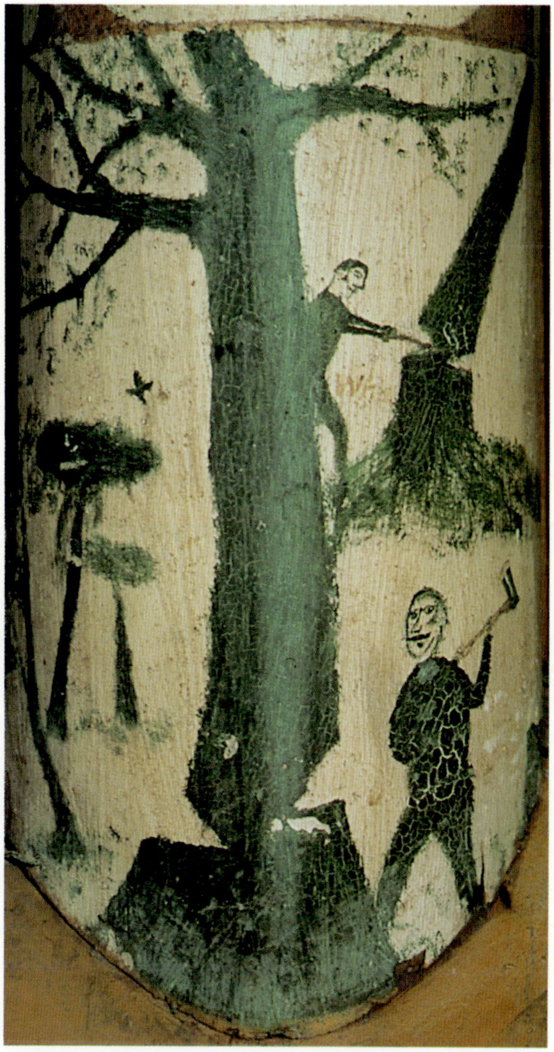

PLATE 13. Tree-felling scene with elements of perspective. Painted on lower rafter end. Tutamure, 1901. Photograph by R. Neich (see chp. 13).

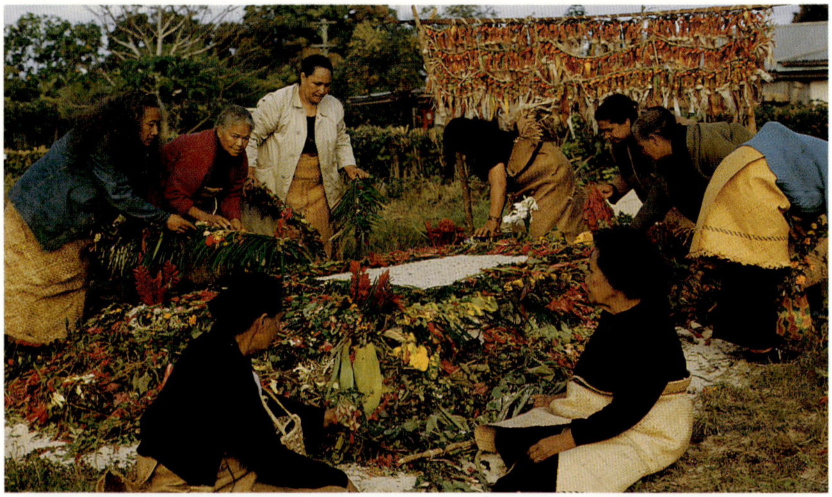

PLATE 14. Neo-traditional decorating of a grave in Nuku'alofa, Tonga, the day after the burial (see chp. 17).

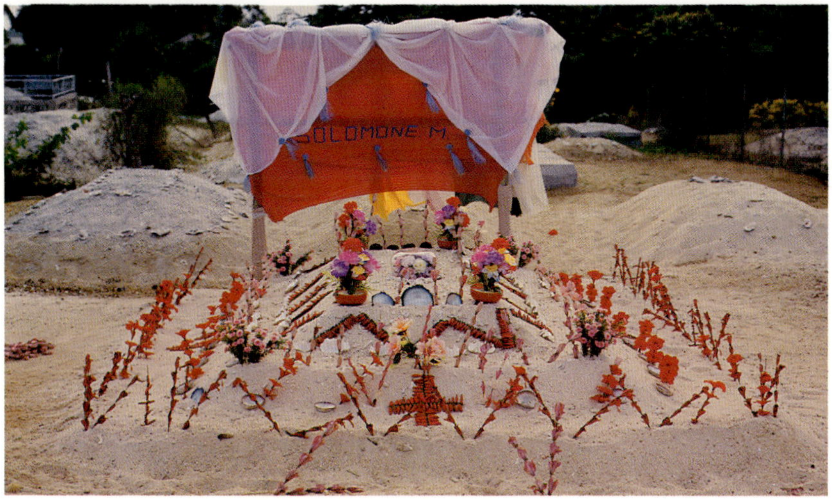

PLATE 15. A grave in Nuku'alofa, Tonga, with the popular red and white symbolic color scheme (see chp. 17).

incorporated among the Tifalmin. Some Tifalmin groups were, in turn, pushed northwest and southwest into Atbalmin and Wopkeimin territories respectively.

Just over one hundred years ago, Ilikimin raiders from Eliptaman to the north of the Telefolmin destroyed the supreme cult house at Telefolip and the Telefolmin revenged this sacrilege by virtually destroying the Ilikimin, driving them out of the Elip and incorporating survivors into their colonies. These colonies extended as far as Ninataman (the upper Frieda River). There are now more Telefolmin in Eliptaman than in their Ifitaman homelands. At the time of European contact, they were beginning to press the Mianmin north of Eliptaman (with inconclusive results) and, to the southeast, their Falamin cousins.

Other Mountain-Ok tribes, not so far advanced in the degradation of their forest environment, have not had an urgent need to develop pig husbandry techniques. The ecological zones available to them are richer because they include a much greater extent of lower montane forest resources where cassowaries and wild pigs are far more abundant than they could ever have been in the intermontane valleys. These tribes are still able to meet their protein requirements by hunting wild pigs and cassowaries, and by capture and subsequent temporary domestication of wild piglets; and, of course, they have access to the wild animal resources of the upper montane forests as well.

Religion, Initiation, and the Male Cult House

The Mountain-Ok venerate their ancestors, make animal sacrifices to them, and beseech them for assistance and success in hunting, warfare, gardening, pig husbandry, and the maintenance of health. This is primarily a male cult and there are several stages of initiation of males into the rituals and mysteries of the cult. Since the rituals and knowledge are to be kept secret from women and the uninitiated, these cult activities take place either in the bush or in special cult houses which dominate the cluster of family houses forming each settlement.

There is a hierarchy of men's houses. At the bottom, for most Mountain-Ok tribes, is the men's club house (*kabelam/ kawelam*)[1] where any male who has at least begun his initiation, and male visitors from other settlements, may eat, sleep and socialize. Men do not normally sleep, with their wives in the family houses (*unangam/wanangam*); such intimacy is permitted and indulged in garden houses (*sebam*).

The club house for ritual leaders, usually aged men, is called the (*katibam/katiwam*). Here the details of rituals can be discussed in privacy. The settlement's cult house, where certain ancestral and other sacred relics and ritual equipment are stored is called the *yolam/yowalam*. Another, more sacred cult house, one for each tribe, is the *amogen/amok*. This contains only the relics of especially important ancestors, usually a male and a female.It is necessary to point out that variations in detail exist among the Mountain-Ok tribes as to the content of initiation rites; how many stages of initiation are conducted; how many cult houses are provided and how they are named; which stages of initiation are conducted in each cult house; exactly what sacred relics, animal trophies, and ritual equipment are stored in them, which houses are decorated by carved and painted boards; which houses customarily contain warshields; and so on. In this paper, however, I am only concerned with the array of sacred human relics and animal trophies.

Relics and Trophy Arrays

MYTHICAL BASIS

There are three extant versions of an episode in the cycle of myths relating to the original, founding ancestress, Afek ("the old woman"). One is from Telefolmin informants, reported by Jorgensen (1981a:404) and is essentially the same as that reported by myself (Craig 1969:53). Another is the Baktamanmin version reported by Barth (1975). The third is the Tifalmin version reported by Wheatcroft (1975).

The Telefolmin version of the episode referred to explains that Afek built the first cult house and the first family house, performed the cult rituals and lived in the cult house, allocating the family house to her younger brother Umoim. However, she did not sleep well and neither did her brother, so she suggested they change places and both slept very well. Since then, men have been in possession of the cult house and its rituals while women look after the children and the pigs in the family houses.

The Baktamanmin and Tifalmin versions add a reference to animal trophies in the cult house. Since Barth reports that the Baktamanmin identify their version as "a story from Telefolmin," it is possible that a reference to animal trophies also exists in some Telefolmin accounts but has not been picked up by any of the ethnographers. It is not likely that the reference to animal trophies is a Baktamanmin gloss, since the Tifalmin also mention them.

The Baktamanmin version is reported as follows:

> The first ancestors were an elder sister and a younger brother. The elder sister built a cult house, put wild pigs' skulls and mandibles there, but the taro did not prosper. She put cassowary pelvises there, but the taro still did not prosper. She would not let her brother into the cult house, but sent him off to hunt and garden. When he objected, she killed him with magic and then exposed his body in a tree. After a while she returned but the body had not decomposed at all. Then she waited a *long* time, and then went and fetched the bones to put in the cult house: skull, mandible, right armbones and finger bones. A *durem* bird [wren warbler = *Malurus alboscapolatus*, a tiny black and white bird] came to eat insects from the roof thatching; she shot it, cooked the breast and gave half to the bones — and then the taro came up terrifically strong.
>
> Her younger (live) brother did not like *her* to do the rituals, *him* to be left out. So he took nettle leaves and spread them all over the floor of the *yolam*. When his sister came and lay down to sleep, she burned herself all over. She went to his house, lay down, and was comfortable. "What a good house you have," she said, "will you change with me?" And so the *men* took over the cult houses. (Barth 1975:278-79)

The Tifalmin version is reported as follows:

> In the beginning when Afekan first created pigs and taro, they were scrawny. They did not amount to much. In those early times Afekan lived in the "men's house" while her husband lived in a "woman's house," exactly opposite to today's practice. Whenever she killed a pig, she merely threw its mandible and skull into the bushes behind the hamlet. She did this time and time again. The taro remained poor. . . . But one day, Afekan decided to change things. She went hunting for marsupials, taking her hunting dog with her. She managed to shoot *nuk delwol, botok, kabang* and *watom* varieties. Returning to the hamlet, she hung them in a string-net bag on a *lupt* tree limb behind her house. Then she came into her husband's house and told him: "I want you to change houses with me. This will become my house; you move into the big house I have been living in. Then kill the big boar I have with the curled tusks. And get the bag of marsupials I have hung on the tree. Butcher the pig, and cook the pork in your new house in a small banana leaf oven. Eat most of it yourself. Thereby, you will develop awareness of the deeper side of things." He did exactly what she told him to do. He cooked the marsupial meat along with the pork. He stuffed himself, after which he did develop new understandings. He went into the forest and cut some hardwood slats which he then lashed into position on the back wall of his new house. On these racks he arranged the numerous old pig mandibles and skulls that he retrieved from the bushes around the hamlet, as well as marsupial mandibles. As he positioned the various mandibles on the racks, he uttered a spell: "*Sisilokkim kawan bon tima tima*!" [*Sisilokkim* = a secret name for pig; *kawan* = a mountainous hunting ground in the parish; *bon* = mandible; *tima tima* = a spell for magical increase]. He put the large mandibles with tusks on the lower racks, and the skulls of the pigs above these. Then he ate the rest of the pork and marsupial meat. That night he slept extremely well, as did Afekan. In the morning he took the fatty flank sections of the pig that he had not cooked the day before and hung them on the firewood drying racks. [Narrator begins to whisper here, to connote secrecy.] The pig fat melted. He took some in his palm and added to it some prepared red ochre (*bogon*) and it produced red paint. This was the first time such a paint has ever been made! He rubbed his face, neck, chest, and shoulders with it first, then rubbed all of his body until his skin glistened! He decorated himself with nose quills topped with the yellow crest of a cockatoo. After he went outside Afekan noticed him, and was attracted to him sexually. He addressed her: "Should I return to my prior house?" But she responded: "No! Continue to develop yourself in these new ways; stay in that house. Gain more insight and awareness. If other men come here, they can live with you in that house; and thenceforth you should instruct them in all your discoveries!" (Wheatcroft 1975:393-94)

The differences between the two versions are interesting. The Baktamanmin version has Afek originating the idea of introducing the animal trophies into the cult house whereas in the Tifalmin version it is her "husband" who originates the practice. In the Baktamanmin version it is the "younger brother" who tricks Afek into handing over the cult house and its rituals to him; in the Tifalmin (as in the Telefolmin) version, it is Afek's own idea. In the Baktamanmin version, it is the offer of sacrificial flesh to the human relics that empowers them to benefit the taro; in the Tifalmin version it is a magical spell uttered by the "husband" that empowers the animal trophies to benefit hunting.

These differences may seem to be substantial but closer examination of the complex of connotations of sacred human relics and animal trophies indicates that the various versions are not making mutually exclusive claims so much as emphasizing certain associations at the expense of others.

A FEGOLMIN RELIC ARRAY

I had casually observed many of the relic arrays over the years, and most seemed to be symmetrically disposed, but it was only when I began to ask for details of the ancestral relics that I perceived a pattern in the arrangement of the various relics and trophies. The pattern was oft-times imperfect, maintenance sporadic, and the identity of items masked by a heavy coat of sooted cobwebs.

On June 8, 1971, I recorded an array of relics and animal trophies (fig. 15.4) on the walls of the *kawelam* at Bolang, the western-most of all Fegolmin villages, on the mid-altitude southern slopes of the Mountain-Ok area. The arrangement had been recently reinstated and was therefore in as perfect a condition as it ever would be. Questioning the men, I obtained information that suggested the array was a symbolic arrangement acting as an ecological model of animal resources in relation to human settlement and gardens.

The Fegolmin inhabit the same ecological zone, or range of habitats, as the neighboring Wopkeimin. Hyndman (n.d.) has reported that the Wopkeimin divide this zone into three ecotones: *gis-dokum-bakan, gis-katep-bakan, and mamin-dokum-bakan.*

Gis-dokum-bakan is the highest and coldest ecotone, abutting the Hindenburg Wall. It is transitional between montane rain forest and montane cloud forest, between two and three thousand meters in elevation. Hunting is the principal subsistance strategy in this ecotone and is directed towards *nuk* (marsupials and rodents) and *maian* (dogs); there are neither wild pig (*samin*) nor cassowaries (*bia*).

Gis-katep-bakan is the ideal ecotone for settlements, for cultivation of taro, and for pandanus orchards. It lies between one and two thousand meters in elevation. The main settlements, while not absolutely permanent, remain for generations within narrowly prescribed areas. Swidden horticulture relies upon a shifting exploitation of extensive tracts of mid-montane rainforest with long fallow periods that prevent the establishment of grassland. Garden areas are not clear-felled and conditions are so wet that very little burning takes place; rather it is a "slash-and-mulch" technique. The men hunt marsupials and the women and children collect a variety of frogs, snakes, lizards, and insects.

Mamin-dokum-bakan is the area below about one thousand meters dominated by foothill rainforest. The people exploit sago and breadfruit and engage sporadically in swidden horticulture, planting taro, cassava, yams, and leafgreens. Both sexes engage in fishing and the men hunt several species of marsupials, including the scrub wallaby and, more importantly, the wild pig and cassowary.

Small-scale pig husbandry for both the Wopkeimin and Fegolmin is considered essential to supply sacrificial animals for certain initiation and sickness-curing rituals. Each household owns one or two pigs. These may be raised from captured wild piglets or from piglets born of sows occasionally impregnated by wild boars. The domesticated pigs are hand fed cooked taro (often substandard tubers) and allowed to forage widely in the mid-montane rainforest and the secondary regrowth of old gardens. Wild pigs may be attracted from their lower-altitude ecotone, as well as to the gardens in the lowest ecotone.

If one accepts that the Wopkeimin categories are true also for the neighboring Fegolmin, then it is possible to see the relationship between the Bolang/Fegolmin relic and trophy array and the ecosystem of the cult-house curator[2] who set it up.

The ancestral relics (*menamem*) are considered to be central in the ecosystem and, being preserved in the male cult houses located at relatively long-term settlement sites centrally placed in tribal territory, it is appropriate that they should be placed centrally at eye level on the rear wall of the cult house. These relics are intimately related to the quality of life of the inhabitants of the settlement, in particular to the activities essential for survival: gardening, hunting, and pig husbandry.

Since domesticated pigs are husbanded in the vicinity of the human settlements, it is appropriate that the jawbones from these animals should be arranged immediately beneath the sacred ancestral relics. The significance of the association of ancestors and domestic pigs is increased further by virtue of the necessity to slaughter domestic

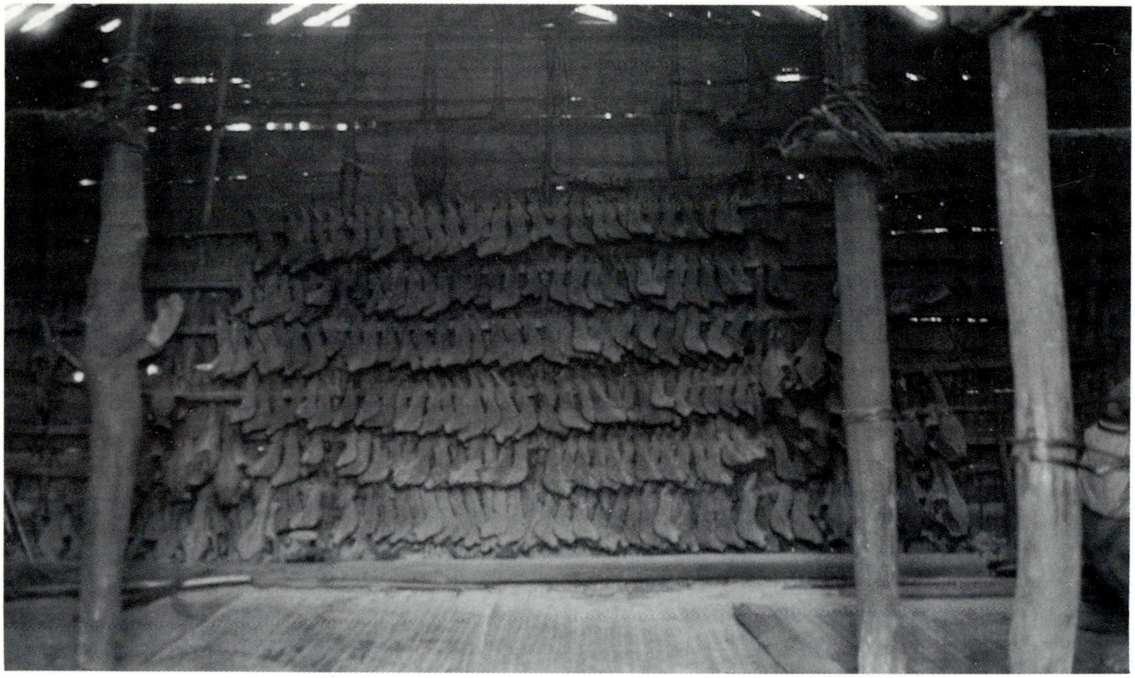

FIGURE 15.4. Relic and trophy array, *kawelam*, Bolang/Fegolmin.

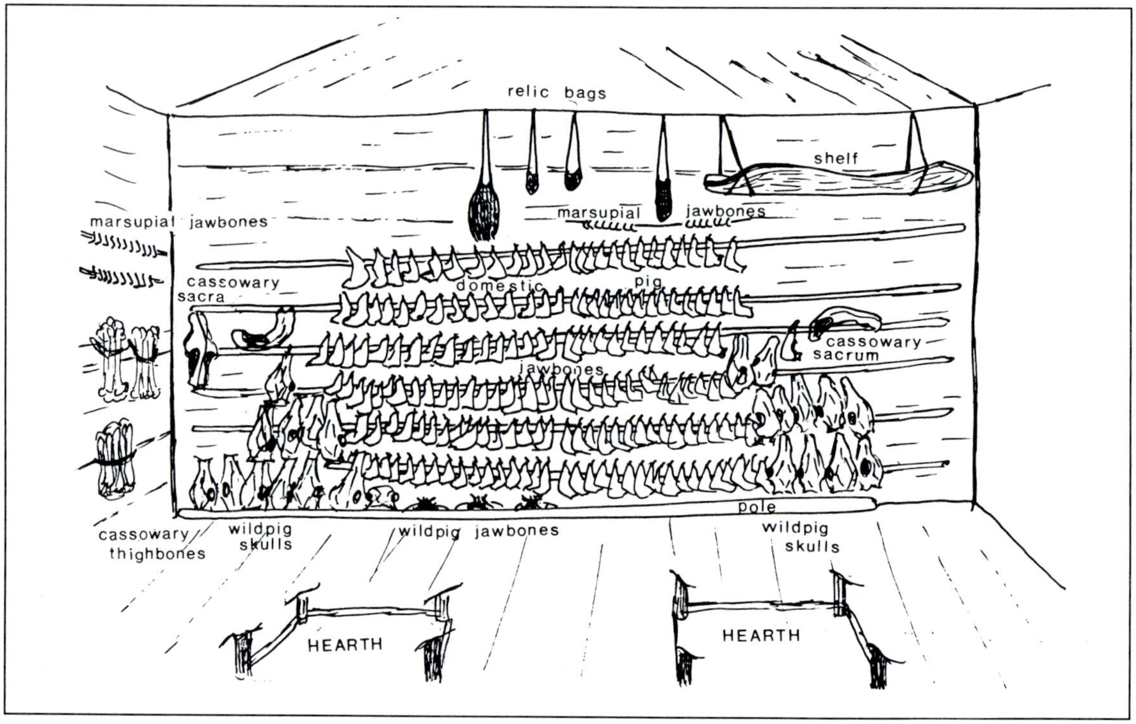

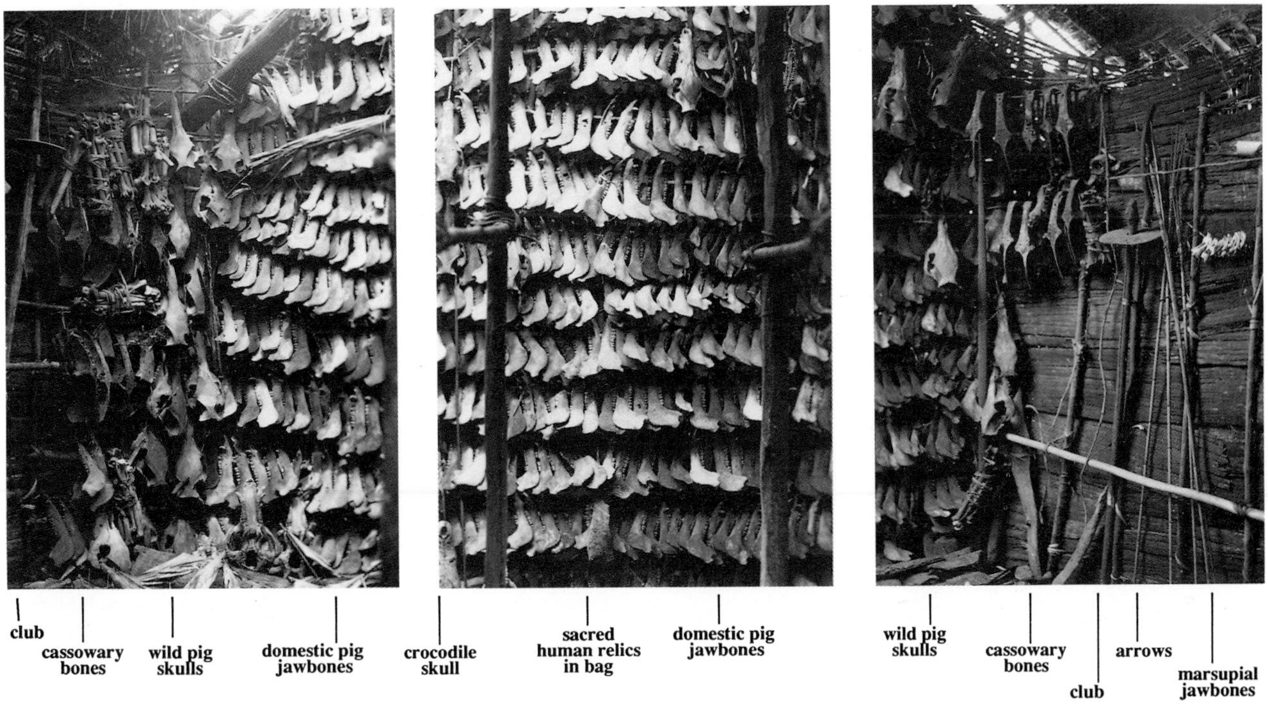

FIGURE 15.5. Interior rear wall of *yowolamem*, Bulolengabip, Tifalmin.

pigs at certain rituals involving the beseeching of ancestors in connection with initiation and the curing of illness. It is also a direct reference to the appeal for the ancestors to provide success in pig husbandry — without such success, the ancestors cannot be fed the "smell" and blood of pig sacrifices!

The grouping of wild pig skulls low down at either side of the domestic pig jaw bones suggests the dependency of the people upon wild boars for semi-domestic stock and for impregnating domestic sows. Wild pig jaw bones lined up against the symbolic garden fence comments on the threat to the gardens by wild pigs. The position of wild pig skulls and jaw bones low down in the array associates the wild pig with the lowest ecotone.

Cassowary pelvis bones are arrayed close to the wild pig skulls, suggesting the coexistence of these two animals in the lowest ecotone. Marsupial and rodent jaw bones are arrayed at the periphery of the display, high above the floor, suggesting their existence in the highest ecotone, at the periphery of human settlement and gardening activity. The Bolang array has a bundle of cassowary thigh bones in association with marsupial and rodent bones on a side wall. Unfortunately, since I did not obtain detailed identification of the marsupial and rodent species present in the array, I cannot clarify this association, or whether indeed those in the two clusters were all of animals of the highest ecotone.

There is no doubt that the identification of the marsupials and rodent trophies would be highly significant for this analysis, not only to clarify the ecological mapping functions of the array[3] but also in terms of symbolic and metaphoric work. As Barth has established for the Baktamanmin, "The various kinds of *nuk* serve the Baktaman [sic] as concrete vehicles for abstract thought; . . . the concepts and thoughts they embody concern qualities and processes of purity/pollution, aggressiveness and, most important, fertility and growth" (1975:187).

Add to this the dense symbolic and metaphoric associations of the relics of ancestors, of wild and domestic pigs, cassowaries, and other sacred materials, and the richness of the significance of the displays may be appreciated.

A TIFALMIN RELIC ARRAY

Wilson Wheatcroft has reported on the relic array in the major cult house (*am-awok*) of Bulolengabip, a Bufulmin parish village of the Tifalmin (fig. 15.5; see also Wheatcroft 1975:pls. 21, 22; Craig 1969:pl. 14).

Men's cult houses usually have two fireplaces — one to the left called *un* (arrow) and one to the right called *iman* (taro) (Jorgensen 1981a:332 ff; Barth 1975:114; Craig 1983:38). This Tifalmin cult house incorporates the entire left-hand flooring salvaged from a cult house of the enemy Wimulapmin driven from the area generations before, to reinforce this division between "arrow" (representing warfare/hunting/killing) and "taro" (representing gardening/domesticity/nurturing). This division into two halves is reinforced in domestic pig trophy arrays throughout the Mountain-Ok area by arranging the curve of the jawbones away from the center line (see figs. 15.4, 15.5). Wheatcroft describes the array in detail:

> The mandibles number just over 700, arranged in 12 horizontal rows. . . . Here and there at the top, but mainly at the top sides, the men have suspended about 60 pig skulls. Some skulls and mandibles were painted with red ochre contrasted by white limestone paint. . . . On both sides of the back wall, the men have arranged about 25 cassowary sacrae (portion of the pelvis). Along the sides advancing towards the front of the house were items used in warfare, such as ancient disc clubs (of which there was one on each side), and a few arrows used to hunt marsupials during initiation ceremonies. Still farther to the front, along the sides, were about 30 pig shoulder blades that the men use during one part of the Kayuban initiation. Along each side wall near the rear were the mandibles of *nuk kabang* and *nuk tifol* marsupials. Along the back wall there were various decomposing, woven string-net bags that once contained some sorts of relics or magical charms. In one bag that was still largely in one piece, I noticed that there was part of a marsupial nest: leaves and small twigs. Buried in this was the skull of a famous hunting dog, and jaw still hinged by ligaments to the skull so it moved. This arrangement was clearly a charm for successful hunting: as the good dog so readily used to find nests (=prey), so men will find the game they seek when hunting. Informants said that this charm's "strength helps all dogs and men when they hunt. . . ."
>
> Down in front of all of the bone relics situated on the floor in a place by themselves, were several old hardwood (black palm) bows and mounted stone adzes of deceased ancestors. These items were also relics, of course, and said to be powerful charms "for the gardens" in their own right. . . . In many ways the most important items in any Tifalmin men's house shrine . . . are the powerful human remains: the *amkun miit awaim*, literally, the sacred house post foundation, symbol, or "root". In the Bulolengabip shrine that I have been describing at some length, in one small string net bag centrally located close to the floor (the typical location) there was a small bamboo tube containing some of the whiskers, one tooth and a fragment of the body-oil impregnated rain cape made from bark cloth: all belonged to one of the older men's father. In another small bag there was another small bamboo tube (*get*) belonging to the head man, Sulukim, the "ritual leader." It contained some of his father's sister's husband's (Apsaiyim's) whiskers, and several of his front teeth and fingernails. Along with it in the bag were the wing feathers of an eagle (*bogol*). . . .
>
> During pre-contact times the Tifalmin (like the Telefolmin and other contiguous groups, today) used to put human bones from famous male ancestors in their men's houses more commonly. They continued this practice until quite recently, apparently. In an earlier pre-contact men's house in the village of Nimnimdumabip, they once had a human skull. But after the house caught fire and was burned down, they never did it again. . . .
>
> When I asked the question, "Why do you call the separate ancestral shrine the *amawok* which means the 'mother-house'?" informants answered: "It is a mother to us since it takes care of us; it makes our taro grow immense and makes our pigs fat." And, "It is called *amawok* because it is the 'home' of the *amkun miit*, which takes care of our gardens." . . . The entire shrine [is] a set of powerful group charms through whose power the taro gardens . . . grow fecund, pigs get big and fat, marsupial hunting is bountiful, and villagers free of sickness. . . .
>
> "When we bring the secretly hunted marsupial species into the *amawok* during ceremonies, we tell the *amkun miit* (human relics) and the pig bones, 'You must take care of us and make our pigs grow fat and plentiful, and our taro immense.' As soon as we tell them this, shortly afterwards we see the results in our gardens. They do just what we petitioned." (1975:401-4)

Wheatcroft points out that only relics associated with males are preserved in the men's cult house.

> Throughout the Mountain-Ok, only fully-initiated, senior men may eat the head of the pig from which mandible and skull is preserved. . . . Marsupials that women and children

may eat never end up as preserved trophies in the men's house; and both cassowary and wild pig are foods only men eat. Thus, everything that ends up as a trophy in the men's house is masculine *par extraordinaire*. (1974:408)

It is not clear from the available literature how the jaw bones of domestic pigs get to be trophies in the male cult house, particularly as Barth records that the jaw and belly of the domestic pig is the cut for women only. Perhaps domestic pigs killed inside the men's house enclosure and cooked in the cult house are entirely eaten by the men and taboo to women; the jaw bone may then be added to the array.[4]

Wheatcroft has attempted to explain the practice of preserving animal trophies in the cult house in symbolic, magical, and "historic" terms:

> Pig mandibles are objects of veneration [because of] the symbolism of pigs as desirable food *par extraordinaire*. (1975:413)
>
> It is the *sinik* [essence] of the ancestors preserved as a [saliva] residue on the bones of animals they relish...that is the main spiritual/magical force in the shrine. (p. 412)
>
> The smoke-preserved bones are a permanent link through tme between the beginning and the present. They become — in both real and magical ways — history itself, encoded in venerated relics....They are the link to Afekan's husband's creative powers (p. 410).

He has not perceived any ecological mapping or modelling function although further enquiry, particularly regarding the identity of the various marsupial and rodent trophies, could provide evidence to support such an interpretation. There are many correspondences between this array and that at Bolang. The existence of a crocodile skull, placed at the base of the array of trophies, is consistent with it being from a creature inhabiting the lowest ecotone known to these people.

TELEFOLMIN RELIC AND TROPHY ARRAYS

Although I have not made detailed records of the contents of all men's club houses and cult houses in the Mountain-Ok area, or even for the Telefolmin, I have recorded brief inventories of a large number. Among the Telefolmin, I have never seen marsupial, rodent, or cassowary trophies in the *yolam* cult houses, though these are to be found in family houses (*unangam*) and men's club houses (*kawelam*). Wild pig skulls and jaw bones I found only in men's club houses and cult houses (which is appropriate since wild pig is forbidden as food for the uninitiated).

Jorgensen lists "wild pig's jaws, with their curving tusks" (1981a:70) along with "cassowary breast bones" and marsupial jaw bones as trophies to be found in the family house. However, some domestic pigs do grow rather long tusks and perhaps it is these he has seen. I have seen domestic pig jaw bones in all three types of house: *unangam, kawelam* and *yolam*; I also found human relics (*menamem*, "bag-sacred"), usually categorized as *un-men* or *iman-men* ("arrow-bag" "taro-bag"), or occassionally *kong-men* ("domestic pig-bag"), in all three house types. Among the Falamin (and I believe it was practiced among the Telefolmin and perhaps Ulapmin as well), the skull of a woman particularly successful at pig husbandry would be kept on a platform near a side wall and beseeched by women for success in pig husbandry.

The typical arrangement of relics and furnishings in the *yolam* are explained by Jorgensen in cosmological terms. The back wall is covered with symmetrically disposed rows of domestic pig jaw bones, often painted in white and red bands. At eye level are hung the blackened net bags (*menamem*) containing the skulls of the *usong* (ancestral spirits). Wild pig skulls and jaw bones may be lined up along the floor at the base of the wall — perhaps with a crocodile skull traded from the Atbalmin. Jorgensen supplies details and analysis:

> The interior of the *yolam* is divided into two halves, the *iman ilo* and the *un ilo* (taro side, arrow side) corresponding to the two divisions of men into taro and arrow spheres (*iman miit, un miit*) respectively. The *usong* and their *men-amem* are likewise so divided into *iman men* and *un men*, and only a man belonging to the taro side may have contact with *iman men* and only men of the arrow side may come into contact with *un men*. The division in the *yolam* of taro and arrow is a reflection of the cosmological separation of nurturing and killing, gardening and hunting, and in most *yolam* the arrow floor and its hearth (*un abiin, un tuul*) are oriented in the direction of enemy territory or hunting grounds (*nuk bagan, saaman bagan*), while the taro floor and hearth are oriented in the direction of major gardening areas (*iman bagan, iman ilang*). Thus within the *yolam* one generally finds the things of gardening — say, the adze (*ubi*) or an *usong* — arranged along the back wall of the *iman abiin*, while the things of war and hunting — shield (*atkom*), arrows (*un*), black palm or stone-headed clubs (*biyal sinam, tingii*), or cane cuirasses

> (*nam*) of the *usong* — along the *un biin*. Here too we find a reflection of the dichotomy between wild and domestic pigs (*saaman* and *kong*), and while the *usong* like the smell and the fat of the pigs, men must take care to cook wild pigs (and eel, *aaningok*) only in the arrow hearth and domestic pigs only in the taro hearth. Should this order be violated, or should the ashes from the two hearths be mixed, entropy would reign free with the flight of taro and domestic pigs and the invasion of wild pigs and enemies. (Jorgensen 1981a:332)

Since the Telefolmin *yolam* arrays lack the cassowary and marsupial/rodent trophies, they are not ecological maps or models in the way the Bolang array seems to be. No one Telefolmin house type is eligible, it seems, for the full range of trophies and relics whereas this did appear to be the case for the Bolang *kawelam*. Rather, to achieve an image like that provided by the Bolang *kawelam*, one would have to consider the totality of arrays in all types of houses among the Telefolmin. My observation of Falmin houses suggest they are consistent with the Telefolmin in this respect, and the Ulapmin also probably are alike.

BAKTAMANMIN RELIC AND TROPHY ARRAYS

Detailed observations published by Barth (1975) make it possible to consider also the Baktamanmin arrays. It is clear that, like the Telefolmin, Falamin, and perhaps Ulapmin, they also have no single examples of an array comparable to that in the *kawelam* of Bolang/Fegolmin.

> The *Katiam* is designated by the Baktaman [*sic*] as Taro House and the Big Sister. Although everything inside its door is equally secret and forbidden to the uninitiated on penalty of death, it is clearly constituted around some central sacred objects: ancestral relics, trophies of the *hunt*, and the sacred fire. Besides this it contains drums, pandanus gouges of cassowary long-bones, pig scapula spoon, cassowary breastbone drinking vessels, and a considerable amount of personal hunting equipment and adornment. . . .
>
> The sacra themselves include mandibles, collar-bones and fingerbones, not skulls or long-bones.
>
> The hunting trophies are cassowary pelvises, wild pig mandibles, and a few skulls. Both male and female wild pig are found; in the Feisabip temple, these are carefully identified and kept separate, while in the Kamsurbang temple they are mixed. These should properly be from all cassowary and wild pigs killed, not just those taken in secret hunt.
>
> The *Yolam*, by contrast . . . is called the War House and the Little Sister. It is constituted around two central relics: the skull and mandible of an ancestor, and the ancestral long-bones and brush turkey foot of the firepost shrine. . . . Other essential sacred objects are two fires, the sacred arrows used to puncture the sacrifice at *wonsa* and the sacred stones for 3rd degree initiation. It also contains trophies of female wild pig killed in secret hunt, war shields, and various minor paraphernalia. (Barth 1975:247-48; see fig. 15.6)

Nowhere does Barth mention the preservation of marsupial and rodent trophies, though it is possible these may be kept in the *kaweram*, whose content he lists briefly as "shields and minor sacra" (1975:247).[5]

Despite the lack of a geographically based ecological schema modelled by the relic and trophy arrays, Barth does claim a conceptually-based ecological schema in the rituals with which the arrays are associated.

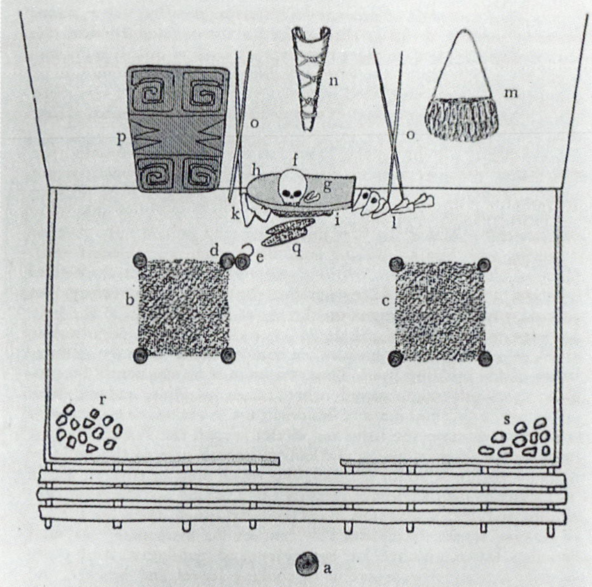

a) Housepost before door, carrying roof-beam b) the more sacred fire c) the less sacred fire d) the sacred fire post e) the long bone sacra f) the ancestral skull g) the ancestor's mandible h) the insect-nest sheet (*Gãím*) i) stone slab k) male pig mandible l) skulls and mandibles of female pigs m) quill bag for ancestral jaw n) pandanus container for bones o) sacred arrow (*bogyōn*) for sacrifices p) fighting shield q) black stones (adzes) for 3rd degree initiation r) cooking stones for pig, marsupial and man s) cooking stones for cassowary and pandanus d) strut for hanging parts of sacrifice

FIGURE 15.6. Interior of Baktamanmin *yolam*. From Barth (1975:114).

What are the major themes that we see codified in *Katiam* and *Yolam* rites respectively? As shown, both play a part in the orchestration of the fertility mystery; but they also constitute distinctive, if partial, alternative codifications. Cast as they are in the structure of an ancestral cult, we may say that each give a substantive codification of the relations Man-Land-Ancestors, and through their inter-relations also a conceptualization of the identity and essence of each part of this triad. Man sustains the fertility of land through his cult of Ancestors, he maintains health and vigour for the population as a whole, and for men specifically in contradistinction to women. The cults further define the essential collectives of men, and their connection to land as resource and territory. . . .

In the *Katiam*, man is related to Ancestors in terms of clan. . . .

This has implications for their relationship to Land: clan membership gives access to clan territories for hunting and gathering; it also comes closest to a ritual expression of lineal rights of succession to fallow lands and to sago and pandanus trees. . . .

In this temple, Man relates to Ancestor through the offering of game in a relatively continuous, everyday flow of prestations, not just on special ritual occasions. In return he obtains taro fertility and plenty. This is a close metaphor to the man-woman relationship of exchange and mutual interdependence in daily subsistence. . . .

In the *Yolam*, on the other hand, the same relations are codified differently. Man is related to Ancestors as a member of a community; the skull symbolises everyone's ancestors. . . .

The central rites whereby Man relates to Ancestors in the *Yolam* are offerings, as in the *Katiam*; but in the *Yolam* these are always solemn sacrifices of meat sanctified through secret hunt and in no way reminiscent of male-female exchanges. The ancestor controls this hunt, not by giving hunting luck but by releasing game, which is a representation of himself; and so the commensual meal becomes a mystery of blessing, conceptualized in imagery such as fur and whiteness, which creates taro fertility in the land.

Yolam rites also relate Man to Land as territory through their warfare potency. (Barth 1975:249-51)

Relic and Trophy Arrays of the Mountain-Ok

It is clear that all the relic and trophy arrays of the Mountain-Ok are associated with the cult of the ancestors, whose rituals are performed to ensure fertility of taro and domestic pigs, success in hunting and warfare, and good health for all members of the community.

It is also clear, however, that there is a great deal of variation, even within certain named groups, in exactly how the relics and trophies are arrayed, precisely which relics and trophies are arrayed in the various houses, and what symbolic/metaphoric connotations (apart from those directly concerned with the ancestral cult) are given the most weight by the men responsible for setting up these arrays.

I have suggested that a geographic/ecological modelling function is consistent with the known facts, as the major modelling function of the Bolang/Fegolmin array, and that this may also be likely for the Bulolengabip/Tifalmin array. Wheatcroft has attempted to demonstrate, however, that the magical aspects of the array (as a model for the manipulation of ancestral power) seem to be paramount in Tifalmin minds. Jorgensen believes that Telefolmin arrays are more concerned with cosmological notion of the distinction between nurturing and killing, gardening, and hunting; that is, they are a model of order versus entropy. Barth interprets Baktamanmin arrays as models of the relations between Man, Land, and the Ancestors.

Some of these variations are no doubt due to the differences in the ethnographers as perceivers and analyzers. But other nuances in cultural detail from group to group suggest that the variations in arrays are real, that other ethnographers could confirm them, and that information from groups I have not mentioned could extend the range of variation.[6]

Relic and Trophy Arrays as Art Works

How may I demonstrate that Mountain-Ok relic and trophy arrays are art works? This must depend upon their conforming to the criteria of an art work. Unfortunately, no clearly stated definition of art is generally accepted by members of the Pacific Arts Association. Judging from the papers delivered at the First and Second Symposia of 1974 and 1978, very few scholars have a definition in mind and even contradict one another when they do. I draw attention, however, to the commendable efforts of both Mataira and Hanson (in Mead and Kernot 1983) to provide the criteria and characteristics of an art work and thereby facilitate a distinction between art and craft.

However, I do not think they have gone quite far enough in exploring their definitions and I offer instead one proposed by Brook (1977) which survives appraisal and ethnographic application better than any other I have come across. This definition is that art is publically accessible, unspecific experimental modelling. This no doubt requires explication but, for the purposes of this paper, I provide the minimum. "Publically accessible" refers to the requirement that an artwork be available for critical appraisal by an audience — not necessarily the whole community, but certainly by persons other than the artist (Brook 1977:15).

The term "experimental" touches on the conventional notion that art is exploratory: "Art activities are experimental in the sense that they venture somehow, however slightly, beyond the familiar and the well-understood" (p. 13). So far as the "unspecific" quality of art is concerned,

> we distinguish between arts and crafts by noticing that a craftsman's goals and problems are specifiable, his techniques are routine and learnable, and there are statable or demonstrable criteria of success. To the extent that these conditions do not apply to some craft-like activity, that activity is, to that extent, an art (or something else) and not a craft. . . . There are *specific* experiments, such as holding out one's hand to see if it is raining; and there are *unspecific* experiments, such as holding out one's hand to see. (p. 13)

"Modelling" suggests that art works not merely in some sense "represent" objects or states of affairs that *are*, but more appropriately, "represent" objects or states of affairs that *might be*.

> The unspecified experimental prospective modelling function is, I believe, fundamental to art. Works of art *may* show how things are, but perhaps no better nor even so well as works of craft, and certainly less well than scientific models. Showing how things *might* be, on the other hand, is always at least one kind of adventure. Speculative models like these enable us to change ourselves, or change the world, in imagination, before and quite independently of whether we set about achieving the alteration in reality. Art, one might say, is the most generalized and characteristically human way of inititiating change, because it generates models of possible futures that we can criticize before we need to act and above all, before we need to act irrevocably. (pp. 14, 15)

Let me now examine the relic and trophy arrays in these terms. First of all, the arrays are accessible for criticism by an audience — admittedly, in most cases, an audience of initiated men, but nevertheless an audience. Barth has recorded specific incidents of critical appraisal relating to relics; I quote one here as an example:

> The ancestral skull in the *Yolam* used to lie on the *gaim* nest (made by the *nap* larvae) directly on the floor of the temple. After participating in a major rite, some guests from Wokfiakmin village criticized this arrangement, pointing out that the *gaim* was clean and should not be placed on the floor, equivalent to the ground (though the temple floor is in fact raised ca. 4' on pillars). Baktaman seniors were suspicious that this might be an attempt to fool them or damage them; but they discussed it and finally decided it was right; so they fetched a flat rock slab and laid the *gaim* on it. (Barth 1975:242)

Barth goes on to generalize from such incidents:

> The purported criteria by which innovations are evaluated by the Baktaman seem to be pragmatic. An agreement that the taro either suffered or prospered entails an authorative conclusion that the innovation must be rejected or adopted respectively. Behind this, however, we can see other processes operate. The most clearly identified is public opinion: pressure and criticism from cult leaders elsewhere . . . rivalry within the community between leaders . . . or the articulated desires of lower initiates. . . . Behind this, again, we may search for factors such as a need for cognitive consistency, and differentials in power sustaining unequal distributions of privilege. (1975:244)

Second, there is the notion of the arrays as unspecific experimental models. It is unnecessary to labor the point, already made, that the arrays do model certain relationships among the conceived entities in the Mountain-Ok universe. Certainly, aspects of the models appear to relate to things as they are; but from the point of view of any individual relics curator, the models are also speculative, since no one model is a copy of another.

In Mataira's terms, the craftsman/artisan "will happily reproduce the products conceived by earlier artists, while the artist working within the traditional norm or drawing inspiration from it, continues to explore new dimensions" (1983:82).

Barth provides an illuminating example of a speculative act in relation to the relic and trophy array in the Baktamanmin *Yolam*. The male wild pig, he explains, is seen by the Baktamanmin as

> an anti-taro and anti-gardening force, an enemy and rival to

> Baktaman male success and thus inimical to the "male" *Yolam*. Yet . . . male boar also clearly embodies virility and aggressiveness, and might be seen as a more impressive analogue to the aggressive marsupials used in warfare rites . . . and thus highly compatible with the *Yolam* as war temple. About 15 years ago, events took a turn in this direction. The (c) set had just been initiated to the 3rd degree; and as he emerged from that seclusion Ngaromnok came upon a very large wild boar in the act of copulating with a domestic sow. He shot it and killed it. When shortly later the (c) set, as novice warriors, joined their first raid they carried the mandible of this formidable animal with them in a net bag. The raid was successful, and Buryep, the cult-master at the time, thereupon incorporated the mandible among the *Yolam* sacra without changing the basic rule banning all other boar meat or bones from the temple. The various codifications of male boar have still not been brought into harmony, nor its connotations as a concrete symbol clarified; and I would expect this to continue to be a matter to puzzle and concern the Baktaman, i.e. one on which their creativity will focus. (1975:241)

This act can be considered an unspecific experiment since it seems to have occurred without any particular intention (or conclusive result). That the results were inconclusive does not disqualify the action as artistic.

While we have such details only for the Baktamanmin, it would be pedantic to suggest that similar examples could not be found among other groups of the Mountain-Ok. As Barth has noted, "it should be remembered that change takes place unrecorded and largely unacknowledged" (1975:240).

Disintegration of an Art Form

The relic and trophy arrays of the Mountain-Ok have been under serious threat since the late 1960s, when the influence of the Baptist mission, based at Telefomin, became stronger. The cult houses and associated rituals were judged anathema by the Christians; individual believers were urged to drop their involvement and to destroy any ancestral relics in their care or possession.

The influence of government and mission-sponsored education has provided the means whereby potential initiates can avoid the rigors of introduction to the cult. This avoidance was supported by a colonial administration that regarded the cult and its leaders as responsible for the killing of two patrol officers and two policemen at Eliptaman in 1953 (see Quinlivan 1954; Gore 1965:chs. 23, 24).

A grassroots based "Rebaibal" ("revival") movement originated by Dios, a Baptist mission trained pastor, led to almost complete destruction of relic and trophy arrays throughout the northern and central areas of the Mountain-Ok by 1979. Only the curators of the supreme cult house at Telefolip, and a few others at Bogalminavip, Abatevip/Kubrenmin, and Yogavip/Falamin resisted the destruction of arrays in their care (Jorgensen 1981b; Craig 1981).

The Roman Catholic mission is more tolerant of traditional cultural forms and the southern curators have not been pressured as heavily as their colleagues to the north of the Hindenburg Range. Nevertheless, many cult houses in the south are in decay, the relics and trophies scattered in heaps on the floor and falling through onto the ground beneath.

The impact of the gold and copper mining operation at Ok Tedi is providing the final blow to the traditional cult system and the associated cult houses. The company has made some attempt to cycle employment opportunities so that villages are not entirely denuded of manpower, but many unemployed men live in squatter settlements on the periphery of the mine site. Indeed, whole villages — men, women and children — have left traditional sites to build adjacent to the mining town of Tabubil or beside the roads to it, and it is significant that these settlements do not include traditional cult houses.

The survival of the Mountain-Ok has been affected radically by factors completely at variance with traditional concerns and strategies. Reliance on a cash income and imported foods (such as rice, tinned meat and fish, coffee, tea, sugar, etc.) has disconnected major sectors of the community from the traditional pursuits of taro gardening, pig husbandry, and hunting. This leaves other sectors of the community to continue the old strategies without sufficient people to support the cycle of initiations believed to be necessary for the success of these traditional pursuits.

The disintegration of the relic and trophy arrays represents the breakdown of the Mountain-Ok universe. The occasional appearance in men's houses of defunct cassette radios, suitcases full of foreign goods, and empty meat and fish cans may be the beginnings of a substitution for the relics of the past.

For almost twenty years, change has been initiated by

exogenous forces — a colonial administration, schools, Christian missions, and now the Ok-Tedi mining operations. Mountain-Ok creativity may have to find completely novel forms to wrest back endogenous control over the initiation of change. And then there will be a new art form.

Notes

1. *Kabelam/kawelam, unangam/wanangam, katibam/katiwam, yolam/yowalam*, and *amogen/amok*: the pronounciation, and sometimes the word, varies from one group to another. Here I provide the two major variants applicable to (1) the Telefol speakers of the central valley, and (2) the Faiwol speakers of the southern slopes.

2. Barth reports that for the Baktamanmin *katiam*: "The cult leader in the *katiam*. . . determines the location of the shrines and the bone trophies from sacrifices" (1975:109).

3. Dr. Thomas Michel advises me that the Kufelmin, on the international border west of the Atbalmin, actually use the trophy arrays to teach initiates where various animal species can be found.

4. Confirmed by Barth, personal communication, November 1984.

5. Confirmed by Barth, personal communication, November 1984.

6. According to Fitz Poole (personal communication, September 1984), the Bimin-Kuskusmin provide further variations on the basic model.

16

Imperatives and Persuasion in the Conservation of Culture: Gender Constraints in Tongan Dance

STEPHANIE REYNOLDS

This chapter examines differences in men's and women's dance forms in the South Pacific island nation of Tonga, in relation to the status of Tongan women and cultural norms regarding them.[1] Theories drawn from visual arts research regarding the role of women artists cross-culturally are applied in Tongan dance. I seek to contribute to these theories of art and to utilize variations and similarities with which constraints in the material arts operate in the performance art of dance, in order to investigate general bases for specific beliefs and practices.

While there is great variance in women's ability to achieve high political and economic status in Polynesia and Melanesia, constraints on their art-making activities appear to be universal in those regions (Teilhet 1983). For instance, women usually do not make figurative images, but produce abstract forms. Also, women are not allowed to produce hieratic, or religio-political art. Women's progenerative powers have been postulated as a basis for this restriction, in order to shield the continuation of the ancestral line from dangerous contact with the spirit world (Teilhet 1978). An additional theory in the study of women's art is that women are carriers of tradition in cultures which are under stress or in flux.[2]

By "constraint," I intend its meanings both as an imperative and a limit. The concept of a constraint resembles that of a cultural *tapu*, which has both a positive and negative charge. "Constraint" conventionally means to compel, oblige, or restrain. All three of these meanings are treated as interdependent functions in the application of custom. This process of compulsion, obligation, and restriction is integral to the operation of culture, so that the cultural significance of particular art forms inheres in the force of the constraints which bind them. Thus, constraints are not treated in this discussion solely as negative limits on women's expressions, but as a part of the form and substance of Tongan culture.

General Background

Tonga is exceptional in that women are allowed to rule, and have higher ceremonial rank than men. However, Bott distinguishes between the Tongan systems of patrilineal authority and ceremonial rank, observing that fathers and brothers control access to land, while sisters have higher ceremonial rank than brothers (1981:8). Women's high status does not always translate directly into utilitarian power, but is often implemented indirectly, through persuasion. For example:

> The father's sister has ritual mystical power over her brother's children. Her curse can make a niece barren. Typically she names her brother's children. She used to choose their spouses. She is an honoured guest at their funerals. In the traditional system, if there were no immediately obvious heirs to a title, her wishes were taken into consideration in choosing an heir. (Bott 1981:18)

In addition to having high ceremonial rank, women in Tonga have traditionally carried out significant art-making activities. There has been a continuing tradition of many women's art forms (such as mats and tapa), while many traditional art forms of men (such as carving) were discontinued following Western contact.[3] Women today are allowed to compose both poetry and dance.

While there have been significant changes in the Tongan culture as a result of Western contact, Tonga has never been completely dominated by Western powers, and the traditional performance arts of music, poetry, and dance have survived. As movement which accompanies poetry, dance was traditionally an inextricable part of an oral tradition which was tied to the ancient religion. It was banned by the Methodist missionaries after Western contact, but not suppressed by the Catholic missionaries, who occupied the village of the sacred line of chiefs, in Lapaha. Consequently, three ancient dance forms were preserved there (*me'etu'upake*, *ula*, and *'otuhaka*) and are still performed, although they are no longer created. In addition, three newer forms (*ma'ulu'ulu*, *lakalaka*, and *tau'olunga*) are performed and choreographed in Tonga today.

Kaeppler (1970) argues convincingly, citing evidence from drawings and descriptions from the early explorers, that these newer dances are evolved versions of indigenous dance types, which were reintroduced through the Methodist missionary schools as hand-action dance enactments of religious stories. An additional dance which was prevalent in 1981 and 1983 was *kailau*, or men's war dance. All of these dances are performed on important occasions in Tonga today, often to honor people of rank or royalty and to entertain visitors.

Conservatism in Women's Dance

The theory that women are carriers of tradition in cultures undergoing crises or transition may be examined in light of historical events as well as contemporary values and practices. The Tongan culture was disrupted due to Western contact, as evidenced by the temporary ban on dancing and the dissolution of the traditional religion. The question of whether women were conservators of traditional values following this disruption may be addressed through an examination of women's current role in dance. In addition, the contemporary production of tourist dances results in continuous pressure for Western adaptation, so that a study of the behavioral values influencing stylistic changes in tourist dance may be examined for gender differences. Greater conservatism toward changes in women's dance conforms to the notion that women are carriers of tradition during periods of cultural change.

When I arrived in Tonga, I observed that the women's dancing embodied the characteristic features of the Tongan form: grace, subtlety and reserve, lack of literality, and minimal spatial and torso movements.[4] Men's dancing, by contrast, was more literal and less subtle, characterized by clear vigorous movements which involved less use of the lower arms and hands to portray abstract images. Often the men acted out fighting with spears, or wrestling, especially in tourist dancing.[5]

I was told that traditionally women's movements have embodied the features of Tongan dance which distinguish it from other forms in general, and other Pacific dances in particular. For instance, Tongans described their dance as graceful, and women's dance as more graceful than that of men. Tongan dance was said to be characteristically abstract, with women's movements more abstract than those of men. It was pointed out that Tongan dance does not move much through space, and that women move less than men.

Kaeppler's ethnography of Tongan dance supports the thesis that women's movements have traditionally been more representative of the Tongan aesthetic. In describing the form in general, she writes: "The most characteristic feature of Tongan dance, and that which distinguishes Tongan from other Polynesian dance traditions, is the extensive use of the rotation of the lower arms. This rotation along with the flexion and extension of the wrist give the graceful, soft movements so much admired by the Tongans." (1970:272)

These qualities primarily characterize the women's style. Kaeppler states that men's actions are equally admired when they are vigorous, and that this derives from less flexion of the wrist and bending of the fingers (1971:181-82).

Grace is another key feature of Tongan dance and Kaeppler, discussing the *me' etu' upaki*, or men's standing dance with paddles, states that "most of the movements are very graceful as Tongans consider this characteristic of the dance" (1970:268). Then, in describing gender differences, she notes that the men perform one set of virile movements while the women perform another set of very graceful movements, so that two dances are happening simultaneously (Kaeppler 1967a:160).

Kaeppler states that the virility and vigor of men's movements and the softness and grace of women's movements reflect the Tongan conceptualization of movements appropriate to the roles of men and women. "The men's movements are bigger, looser, and freer, and quite often the arms are more extended, while the women's movements are smaller, more restrained" (Kaeppler 1971:189). Also, she describes the Tongan dance form as having relatively little spatial movement but with men's movements being bigger and less restrained, and allowing for rolling on the ground (Kaeppler 1972). Thus, from Kaeppler's description, it seems evident that grace and the movements of the lower arm and wrist characterize the Tongan form, and are specifically more characteristic of the women's movements than of those of the men.

From the standpoint of an intra-cultural examination, it would seem impossible to describe the dance style of either gender as more distinctively "Tongan." Certainly, a man's grace is not equivalent to a woman's grace. But the Tongan system of aesthetics seems to be based (in part at least), upon distinctions which Tongans make between their dance form and dances of other Polynesian cultures. In this context it appears that the women's dance style more fully exemplifies the formal properties of the Tongan dance aesthetic.

In addition, I was told that women's dances have been more resistant to change than those of men. While Tongan male dancers import many of their more vigorous movements from other islands, I was told that women dancers who try to adopt the Tahitian or Hawaiian rhythms are always "accused," and instructed not to "behave like Tahitians or Hawaiians." I asked whether the customs were stronger for women than for men, and was told: "Well, I wouldn't say yes, but the men were always freer. They moved around more, and had lighter [clothes] to wear."[6]

It is important to note that a constraint which allows for more range is not necessarily a weaker constraint. But if more freedom in men's movements is traditional, it is possible that women's movements are more purely representative of the formal Tongan aesthetic because, while the men can do movements which are distinctively Tongan, they may also do other types of movement. If women are more limited to distinctively Tongan movements, this could act as a conservative force in the preservation of cultural forms. This conservatism relates to women's proposed role as carriers of tradition, because the greater adaptability of men's styles to non-Tongan movement styles could produce a faster rate of change, leaving women's forms more representative of the traditional aesthetic.

The men's tourist style differed somewhat from the traditional men's dancing. The traditional men's style appeared more graceful and complex, with a quality of energy held in reserve, creating an impression of dignity. There was more utilization of hand movements in traditional contexts, adding range to the expressivity of the powerful masculine form.

With regard to the men's tourist dancing, I was told that when the men act out play fighting

> they get a little rough, and this is not Tongan at all. They just do that for the tourists. . . . When it comes to traditional dance, then they do it in the Tongan way. . . . Yes, the tourist dance is more rough. Although there is a special war dance, the *kailau*, but this type of dance is done exclusively now, whereas before this was only one type.

Two points are relevant here in establishing a difference between men's traditional and tourist dancing: First, that the tourist dancing, with its pantomime fighting, is rougher in quality than the traditional Tongan war dance; and second, that the men are now performing the warlike style exclusively. Thus the predominant performances of war dances have come to characterize the men's tourist style in general, causing it to deviate from the traditional style, which has greater range.

Further, I was told that a growing divergence between men's and women's styles is due to an increased borrowing of movements from other islands on the part of the men.

> I think that it's very pronounced now, this difference. But I don't believe it was that pronounced in olden times, and I think the change has come about through borrowing of motifs from other islands. Those dancers are more energetic than the Tongan dancers . . . the more manly, the more energetic, more athletic movements came from Fiji and other islands. And choreography, of late, is going in that direction, of differentiating more and more, making men's movements more energetic and fierce. I think if you watch for some time, the dance, the *lakalaka* from Lapaha, and the *lakalaka* from Kalonga or any other place, you will see that the men's movements are less energetic with the Lapaha group than with the Kalongans, for example, which is next door to Lapaha (the ancient capital, where the old dances were preserved). But Lapaha has been trying to preserve the more traditional forms. And I know from many old choreographers—they all say that in olden days, in pre-contact and even after contact, the early contact period—that this was the guiding form for choreography, this handwork. More handwork than the fierce, energetic men's movements. But because of the great change that has come over all our art forms, the handwork is being sort of pushed to the background and there are more and more of these warlike stances and poses.[7]

I asked if there was some reason why the women did not show this quality more, and was told: "Well, it suits them. That is the conception of women. They cannot do the poses like war. They can't do that. It doesn't become them. That is the general feeling. Their dancing should be sedate, dignified, and still retain their character, in their movements" (see note 7).

Thus, according to this interpretation, the Tongan male dancers are adopting movements and stylistic qualities from other islands, even in the traditional *lakalaka*. If this is so, it is possible that the increased exposure of Tongan choreographers to other dance forms, and their adoption of these qualities in tourist dancing, is influencing the traditional forms. This would be a way in which men's greater freedom could result in changes to the men's traditional forms, while women's styles remained more exemplary of the formal Tongan aesthetic.

A major exception to the women's retention of a more traditional style in tourist dancing was the occasional performance of Tahitian-style dances by women. The most frequent attitude expressed to me about tourist dancing was a complaint about the Tahitian hip movement. Performances of Tahitian-style dancing were relatively rare,8 and female dancers always wore cloths wrapped around their waists. This sensitivity to the hip movement, which has been described by Kaeppler (1972) could help explain why Tongan women are adopting fewer movements from neighboring islands.

I interviewed a floor show choreographer about the women's perfomance of Tahitian dances, and was told: "This is just to entertain the visitors. Here in Tonga, we do not need the Tahitian movements, and the costumes: being almost naked. The King and the chiefs do not like that kind of dancing because it is not polite. . . . You never do that kind of dancing in the palace or for the chiefs. . . . It does not look well to move the hips. Then the police would come and take that man or woman away."

I asked if more Tahitian dance would be done in Tonga, and he replied: "No, because the chiefs do not like that foreign dance. They especially do not like the Tahitian dance because of the way they move the hips."

While an increase in the frequency of Tahitian-type dancing by women may indeed occur, in order to cater to Western audiences who expect hip movements from Polynesian female dancers, the strong disapproval of Tongans continues to militate against this. The objection to women's hip movements was almost universally expressed, while there was no great offense taken at the roughness of men's tourist dancing. In addition, there was little if any feedback between the Tahitian and traditional Tongan style, as women did not introduce hip movements into the traditional *tau'olunga*.

Bradd Shore (1982) discusses similar qualities associated with gender roles in an analysis of Samoan aesthetics and social structure. He notes the close cultural and historical ties between Samoa and Tonga, so a discussion of these similarities seems relevant (Shore 1982:1). In terms of the dance, he sees associations of center, focus, grace, order, inhibition, and control, for women, as opposed to periphery, aggression, power, expansiveness, and disorder for men (1982:260). Shore describes men's work as emphatically utilitarian, while women's work is more decorative and aesthetic. Also, while growing up girls experience more restraint than boys. For instance, girls "stay put" while boys are free to move around more; girls are expected to be more modest in dress, and this is

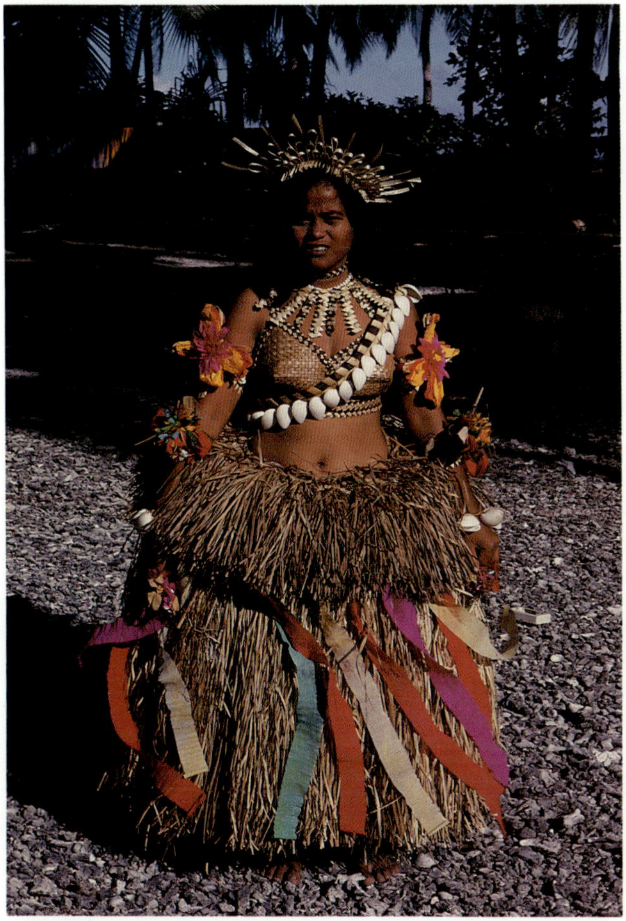

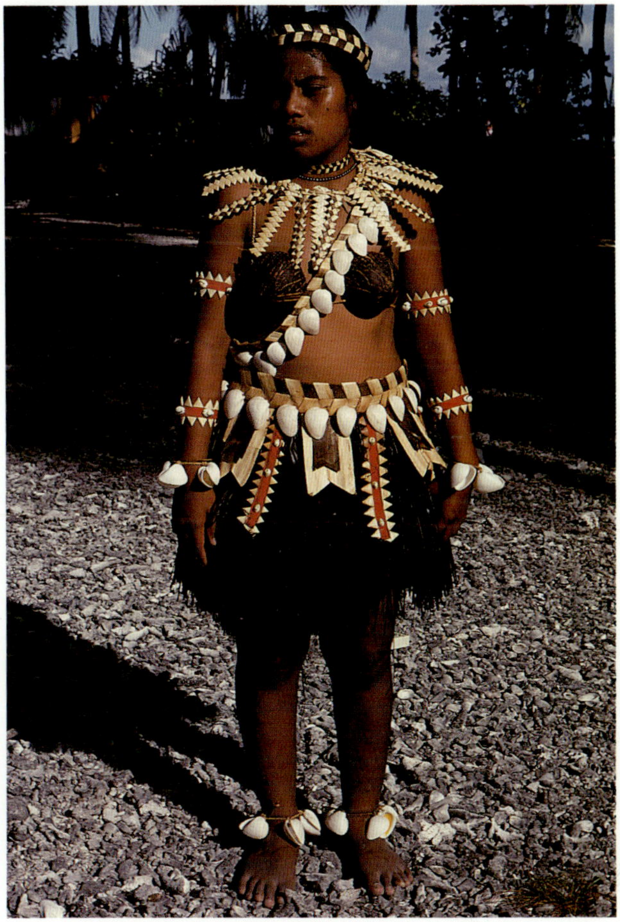

PLATE 16. Ruth Naweir, costumed for dance, Kiribati (see chp. 18).

PLATE 17. Urekei Tonga of Kiribati, costumed for dance and wearing *taona n'riri* belt (see fig. 18.14).

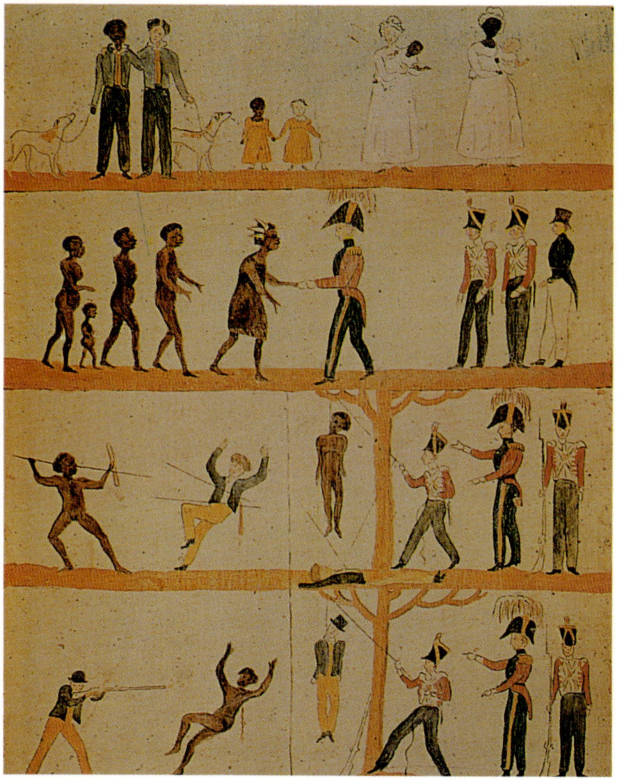

18

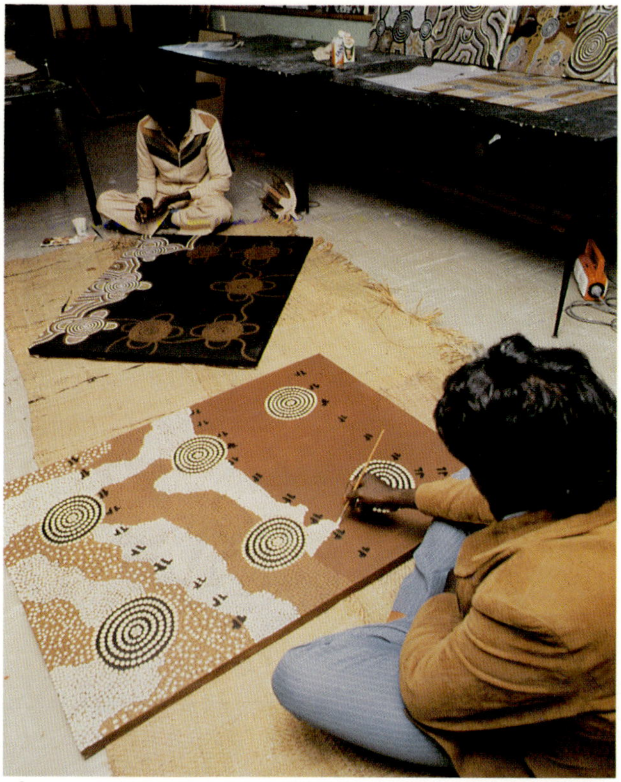

19

20

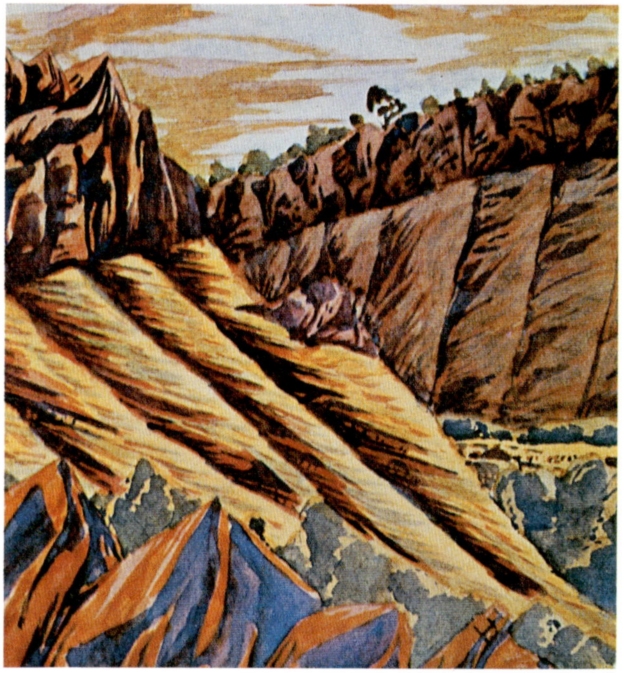

PLATE 18. Lt.-Governor Arthur's Proclamation. Oil on wood, designed for posting on trees in areas where Aborignals remained at large. Reproduced from Dutton (1974: pl. XI) (see chp. 11).

PLATE 19. Turkey Tolsen Tjupurrula (rear) and the late David Corby Tjapaltjarri (foreground). Aboriginal artists-in-residence working in the Visual Arts Studio of Flinders University, South Australia, 1979 (see chp. 20).

PLATE 20. Ewalt Namatjira (Aranda tribe). Untitled, ca. 1970. Watercolor on paper. Photograph from Photographic Service, Flinders University of South Australia (see chp. 20).

associated with a general quality of control (1982:225-28).

As Shore puts it: "In Samoan thought the distinction involves the counterposition of qualities such as movement, energy, change, and diversity with others such as stasis, form, permanence, and accord" (1982:222). The association of stasis, form, permanence, social order, and restraint with women might help explain the greater representation of formal aesthetics in the women's dance style and a greater degree of freedom in the men's style.

Religio-Political Constraints

As some of the traditional dances were reintroduced after European contact, it is difficult to know whether the women's dance embodied the formal Tongan aesthetic prior to contact. It is likely that men's war arts, for instance, held greater cultural prominence in ancient times. Thus, the evidence that women have "carried" the formal aesthetic through a cultural crisis is suggestive, but not conclusive. However, changes in religio-political constraints in women's art forms may also be examined as indicators of a changing role for women.

While women create dance and poetry today, there are indications that men were the producers of hieratic dance in the pre-contact period. Kaeppler (1967) writes that two types of dances were described in the journal of Captain Cook's voyages, one in which men danced holding paddles, (the *me'etu'upaki*) and a hand-action dance done by women or men (the *me'elaufola*). The *me'etu'upaki* was performed on formal occasions, and was associated with the *inasi* ceremony, when food was presented to the sacred king, the Tui Tonga, to insure abundant harvests. The informal dance at the time of European contact was the *me'elaufola*, which was done by men or women, but not at the same time, and with different foot movements. Kaeppler's interpretation is that the current formal dance, the *lakalaka*, is an evolution of the *me'elaufola*, which was reintroduced (as described earlier), with minor variations. These include that the same foot movements are now done by both sexes, and that both men and women dance the *lakalaka* in the same performance, but in separate groups.

Thus, in pre-contact times the men did the formal, or hieratic form, while the current formal dance is performed by men and women, as a result of the disruption brought about by Western contact. This greater participation by women in the formal dance can be seen as an instance of the role of women as carriers of tradition. It is possible that the participation of both sexes in today's formal dance is a result of the breakdown of the traditional religion, and the secularization of dance.

I sought to define more precisely whether dance in Tonga today could be considered a religio-political form, since women's ability to choreograph would then represent an exception to the cross-cultural tendency for only men to produce such forms. In order to isolate factors which are associated with gender constraints in Tongan dance, the term "religious" within this discussion will refer to features related to the supernatural, and "political" will refer to the social powers of rulers. I was told that there is a "political element" in choreography, since if too many new *haka* (dance movements) were introduced which were not related or derived from old *haka*, "then you would be breaking a tradition. Then you would be a revolutionary, and a rebel." I was told that this is why innovation in Tongan dance is accomplished through variation (see note 7).

The presence of a limit to innovation in Tongan dance has been discussed by Kaeppler (1971), who lists appropriateness as one of the aesthetic dimensions of the dance form. This conservative element in innovation in traditional cultures has been discussed by Teilhet: "Heiratic art emphasizes repetition and encourages clever and ingenious manipulation of the iconographic elements, within a given set of iconography" (1983:52).

This evidence would tend to indicate that, while Tongan dance is not a religious form today, it is still an heirarchical, or political form. It is significant that women are currently allowed to create and perform the formal dance, whereas they did not do so prior to Western contact. This isolates the factor of religion, and might suggest that religion is a critical factor in limiting the participation of women.

However, religion, politics, and dance are in no case completely sequestered, so that a discussion of these issues within a contemporary framework is necessarily intricate and complex. Just as traditional Tongan dance reappeared in missionary schools after the Methodist ban, various traditional forms and values have reemerged ineluctably within apparently Westernized structures. While the traditional Tongan religion has ostensibly been replaced by Christianity, there has been some continuity between the ancient religion and the current ruling faction. Rutherford (1977:38) points out that all of the nobles and highest chiefs of Tonga are derived from one of the three chiefly lineages whose origins go back to 'Aho'eitu, the son of the god Tangaloa, founder of the original Tu'i Tonga line. Thus, although the current Tongan government was constructed to resemble the British monarchy,[9] some religious values may persist in the reverence which Tongans display for the king. Certainly, the king's noble and divine lineage is celebrated in formal dance poetry.[10] The presence of religious overtones in formal ceremony may even contribute to the Tongan sensitivity to appropriateness in ceremonial dance, which was discussed earlier.

Moreover, the contemporary Christian church is not entirely apolitical:

> In some ways the church heirarchies, especially the Wesleyans, have taken over the structure and functions of the old chiefly heirarchy, especially on the village level. The concept that the people should give freely of their resources to a higher authority, either from a feeling of *'ofa*, or *loto mafana* (love or warm emotion) or from the honour-conferring acceptance of a *fatongia* (obligation), has largely been transferred from the surviving traditional hierarchy, except when the King is involved, to that of the church. (Marcus 1977:212)

In addition, dance, while it is secular in the sense that it is not a formal aspect of Christian religious practice, is not completely dissociated from the contemporary Christian church. Dances regularly occur for the purpose of church fund raising, in which Tongan traditional values are violated for humorous effect. For instance, an older woman of very high status may dress in rags and dance in a clownish manner, or a young boy may dress up and dance as a girl. Audiences roar with laughter, and liberal donations are made.

However, dance is not a central and essential feature in modern religious practice. And in terms of the ancient Tongan religion, it can be said that the old gods are no longer directly active in current socio-political decision making. There are no longer priestesses or inspirational priests who speak in trances and thus convey divine messages to Tongan chiefs. Thus, in seeking to isolate factors within religion which are associated with gender constraints in dance, two possibilities are: (1) whether dance is a necessary aspect of religious practice, and (2) the immanent nature of gods.[11]

In seeking distinctions relating to gender constraints within a political framework, it may be significant that the formal kava ceremony, when practiced before the king or before chiefs, is exclusively performed by men. The kava ceremony differs from formal dancing in that it can accomplish tangible political changes. The kava movements are not considered a dance form by Tongan definition, as they do not accompany poetry. Still, gender constraints relating to kava movements are relevant from a cross-cultural perspective in an examination of the women's role in movement art. Women perform kava movements in informal contexts, and this is an important women's social art. Kaeppler (1970:275) describes how some of the motifs of the *ula* are derived from the mixing and serving of kava, the ceremonial drink, which is usually done by a beautiful young girl. I was told that it is more important for a woman to know how to make kava properly than to know how to dance well.[12]

Kava is an essential feature in many ceremonies where it is served, as it "clenches the contract" (see note 7). Marcus (1977) discusses this active power of the kava, in describing the Tongan heirarchy. He notes that status, while derived from genealogy, must be recognized by those holding political power. Thus, the royal family and nobility, who hold legally defined status, may recognize and therefore legitimize status which is genealogically accurate but legally undefined, and this is often accomplished in kava ceremonies. Marcus points out that "*'eiki* recognition on a ritual occasion, although only conferring honour, can be very important tangibly, because it can alter relative positions of power and influence of particular individuals, both inside and outside of their immediate family groups" (1977:219). Thus the kava ceremony holds an active (in a sense "immanent") power politically, in its capacity to accomplish status transformations. This ceremonial ability to affect a "real" change may be a critical feature in limiting participation by women in hierarchical art forms.

In any case, the movements in Tongan dance are used as a persuasive element to decorate poetry in accompaniment to an occasion, and this seems coherent with women's role. Bott (1981), for instance, notes that women had the power to request favors of brothers, while men had the power to command. Tongan dance is distinct from forms in which movement itself activiates a worldly change, such as status transformations or abundant harvests. Women in the Tongan case contribute to an adornment of the oral tradition. But for all that, dance remains a potent factor, politically and socially.

It is possible that Tongan women may participate in the creation of dance because it is not as powerful as in some societies, where it initiates important changes. It is also possible that the high status of women in the Tongan culture is responsible for their ability to create in such an important art form.

The relation between women's ceremonial and decorative function and their high rank is coherent with Shore's discussion of rank in Samoa. High rank is associated with qualities of physical stasis and impulse denial, as opposed to impulse expression and utilitarian value (1982:242-43). Shore sees a parallel between men versus women, and ceremonial rank versus political power. He notes Kaeppler's discussion of the Tongan Tui Tonga/Kanokupolu split, in which rank was separated from political power (p. 248). The *ali'i* (nobles) have power in Samoa, and the orators activate power. According to Shore (p. 255) these represent two states of power, potential and kinetic. Thus, the high rank of women and their ceremonial, decorative function, combined with a relative physical stasis and constraint, is consonant with the concept of rank generally.

Another gender distinction occurs in Tongan dance, in that the women's dance forms in general are more detached from the literal meaning of the dance poetry. The *ula*, a standing dance performed by one to eight women, does not interpret poetry, in contrast to other Tongan forms, but "strives for beauty of movement and for displaying the beauty and dignity of the dancers" (Kaeppler 1970:274). In addition, the dancers of the *ula* are chosen because of their skill in dancing, rather than placed according to social status, as in other Tongan dances. Kaeppler also notes that the *tau'olunga*, which she believes is an evolved form of the *ula*, may interpret poetry, but need not do so. She holds that when it is performed by a group, the important factor is an interpretation of beautiful movement (p. 275).

When the above information is examined from the standpoint of women's roles, it suggests that the women's dance form is less an interpretation of the oral tradition than a purely aesthetic expression. If an interpretation of oral tradition on formal occasions can be considered a hierarchical feature in art, then some women's dance forms are less hierarchical than most other Tongan dances. Dancers are chosen for skill rather than rank, and the movements are more abstract and purely decorative.

Abstraction

"The performers scorn realism," observed Kaeppler (1971:183), referring to another principle feature of Tongan dance. Elaborating on this abstractness, she wrote:

> Allusion is also the essence of Tongan dance. Movement motifs do not interpret in a realistic manner. . . . The poetic allusions are usually phrased in terms of nature symbolism, often referring to chiefs and their deeds. The dance motifs, in turn, allude to these allusions rather than to the chief or his genealogy. (p. 179)

It was evident to me that men's movements in tourist dance were much more literal than women's movements, and I was told that

> our men have always been like that. See, if they try to demonstrate the word die, for instance, the girls would go just like this, or like that (she dipped her face, and her hands trembled faintly in front of her face—just a little touch. But the boys, they would fall flat on the floor. And that, and get up. See, they demonstrate it. And women don't do that.[13]

The contrast of male demonstration with female abstraction relates to the visual arts theory that women produce abstract images while men produce figurative forms. Because dance is a form of behavior, the power of literal movements as demonstration is emphasized.

In discussing abstraction in Tongan visual arts, I was told that more traditional designs in women's arts are always highly stylized so that there is very little potential for "rudeness" (see note 7). The abstract designs come from literal objects, but are so stylized that one cannot recognize them. This was said to discourage rudeness by "keeping the suggestion of a real situation to a minimum" (see note 7). My informant also pointed out that the potential for rudeness in the sense of sexual rudeness is much less in the material culture than in dance or poetry. He noted that carving could be potentially rude, but that in women's arts he had not noticed anything that was potentially indecent.

This conception of sexual rudeness relates to progenerative powers and genealogy, but the tendency toward abstraction in women's forms also limits their potential for violating other cultural norms, and for making literal statements about the world. In Tongan dance, both sexes compose in an abstract manner, which communicates through verbally based images, as the movements accompany poetry. The high value placed on abstraction in Tongan dance, and the greater embodiment of this quality by women, may be related to the women's high ceremonial rank. The fact that women create Tongan dance may contribute to its characteristic abstractness.

The tendency toward abstraction may also be linked to the position of dance as an "accompaniment" to poetry, rather than as a central art form around which other arts are elaborated. Kaeppler (1978) considers poetry as the leading part of a performance, with music as a rhythmic dimension, functioning as a drone, and dance as a decorative element. This functioning of dance as an accompaniment is in contrast to dance forms which are believed directly to effect changes in the world, such as insuring good harvests, or accomplishing divine possessions or initiations. In this sense dance forms can be identified as forms which have power, and/or forms which accompany power. Both the abstractness of Tongan dance and women's ability to create and perform it may be related to its function as an accompanying form.

From a cross-cultural standpoint, it is possible that the abstract nature of women's forms would facilitate their retention in situations where there is external domination of a traditional culture, because abstract forms might be less likely to be recognized by the dominant culture as subversive, especially if they are non-hieratic. This factor may be part of women's suggested role as carriers of tradition, if their art forms persist in situations of domination.

Another possible effect of a greater literality in men's movements might be that mimetic movements could more closely resemble other mimetic forms cross-culturally. If, for instance, a war dance contains mimetic movements such as spear thrusts, then the spear thrusts of Tonga might resemble those of other Polynesian islands. This could help explain the willingness of Tongan male dancers to perform warlike movements from other islands.

Progenerative Constraints

In examining constraints on women's art forms which are related to their progenerative powers, it is clear that sexual values which exist in Tongan culture influence appropriate behavior in dance.

> In the earliest accounts of Tongan dance the dancers are described as being clothed only between the waist and the knee. Still today it is not considered in good taste to expose or noticeably move this part of the body. Women especially who move this part of the leg are considered to have very poor taste and are, indeed, even vulgar. In Tongan dance terminology the upper leg does not exist. Movements of both the upper legs and hips are repressed, the traditional costume of tightly wrapped skirt-like covering making it difficult to move this part of the body. This is relaxed in the dancing of young girls and men. (Kaeppler 1972:180)

Kaeppler also observed that "in the Tongan version of sitting cross-legged, the upper legs should be nearly parallel, especially for women. Men and young girls need not keep their legs parallel, although they may do so" (p. 179).

It is significant here that women, more than men or young girls, are strongly compelled by these constraints, and the greater rigidity of this type of constraint upon women may be vital to an understanding of why women's dance forms would be more resistent to change.[14]

An additional aesthetic feature related to progeneration is the use of Tongan oil in the dance. This shiny, fragrant oil is rubbed onto the skin of women dancers, and if it remains on the surface of the skin and continues to glisten throughout the evening as she dances this indicates that she is a virgin.

I also examined rules for innovation in costumes, and found that while new design ideas are considered pleasing as they indicate cleverness and ingenuity, there are rigid rules controlling the shape of the Tongan dance costume. These are explicitly expressed for the women's costume: it must be down over the knee, up over the breast, and the torso must be covered completely, with a belt around the waist. Since these rules apply to what part of the body should be shown, they may well be based in sexual values which arise from genealogical considerations. I was told, for instance, that the costume must be up over the breast because it is *tapu* for a brother to see a sister's breast (see note13). In Tonga, sex-related values appear to play a central role in constraints within dance, and while many of these values apply to both genders, some constraints appear to be more strongly applied or more explicity expressed in the dance behavior of women.

The relationship of sexual constraints on women to a general quality of constraint in which dignity and status are gained from strong limits on activity is also found in Samoa:

> The value placed on premarital chastity for women is one aspect of the control and constraint associated symbolically with female status in general. Much as the male is encouraged tacitly to sexual activity and impulse expression, women gain their prestige from control, from what they manage *not* to do sexually. (Shore 1982:232)

This is clear in the Samoan *aualuma*, or young women's group:

> Functionally, the *aualuma* is more decorative than utilitarian. The *taupou* (leader) is a kind of summarizing symbol for the *aualuma* as a whole, a symbol of the grace, control and negative acitvity seen as appropriate for females. She is sometimes referred to as the *taupou fa'anofonofo* (the sitting/immobile virgin). (p. 232)

The concept of chastity as an aspect of a general role quality of control or constraint is consonant with a more limited movement range in dance. Status is reflected in a relative immobility, in which women's progenerative powers are socially controlled.

Conclusion

While more comparative research is necessary to isolate definitively the major factors determining gender differences in artistic practices, my research indicates that gender constraints which operate in visual arts also operate in dance. Tongan culture appears to be an instance where women are carriers of tradition, for prior to Western contact only men performed the "formal" (or hieratic) dances, whereas the current "formal" secular form is performed by both sexes. But only men perform the formal kava ceremony, in which status transformations are accomplished and social contracts cemented. This isolates the factors of religion and active transformation in association with constraints on women's participation.

The women's dance style more faithfully represents the distinctive features of traditional Tongan dance since its reintroduction following the Methodist ban, and with the influence of tourism on cultural values the men's style appears to be more readily adapting to the different aesthetic of tourist audiences. This element of conservatism in women's dance, in which movement constraints on women are stronger, could help account for the notion of women as carriers of tradition. Also, the presence of more literal demonstration in the men's traditional form (more mimetic movements) may lead it to resemble mimetic dance in other societies, and hence be less uniquely Tongan. This could result in a greater willingness to utilize elements of other mimetic dance forms, and also facilitate some crossover between men's contemporary traditional dance and tourist dancing.

Summarizing my other results, female progenerative powers are significant in gender differences in dance, due to values defining sexual decency in movement behavior and costume. Some of these constraints are explicity emphasized for women. Women's high ceremonial status in Tonga is doubtless connected with the fact that women may compose dance. Tongan dance is a secular form which acts as an accompaniment to poetic performances, and which places a premium on abstractness, allusion, and subtlety. Within that abstract form, there is a tendency for men to act out graphically and for women to dance in a more abstract and purely aesthetic manner.

Notes

1. This paper utilizes information gathered during two research trips to Nuku'alofa, on the island of Tongatapu, Tonga (summer 1981 and fall 1983), as well as published ethnographic materials — particularly those of Adrienne Kaeppler — on Tongan dance. Nuku'alofa is the capital of Tonga, the residence of the king, and the site of many ceremonial and tourist performances. Field observations, interviews, and video documentation have been combined with previous ethnographic materials in order to verify findings.

The initial field research for this paper was carried out under a University of California Grant for Humanities and Interdisciplinary Studies obtained from the University of California, Irvine in 1981. All research on Tonga was performed in the company of Dr. Jehanne Teilhet, whom I wish to thank for her valuable support and guidance. In addition I would like to express my appreciation to Dr. Joseph G. Jorgensen for his critical reading of this paper.

2. Jehanne Teilhet, lectures in art history, University of California, San Diego, 1980.

3. Jehanne Teilhet, personal communication.

4. I interviewed Va Taumalolo, winner of the Miss Heilala contest, put on for the king's birthday. I asked if there were any rules for the movement motifs, and she said: "No, there are not rules at all but if you

are moving hands, for instance, for Tongans it would look silly if you opened your fingers too much, so that the woman would try to keep her fingers together." She said that when you move your hand you have to just keep every finger held together whenever you are telling someone something. She added: "Also, for women, they must keep their feet fairly close together. Only the men are allowed to put their feet apart. But ladies have to keep their feet together. And you can't just dance like this — with your whole body. You have to go like this — (keeping her torso still) — so it looks gracious."

She also told me about the Tongan oil, which is applied to the skin of women dancers. When the oil is not soaked in and stays on the skin it means that the girls is a virgin, whereas the skin will absorb the oil if she is not. The oil should shine and actually drip off the fingers, to demonstrate that the girl is still a virgin.

The *tau'olungas*, or women's solo dances, which were performed at the beauty contest closely resembled those done for tourists, and in both cases the features just described were in evidence. The keeping of the fingers together, for instance, gave a striking flavor of restraint, and artistic "remove," when combined with the incredibly sensitive articulation of the hands, in conveying the verbal images. Keeping the fingers together accentuated the feeling of accompaniment, as the hand movements were necessarily more abstract and subtle, rather than literal, in portraying images, due to the increased limitation of movement. The men did not keep the fingers together as much, and they also more often held objects, such as spears or bamboo sticks.

The women's ankles were always kept closely together, and, while occasionally there were little jumps from both feet, there was less spatial movement in the vertical or lateral planes, compared to the men. The holding of the ankles and knees together created a bound feeling, but at the same time there was a lightness and subtlety caused by the generation of multiple rhythmic patterns from the feet which were so held in place. At times the toes would come off the ground, and the slightly bent knee was maintained, so that the feet were delicate and alive, and full of the strength and sensitive articulation which was necessary to hold them in place. Tremendous subtlety resulted from this limitation of movement, and yet the generation from the feet, of all these various rhythms and expressions was very delicate, and an observer would have to look deeply into it and become sensitive to the motions, because they are not blatant or obvious. It seemed very feminine to keep the feet so contained and the ankles so close together, with the slightly bent knees held almost touching, through the slight swaying and turning of the steps. It felt very respectful and the lightness and held feeling was almost like an expectancy, because so many trembling rhythms came out of it. It felt very birdlike and always on the verge.

Grace was said to be a key quality for women, and the women's movements were graceful and slow, so that the eloquent, restrained, subtle, multifaceted, rhythmic expressionality had a feeling of nobility because of its grace and restraint. It was refined and yet proud. Because the head movement and eye contact is left to the individual dancer, the form is also personal, while publicly accompanying a poem, and an event. Miss Heilala said that the feet were held together because it looks gracious, and this quality was accentuated by constantly facing to the front, continually smiling, holding the arms out from the body, and holding the body supple and responsive to the steps, but with the hips still.

5. There was a wide variance of skill in male tourist dancing, and at times the men would simply clown around, while playing at wrestling or fighting. Some of the male tourist dancing *was* highly skilled, and the performance message was a demonstration of male aggressive prowess. The movements were generally fast and sudden, with strong body tension, and forceful steps, lunges, and jumps, into the ground. There were sudden still poses at times (e.g., as if to throw something) and direction shifts, contrasting a quality of active suspension to the fast aggressive, forceful movements. The men often shifted levels, from sitting to standing, to lying on the ground, rolling over, or going down on one knee. The legs were generally turned out, with the feet apart, and knees slightly bent. (I was told at one rehearsal that a dance was done to please Hiva, a female goddess, as she liked men to perform masculine dances, to entertain her.) The men often held spears or sticks, and there was little use of the lower arms and wrists, and little communication with the hands.

In more traditional contexts, the men's style was much more complex, with a more "held" energy behind the aggressive lunges and stances. This impression of energy held in reserve, together with a graceful dance style, created a sense of dignity. There was much more utilization of hand movement in traditional dancing, adding range to the expressivity of the form, by allowing the dancers to combine a graceful, noble, sophisticated communication, as hands conveyed images, with their demonstration of masculine physical prowess. The traditional stamps and jumps had a more aerial quality, being lighter and more suspended. A greater impression of power was created by the traditional form, and this derived from the dense, yet aerial springs, as opposed to the more blatant and aggressive leaps in the tourist dancing. In the latter form, the energy of a lunge or jump poured out of the movement and was lost, while in the traditional dancing, the force was more contained within the dancer.

6. The Honorable Ve'ehala, personal communication. Ve'ehala is a Tongan noble, who was a Keeper of the Queen's Records, and the first Secretary of the Tonga Traditions Committee.

7. Helu, I. Futa, personal communication. Futa is the founder and head of Atenisisi Cultural Institute in Nuku'alofa, and has published numerous articles on Tongan arts. I attended his lectures on Tongan dance.

8. There were more performances of Tahitian style dancing in 1983 than in 1981, however.

9. Marcus (1977:216) states that "the decision to preserve a limited number of major traditional chiefs in the form of Western-styled noble landlords in the nineteenth century was partially motivated by a need to conform to European views of what the basis of a modern constitutional monarchy should be, since it appears that the independence of Tonga at the time was dependent on a self-transformation which courted Western views of 'civilized' institutions." Rutherford (1977:154) points out that through this strategy, King George Toupou I was uniquely successful in defending Tonga from the powerful European forces which surrounded it. He prevented Tongan land from being alienated (Rutherford 1977:157). "Tonga was the only one of the Pacific island kingdoms founded in the nineteenth century that survived into the twentieth" (Fusitu'a and Rutherford 1977:173).

10. Marcus (1977:218) describes how the present Tupou dynasty, though derived from the Tu'i Kanokupolu line of secular rules, has

accomplished through strategic marriages various connections with the direct blood descent line of the defunct Tu'i Tonga line, so that the mystique of this noble bloodline has been assimilated by the current ruling line.

11. Of course, multiple factors come into play in cross-cultural analysis, and such associations are measured by various statistical procedures.

12. This was first suggested to me by Lata Soakai, and later discussed with various informants.

13. Fanua, Tupou Posesi, personal communication. Tupou is a researcher for the Tonga Traditions Committee, and a past research fellow at the University of Auckland, New Zealand.

14. It is important to note that it is not contended here that sexual constraints are absent for men. A virtually unlimited potential exists in the dance behavior of both genders for violating Tongan sexual mores. The focus here is on explicitly formulated values and constraints.

17

Tongan Grave Art

JEHANNE TEILHET-FISK

The Kingdom of Tonga, located in Western Polynesia, is a constitutional monarchy which still maintains principles of social status and rank. These principles of status and rank become most evident and visibly reinforced in the complex funeral ceremonies, in contrast with the decoration and maintenance of graves, where rank plays a less overt role. Funerals are Tonga's most important social events in that they affirm and even celebrate the deceased's rank in life, clarify how the extended family is related to the deceased, and, of course, offer comfort and love, as well as providing a formal burial (Kaeppler 1971b:177; Gifford 1929:196-203; Rogers 1977: 157-82; Helu n.d.).

The cycle of ceremonies beginning at the death of an individual reflects some changes since the arrival of the first Methodist missionaries in 1826, yet they still convey a sense of stability and tradition. Tongan funerals are culturally transmitted codes that are learned and more or less followed. One of the dramatic social changes that took place after the arrival of the missionaries was the widespread use of graves by commoners. Before the emancipation of the people in 1862, commoners died uncommemorated. Only those with societal ranking — the *tu'i* (king) and *'eiki* (chiefs and nobles)—had marked graves sculpted from cut coral and adorned with white sand.[1]

This study, however, focuses on the graves of the commoners. The term *fa'itoka* refers to an individual grave, graves, or even the whole cemetery rather than to a particular structural shape or style. Graves in the Tongan Islands and in the Fijian Lau group[2] reflect the synthesis of neo-traditional forms with new materials from industrial societies. These materials are applied in a most innovative manner that rarely disturbs the original meaning. The Tongan grave decorator is a perfect example of Lévi-Strauss' *bricoleur*, using bottles, aluminum cans, tinsel, candy wrappers, fabrics, and plastics, or whatever is at hand, in a unique way. The grave is not only a visual statement of the maker's attitude towards death, but is also an art form that clearly reflects Tongan ethno-aesthetic values.[3] It is difficult to find, in contemporary Third and Fourth World societies, art forms that *do* reflect purely ethno-aesthetic values. Unlike the tapa objects that Tongan women make primarily for tourist consumption and that have a definable ethnicity that satisfies the tourist's sense of aesthetics and authenticity, grave art is not directly affected by Western aesthetic judgment.[4] In fact, grave art has managed to survive the critical and often

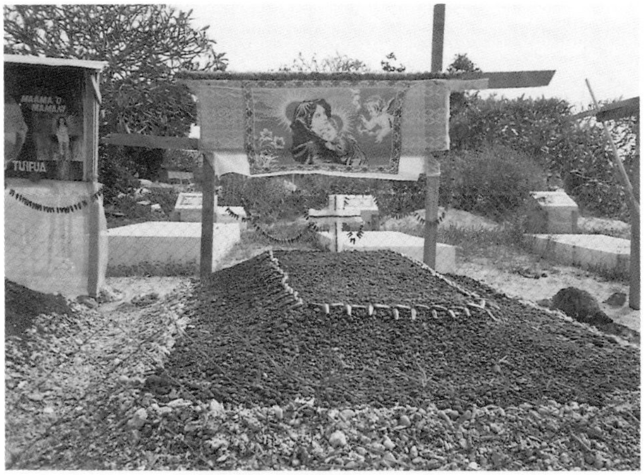

FIGURE 17.1. A Tongan cemetary, showing some of the variety of grave forms and decorations.

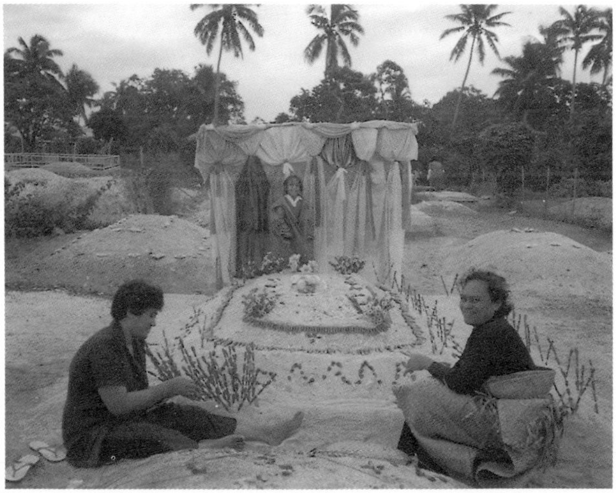

FIGURE 17.2. Women decorating a sand-covered grave.

derogatory comments of tourists and *palangi* (Caucasian) missionaries who dislike its decorative form.

In many present-day Polynesian societies graves have become acculturated forms based on a Christian headstone, often imported and purchased as a commercial commodity of some expense.[5] These graves do not necessarily reflect the ethno-aesthetic values of the Polynesian peoples, but are manifestations of generic Christian graves. Contemporary cemeteries found, for example, in Tahiti, Rarotonga, Hiva Oa, Easter Island, and New Zealand, are essentially the same as their counterparts in the Western world; the cultural distinctions are only apparent on Christian holy days when individuals will often decorate the graves with perishable items.

Within this context, Tongan graves are unique. They are shaped mounds of glistening white sand that are mainly adorned by women (fig. 17.2). It was, until recently, exclusively a female art form. These women are not formally trained artists, but the product of their work is aesthetically pleasing and valued by the society. Graves are an ephemeral art form that needs attention and refurbishing by their makers. Most interestingly, their decorative elements are affected by historical movements and respond quickly to cultural change and prevailing taste. As assemblages of decorative elements shimmering with new vitality, these graves celebrate death and, I feel, deliberately call attention to themselves and broadcast a new ordering of social relationships where anyone can aspire, through the hubris of art, to be a noble. Grave art transgresses the Tongan system of rank, balances out the inequitable class system, and announces the emergence of a rising middle class among the commoners.

My study of this phenomenon is diachronic, beginning in 1972 and continuing through five subsequent visits to Tongatapu — each lasting a month or more during different seasons. Although I have documented graves from the islands of Vava'u, Ha'apai, 'Eua, and Tongatapu, germaine to this paper are the twelve cemeteries I studied in Nuku'alofa, particularly Takaunove and Telekava. A synchronic study of graves would not, in my opinion, be as effective for predicting and diagnosing the evolving changes in form and meaning found in grave art.

Before analyzing the process of change in Tongan grave decorations, it is necessary to highlight some of the ceremonial elements of a commoner's funeral, *putu*, and to clarify the status structure. In contrast to grave art, funeral ceremonies *do* reflect and confirm the deceased's rank in life, as well as identifying and maintaining the participant's position in relation to the deceased, and society as a whole (Kaeppler 1987).

Commoners, *tu'a*, are differentiated (within the society as a whole), from the chiefly ranks. Membership in the traditional class structure consisting of king, chiefs and nobles, ceremonial attendants, and commoners is ascribed by birth.[6] Hierarchical ranking also exists within the kinship group or extended family, the *kainga*. The descent system is agnatic and sisters outrank brothers, whereas the father's side outranks the mother's.[7]

When a person dies a number of mourning prohibitions or taboos (*tapu*) are observed by the deceased's family, larger kinship group, and even the village or district.[8] Among the first of these is the taboo against any loud noises. The most notable and symbolic noise to cease is the rhythmic drum sound produced by women beating tapa, the *tutu* process. Metaphorically, *tutu* is considered the heartbeat of Tonga and its silence is one way of announcing to all that someone in that village has died. The deceased's rank within the kin group determines the length of the prohibition against loud noises. The ban is lifted by a *tukipotu* ceremony where tapa is ritually beaten.

Mourners reidentify themselves in relationship to the deceased by following prescribed codes of appearance and dress. If, for example, a father dies, his daughters will not decorate themselves by wearing makeup, earrings, and fine dresses. In fact, Tongans find our present-day American custom of "dressing up" for funerals strange; to them, our appearance hides our grief whereas their appearance is a visible statement of grief. Upon learning of the death, relatives of lower rank will *fakalafua'a*, paint themselves with ashes. The deceased's children will not wash their bodies or comb their hair, and the father's eldest sister, the *fahu*, may cut the daughter's hair (traditionally human hair is considered sacred in Tonga). This is a further sign of respect and honor for his power and authority, as the head of the family. All participants wear black mourning clothes, *tauanga'a*, an accommodation to Christianity, especially as Tongans do not find black an attractive color.

However, worn over Western dress are the neo-traditional pandanus fiber waist mats, *ta'ovala*, the symbol of respectability. Within the funerary complex, the waist mat plays an important role by ritually marking the wearer's rank in relationship to the deceased. Those who are of the lowest rank wear the *patetele* mat. This is a single or double fiber off-white mat made from *lo'akau* (pandanus) using the simple *tofua* process. It is coarsely woven and usually ragged and dirty because it is often taken from the floor. To wear this is an act of degradation particularly as it has been walked on and feet are sources of pollution. The largest of these mats wraps around the entire body and is tied at the waist (fig. 17.3). It is usually worn by the deceased father's youngest child. Those of somewhat

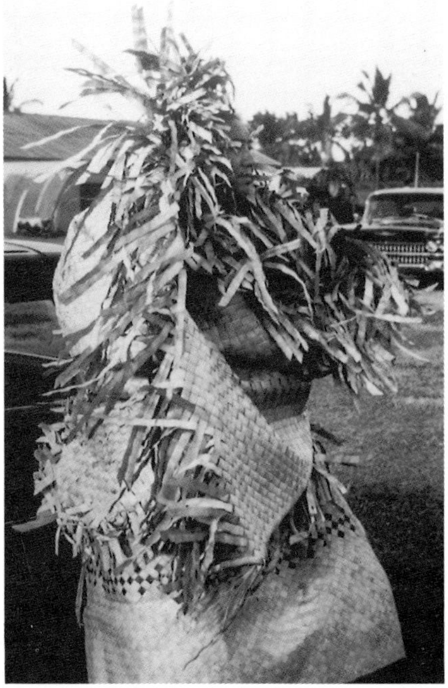

FIGURE 17.3. Mourner wearing a large *paatetele* mat.

higher rank may wear a *lotaha* or *motumotu* mourning mat, which is less coarsely woven and smaller than the *patetele*. The mourners who are higher in rank still wear a finer mat, *ta'ovala*. This is a smaller waist mat made from *pa'ongo* (dark brown or red-brown pandanus) that is tightly woven, about thirteen to seventeen wefts to the inch. The finest mat, a *kiekie* or *kie* (soft, top layer of pandanus leaf which is boiled, placed in the sea for two weeks, rain-water washed and sun-dried) might be worn by the deceased's eldest sister's children, or a noble paying his respects to his subordinates.[9] The closeness of a person's relationship to the deceased determines the length of time one would wear a mourning mat: approximately six months for a daughter, and only a few days for a distant cousin. These mats are always worn in public and their ragged, dark appearance is in direct opposition to the clean, vibrant graves.

In coming to honor and mourn the deceased, the Tongans, women in particular, bring gifts (*koloa*). Different forms of gifts appear on the grave. These have specific names according to the content and/or bearer's relationship to the deceased. For example, it is the duty or *hala* of the close female relatives of rank to prepare a *teu*. A

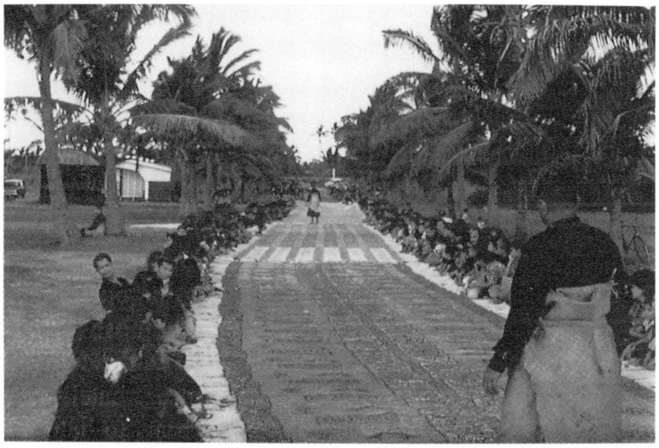

FIGURE 17.4. The streets were lined with tapa for Queen Salote's funeral.

complete *teu* usually consists of a blackened ceremonial basket, *kato alu*, containing a small piece of tapa, *ngatu*, Tongan oil, perfume, and powder. All this rests on a larger piece of tapa which is carried into the room where the body lies in state and is used to enhance the deceased. Another woman follows carrying a large bouquet of cut flowers, *pale*, which are placed on several yards of brocade or fine imported cloth of bright hues. The *teu* is completed by a large piece of tapa wrapped in a fine mat. Today, the *teu* is still largely composed of indigenous elements, but the use of store-bought goods is increasing.

Tongans rank the funerary gifts.[10] Tapa and fine mats of any size always outvalue imported cloth and velveteen rugs. Tongans esteem the fine quality of the workmanship and respect the time and effort it takes to make the object: this standard of aesthetics seems fairly universal. However, Tongans will rank a large tapa (especially a *ngatu' uli*, black tapa) above a fine mat. This is because the notion of scale, which is fittingly called *'eiki* (noble), becomes more important than fine workmanship. This understanding of the system of ranking clarifies why women, when painting over the stenciled tapa design, *kupesi*, do not pay great attention to small details. Contemporary tapa is not meant to be examined closeup; its impact and grandeur derives from its sheer size, which may be some one hundred yards in length (fig. 17.4).[11] Should a tapa and fine mat be of comparable size however, then the fine workmanship of the mat takes precedence over the tapa. (The fact that tapa is the product of a group of women, while fine mats are made by individual women, may have a subtle influence on ranking preferences.) Today, brocade and fine cloths are replacing tapa. Tapa has become a cash product with a growing market. It is exported abroad as well as being consumed for neo-traditional uses in Fiji and Samoa. Tongans complain that they cannot afford to purchase tapa when someone dies, nor can they afford not to sell the tapa they make. It is a no-win situation which generates a good deal of shame because they may have no tapa to present as funerary gifts, and yet they still feel that tapa and fine mats should be given by close relatives in order to show proper respect for the deceased.

Other gifts of sympathy and respect include a sacred decoration which is called *tapu*. This is often confusing to outsiders who only associate this term with taboo or prohibition. In Tonga, *tapu* signifies that which is set apart either because it is sacred or a corrupt, polluting negative

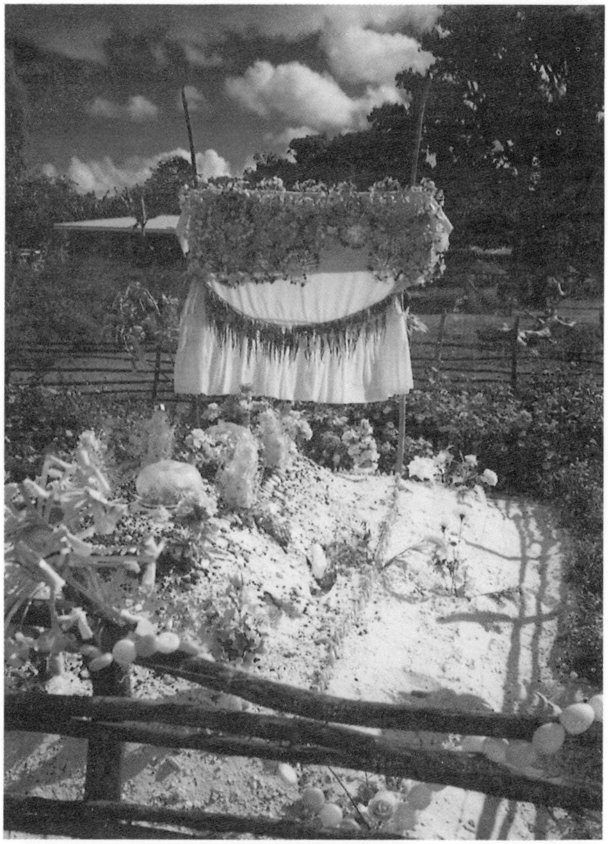

FIGURE 17.5. A cloth *tapu* at the head of a deocrated frave.

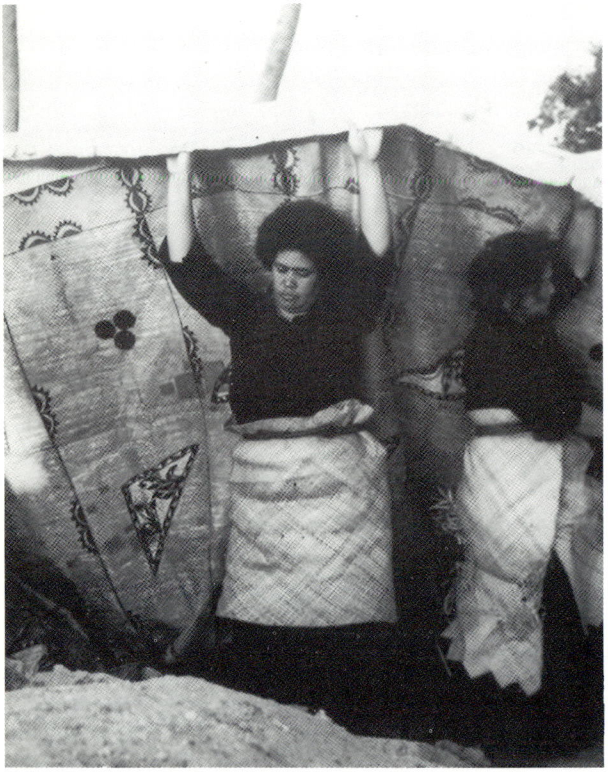

FIGURE 17.6. Screening the burial with tapa.

force. *Tapus* aid in conserving and even protecting *mana*, an important Polynesian concept that may be thought of as a "natural force" that keeps the world going. Sacred decorations are placed within the funerary complex. They are named *tapu* because they mark the grave as sacred and signal to others that it is forbidden to take anything from it. They consist of two upright posts, with a single or double cross-piece upon which is fastened the decoration: tapa, fine mats, fine cloths or other materials (fig. 17.5). At a large funeral for an important commoner it is common for some thirty or forty sacred decorations to be presented. These are impressive gifts of great honor because they are made only after hearing of the death. This means that the women making them must work for hours, late into the night.

All the funerary gifts are first presented to the *mata kali* relative or *mata pule*, the ceremonial attendant who formally receives and duly records them. Then the gifts are taken to the room where the deceased lies in state. The ranking woman of the family receives the gifts and redistributes the majority of them at a later time to those of superior rank to the deceased. The remaining gifts will be kept by the nuclear family and/or placed on the grave.

The deceased must be "fare welled," *faka mavae* or *me'a'ofa*, for at least twenty-four hours before being taken in a coffin draped with tapa and fine mats to a church service.[12] The final burial is screened by a large tapa held high by some thirty people surrounding the open grave (fig. 17.6). This is done in order to protect those present from spirits of persons previously buried in the cement-block vault. The vault (*fonualoto*) is approximately four feet deep and lined with tapa and fine mats to help the deceased rest comfortably. The body is interred with the head lying east, symbolic of the sunrise.

Men who rank above the deceased place heavy cement or cut coral slabs over the vault, onto which they then pour bags of sand. Once the men have completed this task, women who are superior in rank and/or closest in direct lineage to the deceased begin smoothing the sand into a mound shape. When this is finished all the cut flowers that were presented as gifts are randomly placed by women and children over the grave (fig. 17.7). The use of cut flowers may reflect Western funerary practices, but there are a number of references to Tongans traditionally placing flowers on chiefly graves. William Mariner, who recorded his stay in Tonga (1806-10), explains how Foonagi, Finow Fiji's wife "was most attentive in decorating with flowers planted by her own hand, and with the utmost solicitude keeping in order, the *fytoca* (*fa' itoka*) where lay the body of her deceased friend" (Martin 1827 II:10-11). Tongans also believe that the spirits of the deceased like aromatic sweet smells.

The burial marks the beginning of the temporal divisions of mourning and associated ceremonies, such as the *pulua*, a ritualized kava ceremony that gives honor to the deceased and the societal groupings. Another way of marking temporal divisions of mourning that has not been formally studied, is the process of decorating the graves. Most of the literature on Tongan funeral ceremonies ignores the decorated graves. The graves are monuments to the deceased, but they also provide a means for the women to make a visual statement about the disruption of the nuclear family. Whereas the funeral ceremony adheres to a culturally prescribed form predicated on maintaining rank within the kinship group and society at large, the graves make no such pretense. The funerary arts — mourning mats, tapa, fine mats, sacred decorations — reinforce the principles of rank in contrast with grave art, which emphasizes equality. There is virtually no way to discern the age or rank of the deceased once interred, and if his or her name is not on the sacred decoration then even the gender cannot be determined. In a society where the commoner class is socially inferior, grave art manifests egalitarian values.

The actual process of decorating the grave usually begins the day after burial. Initially female relatives and friends will gather at the grave to help the nuclear family. Men may also help by weeding or sweeping the plot around the grave. Although the deceased has been buried, gifts continue to be presented to the family (*feitu'ui*) and redistributed as family and friends come from a distance to pay their respects. The grave is an informal, pleasantly neutral area to gather and renew family ties; memories are exchanged and stories are told about other family members who are buried nearby.

After the first week or two the group thins, but the wife, mother and/or daughters and nieces will continue to decorate the grave. They clean and tend it early in the morning or late in the afternoon and leave at dusk because there are some Tongans who believe the spirits wander at night and may cause harm. Graves are not decorated on Sunday, which is reserved for prayer and visiting the graves of the recently deceased.

If the immediate family lives near the cemetery, the women will continue to decorate the grave for a year, and, in some cases, longer. However, once regular decoration of the grave has ceased, it will be refurbished only on special occasions. These vary among individuals and include the deceased's birthday, Christmas, New Year's Day, Easter, All Saint's Day, and Mother's Day (special days that are, interestingly, Western in origin). It is also considered proper to embellish a grave when another member of the deceased's family dies and is buried nearby.

Tongans, including devout Christians, have ambivalent feelings towards the dead. To neglect the dead is to court discomfort, sickness, and even death.[13] According to Tupou Posesi Fanua, "the love from the graveyard is poison. Our people still believe that the dead are not gone and they can do harm to the living." Should a woman begin decorating a grave anew and for no special occasion, it is believed that she wishes someone dead.

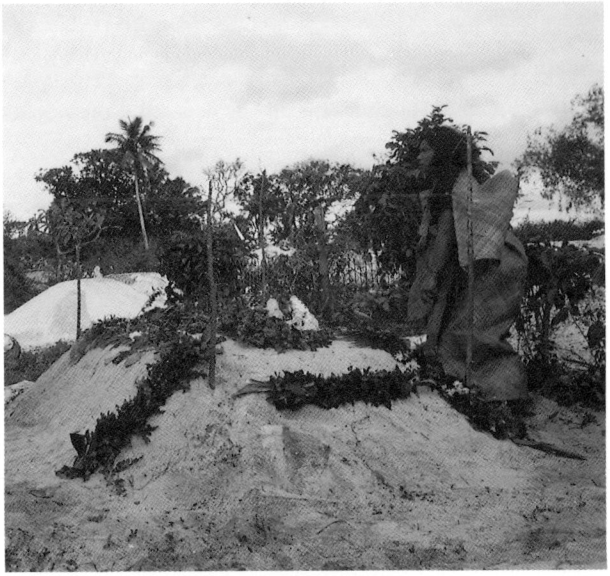

FIGURE 17.7. Grave mound with flowers.

Out of respect, devotion, and fear there are prescribed codes of behavior at cemeteries: one should not run, play, eat, smoke, shout, or turn on loud music. These learned codes regulate social behavior and conform to a behavioral norm that the *hou'eiki* (aristocratic class) have come to expect from the commoners, their subordinates. The values promoted are not egalitarian in nature, but submissive, respectful, and loyal. But it is becoming apparent that the younger generation is challenging these codes of behavior in the cemeteries precisely because of the implied subordinate position; and it is here they can take their first stance.

Within the praxis of art history, Tongan grave art falls into the category of folk art. Folk art is an umbrella term that often places too much emphasis on who the folk are and whether they make art. In Tonga, these issues are simplified. The commoners are the "folk" and they do make and consume products that can be termed art, in that they are aesthetically pleasing, and demonstrate "style" and "influence." The artists may not be formally trained, in an academic sense, which may, in part, account for its immediate appeal and lack of pretention. It is a decorative art form that is usually produced outside of, or as a minor offshoot from, the mainstream of high or traditional art, as it lacks an active intellectual discourse. Tongan folk art is a "living art." As such it reflects the changing ideologies and taste of the contemporary majority and has no imperious liturgy. Again unlike traditional or tourist art, grave art is not part of the market economy or gallery scene. But the graves demonstrate Thorstein Veblen's notion of conspicuous consumption and Robert Trent's display of blood and treasure: Considering the labor spent, it is a good value for the money.

Within a year after its construction, a grave may undergo a sequence of stylistic changes. I have heuristically classified these changes into three major styles. The first is labeled "neo-traditional" because it reveals what the women consider to be, through manipulation and contemplation, traditional. The neo-traditional style achieves its legitimacy through traditional forms used by the aristocratic class; it reflects the dimensions of that burial tradition which was formerly denied to the commoner class. The neo-traditional style, when used, is appropriately first in the evolution of grave art and temporally parallels stages in the funerary complex. Therefore, the neo-traditional style marks the formal mourning period for the recently deceased. The style is characterized by the use of local, traditionally influenced materials: sacred decorations of tapa, mats, and woven sweet smelling plants adorn the sand mounds (figs. 17.8 and 17.13).

The second style, "art trouvé," bears a striking resemblance to contemporary Western art movements: "pop art," "adhocism," and "bricolage." The distinctions between all these classifications can boil down to appropriateness and artistic intent. On the one hand, art trouvé reflects the impact that the mass culture of dominent powers has had on Tongan art forms. On the other hand, art trouvé is not some mindless, accidental substitution of one item for another; it is purposeful creativity. Art trouvé is the self-conscious contextual manipulation of often popular, usually mundane, and mostly found, objects. Whether the objects are found or not, it is the artist's intent, her act of designation, that creates its "foundness." In 1917 Marcel Duchamp demonstrated with his sculpture Fountain, a common urinal, that art can be made out of anything, even objects that are found in the seemingly mundane. Most people, particularly middle class Americans, are culture specific when it comes to art and do not appreciate the artistic genius of Duchamp, nor are they open to art trouvé or, for that matter, to pop art as legitimate forms of art.

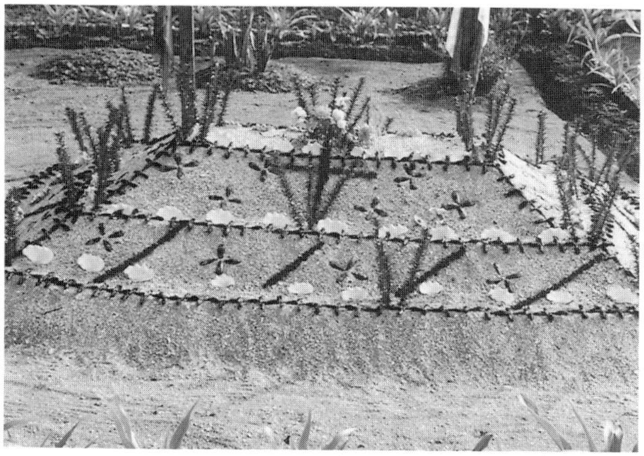

FIGURE 17.8. A neo-traditional style grave. This stepped shape is considered beautiful.

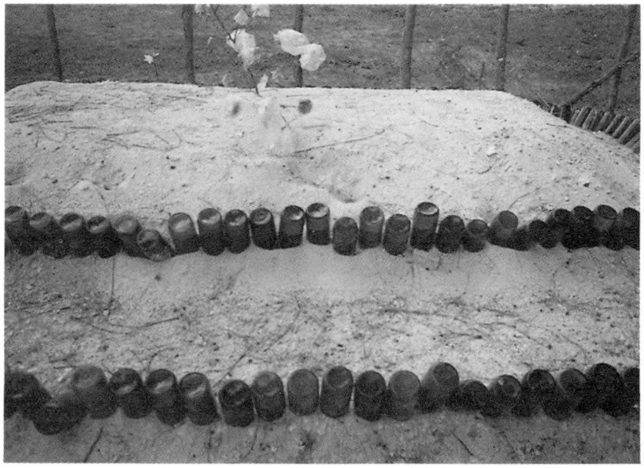

FIGURE 17.9. A beer bottle border in the art trouvé style.

Art trouvé is characterized by the use of new, mass-produced, commercial materials which are placed outside their usual context and yet retain their traditional structural forms (figs. 17.9 and 17.17). A sacred decoration may be made from brocade, tinsel, and plastic syringes, and the sandy gravel may be outlined with beer cans. The meaning of the decoration and purpose of the cans, to hold the sand and mark the grave, remains intact. The art is joyous and playful, the colors are bright and often gaudy;

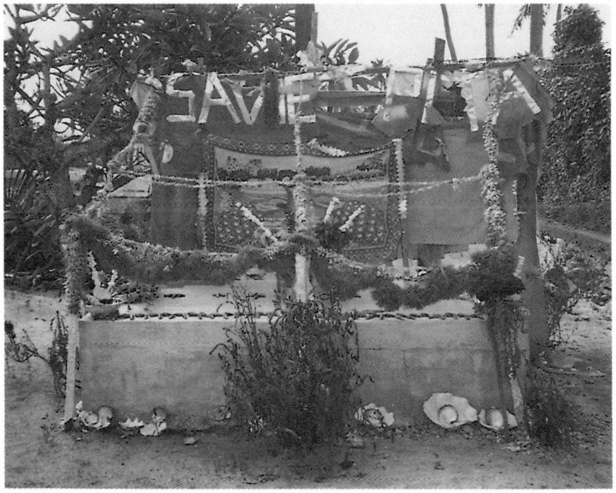

FIGURE 17.10. An example of the concretism style.

the grave has decorative concinnity. It is a part of the economic market, but only in that some of the objects are now purchased and thereby demonstrate financial power and increased status in the kinship group. Art trouvé may co-occur with aspects of the neo-traditional style. For example sand, a neo-traditional element, is commonly found on graves decorated in the art trouvé style.

The placing of crushed coral (*patapata*) on the grave usually marks the beginning of the art trouvé style. In former times, and often today, the addition of crushed coral signifies the transition from the formal to the informal mourning period.[14] At the conclusion of the informal mourning period the family will often make or do something "special" for the grave. This should be something lasting and should require family assistance in the form of group effort or money expended. Within the neo-traditional style, the family might place the rare and highly prestigious *kilikili* stone on the grave or they might build an art trouvé style roof or house over the grave (see fig. 17.1).

The third style, unlike the other two, is a non-continuous form that has no ethno-aesthetic connection with the Tongan past. Its model is taken from dominent Christian cultures and is labeled concretism. This style is characterized by the use of materials and objects that conform to Western notions of proper grave art. Here a foreign style takes precedence over Tongan ethno-aesthetics and cultural traditions. Grave art should not be made from ephemeral elements, reflect joyfulness, or display prismatic verve. Concretism is a style that is made from permanent commercial materials such as cement, metal, or hard stone. The material takes the shape either of a Christian cross or tumulus, and is fashioned by a professional male artisan (fig. 17.10). Concretism may interface with the other styles. It is a recent style and, at the moment, is usually employed last. However, I believe that this may change and that concretism could even replace the other styles, particularly as it is part of the market economy and, more importantly, is sanctioned by all the Christian religions.

The style concepts, as presented here, are not hermetic. They can and do overlap and interface. The funerary complex is a stylized ritual, structured with a beginning, middle, and end. The grave art can signal, by its stylistic attributes, these stages of the funerary ritual. In addition, the style concepts are methodological categories in terms of which it is possible to analyze some of the specific elements found in Tongan grave art.

Traditionally the deceased's societal rank determined the location and size of the grave. In ancient times (ca. a.d. 950 to 1845) the Tu'i Tonga line was buried in a *langi* (sky-tomb for the sky god-king). There are some twenty-eight of these royal tombs in or near the ancient capitol of Mu'a on Tongatapu (McKern 1929:30). The *langi* tombs found on Tongatapu, the Ha'apai group, and Vava'u vary structurally, but in general share an imposing, massive size that provides, at least on Tongatapu and Ha'apai, a

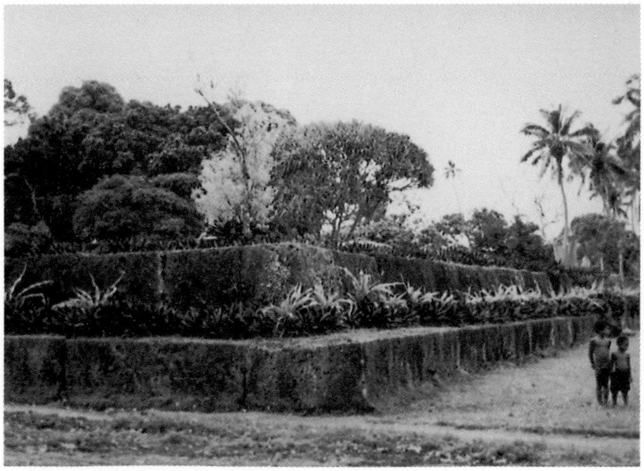

FIGURE 17.11. A *langi* tomb.

dramatic visual contrast to the flat terrain (fig. 17.11).

Prior to the arrival of the missionaries in 1797 there were three separate royal lineages ruling and fighting in Tonga. The oldest was the Tu'i Tonga dynasty, next was the Tu'i Ha'atakalaua, and in 1610 the Tu'i Kanokupolu dynasty was founded. The Tu'i Ha'atakalaua's burial ground is called Mala'e. The royal tombs of the pesent Tu'i Kanokupolu are called Mala'e or Mala'ekula, and are located in Nuku'alofa. Several smaller cemeteries are reserved for deceased chiefs and nobles. One such cemetery, Mala'e'aloa, is marked by a row of sacred *toa* (casuarina) trees and is within walking distance of the palace.

Given that grave art is a modern form without traditional antecedents, it seems that the commoner class chose, in 1862, the "chiefly" grave style that they were familiar with, rather than adopting the recently introduced Christian tombstone. By selecting this style, I suggest that the commoners were implicitly stating that they wanted to be like their chiefs, and asserting that here, in this small area, they could be.

The use of sand has always been a traditional material and dates back to the royal tombs of the Tu'i Tonga dynasty. According to Lua Mafoa, "Our people have a belief that you must put something clean over the top of the deceased, that is why we use sand. In former times, people were buried on the *tuo'ao* or coastal side of Tongatapu where the beaches are. Now each district has its own area reserved for the dead."

Most Tongans call sand by its common name, *'one'one*; a few women call it *koloa*, gift, and several women referred to sand as *teuteu*, decoration. Whatever the women term it, they all stress the importance of using sand as a material distinct from earth, which is "dirty," "common," and "dull."[15] Tongans are critical about the sand they use: it must be white, not grey or brownish, and it must sparkle and shine. "White is the opposite of black, darkness. We wear black, which, I think, we got from the missionaries. They probably associated black with death because down there it is black as anything. Also in our hearts it is black as anything."

The finest and most prestigious sand comes from Tuitui'atamale on the far eastern side of Tongatapu. It is not permissable to take sand from the Nuku'alofa coast because "the government thinks that everyone would take it and no sand would be left." Most people buy sand. "We must buy sand and it is expensive, a truck load is seven *pa'anga* (in 1985, US $1 = 1.48 *pa'anga*) and enough sand for a proper grave will cost at least twenty *pa'anga*. We buy sand because it is the old way. Sand is clean and looks beautiful, we don't want to bury our loved ones in the soil. We want to bury them in something which is beautiful."[16] In addition, the women like the texture of sand, which they say is easier to work with than soil. If the women can select their sand, they will use the coarser sand first, reserving the fine sand from Tuitui'atamale for the exterior surface. This is also practical because the coarse sand holds the initial shape better.

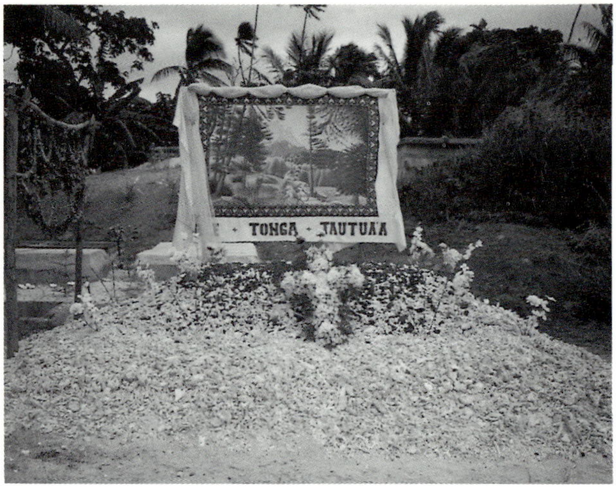

FIGURE 17.12. A grave covered with crushed white coral.

The sand is sculpted into a mound "so that one can easily see that it is a grave." We must make the mound high so it will stay there. An average grave measures ten feet, seven inches by nine feet, one inch, at the base where the sand is loose, and seven feet, six inches, by five feet at the top and stands two feet, nine inches, high. The mounds, called *funga* are sculpted into several shapes: rounded, truncated, or stepped. The top of the grave is flat. Many women find the stepped or stair design, *faka fungavaka*, the most beautiful (fig 17.8). It is also the most difficult to execute and maintain.

The graves emulate, on a smaller scale, the *langi* tombs of the ruling aristocracy. In fact, the main distinctions between a common grave and a royal are the location and the size. The royal grave Paepae'otele'a at Mu'a is eight feet, four inches high, and one hundred thirty-five feet,

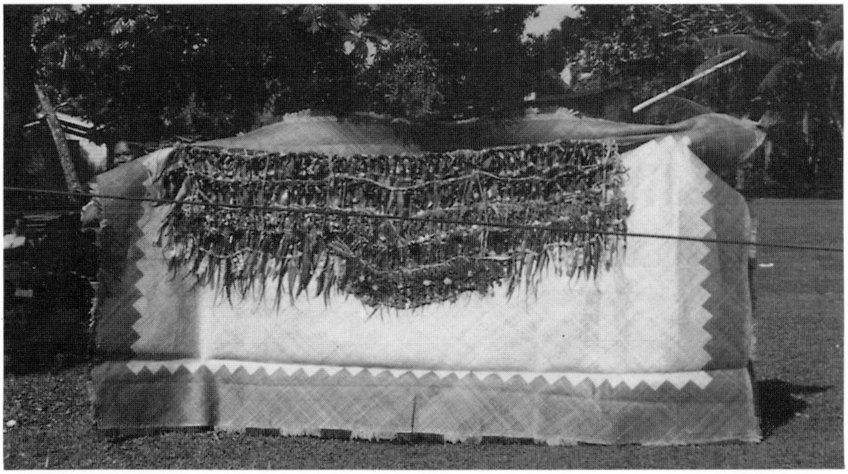

FIGURE 17.13. A neo-traditional *tapu kakala*.

five inches (western wall) by ninety-two feet, five inches (southern wall); it is fashioned from coral reef and limestone retaining walls (McKern 1929:53).

Another material that is used on graves is *patapata*: small, broken pieces of white coral (fig. 17.12). It is heavy and helps hold the fine sand, especially in the heavy rains. White coral usually marks the beginning of the art trouvé style; it should be placed on the grave before the tenth night of mourning. This coincides with the end of the most important ceremonial observances, which occur during the first ten days of mourning. These include the serving of ritual foods, kava ceremonies, and the distribution of the funerary gifts. Today, under the influence of the different religious organizations, the formal mourning period is being shortened and coral may be placed on the sand as early as the second or third day after burial.[17] However, before the coral is placed on the grave, it is adorned with one or more sacred decorations (*tapu*).

The *tapu* is called that precisely because it is a sacred decoration that is *tapu* or forbidden for others to take; it is also a sign designating the particular area as *tapu* ("keep out!"). According to the Honorable Ve'ehala, the placing of sacred decorations on the graves is an ancient custom. They were used on the graves of the Tu'i Tonga and his chiefs and, after 1862, commoners started to copy the practice.

The sacred decoration is an excellent example of change and acculturation, as one can often see many forms that co-exist on a single grave over a period of time. These sacred decorations are usually presented as funerary gifts, the majority of which are subsequently given away to honor those who are superior in rank to the deceased. A few sacred decorations, however, are kept to be placed on the deceased's grave. The first of these should be a *tapu kakala* (fig. 17.13). This is an example of the neo-traditional style. It is made from local materials that are woven together to form a banner, about four feet six inches wide by two to four feet long that hangs from a crosspiece some six to seven feet high. Sacred decorations of this sort are composed of sweet smelling, colorful local plants. Some *tapu* are made from rows and rows of sewn *sisi* (local flowers, variegated leaves, processed hibiscus fiber). *Sisi* are also worn around the waist of dancers as formal festive dress over their costumes or wrap around skirts. This type of sacred decoration is often backed with a woven pandanus mat or tapa.[18] Sacred decorations simply made from tapa are also common.

All of these sacred decorations are labor intensive and made from local, ephemeral materials; they are neo-traditional and valued as such. In contrast, the art trouvé style *tapus* are valued because they are not labor intensive, and are less perishable, more colorful, and contemporary. The replacement of, or covering over of, the neo-traditional sacred decorations with the art trouvé style usually marks the end of the formal mourning period.

Initially, women may adorn the grave with a *tapu* that is made by someone else to honor them, or a relative from abroad might later send or bring one. For the most part,

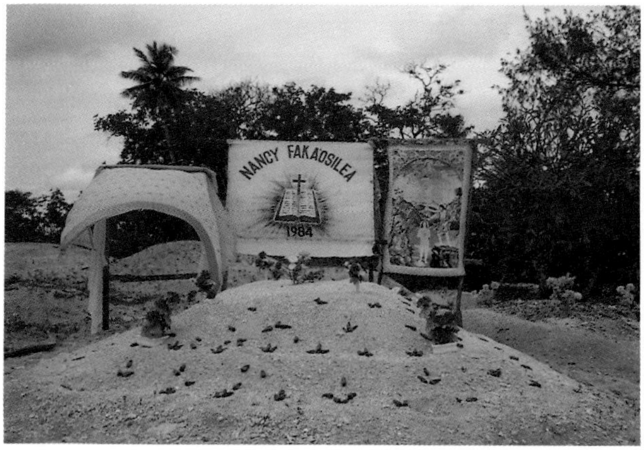

FIGURE 17.14. A grave with several *tapus*.

however, the woman who decorates the grave will also make the *tapu*. It is common to find anywhere from one to three *tapus* on a single grave (fig. 17.14). During the informal mourning period, a woman might place several sacred decorations of different materials on the grave, or she might continue to embellish the same one with applique, cloths, sashes, embroidery, tinsel or whatever is suitable. Sacred decorations in this phase are changed when they become torn, ragged, dirty, or faded.

Within the art trouvé category, fine imported cloth *tapus* of brilliant colors are the most prevalent form. It is difficult to document when cloth first became popular. The older women note that it has been used as long as they can remember, and one said that Tongans have liked cloth ever since Captain Cook brought it in 1777. Will Mariner gives a different account of cloth being used in a funeral. In this case the deceased was "wrapped up in fourteen or fifteen yards of fine East India embroidered musil . . ." (Martin 1827 I:296). The popular belief is that cloth was initiated by relatives who were overseas and could not send tapa; instead, they sent a likely substitution of intrinsic value: an expensive, fine cloth. Like tapa, cloth flows gently in the wind and is soft and graceful like the hands of a woman dancer. The Tongans have come to prefer cloth over tapa only because they admire its durability. Cloth lasts longer than tapa, which tears and spoils in a tropical rain storm; and it maintains a clean and fresh appearance (figs. 17.2, 17.5, 17.14, 17.16, 17.20, 17.21).

Quilts are occasionally used as sacred decorations, although they are not a prominent form. These quilts are made by the mother or wife of the deceased, for his or her use while still living. It would appear that women do not make quilts solely as sacred decorations; instead they feel it is more appropriate that the quilt now function as a *tapu* for the deceased in everlasting sleep.

In the last decade, a sacred decoration which has gained popularity is the velveteen rug with religious or secular scenes (figs. 17.1 and 17.14). These rugs are a perfect syncretism: the size is ideal, the colors bold, and the symbolic religious scenes, though novel, seem proper. These pictorial rugs were originally sent by relatives from abroad, but the local stores are now doing a brisk business selling them. The rugs are not inexpensive; prices vary according to the size and quality, ranging from thirty to sixty *pa'anga*. The most sought after rug imagery depicts the Last Supper and the Twenty-Third Psalm. However, any subject may be used as long as it is not funny and does not show people fighting. To the Tongans, these rugs resemble paintings and are valued as an introduced form of high art. The fact that they depict religious themes enhances their value, especially as a number of Tongans, men and women, are sensitive to the fact that most Westerners feel their graves are not Christian in form.

In the early 1970s, a novel *tapu* appeared, which I designated the "billboard" type (fig. 17.15). It is inspired by the increasing number of billboards placed on the road from Nuku'alofa to the airport advertising hotels, products, and services. By the nature of the material, gender contraints now apply to its manufacture. Women have always been the makers of *tapu*. Men might help dig the hole and make the scaffolding, but they do not work in soft materials and women do not work in hard materials.[19] As the billboard *tapu* is made from wood and painted with commercial paints the women will usually ask a nephew or brother to make it; otherwise they must pay a professional sign painter. The billboard *tapu* can be erected at any time during the art trouvé phase, but because it is permanent and formal it is usually put up later to mark the end of the informal mourning period. It is not a very popular style because it requires male collaboration. A compromised form is seen in securing the cloth to a bottom cross-piece. The cloth *tapu* is no longer free to billow in the wind; it has become a soft billboard. Many women like this form, only because it keeps the cloth from tearing. Practicality takes precedent over the flowing soft lines.

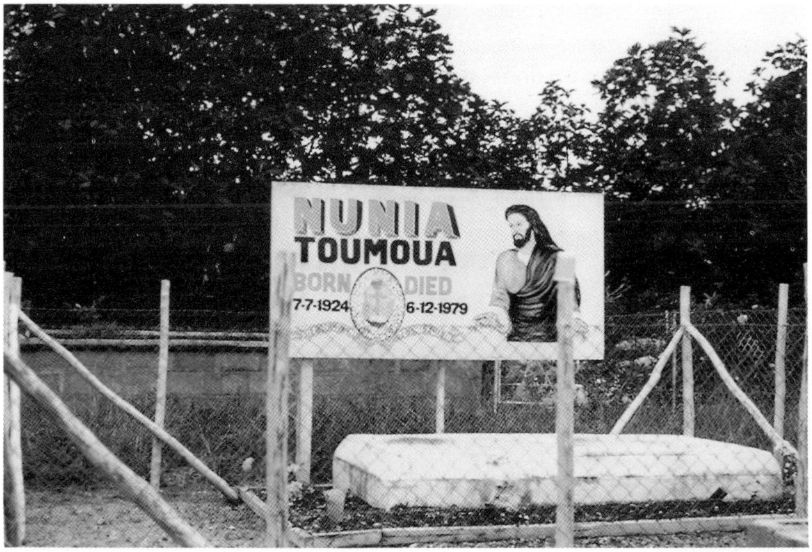

FIGURE 17.15. A "billboard" *tapu.*

The placing of the deceased's Christian name on the *tapu* (figs. 17.10, 17.12, 17.14, 17.15) has been in vogue for only about fifteen years, which is curious since the Tongans had been familiar with headstones with names and birth/death dates in Catholic cemeteries dating from the turn of the century. One woman explained: "People have become more fond of putting up the names of the dead on the *tapu* because there are a lot of graves and it is becoming more crowded. The graves are not as easy to locate or notice. Anyone can say that it is just another pretty *tapu*, but if you put the name of the deceased on it, that makes it more attractive and it attracts attention." The names are sewn, fastened, woven, or painted, usually in large block letters. Clearly displayed, they add to the status of the graves which in turn reflect back on the immediate family. The use of Christian names on *tapu* is an example of social change. Names signal the rise of the nuclear family over the larger kinship group and the importance of the individual.

Below the stately *tapu*s, flowers are arranged on the grave like frosting on a white wedding cake. Tongans love flowers and use them in everyday life as well as for all ceremonial occasions. Some women say that the custom of decorating the grave with flowers is very old and stems from the *sisi*. *Sisi* are made of *falahola* and *pua tonga* flowers, *fa* and *pa'ongo*, the red orange fruit of the pandanus.[20] The *sisi* is cut and arranged in a variety of geometric shapes that can imitate flowers and rare, sought-after bird feathers.

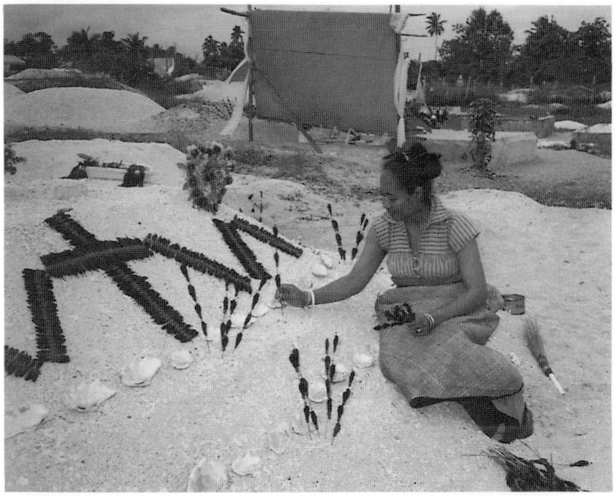
FIGURE 17.16. Decorating a grave with threaded hibiscus flowers.

The most commonly used flower is the *kaute*: the red hibiscus which is picked when the petals are closed. These flowers are used in the first and second decorative phases. The hibiscus grow everywhere, the women gather and thread the flowers onto thin sticks. The threading process is a time-consuming "labor of love," especially because flowers must be replaced with fresh ones every other day (fig. 17.16). On the other hand, it is a pleasant form of busy-work and helps pass the time spent at the grave. The dominant color theme, red and white, is consciously chosen as symbolic of modern national identity. These are the colors of Tonga, under which all classes are united in their allegiance.

Faina and/or *moko* plants may be planted by the women to mark the boundary of the land that encloses the grave. Some families plant the fragrant *heilala* tree, the national flower which was formerly worn only by women of rank. One woman said: "We are making an area that is special, a special garden for the dead to make the spirit feel at home." When you see a grave surrounded by beautiful flowers, you can be certain that the maker has a beautiful garden at home.

After a period of several weeks or months, most women will replace the fresh flowers with plastic versions because they last longer and appear fresher and brighter.

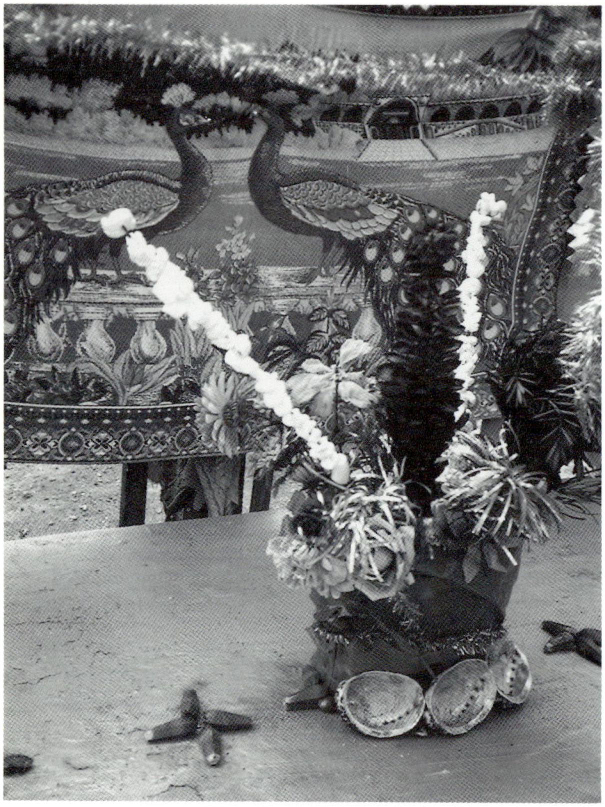

FIGURE 17.17. Flowers of tinsel, plastic, and styrofoam.

Plastic flowers are expensive; a single rose may cost nearly two *pa'anga* and the selection in Nuku'alofa is limited. Women will often ask close relatives living in New Zealand or Australia to send them specific lusters of artificial flowers. But, in the last two years, women have created extraordinary flower clusters from cut aluminum cans with petals made from multi-colored bits of crepe-paper, cloth, or candy wrappers. These flowers are an ingenious solution to the commercial plastic flower and rival in innovation and beauty the flowers the women fashion from twisted wire and styrofoam or eggshells (fig. 17.17). These flowers require hours to make, but it reduces the time the women would have to spend at the grave replacing the dead flowers. This move to more permanent, often commercial materials, signals the weaning process whereby the maker begins to separate herself from the grave.

The graves are always framed in some decorative manner to keep the sand and crushed coral in place, to mark the family plot, and to protect the grave from roaming dogs, pigs and horses. In former times the Tongans used large pieces of cut sandstone coral (*pae*) to frame the graves. When I first arrived in Tonga in 1972, I saw brown beer bottles with the necks stuck into the ground encircling graves (fig. 17.9). A number of white missionaries thought this practice was loathsome; a Mormon complained, "I will never understand why they insist upon putting beer bottles around the graves." But, as the Tongans say, "there is almost nothing that should not be put on the grave; it depends on how you see it."[21]

The Honorable Ve'ehala tells a famous story about some missionaries that arrived on Ha'apai. "When the missionaries walked by the cemetery they opened their eyes in amazement as they saw that the graves were decorated with gold coins. They exclaimed: 'We thought we came here first, but we see that the Devil arrived before us.'" The Honorable Ve'ehala went on to explain that a ship was carrying gold when it fought its last battle at Ha'apai. The Tongans took the gold and placed it on the graves. They did not know its value as money but loved the gold because it was shiny and beautiful. The village is now called Koula, gold.[22] Throughout the islands of Tonga, there are stories about ships running aground and of people taking what they liked to decorate the graves of their chiefs.

In the winter of 1983, I noticed that the women were no longer using beer bottles as borders, and, in fact, had replaced some of the older bottles with other objects. I inquired, thinking that perhaps the missionaries had won their battle. But no, it was that art had lost out to economics as the Tongans now received two cents on the bottle. The bottles were replaced with aluminum beer cans. However, when I returned in the summer of 1985, I was puzzled to find that the bottles were in vogue again. It seems that many Tongans frowned upon the use of cans because they clearly advertised beer, whereas the brown bottles were without labels and were also used to hold lemonade and Tongan oil. In addition, non-refundable bottles are in use once again. The economic factor is important, but a number of Tongans also complained that the cans weathered poorly. The shiny surface becomes rusty and dull, which they consider unattractive. Furthermore, the cans are too malleable to function properly as borders. Nevertheless, some of the Tongans continue to use the cans because they are free, whereas others prefer the shiny bottles.

Seashells of various sizes, colorfully painted by the women or left plain are used as borders, as are cement bricks and even steel girders remaining from World War II. Among a number of unique borders is one constructed entirely of miniature license plates purchased from a toy store in the United States. Many of the materials used on the graves are also used to form decorative borders in the family flower garden.

At the conclusion of the informal mourning period and associated art trouvé style, the women often decide, with the immediate family's consent, to make something "special." The result is usually expensive, permanent, difficult to make or to obtain, and requires some sort of assistance from the family. Time is also an important factor. Tongans need time to save the necessary money, they need time to gather the materials, and they need the psychological time to separate themselves from the mourning process. Thus, this stage can begin as early as after the traditional one hundred nights (*faka po-teau*) or as late as a year after the burial.

Traditionally this stage, announcing the end of formal mourning, was marked by placing oiled, black volcanic stones (*kilikili*) on the grave. "In the old days, *kilikili* was reserved only for chiefs." These stones are still considered to be the most prestigious traditional element found on graves, and not many graves have these them. They are difficult to obtain, being found only on the volcanic islands of Tofua and Kao. Tongans wait months to get the stones. "It is very rare and expensive, our relatives must help pay for the *kilikili*. Men must dive for the stones, bring them up, bag them and then send them to Nuku'alofa by ship."

When the shipment finally arrives, the women gather in the deceased's home to sort out the inferior stones. "The stones should be black, not grey and smooth, not pitted, and of the same relative size," an older woman explained.

> It can take days to sort the stones, after that we bathe the stones in sea water and then we place them on a large fine mat to oil them. The Tongan oil makes them glisten. Once

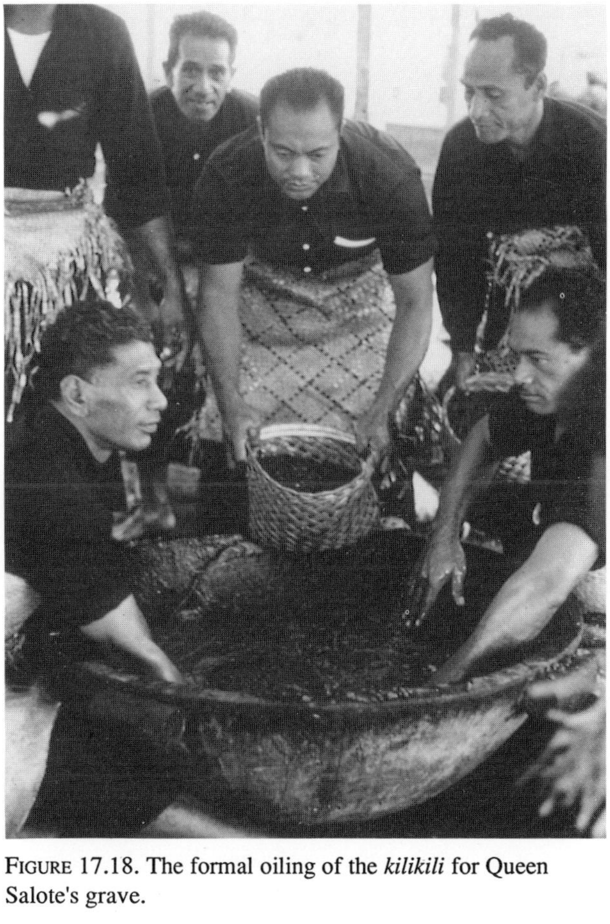

FIGURE 17.18. The formal oiling of the *kilikili* for Queen Salote's grave.

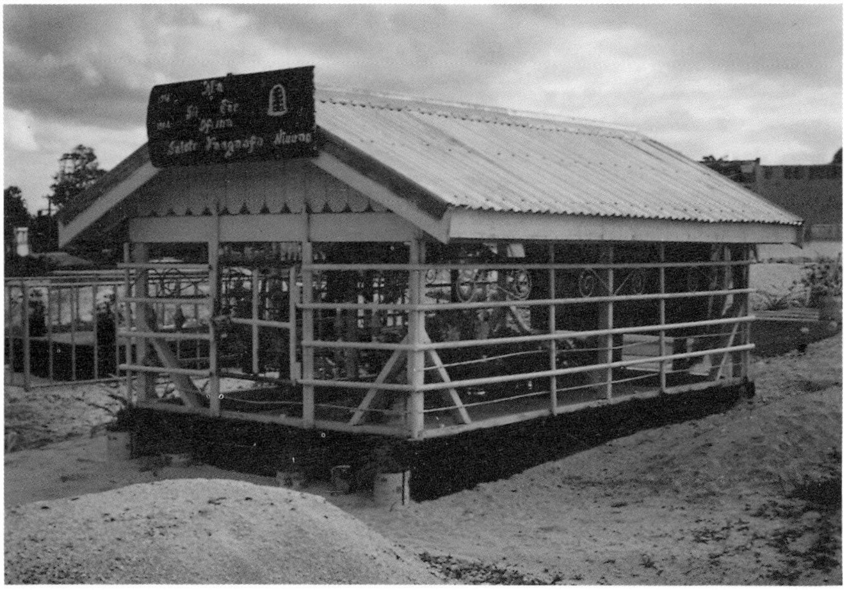

FIGURE 17.19. A small house built over a grave.

> oiled we place the stones in one or more coconut leaf baskets [fig. 17.18]. We take the baskets filled with stones to the grave on Saturday, our day off from work, and decorate the grave.[23] If you have only a few stones, you will just make the name of the deceased on the grave. When you more stones you will place them on top of the grave, outlining the body. If you have plenty of stones, you will put them all over [fig. 17.1]. The oil dries up after several months, so one should oil the stones at least twice a year. I can't tell you why we put stones on the graves, but I can say it is just for beauty. The stones are black and shiny and they help make the sand firm and keep it from washing away.

The placing of black stones on the grave is a claim for upward mobility. It is one of the few materials that seems to be reserved for the upper middle class. Children's graves are rarely adorned with these stones.

An oiled or shiny surface (*ngingila*) is an important aesthetic criterion in Tonga. Dancers' bodies always glisten and shine with Tongan oil, as do the deceased, and if a bride does not shine when oiled, it implies she is not a virgin. Bottles are shiny, aluminum shines but rust spoils the surface. Also of interest is that the few Tongan sculptures that remain in museum collections and pre-date Christianity all have a shiny surface. This might have other levels of meaning, but it is obvious that it has a long-standing aesthetic value. I was told that at one time Tongans used red coral to make designs against the black stones, but red coral is not now available.

Certainly one of the most elaborate forms of grave decoration is the small house (*fale toli'a*) built entirely over the grave (fig. 17.19). The brightly painted houses are usually made from wood and/or cement with tin roofs. They are a collaborative effort: The men build and paint them and the women offer advice and decorate the interiors. And, as with the oiled black stones, these houses are expensive and require family assistance. Less expensive substitutes are the roofs (*'ato*) constructed over the grave.

Some Tongans believe that these houses are influenced by sarcophagi or mausoleums seen abroad; other say that the idea came from the houses used for a dead chief lying in state near the grave. However that may be, all view these structures as miniature homes for the dead.

These houses seem to have been made in the last twenty years and not many exist. They are usually painted in bold, primary colors. The construction, essentially rectangular, is often fanciful in design as the mourners must be able to see in and walk or crawl in to arrange the interior. Some houses are made from ornate slats, others use decorative iron grill-work and a number are glassed in. The interiors often vie with the exteriors. They are embellished with the same neo-traditional or art trouvé styles, but perhaps more excessive because they are protected.

The houses are sumptuous and practical; they protect the dead in comfort and beauty against the elements. However, a permanent house for the dead also implies that the spirit lingers on earth rather than passing to heaven. This may be one of several reasons why these houses are less common; another may be expense. Some Tongans expressed the opinion that the house "is too modern, and furthermore, it is too dusty and dirty inside." Some of the families who built these houses live abroad and the houses are left unattended and become dirty. They built them knowing that they might never return, but they did not realize just what an eyesore they would become to other Tongans. A few Tongan women exclaimed their dislike of these houses: "They block our view of the sacred decorations; we like to see the colorful *tapu* as we pass by the cemeteries."

Some of the families ask the men to mark this special stage with a wrought-iron fence, handsomely made, and with a gate bearing the initials of the deceased. These fences are a recent innovation; they are also permanent and practical and people paint them to keep them from becoming "dull." Some families will have a special *tapu* made. For example, they might commission a weaver from Ha'apai to make a woven decoration with the deceased's name on it. Women may choose to put up a decoration such as a pictorial rug, but now they will place this under glass or plastic. All of these last "special" decorations share a common notion: an attempt at permanence. The women are aware that they are spending less and less time decorating the graves and yet they do want them to look beautiful, and to last. This is not an easy task, given the impermanence of the materials.

Recently, a different type of grave has come to the fore and is, I think, destined to remain. This grave replaces the mound of sand. It is called by some *fonualoto* and is a cement-lined vault that receives the body and is in the style I label concretism. This grave form is an extension of the cement-block vault built above ground with a cement slab lid (fig. 17.10). Being made from cement, gender-based constraints apply, and men must make the grave. As there is no sand, the women's role becomes obsolete.

The Tongans I interviewed, both men and women, had mixed feelings toward the cement grave. There was a general consensus that this type of grave was "Not the Tongan style and it was dull, it lacked *'eiki*." One woman remarked, "It is very new to us. I don't like it. I know that is not a nice thing to say." Another woman said, "You know when I was in Samoa, do you know the cemeteries in Samoa? Well, they bury their dead in cement graves and cover them with cairns of large rocks. It is terrible! The first time I visited Samoa, I remember we drove past a cemetery and I hated it, it looked so ugly and hard." In 1974, the Honorable Ve'ehala told me that "The Samoans buried their dead with rocks so the body won't come back: stay there and don't come back! Tongans don't feel this way." Times have changed and some of the younger Tongans seem to share the Samoan attitude.

Change, particularly from a shiny, decorative ephemeral art form to a permant hard-edged shape that is clearly modeled after the tombs of dominant Christian cultures, is difficult for some Tongans to accept. But it is obvious, by the increasing number of cement tombs that Tongans have decided to adopt this form.[24] They say it is much easier to maintain: "We don't want the grave to be disrupted or destoyed by animals and hurricanes." Implicit is the fact that the deceased is also safer in a cement grave. Many women expressed their sadness and horror in hearing that some graves were opened by the last hurricane. Economics has again induced change. "If sand were available, as it was, say five or ten years ago, I would still prefer sand because it looks more beautiful. But, as the male head of the family, I decided that cement was the best way." Cement is more expensive initially, but it is cheaper in the long run.

The concrete tomb is also a sign of modernity and education, as well as indicating that the family has some wealth and status. To soften the harsh, grey tone (and, perhaps, the acculturation transition) women encourage the men to paint the cement. The most common color is white, the color of the shiny sand. But I have seen a variety of bold color combinations and a few are very creative. One artist has used the grave as, so to speak, a canvas. He has painted a traditional tapa design (*tokelau feletoa*) in blue, as well as depicting people and objects (fig. 17.20). Another artist painted a palm tree. Some of the men are not following the prescribed rectangular shape, but are sculpting the cement tombs into the form of a large cross (fig. 17.21). Women also soften and brighten them by using the same decorative elements they would use on a sand grave, including the *tapu*. This experimentation with the new

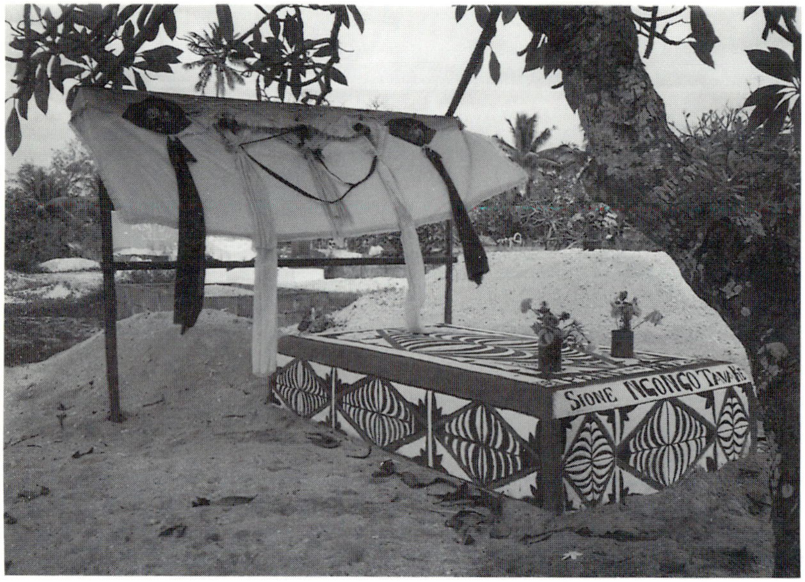

FIGURE 17.20. A painted cement grave.

material and form visually depicts the effect of acculturation on tradition. In addition, the cement grave signals the fact that Tongans are changing their attitude toward the dead. Many people no longer associate the grave with the deceased. As one professional woman said, "I am sure my father is not in his grave; he is alive in heaven. My mother still goes to his grave to talk with his spirit. She also respects the grave because it is the last place he was. My generation is different, we think differently about the grave."

Coupled with the increased use of cement graves is the adoption of memorial stones, which truly fits the concretism style. When I returned to Tonga in 1985, I was stunned by the number of commercial memorial stones (*maka fakamanatu*) marking both new and old graves (fig. 17.22). These memorial stones have no reference to Tongan burial customs. They conform to an established Western style of grave art rather than any Tongan aesthetic standard. They are purchased commodities replete with engraved names and, if desired, color photographs of the deceased. And, as of yet, no Tongan has tried to soften the memorial stones with paint or tinsel. I questioned the increase in memorials and was told that Tongans could buy these locally, since 1984, rather than ordering them from New Zealand. An enterprising Tongan, named Saia Sevele makes them and even advertises locally. The price depends upon the type of stone, color, and size. A small monument costs about two hundred fifty *pa'anga*, whereas a large one can run as high as four hundred *pa'anga*. This is expensive for those who opt for the concretism style. At present, because of its newness and expense, the memorial stone is, in the temporal sequence, placed last. It is used most commonly with traditional grave forms, but I have seen a few juxtaposed with cement tombs.

After the special grave art has been erected, the women might return to the grave site on Saturday to sweep or weed in preparation for the family's visit on Sunday. These visits become less frequent with the passage of time. The grave will probably be decorated on special occasions, such as Christmas. Some women will hang electric Christmas tree light from a new *tapu*, especially if it is the first Christmas following the burial. Otherwise tinsel, plastic wreaths, tree ornaments, and Merry Christmas banners festively adorn the grave. A few families will actually spend Christmas Eve at the grave. In time, especially if the family lives far from the cemetery or has moved away, the grave, being an ephemeral form, will become a low mound of sand. After a set period, usually two to five years, another deceased of similar lineage may be buried there and the cycle of grave art begins anew.

Some graves, regardless of the age, gender, status, and rank of the deceased, are more elaborately decorated than

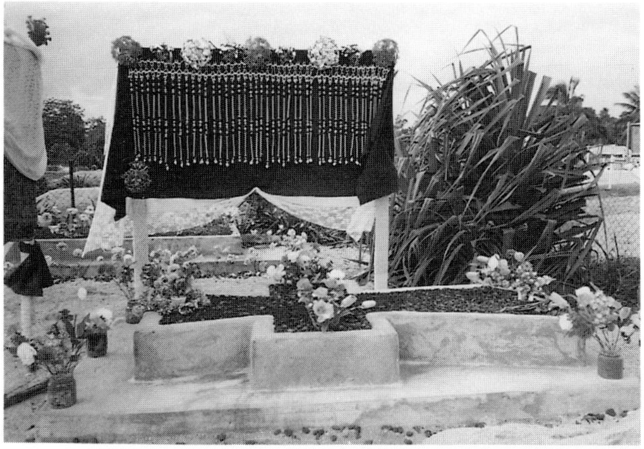

FIGURE 17.21. A cement grave in the shape of a cross.

others. One Tongan woman said, "It all depends on how much you love that person and if you have the means to do something. No matter how much you love that person, if you can't afford to do something, you won't have anything there except flowers. There are no laws that say you must do this or that. I only go and put what I feel. I feel contented to put something on, but some day when my kids get some money I will do more for my mother's grave."

This statement typifies the responses the women would give to my questions about what is placed on the graves. There are, in fact, culturally agreed upon criteria. "If the objects are considered bright, shiny and beautiful, then these items can be used for the grave and that is the Tongan way!" exclaimed an older woman. In addition, no matter how beautiful and complete a grave appears to an outsider, its maker always has a desire to do more, whether or not she actually does so.

In carrying out a diachronic study of graves, I became acutely aware that my return to a particular grave after a year or more might cause embarrassment to its maker. More than one woman has accused the deceased of sending me back to make certain that she has, at the least, kept the weeds from growing around the grave. Others greet me with open pleasure, knowing I will notice any new decorations or other additions to the grave, including memorial stones. But these same women are reluctant to discuss the grave art, unless they are actually at the grave site.

The process of decorating the grave is almost always under the charge of one person, usually a woman. If a child dies, it will be the mother; should the father die, it may be

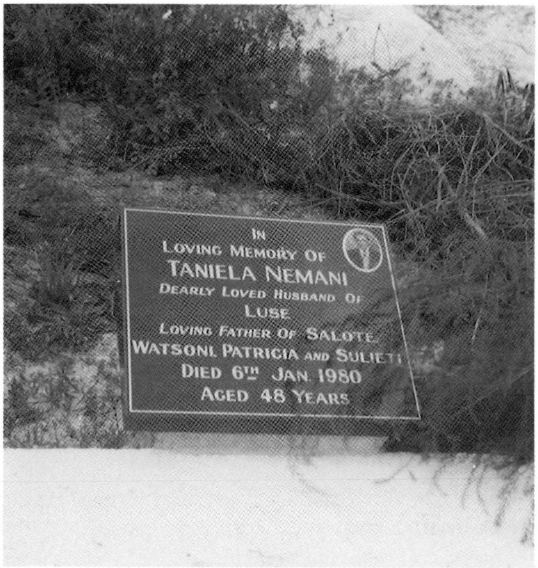

FIGURE 17.22. The new memorial stones that are replacing the neo-traditional graves.

the wife and/or the husband's eldest sister and his daughters and nieces; should a mother die it will be the daughter or nieces, and on rare occasions a son or husband might decorate the grave.

When questioned about the source of the designs they make from flowers, shells, or whatever is available, the women always replied that "the designs come from the head." There is little variation in the design applied to the sand graves, bilateral symmetry with repetitious units based on geometric shapes is the norm (figs. 17.2, 17.8, 17.16). Variegation is achieved by the placement and range of materials used on the sand or cement background: *paongo* fruit, flowers, buttons, tinsel, marbles, shells, oiled black stones, styrofoam, and small toys, to name a few. The designs may outline or accentuate the shape of the grave, making the sides simpler and less busy than the pattern on the top.

The designs made by the women are abstract, with the exception of the cross and the heart, commodities which may be purchased. The men, in contrast, paint representational or abstract motifs on the cement tombs. The style and quality of their work varies considerably,[25] whereas the women's designs are stylistically more homogeneous.

The more I examine the designs found on tapa cloth, the

more I am convinced that grave designs have evolved from the more geometric, neo-traditional tapa designs. This notion seems appropriate because the women have been brought up watching or making tapa and this aesthetic socialization would explain the similarities in their designs and why that design is "in the head." In addition, tapa plays several important neo-traditional roles within the funeral complex: Tapa is a common neo-traditional funerary gift, the deceased is laid out on it, the vault is lined with tapa, and if there is a previous body in the vault tapa is used as a protective covering. If a woman dies in childbirth she may be buried with a tapa mallet (*'ike*), and the mallet is used in the *tuki potu* ceremony to announce the end of the prohibition against loud noises and mourning.

In contrast with the somber neo-traditional mourning dress (of black, worn under a large ragged mat) that so poignantly expresses, in visual terms, the wearer's grief, the graves are playful and joyous. The art trouvé colors shimmer with a vitality; primary colors contrast against the dominant white background.

When I ask Tongans if they think of their graves as being beautiful, the response is always affirmative. One woman said, "I know it is beautiful!" Another woman responded, "Yes, we admire our graves and behind the admiration is the thought that these people really care for the dead person. Tongans admire the beauty of the grave but they also admire the fact that the family are tending the grave continually and that ties in with a certain amount of respect. If you don't look after the grave, after a while that is considered uncaring. Sometimes people will make excuses for these uncaring people by saying that they must all be living abroad." I also asked whether they think the deceased like beautiful graves. "Yes! If you don't decorate the grave it is considered more likely that the deceased is going to haunt you. Some people believe that the roots of the weeds will cause the deceased discomfort and that is why they keep the graves so clean."

There are a few women who do not decorate the grave in the art trouvé or concretism style but use the essential neo-traditional elements, such as white sand and crushed coral. One progressive working woman acknowledged that the graves were pretty, "But my family never decorates my husband's or son's graves. I think it is a waste. I have no time to come and spend all day Saturday on the grave. An officer yelled at me to weed my graves. What for? Why should I go and weed; my husband doesn't know anything. They say I am stupid and leave me alone. Well, I might go and clean it up, but to put a new *tapu*, no. I can give the cloth for the *tapu* to a person who needs it to clothe their kids, rather than hang it out in the sun. For what?" This woman's attitude is unusual; she has broken from the cultural norm.

The uniqueness of Tongan grave art lies in the fact that it was, and for the present still is, almost exclusively a woman's art form. These women are not formally trained artists, but the product of their work is aesthetically pleasing and valued by the society. Gender-based restrictions have prevented women from working with the graves constructed from permanent, hard materials such as the cement tombs. At present, however, the men are collaborating with the women on the choice of color and design. I inquired why grave art is predominantly women's work, especially as only men with special training and lineage can be undertakers (*ha'atufunga*) and keepers of graves for the chiefly ranks. One family I interviewed said, "it is the custom; ladies do it every time. Probably, like my father said, it is *the* work for women. My mother says it is women's work because there is nothing for them to do. The men go to work; the women are more free. The women have more spare time, but it could be that women have more love in their hearts, whereas the men seem harder inside."

All the Tongans I spoke with agreed that grave art was women's work. After all, caring for the grave is similar to caring for one's home — the domain of the women. As more Tongan women join the labor force, this custom may well change, particularly as there is no financial return for their time and effort. The artistic graves do beget other forms of return for women's effort, such as personal and public expressions of family honor and rank. Beautiful graves advertise, through the expenditure of time and money, the family's social achievement. Wealth and education are signs of achievement, and this can take precedence over primogeniture and age in the kinship group.

It seems that initially more emphasis was placed on the traditional funerary ceremonies, which were scaled down proportionately for commoners. Nevertheless funeral ceremonies, be they for the chiefly ranks or commoners, maintain and regulate Tonga's socio-political system which is still based on societal rank. To reiterate, funerals are still Tonga's most important social event and that is why the Tongans have managed to keep them relatively intact despite the desires of certain educated commoners who dislike their inequality. Some religious groups, such as the Mormons and Seventh Day Adventists, argue that the funerary ceremonies place a serious economic burden on the family and are not compatible with their teachings.

The funeral ceremonies and ritual markers, such as the black dress and coarsely woven mourning mats are slowly changing in response to Christianity and pressure from the nuclear family. The Seventh Day Adventists do not like members of their congregation to wear the "dirty mats" to services. But the changes are slow in contrast with grave art. This can be explained in part by the fact that the funerary ceremonies are embedded in a traditional form, whereas grave art is a borrowed form. Grave art does not reflect or confirm the deceased's actual societal rank. If anything, it generates a new ordering of social relationships where anyone can aspire, through the hubris of art, to be a noble. Grave art transgresses the Tongan system of rank, balancing out its inequality and announcing the emergence of a rising middle class.

In examining grave art as an art form, it is evident that it has distinctive properties. Within the funeral complex, it is the most innovative aspect of the decorative process (*teuteu*). The Tongan's say that grave art is *teuteu* because it is not essential to the actual function of burying the body. It is innovative because its purpose does not directly bear on the function. The decoration serves an aesthetic and social function. It communicates ideas about social changes in the here and now: gender distinctions and societal ranking. Furthermore, the art is made by women and, unlike tapa, is not strictly bound to any formal tradition. Therefore it is more free to experiment with innovation and to reflect the Tongans' changing notions of aesthetic taste. This is seen especially in the art trouvé style.[26]

Grave art is a primary source for studying contemporary Tongan ethno-aesthetics. My analysis suggests that certain aesthetic criteria are culture bound and unchanging: shininess, brightness, and the notion of scale. In addition grave art is unusual in that it is not yet part of what I call the "econo-art" syndrome of marketing. Unlike the various categories of tourist art, graves cannot be purchased. They are made exclusively by Tongans for Tongans. However, like tourist art, economics can induce changes in the materials used. In the field of economics, this is called "substitution effect."

The replacement of traditional graves with cement tombs and memorial stones reflects changing attitudes toward spirits of the dead and an affirmation of Christian beliefs.[27] Furthermore, the adoption of permanent materials and processes makes it easier for Tongans to be less preoccupied with graves. This is part of a general process in which the role of chiefs and nobles is de-emphasized in favor of increased significance of the nuclear family and a rising middle class. Change is occurring all over the Pacific and visual art, such as that of Tongan graves, is one way this process is being recorded.

Notes

I wish to acknowledge and thank the many Tongans who have helped me with this study on grave art. *Malo 'aupito* to all the women, over the years, with whom I sat on their *fa'itoka*. I would like to extend a special "thank you" to the Tongans I quote in this text: The Honorable Ve'ehala, Tupou Posesi Fanua, Futa Helu, Papiloa Foliaki, Manu Faupula, Latai Finau, Viki Tu'ifua, Lata Soakai, Tupou Tonga, Limulaki Havea, and Maile Savieti Pita. Rev. Dr. Tevita Tonga Mohenoa Puloka graciously read a previous draft of this paper. I am indebted to him for calling to my attention a number of spelling errors. Dr. Saral Waldorf and Dr. Diane Rothenberg further assisted me with their critical comments and enlightened suggestions. And one cannot write about Tonga without acknowledging Adrienne Kaeppler's seminal works on Tongan dance, art, and culture. It is necessary to add that all this invaluable assistance in no way entails that any of these people necessarily agree with my interpretations of the data. I would like to acknowledge the University of California at San Diego for grants which enabled me to travel and work, and the University Research Expeditions Program for financial assistance. Finally, gratitude is extended to my daughter Samantha and my husband Zach, who share my affection and admiration for the people of Tonga.

1. The Honorable Ve'ehala, former Governor of Ha'apai, First Keeper of Traditions, personal communications, July 1981 and July 1985. I want to stress that commoners were buried but they did not own land. Therefore the graves were unmarked. "Chiefs owned the land and could take what they pleased from their tenants and even kill them" (Gifford 1929:127).

2. Simon Kooijman writes about the contextual role the arts played in the funeral of a young girl on the island of Moce, in the Lau group, Fiji (Kooijman 1979:368-71).

3. For a more comprehensive analysis of the term "ethno-aesthetic" see Silver (1979).

4. Graburn (1984:74, 75, 88). For a comprehensive study of tourist art, see Graburn (1976).

5. Christian headstones are prevalent in the South Pacific. I have

visited and photographed cemetaries in the Society Islands, Marquesas, Cook Islands, New Zealand, Fiji, Easter Island, and Samoa.

6. Kaeppler (1978).

7. "The father's sister has ritual mystical power over her brother's children. Her curse can make a niece barren. Typically she names her brother's children. She used to choose their spouses. She is an honoured guest at their funerals (Bott 1981:18).

8. There are a number of death restrictions on Tonga. Mourners must not smoke near the deceased laid in state, and respect demands that they enter through the back door (Latai Finau, personal communication, June 1981). Writings on mourning restrictions include Beaglehole and Beaglehole (1941:100-4), Kaeppler (1978:180-81) and Martin (1827 I:303-29).

9. Informants also say that the *fakalala* is a special costume worn by the chief's children, for instance at weddings. For descriptions of funeral dress see Beaglehole and Beaglehole (1941), Kaeppler (1978:176, 179, 180, 181) and Martin (1827). Gifford writes: "Old, torn mats (*tauanga'a*) are worn as a sign of mourning for a near relative. For a remote relative who is not a chief a good mat may be worn. The mourning mat worn by a chief over his tapa garment is called *fakangafingafi*. The general term *ta'ovala* applies to *tauanga'a* and *fakangafingafi*. Neither tapa nor modern textile cloth may be so worn" (Gifford 1929:200). *Fakangafingafi* is a fine mat worn by the *hou'eiki*. The *motumotu* is an old mat worn by the lowest ranking person who is not a "blood tie" to the deceased, while *patetele* is the lowest "blood tie." Unless I know the family lineage I cannot always distinguish the differences in the mats. The names of the mats may change according to whom is wearing what, when, and the process of preparing the different species of pandanus.

10. I video-taped two funerals to document the funerary gifts and to clarify my notes. I am indebted to Lata Soakai, Papiloa Foliaki, and Vika Tui'ifua for their assistance. The foods presented as funerary gifts are ranked as well as being distinguished by the gender of the giver. Women give the lesser ranked foods of sweet cakes and bread loaves. These are also non-traditional foods, innovative adaptations. The men present the traditional, ritual foods of kava, sugar cane, pig, and beef. Food is never taken to the room where the deceased lies. It is redistributed according to rank at a later time.

11. Futa Helu and the Hon. Ve'ehala confirmed my idea that scale is an important criterion in the ranking of material culture. The notion that Tongans rank their material culture is not new. See Kaeppler (1971a).

12. They must wait twenty-four hours to make certain that the deceased is in fact dead.

13. In former times, and even today, the role that the spirit of the dead plays cannot be overestimated, although I have glossed over it in this paper. Rev. Tremblay wrote: "You see, the Tongan regards his dead with a mixture of devotion, respect and superstition. If you saw one of their grave yards you would be astounded. It looks like a field of beautiful white sand covered with huge birthday cakes" (1954:202). According to Collocott, "Neglect of the dead is a fruitful source of discomfort and sickness to the living. Many ghosts, however, do not seem to merit so much fear as pity. . . . People are rather ashamed of having their dead relatives walking about. Neighbours are inclined to judge harshly, and to conclude that the spirit is failing to make good its entry into heaven, and is exhibiting a not unnatural reluctance to take the final plunge into the other place" (1923:137-38). Tongans were upset when my daughter, then two years old, showed up in the Takaunove cemetery with bruises on her legs. The women said that the dead were grabbing her and requested that she not be brought back.

14. "The laying of the *pata* signifies the end of formal mourning. From that time onward the unbroken vigil ceases and only periodic visits for grave tending are then paid" (Bain 1967:136).

15. Futa Helu, personal communication, December 1983. According to Tremblay, "To them, it would be a sacrilege to bury a person in firm soil. The graveyards are always on the beach or at least in sandy soil. In the latter case, as much soil as possible is dug out and the grave is filled with pure, white sand. . . . The depth of the grave varies, those who were much loved being buried deep while a poor person who wasn't particularly well liked is put in a shallow grave" (1954:202-3). The depth of graves today is basically the same, some three to four feet.

16. There is a proverb that is appropriate, although not used today: *matamatalelei fakafaitoka*, meaning "beautiful like a cemetery" (Collocott and Havea 1922:128). A common interpretation would be the idea that beauty is only skin deep.

17. See footnote 14. Most of the women agreed with this statement, and I have photographed sacks of crushed coral left by the grave, awaiting the proper time. However, in retrospect, no woman ever volunteered that information about the crushed coral.

18. Several women have helped me to identify the different types of sacred decorations: Tupou Posesi Fanua, Manu Faupula, Lata Soakai, and Vika Tu'ifua. There is a rare sacred decoration, *tapu tuitui*, which is difficult to make and takes more than the usual five to eight hours, with several women working. I only saw this presented at the funeral for the Bishop's mother.

19. "In most Oceanic cultures women are rarely allowed to make anthropomorphic or zoomorphic forms; this is the prerogative of men. In most Oceanic cultures women are rarely allowed to make objects which require the knowledge or ritual process or the skill and knowledge of manipulating certain specialized tools. Also, there seems to be a universal taboo restricting women from sculpting in hard materials such as wood, bone, ivory or stone; these materials are used exclusively by men. Women can only work in soft, malleable materials, such as clay, gourds, tapa, skins, and weaving substances" (Teilhet 1983:46).

20. The *sisi* and *salusalu* are also worn around the waist in place of the *ta'ovala* or *kiekie* for special celebrations and dances, but not funerals. Sometimes a woman will hang a *sisi* or *salusalu* on the *tapu* after wearing it for a celebration.

21. Alfred, who was helping with his auntie's cement tomb, said: "When I was in high school, the people from the tourist ships would always ask us why we put beer bottles around the graves. We always told them that the bottles were not empty, but full, and at night the dead would drink them."

22. This is a popular story, especially as the white men took the gold pieces and anything of value from these graves. They realized the Tongans did not know its worth, and risked breaking the *tapu* to steal.

23. The process of oiling the stones is ritualized for royal funerals, such as that of Queen Salote. The process is elaborated, *kava* bowls are used to wash and oil the stones and this is done under the supervision of the undertakers. There is no ritual form that the commoners follow. In

fact, some women will oil the stones at the grave site.

24. I was curious to see if the cement grave was larger than the traditional grave, so I measured the different forms. The difference in size is negligible, implying that the size of the grave is based on a standard sized coffin. Taniela Nemani's cement grave measured nine feet, four and one-half inches, by four feet, eight inches. Nancy Fakaosilea's traditional grave measures nine feet, six inches, by five feet at the top.

25. One abstract motif is the previously mentioned *tokelau feletoa*. This is undoubtedly the most popular pattern and it is found on everything: houses, bags, tourist products, and even match covers. Originally, this pattern was reserved for the *hou'eiki* and only found on tapa.

26. "I suggest that the study of style and technique in the arts produced by women would be as valid an indicator of the society's changing notion of aesthetics as the arts produced by men. The objects made by women are generally used by everyone: as the culture's aesthetic norm changes, the women's art should immediately reflect this since these arts are non-hieratic. In the hieratic arts of men, an innovation conjoined with an aesthetic change introduces a state of anxiety as the artists risk losing their religio-political position of status from these new aesthetic elements which might offend the ruling chiefs, and the realm of the supernatural. As women's art is secular bound, the risk factor is greatly reduced" (Teilhet 1983:52-53).

27. Pastor Lee, a Seventh Day Adventist, told me that he believes the decorating process reflects the notion of life after death. This is contrary to his religion because it is a form of animism. "The simple fact is that those people sit and talk to the grave. It is a belief that a person is, in some way, able to receive the message. This leads to a form of spiritualism. The person who says there is no such thing as spiritualism doesn't know what he is talking about. I have to deal with it." In the summer of 1985 Pastor Lee did note that spiritualism, at least in his congregation, was on the decline, although not fast enough to suit him. Lua Mufoa's mother told her not to tend her grave. "I am not here. I am nothing. Stay home!"

18

Tomorrow's Heritage is Today's Art, and Yesteryear's Identity

PHILIP J. C. DARK

There seems to be a general concern among Pacific islanders for the restoration of their heritage. Recently, in preparation for the Fourth Festival of Pacific Arts, this concern found expression, for example, in the quarterly review, *Pacific 2000* (no.2 1983:17), the editors of which had just produced a book *Kanak Artefacts*, based on the work of Roger Boulay. The stated objectives of this work are, first, "to help restore their heritage to the Kanak people (in picture-form at least) so that the latter may come to know it for the first time or rediscover it and gain inspiration for the creation of contemporary art," and, second, "to be given for presentation to artists and traditional Melanesian authorities for the verification of an artistic cultural and historical commentary on each object, so that a new revised version of this book may be put together and released to what is commonly known as the general public."

The two concerns expressed here are for heritage and its authentication, to restore what is inherited and verify its past by contemporary opinions and understandings of that past. "Restore" means to give back, to make restitution of things taken away. In various ways some things have been returned, whether an object or an illustration of it, skills that had been abandoned have been revived, knowledge that might slip away has been sought and recorded. I hope all these, however inadequate and deficient some may feel them to be, add up to forces which are helping to heal and restore pride in reshaping and redefining Oceanic cultures so that new cultures and a new Oceania arise, to paraphrase part of Albert Wendt's (1983:198) opening statement in his presentation at the 1978 symposium of the Pacific Arts Association. "New cultures" and "a new Oceania" will undoubtedly arise, but there are other forces at work in the Pacific which may be thought by some as devisive and fragmenting but which come from changes occurring in the modern world, a world dominated by technology and the supply and demand of its resulting products; a world shrinking in scale so that all human beings are in communication with all others. These forces, while cutting across national boundaries and breaking them down, are also reinforcing them. There is no escaping but there is no isolation. The result? A form of Pan-Pacificism, a Pan-Pacific culture, perhaps, effected in much the same way as American culture in many of its physical features has permeated the Western world and left impressed on it its supermarket culture with its conformities, sameness, standardization of products and means of consumption, and depersonalization of community relations; a catering to the individualness of the person though thereby divorcing him from the fraternalness of his fellow human beings.

But the restoration of a heritage includes accumulating old things and putting them in museums or cultural centers, or securing them as cultural monuments. What is the significance of this? For storage, conservation and research, of course, but why do people go to museums? Why would they want to? Curiosity? Inquisitiveness? To learn about something? To learn about things of their past and the past of others?[1] Dirk Smidt, writing of the role of museums in a Pacific context, noted that they are a means of reaffirmation of the value of cultures and of great artistic traditions and spiritual achievements, serving as a way to regain identity and the return of cultural heritage (quoted in Godin 1983:21).

In the Marshall Islands, the Alele Museum sponsored last year its first annual Folk Arts Festival. The aims of the festival were "to stimulate cultural identity; celebrate the traditional; provide an opportunity for contemporary expression, and encouragement toward a national goal of self-reliance."[2] The festival was also an occasion for the marketing of handicrafts.

In 1979, in Malaita, Solomon Islands, the Kwaio Cultural Centre was established inland from Sinalagu Harbor. The aim of this Centre, the Akins (1981:31) wrote in *Pacific Arts Newsletter*, was "to foster rural development as well as to revive and maintain traditional art work." Revival meant learning about art forms and how to make them from those elders who still remembered the old ways. But the viability of the cultural centre in this modern world depended on the sale of what it produced, not forgetting the artists who had to live too. Initially, the centre was sustained, at least in part, by an Australian Government grant as well as by the business it generated. This business, like so many others, was directed outward from the community towards the rest of the country, and to commercial enterprises overseas. The *raison d'être* for continuing to produce traditional art is projected away from the tradition that produced it toward an alien context which nurtures it, and which, in so doing, inevitably changes it. It would be contributing to what Wendt (1983:200) has referred to as a "fake tradition." Be that as it may, it exists. Indeed I see the process at work as being, in a sense, Pan-Pacific, though the resulting ties — or relationships — are beyond (hopefully, in this context, not pancosmismatic or entirely materialistic in nature).[3] Eventually, though accretively, the result may be an established tradition in which many individual artists will have their roots. Perhaps they will be the members of the "academy" and no doubt there will always be rebels around.

In the Kingdom of Tonga there is no museum, though I understand there were hopes of creating a Tongan arts association and National Dance Theatre. To that end the government had agreed to establish four new posts in the Teacher Training College: in dance, in arts and crafts, in Tongan music, and in Tongan language and culture. The idea of establishing a National Dance Theatre expresses the orientation Tongans have toward the arts. The post in arts and crafts has been filled by an Australian artist.

Of those who are interested today in the arts of the Pacific, some tend to confine their interests to what has passed, any attention they give the present being largely a means of enlightening that past. But what is produced today is tomorrow's heritage. What is that likely to be? In trying to answer this question I will present some observations, limited though they are, which I made in several Pacific countries in 1983 together with data deriving from earlier contact with Pacific peoples. I do this hesitantly, knowing that those who live and work in the Pacific know more about the matters I shall discuss than I do and that some of them have written on the contemporary scene with passionate conern.[4] However, what I want to say is but an outsider's view and perceptively suffers accordingly. Present happenings and trends in Pacific affairs can be decried or acclaimed. The stage on which they occur represents today, this point in time. Tastes change hand in hand with fashions: Perhaps it will take over two hundred years for full cognition to occur that the works of some contemporary artists are those of geniuses, as was the case, for example, in Europe of the work of Diego Velazquez, sorely neglected until a hundred years ago. I shall restrict myself to the visual arts and some references to the dance.

My observations suggested that several different trends were taking place in the development of Pacific arts, using the term art broadly.[5] During the 1978 Pacific Arts Association symposium at Wellington, Nelson Graburn (1983) suggested theoretical approaches which might help clarify the contemporary scene in the Pacific. He pointed out how wide ranging were the artistic activities being pursued and suggested modifications to his earlier (1976) classificatory scheme for putting order into the changes to which ethnic and tourist arts generally were being subjected. His schema is significant to the pursuit of theoretical interests in art in culture and should be born in mind, but I did not have it in mind when trying to put some order into my observations which grouped into the categories presented below. I hope these may add something to what has been advanced by others. The categories or trends concern artistic activities:

1. Which have a continuing link with the past even if modified. They can be divided into:
   1.1. those which produce art mainly for internal consumption, in the culture
   1.2. those which produce art for consumption outside the culture as as well
2. Which are devoted to the copying of old forms for commercial purposes
3. Which create new forms out of old Pacific ones, producing a Pan-Pacific style
4. Which create new forms out of old Pacific ones in a synthesis with non-Pacific forms and sometimes in non-Pacific media, producing a Pan-Pacific art

The third of these I see as a kind of internal Pacific eclecticism, largely lacking originality, which is manifest in a uniformity of style. The fourth category is both original and derivative — all art is — and being at an early stage of development it has no uniformity of style, although it does have a Pan-Pacific commonality; however, its inspirations are internal and external to the Pacific. Indeed, there are perhaps three trends which are Pan-Pacific in nature, for some of the art produced in my first category — art which continues from the past — will, no doubt, continue, even if modified, to function in indigenous contexts, but some of it will serve more and more in applied fields of furnishings, textiles, household utensils, and buildings, which may reflect national origins in design but be used internationally.

Artistic Activities with a Continuing Link with the Past

Included here are those artistic activities some of which may have become modified but which have a continuing existence; generally old forms are still being produced in old ways though some may have been dropped from the repertoire. Sometimes new materials are used in old ways. It is difficult to establish any hard and fast categories because the links with the past in some artistic activities may be tenuous or even broken in some cultures but not in others. Or an activity may be revived after it had ceased for a period in terms of production, the knowledge and skill of it being retained by one or two artists who had practised it in the past.

REVIVALS

A recent, outstanding example of revival is the 1980-81 construction of a *binabina* or Gela war canoe by the canoe makers of Haroro Village on Big Gela (Florida Island), a record of which was made by Robert Pule (1983), who coordinated the project, and published it in the Solomon Islands. A further revival, which was remarkably fruitful and to which particular attention should be drawn, is that of Gogodala of the Aramia River under the sponsorship of the National Cultural Council, Papua New Guinea; a revival so well documented by Tony Crawford (1981) in his remarkable book, *Aida, Life and Ceremony of the Gogodala.*

Revivals flow from a variety of circumstances and stimuli. Mention has been made of those instigated by the Kwaio Cultural Centre. In Fiji, pottery used to be made at Nasilai on Viti Levu. The practice ceased, but as tourists could reach the village it started up again. The same circumstances occurred with two potters, Vesina and her daughter-in-law, Amilia, who lived near the ferry crossing on the Rewa River, opposite Lomanikoro, and who returned to making old forms in the traditional manner because they could sell them to tourists.

When working among the Kilenge, West New Britain, in 1966-67, my quest for knowledge about past ceremonial was sufficient stimulus to cause three artists to carve masks of a type which had not been produced for some while. The result was the revival of the ceremony in which they functioned. The next step was for one or two artists to carve masks for direct sale outside Kilenge. Indeed, they happily found their way to the Field Museum in Chicago. But the possibilities of cash returns induced someone not recognized as an artist to produce a mask — a poor one indeed — and this was regarded by one or two master artists as an offense. It was all right for somebody to carve coconuts for sale, which one or two did, but that certain standards in carving a mask were not maintained was disapproved and insulting. The sale of the masks was not a direct matter between artist and customer. Partly because of logistics a non-artist took on an entrepreneurial role, which signaled the beginnings of the middleman in commercial transactions.

RETENTIONS

When the press of change is strong, activities drop out unless they are economically viable or there is some very strong cultural cause for their retention. Apparently there is one island in the Vava'u group where traditional Tongan canoes are still made, but elsewhere new craft with new propulsion methods provide better returns than the old ones. On the other hand, in Kiribati, though a few fishermen use imported hulls and motors, sailing, with its skills and the production of outrigger canoes as works of art, is fundamental to the *weltanschauung* of the Kiribati and their aesthetics, so much so that I found these arts to be very much alive and part of the contemporary culture. The observations in Grimble's excellent paper on Kiribati canoes (1972:152) hold true today: "The love of his canoe still amounts to a passion with the Gilbert Islander. It ranks second only to the feeling he has for his paternal lands. . . . For the shipwright's and the yachtsman's arts were gifts of the gods, entitling a man to freedom and a competence."[6]

May and Tuckson (1982:145) concluded that all pottery in Papua New Guinea is on the decline save that of the Azera. Even though they had ceased making some old forms, the stimulation and industry of one individual turned pot making into "a thriving, growing industry." In some instances the impetus to retain clay pots in favor of modern substitutes, May and Tuckson noted, arose from culinary preferences — food cooked in clay vessels was considered tastier than that cooked in aluminium ones.[7]

HOME AND FOREIGN CONSUMPTION

In many Pacific cultures, traditional handicrafts are still pursued and consumed in the community or culture, or partly within and partly without. In reference to mat weaving in Fiji, Ewins (1982:iii) notes that "in contrast with the steady decline in both activity and artefact quality in most Fijian crafts today, mat production has grown in quantity and regional distribution, and quality, demonstrably lower than that of some museum pieces, remains quite reasonable." He goes on to point out that the skills involved are known more widely today than before because the traditional district proprietary rights in various crafts no longer hold. In contrast, I do not know how far traditional pottery forms are used locally, but it is clear that, in the two areas I visited, they are still made and fired in the old manner even though they are intended for tourists to buy. For example, Maria Rawaci of Naiawa village, Sigatoka, told me that she makes various traditional forms: three kinds of cooking pots (*kuro lailai, al vakiriri/alriri, vaka sangqa*), earthenware pot stands (*sue qaqi*), various finger bowls (*al vuluvulu/darim vuluvulu*) and drinking vessels (*saqa moli, sangqa ni wai*), a big mouthed pot (*ravarava*) for cooking oil, and a number of non-traditional pieces for sale too, such as frogs, pigs, dogs, and ashtrays; all are low fired.[8] Diana Bawa of Nakambuta, on the Buta River, also made a similar range of pots including finger bowls and a form of oil pot (*koroniwaiwai*), but she had also made some innovations to traditional forms such as adding legs (*huwe*) of clay to a globular vessel (*koroniviti*), adding a lip to a water pot and a base to a dish. Her new forms included pigs, turtles, piggy banks, ashtrays, and small bowls for nuts, all items that tourists bought when they came to watch her give demonstrations.

The movement away from producing art forms solely for home consumption to selling them outside the community reflects various stimuli at work and different balances of contrasting and opposing factors. Initially, in a situation of social change, the first step is to sell "old" things for which there is no longer a need in the culture or, at least, where the need for cash, or its equivalent in "external" goods, tips the balance in favor of getting rid of the old. It is a situation where the avarice of the collector perhaps outdoes the cupidity of the owner. But the beginnings of commercialism may also stimulate production of "old" forms before they have disappeared from use in the culture. Then an art form may be produced partly for home consumption and partly for sale externally. For example, in Tonga, *ngatu*, tapa, and mats particularly continue to be intertwined in the daily lives of the people, functioning in various ceremonies connected with the life-cycle of the individual. Various baskets too continue to be made for home use. But a proportion of these traditional crafts are made for sale and are bought by tourists, or exported to suitable markets, such as museums in the Western world.

In Vava'u, according to the Government Handicraft Advisor, at least 60 percent of handicrafts produced were kept for home use, including mats and *ngatu* for funerals and weddings, and it is in these items that quality is maintained. Two channels are available for selling outside the community: either the individual, or someone for her, sells directly, or the craftswoman may market her wares through a women's cooperative, *langa fonua*. In the former instance, production in Vava'u is keyed to the appearance in the harbor off Neiafu of one or two cruise ships a month, each of which may disgorge a thousand passengers. For a few days before the appearance of a ship women in some of the villages will be making baskets, hampers, coiled mats, sewing baskets, waste-paper baskets, and circular basketry discs with tapa on them (indeed, pieces of tapa are made to cover decoratively handbags and the like), all to be sold to the tourists from the ship. The kinds of items produced can be gleaned from the very nicely produced booklets compiled by the Ministry of Work, Commerce and Industries.[9]

Alternatively, a woman may belong to a *langa fonua* (cooperative), which has a shop. She may leave her work there, and if it does not sell after a certain period she may remove it. While the tourist industry promotes the production of new forms, such as hats, sandals, napkin rings, model plaited horses, trays, and so on, as well as the occasional introduction of foreign materials, it also fosters the traditional use of traditional materials.[10] Six forms of pandanus are distinguished on Vava'u in making baskets for sale (*pauongo*, *tafua*, *utuila*, *fafa*, *tawtawlo*, and *tapahina*). The trade can be a stimlus to craft specialization; the cooperative at Neiafu, for example, has one member on Farivai Island producing necklaces of small coral beads, similar to some shell curencies, and another on Orfu Island, Anna Totohea, who makes cowrie necklaces. Occasionally the commercial stimulus leads to someone with a particular skill producing exceptionally fine work, and, in this contemporary scene, such a person becomes an artist recognized outside the traditional community context and in the new. In this respect, the work of Kalo Taumalolo of Panga Motu village, Vava'u Island, is particularly noteworthy.

An event such as the Pacific Basketmaker's Symposium and Exhibition (Jones 1983), which took place in Alaska at the Anchorage Historical and Fine Arts Museum, draws attention to the changing roles of Pacific basket makers. A number of basket makers from Hawaii, Guam, American Samoa, and the Commonwealth of the Northern Marianas, as well as from California and Alaska, gathered together to demonstrate their skills and discuss their art in a completely new context which required a change of traditional role, giving new emphasis to the artist as an individual. Somewhat in contrast to this is the role that one or two basket and mat makers have been led to play in Fiji by advertising their skills more for commercial than purely artistic purposes. This is visible in Fiji's Handicraft Development Project, which was represented in 1982 at trade fairs in New Zealand and Australia, and in 1983 in Australia, the United States, and Canada. In February 1983, I met two Fijian women who spoke no English and who were being sent to the Fiji Visitors Bureau in Auckland for one week to demonstrate their skills in making mats and baskets. The emphasis here was on encouraging people to buy traditional crafts. The craft, the object, had precedence, it would seem, over the individual as an artist. The anonymity or identity of the artist depends, I would suggest, on the context emphasized, and this, in turn, depends not only on the interests of the observer of the context, but on the viability of the activity. How far, in fact, do the returns maintain the artist in his or her work? In the case of the Alaskan basketry symposium, it was sponsored by the Consortium for Pacific Arts and Cultures and the returns were not pecuniary; in the case of the two Fijian women going to Auckland for a week's demonstration, it was the Fijian government investing money to create returns.

In Kiribati there is no tourism, only occasional visitors and a small population of expatriates, who are gradually being phased out of their various employments. Apart from the major Kiribati art forms of dancing and poetry, navigation and watercraft, items produced either for local consumption or for export include baskets, mats (fig. 18.1), various ornaments and a few other objects. Two organizations function to encourage production and distribution. The first, the National Women's Federation of Kiribati, fosters local production of baskets, mats, handbags, belts, and similar items but also serves to distribute

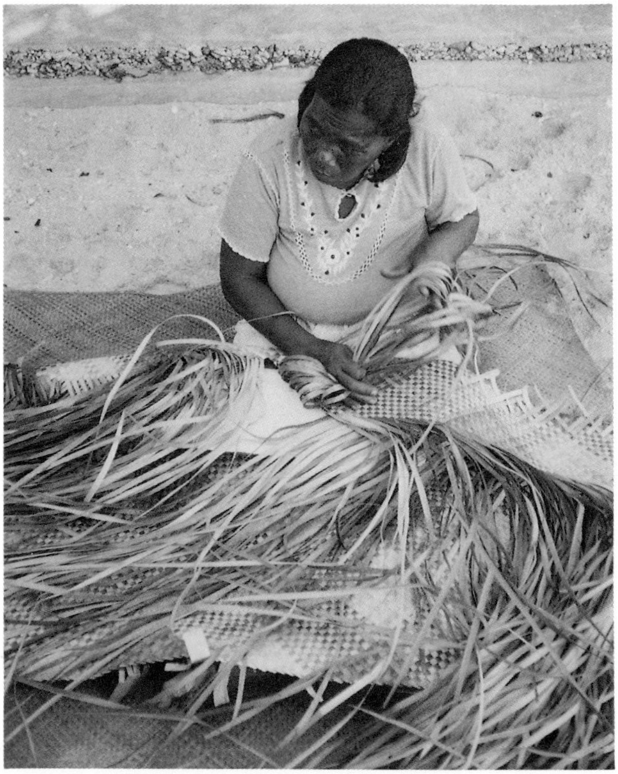

FIGURE 18.1. Mrs. Toti Noran, Kiribati, weaving a mat.

them, for they are brought from the various islands to Bikenibeu where the Women's Federation has a store.[11] There they are sold to people who are working and who no longer have any time to weave their own.

The form of handbags being produced and the designs on them are in the tradition of earlier forms and designs, recorded by Koch (1965:t.9, 15) twenty years ago, although he illustrates a greater variety than seem to be made today. I noticed at Sunday morning service in the Lutheran church in Bikenibeu that these bags were worn by many women, some of whom also brought mats, the whole congregation being seated on the floor of the church. New forms seem to be cushions, place mats, and laundry baskets, perhaps instigated by expatriate residents' demands. The quality is excellent, and explicit steps are taken to maintain it. This is done by community workers, who tour the islands.

Mrs. Yaneta Paiitekei, the head of the National Women's Federation of Kiribati, said that they were always encouraging "our" women, and "keep on reminding the women not only for the money (they will get) but to maintain our own skills in handicrafts and weaving." Craftswomen do send in things regularly from certain islands, such as Makin, Beru, and Tamana, but it is easier to do so from some islands than from others. In an island country like Kiribati, which is so spread over the vast ocean, transport and communications forever pose problems. Once received, the articles are paid for but if the work is carelessly done it is sent back. "We want something really good," Mrs. Paiitekei said, "not its commercial business." The work is judged by a senior community officer, who, if in doubt, checks with other colleagues. They "see the way the weave [goes], not just the outside but inside as well." Technical standards are thus maintained; rough and ready work is not acceptable.

Certain women are recognized as particularly skillful; they are "noted for the art of weaving" and the community workers ask them to make things. Very fine sleeping mats are still made. Although designs still belong in clans and families, Mrs. Paiitekai said that recognition of this custom "has been dying out now. You can see the same patterns now coming from different islands." The change would seem to be away from individuality to general similarity, at least within the Kiribati idiom. But even if the use of the range of Kiribati designs becomes common to all — and probably less various — there are plans afoot to extend the number of forms produced. The aim, however, is to export them, something which is not currently done. The Federation has plans to send skilled weavers overseas to other Pacific countries in order to learn new forms and thus increase the current Kiribati range.

These plans seem to stem, at least in part, from concern that there were very few women producing handicrafts. The women realize that their skills are disappearing and they feel that something must be done about it. Women were encouraged to bring things for sale in the small shop at the National Women's Federation Centre, which was advertised on the radio. However, it seems that more than 50 percent of the handicraft items were not sold. Of those that did sell, more than a third were bought locally. Apart from what they use themselves, the Kiribati buy mats, swords, and other items as going away gifts.

Export of Kiribati handicrafts is currently undertaken only by one organization: the Kiribati Cooperative Whole-

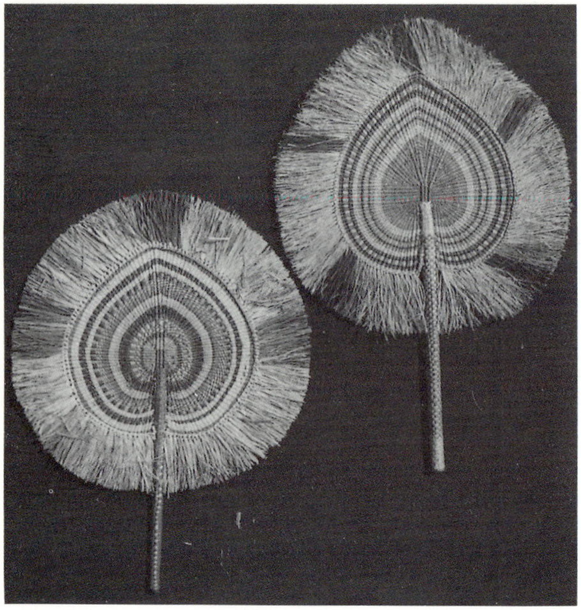

FIGURE 18.2. Coconut fiber fans, Arorae Island, Kiribati.

sale Society Ltd., located on Betio, Tarawa. It has agents in the outer island cooperative societies, who buy items from the people. The people bring them to the Cooperative's manager, who buys the articles after consultation with a local committee — of which he is a member — which judges the quality of the work produced. The purchased articles are sent to the Kiribati Cooperative on Betio, where they are checked by the manager and his assistants. Most items come from the southern islands, particularly Beru Island whose inhabitants were judged "the most proficient in making handicrafts," especially swords, sleeping mats, table mats, trays for food, hats, and all kinds of baskets.[12]

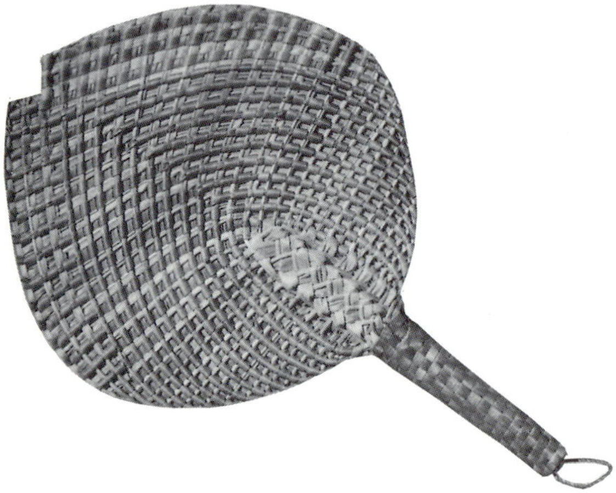

FIGURE 18.3. Coconut frond fan, Arorae Island, Kiribati.

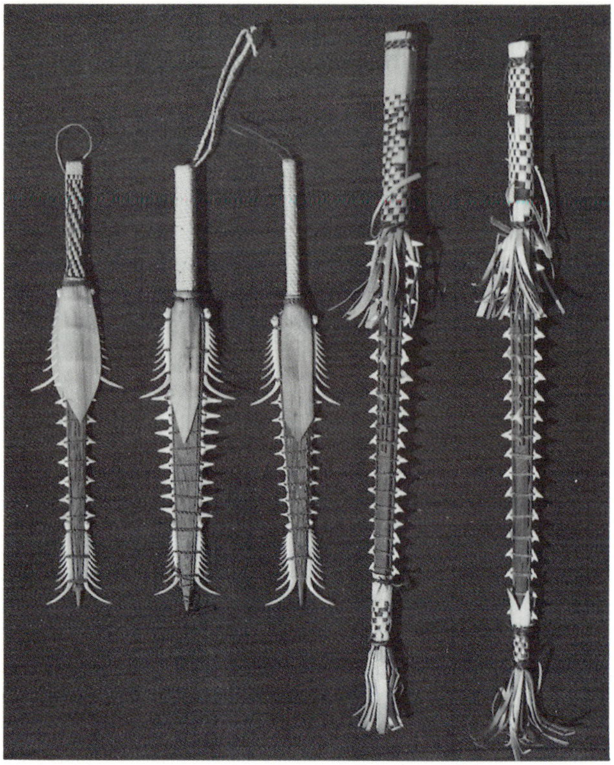

FIGURE 18.4. Sharks' teeth swords and daggers, Kiribati.

Panama-style hats are made for men and women, and the fisherman's hat (*teipura nakowa*)—which is basically conical in form, with the front extending forward — is worn widely in the islands as well as being produced for export. Hats are made from pandanus, have brims (*teitoma*) of coconut rib and are stitched with human hair and coconut fiber. They are largely made on Onotoa and Tamana islands and recall the shape of the hats worn by hunters of the Aleutian Islands.[13]

Circular fans, woven of colored coconut fibers, are made on Arorae Island and showed great diversity in

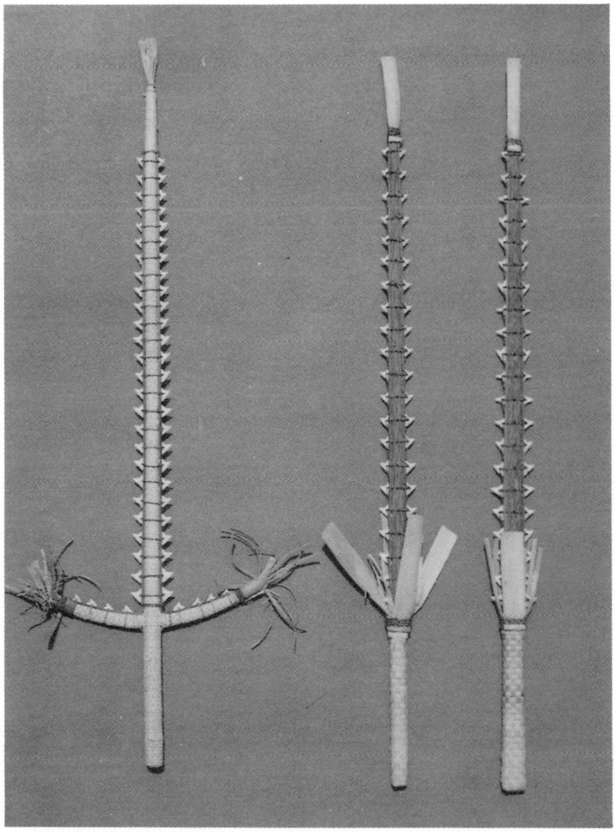

FIGURE 18.5. Swords, Kiribati.

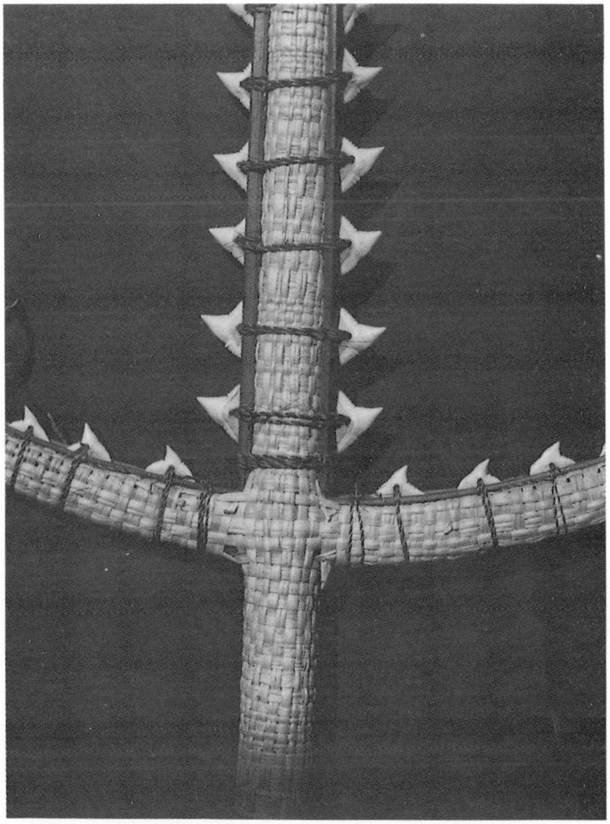

FIGURE 18.6. Hilt of sword pictured in figure 18.5.

designs: In examining some twenty or more I found no two the same (fig. 18.2).[14] Other fans are pleasingly plaited of bleached coconut fronds (fig. 18.3). Swords copy in miniature the deadly weapons of the past (figs. 18.4-18.5). Traditional binding materials of human hair and sennit are still used to attach the shark's teeth to the edges of the blades, demonstrating the virtuosity of the maker in a technologically most exacting skill (fig. 18.6).[15]

The government-controlled Kiribati Cooperative Wholesale Society exports the crafts it has bought locally to Tonga, Honolulu, Norfolk Island, Auckland, Fiji, the Marshall Islands, Nauru, and England, although to this last they send only floor mats. Other government-sponsored cooperatives, like that of Kiribati, have similar outlets for export, which are not all outside the Pacific. A number of companies located in Honolulu buy widely in the Pacific and there is considerable movement of artifacts on a commercial basis between Pacific countries. Western Samoa buys mother-of-pearl and turtle shell brooches and pendants from Fiji, although they are also made locally. Fiji buys placemats and baskets from Samoa and tapa from Tonga. Various carved items in wood find their way from the Philippines to Western Samoa.

The continuing production of various handicrafts seems to be of concern to all Pacific island governments who, in varying ways, have set up organizations to encourage production and market the products; they are, after all, local industries. The products represent the results of the application of the skills and tastes of the artists and craftsmen to various media in traditional ways, ways which were those of their forebears and which represent an important part of a heritage which has been buffeted and changed, and of which much has been lost. Arts and crafts, like the Terpsichorean arts, are visible manifestations of the past, and there is general concern to maintain their quality. I have drawn attention to this with respect to Kiribati. Other examples are in Fiji, where it is the concern of the government's Handicraft Development Project; in Western Samoa it is that of the Western Samoan Handicrafts Corporation; in Papua New Guinea, of the National Cultural Council (Brown, n.d.). While Pacific Islanders know their own standards of quality, those to whom they sell may know nothing about what they are buying, save that it originates from some context they have learned to regard as exotic or quaint. This is hardly a situation likely to support maintenance of standards of quality if quick cash can be made by obviating some of the requirements of those standards.

INNOVATIONS AND BORROWING

It is to be noted that producing for a commercial outlet provides opportunity for innovation in the arrangement of design features, or the creation of new ones, and the introduction of new materials, but it also sets demands on ingenuity to produce new objects that suit the new market and will sell. Indeed, the market — the tourists, mainly — expect certain forms and they have to be produced. But, in all this, quality and aesthetic features of art can and are maintained. Where *ngatu*/tapa or baskets are largely consumed at home, the required standards can carry over to work made for sale, though some fudging may occur. In some instances the freedom provided by the commercial market can allow experiment and new designs which would not be appreciated if served in a home context. In Nuku'alofa, direct cash sales of a variety of handicrafts to tourists and visitors but not to Tongans take place at the

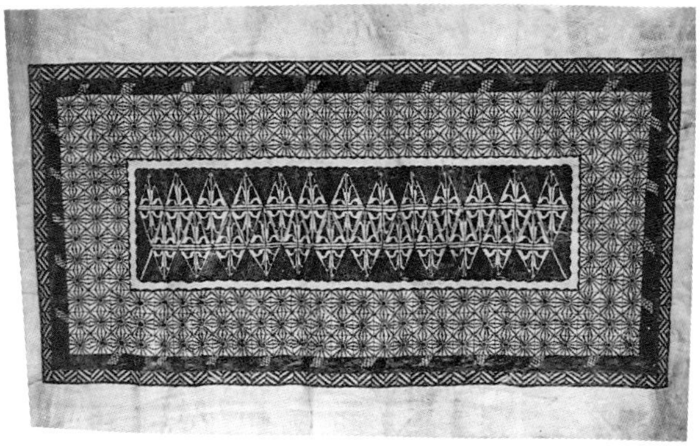

FIGURE 18.7. Tapa by Luisa, Sapu village, Koromutua, Tonga.

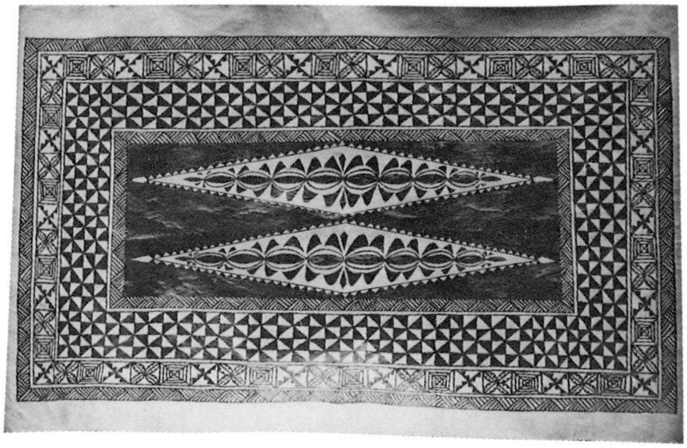

FIGURE 18.8. Tapa by Tupou, Sapu village, Koromutua, Tonga.

Langa Fonua'oe Fefine Tonga, the women's cooperative of Nuku'alofa. While the range of items for sale includes novelties and various tourist attractions, a number of the members contribute high quality tapa for sale. Some of the designs are traditional, such as done by Olivia of Nuku'alofa, but some new ones, such as work by Luisa (fig. 18.7) and by Tupou (fig. 18.8), both of Sopu village, Kolomotu'a, show new directions of inventiveness of designs, more elaborate than older ones but executed with great skill and taste.

Will these trends depend solely on support from outside the culture to insure their continuity and further evolution? Old techniques can be used to produce new forms that are of the traditional idiom. But old techniques may also be used to produce forms which are alien to the indigenous tradition: hats, sandals, laundry, wastepaper and sewing baskets, various non-traditional forms of shell and turtle shell jewelry, and other items. In Kiribati, the lining used in some baskets is cardboard, or black plastic taken from building materials bags. Plastic is also stitched on the inside of Tongan baskets. Materials imported from outside the Pacific must be endless in number but their commonality in the Pacific and their suitability for use to meet similar technical and decorative needs leads to a blandness or sameness of objects made with them.

On the other hand, some introductions conserve, which can perhaps be considered beneficial. For example, in Tonga tapa is being painted in Vava'u with scenes and figures — a nose flute player, Maui pulling up the land, a kava-drinking party or a man drinking it — are glazed to

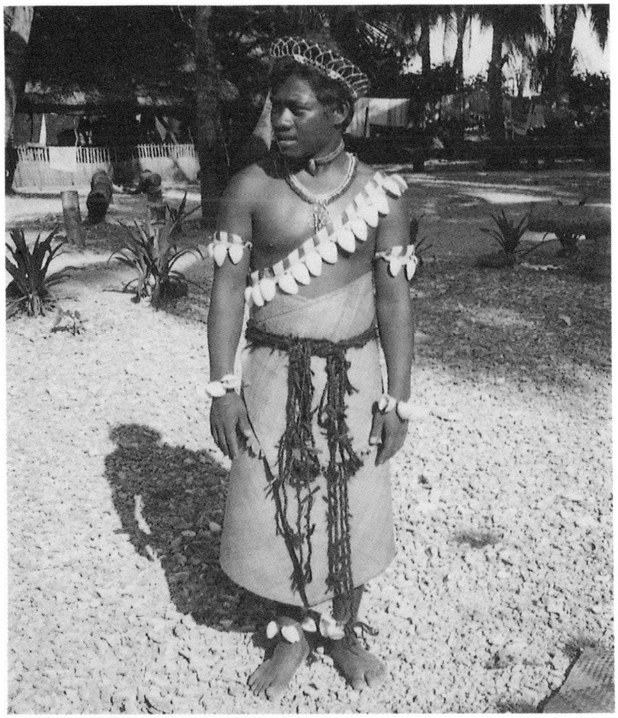

FIGURE 18.9. Bito Faiitwa, costumed for dance, Kiribati.

make them waterproof. Such pieces are stitched to pieces of masonite to form trays, or to plaited discs of pandanus. The work, tastefully executed by an artist called Sinisia, is, however, derivative, the kava drinker being a design created by a New Zealand woman living in Vava'u rather than a traditional one. If such introductions become established, new dimensions follow.

The juxtaposition of the new and the old are manifest marks of change; the contemporary display of Motu bride payments mixes currency notes with traditional shell armbands. Collars, headbands, and armbands made of imported beads are worn side by side with traditional ones made of shells, turtle shells, plants, and beetles, or the new may displace the old altogether (fig. 18.9). The press of fashion, or missionary urging, leads to the adoption of items of foreign dress, such as the white cotton bra, which is worn with traditional necklaces, leaves, and plant sachets, providing a note of change albeit an incongruous one.[16] The next step can be to copy the form in indigenous materials, as Kiribati dancers have done in plaited pandanus (fig. 18.10), or by cutting a coconut in half to provide suitable cups for breasts that were previously left bare (fig. 18.11); alternatively, traditional dances can be performed in modern costume.[17]

As in the Kiribati dance itself (discussed below), changes in costume have occurred in recent years as a result of the introduction of new materials and techniques. Any good troop has a large number of dances in its repertoire, and the costumes appropriate to each vary. In his study of Kiribati material culture Koch (1965:t16-20, Abb. 82-3) illustrates many old forms which are no longer made.[18] Bwere Eritaia told me that these forms have been abandoned because people are either no longer interested or they do not have the time to make them. Having watched some costume items being made, I can testify to the processes requiring considerable time and patience as well as skill in order to achieve a satisfactory result.

A number of costume innovations were employed by dancers of a troop trained and directed by Biteti Tentoa of Abarao, Tarawa. A new form of headband, or headdress, *temai nassu* (fig. 18.9), like a crown, was made of round

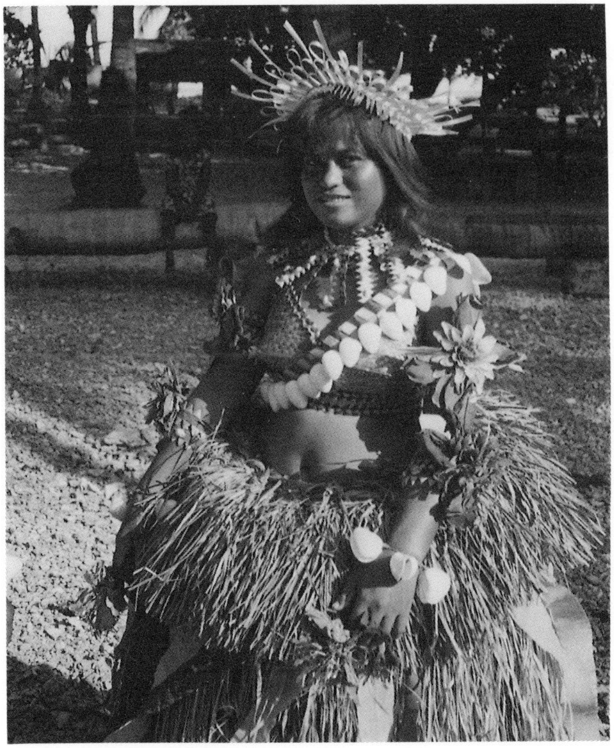

FIGURE 18.10. Ruth Naweir, costumed for dance, Kiribati.

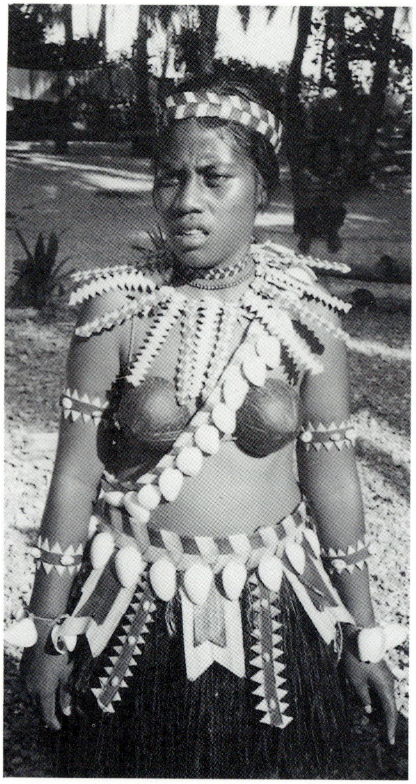

FIGURE 18.11. Urekei Tonga of Kiribati, costumed for dance and wearing *taona n'riri* belt (see fig. 18.14).

glass beads obtained from a Chinese store. It was copied from the Gilbertese type referred to as *tebuwai ton* (fig. 18.10), which was traditionally made from stalks of a certain grass, *makeimakei*, scraped until white.[19] The *tebuwai ton* headdress is used in a hip dance in which the dancer wears a big skirt, *terri ni buki*, which weighs some twenty-five kilograms and "has to be waved around, like the sea, come over onto the head and knock off the headdress" (fig. 18.10). This used to be danced by women, but the new beaded headdress was heavier and firmer on the head than the *tebuwai ton* and it became too difficult for them to knock it off. Now the dance is done by boys dancing in a group, "because they are stronger." The personnel of an activity has thus been completely changed by the introduction of a new material.

New materials have been introduced into other items of costume partly because they are more durable than natural materials and partly because of an enhancement of aesthetic values. For example, armbands (*teikaruru*) made of flowers are worn for slow dances in which the arms make weaving motions. They are now made from pandanus leaves (*tamathr*), with crepe paper serving as petals and the flowers are of plastic (fig. 18.10). Some are made from "shiny Christmas papers: when the people [are] watching they see the shining movements."[20] Plastic strings and crêpe paper, which are kept rolled up, are let down all round the *terri ni buki*, the big dance skirt, when it is worn (fig. 18.10). Formerly, these strings, *teiton' ndidi*, were of shredded coconut fronds. The *karaebari*, a chest ornament, used to be made from flowers and leaves, I was told, but is now made of plain and black-dyed pandanus (figs. 18.10-18.12) and used for all types of dances except those grouped as *teitaupas* and *tereipei*, in which all the dancers stand and clap with up and down movements, which would break the *karaebari*. The form of the *karaebari* in pandanus does, however, vary (fig. 18.13). Going back twenty years, Koch (1965:135, Abb. 82) notes a *karaebari* of pearl shell discs and he collected a beautiful old one made of the bases of a conus shell from Teuabu/Nonouti.

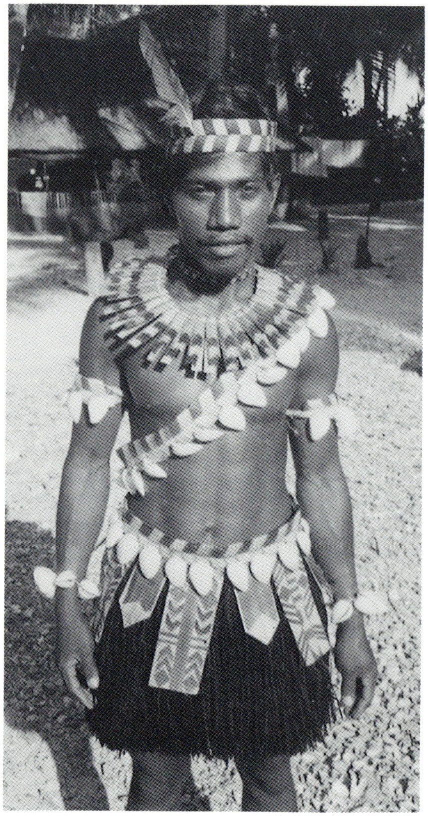

FIGURE 18.12. Richard Drisetta of Kiribati, costumed dance and wearing *kamakorokoro* waistband detailed in figure 18.14.

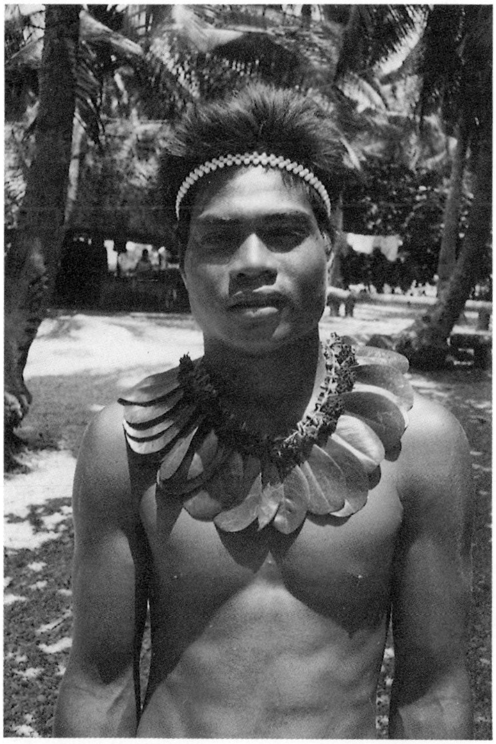

FIGURE 18.13. Antonio At r, wearing traditional *karaebari*, Kiribati.

In fact the practice of using flowers and leaves for a *karaebari* continues, for I watched one being made (fig. 18.13).

A considerable change has occurred in the *ririko*, a kind of sash worn across the chest from the left shoulder to the right side, and up across the back, rather like a bandolier. The *ririko* is made of braided alternating lengths of light and black pandanus, forming a strip some eight centimeters wide which covers the front of the body; lengths of sennit are tied to each end and joined at the back. On the front of the braided piece, white scallop shells, carefully selected to match, are attached (figs. 18.9-18.12). These shells (*sumara*) are the same as those that ornament a waistband, *tekatao sumara*, for which the *ririko* can be substituted. In earlier times the *ririko* was made of dolphin teeth (cf. Koch 1965:137, t.19c).[21] It is worn for dances known as *kabus*, *kaiteitei*, and *kainimiyang*.[22]

Belts and waistbands, worn over the top of the dance skirt round the hips, were made of different materials — shells, coconut shell, pandanus — depending on the costume and the dance they were intended for. Belts, or girdles, which were made in the past of many discs from coconut shells (e.g., Koch 1965:t.17) are still made on the outer islands, and even on Tarawa. A belt in fashion today, the *taona n'riri*, is made of braided pandanus strips with little cowrie and scallop shells stitched to it (figs. 18.11 and 18.14, top). In the old days this belt was made of plain white pandanus fringed in wide natural colored strips and not ornamented with shells at all (cf. Koch 1965:t.16a).

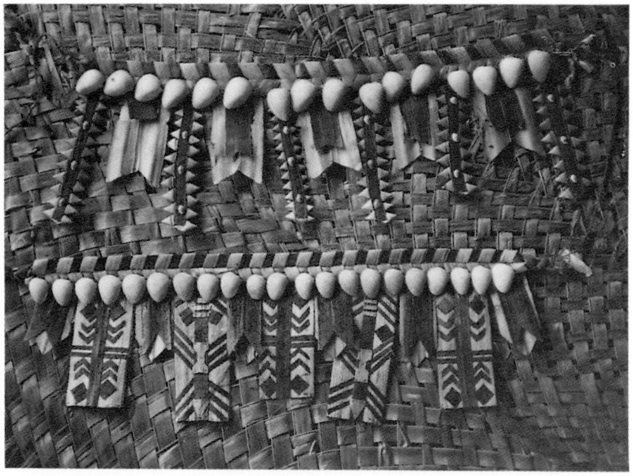

FIGURE 18.14. Top: *taona n'riri*, as pictured in figure 18.11; bottom: *kamakorokoro*, as in figure 18.12.

The *kamakorokoro* is a waistband that used to be made of plain pandanus strips, cut to two points at the end, and placed across each other, projecting down from a plaited base (see Koch, 1965:t.16e). This was the type worn by the Kiribati troop which danced at the South Pacific Festival of the Arts at Port Moresby in 1980. On top was worn a *tumara*, a belt made of small shells.[23] In the costume repertoire of Biteti Tentoa's dance troop this has been replaced by a much more elaborate *kamakorokoro* (figs. 18.12, and 18.14) than any that would appear to have preceded it, though it is very similar to the *taona n'riri* illustrated in figure 18.11. Made of pandanus and shells, it is of interest as an innovation on two counts. First, the design came to Biteti from a vision brought to him "by a devil."[24] Second, the *kamakorokoro* is made from both indigenous and imported materials. The latter consists primarily of flannelette, a blue form, which is used as backing for the elaborate pieces of the costume, and which is stitched on with cotton by a sewing machine. In fact the elaborateness requires the strength of flannelette or the *kamakorokoro* would tend to come apart in vigorous dances. Flannelette, or some other imported material, is also used to line the plaited pandanus bras, noted above, which are now de rigueur for dancers (fig. 18.10).

I have discussed in some detail changes which may appear small, but nevertheless they do represent the effect of new circumstances. Perhaps they parallel other trends and developments occurring elsewhere in the Pacific. I suspect they do.

CHANGES IN CONTEXTS

In times of rapid change items shift contexts as the context becomes obsolete or is no longer binding as a structure for a particular activity. In Papua New Guinea, masqueraders may appear on public occasions, such as at the South Pacific Festival of the Arts, which they would not have done in their own culture in the past without restrictions on who could be present. The abandonment of restrictions seems to stem from a desire to represent the past in the context of the new age, and the result is the production of folk art forms. Changing the context of an object removes something of the pressures of stereotyping it when making it, thus allowing the substitution or addition of new materials and consequent changes in form.[25]

Copying Old Forms

The copying of old forms seems to be undertaken for two purposes: for educational needs, and for commercial ends.

EDUCATIONAL PURPOSES

The need of museums and cultural centers to sustain themselves has led to the revival of old forms and techniques as, to give an example already mentioned, at the Kwaio Cultural Centre. But there is concern among some school teachers to see that the old crafts are taught by the old to the young before those who still know them have all died off. I reported an instance of this in the *Pacific Arts Newsletter* (Dark 1979:24). When in Aitutaki (Cook Islands) the vice principal of Ararua College, Kirore Charley, recounted in 1978 that he was about to start a project in which the children would learn some of the local crafts from old women. But he indicated that it would help the project if he could acquire Te Rangi Hiroa's (1944) record made at the time the crafts were widely known. A similar concern for traditional handicrafts and their preservation finds expression through the Fiji Art Teacher's Association, which printed a newsletter in which various of them are discussed.[26]

COMMERCIAL PURPOSES

The main aims of reproducing old forms are directed toward obtaining cash, though exchange may also be sought. The beginnings of commercialization have been touched on earlier. Mention was made of the Kilenge revival of the carving of masks for local purposes leading to their reproduction for sale, and the consequent opening of the door to change in standards when a non-artist in the society attempted what was formerly only the work of those recognized as artists. These sales extended outside the traditional trading network to the larger national, and indeed international one. Initially, if there is an entrepreneur in the community, as there was in the case of the Kilenge, he serves as a buffer between the outside world and the artists, who tend to remain anonymous. This also pertains when, at a national level, a cooperative or government handicrafts center acts as intermediary between the artist and those to whom he sells. Records may be kept in the cooperative of which member produced what, but these are seldom acquired by outside buyers unless the artist's identity is specifically sought. Commercialization means anonymity.

Where there are sufficient commercial demands, and the right kind of enthusiastic stimulation is given, reproduction of old forms can receive the same kind of revitalization as occurred on the Pacific Northwest Coast of Canada some twenty years ago. In Fiji, Emele Vulaca, director of the Handicraft Development Project, spends 75 percent of her time in the field, working with elders to encourage them in the work that they produce but seeing that standards are maintained. To this end she suggests that the craftsmen refer to the specimens in the Fiji Museum for their models. Her insistance on this, in the case of carvers, has even led in some instances to the reproduction of breaks or cuts in old specimens in the excellently executed copies. The carvers of Kandavo supply about 25 percent of the pieces sold and those of Fulunga, Lau Province, the remaining 75 percent.

In Western Samoa a very hard wood, *pau*, which is scarce and not available for commercial use, is found in the area of Falealupo, in the western part of Savai'i. Joe Hunter, the manager of the Western Samoan Handicrafts Coropration, told me that it can only be worked with a very sharp knife. "Power saw blades become dulled in minutes by its hardness. At present there is a woodcarving cottage industry project at the Falealupo Catholic mission where there is wood available to the residents of the village. We try and bring back the original design of artifacts used in ancient times, such as weapons and other wood carvings. The tools used are a Samoan adz and knives." The items produced, which are sold by the corporation on commission, include combs and copies of various types of clubs with serrated edges and some with a hook at the end: *nifo otitala valu, talavalu, lapalap, tala-oldo, nifo oti.* Necklaces imitating pigs' tusks are made from the leg bones of cows, technically quite a task to achieve an elegant curve; the tusks are highly polished and have the look of pearl shell. At Fanga Loa, near Apia, carvers make kava bowls in a large range of sizes from *ifileilei* wood. These are sometimes bought by Samoans to send to families living in New Zealand. Indeed, other replicas are bought sometimes by Samoans as well as the modern versions of ordinary crafts. I was told, too, that when a man gets a new title he will come and buy a staff and fly whisk in the shop, though he will make his own sennit handle.

As well as access to examples of traditional work kept in museums, as in Fiji, local artists may also benefit from books. An example of this occurred in the 1960s when one or two Tami carvers revived the style — which had ceased as the work of Tami artists for a long while, the production having shifted to the Siassi Islands — using Bodrogi's (1961) study of Tami-Huon Gulf art as a source book.[27] No doubt local potters would like to refer to May and Tuckson's (1982) splendid study of the pottery of Papua New Guinea, but what village can afford the price?[28]

While recourse to Pacific models is made by artists in the Pacific, in February 1983 I saw in BP's in Nuku'alofa three copies of a Tongan diety with a label *Ofa Atu* (meaning *aloha*) on it, the original of which is in the Field Museum of Natural History, Chicago. They had been imported by the Tonga Trading Company of Honolulu. Who carved these "Genuine Reproduction[s] of Museum Artifact[s]"?[29] I drew their attention to the carver, David Fisi'ia, who, a week later produced his miniature copy of the copy which, alas, was an ill-conceived, insensitive stereotype.

Illustrations of copies of old forms and modern versions of them, as well as other arts and crafts for sale, are to be seen in a number of smartly produced publications printed for the handicrafts organizations of different Pacific governments.[30] Their principal aim is the sale of their products, whether locally or by export to countries inside and outside the Pacific. The main consumers are tourists although, as I have indicated earlier, some native artifacts are bought by local inhabitants and it would seem not unlikely that they also buy items originating from countries other than their own. For example, as noted before, the Western Samoan Handicrafts Corporation occasionally obtains brooches and pendants of mother-of-pearl and turtle shell from Fiji even though they are made locally in Western Samoa. In return, place mats, basketry, tapa — nearly all produced on Savai'i — go to Fiji. The indigenous origins of craft skills get muddled up, and perhaps even cease to matter. Tongan tapa is sold in the market in Fiji as Fijian tapa. Who made it is not important. That it is tapa is what matters to the buyer, if he is not a Pacific islander. Fijians and Tongans may be able to tell the difference today, but will the majority of them in years to come? Part of the mechanics of Pan-Pacificization in the arts can develop on these lines.

Pacific tourist arts and crafts have attracted the attention of a number of scholars (e.g., Wendt 1983; Tausie 1980; Bolabola 1980; Horoi 1980). In the business of replication and quantity production, indeed, of mass production of crafts made by hand, standards change, and quality depreciates when taste and commerce become bedfellows. A threat to standards generally produces some concern: Pacific island governments have expressed this, as I have indicated before. Some have sought help of international organizations, such as the International Labour Organization and the United Nations Development Program . A quality control assistant was funded for a year in Western Samoa by a grant from the Commonwealth Fund for Technical Cooperation. Such concerns for maintaining standards of traditionally produced arts and crafts are admirable, and these may even include forms which are solely for commercial contexts. However the copying or utilization of old forms in new media for new contexts is beginning to produce what might be termed "instant art" or arts in the applied field. Many of these appear to manifest high standards, though there are some aberrations.

I would think that this area of art will develop. It certainly has rich source material to draw on. Some examples of applications which have been made are in silk screening in Papua New Guinea, when, in the 1960s at Lae, copies of old forms were printed on linen and silk. Of the forms reproduced there were *gope* boards of the Papuan Gulf, a painting from the cult house at Kambrambo, Lower Sepik, and a wooden shield, which would have been placed on a cult house, from Tambunum, Middle Sepik.[31] The use of tapa as a substitute for a painting on a wall as part of a room decoration was observed in Nuku'alofa (Tonga) and perhaps is so used elsewhere; it is also used to cover cushions (e.g., Western Samoa) or waterproofed for use in bags or coverings of trays (e.g., Tonga). A further step has been to reproduce tasteful tapa designs in plastic as mats for trays, observed in Western Samoa, and as headboards for beds, as seen in Fiji. Perhaps the best known application of a traditional form for a variety of new purposes is the Cook Island carving of the deity Tangaroa, which has been used on the face of the dollar coin, on stamps, on T-shirts, and reproduced as carvings of varying sizes and qualities for sale.[32]

The directions just described which some visual art is taking causes the public image of art itself to become diffused; it gets a generalized identity sans social energy which becomes defused. The mystery of art is taken away and it becomes chargeless; it loses its "unexpected imminent significance"; it is instant art and everyone can fill the cup and throw it away after drinking.[33]

Western forms and techniques of pottery making, particularly with respect to firing, have been introduced into the Pacific. In Fiji, for example, a glazed ware is sold by the Handicraft Development Project, and in Papua New Guinea, Jorgen Petersen, the Danish potter, worked for the International Labour Organization in 1967-71.[34] Outside the Pacific forms from different Pacific cultures have been used indiscriminately in commerce to symbolize the Pacific in general. This negates the particular identities of its cultures and peoples, creating a false image of uniformity. One thinks of so-called Pacific restaurants in the United States A St. Louis hotel I visited in the 1960s featured plastic swizzle sticks in the shape of Fijian clubs, a logo on sugar packets and matchbook covers consisting of an Abelam mask with two forms of Samoan clubs, and original works of art from Papua New Guinea nailed to the walls and doors . . . applied art par excellence.

Creating New Forms out of Old Ones

The activity of making new forms out of old ones, which seems to be done mainly for commercial purposes, is a kind of eclecticism that largely lacks originality and results in a rather tasteless style poised between a locally trite expression and a generalized statement Pan-Pacific in extent. It is what I understand Wendt (1983:200) would call a "fake tradition," referred to earlier. Its local expression would be exemplified by the hackneyed figures of chiefs initially carved by Svenortquist, who lives in Apia, Western Samoa. Its generalized Pan-Pacific expression, which is distinct from art forms of the past, draws on them literally to make its concoctions. But I should perhaps be cautious, for the style is largely derived from Polynesian sources, though it is beginning to incorporate New Guinea forms. In terms of the dance perhaps a broader pervasiveness for melding of Polynesian, Melanesian, and Micronesian forms is taking place, although particular interpretations are strongly local in color.

The hypothesis is advanced that this generalized Pan-Pacific style began twenty-five or more years ago in Hawaii with a number of highly skilled craftsmen, who were copying not only old Hawaiian sculptures but those of other Pacific countries. One of these was Phil Hooton, who is pictured in his studio in Hawaii in about 1970 in a book by William Graves (1970:107). The caption to the illustration reads:

> Products of the woodcarver's art, Polynesian gods grimace, outrigger canoes wait as if to sail legendary seas, plump birds roast, and a whale swims overhead in the Hawaii studio of Phil Hooton. An expert on early Polynesian art and culture, Mr. Hooton wields knives and chisels to help preserve Hawaii's artistic heritage. Here he carefully fits a limpet shell lid on a jewelry box.

In the studio can be seen not only copies of Hawaiian forms but three carvings in the Marquesan style. In enquiring about Phil Hooton and his work, I learned that there were others who might have been involved in similar activities, but I could not discover any further information about Hooton himself.[35]

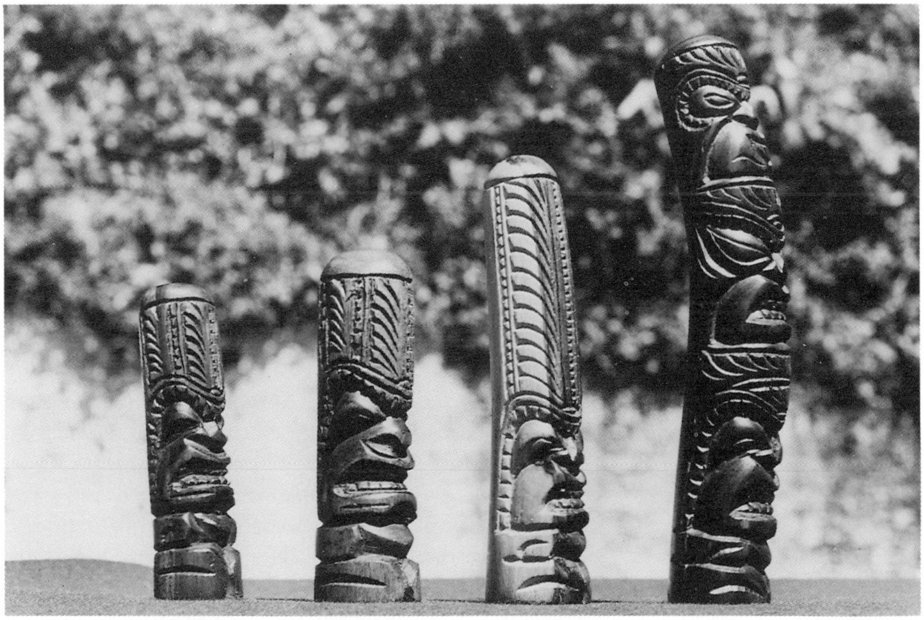

FIGURE 18.15. Two carvings by David Fifi'ia and two by Niu Tuitupo, Nuku'alofa, Tonga.

Did the imitation of Hawaiian and other Pacific forms some years ago lead to the production of the kind of composite carving which seems to be widespread today, for example, in Tonga (figs. 18.15) and Western Samoa (figs. 18.17, 18.18)? The emphasis is on the grimacing mouth, which would appear to have its origins in Hawaiian carvings, such as those of the god Kuka'ilimoku, as seen in Honolulu's Bishop Museum or in the Peabody Museum, Salem. Various distortions of those forms have been made, and no doubt are still being made. The 1969 restoration of the "City of Refuge" at Honaunau, Hawaii, by the U.S. National Park Service included carvings copying ancient forms with varying emphasis on early features. These are further stressed and distorted in carvings made in Tonga which can be combinations of heads (fig. 18.15d) or heads alone, figures with disproportionately large heads and bodies in a squatting Marquesan manner, with poor imitations of the headdresses of the type of the Hawaiian sculptures at Honaunau (e.g., fig. 18.15a-c),[36] or be wildly inventive in combining two gaping mouths yet retaining the Hawaiian distorted facial features (fig. 18.16). Did the growing activity of reproducing Polynesian forms in Hawaii follow the route to Tahiti, Western Samoa, Tonga, and Fiji as communications in the Pacific intensified as the result of increasing local air

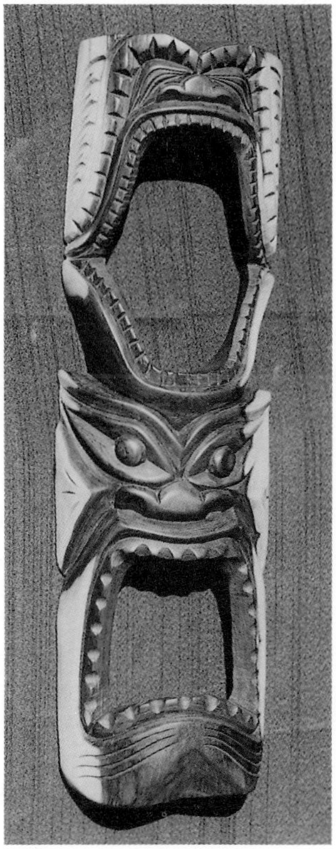

FIGURE 18.16. Carving by Tua Alau, Vavau, Tonga.

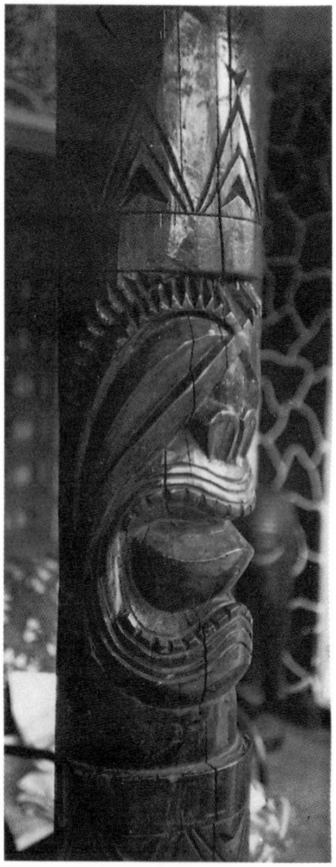

FIGURE 18.17. Carving by Timu, Latongo, Western Samoa.

services? What has been the role of Easter Island in this? In the Cook Islands I gained the impression, in 1978, that reproductions of Tangaroa predominated and his prominence in the culture prevented outside distortions or substitutions. But what trends are to be found elsewhere?

In the public image, the Tahitian style is sometimes blended with Marquesan forms. For example, the leader of the Tahitian contingent to the South Pacific Festival of the Arts at Port Moresby carried a wooden staff carved with a figure at the top which resembled a Marquesan *tiki* in style rather than any known Society Island carving.[37] In Western Samoa the Handicrafts Corporation sells Hawaiian-style figures, and pseudo-Marquesan tikis; the latter sell for eight dollars a foot. The figures are carved by Samoans who make them up from books. Indeed, they were being produced before the Handicrafts Corporation was established in 1965. Apparently, they appeal to Americans, Japanese, and Europeans. The Handicraft Corporation received orders for them from American Samoa, Fiji, Rarotonga, New Zealand, Australia, various parts of the United States (including New York and Seattle), and the Corporation has also supplied them to the Museum für Völkerkunde, Hamburg.[38]

Similar manifestations of Hawaiian and Marquesan styles are to be found among the large numbers of figures and posts in Aggie Gray's Hotel in Apia, Western Samoa (figs. 18.17, 18.18), which were commissioned some sixteen or seventeen years ago when the hotel hosted the first tourist conference, The Heart of Polynesia. The hotel managers were worried that the poles for their f*ale* were too bare. In consequence, Timu of Latongo carved the inside poles of the hotel f*ale*. At that time he was a young man, who had had no training, but he started, I was told, with dinner gongs and then went on to make masks, tikis, monkeys, and even carved the statue of a Catholic saint. The sources for his carvings were photographs in books, and his work included not only his interpretations of Marquesan and Hawaiian figures but extended to producing a Pacific Northwest Coast style totem pole.[39] Masks suggestive of New Guinean origins are also carved by Samoans for sale. In American Samoa I have seen large wooden figures in the Hawaiian idiom, carved and blackened masks and heads produced in Fiji, and Marquesan style carved tiki figures.

In Tonga the market for tourist carvings is sufficient to support some carvers working full time to produce figures, heads, and various other concoctions, much of it in a semi-Hawaiianized style, though some of them are probably derived from Marquesan forms. Sources of inspiration used by the carver, David Fisi'ia, were two carvings in the Tourist Office at Nuku'alofa, and illustrations in a book. Those he referred to were of a mask from Fiji and works from Tahiti and Hawaii, and he recognized that his carving was a little bit different from the last. But a Tahitian, he said, had come to work in Tonga and shown him photos of Tahitian carvings. This Tahitian may well have been the person with whom Tua Alau (a carver working, in 1983, in Neiafu, Vava'u) went to Tahiti in 1977 with a load of carvings to sell. Tua was apparently amazed at the high prices carvings fetched in Tahiti and, on his return, abandoned his job as a carpenter for the Commodities Board and turned his hand to producing carvings for tourists in Nuku'alofa. For the first months he mostly copied the figures other carvers were producing, and the dolphins in the town's fountain. "I'm good at proportion. I like people best, fish, and mermaids." During the festival week of Heilala in 1980, the Tourist Board held the first carving competition. About one hundred carvers took part and Tua won. He subsequently returned to Vava'u.

The whole families of some full time carvers become involved in production of items. For example, David Fisi'ia would start a piece and Mahu, his second son, who works full-time, would continue to rough it out. It would then be returned to David for marking out the forms in greater detail. Mahu would take it further, then back to David who would smooth the forms with a file, and then to John, the oldest boy, who would carve the decorative details. The piece would be further smoothed with sandpaper by Au'tapa, David's wife, who might use a chisel to refine the design. The third son, who attends school, might be made to help with the sandpapering. Finally, floor wax or shoe polish (Nugget or Kiwi) would be used to give a dark tan coloring and shine to the piece.

The family style of production is geared to the needs of the market, composed mainly of those who visit Tonga by air and those who come on cruise ships. For the former the sizes must be such that the carvings will fit into suitcases, but the latter buy bigger pieces. That the pursuit of this type of art is economically viable is attested by the fact that a number of carvers work at it full time. However, it has its ups and downs as a means of livelihood. On some days, I was told, a carver might sell four or five pieces, ranging in price from three to four dollars up to twenty, and on other days, nothing. As the carver Niu Tuitupo said, "This business is like fishing: one day you try and try and catch nothing; then one day you have luck."

Though emphasis has been given to the apparent influence of a Hawaiian style in the Tongan carvers' work, I have seen pieces which suggest that carvings of Tangaroa from the Cook Islands provided prototypes, and the presence at one time of an artist from Bali also left its effect.[40] Extraneous influences in the development of art in these days of intensified intercommunication between peoples must be expected. A young carver in Vava'u, Ilee'skili, who is only fifteen years old, interprets what he sees in books as well as producing miniature carvings of the Nuku'alofan-Hawaiian style. Once he was inspired by a bear on a U. S. postage stamp commemorating the indians of Alaska.

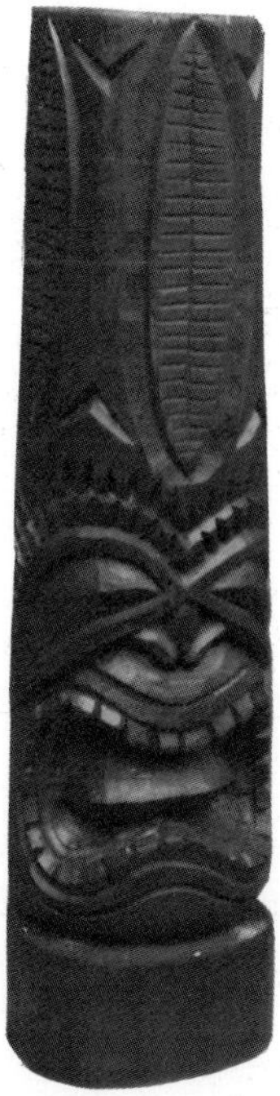

FIGURE 18.18. Carving by Timu, Latongo, Western Samoa.

Bolabola (1980) has written of "the impact of tourism on Fijian wood carving," which only became a commercial concern during the 1960s. On the one hand, in its growth, it produced carvings for souvenirs for tourists. On the other, the tourists provided the stimulus for some Fijians to exploit the work of local carvers for applied needs, such as decorating hotels with appropriate Fijian and Pacific symbols to attract more tourists. The "gun-stock" form of a Fijian club is a widely familiar old form and its reproduction and exhibit adds a note of authenticity wherever it is displayed. Authenticating identity is a first step in transforming old forms into new ones to serve new economic purposes, or new spiritual directions. Folk arts gradually reconstitute themselves even if the way is fraught with shifts in the use of indigenous forms and the adoption of new ones from outside the culture. The carved podium of the conference center in the Travelodge Hotel, Suva, for example, seems to combine a mouth form and eyes perhaps derived from the Hawaiian style with a Marquesan nose — the result, however, being a satisfactory Pacific emblem.

Making new forms out of old ones for commercial

purposes in order to have a major impact on public taste has been an undertaking of the Polynesian Cultural Center at Laie, Hawaii. The imagery presented sometimes uses forms of diverse origins but presents them in a non-traditional manner, though the impression of the general idiom is that it is Pacific, even if executed mechanically and, perhaps because of its eclecticism, lacking vitality. Indeed, university courses in Polynesian carving — enrollment being restricted to twelve students — are given at the Center, surely a form of Pan-Pacificization.

I sounded earlier a note of caution as to the sources upon which the generalized Pan-Pacific expression I have been describing might be based. Peter Gathercole pointed out to me that generalized Pacific artifacts were produced for sale on Pitcairn Island soon after the opening of the Panama Canal in 1914. Perhaps, therefore, my particular projection of a generalized Pan-Pacific expression should be advanced with twofold caution. Or might it be that there have been several waxings and wanings of a Pan-Pacific style, and that the one I am hypothesizing as beginning in Hawaii relatively recently occurred after an earlier one, or earlier ones, with origins elsewhere had come and gone? If so, how local was their generalized expression or how general their local interpretation?

Song and dance seem to be Pacific art forms which are both resilient and adaptable to change but able to express vigorously new forms. Reasons for differences in changes in the arts in the Pacific must be sought in the differing functions they serve in society. The persistant vitality of Pukapukan music, for example, rests in the role it plays in regulating conduct, both serving to check antisocial behavior and permitting rivalry between groups within controllable limits (Salisbury 1984).

In Kiribati, music, poetry, and the dance were bedfellows in an art form which covered "the whole range of experience that may befall an island people" (Grimble 1957:206). Today the dance is still the major form of aesthetic expression even though performances are put on for commercial purposes. One dance troop created, choreographed, and managed by Biteti Tentoa of Eita, Tarawa Island, has spent up to a year travelling overseas — in Vanuatu, Honiara, and Nauru — and at home earns some of its support from paid appearances, such as at weddings, a community social, or the president's inauguration. It performs traditional dances, such as the "stick" dance, as well as some modern ones. Biteti said, "we are adding Pacific movements," and he has incorporated Hawaiian movements into some dances, using the guitar for accompaniment. They acquired a hula from Tahiti and obtained a dance called *damorei* from Rarotonga, but nothing from Samoa. The dancers like performing the Tahitian and Rarotongan dances in the Gilbertese style, and they enjoy mixing these old dances in their performances. When dancing they think first of the movements of the dance, "the movements have to be mixed with the sweet actions," and they remember the old words of the song which is danced, for, Biteti said, the words come first and then the movements are put to them. This is exactly the sequence which Grimble (1957:204-5) described so beautifully — how the poet creates his poem, tries it out on his peers but only achieves its complete aesthetic expression when it is sung and conveyed in the movements of the dance. For the Tahitian and Rarotongan dances they use the Tahitian and Rarotongan words which go with them but put them into Gilbertese timing.

Biteti's repertoire of ninety traditional dances testifies to the continuing importance of the song-dance as the major form of aesthetic expression in Kiribati culture.[41] Exposure to dances from other Pacific countries has led to their adaptation to the Gilbertese idiom, and no doubt more will be absorbed. It would seem probable that eventually the basic forms of some dances, and their musical accompaniments, will be taken over by all Pacific cultures, even if expressed with local touch and flair.

New Manifestations

This category embraces works of art by Pacific artists which show varying originality and ingenuity but often represent a kind of eclectic synthesis of Pacific and non-Pacific traditions. New forms seem to stem from combining old Pacific ones, or new interpretations of them, with non-Pacific ones, sometimes in non-Pacific media. Some of the resulting works have a distinct Pacific flavor while others seem to be Pacific artists' versions of Western traditional art. Both seem to represent the beginnings of a Pan-Pacific art. A number of trends are to be observed.

OLD ART ADAPTING TO THE NEW

Some indigenous artists, who have been continuing to produce art in a traditional manner, have been faced with

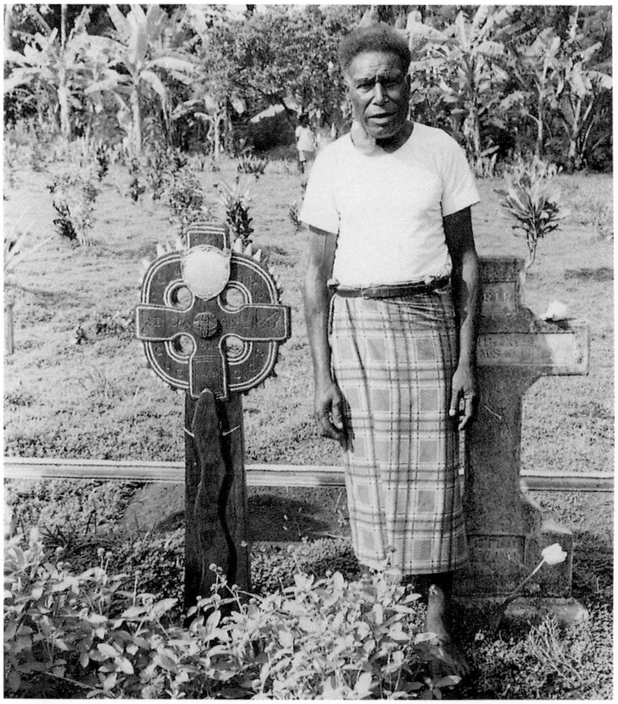

FIGURE 18.19. The late Ganor Aiingei, Kilenge, posing with serpent and cross carving.

commissions for work outside their traditional style. The churches have sometimes sought local artists to meet their need for a Christ figure, a saint, or a cross. Among the Kilenge of New Britain, Aisapo, a master artist of Ongaia, produced a cross for the grave of a priest who died of a heart attack when he fell overboard from a launch. The carving combined the Western symbol of the cross with that of a serpent, which, Aisapo related, represented a culture hero of the Kilenge named Mooro (fig. 18.19). Talania, another master artist of Ongaia, was asked to carve a statue of the Virgin Mary, which he produced satisfactorily in a foreign Western idiom (figs. 18.20, 18.21). These two works prove well how skillful the Kilenge artists can be in expressing a different tradition.

NEW CONTEXTS

New contexts for art can produce new artists. Though Tongan carvers are largely impelled by the economic returns they receive for the kinds of carvings they do for tourists — as considered in the previous section — some are capable of producing works that reflect Western art as

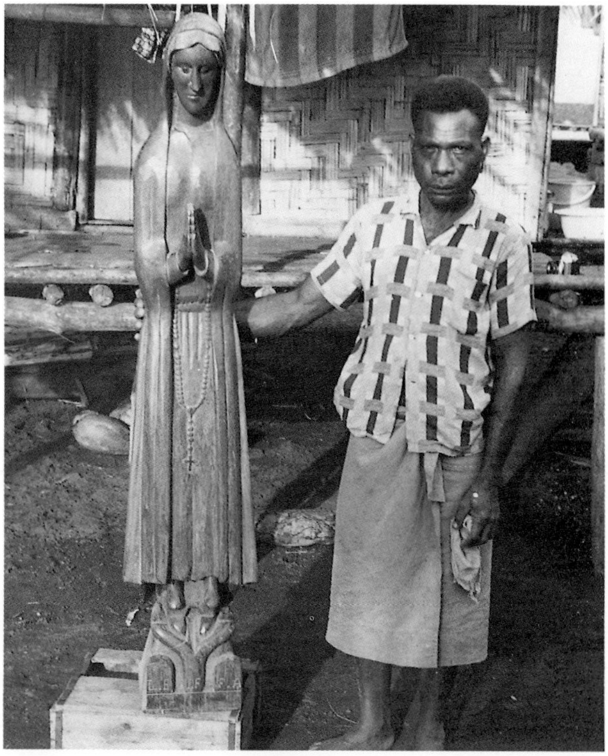

FIGURE 18.20. Talania of Ongaia, Kilenge, stands by his carving of the Virgin Mary.

their source, forms that are not traditional but for which a need has developed or for which there are new contexts. The carved posts of the new museum in American Samoa combine original or new forms with traditional ones. Lionati Jaka Tava, a fine jeweller of Vava'u, Tonga, works some forms in black coral that are not Tongan but can only be described as Pacific in style. Carvers at Arutanga, Aitutaki, Cook Islands, mass produce bowls which are sent to Rarotonga to be marketed to tourists. Outside their workshop are two poles each carved with a figure of a human being, plants, animals and other forms, made by an old man of Rarotonga — a spontaneous modern work? It is a most satisfactory sign for a carvers' shop, in a style that can perhaps be said to be Pacific; and certainly the carvers did not know what the forms represented.[42] In Papua New Guinea many new contexts, such as public buildings, offices, and libraries, have arisen requiring new works by new Papuan New Guinea artists.[43]

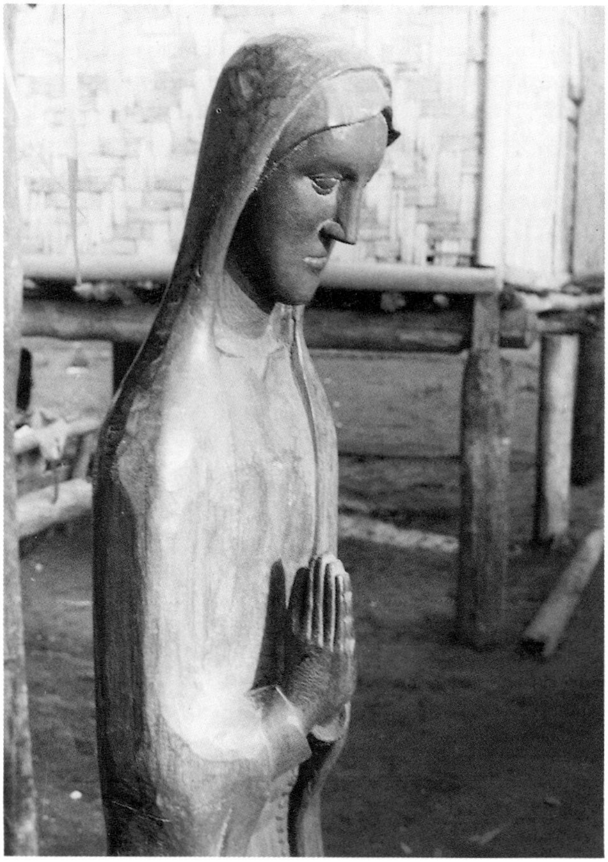

FIGURE 18.21. Close up of carving of the Virgin Mary.

NON-PACIFIC TRADITIONS IN THE PACIFIC

A major modern source of art in the Pacific has been, and is, the all-pervading tradition of Western art. Its penetration of Pacific cultures has been, it would seem, largely through the educational systems they inherited under colonialism. Today, Western art is part of teacher training in many Pacific countries. An Australian artist is employed in Nauru and another in Tonga. An English artist teaches in the King George V High School in Kiribati, which has over five hundred students. European teachers in Papua New Guinea have taught art in high school and at art-school level.[44] The prospectus of the National Arts Schools in Boroko, Papua New Guinea, indicates the same structuring of the arts as in an English art school and the same length of study, starting in a similar fashion with a foundation year. In Fiji, some school teachers have received overseas training, resulting in a blend of ideas and the potential to change traditions. Mrs. Mereisi Tabualevu, a teacher and potter, has had such training; her work in ceramics reflects a synthesis of Fijian ideas with those gleaned in Australia and she uses non-Fijian firing techniques.

Some Pacific artists are experimenting with the execution of local forms in non-traditional media, such as the welded metal sculptures of Gickmai Kundun and Bennny More (n.d.), the beaten copper plaques of Kauage (surely West African, derived via Uli Beier?) or his acrylic and enamel paintings on masonite and color prints, and the screen prints of David Lasisi,[45] four Papuan New Guineans, or the murals in cement with glass[46] and the taspestries of Aloi Pilioko, which he calls "needle paintings."[47]

> In Rotuma I ran out of paints and so I came up with the the idea of needle painting. I saw the Rotumans decorate their mats with coloured wool. I used a copra bag needle and wool to draw on hessian in the way Cecile Varin taught me a few years before on Futuna. The first design was the tapa design but gradually faces and fowls appeared on the hessian and I felt I had discovered my way of expressing myself. (Michoutouchkine n.d.:27)

Nicolai Michoutouchkine produces what he calls "art clothing": "walking paintings, highly coloured, bearers of a message of joy in our tormented world," expressing "les couleurs de l'art primitif océanien," according to *30 Jours* (no. 24). In this same magazine he is pictured painting by causing a nude girl to roll around on a canvas with paint on it, a technique employed not long ago in Western art. Michoutouchkine and Alio Pilioko hosted a two week workshop in May 1984 at Port Villa, Vanuatu. It was sponsored by the Institute of Pacific Studies of the University of the South Pacific and the South Pacific Creative Arts Society, Suva, and was attended by artists from the Cook Islands, Fiji, Kiribati, New Caledonia, Solomon Islands, Wallis, and Western Samoa.[48]

Of considerable prominence in Pacific countries has been the non-Pacific panoply of vestments worn by some Christian priests and their acolytes, in the past almost medieval in display although recently more adapted to changes blowing through the Pacific as well as through the church itself. A guitar accompaniment is used in the Catholic cathedral in Apia, Western Samoa, and robes are kept simple. In Kiribati, the architect of the Catholic

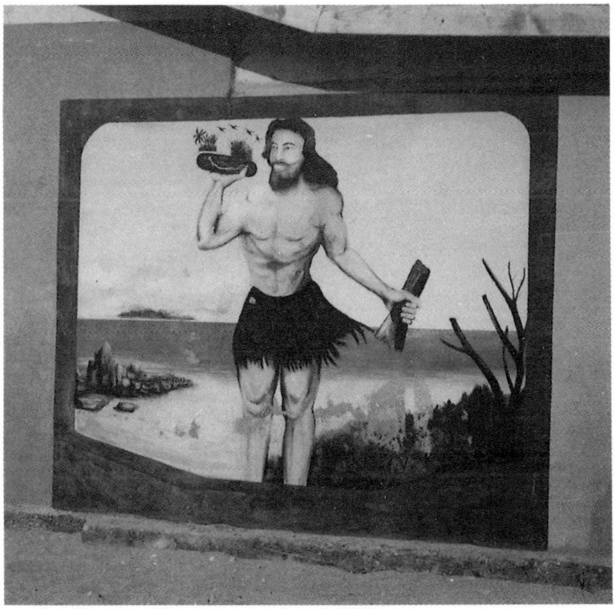

FIGURE 18.22. Painting by Tekiraua Urio.

church on Tarawa Island has incorporated windows of stained glass, some with blues and greens predominating, others with yellows and oranges, the colors made powerfully vibrant from the intense sunlight cast over the atoll setting. It is an eminently suitable inspiration, perhaps deriving from Matisse's masterpiece, the Dominican Chapel of the Rosary at Vence, or from Piper's huge window that illuminates Coventry Cathedral.

Sometimes forms which have no Pacific connotations and which are made outside the Pacific, or copied within it, are transformed from general symbols of the exotic to Pacific ones, provided they are used in appropriate contexts. Examples are masks seen in Neiafu or the so-called totem pole at Aggie Grey's, mentioned above.

NEW ARTISTS[49]

Some new artists have been initially inspired solely by Western art. I reported briefly (Dark 1983:26) on the Gilbertese artist, Tekiraua Urio, who has done paintings for churches, the government, signs for stores, and decorations for graves, and has gradually built up a reputation as an easel painter of stories and fantasies (fig. 18.22). His public works are completely within a Western idiom. In contrast, the work of the late Kuai Maueha, whom Kernot (1984:12) refers to as a "towering enigma" of Pacific art, drew on traditional and biblical themes which he expressed in woodcarving in a most tortuous manner.

Some Pacific artists have found ways, through exposure to the Western manner of execution in various nontraditional media, of expressing dynamically new ideas on life with remarkable inventiveness and power. One thinks of the passion and pathos in the surreal drawings of Joseph Nalo (1978), of the commentary of Akis (1977, 1978), and the ingenious recasting of an old tradition of design in a completely new and exciting direction as in the drawings of the Trobriand artist, Matin Morububna, or the New Ireland artist, David Lasisi.[50] It would seem that to such artists the opportunity to express themselves in new ways and in new media was fortuitous: There was concern in the early 1970s in the four National High Schools in Papua New Guinea for "expressive arts" and a National Arts School was founded in Papua New Guinea which provided a completely new direction for art to be pursued outside the community. But what of carvers such as Tua Alau of Neiafu, Tonga, who has remarkable facility? His only way of earning a living is in his present mold, which prevents him from expressing his skills in directions too new, too different.

COMMENT

Are not the new visual arts in the Pacific growing in a Western pattern? A pattern in which the new painters and carvers form an elite expressing, perhaps, the beginnings of a future Pan-Pacific tradition? But what of the arts of the hoi polloi? Some objects are no longer made and others will be replaced by manufactured imports. But still others continue, even if changed, because they are at the heart of culture—tapa making, basketry, mat making, ornamental lashings, canoe building, and dance and song. Tomorrow some will continue and some not, but they will be tomorrow's identity of today, the markers of earlier times and perhaps continue in what in the West are applied fields, or just become folk arts. Perhaps the genius of the painter, poet, and novelist penetrates the heart of a culture to lay bare its mystery and beauty, but the quality of its life is maintained by the good taste of its artist-craftsmen and the manifestations of their skills.

New artists tomorrow will provide tomorrow's heritage, moving one suspects in a Pan-Pacific stream of artistic expression, no doubt manifesting an individuality and personal stamp of expression on their work, and new symbols of identity will be added to those of yore, and perhaps replace some.

Notes

I am most grateful to the Wenner Gren Foundation for Anthropological Research for a grant which allowed me to seek out trends in the production of art in certain Pacific countries in 1983. I am grateful too for the help and kindness extended to me by many people in the Pacific. Some, particularly, gave me considerably of their time and I wish to thank: J.D. Hunter, John Brown and Mrs. Marina Grey, Western Samoa; Paul Bloomfied, Robert Greer, Futa Helu and David Bisi'ia, Nuku'alofa, and Kevin O'Connor, Tua Alau, Miss Kalo Taumalolo and Mrs. Tina Finneran of Neiafu, and Mrs. Eitita Saresi and Mrs. Helena Martin of Utui village, Vava'u, Kingdom of Tonga; Fergus Clunie, Paul Geraghty, Emele Vulaca, Ivan Williams, Mrs. Vesina Simonei and Amilia, and Mrs. Maria Rawaci, Fiji; Philip Matthews and Prez Nimes, Nauru; Tony Whincup, Peter Kanere Koru, Aristiera Bauro, Bonny Isaia, Mrs. Claire Yaneta Paiitekei and Mr. Donald Rose, the British high commissioner, Kiribati. I wish to record special thanks to Bwere Eritaia and to Peter Biteti Tentoa and his dancers, of Tarawa, Kiribati, and to Peter Gathercole for his helpful comments.

1. See van Wengen (1980:140) for Professor Pott's three motives for visiting museums.

2. See *Pacific Arts Newsletter*, no. 19:11.

3. Bryan Cranstone (1984:20), in reviewing *Art and Artists of Oceania* (Mead and Kernot 1983) and referring to Wendt's (1983) paper, suggests that Wendt seems to be ignoring "the danger of the artist losing his social roots. In Europe, art has not been integrated with daily life, as it formerly was in Oceania, since the Renaissance." The dilemma is how to reconcile domicilary and occupational identity with original roots if they are different.

4. For example, Wendt (1980 and 1983).

5. When man makes various applications of his skill and knowledge according to institutionalized canons of taste the results are forms of art.

6. In the third paragraph he continues "Notice the loving care with which a Gilbertese canoe-maker chooses a name for his boat; were it a son he could not show more solicitude. . .".

7. See *Pacific Arts Newsletter*, no. 18:20-21.

8. One dish I saw fired took approximately half an hour, from the time of lighting the fire to withdrawal of the vessel. The fuel consisted of bits of wood and palm rib, and some sticks, but mainly the husks of coconuts, which, when well lit, gave off an intense, concentrated heat.

9. For example Anon. a (n.d.) or Anon. b (1980).

10. The range of products sold through this cooperative is indicated by the 124 items illustrated in Anon. a (n.d.).

11. Items seen in the store are: large basket, of coconut, made on Beru; coiled trays made on Beru; large mats, pandanus, made on Tabiteuea and Nonouti; small mats, made on all islands; belts of shells, made on Maiana; coils of sennit, made on the southern islands; cushions, of pandanus, made on Tabiteuea, Tamana, and Nikunau; laundry basket, made on Beru; round and oval table mats, made in Beru; handbags with lids, of pandanus, made on Beru; handbags with flaps, made on Beru; necklaces of shell made on Tabiteuea and to the north; and shell hair-clips with coconut strips made on Tabiteuea, and to the north.

These items are similar to those illustrated in a catalog, *Gilbert Islands Handicrafts*, photographs by A. Whincup, put out by the Gilbert Islands Cooperative Federation Ltd. (see Anon. c).

12. The range of items produced can be gleaned from *Gilbert Islands Handicrafts*, Anon. c (n.d.). Some islands produce quite a wide variety of items. For example, Tamana Island products include hats, swords, sleeping mats, floor mats, different kinds of baskets, and walking sticks (*thiokrr*) made from shark's vertebrae (*ria bakra*).

13. Cf. Koch (1965:Abb. 78).

14. for example, in Anon. (n.d.:15) The fans (*tei' lipr*) are made from coconut fibers. Colours used today are not vegetable dyes but imported ones, although they are said to have been made from boiled leaves: red from *teiperu*, yellow from pandanus roots, and I have no information for green. Fans of plaited palm fronds, as illustrated in Koch (1965:Abb. 102), are no longer made.

15. A form of dagger, *sau*, has a blade of coconut rib with sharks' teeth mounted on either side and bone spikes on either side near the tip and on either side near the hilt. The handle is covered with finely plaited, thin strips of colored frond. They are made on Nonouti Island by both men and women (see fig. 18.4). Four kinds of miniature swords of palm rib (*piri*) are made, all mounted with sharks' teeth and using human hair and sennit binding: one is straight bladed, with shark's teeth on either side (fig. 18.5); one has four edges of sharks' teeth (figs. 18.5 and 18.6). This last type is made on Beru Island. The straight swords are made on Arorae and Onotoa islands, those made on the latter being elaborately covered with designs of plaited, colored coconut fibers. See Anon. (n.d.:11); cf. Koch (1965:t.38). An excellent exhibit of old sharks' teeth weapons of Kiribati may be seen in the Fiji Museum.

16. For example, the Cook Island dancer at the South Pacific Arts Festival in Papua New Guinea (see Holdsworth 1982).

17. For example, Hawaiian dancer in Holdsworth (1982).

18. In discussing Koch's (1965:t.16-20, Abb.82) record of costume items made twenty years ago with Bwere Eritaia, he made some observations, which I record herewith: *Wini bakoa* (as in Koch, 1965:t.19e) is the correct term for necklaces. It is the name of the shape of the pattern, which was serrated on either side: it is made of pandanus and it is tied across the girl. In the old days it would have been made of dolphins' teeth. Then the idea of substituting sharks' teeth came in, hence the serrated nature of the pattern. However, those worn by the dancers in figures 18.10-18.12 are no longer serrated, making the serrated ones look longer than the simple bands shown.

Eiteitei or *teitei* (as in Koch 1965:t.20e): the general terms for arm decorations though *eiteitei* are also worn on the fingers (fig. 18.10). Those that go on the forearm are called *namata ni burei*; those on the upper arm *teburei*. Today, these are substitutes for what would have been *ovulae ova* (white cowries) in the past. *Teitei* enable the dancer to check that his or her arms are correctly positioned during the dance.

Tumara, *kamakorokoro*, and *katau*, as in Koch (1965:t.16b, e; t.17), have all now been superceded by the belt *taona n'riri*, as in figure 18.11.

Tekatao sumara, a waist band with black stripes and white shells, can be substituted for *katau*, as in Koch (1965:t.17a). The black and white stripes are regarded as substitutes for the pieces of coconut shell of which the *katau* were made. (*sumara* is the white shell).

Mae, a general term for something hanging from the neck.

Bunna, something made of human hair (e.g., Koch 1965:t18b, c, e-h, Abb.82), something tied around the person, the neck, wrist, ankle, arm. "It has magical properties for protecting you." It derives from the family; the family spirit goes into it. It is cumulative over generations. It is "the force of the spirit"; the force is protective.

19. Shown on Gilbertese dancers in Holdsworth (1982) and Kaeppler (1983:11). The dancers pictured are those with whom I worked in Kiribati.

20. Shown in Holdsworth (1982).

21. I was told that the *ririko* can also be made of leaves and shells.

22. Of group of dances type eight; see note 41, part 3.

23. Shown in Holdsworth (1982). See Koch (1965:t.16b).

24. The design on the three similar panels have eyes and brow "just the same [as]the head — when he's ugly he is looking at you this way." The vision Biteti Tentoa recounted to me occurred as follows:

> After he had been specially prepared for the occasion, he was taken and "they stand you on the edge of a reef, sing a special song, whispering," "they take the ends of a special young leaf together with fresh water from the sea which they put on it and tap you on the chest with it." The leaf is called ukini peneipenei. "They are special magicians; they sing a poem, keep on tapping you with the leaf, when the water rolling over you; they flick fresh water from the ocean on you. They repeat the poem three times." "When this is finished you must look at the other side of the breaking waves and you will see the whales jumping round on the other side." "Go back to house." "The second day the same; the same the third day." At the end of the third day "you will see the proof; the frigate bird will fall down and die or the turtle will come ashore, or the whales will be washed ashore." After that "I could be attacked or visited by those devils." I could be visited "straight after the third day; maybe mostly midnight till morning. If they visit you in the daytime that means very urgent, very special." What happens when they visit you? "They can tell you something, or give you a dream about what you are going to do or where you are going to go. It was then that he came with this belt in his hand; actually it was a woman; the devil appeared to me in the body of my grandmother. She was standing on the side of the bed I was sleeping on. 'Peter,' she said, 'wake up, we are going to attend the dancing in Muckin [north of Tarawa] and this is the costume we take with us but we want you to use it for the costume of your group.' She held it behind her back and then brought it out and said, 'you must look at it carefully as I must take it to Muckin to dance with.' A very tall man was the leader of the trip; you would only see him from the knees down because his body was right up hiding in the house. 'Leave that costume with us,' I said [Peter]. 'No,' she said, 'look at it carefully, how it is made, and when you get up you will make it straight away for yourself.' 'How do you know the design?' I asked. 'That's how they explained it to me,' Peter said. Then he went on: 'After I woke up in the morning, and they left, this one [design] was hanging in [front of] my face; after I rub my eyes it hangs there.'" "When I got up I take a walk, half a mile from my home; how can I find a leaf black and white? Something made me approach the people of a house I had not been to before. When I got in the house I asked, 'Did you have any flat leaves, the white one and the black one?' The couples said, 'No,' then the old lady spoke up and she said 'I have two rolls left behind from my baskets I've done last month. If you want to see I will get them.' I said thank you that is enough for one. The tall man said the belt shouldn't be used by women and they don't. And that's the story of that complete one. It is 'only worn at our dancing.'"

25. Examples can be found in a number of contemporary books illustrating district, national, and international festivals (e.g., Holdsworth 1982).

26. See *Pacific Arts Newsletter*, no 11:14, June 1980.

27. See Dark (1979:24).

28. See *Pacific Arts Newsletter*, no. 18:18-22.

29. On a label attached to one of these figures was the following:

> "Genuine reproductions of Museum Artifact." *Tongan Goddess*. Less than ten pre-European are known to exist. One of these is in the Fuller Collection, the shell inlay is missing from the eyes of the original and, so, has been left from this reproduction, hand carved original in the Field Museum of Natural History, Chicago. Imported by the Tonga Trading Co., Ltd., Honolulu.

On one side of a gold label attached to the piece was "O A T" and on the other "G W C H." The catalog number was given as no. 206. The original carving is in Force and Force (1971:no. 152).

30. For example Anon. a(n.d.), Anon. c(n.d.), Brown (n.d.), McBean (1964 and 1976), and Bollard (1979).

31. The printing is illustrated in Bühler et al. (1962:54), the shield in the same, on p. 58.

32. See reproduction in Okotai (1980:55).

33. It was Robert Louis Stevenson who wrote that art was "an unexplored imminent significance." This was before ideas of "significant form" which Roger Fry and others employed.

34. See *Pacific Arts Newsletter*, no. 18:20, and further in May and Tuckson (1982).

35. I was told in January 1983 in Honolulu of Wright Bowman, Senior, who taught woodworking at Kamehameha Schools but was retired, and Cecil Martin, who was at the Mid-Pacific Institute but who had retired a long time ago.

36. According to David Fisi'ia, the headdress design on fig. 18.15, a and b, represents a tapa design called *hala paiini*, *hala*, meaning road, and *paiini*. pine tree.

37. See illustration in Holdsworth (1982).

38. I was told this by Mr. J. D. Hunter, the manager of the Corporation.

39. The information included here derives from Mrs. Marina Grey.

40. I saw in Neiafu two versions of an elongated figure drinking from a coconut shell carved by Tua. Adrienne Kaeppler told me that a Balinese carver had visited Tonga. Perhaps Tua was influenced by him to produce these two pieces.

41. Bitetei noted eight major groupings of dances:

1. *Tekateitei*: always done by men and women standing; an appropriate costume is that shown in figure 18.12 or as in Koch (1965:Abb.82).
2. *Tekabus*: done only by one or more women, standing, with fast

movements (*tekabus*); appropriate costume is that shown in figure 18.11 or in Koch (1965:Abb.82), and headdress, *tawanido*, as in figure 18.9, or *teimae*, which is similar.
3. *Tebuki*: a woman's dance which more than one can perform, requiring hip movements with a big skirt, *terri ni buki*, weighing twenty-five kilos, and costume accoutrements as shown in figure 18.10.
4. *Tebino*: danced by women and men with different actions, the dancers seated with a mat on the lap.
5. *Teitaupas* and *tereipei*: all the dancers stand and there is clapping with up and down movements and also jumping with the clapping.
6. *Tekameii*: the dancers, usually men but it can be both sexes, stand and wear mats around the waist, as in figure 18.9.
7. *Teiwan'tarawa*: dance for men standing.
8. *Tekaii nimeiang*: only known on the two northern-most islands. Some dances are sexually expressive in manner. Those that are performed at a wedding could lead, sometimes in the past, to intercourse on the ground, the couple being covered with mats. Biteti's groups have a standing dance in which copulation is simulated. There are dances in which old and young are imitated to make fun of them, and dances in which Europeans and a wide variety of animals are mimed. Some of these are frigate bird (*teitei*), sandpiper (*tekeiwei*), chicken (*temwo*), cock (*temeomai*), black tern (*teiyo*), white tern (*kaiaukiau*), dog (*tekiri*), cat (*katamo*), and there are dances imitating the sea (*marowwa*) breaking on the reef, the wind (*tiung*), the rain (*karowa*), wind and rain (*tekaimetwa*), thunder (*tepa*), lightening (*teiis*), the moon (*namakaiing*?), and the moon and Venus (*teitoingaiingr*).

42. See Dark (1979:23).

43. See, for example, Heermann (1979).

44. For example, Ison (1975), Baker (1980), and Dark's (1982) review of the latter.

45. Examples of Gickmai's work are illustrated in Heermann (1979:163, 165) and of Kauage's plaques in the same, p. 136; also see Kauage (1977 and 1978); examples of Lasisi's work are in Heermann (1979:175, 179, 181, 184).

46. Examples decorating the Vila Post Office, Vanuatu, are illustrated in Michoutouchkine (n.d.:37-38).

47. Examples of Pilioko's tapestries are in Michoutouchkine (n.d.:after p. 16, in color, 25-26, 33) and in *30 Jours*, no. 24.

48. Reported in *Tam-Tam*, December 5, 1984.

49. Wendt (1983) comments on some new Pacific artists, including Aloi Pilioko, Iosua Toafa, and Kuai Maueha.

50. See Heermann (1979:167, 170, 171) for examples of the work of Martin Morububna, and note 45 for others.

19

Tribal Art as Symbols of Identity

Hirini (Sidney) Moko Mead

In this chapter I describe different degrees of identification with tribal art when considered at various levels of generalization. Tribal art is taken here to mean the art of tribal groups. In the case of New Zealand there are three main levels of tribal art. The first level is that of the nation or collection of Maori tribes, and is important in several contexts. The Te Maori Exhibition in the United States illustrates some special degrees of identification among the different members of the national population. In an international context the art objects on display carry a heavy burden of representing us, our heritage and our nation. The second level is the art of specific *iwi* (tribes), and is meaningful for a large number of Maoris. Often a tribe has a distinctive style of art and a reputation to uphold. The third level is the *hapu* (sub-tribe). In most cases this is the art-producing and art-owning group. I focus upon *hapu* art because for us identity with this art is strongest, not just with woodcarving but with traditional dances and music, with cloak making, basketry, and so on. At this level tribal art is very close to the individual members of the *hapu* and it forms an essential part of one's sense of being human and cultured.

It would be reasonable to propose as a characteristic of all tribal art that it is closely bound up with the social identity of members of the community. All such art is symbolically rich and meaningful in terms of a group's self-image and how the group presents itself to others. Such art therefore, is not meant for contemplation at a distance but rather is to interact with and to touch.

When we speak of a Pacific or Oceanic art we are referring to a category that is at once concrete and abstract. It is concrete inasmuch as Oceania is a geographical place which can be located on a map, and where parts have been visited by countless people. While there are arguments about the boundaries of Oceania, such as whether Indonesia should be included, by and large we know what the geographical term means. It is, however, quite another thing to be able to define the art of Oceania. Are we able to pinpoint its main characteristics? Can we picture an example that is typical of all Oceania? Probably not, because such art does not exist. What we end up doing is defining a body of art which is produced in particular countries and islands. This sort of definition is tied to culture areas but the art remains abstract and somewhat amorphous.

It is possible that people who belong to the culture area

and part of whose general culture we are discussing will warm to the category called Oceanic art and come in droves to our discussion. This is, however, not the case. Relatively few persons who are linked to Oceanic art both geographically and culturally are seen at art conferences. Rather what we are more likely to see are persons whose identification may be geographical but not cultural, or neither of these. Instead their interest is vocational, academic, and sometimes commercial as well. In some cases the choice to become interested in one culture area or another is related to non-academic matters such as travel, television, or family influence. This sort of identification involves a conscious choice — it is intellectually comfortable and permits easy cooperation among diverse nationals. Only a few persons who identify closely with Oceanic art and who take part in conferences are associated for reasons of culture and heritage.

At the outset, therefore, the analysis of identification and association with the arts requires us to make certain distinctions. For example, the geographic factor operates when an individual is resident within Oceania, and the cultural dimension comes into play when a person belongs to an Oceanic society. Association can be by vocation, which accounts for nearly all of the museum, art gallery, and university personnel; or commercial, which includes all of the collectors and some museum curators. These varied associations center around three main sorts: cultural, vocational or political. The weakest link is the vocational, and strictly commercial one, for the persons associated in this way may not, in fact, want to become involved with the people of Oceania. Their interest is job related. For the person who identifies by reason of cultural association, the art tradition is part of one's heritage. As the focus of attention moves closer and closer to their own art tradition the relationship to art undergoes a qualitative transformation and intensification. Translated into the language of feelings this means that we feel close and warm towards such art and our self-esteem increases.

The people who identify politically with the art of Oceania appeal largely to residence within the region as the main reason. Such a person has become a new Pacific islander, and is very aware of symbols which distinguish Oceania from other regions. The arts of Oceania become part of their new culture and their new identity. An important aspect of this sort of association is that the art of one's own heritage is suspended in various social contexts and certainly in discussions of the tribal arts of Oceania. The new Pacific islanders are able to move in and out of the art heritages to which they are linked. While this might be seen as an advantage by the new recruit it is viewed with some suspicion by the native peoples of the region.

If we want to see what Oceanic art really is we need to focus on examples that belong to a group of people of a particular region. But before we can do so we have to deal with a hierarchy of terms of descending degree of generality. Thus at the level immediately below Oceania we can distinguish the arts of Australia, Melanesia, Micronesia, and Polynesia. These culture area designations are still very broad and unify many political and sometimes linguistically distinctive groups. If we asked members of the conference to divide themselves by the culture area corner to which they most strongly identify, I would expect all the Australians to choose Australia, the Solomon Islanders and Papua New Guineans choose Melanesia, and the Americans and the New Zealanders choose the Polynesia. The reason is obvious enough. Cultural and political affiliations outweigh vocational and scholarly interests when one's loyalty is tested in an exercise such as this. Interestingly, some individuals will find themselves excluded because they do not belong to any of the regions specified and they feel no sense of political, social, or symbolic relationship to any one political entity. Their defense would be that as outsiders they are interested in all of the regions of Oceania and cannot favor one over another. In fact, they are likely to resent being put to the test in this way because no one enjoys exclusion on the ground of residence, culture, and ethnic eligibility. It is a fact that as we deal in turn with the hierarchy of art terms the political dimension becomes increasingly important and exclusiveness more marked. The microscope, as it were, is focusing increasingly on the ethnic group that actually produced the art works we admire.

Within the culture area of Polynesia we come to labels such as Maori or Hawaiian, which still are general terms. From the perspective of a Chinese or American the category "Maori art" constitutes only a small corner in the universe of art. The New Zealand Maori point of view is very different. The term Maori includes within it some twelve "canoe" divisions which are combinations of several tribal groups, about eighty actual tribes (each a political unit in itself), and well over two hundred *hapu* or sub-tribe groupings. Maori art is a collective term encompassing a host of tribal groups which are politically distinct from one another. While all tribes speak dialects of the same language, and while from an outsider's point of view all Maori art may look the same, each tribal group has its own history and sometimes a distinctive art style.

The exhibition of Maori art, which has been shown in New York, Saint Louis, San Francisco and Chicago, is a combined effort with all except one main tribal group participating. The emphasis is upon the art of the combined whole, of the Maori nation. Tribes without examples of great art in the exhibition can bask in the glory of the nation. Thus every New Zealand Maori out of a population of 385,000 can identify with the exhibition and enjoy the praise which critics write and commiserate with the rest of the population if there is adverse criticism. Here our self-esteem is very closely associated with examples of our art included in the exhibition. That the bulk of Maori art is at home in New Zealand does not matter. Any part of the national heritage carries the extra symbolic burden of representing the whole body of art and culture. In addition, these few pieces were selected because of their excellence and carry the *mana* (prestige, power, self-image) of all the tribes of New Zealand. There is thus a special sort of identification with this art; our ideas of self-image, self-esteem, and ethic identity are at stake.

As national art the examples of Maori art in the Te Maori exhibition also have meaning for all citizens of New Zealand regardless of ethnic origin. Thus every New Zealander identifies in varying degrees of intensity with Maori art — more so for New Zealanders abroad in the United States at this time, and less for those at home. There is a positive feeling of pride at the achievements of the ancestors and there is an expectation that the art objects will do great things for our national *mana*. Thus the category "Maori art" is still a unifying concept. The identification was very strong for those New Zealanders who were in New York while Te Maori was on exhibition at the Metropolitan Museum of Art.

At this level of identification the face of the Arawa ancestor, Tutanekai, which was used in New York for exhibition posters as well as for the cover of the Te Maori catalog (fig. 19.1), is not seen as a tribal face as such (namely, Ngati Whakaue, sub-tribe of Te Arawa) but as a Maori face. In this latter sense Tutanekai represents a Maoridom for the Maori population and all of New Zealand for the non-Maori population of the country. Because of the great success of the exhibition in New York, Tutanekai, an ancestor who died generations ago, became transformed into a national symbol. In effect he became the face of the nation — a remarkable achievement for Maori art. Even more noteworthy is that Tutanekai is now known as a named face to many pre-school Maori children. The same thing has happened to Te Kauru-o-te-rangi (fig. 19.2) from Ngati Kahungunu. He, too, is a national ancestor as well as being a local hero who has been "rediscovered" because of the Te Maori exhibition.

Personal commitment to art, as well as identification with it, increases dramatically the moment we talk about the art of "our" tribe. For us in New Zealand, the term *taku iwi* (my tribe, my people) has deep significance. The *iwi*, meaning literally "bone," is the group of people who are

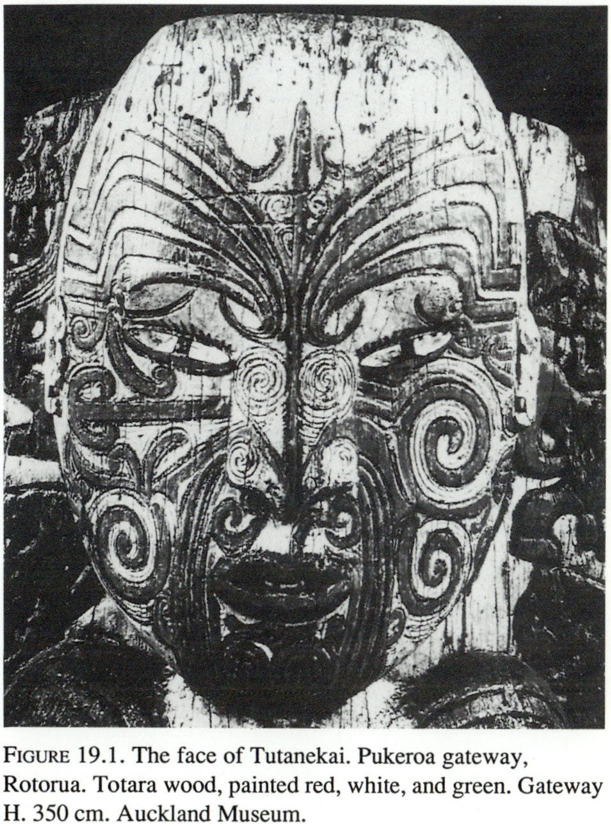

FIGURE 19.1. The face of Tutanekai. Pukeroa gateway, Rotorua. Totara wood, painted red, white, and green. Gateway H. 350 cm. Auckland Museum.

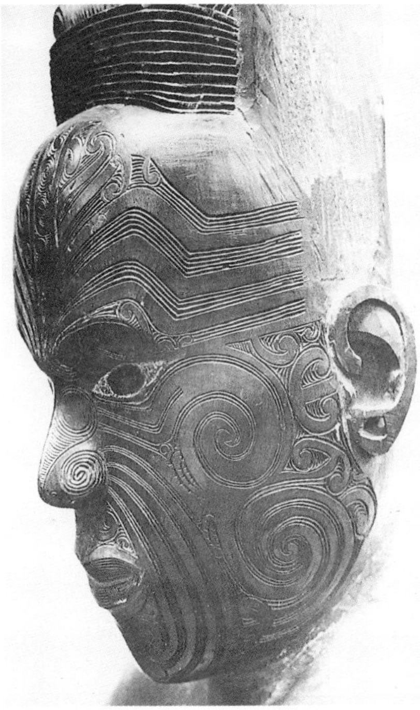

FIGURE 19.2. The face of Te Kauru-o-te-Rangi. Centre-post carving from a meeting house that once stood at Pakowhai, Napier (Hawkes Bay). H. 144 cm. Hawkes Bay Art Museum.

descended from the particular ancestor for whom the tribe is named. I use my own tribe as an example. Awanuiarangi is our founding ancestor, hence I am Ngati Awa. But there are other necessary symbols of identity required to complete my credentials of belonging. The mountain of the tribe is Putauaki (Mt. Edgecumbe) (fig. 19.3), its rivers are Rangitaiki and Whakatane, and our canoe is Mataatua. Hence we are listed on the map as a Mataatua tribe (fig. 19.4).

Like all other tribal groupings in New Zealand, Ngati Awa consists of a collection of some sub-tribes called *hapu* ("pregnancy"). The more important ones are Ngati Hokopu, Taiwhakaea, Ngati Pukeko, Patuwai, Te Rangihouhiri, Ngati Hikakino, Rangataua, Ngati Wharepaia, Ngati Pahipoto, Ngati Hamua, Nga Maihi, Ngai Tamaoki, and Warahoe. These divisions are important because each is potentially an art-owning and art-producing group. Carved meeting houses characteristically belong to a sub-tribe (*hapu*) rather than to a tribe (*iwi*). To illustrate the points made above I shall examine some of the art works that are attributed generally to Ngati Awa and provide more specific information relating to who actually produced and owned such works or who the likely owners might be.

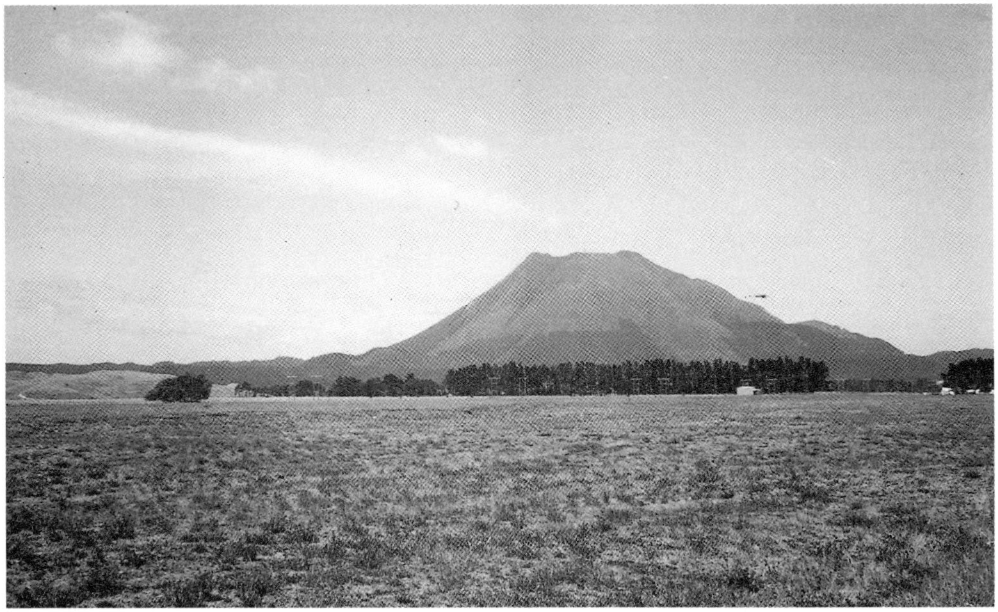

FIGURE 19.3. Mount Putuaki (Edgecumbe), the symbolic mountain of Ngati Awa of the Bay of Plenty region. Photograph by H. Mead.

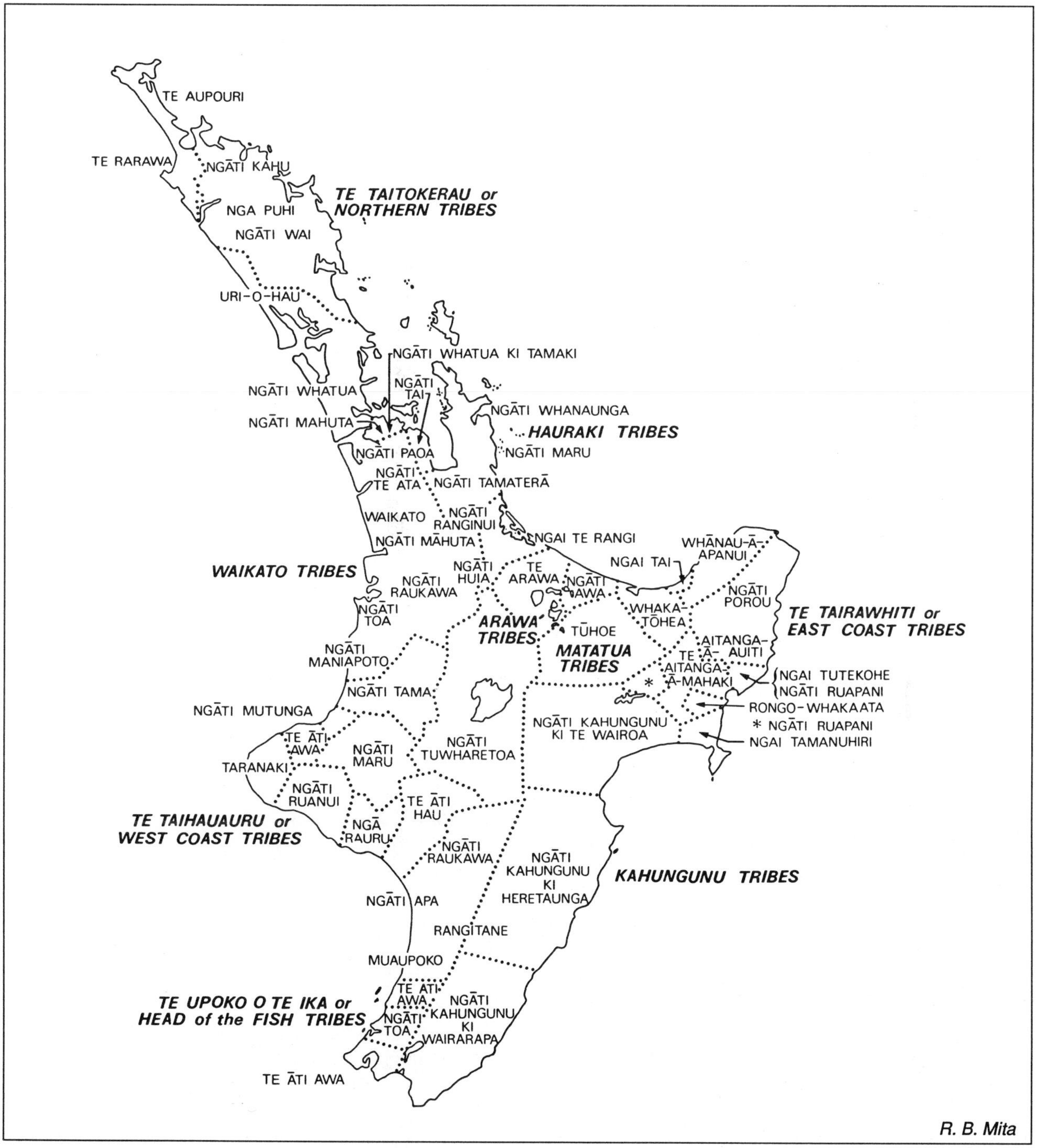

FIGURE 19.4. Tribal regions in the North Island. Maori Studies, Victoria University.

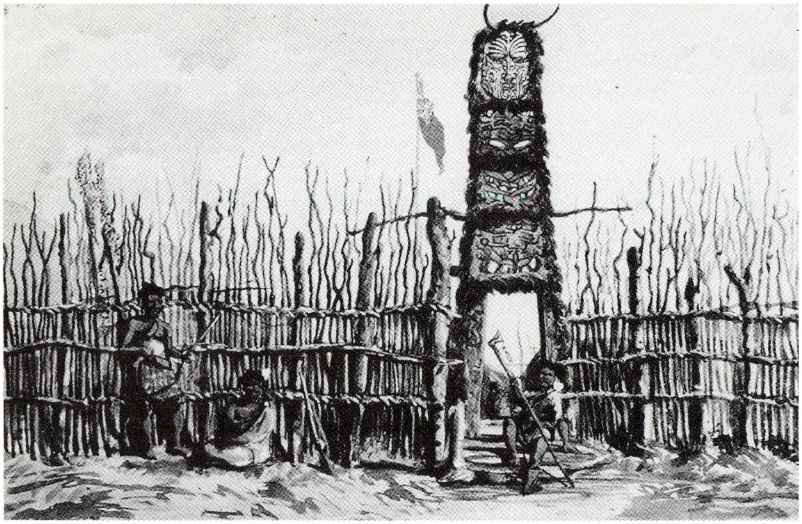

FIGURE 19.5. Gateway to the fortified village of Ngati Te Rangihouhiri, at Matata. Painted by Major General Robley in 1865. Bernice P. Bishop Museum collection.

Example 1. As a hapu, Ngati Te Rangihouhiri is hardly known today but before the Land Wars of 1865-66 it had a large village in Matata and could muster a fighting force under its chief, Te Hura. Nothing is left of Ngati Te Rangihouhiri's former possessions at Matata because the land was subsequently confiscated by the New Zealand government and most of it given away as a reward to the "friendly" tribes. But some details of their art works remained because Major General Robley (1896), a soldier and ethnographic artist, was in the region during the wars. He painted a scene of the wartime village with its rim completely covered with defensive works. Within the palisading was a collection of houses, one of which (a chief's house or meeting house) had a carved gable figure (*kokuru*). Of great interest is the detail shown in another sketch, this time by J. McDonald (reproduced in Best 1975:397). This shows one particularly large meeting-house type of structure and five smaller structures near it, suggesting a fairly large population. Fortunately Robley went to great pains to paint the carved gateway of the village. The original is no. 50 in the Robley sketches at the Bishop Museum in Honolulu. It is reproduced here (fig. 19.5) as evidence that Ngati Te Rangihouhiri sub-tribe of Ngati Awa, which formerly lived at Matata, was an art-producing and art-owning group. Since in the Land Wars Te Arawa fought against Ngati Awa it is most unlikely that the gateway was Arawa work. Rather it is safer to assume that it was Ngati Te Rangihouhiri's own work. It features a larger-than-life male ancestor with a large head painted in white and decorated with black tattoo. The body is red.

Example 2. The carved meeting house called Mataatua built 1872-1874 is reasonably well known in the literature (Phillipps and Wadmore n.d.). For example it is featured on the cover of the first occasional paper of the Pacific arts Association. It was reputed to have been gifted to the Queen of England and thus owned by the Crown, that is, the Government of New Zealand. Subsequent research has revealed that there was never any transaction whereby a property was transferred to the Crown. Thus in legal terms the house still belongs to Ngati Awa, but it stands in the Otago Museum (fig. 19.6) where it is regarded as part of the ethnological collection of that institution.

The house, described by Phillipps and Wadmore (n.d.) actually belonged to a *hapu* or sub-tribe and in this case Ngati Hokopu, the *hapu* of the Chief Wepiha Apanui is the best candidate. Some would argue that the house was in fact a tribal one and thus belonging to all of Ngati Awa. The reason to arguing in this way is because all sections of Ngati Awa assisted in building Mataaua, in collecting money for it and in opening it. Nonetheless it was built on *hapu* land and it was located in a village. Today there is some confusion about whether the house stood in the village of Ngati Hokopu or of Ngai Tonu, a *hapu* of Ngati Pukeko.

The house was carved by Wepiha Apanui and assisted by carvers from Ngati Patuwai and Ngati Pahipoto of

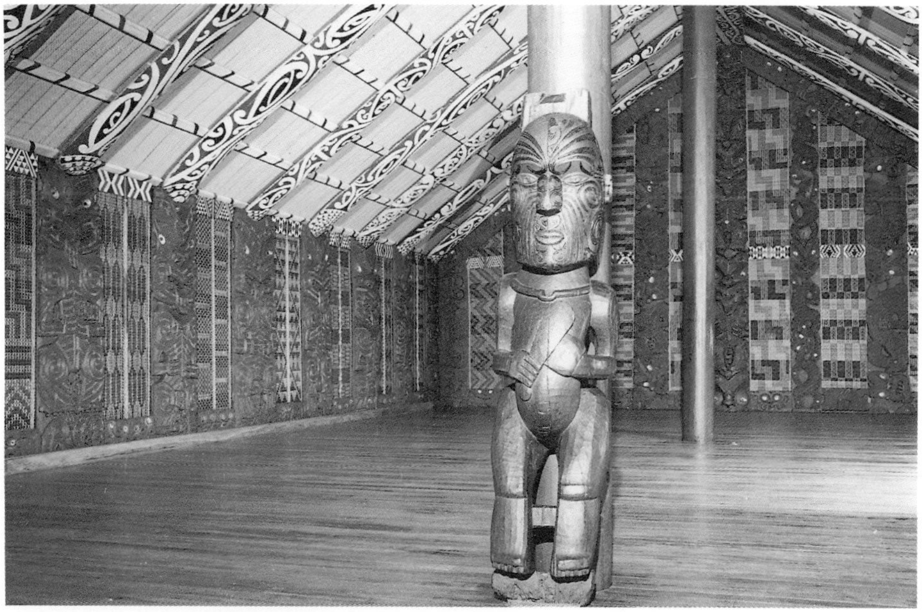

FIGURE 19.6. Interior of the carved house Mataatua, now in the Otago Museum. Otago Museum.

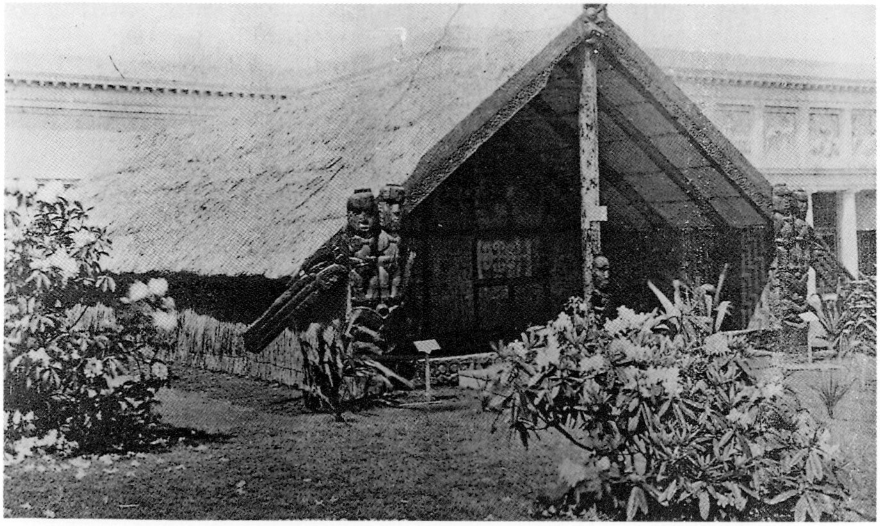

FIGURE 19.7. Mataatua house as it appeared at the British Empire Exhibition, London, 1924. Whakatane Museum.

Ngati Awa and by Te Whanau-a-Apanui carvers. The house was erected on land that had been returned to Ngati Awa following wholescale confiscations in 1866. It was opened with full traditional and modern ceremonies in March 1875 and the event was described in detail in the local newspaper.

Under most unusual circumstances Mataatua was allowed to be taken to Sydney in 1879 tor an exhibition. From there it began a series of journeys that took it to Melbourne and eventually to London where it was exhibited in 1924 at Wembley Park (fig. 19.7). Later it was returned to New Zealand for the New Zealand and South Seas Exhibition held in Dunedin in 1925-26. It stayed in Dunedin and it is there now. Today Ngati Awa is attempting to have the house returned to its tribal domain. An important consideration from an art point of view is that

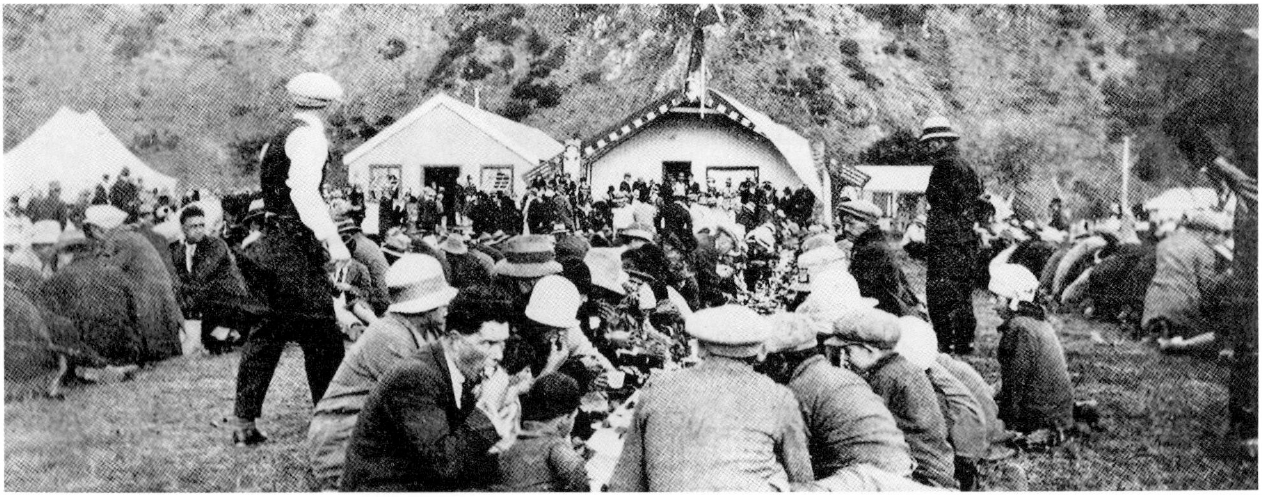

FIGURE 19.8. A 1926 feast at the *marae* of Ngati Hokopu, Whakatane. Whakatane Museum.

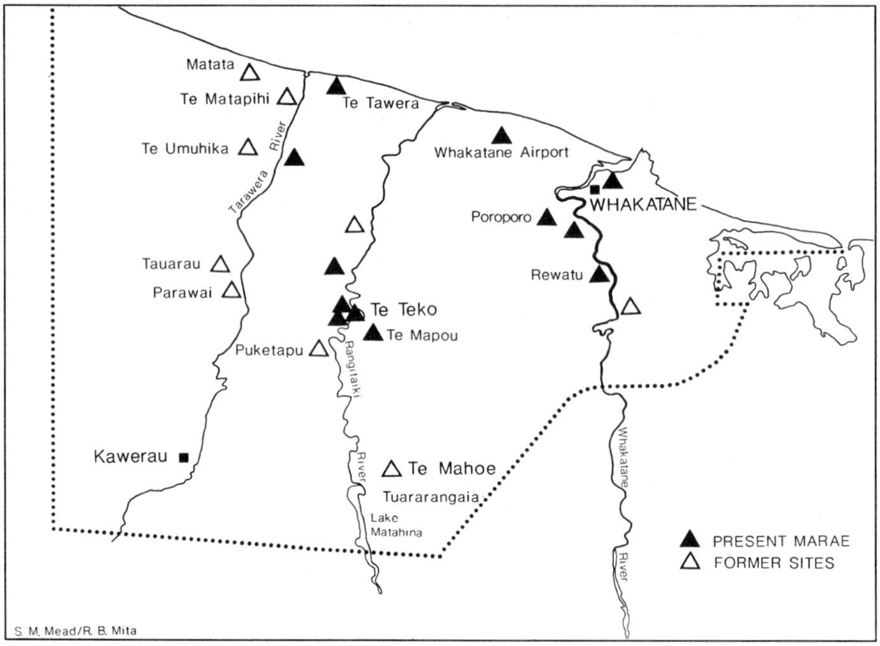

FIGURE 19.9. *Marae* complexes in the Ngati Awa territory, Bay of Plenty region.

the house is a model of the carving style of Ngati Awa in the 1870s and artists want to study their art style as captured in Mataatua.

Example 3. After Mataatua had been given away, Ngati Hokopu and Wharepaia resolved to build a second decorated meeting house. Though many of its carvings were done at Whakatane in Ngati Awa territory, the house itself was built in Thames, again by Wepiha Apanui, assisted by his aged father Te Hamaiwaho Apanui. The house was built as a marriage gift for Mereana Mokomoko, Wepiha's sister, who was given as a wife to Hoterini of Hauraki. This house is called Hotunui, and it now stands in the Auckland War Memorial Museum. There are thus two reasonably early houses that are part of the Ngati Awa art tradition and

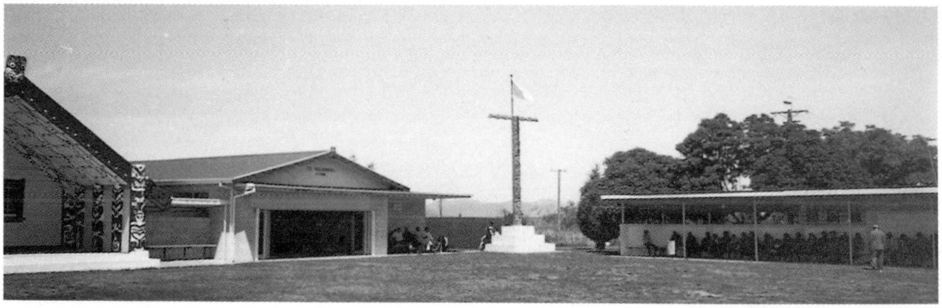

FIGURE 19.10. The carved house Ruataupare, a mourning house (*whare mate*), carved flagpole, and shelter shed on the *marae* of Ngati Pahipoto. Photograph by H. Mead.

were built by the same two *hapu*. This fact attests to Whakatane having been a carving center after the Land Wars of 1865-66, and by inference it must have been a carving center even before the wars — carvers do not suddenly emerge in a community and an art tradition does not begin from nowhere.

Example 4. Ngati Hokopu subsequently established a *marae* for itself near the beach at Whakatane. Known as Wairaka, the *marae* and house are clearly established in Maoridom as the headquarters of Ngati Hokopu. Since the photograph (fig. 19.8) was taken the *marae* has been updated and new facilities added, but the meeting house Wairaka remains.

Example 5. On the inland side (*taha ki uta*) of the tribal boundaries is the headquarters of Ngati Pahipoto which is located at Te Teko (see fig. 19.9). Known as Kokohinau, its present *marae* has been in existence since 1882 (Mead and Phillis 1982). The earlier *marae* sites were even farther away from the coast. The carved meeting house, Ruataupare, was opened in 1882 (fig. 19.10) and is third in the sequence of large decorated meeting houses built by Ngati Awa carvers, the first two being Mataatua and Hotunui. The *marae* of Ngati Pahipoto has been improved several times and has had several facilities added over the years. It is now a very large *marae* capable of holding large gatherings of more than a thousand people.

Example 6. Ngati Wharepaia, mentioned in examples 1 and 2, became extinct and only in 1984 was it thought possible to revive the sub-tribe. Another formerly extinct sub-tribe was Ngati Warahoe. Interestingly, the Te Maori exhibition features an artwork belonging to Warahoe (Catalog item no. 86 in Mead 1984b). These two *hapu* were reestablished when a newly formed tribal authority known as the Ngati Awa Trust Board made it possible to do so by public declaration and by payment of a tribal tax of NZ $1,000. Members of these *hapu* were still living but they had for all intents forsaken their ancestral *hapu* and affiliated with another to which they also had genealogical links. The old link was destroyed when their lands were confiscated in the 1865 Land Wars. All that seems to have survived of its body of art was the carved front end of a

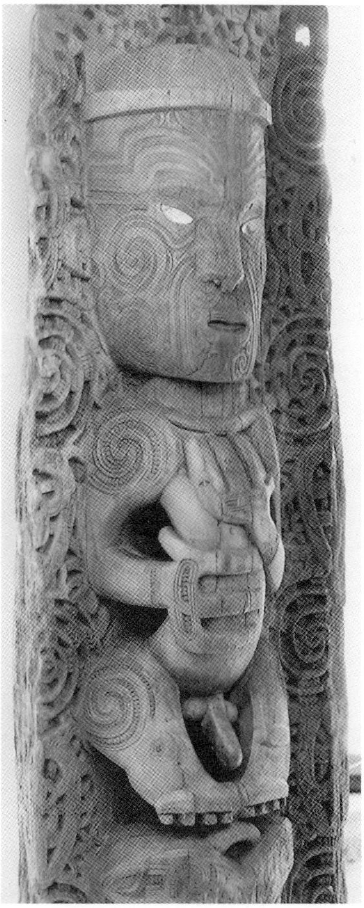

FIGURE 19.11. Ridge-pole carving of Tuwharetoa, belonging to Ngati Warahoe. Auckland Institute and Museum.

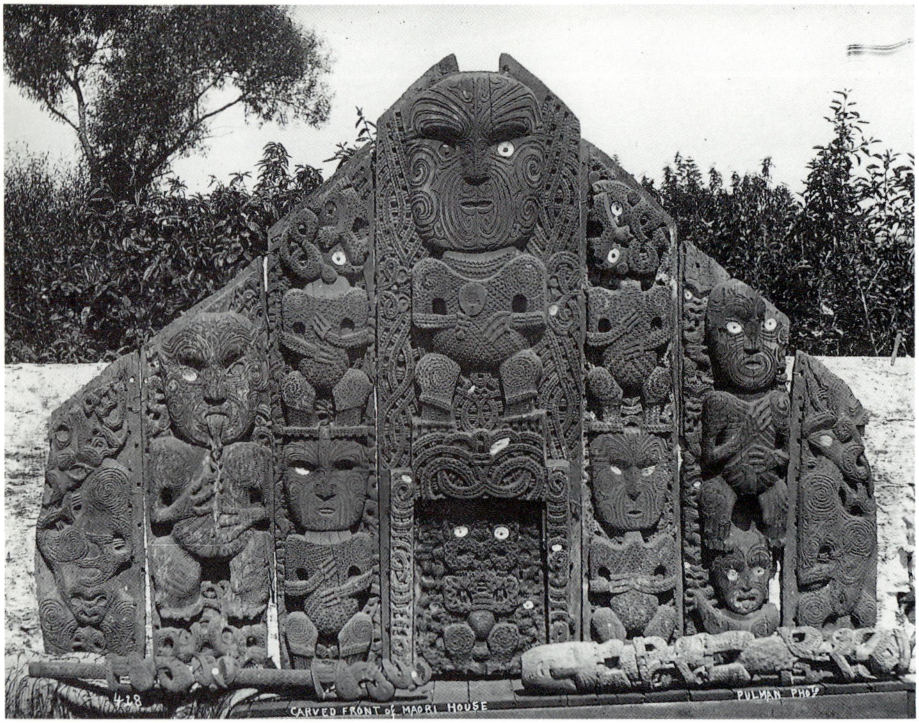

FIGURE 19.12. *Pataka* (storehouse) facade, probably belonging to Ngati Patutatahi. Bernice P. Bishop Museum collection.

ridgepole belonging to a house that was built about the late 1840s (fig. 19.11). According to David Simmons of the Auckland Museum, where the piece has been housed, the carver was Owaihaputangirangi and the ancestors depicted are Tuwharetoa and Kahungunu. Ngati Warahoe's territory was at Tuararangaia (see fig. 19.9).

Example 7. A major piece of Ngati Awa art now rests in the Bishop Museum in Honolulu (fig. 19.12). It is the carved frontage of a storehouse that fell into the hands of the dealer Craig some years after the Land Wars. Because of its richness in decoration, few *hapu* can claim it. Ngati Hokopu, headquarters of the chiefly line of the Apanui family, is a strong contender, but can probably be ruled out in this case because the carvings do not show a sufficiently strong Te Kaha influence. Te Whanau-a-Apanui people of Te Kaha had a distinctive style of carving which is illustrated in the Te Maori exhibition catalogue, item 91 (Mead 1984:204-5). The most likely former owners of the storehouse are Ngati Patutatahi. This sub-tribe became extinct after the Land Wars, but some of its members reformed under the name of Te Whanau-a-Taiwhakaea. Today Taiwhakaea has its own large *marae* complex which is near the Whakatane airport (see figs. 19.9 and 19.13).

Several other *hapu marae* with carved houses, flagpoles and large dining rooms in the tribal region of Ngati Awa (as in fig. 19.10) might be discussed, as well as further examples of our art in museums, but I believe the point is made. The sub-tribe unit, called *hapu*, is first and foremost the art commissioning group and it owns the resulting work. Even when a non-*hapu* carver is commissioned to build a meeting house or storehouse, the bulk of the required labour is local. In some cases a *hapu* may not be able to supply its own carvers and must ask someone else to assist them. Certainly it is the responsibilty of such a group to provide food and hospitality for the carvers until the job is finished. Thus the group's investment in its artworks is considerable, consisting of labor, food from land, forest lakes, and ocean, and hours of hospitality.

The *hapu* remains the predominant art-owning group in the Maori world. These are the social and economic units which build and maintain decorated structures and which keep in group ownership a stock of art works such as woodcarvings, paintings (*kowhaiwhai*), latticework

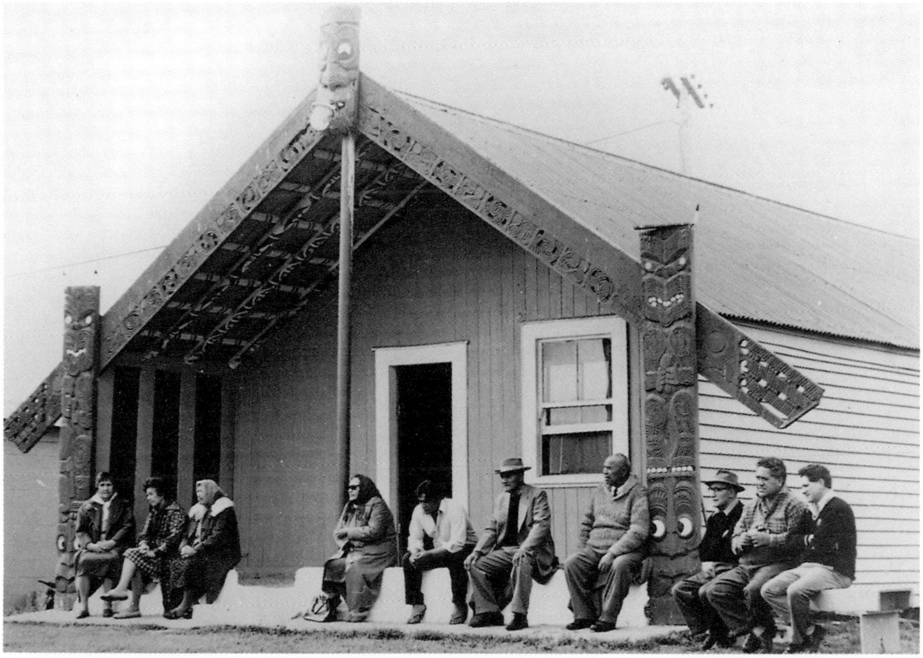

FIGURE 19.13. The house Puawairua, belonging to a section of Taiwhakaea in Whakatane. Eruera Manuera, chief of Ngati Pahipoto, is sitting near the upright front carved post. Photograph by H. Mead.

(*tukutuku*), basketry in the form of floor mats, kits, and weaving in the forms of cloaks. In fact, art works handed down from the ancestors are thought of as belonging more appropriately to the group rather than to an individual even when legal custody might be vested in one person.

It follows that what we really mean by the term Ngati Awa art is the sum total of all art works belonging to every *hapu* of the tribe. The corpus includes all works from earliest times up to the present in the various domains of art such as sculpture, tattoo, painting, weaving, lattice-work, and so on. The term unites all sections of the tribe and gives every individual member equal rights to the heritage. But in unifying the tribe a consequence is the creation of some distance between the individual and the art heritage. The collective tribal term Ngati Awa is an abstration which has the advantage of drawing together all members of the tribe, the rich and the poor, to enjoy the best of the group's art works. From the point of view of the individual members of the tribe, Ngati Awa art or the Ngati Awa art style represents a distillation of the best examples of art actually produced over time and is a summary of the characteristics of that highest quality portion. In this instance I have tried to gather together the various examples of Ngati Awa art as a step preliminary to describing its characteristics.

It would be true to say that for most Maori adults the most meaningful category of art is that of their sub-tribe, their *hapu*. Identification focuses upon the carved house, the *marae* or courtyard, the people of the group, the activities which go on at the village, the close relatives who passed on, and the cemetery where they all lie. Thus, for me, I cannot help but warm towards the house Rua-taupare and the whole *marae* complex because it is there that my roots are anchored. Built in 1882 the house has stood for just over a hundred years and has witnessed some remarkable changes in that time. The *marae* on which it stands has itself changed a great deal since 1882 so that its facilities are modern, very large, and appropriate to meet the needs of the people in the 1980s.

The bond established with the meeting house is through people who are our relatives near and distant (fig. 19.13). In a lifetime we see many of them at numerous functions and at some large meetings (*hui*) when other tribal groups are present. We see our *iwi* or "bones" at the house and we welcome and bid farewell to many friends there. For men of the sub-tribe, the greatest honor (which is also fraught with difficulties) is to be able to stand on one's own *marae* to welcome visitors. This act reflects the importance of the concept of *turangawaewae* (place for the feet to stand). One's right to stand on the ground and speak is never greater than at one's ancestral *marae* . It is rich in history. Here stood our grandfathers and uncles. In their day they represented the sub-tribe and spoke on its behalf. The greater the prestige (*mana*) of the visitors the more it rests on the shoulders of the speakers to uphold the reputation of the local group.

For women the honor of doing the ceremonial call (*karanga*) is a similar privilege that is not taken lightly. The singing of traditional songs (*waiata*) at the end of the speeches also draws upon the heritage of the group. The act of performing them brings one into contact with the ancestors who, in their day, sang the same songs on behalf of the same group and in front of the same house.

These activities at the *marae* sometimes occur outside and at other times inside the meeting house with its rich array of ancestor figures. If outside, people are interacting with the house, the flagpole, and any other decorated structures present. During the funeral ceremony, called *tangihanga*, there is even more interaction in a particularly charged atmosphere. By the time our elders die, the bond to the structures of the *marae*, to the ground, and to the artwork is already established.

At the cemetery lies the dead of the sub-tribe: the mothers, fathers, grandparents, the aunts and uncles, sisters and brothers, the children and grandchildren. Their headstones are marked; some are decorated in the form of stone work and others reflect the traditional styles of carving and the traditional memorial post. The cemetery is becoming an increasingly beautiful place in its layout and its decorations. Thanks to the Western art of photography we can see images of personalities who are now only bones in the ground. But these are the people who give meaning to our identity as persons. As individuals we are nothing and we are no one. The sub-tribe group, our relatives, the *marae*, the ancestral mountain, the rivers, the carved house, and all of the artwork of the group, including family heirlooms, define us as persons. I cannot be understood as a mere individual who is cut adrift from my cultural roots. The roots help me stand like a tree.

The carvings inside the house portray relationships in the realm of the ancestor world and the gods. In a way the house is a recreated cemetery in which the ancestors represented are selected for a purpose. Some ancestors are

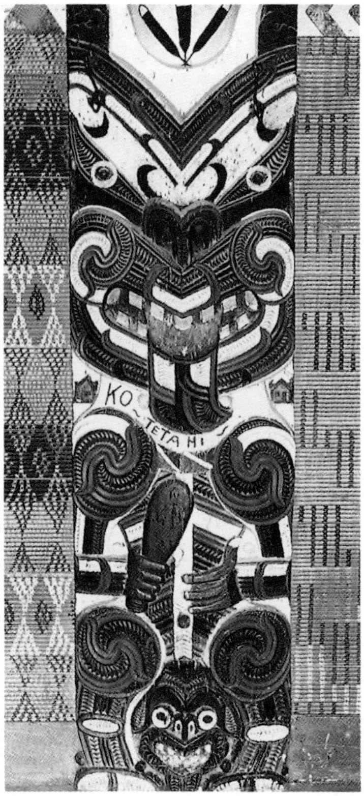

FIGURE 19.14. Te Tahi, a popular legendary figure of Ngati Awa. Rafter support post in the carved house Te Tokanga-nui-a-Noho, at Te Kuiti. Photograph from Australian National Gallery.

legendary figures such as Te Tahi-o-te-rangi, who is well known among the people of Ngati Awa (fig. 19.14). His exploits are told over and over again and his proverb *Waiho ma te whakamaa e patu* ("Let shame do the punishing") is often quoted to make a point.

Tuwharetoa, illustrated in figure 19.11, is also an important ancestor of many Ngati Awa sub-tribes. Although he is recognized as the founding ancestor of Ngati Tuwharetoa of the Taupo region, he happens also to be a Ngati Awa ancestor. The sub-tribes Warahoe, Pahipoto, and Ngati Te Rangihouhiri, to mention but a few, can all trace relationships to him. Thus his presence in Ngati Awa houses can be explained easily on kinship grounds. Numerous other ancestors, such as Awatope, Te Rangikawehea, Nukutaimemeha, Tukere, Tamatearehe, Tuteao, Iratumoana, and Taiwhakaea appear in the tribe's meeting houses. The historically important ancestor Te Maitaranui is shown at the base of the center pole in Mataatua house (fig. 19.6). They are all in the beautifully recreated ancestor world, standing between their living descendants and the gods.

By filling a house with named ancestors the whole character of the house is charged with significance and with genealogical points to which individuals can relate in varying degrees of closeness.

Certain ancestors of the caliber of Tuwharetoa stress interrelationships with a wider universe of kin and political and historical associations that reach far back in time. Thus, in addition to being a focus for sub-tribal identity, the carved house is also a reminder to members of the *hapu* (sub-tribe) of their many links of intermarriage with other tribal groups. Ultimately, we are always more than we seem because people marry, they bring up children, or give children to others to bring up, they travel, they meet stangers from other tribal lands, sometimes overseas, and they bring them back home. Ngati Pahipoto people such a myself have many tribal links and relationships with other people and with other lands.

There are always ancestors in the house who tie us to the land on which the house stands. In this case those ancestors are Irapeke, famous ancestor of Ngati Awa, the twins Iramoko and Manukorihi, Tuwharetoa, Tuhoe-Potiki, and Iratumoana. These ancestors are anchor points of local genealogical connections. They say something about the owners of the house, and about how genealogical branches stretch out to connect the group called Ngati Pahipoto with other well-known tribal groups. They identify some of the political alliances of the past and hence say something about the *mana* (prestige) of the group today. Certainly, there is no doubt that Ngati Pahipoto people are proud of their identity and very proud of their *marae*, its facilities, and its artwork.

Thus at the level of sub-tribe (*hapu*) our identification with our artwork is very close. Indeed, since one of the basic themes of Maori art is commemoration of the ancestors, individual pieces of art are more than just art objects. They are ancestors who are symbols of our identities as persons and as members of particular social groupings. To see the house Ruataupare (fig. 19.10) is to touch a chord of immediate sympathy and to set off a chain of associations which are nostalgic, both happy and sad. To see it is to remember those who are no longer here.

After being away from the tribal heartlands for many years one of the greatest experiences for us is to stand before our tribal house and then to go inside it. Many alienated Maori men and women have shared this feeling of delight, of rediscovery, of poignant reunion with their heritage, their cultural roots, and their arts. It is a proud moment when one can say: "This is my house, these are my ancestors, and this art work is part of my heritage."

Of all the different sorts of association with art that I mentioned there is none more fundamental to a person's sense of identity and self-worth than *hapu* art. Perhaps the meaning of *hapu* as "pregnant" is apt, for pregnant art is a necessary part of every cultural person. We all need this sort of art to give us a sense of self-worth. We need meaningful and beautiful architecture that we can call our own. We need richness in art and artistically created environments in which we do our living, our work, our coming together, and our play; in which we recover when we are ill and in which we die and are farewelled from this earth. Art should be pregnant in the sense that it helps define our identity and gives birth to feelings of self-worth and self-esteem, is rich in meaning, links us to our cultural roots, and makes us proud to be part of the human race.

20

Art as Identity: Aspects of Contemporary Aboriginal Art

J. V. S. MEGAW

I should commence this chapter with a clear statement of what it is not: Despite my concern to argue for the cultural significance of certain types of material culture I do *not* attempt to offer here a definition of art itself either as recognized within a single culture or across cultures or institutions (see, for example, Brook 1980, 1982). Though cogent arguments have been advanced at this symposium as to why we should spend more time defining our terms, what is — or is not — regarded as "art" is of less concern to my theme than the fact that almost everything discussed here has at some time or other been considered by someone, usually the consumer, as "art." I for my part would be wholly satisfied with substituting "product x" for every appearance of the word "art" in the following pages. Since, however, one cannot avoid using some sort of terminology I have borrowed here the distinctions usefully made elsewhere between various grades of indigenous arts from "tourist" to "fine" arts (Graburn 1976, Morphy 1980). Such divisions have been established largely on the basis of market forces and the perceived purchasers.

In the following pages, I shall give one person's view — the view, I should add, of one white Australian regarded by at least some black Australians as reactionary and irrelevant (Megaw 1984b) — of the ways in which Aboriginals in the 1980s are perceiving their own arts; such perceptions are, of course, independent of how such arts may be categorized by cultures and cultural values outside their own — or are they? I also contend that there is a basic dilemma in the wholly legitimate fostering of the production for cash of art works by communities of the Third and Fourth Worlds in order to gain greater economic independence. This is that in joining the international art market such communities run the risk of being controlled by it.

Sidney Mead recently commented:

> However one views the Pacific, it has made a valuable contribution to the cultural wealth of the world and it is entitled by various internationally recognized rights to continue making that contribution. Its various cultures, which have added their own measure of human creativity to the arts of the world, need to to be encouraged to hold on to their art systems and to develop them for the benefit not only of their citizens but also for the world at large. (Mead 1984:3)

Although already in Australia in the 1960s one or two

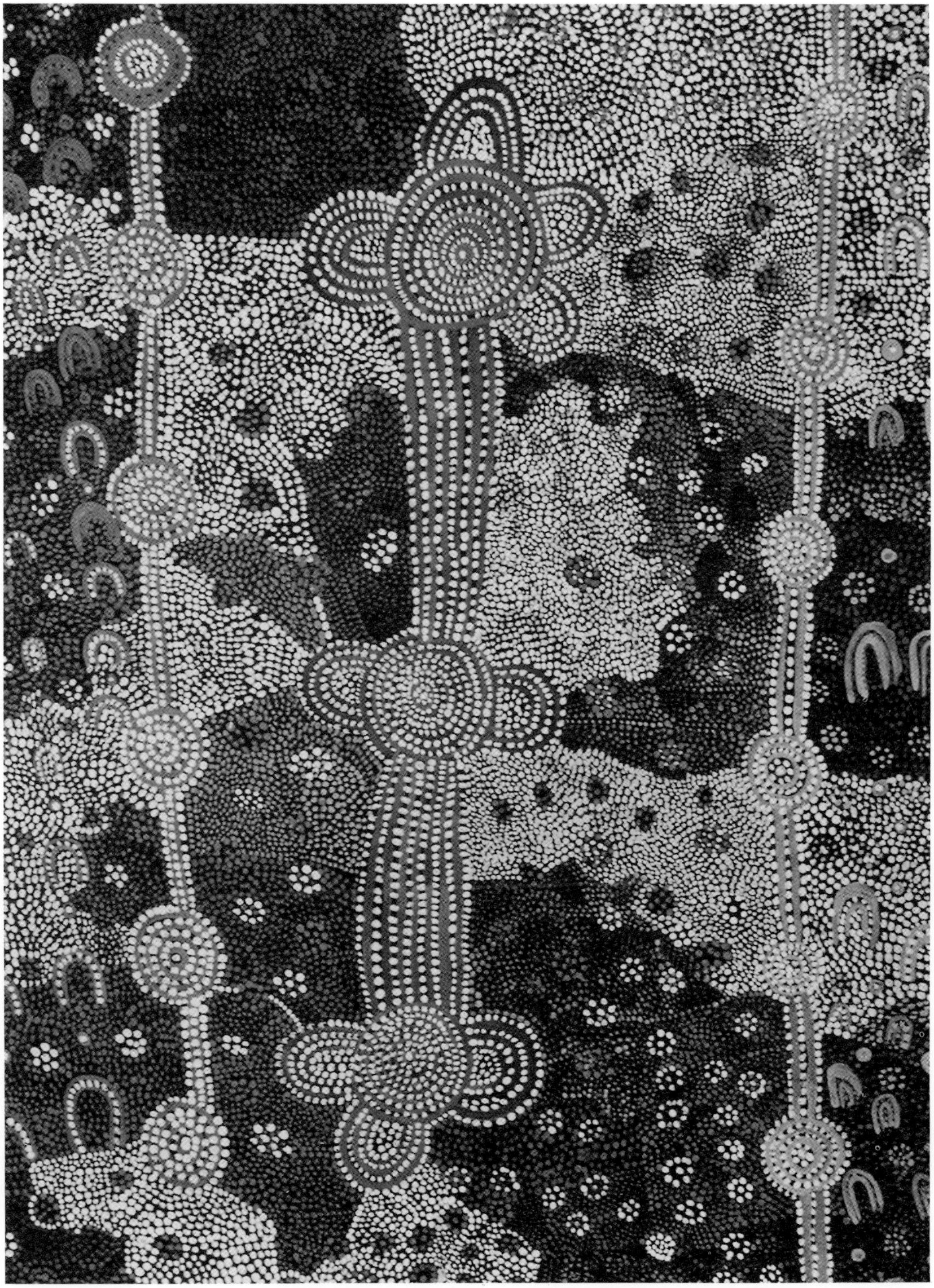

FIGURE 20.1. Old Mick Tjakamarra (Loritja tribe). Honey ant dreaming, 1973. Synthetic polymer paint on composition board. (Photograph from Australian National Gallery.)

individual curators, anthropologists, and critics were promoting the importance of Aboriginal culture in any public overview of the visual arts — notably Tony Tuckson at the Art Gallery of New South Wales, himself an artist (Tuckson 1964) — it is only comparatively recently that contemporary ethnographic fine arts have been generally recognized as fulfilling any role other than that either of cash crops[1] or, in an age of cultural pluralism, as extensions of the investment potential of the capitalist art market. Unlike those well-established modes of entry for minorities to international recognition, sports and entertainment, the arts of the Fourth World are only beginning to confer prestige and status on their producers. Like sport and entertainment, success in the arts offers no obvious threat to the political and economic power of the dominant cultures. Equally it is the artistic hierarchy of the latter which has emerged as being the arbiter of taste in ethnographic arts as well as in its own. Several years ago, in a review of art museums in the United States, Joshua C. Taylor succinctly pointed out the interesting transition from cultural artifact to art object, which resulted in the 1950s and 1960s from increasing interest by art galleries in what had been previously considered almost exclusively the territory of the ethnographic museum (Taylor 1975:56ff).

In North America, the government-sponsored Indian arts and crafts projects of the 1930s were guided largely by white policies which saw the need not only for "cash crop art" but also for a kind of ethnographic cultural salvage archaeology, a reaffirmation of Indian communal cultural indentity in a world ecnomic crisis which seemed to demonstrate the weaknesses of individualistic capitalism. This was not really the fostering of Fine Arts, in capital letters. Up to a point, this is also the case even with the most successful contemporary descendents of such projects as the K'san community development in British Columbia.

In Australia, a multicultural nation where the indigenous population numbers 1.4 percent of the total and represents in every sense an insignificant minority, the tyranny of distance and continuing provincialism has always led to cultural time lags in the acceptance of new trends and attitudes. Nowhere is this more clearly seen than in the changing attitudes of those concerned with establishing the acquisition policies of the developed world's newest national repository for the fine arts, the Australian National Gallery. Thanks largely to the expert advice of Douglas Newton, from the outset the traditional ethnographic arts of Africa and the Pacific region have had a significant if minority role in achieving what James Mollison, the foundation director of the gallery, sees as its main role: "To chart from antiquity through to the present the cultural development of pretty much the whole of mankind."[2] This, however, enunciates a policy which initially at least did not give any priority to certain examples of what were not considered to be part of the mainstream of tribal Australian Aboriginal art, notably what is now arguably the most internationally regarded contemporary manifestation of Aboriginal art, the acrylic paintings of the Western Desert. As was observed at the time, no work of this category "was selected for hanging for the Gallery's opening celebrations" (Burn 1983:41). One example of a so-called "Papunya painting" (fig. 20.1) was purchased in 1980 (Mollison and Murray 1982:192). More recently, following the first extensive purchases in this area, Mollison has stated that "it is apparent the achievements of Aboriginal artists are possibly the finest art achievements to date in Australia."[3] A cautious statement, but one which certainly suggests growing acceptance of such works.

The obvious question to ask is what has brought about this change? Various conflicting and at times cynical reasons have been advanced by those in authority for advocating — usually too little and too late — that some recognition is necessary for the political, economic, and social claims of indigenous communities within their control. In comparison with the United States, the link between art and politics in Australia has perhaps seemed easier to ignore in so-called ethnographic contexts, particularly when, as one reviewer has commented, "there appears to be an all-too-ready tendency to equate the Aboriginal contemporary fine art tradition simply with that art being made in the tradition-oriented communities" (Hill 1983).

This current denial of artistic status to even firmly established fine arts such as the Hermannsburg 'school' watercolors of the Centre of Australia (fig. 20.8) is not shared by all non-Aborigines. Again there is probably a familiar ring in the pronouncements of the current director of the Aboriginal Arts Board of the Australia Council —

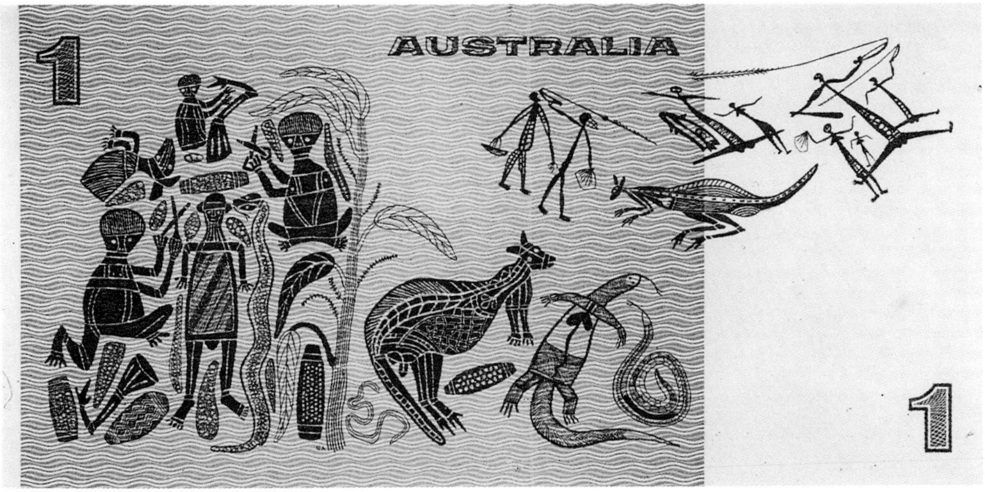

FIGURE 20.2. Australian one dollar note, reverse. Photograph courtesy of Commonwealth Reserve Bank.

the federal body responsible for funding all aspects of the arts. Gary Foley, first Aboriginal director to be appointed to the all-Aboriginal Board, participated in an open forum entitled "Aboriginal Art: the Politics of Consumption and Display" held as part of the 1984 Adelaide Festival of Arts. There he stated: "Aboriginal art today is a whole range of different life experiences, and each of those different life experiences . . . is part of the continuing political struggle" (quoted by Hoffberg 1984).

What is not so generally realized amongst the current turmoil of land rights claims and sometimes conflicting Aboriginal views as to the propriety — or perhaps economic usefulness — of mineral exploration and exploitation, is that many forms of both "traditional" and "transitional" Aboriginal art contain what in reviewing a recent exhibition of Western Desert acrylics Barry Craig has referred to as a non-violent but "significant event in the recent history of assertion of Aboriginal culture and land rights" (Craig 1984).

Since in many (non-Aboriginal) people's eyes it is the bark painting of Arnhem Land which epitomizes "traditional" ethnographic fine arts in Australia (although bark paintings are as much a product of art in transition as their earliest obviously European influenced forms), I may take Craig's point a step further by citing an until-very-recently literally ubiquitous example of artistic appropriation of Aboriginal art by the dominant white culture for financial purposes. On the reverse side of the one dollar note, withdrawn from circulation in 1984, is a pastiche of Aboriginal motifs from various parts of Arnhem Land (fig. 20.2). Included as its left-hand element is an adaptation of a bark painting by David Malangi, a member of the Urgiganjdjar clan now living in a small community near Ramingining in eastern Arnhem Land. Although the bark painting was first exhibited in Paris in 1963, its source and ownership was not officially recognized until 1967. This was despite frequent copying by its "onlie true begetter" which led to his subsequently being nicknamed "Dollar George" (Bennett 1980). The scene depicted refers to the mourning rites which commemorate the killing of the ancestral hero Gurrumiringu. Such rites are followed to this day on the death of any member of Malangi's clan. In the painting, a version of which was painted by Malangi for Flinders University on the occasion of his visit to Adelaide during National Aborigines Week in 1982 (figs. 20.3 and 20.4), the two flanking trees represent the artist's Dreaming sites on the two sides of the Glyde River as it flows out into the Arafura Sea. The rectangular area of fine cross-hatching at the base of the painting — notably absent from the design on the dollar bill — again represents Malangi's ancestral land (and it may be added that it was not until 1983 that his clan was granted title to this land).

The inextricable link between the land and all contemporary living things with those of the Dreamtime lies at the root of Aboriginal claims to that land — one other point of contact with native Americans. This has led the craft-adviser at Ramingining, John Mundine, an Aboriginal

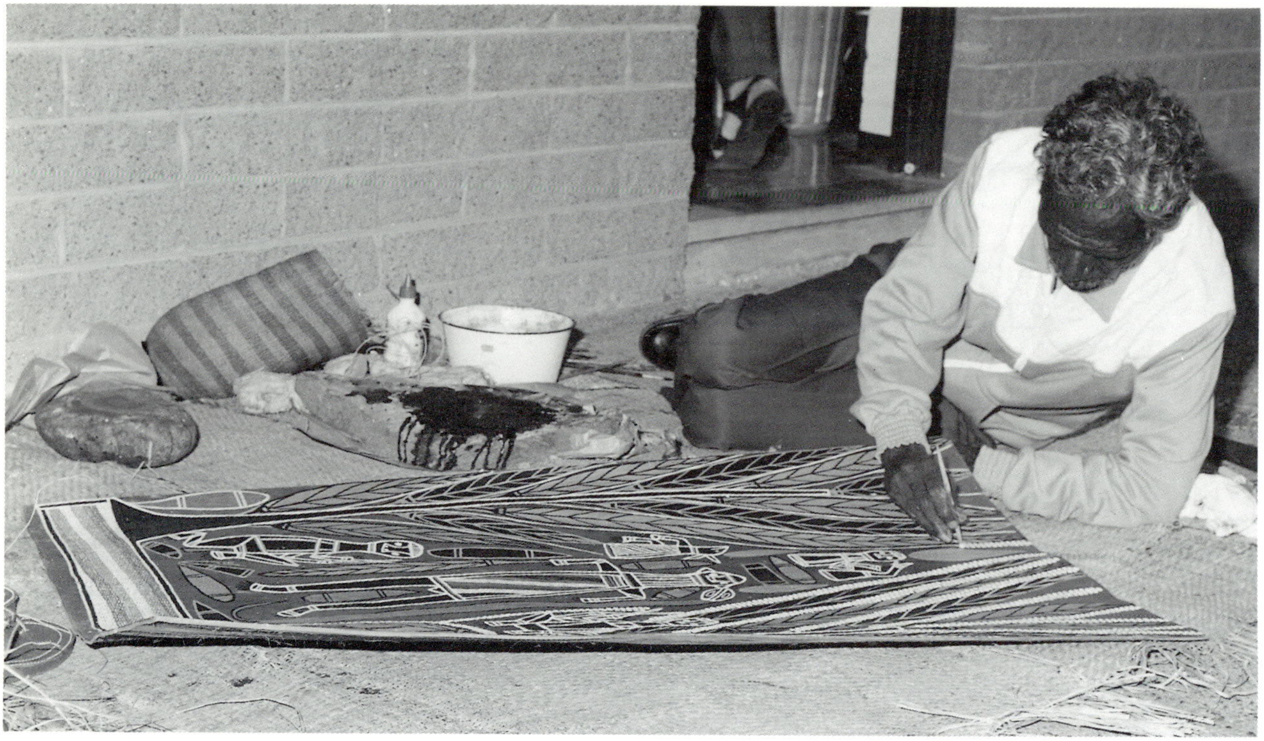

FIGURE 20.3. David Malangi (Urgiganjdjar clan). Artist painting the death of Gurrumiringu, 1982. Ochres on eucalyptus bark. Photograph from Photographic Service, Flinders University of South Australia.

from New South Wales, to claim (*in litt.*) such works as the Malangi bark as the equivalent of land title documents. Other bark paintings, such as that now in the collection of the Faculty of Arts at the Australian National University by Banapana Maymuru of the Manggalili clan at Yirrkala in northeast Arnhem Land (fig. 20.5), translate the forms of ground sculptures into two dimensions. Such highly complex compositions again codify the stories behind the necessary rituals and also mark the claims of individuals and their clans to certain geographical features which today mark the spots where sacred beings have left their imprints on the landscape; thus "clans, countries, song series, dances and sand sculpture designs are related" (Keen 1977:179). It is interesting, indeed, to see how the laudable efforts of the Reverend Wilbur Chaseling, the Methodist missionary at Yirrkala in the 1930s, to promote the production of bark paintings as a method of bringing much needed capital into the Aboriginal communities of Arnhem Land should have progressed from "cash cropping" to an integral part of contemporary "traditional" Aboriginal society (Williams 1976; Morphy 1977).

Images such as the land rights poster designed by a non-Aboriginal but produced by Mimi Arts, the cooperative serving the Katherine region, could be regarded, then, as no more than translations into European iconographic terms of much more specific statements whose true meaning only ignorance fails accurately to read (fig. 20.6). It is true that to my mind such European-inspired images of Aboriginal identity teeter perilously close to the edge of Aboriginal kitsch (see Pearson 1984), but here is dangerous ground indeed.[4]

I have referred above to "Papunya painting," as the acrylics of the Western Desert continue somewhat over-restrictively to be termed. These were initially inspired and encouraged by Geoff Bardon, then art teacher at the government settlement school at Papunya, 250 kilometers. due west of Alice Springs (Bardon 1979). The movement has only comparatively recently won institutional

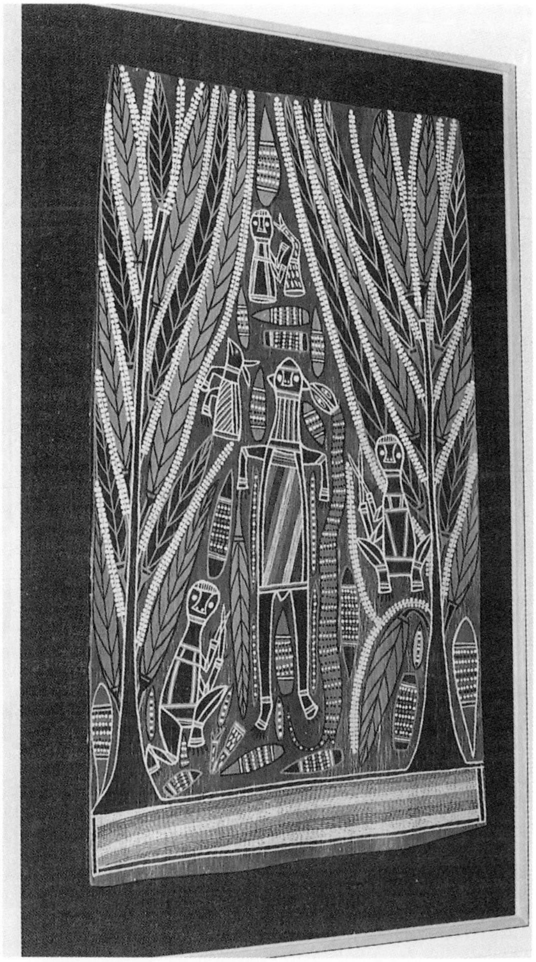

FIGURE 20.4. The finished bark painting depicted in figure 20.3. Photograph from Photographic Service, Flinders University of South Australia.

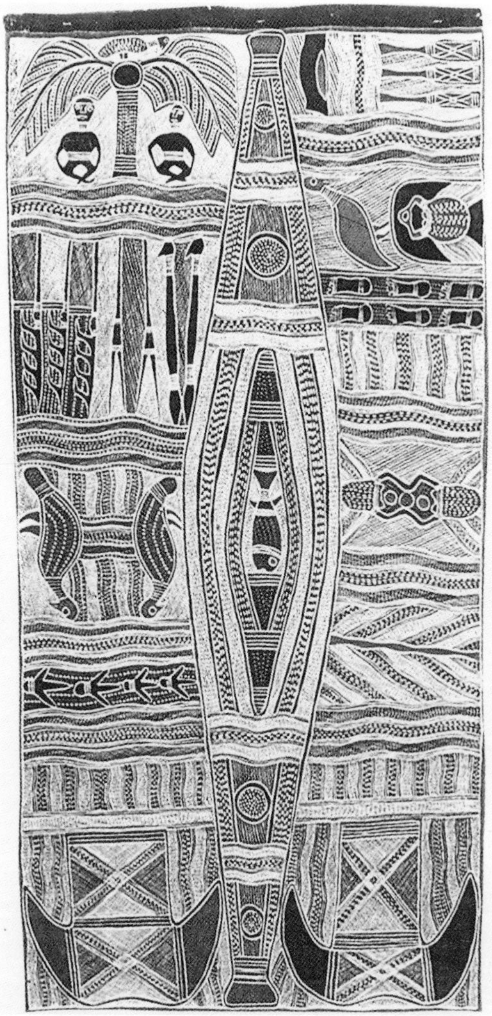

FIGURE 20.5. Banapana Maymuru (Mangalili clan). Yingapungapu ground sculpture, 1976. Ochres on eucalyptus bark. Photograph courtesy of Faculty of Arts, Australian National University.)

recognition. Only with this recognition, together with purchases by wealthy private collectors both in Australia and elsewhere, has Papunya art gained anything approaching a firm financial footing — in other words, begun to reap the real benefits of cash crop art. The art is more closely related to body painting than to traditional ground designs, although there are often visual references to both. It does not necessarily present "cognitive maps" of readily identifiable localities, as I among others have sometimes claimed. However, nothing has advanced so far so quickly in recent years in critical acclaim as the acrylics (Megaw 1982, 1984a; Maughan 1986).

Much of this is due to factors which have a great deal more to do with contemporary European and white American aesthetics than with the significance of this art within the society that is producing it. Also it indicates not a little about official support for what is seen as politically "safe" art which happens conveniently also to be art produced by Aborigines (see Marrie 1985).

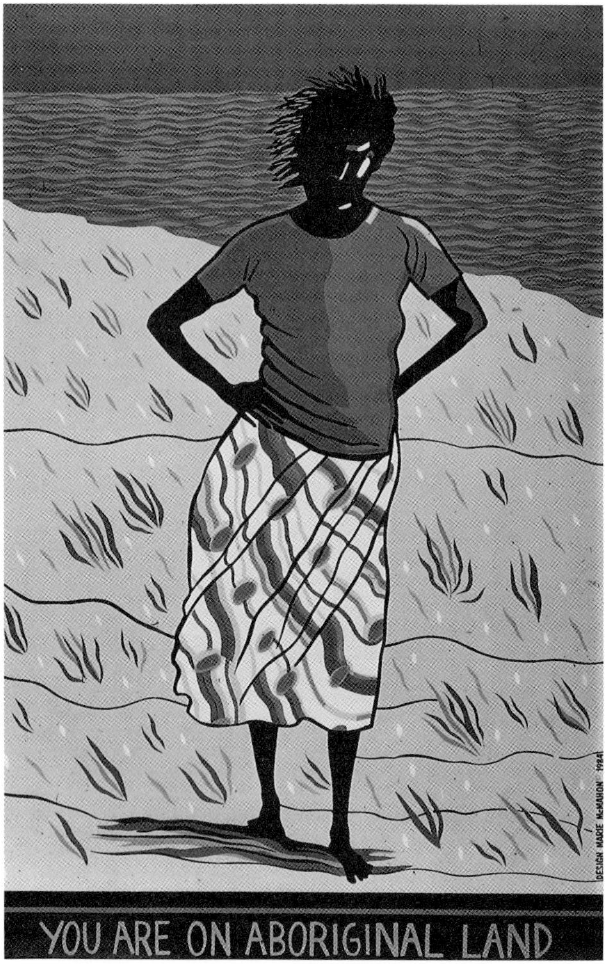

FIGURE 20.6. Marie McMahon. You are on Aboriginal Land, 1984. Land rights poster. Silk screen. Photograph courtesy of Mimi Aboriginal Arts and Crafts, Katherine, N.T.

Somewhat paradoxically, in view of current Aboriginal hostility toward any government agency, state or federal, the Federal Department of Aboriginal Affairs was the first to use an acrylic design to publicize the introduction of procedures for legitimizing land claims. The "stories" behind each painting — and even the most abstract-appearing of designs cloaks a particular Dreamtime event sometimes explicitly and generally revealed, sometimes so restricted to the ritually mature that only the briefest details of location and event can be recorded — may indeed be regarded as making explicit statements about land and people to those who can read them. In 1984 the National Aborigines' Day Observance Committee also used a Western Desert acrylic to make the same statement.

It is reasonable enough to question the role that such paintings are filling. To quote again from Craig (1984):

> Who . . . are the intended audience for these works? And since much of the symbolism is esoteric, why do these artists employ it if they intend their works for sale primarily to non-Aboriginals (which they clearly do)?

To these I may, following another reviewer (Kesteven 1983:198-99), add further questions:

> How do Aborigines view their art? . . . It is not sufficient to say that they are awarded status for being artists, because one then has to ask what validity that status has in Aboriginal contexts, and if the status comes from having money or recognition in non-Aboriginal eyes, why is that important?
>
> This reviewer continues:
>
> There [has been] no discussion as to whether Aborigines divide art into "fine" and "tourist" art. Or, if they do make distinctions about art, what types of distinctions do they make. If Aboriginal and non-Aboriginal classifications do not coincide, then what value is there in making distinctions of the "fine" and "tourist" variety? To increase the values of individuals' and museums' collections?

In a brief paper such as this all I can attempt to do is to suggest that one cannot adequately assess the arts of other peoples by the economic principles and aesthetics of our own society. Mead, in his Dunedin paper cited near the beginning of this chapter, recounts the surprised reactions of a German visitor to the manner in which Pakeha New Zealanders seem to have control over all aspects of Maori culture. Mead notes, correctly, that as in New Zealand, Australian Aborigines also exercise little or no control over the sources of power — tourism and government (Mead 1984:7ff). To this one must add the sale of art works. A recent report commissioned by the Commonwealth government to look into the whole question of marketing Aboriginal arts and crafts has pointed up the way in which current pricing policies from original payment to the artist to final sale widely fluctuate. Such factors as the initial subjective assessment of quality by Europeans and differing attitudes to "fine" as opposed to "tourist" arts inevitably lead the artists themselves to observe wide discrepancies between the price they receive

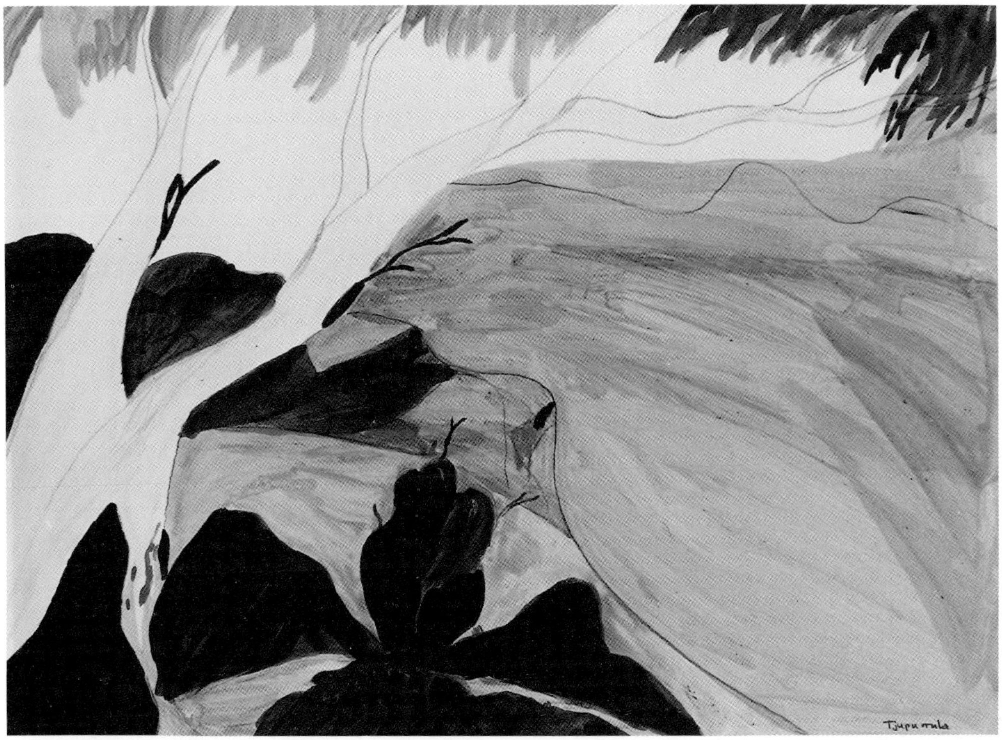

FIGURE 20.7. Turkey Tolsen Tjupurrula (Pintupi tribe). Untitled, 1980. Photograph from Photographic Service, Flinders University of South Australia.

and that achieved in the sale room or art gallery.[5] What the report does not indicate is that current discontent amongst, for example, Western Desert artists is centered on what is regarded as the insufficient value which is placed on the stories contained in their paintings, that it is the medium rather than the message which is employed as the monetary yardstick.

When I first went to Australia some twenty years ago, amongst contemporary artists one Aboriginal name was as well known internationally as nationally — Albert Namatjira, Aranda painter who learned much of his watercolor technique and style in the 1930s at the Lutheran mission of Hermannsburg from the Sydney "bush painter" Rex Battarbee. Namatjira, who frequently visited Papunya and painted there the desert landscape now altered only superficially by the "improvements" of the 1970s and 1980s, once said, in response to the question as to why he painted, that he wanted to paint like a white man. But he did *not* say that he wished to *be* like a white man. An ironical comment from a black eventually killed by whitefella's alcohol. While original Namatjiras still hold their value, by and large the school has suffered from what many critics perceive as its Europeanized non-Aboriginality as well as the perhaps inevitable decline in quality which has followed quantity. Today, however, it is the standard iconography of the Namatjira landscape — gum tree to the left, red-blue hills in the distance — which has become a kind of Aboriginal visual *lingua franca* throughout Central Australia (fig. 20.7). One should also observe that the concern to depict and integrate images of the land — tribal land — is at one with all other visual expressions of Aboriginal culture and beliefs.[6]

Every art form comprises elements of technique, style, and content. To my mind, for those who would be concerned with analyzing contemporary aspects of art as identity amongst communities of the Third and Fourth Worlds it is the last of these three categories, content, which is the most significant. While much of the contemporary output of the Hermannsburg School has undoubtedly degenerated in quality to the lowest level of tourist art, the earliest works of Namatjira and those of his immediate family as well as his most recent followers

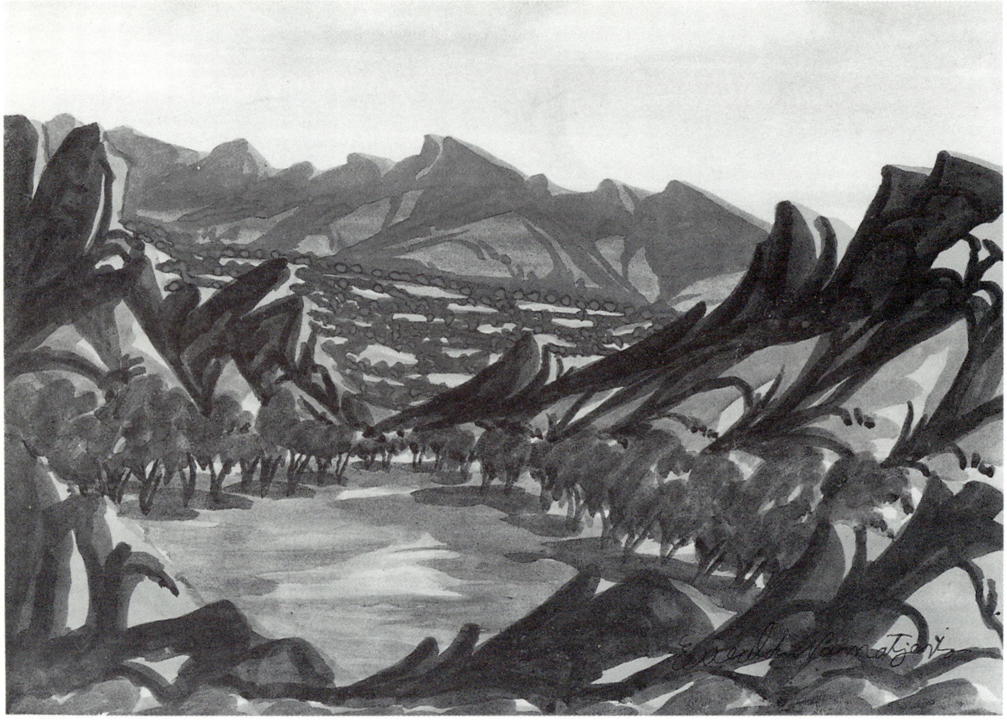

FIGURE 20.8. Ewalt Namatjira (Aranda tribe). Untitled, ca. 1970. Watercolor on paper. Photograph from Photographic Service, Flinders University of South Australia.

show a distinctive stylistic abstraction of forms and colors which I believe merits recognition as a unique and important example of "transitional" art and does not deserve critical dismissal as second-rate European-influenced rubbish (fig. 20.8). That they remain, quality apart, a regular selling line throughout the tourist shops of Australia opens other areas which I must leave for another time and another place.

In Paris, during the winter of 1983, the Musée d'Art Moderne mounted a survey of contemporary Australian art subtitled "L'Australie; le rêve et le réel. As part of this exhibition, which one critic dubbed "Australia — the French discovery of 1983," a group of Warlpri tribesmen from the Centre of Australia executed a ground design and choreographed for their European audience a series of dances and songs based on traditional forms (Montgomery 1984). Another reviewer noted with approval, as applicable to Aboriginal and non-Aboriginal art alike, a contributing white Australian artist's quotation of a statement from Alain Robbe-Grillet's *A futur*:

> Let it be first of all by their presence that objects and gestures establish themselves and let their presence continue to prevail over whatever explanatory theory that may try to enclose them in a system of references, whether emotional, sociological, Freudian, or metaphysical. (Spens 1983)

But this smacks more of dream than reality and certainly will help few who wish to regard art — any art — as an expression of identity.

One Western Desert artist, who died tragically as do so many of his people, once said to me in answer to the question as to why he continued to paint: "I learnt these drawings, these stories from my father; he has passed away. I teach my stories, my pictures to my son so, when I pass away he too can paint them for his children" (quoted in Megaw 1982:211).

Just how universal a response this may be to the previously posed questions as to how Aborigines view their art is arguable.[7] But it is clear that for Aboriginals, who claim an affinity with the harsh land of Australia and its living creatures, many of the images they create reflect their sense of a separate identity. It is totally indefensible to

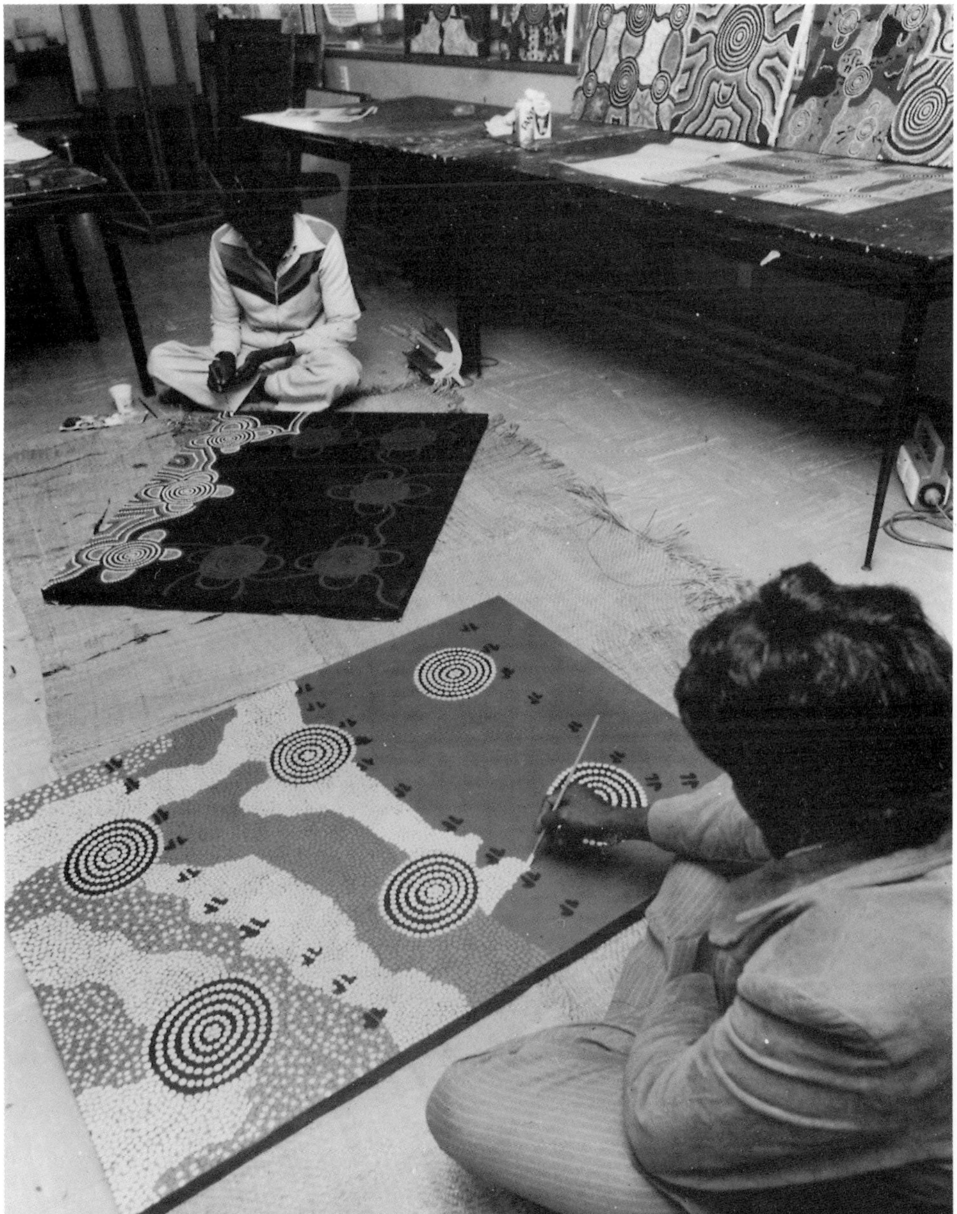

FIGURE 20.9. Turkey Tolsen Tjupurrula (rear) and the late David Corby Tjapaltjarri (foreground). Aboriginal artists-in-residence working in the Visual Arts Studio of Flinders University, South Australia, 1979.

deny that this is true even of urban Aboriginals. The art also reflects the search for sources of livelihood in a land whose economy has been irretrievably transformed by the coming of the white man, where art has a market as well as a spiritual value. It may also indicate a desire for recognition and status, since "fine" art carries status in white-fella's culture; in traditional Aboriginal society painting is also a recognition of status, being generally confined to the older, initiated men. So far as form and technique are concerned, Aborigines are both willing and able to adapt and adopt from the white man's traditions as well as from their own to create something which expresses their roots, their social, economic and political present, and their hopes for the future.

Notes

I am indebted to Dr. M. Ruth Megaw for her critical reading of the text of this paper, which has gained over its spoken New York version from the knowledge of an American cultural historian.

1. The phrase is borrowed from William Feaver, the art critic writing of the exhibition "Art from Africa" in *The Observer* (London), January 23, 1981.

2. Quoted in *The National Times Celebrates the Opening of the Australian National Gallery*, color supplement to *The National Times* (Sydney), October 1, 1982, p. 30.

3. Quoted in *The Sydney Morning Herald*, January 26, 1984.

4. During the New York Symposium, Katerina Mataira made the valid point not infrequently heard from Third or Fourth World artists in an urban context, that if such artists wished to innovate or borrow from other styles then they should do just that.

5. Logistics International, *Aboriginal Arts and Crafts: Supply, Distribution and Marketing*, 1983, Chatswood, New South Wales.

6. I am indebted for much illuminating discussion to Mrs. Helen Burns, daughter of Pastor F. W. Albrecht, superintendent of the Finke River Mission and champion of Namatjira and his family. There still is no thorough analysis or survey of the *oeuvre* of the Hermannsburg school, but see Amadio (1986) and, for the genesis, Mountford (1949), Strehlow (1956), and Batty (1963).

7. This strikes me as the kind of problem missing from the fascinating — one cannot state "definitive" — 1984 exhibition of *"Primitivism" in Twentieth Century Art* at the New York Museum of Modern Art and its companion publication (Rubin 1984).

8. The position of women as artists is only now beginning to receive due recognition and study.

Contributors

George A. Corbin is Associate Professor of Art and Chairman, Department of Art, Lehman College (CUNY). He received a B.A. from Oakland University, an M.A. from Bucknell University, and an M.A. and Ph.D. (1976) from Columbia University. He has done fieldwork in Papua New Guinea among the Baining, Tolai, and Sulka peoples of East New Britain. His publications include "The Art of the Baining: New Britain" (1979), and "A Brief Note on a Tolai Mask Called Alor" (1977). Currently, Corbin is writing a textbook on the art of Africa, North America, and the South Pacific.

Barry Craig is a Ph.D. candidate at Flinders University in South Australia. He has an M.A. in anthropology from the University of Sydney, and has carried out several ethnographic research and collecting expeditions in the Mountain-Ok and Sepik areas of Papua New Guinea as well as New Britain and New Ireland. He has held the position of Curator of Anthropology at the Papua New Guinea national museum. Among his publications are "The Houseboards of the Telefomin Sub-district of New Guinea" (1967), "The Keram Style in the Abau Area of the Upper Sepik, New Guinea" (1976), and *The Telefolmin: People of Papua New Guinea* (1975).

Philip J. C. Dark is Emeritus Professor of Anthropology, Southern Illinois University at Carbondale. He holds a diploma. in fine art from the University of London and an M.A. and Ph.D. from Yale. His field research was conducted in West Africa, Irian Jaya, Papua New Guinea, and the Central Pacific. Among his publications on Oceanic art are "Among the Kilenge 'Art is Something Which is Well Done'" (1983), "The Art of the Peoples of Western New Britain and their Neighbors" (1979), and "What is Art for Anthropologists?" (1978). Since 1975, Professor Dark has been Editor of the *Pacific Arts Newsletter*. He was awarded the Manu Daula Frigate Bird Award by the Pacific Art's Association in 1984.

William H. Davenport is Professor of Anthropology in the Department of Anthropology and Curator, Oceanian Section, at the University Museum of the University of Pennsylvania. His Ph.D. is from Yale University (1956). Davenport has conducted extensive field research in several areas of the Solomon Islands. His publications include *Hawaiian Sculpture* (with J. Halley Cox, 1974), *Hawaiian*

Petroglyphs (with Edward Stasack, 1970), the exhibition catalog *Melanesian Art* (1967), and "Sculpture of the Eastern Solomons" (1968).

Lawrence Foanaota is Director of the National Museum, Honiara, Solomon Islands. He holds a B.A. in anthropology/archaeology from the University of Auckland, completed the UNESCO Fellowship Course in Resource Management and Protection at Auckland in 1976, and holds a Museum Management Certificate from the East-West culture Learning Institute, Honolulu, Hawaii. He has written "Burial Sites on Vella Lavella Island" (1974) and "Solomon Islands Museum, 1971-1973" (1974). Foanaota serves on the South Pacific Art Council.

Allan Hanson, Professor of Anthropology at the University of Kansas, was educated at Princeton and the University of Chicago. Among his publications are *Rapan Lifeways: Society and History on a Polynesian Island* (1970), *Meaning in Culture* (1975), "Art and the Maori Construction of Reality" (1983) and "When the Map is the Territory: Art in Maori Culture" (1983).

Louise Hanson is Executive Director of the Association of Kansas Theatre and has held positions as Research Associate in the Museum of Anthropology, University of Kansas and Assistant Director of Libraries and Reference Librarian, Baker University. She holds a B.A. from Douglass College of Rutgers University and M.L.S. from the University of Pittsburgh. She has published a bibliography of the work of the American author James Norman Hall.

The Hansons have carried out research in French Polynesia and New Zealand. Jointly they have published "The Cybernetics of Cultural Communication" (1981), *Counterpoint in Maori Culture* (1983), and *The Art of Oceania: A Bibliography* (1984).

Phillip H. Lewis is Curator of Primitive Art and Melanesian Ethnology at the Field Museum of Natural History in Chicago. He earned a B.F.A. from the Art Institute of Chicago and an M.A. and Ph.D. from the University of Chicago. His initial fieldwork in New Ireland was undertaken in 1953 and he has returned to that area in 1970 and 1981 to continue his longitudinal study of the social context of art. His publications on New Ireland art include "Art in Changing New Ireland" (1979), "The Artist in New Ireland Society" (1961), and "Changing Memorial Ceremonial in Northern New Ireland" (1973).

John A. McKesson is Professor of International Relations at the Institute of French Studies at New York University. He holds a B.A. and M.A. in Political Science and Art History respectively from Columbia University and an honorary LL.D. degree from Eastern Michigan University. McKesson has served as American ambassador to Gabon and has held a number of posts abroad and in Washington, D.C. with the U.S. Foreign Service and the State Department. His publications have appeared in *Political Science Quarterly, UN Plaza Magazine*, and in *Arts d'Afrique Noire*, of which he is currently the associate editor.

Hirini (Sidney) Moko Mead is Professor of Maori at Victoria University, Wellington, New Zealand, and President of the Pacific Arts Association. He received a B.A. and M.A. from the University of Auckland and a Ph.D. in anthropology from Southern Illinois University (1968). His research has included the Star Harbor region of the Eastern Solomon Islands and Fiji in Melanesia as well as the New Zealand Maori. He edited the proceedings of the first two international symposia on the arts of Oceania: *Exploring the Visual Art of Oceania* (1979) and, with Bernie Kernot, *Art and Artists of Oceania* (1983). He produced the catalog for *Te Maori*, the exhibition of Maori art that recently toured American cities, and another book about the exhibition, *Magnificent Te Maori* (1986).

J. V. S. Megaw is Head of the Discipline of Visual Arts at the Flinders University of South Australia. He received his professional training at Edinburgh University in prehistoric archaeology and prehistory of art. His interests include Celtic art and archaeology and contemporary developments in the art of the Third and Fourth Worlds as well as Oceanic art. Among his publications are *Art in Society: Studies in Style, Culture and Aesthetics* (edited with Michael Greenhalgh, 1978), "Art Styles and Analysis" (1967), and "Western Desert Acrylic Painting — Artefact or Art?" (1982).

Roger Neich was the Ethnologist at the National Museum of New Zealand for several years and is now the Curator of Ethnology at the Auckland Institute and Museum. He holds an M.A. in anthropology from Victoria University, Wellington, and has recently completed his Ph.D. dissertation for the University of California at Berkeley. He has carried out fieldwork in Western Samoa, Papua New Guinea, and New Zealand. His publications include "A Semiological Analysis of Self-Decoration in Mount Hagen, New Guinea" (1982) and "The Veil of Orthodoxy: Rotorua Ngati Tarawhai Carving in a Changing Context" (1983). He was International Executive Secretary of the Pacific Arts Association from 1978 to 1984.

Stephanie Reynolds is a Ph.D. candidate in the Program in Comparative Culture, School of Social Sciences, University of California, Irvine. She has been a professional dance artist and teacher. Her research interests focus on comparative worldview and dance as well as other art forms. She has carried out fieldwork in Polynesia, Mexico, and on American Indian reservations. Among her publications is "Concepts of Nature and Power: Environmental Ethics of the Northern Ute" (1985).

Roger G. Rose is Anthropologist and Curator of Ethnology and Hawaiian Historical Collections at the Bernice P. Bishop Museum, Honolulu. He holds a B.A. degree from the University of Kansas and an M.A. and Ph.D. degrees from Harvard University. His archaeological field experience includes expeditions to the Marquesas, Tuamotu, and Society islands, and France and Afghanistan. Among his publications in Oceanic art are "The Cave of Images: New 'Discoveries' in Hawaiian Art" (1983), "On the Origin and Diversity of 'Tahitian' Janiform Fly Whisks" (1979), *Symbols of Sovereignty: Feather Girdles of Tahiti and Hawaii* (1978), and *Hawaii: The Royal Isles* (1980).

Edward L. Ruhe was Professor of English at the University of Kansas, specializing in English literature, in particular Johnsonian studies, the eighteenth century Milton tradition, and the career of Edmund Curll, bookseller. He holds a B.A. from Swarthmore College and an M.A. and Ph.D. from Columbia University. Professor Ruhe became interested in Australian Aboriginal art while holding a Fulbright Lectureship at the University of Adelaide in 1965. Since that time, he has been an avid student and collector of Aboriginal art and has exhibited his collection in twenty shows. He served from 1972-81 as Editor of the University of Kansas Humanistic Studies series and, in addition to his numerous publications in English literature, has compiled a number of catalogs on Aboriginal bark art. Professor Ruhe died in June, 1989.

Tobias Schneebaum made his first visit to the Asmat of Irian Jaya in 1973. He was Assistant to the Curator of the Asmat Museum of Culture and Progress, in Agats, Irian Jaya, for ten years and during that time traveled extensively in the Asmat region on research and collecting expeditions. He has published two catalogs on Asmat art collections, one featuring the collection in the Asmat museum and the other describing the holdings of Ursula and Gunther Konrad now at the University of Heidelberg. He is author of the autobiographical triology *Keep the River on Your Right, Wild Man*, and *Where the Spirits Dwell.*

Eric G. Schwimmer is Professor of Anthropology at Université Laval, Quebec. He holds a Ph.D. from the University of British Columbia. He resided in New Zealand for many years where he was editor of *Te Ao Hou.* During that period, he wrote two books and numerous articles on the New Zealand Maori. His recent publications focus on the ethnography of the Orokaiva, Papua New Guinea and on cultural semiotics. In progress are works on spirit impersonation and on folk festivals.

Dirk Smidt is Curator of the Department of Oceania at the Rijksmuseum voor Volkenkunde in Leiden, The Netherlands. He received his doctorate from the University of Leiden where he specialized in the art of New Guinea. From 1970 to 1980 he held several positions at the National Museum and Art Gallery in Papua New Guinea. He has undertaken fieldwork in several areas of Papua New Guinea, especially among the Kominimung and neighboring peoples in the Middle Ramu River region of the Madang Province. His publications include *The Seized Collection of the Papua New Guinea Museum* (1975), "Establishing Museums in Developing Countries: The Case of Papua New Guinea" (1979), and "Kominimung Shields" (1983).

Jehanne Teilhet-Fisk is Associate Professor of Art History at the University of California, San Diego. Her initial foray into Polynesian art was in 1973, when she guided her undergraduate students in mounting an exhibition — and edited the resulting book, *Dimensions of Polynesia.* A series of publications followed: "The Equivocal Nature of a Masking Tradition in Polynesia," "The Role of Women Artists in Polynesia and Melanesia," and *Paradise Reviewed: An Interpretation of Gauguin's Polynesian Symbolism.* She has also worked in Nigerial, Nepal and Suriname on gender considerations in the creation and reception of works of art.

Deborah B. Waite is Professor of Art History in the Department of Art at the University of Hawaii. She received a Ph.D. in art history from Columbia University where she specialized in Melanesian art and, in particular, the art of the Solomon Islands. She has published many articles and two books on art from the Solomons: *Art of the Solomon Islands: Barbier-Müller Collection, Geneva* 1983) and *Artifacts from the Solomon Islands in the Julius L. Benchley Collection* (forthcoming).

References

Chapter 1

Holmes, Lowell D. 1987. *Quest for the Real Samoa: The Mead/Freeman Controversy & Beyond*. South Hadley, Massachusetts: Bergin & Garvey.

Chapter 2

Arnheim, Rudolf. 1954. *Art and Visual Perception*. Berkeley: University of California Press.

———. 1966. *Toward a Psychology of Art*. Berkeley: University of California Press.

Artaud, Antonin. 1964. *Le théâtre et son double*. Paris: Gallimard.

Auge, Marc. 1982. *Génie du paganisme*. Paris: Gallimard.

Barthes, Roland. 1970. *S/Z*. Paris: Seuil.

Bateson, Gregory. 1973. Style, Grace and Information in Primitive Art. In *Primitive Art and Society*, ed. Anthony Forge, 235-55. London: Oxford University Press for the Wenner-Gren Foundation for Anthropological Research.

Chabert, Pierre. 1976. Le corps comme matériau de la représentation théâtrale. *Recherches Poiétiques* 2:298-325.

Duvignaud, Jean. 1972. *Sociologie de l'art*. Paris: Presses Universitaires de France.

Eco, Umberto. 1962. *Opera aperta — Forma e indeterminazione nelle poetichi contemporanee*. Milan: Bompiani.

———. 1978. Le concept de signe iconique. *Communications* 29:141-91.

———. 1979. *The Role of the Reader*. Bloomington: Indiana University Press.

Forge, Anthony. 1966. Art and Environment in the Sepik. *Proceedings of the Royal Anthropological Institute for 1965*, pp. 23-31. London: Royal Anthropological Institute.

———. 1973a. Introduction. In *Primitive Art and Society*, ed. Anthony Forge, xiii-xxii. London: Oxford University Press for the Wenner-Gren Foundation for Anthropological Research.

———. 1973b. Style and Meaning in Sepik Art. In *Primitive Art and Society*, ed. Anthony Forge, 169-92. London: Oxford University Press for the Wenner-Gren Foundation for Anthropological Research.

———. 1979. The Problem of Meaning in Art. In *Exploring the Visual Art of Oceania*, ed. Sidney M. Mead, 278-86. Honolulu: University Press of Hawaii.

Fortune, R. F. 1935. *Manus Religion*. Philadelphia: American Philosophical Society.

Francastel, Pierre. 1965. *La réalité figurative*. Paris: Gonthier.

Geblesco, Nicole. 1976. Poiétique et masques. *Recherches Poiétiques* 2:273-91.

Geertz, Clifford. 1983. *Local Knowledge*. New York: Basic Books.

Gell, Alfred. 1975. *Metamorphosis of the Cassowaries: Umeda Society, Language and Ritual*. London: Athlone.

Gombrich, E. H. 1960. *Art and Illusion*. Oxford: Phaidon.

———. 1972. *Symbolic Images*. Oxford: Phaidon.

Herdt, Gilbert H. 1981. *Guardians of the Flutes*. New York: McGraw Hill.

Iteanu, André. 1983. *La ronde des échanges*. Cambridge: Cambridge University Press.

Joseph, Isaac. 1984. Gabriel Tarde. Le monde comme féerie. *Critique* 40 (445-46):548-65.

Leach, Edmund. 1954a. Aesthetics. In *The Institutions of Primitive Socity*, ed. E. E. Evans-Pritchard, et al., 25-38. Oxford: Blackwell.

———. 1954b. A Trobriand Medusa. *Man* 54:103-5.

———. 1973. Levels of Communication and Problems of Taboo in the Appreciation of Primitive Art. In *Primitive Art and Society*, ed. Anthony Forge, 221-34. London: Oxford University Press for the Wenner-Gren Foundation for Anthropological Research.

le Marinel, Jacques. 1981. *La mise en question du langage dans le "nouveau théâtre."* Lille: Presses Universitaires de Lille.

Lévi-Strauss, Claude. 1950. Introduction. In *Sociologie et anthropologie*, by Marcel Mauss, ix-lii. Paris: Presses Universitaires de France.

———. 1958. *Anthropologie structurale*. Paris: Plon.

———. 1962. *La pensée sauvage*. Paris: Plon.

———. 1975. *La voie des masques*. 2 vols. Genève: Éditions Albert Skira.

———. 1983. *Le regard éloigné*. Paris: Plon.

Mauss, Marcel. 1950. *Sociologie et anthropologie*. Paris: Presses Universitaires de France.

Mead, Sidney M., ed. 1979. *Exploring the Visual Art of Oceania*. Honolulu: University Press of Hawaii.

Merquior, José Guilhelme. 1977. *L'esthétique de Lévi-Strauss*. Paris: Presses Universitaires de France.

Moles, Abraham. 1972. *Théorie de l'information et perception esthétique*. Paris: Denoel/Gonthier.

Mukarovsky, Jan. 1977. *Structure, Sign and Function*. New Haven: Yale University Press.

Panofsky, Erwin. 1955. *Meaning in the Visual Arts*. New York: Doubleday.

Prudhomme, G. 1976. Le corps humain matériau du danseur. *Recherches Poiétiques* 2:293-97.

Read, K. E. 1965. *The High Valley*. London: Allen & Unwin.

Redfield, Robert. 1959. Art and Icon. In *Aspects of Primitive Art*, by Robert Redfield, Melville Herskovits, and Gordon F. Ekholm, 12-40. New York: The Museum of Primitive Art.

Schwimmer, Eric G. 1979. Aesthetics of the Aika. In *Exploring the Visual Art of Oceania*, ed. Sidney M. Mead, 287-92. Honolulu: University Press of Hawaii.

———. 1981a. Power and Secrecy: The Semiotic of Manipulation and Detection. *Semiotic Enquiry* 1:214-43.

———. 1981b. Presentation — La dérision des pouvoirs. *Anthropologie et Sociétés* 5(3):1-10.

Sieber, Roy. 1962. Masks as Agents of Social Control. *African Studies Bulletin* 5(11):8-13.

Smith, Marian W., ed. 1961. *The Artist in Tribal Society*.

London: Routledge & Kegan Paul.

Somare, Michael T. 1979a. Our Pride, Our Strength. In *Arts of the People*. Special Issue, *Papua New Guinea Post-Courier*, p. 2. September, 1979.

———. 1979b. Foreword. In *Exploring the Visual Art of Oceania*, ed. Sidney M. Mead, xiii-xv. Honolulu: University Press of Hawaii.

Strathern, Andrew. 1971. *The Rope of Moka*. Cambridge: Cambridge University Press.

——— and Marilyn Strathern. 1968. Marsupials and Magic. In *Dialectic in Practical Religion*, ed. E. R. Leach, 179-202. Cambridge: Cambridge University Press.

and Marilyn Strathern. 1971. *Self-Decoration in Mount Hagen*. London: Duckworth.

Tamba, Akira. 1976. Poiétique du No. *Recherches Poiétiques* 2:253-71. Tarde, Gabriel. 1890. *Les lois de l'imitation*. Genève: Slatkine.

Turner, Victor W. 1969. *The Ritual Process*. Aldine.

———. 1974. *Dramas, Fields and Metaphors*. Ithaca: Cornell University Press.

Villiers, Andre. 1976. Mise en scène et création. *Recherches poiétiques* 2:327-46.

Chapter 3

Bascom, William. 1969. Creativity and Style in African Art. In *Tradition and Creativity in Tribal Art*, ed. Daniel P. Biebuyck, 98-119. Berkeley: University of California Press.

Batkin, Jonathan. 1981. Introduction: The Art of New Guinea. In *Ritual, Power and Function: Oceanic Art of the Sepik River and Papuan Gulf*. Oklahoma City: Oklahoma Museum of Art.

Bruce, Les. 1984. *The Alamblak Language of Papua New Guinea (East Sepik)*. Pacific Linguistics Series C, No. 81. Canberra: Department of Linguistics, Research School of Pacific Studies, The Australian National University.

Cochrane, Renata. 1974. *Dangers of the Reef and Sea*. Milton, Queensland: The Jacaranda Press. (First published in 1968.)

Damm, Hans. 1962. Sacrale Statuen aus dem Gebiet der Arawe (Arue) in Süd-Neubritannien, Südsee. *Annals of the Naprstek Museum* 1:29-36.

Forge, Anthony. 1960. Three Kamanggabi Figures from the Arambak People of the Sepik District. In *Three Regions of Melanesian Art*, by Anthony Forge and Raymond Clausen, 6-11. New York: The Museum of Primitive Art.

Gerbrands, Adrian A. 1967. *Wow-Ipits*. The Hague: Mouton.

Gordon, R., K. Waiko, B. and W. Heaney. ca. 1982. Intensive Ethnographic and Sociological Studies. In *Papua New Guinea Atlas*, ed. David King and Stephen Ranck, 106-9. Waigani: The University of Papua New Guinea.

Haberland, Eike. 1964. Zum Problem der 'Hakenfiguren' der Südlichen Sepik-Region in Neuguinea. *Paideuma* 10:52-71.

———. 1968. *The Caves of Karawari*. New York: D'Arcy Galleries.

——— and Siegfried Seyfarth. 1974. *Die Yimar am Oberen Korowori*. Wiesbaden: Franz Steiner Verlag.

Kasprus, Aloys. 1973. *The Tribes of the Middle Ramu and the Upper Keram Rivers*. St. Augustin bei Bonn: Verlag des Anthropos-Instituts.

Kaufmann, Christian. 1974. Ethnographische Notizen zur Basler Korewori-sammlung. *Verhandlungen der Naturforschenden Gesellschaft in Basel* 84:711-25.

Laycock, D.C. 1973. *Sepik Languages — Checklist and Preliminary Classification*. Pacific Linguistics Series B, No. 25. Canberra: Department of Linguistics, Research School of Pacific Studies, The Australian National University.

Mangal, Pita, and Dirk Smidt. 1980. *The Kominimung*. Boroko: National Cultural Council in association with Robert Brown & Associates of Australia.

Mihalic, F. 1971. *The Jacaranda Dictionary and Grammar of Melanesian Pidgin.* Milton, Australia: The Jacaranda Press.

Moyne, Lord. 1936. *Walkabout.* London: William Heinemann.

Paijmans, K., ed. 1976. *New Guinea Vegetation.* Canberra: Commonwealth Scientific and Industrial Research Organization in association with The Australian National University Press.

Smidt, Dirk. 1975. *The Seized Collections of the Papua New Guinea Museum.* Port Moresby: Creative Arts Centre.

———. 1983. Kominimung Shields. In *Art and Artists of Oceania*, ed. Sidney M. Mead and Bernie Kernot, 137-61. Palmerston North, New Zealand: Dunmore Press.

———. forthcoming a. Kominimung Art and Artists. In *The Language of Things*, ed. Sandy Roels and Dirk Smidt. Leiden: Mededelingen van het Rijksmuseum voor Volkenkunde, No. 25.

———. forthcoming b. Symbolic Meaning in Kominimung Masks. In *Sepik Heritage: Tradition and Change in Papua New Guinea*, ed. Nancy Lutkehaus et al. Durham: Carolina Academic Press.

Wurm, Stephen A., and Shirô Hattori, eds. 1981. *Language Atlas of the Pacific Area.* Pacific Linguistics, Series C., No. 66, Canberra: The Australian Academy of the Humanities in collaboration with the Japan Academy.

Z'graggen, J. A. 1975. *The Languages of the Madang District, Papua New Guinea.* Pacific Linguistics, Series B, No. 41. Canberra: Department of Linguistics, Research School of Pacific Studies, The Australian National University.

Chapter 4

Konrad, Gunter, Walter Böhning, and Alphonse Sowada. 1975. On Two Shield Types of the Asmat Region. *Irian: Bulletin of Irian Jaya Development* 4(3):1-11.

Chapter 5

Amherst, Lord William, and Basil Thomson. 1901. *The Discovery of the Solomon Islands by Alvaro de Mendana in 1568.* Translated from the original by Amherst and Thomson. 2 vols. London: Hakluyt Society.

Barraud, C. 1972. De la chasse aux têtes à la pêche à la bonite. *L'Homme* 12:67-104.

Beti, G. O. 1977. Kesoko Pature. *The Journal of the Cultural Association of the Solomon Islands* 5:40-46.

Brown, G. 1908. *Autobiography of a Pioneer Missionary.* London: Hodder & Stoughton.

Codrington, R. 1891. *The Melanesians: Studies in their Anthropology and Folklore.* Oxford: The Clarendon Press.

Davenport, W. 1985. The Canoes of Santa Ana and Santa Catalina Islands, Eastern Solomon Islands. Paper presented at the Wright Symposium on Primitive and Pre-Columbian Art, the Israel Museum, Jerusalem, January, 1985.

Edge-Partington, J., and C. Heape. 1890. *An Album of the Weapons, Tools, Ornaments, Articles of Dress of the Natives of the Pacific Islands.* 3 vols. Manchester: J. C. Norburg.

Elkington, E. W. 1907. *Savage South Seas: Painted by N. H. Hardy.* London: Black.

Festetics de Tolna, R. Cte. 1903. *Chez les cannibales. Huit ans de croisière dans l'Océan Pacifique à bord du yacht 'Le Tolna'.* Paris: Librairie Plon.

Fleurieu, C. F. Claret de. 1791. *Discoveries of the French in 1768 and 1769 to the Southeast of New Guinea.* London: Printed for John Stockdale.

Gathercole, P., A. L. Kaeppler, and D. Newton. 1979. *The Art of the Pacific Islands.* Washington, D.C.: National Gallery of Art.

Haddon, A. C., and J. Hornell. 1937. *Canoes of Oceania. Vol. II: Melanesia, Queensland, and New Zealand.* Bishop Museum Special Publication No. 28. Honolulu: Bishop Museum.

Hocart, A. M. 1922. The Cult of the Dead in Eddystone of the Solomons. *Journal of the Royal Anthropological Institute* 52:71-112, 259-305.

———. 1931. Warfare in Eddystone of the Solomon Islands. *Journal of the Royal Anthropological Institute* 61:301-24.

———. 1935. The Canoe and the Bonito in Eddystone Island. *Journal of the Royal Anthropological Institute* 65:97-111.

———. *Unpublished Manuscript*. MS Papers 60. A. M. Hocart. The Alexander Turnbull Library, Wellington, New Zealand.

Lanyon-Orgill, P. A. 1969. *The Language of Eddystone Island*. Balmain, Stanley, Perthshire: The Crichton Press.

Log of H. M. S. "Rapid" Commanded by Cm. John Casement for the Period Commencing 17 of May 1890. 1897. Public Record Office ADM 53, 15272. London: Waterloo & Sons.

Miller, D. 1978. An Organizational Approach to Exchange Media: An Example from the Western Solomons. *Mankind* 11:288-95.

Penny, A. 1888. *Ten Years in Melanesia*. London: Wells, Gardner, Darton.

Ribbe, C. 1895. *Zwei Jahre unter den Kannibalen der Salomo-Inseln*. Dresden-Blasewicz: Beyer.

Salisbury, E. A. 1922. A Napoleon of the Solomons. *Asia. The American Magazine of the Orient* 22 (9):707-12.

Scheffler, H. W. 1962. Kindred and Kin Groups in Simbo Island Social Structure. *Ethnology* 1:135-57.

A Short Guide to the Material Culture of the Solomon Islands and the Collection in the National Museum. n.d. Honiara: Cultural Association of the Solomon Islands.

Somerville, B. A. 1897. Ethnographical Notes in New Georgia, Solomon Islands. *Journal of the Royal Anthropological Institute* 26:357-412.

Stöhr, W. 1972. *Schwarze Inseln der Südsee: Melanesien*. Cologne: Rautenstrauch-Joest Museum.

Tedder, M. M., with S. Barrus. 1976. Old Kusaghe. *The Journal of the Cultural Association of the Solomon Islands* 4:41-93.

Thorpe, W. W. 1923. A *Tomako* or Headhunter's Canoe from the Solomon Islands. *Australian Museum Magazine* 1:289-92.

Thurwald, R. 1910. Im Bismarckarchipel und auf den Salomoinseln, 1906-9. *Zeitschrift für Ethnologie* 17:98-147.

Turner, V. W. 1964. Betwixt and Between: The Liminal Period in *Rites de Passage*. In *Symposium on New Approaches to the Study of Religion*. Proceedings of the 1964 Annual Spring Meeting of the American Ethnological Society, 4-20. Seattle: University of Washington Press.

Waite, D. 1969. Solomon Islands Art. Ph.D. dissertation, Columbia University, New York.

———. 1979. Aspects of Style and Symbolism in the Art of the Solomon Islands. In *Exploring the Visual Art of Oceania*, ed. Sidney Mead, 238-64. Honolulu: The University Press of Hawaii.

———. 1983. Form and Function of Tridacna Shell Plaques from the Western Solomon Islands. *Empirical Studies of the Arts* 1(1):55-74.

War-Canoe (Toitoko) of Choiseul, Northern Solomons. n.d. Accession file information for canoe E.173.627, Canterbury Museum, Christchurch, New Zealand. 4 pp.

Waterhouse, J. H. L. 1928. *A Roviana and English Dictionary with English-Roviana Index and List of Natural History Objects*. Guadalcanal, Solomon Islands: Melanesian Mission Press.

White, G. 1983. War, Peace, and Piety in Santa Isabel, Solomon Islands. In *The Pacification of Melanesia*, ed. M. Rodman and M. Cooper, 109-42. ASAO Monograph No. 7. London: University Press of America.

Woodford, C. M. 1905. Further Note on Funerary Ornaments from the Solomon Islands. *Man* 5:38–39.

———. 1909. The Canoes of the British Solomon Islands. *Journal of the Royal Anthropological Institute* 39:506-16.

Zelenietz, M. 1983. The End of Headhunting in New Georgia. In *The Pacification of Melanesia*, ed. M. Rodman and M. Cooper, 91-109. ASAO Monograph No. 7. London: University Press of America.

Chapter 6

Bateson, G. 1928. Field diaries and notes from 1928 field research among the Sulka. 7 vols. (Handwritten MSS with drawings.) Currently housed at the Library of Congress, Washington, D. C.

Bodrogi, T. 1959. *Oceanian Art*. Budapest: Corvina.

Bühler, A., T. Barrow, and C. P. Mountford. 1962. *The Art of the South Sea Islands*. New York: Crown.

Chowning, A. 1976. Austronesian Languages: New Britain. In *New Guinea Area Languages and Language Study. Vol. 2. Austronesian Languages*, ed. S. A. Wurm, 365-83. Pacific Linguistics Series C, no. 39. Canberra: The Australian National University.

Corbin, G. A. 1983. Field diaries among the Sulka, Wide Bay, East New Britain, Papua New Guinea. 3 vols. (Handwritten MSS, with drawings, black and white photographs, and color slides.)

———. 1984. The Central Baining Revisted: 'Salvage' Art History Among the Kairak and Uramot Baining of East New Britain, Papua New Guinea. *Res* 7/8:44-69.

Craig, B. 1982. Report of Field Trip to Sulka Area, Wide Bay, East New Britain Province, 3rd-10th January, 1982. (Typed MS report to the National Museum and Art Gallery, Boroko, Papua New Guinea. 15 pp. with maps and illustrations.)

Eichhorn, A. 1916. Zur Pur Mea (Todeszauber) der Sulka. *Baessler-Archiv* 5:296-97.

Fraser, D. 1962. *Primitive Art*. Garden City: Doubleday.

Hill, R. 1982. Trip to the Sulka Area of Wide Bay, East New Britain. Unpublished manuscript, National Museum and Art Gallery, Papua New Guinea.

Laufer, C. 1952. Notes on New Britain Religion. *Mankind* 4:381-82.

———. 1955. Aus Geschichte und Religion der Sulka. *Anthropos* 50:32-64.

———. 1962. Notizin zur materiellen Kultur der Sulka. *Acta Ethnographica* 11:447-55.

Lewis, A. B. 1909-1913. Field Diary of the Joseph N. Field Expedition, 1909-1913. (Typed MS diary. Housed at the Field Museum of Natural History, Chicago.)

———. 1934. Sulka Masks. *Field Museum News* 5(4):2.

Linton, R., P. S. Wingert, and R. d'Harnoncourt. 1946. *Arts of the South Pacific*. New York: Museum of Modern Art.

Luschan, F. von. 1900. Schilde aus Neu-Britannien. *Zeitschrift für Ethnologie* 32:496-504.

Meier. P. J. 1911. Zur Ethnologie der Sulka, Neupommern, Südsee. *Anthropos* 6:1039.

———. 1914. Ehemaliges Vorkommen des Plankenbootes bei den Menen und Sulka auf Neupommern (Südsee). *Anthropos* 9:657.

Müller, H. 1915/1916. Erster Versuch einer Grammatik der Sulka-Sprache, Neu-Pommern (Südsee). *Anthropos* 10/11:75-97, 523-552.

Nevermann, H. 1933. *Masken und Geheimbünde in Melanesien*. Berlin: Reimar Hobbing.

Parkinson, R. 1907. *Dreissig Jahre in der Südsee*. Stuttgart: Strecker and Schröder.

Powell, W. 1883. *Wanderings in a Wild Country; or Three Years Amongst the Cannibals of New Britain*. London: S. Low, Marston, Searle and Rivington.

Rascher, M. 1904. Die Sulka. Ein Beitrag zur Ethnographie von Neu-Pommern. *Archiv für Anthropologie* 29:209-35.

Schmidt, W. 1904. Eine Papuasprache auf Neupommern. *Globus* 86:79-80.

Schmitz, C. A. 1971. *Oceanic Art: Myth, Man and Image in the South Seas*. New York: Harry N. Abrams.

Schneider, J. 1954. Über den Feldbau der Sulka auf Neubritannien. *Anthropos* 49:276-89.

Speiser, F. 1932. Über Keulenformen in Melanesien. *Zeitschrift für Ethnologie* 64:74-105.

Tischner, H., and F. Hewicker. 1954. *Oceanic Art*. New York: Pantheon.

Wingert, P. S. 1946. *An Outline Guide to the Art of the South Pacific*. New York: Columbia University Press.

———. 1953. *Art of the South Pacific Islands*. London: Thames and Hudson.

———. 1962. *Primitive Art: Its Traditions and Styles*. New York: Oxford University Press.

Wurm, S. A. 1975. The New Britain Stock. In *New Guinea Area Languages and Language Study. Vol. 1. Papuan Languages and the New Guinea Linguistic Scene*, ed. S. A. Wurm, 789-91. Pacific Linguistics, Series C, no. 38. Canberra: The Australian National University.

Chapter 7

Fraser, D. 1966. *The Many Faces of Primitive Art*. Englewood Cliffs, N.J.: Prentice-Hall.

Graebner, F. 1909. Die Melanesische Bogenkultur und ihre Verwandten. *Anthropos* 4:726-80.

Guiart, J. 1955. *Contes et légendes de la Grande Terre*. Nouméa: Éditions des études mélanésiennes.

———. 1966. *Mythologie du masque en Nouvelle Calédonie*. Publications de la Société des Océanistes No. 18. Paris: Société des Océanistes.

Lambert, R.P. 1900. *Moeurs et superstitions des Néo-Calédoniens*. Nouméa: Nouvelle Imprimerie Nouméene.

Leenhardt, M. 1933. Les masques néo-calédoniens. *Bulletin du Musée d'Ethnographie du Trocadéro* 6:3-21.

———. 1937. *Gens de la Grande Terre: Nouvelle Calédonie*. Paris: Gallimard.

———. 1954. Le masque et le mythe en Nouvelle Calédonie. *Études mélanesiennes*, No. 8, pp. 9-20.

Sarasin, F. 1929. *Ethnologie der Neu-Caledonier und Loyalty-Insulaner*. Munich: C.W. Kreidel.

Chapter 8

Green, R.C. and H.H. Cresswell, eds. 1976. *Southeast Solomon Island Cultural History*. Bulletin no. 11. Wellington: Royal Society of New Zealand.

Kirch, P.V. 1978 Test Excavation of a Coastal Midden Graciosa Bay, Santa Cruz, Eastern Solomon Islands. Unpublished manuscript.

McCoy, P.C., and P.L. Cleghorn. 1978 Summary Report of Recent Archaeological Investigations on Santa Cruz (Nendö). Unpublished manuscript.

Chapter 9

Davenport, William H. 1962. Red-feather Money. Scientific American 206(3):94-104.

———. 1965. Sculpture of the Eastern Solomon Islands. Expedition 10(2):4-25.

———. 1981. Male Initiation in Aoriki. Expedition 23(2):2-19.

Edge-Partington, James. 1890. An Album of the Weapons, Tools, Ornaments, Articles of Dress, etc. of the Native of the Pacific Islands, vol. 1. Manchester: J. C. Norbury.

Gillett, Joyce. 1939. 'Dukas' of Santa Cruz. Man 39:153-54.

Graebner, F. 1909. Völkerkunde der Santa-Cruz-Inseln. Ethnologica 1:71-184.

Koch, Gerd. 1977. Materielle Kultur der Santa Cruz-Inseln. Berlin: Museum für Völkerkunde.

Rivers, W. H. R. 1914. History of Melanesian Society, Vol. 2. Cambridge: Cambridge University Press.

Waite, Deborah. 1983. Art of the Solomon Islands. Geneva: Musée Barbier-Müller.

Chapter 10

Coombe, Florence. 1911. *Islands of Enchantment: Many-sided Melanesia*. London: Macmillan.

Codrington, R. H. 1891. *The Melanesians, Studies in Their Anthropology and Folk-lore*. Oxford: Clarendon Press.

Crowe, Peter. 1984. The Matriality of Maewo Song. Paper read at the Third International Symposium on the Arts of Oceania, Metropolitan Museum of Art, New York, September 4-8, 1984.

Davenport, William. 1964. Notes on Santa Cruz Voyaging. *Journal of the Polynesian Society* 73:134-42.

———. 1968. Social Organization Notes on the Southern Santa Cruz Islands: Utupua and Vanikoro. *Baessler-Archiv*, n.f. 16:207-75.

Dillon, Peter. 1829, *Narrative and Successful Result of a Voyage in the South Seas to Ascertain the Actual Fate of La Perouse's Expedition, Interspersed With Accounts of the Religion, Manners...of the South Sea Islanders*. London: Jurst, Chance. 2 vols.

Discombe, Reece, and Pierre Anthonioz. 1960. Voyage to Vanikoro. *Pacific Discovery* 13:4-15.

Dumont d'Urville, J. S. C. 1833. *Voyage de la corvette l'Astrolabe...1826-9. Histoire du Voyage...* Paris: Tastu.

Foanaota, Lawrence. 1977. Melanesian Cultural Council. *South Pacific Bulletin*, Fourth Quarter (offprint).

Goodenough, James Graham. 1876. *Journal of Commodore Goodenough...During his Last Command as Senior Officer of the Australian Station, 1873-1875*. Ed. V. H. Goodenough, London: Henry S. King.

Ivens, W. G. 1931. The Place of Vui and Tamate in the Religion of Mota. *Journal of the Royal Anthropological Institute of Great Britain and Ireland* 61:157-66.

Kirch, Patrick K. 1983. An Archaeological Exploration of Vanikoro, Santa Cruz Islands, Eastern Melanesia. *New Zealand Journal of Archaeology* 5:69-113.

Montgomery, H. H. 1896. *The Light of Melanesia. A Record of Thirty-five Years' Mission Work in the South Seas*. London: Society for Promoting Christian Knowledge.

Rivers, W. H. R. 1914. *The History of Melanesian Society*. 2 vols. Cambridge: Cambridge University Press.
Solomon Islands Annual Report. 1976. Honiara: Government Printer.

Tua, Ben. 1979. *Our Custom Way Vanikoro*. Ed. Peter C. Lincoln. Auckland: University of Auckland Bindery.

Wench, Ida. 1961. *Mission to Melanesia*. London: Elek Books.

Yonge, Charlotte Mary. 1874. *Life of John Coleridge Patteson, Missionary Bishop of the Melanesian Islands*. 2 vols. London: Macmillan.

Chapter 11

Baudin, Nicolas. 1974. *The Journal of Post Captain Nicolas Baudin: Commander-in-Chief of the Corvettes Géographe and Naturaliste*. Adelaide: Libraries Board of South Australia.

Berndt, Ronald M. 1964. *Australian Aboriginal Art*. Sydney: Ure Smith.

——— and Catherine H. Berndt. 1982. *Aboriginal Australian Art: A Visual Perspective*. Sydney: Methuen.

Bischoff, James. 1832. *A Sketch of the History of Van Diemen's Land*. London: John Richardson. (Reprinted 1967, Adelaide: Libraries Board of South Australia.)

Bonwick, James. 1870. *Daily Life and Origins of the Tasmanians*. London: Sampson Low, Searle and Rivington. (Reprinted 1967, New York: Johnson Reprint Corporation.)

———. 1870. *The Last of the Tasmanians*. London: Sampson Low, Son, & Marston. (Reprinted 1969, Adelaide: Libraries Board of South Australia.)

———. 1884. *The Lost Tasmanian Race*. London: Sampson Low, Marston, Searle & Rivington.

(Reprinted 1970, New York: Johnson Reprint Corporation.)

Bunce, Daniel. 1857a. *Australasiatic Reminiscences of Twenty-Three Years Wandrings in Tasmania and the Australias.* Melbourne: J. T. Hendy.

———. 1857b. *Twenty-Three Years Wandering in the Australias and Tasmania.* Geelong: Thomas Brown.

———. 1859. *Travels with Dr. Leichardt in Australia.* Melbourne: The Booksellers. (Reprinted 1979, Oxford: Oxford University Press.)

Calder, James Erskine. 1849. Some Account of the Country Lying Between Lake St. Clair and Macquarie Harbour. *Tasmanian Journal of Natural Science* 3:415-29.

———. 1874. Some Account of the Wars of Extirpation, and Habits of the Native Tribes of Tasmania. *Journal of the Anthropological Institute of Great Britain and Ireland* 3:7-28.

———. 1875. *Some Account of the Wars, Extirpation, Habits, &c., of the Native Tribes of Tasmania.* Hobart: Henn & Co.

Clark, Julia. 1983. *The Aboriginal People of Tasmania.* Hobart: Tasmanian Museum and Art Gallery.

DeTeliga, S., and W. Bryden. 1958. A Note on Tasmanian Aboriginal Drawings. *Papers and Proceedings of the Royal Society of Tasmania* 92:190.

Dutton, Geoffrey. 1974. *White on Black: The Australian Aborigine Portrayed in Art.* Sydney: Macmillan.

Fenton, James. 1884. *A History of Tasmania from its Discovery in 1642 to the Present Time.* Hobart: J. Walch and Sons.

———. 1891. *Bush Life in Tasmania Fifty Years Ago.* London: The Booksellers.

Flood, Josephine. 1983. *Archaeology of the Dreamtime.* Sydney: Collins.

Forge, Anthony. 1977. Schematization and Meaning. In *Form in Indigenous Art*, ed. Peter J. Ucko, 28-32. Canberra: Australian Institute of Aboriginal Studies.

Gallus, A. 1977. Schematization and Symboling. In *Form in Indigenous Art*, ed. Peter J. Ucko, 370-86. Canberra: Australian Insitute of Aboriginal Studies.

Grey, George. 1841. *Journal of Two Expeditions of Discovery in North-West and Western Australia, During the Years 1837, 38, and 39.* 2 vols. London: T. and W. Boone. (Reprinted 1964, Adelaide: Libraries Board of South Australia.)

Groger-Wurm, Helen. 1973. *Australian Aboriginal Bark Paintings and their Mythological Interpretation.* Canberra: Australian Institute of Aboriginal Studies.

Hamy, E.-T. 1891. L'oeuvre ethnographique de Nicolas-Martin Petit. *Anthropologie* 2:601-22.

Jones, Rhys. 1974. Tasmanian Tribes. In *Aboriginal Tribes of Australia*, ed. Norman B. Tindale, 317-54. Berkeley: University of California Press.

———. 1977. The Tasmanian Paradox. In *Stone Tools as Cultural Markers*, ed. R. V. S. Wright, 189-204. Canberra: Australian Institute of Aboriginal Studies.

Kupka, Karel. 1972. *Peintres aborigênes d'Australie.* Paris: Musée de l'Homme.

McCarthy, F. D. 1957. Theoretical Considerations of Australian Aboriginal Art. *Journal and Proceedings of the Royal Society of New South Wales* 91 (Part 1):3-22.

McCulloch, Alan. 1968. *Encyclopedia of Australian Art.* New York: Praeger.

Moore, David R. 1977. The Hand Stencil as Symbol. In *Form in Indigenous Art*, ed. Peter J. Ucko, 318-24. Canberra: Australian Institute of Aboriginal Studies.

Mountford, Charles P. 1956. *Art, Myth and Symbolism.* Records of the American-Australian Scientific Expedition to Arnhem Land. Melbourne: Melbourne University Press.

Mulvaney, D. J. 1969. *The Prehistory of Australia.* London: Thames and Hudson.

Oxley, John. 1820. *Journals of Two Expeditions into the Interior of New South Wales*. London: John Murray. (Reprinted 1964, Adelaide: Libraries Board of South Australia.)

Péron, François. 1807-1816. *Voyage de découvertes aux terres australes*. 2 vols. Paris: L'Imprimerie royale.

———. 1809. *A Voyage of Discovery to the Southern Hemisphere*. London: Richard Phillips. (Reprinted 1975, Melbourne: Marsh Walsh.)

———. 1812. Historical Relation of a Voyage Undertaken for the Discovery of Southern Lands. In *A General Collection of the Best and Most Interesting Voyages and Travels in All Parts of the World*, ed. John Pinkerton, 793-952. London: Longmans.

———. 1824. *Voyage de découvertes aux terres australes*. 2nd ed., 4 vols. Paris: A. Bertrand.

Pfeiffer, John E. 1982. *The Creative Explosion: An Inquiry into the Origins of Art and Religion*. New York: Harper and Row.

Plomley, N. J. B. 1983. *The Baudin Expedition and the Tasmanian Aborigines 1802*. Hobart: Blubber Head Press.

Robinson, George Augustus. 1966. *Friendly Mission: The Tasmanian Journals and Papers of George Augustus Robinson*, ed. N. J. B. Plomley. Hobart: Tasmanian Historical Research Association.

Robson, Lloyd L. 1983. *A History of Tasmania*. Melbourne: Oxford University Press.

Ross, James. 1836. The Settler in Van Diemen's Land Fourteen Years Ago. In *Ross's Hobart Town Almanack, and Van Diemen's Land Annual for 1836*, by James Ross. Hobart Town: James Ross.

Roth, H. Ling. 1890. *The Aborigines of Tasmania*. London: Kegan Paul, Trench, Trubner and Company.

———. 1899. *The Aborigines of Tasmania*. 2nd ed. Halifax: F. King & Sons. (Reprinted 1968, Hobart: Fuller's Bookshop.)

Ruhe, Edward L. 1966. *Bark Paintings from Arnhem Land*. Lawrence: University of Kansas Museum of Art.

Schneckenburger, Manfred. 1984. Untitled introductory essay. In *Resonanzen: Naturvolkkunst-Moderne Kunst/ Resonances: Tribal Art-Modern Art*, by Suzanne Greub. Basel: Galerie Greub.

Sims, Peter. 1977. Variations in Tasmanian Petroglyphs. In *Form in Indigenous Art*, ed. Peter J. Ucko, 429-38. Canberra: Australian Institute of Aboriginal Studies.

Smith, Bernard. 1960. *European Vision and the South Pacific 1768-1850*. Oxford: Clarendon Press.

Spencer, Baldwin. 1928. *Wanderings in Wild Australia*. 2 vols. London: Macmillan.

Thomas, Daniel. 1878. Aboriginal Art as Art. In *Aboriginal Art in Australia*, ed. Robert Edwards, 29-31. Sydney: Ure Smith.

Tuckson, J. A. 1964. Aboriginal Art and the Western World. In *Australian Aboriginal Art*, ed. Ronald M. Berndt, 60-68. Sydney: Ure Smith.

Walker, James Backhouse. 1900. *The Tasmanian Aborigines*. Hobart: John Vail.

West, John. 1852. *The History of Tasmania*. 2 vols. Launceston: Henry Dowling.

Chapter 12

Abramson, J. A. 1976. Style Change in an Upper Sepik Contact Situation. In *Ethnic and Tourist Arts*, ed. Nelson Graburn, 249-65. Berkeley: University of California Press.

Graburn, Nelson H. H., ed. 1976. *Ethnic and Tourist Arts*. Berkeley: University of California Press.

Kelm, Heinz. 1968. *Kunst vom Sepik*, Bd. 3. Veröffentlichungen des Museums für Völkerkunde, 15; Abteilung Südsee VII. Berlin: Museum für Völkerkunde.

Lewis, Phillip H. 1961. A Definition of Primitive Art. *Fieldiana: Anthropology* 36:221-41. Chicago: Chicago Natural History Museum (Field Museum of Natural History).

———. 1969. *The Social Context of Art in Northern New Ireland. Fieldiana: Anthropology* Vol. 58. Chicago:

Field Museum of Natural History.

———. 1979. Art in Changing New Ireland. In *Exploring the Visual Art of Oceania*, ed. S. M. Mead, 378-91. Honolulu: University Press of Hawaii.

Schmitz, Carl A. 1971. *Oceanic Art: Myth, Man and Image in the South Seas*. New York: Henry N. Abrams.

Chapter 13

Amoamo, T., R. Neich, and T. Tupene. 1984. The Complementarity of History and Art in Tutamure Meeting House, Omarumutu Marae, Opotiki. *Journal of the Polynesian Society* 93:5-37.

Angas, G. F. 1847. *The New Zealanders Illustrated*. London: McLean.

———. 1972. *Portraits of the New Zealand Maori Painted in 1844*. Text by G. C. Petersen and S. M. Mead. Wellington: A. H. and A. W. Reed.

Barrow, T. 1965. *A Guide to the Maori Meeting House, Te Hau-ki-Turanga*. Wellington: Dominion Museum.

Best, E. 1925. *Tuhoe. The Children of the Mist*. Memoirs of the Polynesian Society, vol. 6. Wellington: The Polynesian Society.

———. 1928. The Story of Rua and Tangaroa. An Origin Myth. How the Art of Woodcarving Was Acquired by Man. *Journal of the Polynesian Society* 37:257-60.

———. 1982. *Maori Religion and Mythology*. Part II. Wellington: Dominion Museum Bulletin No. 11.

Binney, J. 1984. Myth and Explanation in the Ringatu Tradition. *Journal of the Polynesian Society* 93:345-98.

Clarke, G. 1903. *Notes on Early Life in New Zealand*. Hobart: Walch.

Colenso, W. 1892. Vestiges: Reminiscences, Memorabilia of Works, Deeds and Sayings of the Ancient Maoris. *Transactions and Proceedings of the New Zealand Institute* 24:445-67.

Editor. 1852. Brief Reviews of the Past History of the Mission. *Church Missionary Intelligencer* 3(2):42-48.

Fowler, L. 1974. *Te-o-Mana*. Auckland: Penrose

Hamilton, A. 1896-1901. *Maori Art. The Workmanship of the Maori Race in New Zealand*. Dunedin: Ferguson and Mitchell, for the New Zealand Institute.

Hanson, F. A. 1983. Art and the Maori Construction of Reality. In *Art and Artists of Oceania*, ed. S. M. Mead and B. Kernot, 210-225. Palmerston North: Dunmore.

Misur, G. Z. 1975. From Prophet Cult to Established Church: The Case of the Ringatu Movement. In *Conflict and Compromise. Essays on the Maori Since Colonisation*, ed. I. H. Kawharu, 97-115. Wellington: Reed.

Orbell, M. 1968. *Maori Folktales in Maori and English*. Auckland: Blackwood and Janet Paul.

Phillipps, W. J. 1944. Carved Maori Houses of the Eastern District of the North Island. *Records of the Dominion Museum* 1(2):69-119.

Robley, H. G. 1896. *Moko; or Maori Tattooing*. London: Chapman and Hall.

Salmond, A. 1978. Te Ao Tawhito: A Semantic Approach to the Traditional Maori Cosmos. *Journal of the Polynesian Society* 87:5-28.

Schwimmer, E. 1966. *The World of the Maori*. Wellington: A. H. and A. W. Reed.

Simmons, D. R. 1976. *The Great New Zealand Myth*. Wellington: A. H. and A. W. Reed.

———. 1983. Moko. In *Art and Artists of Oceania*, ed. S. M. Mead and B. Kernot, 226-43. Palmerston North: Dunmore.

Smith, S. P. 1913. *The Lore of the Whare Wananga, Part I: Te Kauwae-Runga*. Memoirs of the Polynesian Society, vol. 3. New Plymouth: The Polynesian Society.

Tovey, A. G. 1961. *The Arts of the Maori*. Wellington: Department of Education.

Ward, A. 1980. Documenting Maori History: The Arrest of Te Kooti Rikirangi Te Turuki, 1889. *New Zealand Journal of History* 14:25-44.

Wolff, J. 1981. *The Social Production of Art*. London: MacMillan.

Chapter 14

Archey, Gilbert. 1933. Evolution of Certain Maori Carving Patterns. *Journal of the Polynesian Society* 42:171-90.

———. 1936. Maori Carving Patterns. *Journal of the Polynesian Society* 45:49-62.

———. 1937. *South Sea Folk*. Auckland: Auckland War Memorial Museum.

———. 1960. *Sculpture and Design: An Outline of Maori Art*. 2nd ed. Auckland: Auckland War Memorial Museum.

———. 1962. Spiral Dominated Compositions in *Pare* (Door Lintels). *Records of the Auckland Institute and Museum* 5:271-81.

———. 1965. *The Art Forms of Polynesia*. Bulletin of the Auckland Institute and Museum No. 4. Auckland: Auckland Institute and Museum.

———. 1967. Maori Wood Sculpture: The Human Head and Face. *Records of the Auckland Institute and Museum* 6:229-49.

———. 1977. *Whaowhia: Maori Art and its Artists*. Auckland: Collins.

Barrow, Terrence T. 1956. Maori Decorative Carving — An Outline. *Journal of the Polynesian Societyr* 65:305-31.

———. 1967. Material Evidence of the Bird-man Concept in Polynesia. In *Polynesian Culture History*, ed. Genevieve Highland et al., 191-213. Bernice P. Bishop Museum Special Publication 56. Honolulu: Bishop Museum.

Bechtol, Charles O. 1967. Hei-tiki. *Journal of the Polynesian Society* 76:445-52.

Best, Elsdon. 1915. Maori and Maruiwi: Notes on the Original Inhabitants of New Zealand and Their Culture. *Transactions and Proceedings of the New Zealand Institute* 48:435-47.

Binney, Judith. 1980. The Last Drawing of Nukutawhiti. *New Zealand Journal of History* 14:3-24.

Brown, J. Macmillan. 1907. *Maori and Polynesian: Their Origins, History and Culture*. London: Hutchinson.

Edge-Partington, James. 1900. Note on a Pataka in the Auckland Museum, New Zealand. *Journal of the Royal Anthropological Institute* 30:34-35.

Hamilton, Augustus. 1901. *Maori Art*. Wellington: New Zealand Institute.

Hanson, F. Allan. 1983a. Art and the Maori Construction of Reality. In *Art and Artists of Oceania*, ed. Sidney M. Mead and Bernie Kernot, 210-25. Palmerston North: Dunmore Press.

———. 1983b. When the Map is the Territory: Art in Maori Culture. In *Structure and Cognition in Art*, ed. Dorothy K. Washburn, 74-89. Cambridge: Cambridge University Press.

———. 1985. From Symmetry to Anthropophagy: The Cultural Context of Maori Art. *Empirical Studies of the Arts* 3:47-62.

Hanson, Louise, and F. Allan Hanson. 1984. *The Art of Oceania: A Bibliography*. Boston: G. K. Hall.

Hiroa, Te Rangi (Peter H. Buck). 1950. *The Coming of the Maori*. 2nd ed. Wellington: Whitcombe & Tombs.

Jackson, Michael. 1972. Aspects of Symbolism and Composition in Maori Art. *Bijdragen tot de Taal-, Land- en Volkenkunde* 128:33-80.

Kernot, Bernie. 1983. The Meeting House in Contemporary New Zealand. In *Art and Artists in Oceania*, ed. Sidney M. Mead and Bernie Kernot, 181-97. Palmerston North: Dunmore Press.

McEwen, J. M. 1966. Maori Art. In *An Encyclopaedia of New Zealand*, ed. A. H. McLintock, vol. 2, 408-29. Wellington: Government Printer.

Mead, Sidney M. 1975. The Origins of Maori Art: Polynesian or Chinese? *Oceania* 45:173-211.

Neich, Roger. 1983. The Veil of Orthodoxy: Rotorua Ngati Tarawhai Carving in a Changing Context. In *Art and Artists of Oceania*, ed. Sidney M. Mead and Bernie Kernot, 245-65. Palmerston North: Dunmore Press.

Phillipps, William J. 1939. Taranaki Carving. *Public Service Journal* 26:235.

———. 1955. *Maori Carving Illustrated*. Wellington: Reed.

Pitt-Rivers, George. 1924. A Visit to a Maori Village. *Journal of the Polynesian Society* 33:48-65.

Rout, Ettie. 1926. *Maori Symbolism*. London: Kegan, Paul, Trench, Trubner.

Rowe, W. Page. 1935. Some Unorthodox Reflections on the Spiral in Maori Ornament. *Journal of the Polynesian Society* 44:112-23.

Shirres, Michael P. 1987. Review of D. R. Simmons, *Iconography of New Zealand Maori Religion*. *Journal of the Polynesian Society* 96:520-23.

Simmons, David R. 1983. Moko. In *Art and Artists in Oceania*, ed. Sidney M. Mead and Bernie Kernot, 226-43. Palmerston North: Dunmore Press.

———. 1985. *Whakairo: Maori Tribal Art*. Auckland: Oxford University Press.

———. 1986. *Iconography of New Zealand Maori Religion*. The Netherlands: Brill.

Skinner, H. D. 1921. Comment to The Awanui (Kaitaia Carving) Lintel, by F. Waite. *Journal of the Polynesian Society* 30:246-51.

———. 1922. The Kaitaia Carving. *Journal of the Polynesian Society* 31:57-58.

———. 1924. The Origin and Relationship of Maori Material Culture and Decorative Art. *Journal of the Polynesian Society* 33:229-43.

———. 1931. A Kaitaia Carving from South-east Polynesia? *Journal of the Polynesian Society* 40:253-54.

———. 1951. Some Aspects of the History of Polynesian Material Culture. *Journal of the Polynesian Society* 60:40-46.

———. 1974. *Comparatively Speaking: Studies in Pacific Material Culture 1921-1972*. Dunedin: University of Otago Press.

Smith, S. Percy. 1917. Note on the Manaia in Maori Carving. *Journal of the Polynesian Society* 26:130-31.

———. 1919. An Ancient Carved Pare. *Journal of the Polynesian Society* 28:160.

———. 1921. The Kaitaia Carving. *Journal of the Polynesian Society* 30:91-95.

Tregear, Edward. 1899. Maori Spirals and Sun Worship. *Transactions and Proceedings of the New Zealand Institute* 32:284-93.

———. 1920. Three Fingers in Maori Carving. *Journal of the Polynesian Society* 29:224.

Chapter 15

Barth, F. 1975. *Ritual and Knowledge Among the Baktaman of New Guinea*. New Haven: Yale University Press.

Brook, D. 1977. *The Social Role of Art*. Adelaide: Experimental Art Foundation.

Brookfield, H. C., and D. Hart. 1971. *Melanesia*. London: Methuen.

Craig, B. 1969. Houseboards and Warshields of the Mountain-Ok of Central New Guinea. Master's thesis, University of Sydney.

———. 1981. Report of Mountain-Ok Field Survey, 1981. Submitted to the Trustees of the Papua New Guinea National Museum.

———. 1983. Report of Mountain-Ok Field Survey, 1983. Submitted to the Trustees of the Papua New Guinea National Museum.

Gore, R. T. 1965. *Justice Versus Sorcery*. Brisbane: Jacaranda Press.

Hanson, F. A. 1983. Art and the Maori Construction of Reality. In *Art and Artists of Oceania*, ed. S. M. Mead and B. Kernot, 210-25. Palmerston North: Dunmore Press.

Healey, A. 1964. A Survey of the Ok Family of Languages. Ph.D. dissertation, Australian National University.

Hyndman, D. 1975 The Ecology of Subsistence of the Wopkaimin, Mountain-Ok People of the Western District, Papua New Guinea. In *Occasional Papers in Anthropology* 4:41-54. University of Queensland Museum.

Jorgensen, D. 1981a. Taro and Arrows: Order, Entropy and Religion Among the Telefolmin. Ph.D. dissertation, University of British Columbia.

———. 1981b. Life on the Fringe: History and Society in Telefolmin. In *The Plight of Peripheral People in Papua New Guinea*, ed. R. Gordon. Cambridge, Mass.: Cultural Survival.

Mataira, K. 1983. Negative and Positive Influences in the Development of Oceanic Art. In *Art and Artists of Oceania*, ed. S. M. Mead and B. Kernot, 80-87. Palmerston North: Dunmore Press.

Mead, S. M., and B. Kernot, eds. 1983. *Art and Artists of Oceania*. Palmerston North: Dunmore Press.

Morren, G. 1977. From Hunting to Herding: Pigs and the Control of Energy in Montane New Guinea. In *Subsistence and Survival: Rural Ecology in the Pacific*, ed. T. Bayliss-Smith and R. Feachem, 272-315. London: Academic Press.

Quinlivan, P. J. 1954. Afek of Telefolmin: A Fabulous Story from New Guinea Which Led to a Strange Tragedy. *Oceania* 25:17-22.

Wheatcroft, W. 1975. The Legacy of Afekan: Cultural Symbolic Interpretations of Religion Among the Tifalmin of New Guinea. Ph.D. dissertation, University of Chicago.

Chapter 16

Bott, Elizabeth. 1981. Power and Rank in the Kingdom of Tonga. *The Journal of the Polynesian Society* 90:7-81.

Fusitu'a, 'Eseta, and Noel Rutherford. 1977. George Tupou II and the British Protectorate. In *Friendly Islands, A History of Tonga*, ed. Noel Rutherford, 173-89. Melbourne: Oxford University Press.

Kaeppler, Adrienne. 1967a. Folklore as Expressed in the Dance in Tonga. *Journal of American Folklore* 80:160-68.

———. 1967b. Preservation of Evolution and Function in Two Types of Tongan Dance. In *Polynesian Culture History*, ed. Genevieve Highland et al., 503-36. Bishop Museum Special Publication 56. Honolulu: Bishop Musem.

———. 1970. Tongan Dance: A Study In Cultural Change. *Ethnomusicology* 15:175-85.

———. 1971. Aesthetics of Tongan Dance. *Ethnomusicology* 15:175-85.

———. 1972. Method and Theory in Analyzing Dance Structure with an Analysis of Tongan Dance. *Ethnomusicology* 16:173-217.

———. 1978. Melody, Drone and Decoration: Underlying Structures and Surface Manifestations in Tongan Art and Society. In *Art and Society: Studies in Style, Culture and Aesthetics*, ed. Michael Greenhalgh and Vincent Megaw, 261-74. London: Duckworth.

Marcus, George. 1977. Contemporary Tonga: The Background of Social and Cultural Change. In *Friendly Islands, A History of Tonga*, ed. Noel Rutherford, 210-27. Melbourne: Oxford University Press.

Rutherford, Noel. 1977. George Tupou II and Shirley Baker. In *Friendly Islands, A History of Tonga*, ed. Noel Rutherford, 154-72. Melbourne: Oxford University Press.

Shore, Bradd. 1982. *Sala'ilua, A Samoan Mystery*. New York: Columbia University Press.

Teilhet, Jehanne. 1978. The Equivocal Role of Women Artists in Non-literate Cultures. *Heresies* 4:96-102.

———. 1983. The Role of Women Artists in Polynesia and Melanesia. In *Art and Artists of Oceania*, ed. Sidney M. Mead and Bernie Kernot, 45-56. Palmerston North: Dunmore Press.

Chapter 17

Bain, Kenneth. 1967. *The Friendly Islanders*. London: Hodder & Stoughton.

Beaglehole, Ernest, and Pearl Beaglehole. 1941. *Pangai, Village in Tonga*. Memoirs of the Polynesian Society, vol. 18. Wellington: The Polynesian Society.

Bott, Elizabeth. 1981. Power and Rank in the Kingdom of Tonga. *Journal of the Polynesian Society* 90:7-81.

Collocott, E. E. V. 1923. Sickness, Ghosts and Medicine in Tonga. *Journal of the Polynesian Society* 32:136-42.

Collocott, E. E. V., and John Havea. 1922. *Proverbial Sayings of the Tongans*. Occasional Papers of the Bernice P. Bishop Museum, vol. 8, no. 3. Honolulu: Bernice P. Bishop Museum.

Gifford, Edward Winslow. 1929. *Tongan Society*. Bulletins of the Bernice P. Bishop Museum, no. 61. Honolulu: Bernice P. Bishop Museum.

Graburn, Nelson. 1984. The Evolution of Tourist Arts. *Annals of Tourism Research* 2:393-419.

———, ed. 1976. *Ethnic and Tourist Arts: Cultural Expressions from the Fourth World*. Berkeley: University of California Press.

Helu, Futa. n.d. Tongan Culture Lecture Summaries.

Kaeppler, Adrienne L. 1971a. Eighteenth Century Tonga: New Interpretations of Tongan Society at the Time of Captain Cook. *Man* 6:210-13.

———. 1971b. Rank in Tonga. *Ethnology* 10:174-93.

———. 1978. Me'a Faka'eiki: Tongan Funerals in a Changing Society. In *The Changing Pacific: Essays in Honour of H. E. Maude*, ed. Niel Gunson, 174-202. Melbourne: Oxford University Press.

Kooijman, Simon. 1979. Traditional Handicraft in a Changing Society: Manufacture and Function of Stenciled Tapa on Moce Island. In *Exploring the Visual Art of Oceania*, ed. Sidney M. Mead, 363-77. Honolulu: University Press of Hawaii.

Martin, John. 1827. *An Account of the Natives of the Tonga Islands...from the Extensive Communications of Mr. William Mariner*. 2nd ed. Edinburgh: Constable & Co.

McKern, W. C. 1929. *Archaeology of Tonga*. Bulletins of the Bernice P. Bishop Museum, no. 60. Honolulu: Bernice P. Bishop Museum.

Rogers, Garth. 1977. The Father's Sister is Black: A Consideration of Female Rank and Power in Tonga. *journal of the Polynesian Society* 86: 157-82.

Silver, Harry R. 1979. Ethnoart. *Annual Review of Anthropology* 8:267-307.

Teilhet, Jehanne. 1983. The Role of Women Artists in Polynesia and Melanesia. In *Art and Artists of Oceania*, ed. Sidney M. Mead and Bernie Kernot, 45-56. Palmerson North: Dunmore Press.

Tremblay, Rev. Edward A. 1954. *When You Go to Tonga*. Boston: Daughters of St. Paul, Apostolate of the Press.

Chapter 18

Akin, David W., and Kate Gillogly-Akin. 1981. Traditional Arts of East Kwaio, Malaita. *Pacific Arts Newsletter*, no. 13, pp. 31-34.

Akis. 1977. *Catalogue of an Exhibition*. Boroko: National Arts Schools.

———. 1978. *Catalogue of an Exhibition*. Boroko: National Arts Schools.

Anon., a. n.d. *Artisanat de Tonga*. Nuku'alofa, Kingdom of Tonga: Ministry of Work, Commerce and Industry.

Anon., b. 1980. *Tongan Handicrafts*. Canberra: Australian Government Publishing Service.

Anon., c. n.d. *Gilbert Islands Handicrafts*. Auckland: Unity Press.

Baker, Catherine. 1980. *The Innocent Artist, Student Art from Papua New Guinea*. Poole, Dorset: Blandford Press.

Bodrogi, Tibor. 1961. *Art in Northeast New Guinea*. Budapest: Hungarian Academy of Sciences.

Bolabola, Cema A. B. 1980. The Impact of Tourism in Fijian Woodcarving. In *Pacific Tourism, As Islanders See It*, ed. Freda Rajotte and Ron Crocombe, 93-97. Suva: The Institute for Pacific Studies of the University of the South Pacific with the South Pacific Social Sciences Association.

Bollard, Alan. 1979. *T-Shirts and Tapa Cloth*. Nouméa: South Pacific Commission.

Brown, Nicholas. n.d. *The Crafts of Papua New Guinea, a Guide for Buyers*. Waigani, Papua New Guinea: Office of Business Development, Ministry of Labour, Commerce and Industry.

Bühler, Alfred, Terry Barrow, and Charles P. Mountford. 1962. *Oceania and Australia: The Art of the South Seas*. London: Methuen.

Cranstone, B. A. L. 1984. Review of *Art and Artists of Oceania*. *Pacific Art Newsletter*, No. 19, pp. 19-21.

Crawford, A. L. 1981. *Aida, Life and Ceremony of the Gogodala*. Bathurst, New South Wales: Robert Brown & Associates with the National Cultural Council of Papua New Guinea.

Dark, Philip J.C. 1979. Old Arts Anew? Some Comments on a Visit to the Cook Islands. *Pacific Arts Newsletter*, no. 9, p. 23.

———. 1982. Review of *The Innocent Artist*. *Pacific Arts Newsletter*, no. 14, pp. 19-20.

———. 1983. Shop Signs in Kiribati: Today's Folk Art. *Pacific Arts Newsletter*, no. 17, pp. 25-26.

Ewins, Rod. 1982. *Mat-Weaving in Gau, Fiji*. Fiji Museum Special Publication No. 3. Suva: Fiji Museum.

Force, Roland W., and Maryanne Force. 1971. *The Fuller Collection of Pacific Artifacts*. New York: Praeger.

Godin, Patrice. 1983. Why Museums in the Pacific? *Pacific 2000*, no. 2, pp. 21-28.

Graburn, Nelson H. H. 1976. Introduction: Arts of the Fourth World. In *Ethnic and Tourist Arts, Cultural Expressions from the Fourth World*, ed. Nelson H. H. Graburn, 1-32. Berkeley: University of California Press.

———. 1983. Art, Ethno-Aesthetics and the Contemporary Scene. In *Art and Artists of Oceania*, ed. Sidney M. Mead and Bernie Kernot, 70-87. Palmerston North: Dunmore Press.

Graves, William. 1970. *Hawaii*. Washington, D.C.: National Geographic Society.

Grimble, Arthur. 1957. *Return to the Islands*. London: John Murray.

———. 1972. *Migrations, Myth and Magic from the Gilbert Islands*. London: Routledge & Kegan Paul.

Heermann, Ingrid, ed. 1979. *Tingting bilong mi/ Zeitgenössische Kunst aus Papua Neuguinea*. Stuttgart: Institut für Auslandsbeziehungen.

Hiroa, Te Rangi. 1944. *Arts and Crafts of the Cook Islands*. Bulletins of the Bernice P. Bishop Museum, no. 179. Honolulu: Bernice P. Bishop Museum.

Holdsworth, David. 1982. *Festivals and Celebrations in Papua New Guinea*. Bathurst, New South Wales: Robert Brown & Associates.

Horoi, Stephen Rex. 1980. Tourism and Solomon Handicrafts. In *Pacific Tourism, As Islanders See It*, ed. Freda Rajotte and Ron Crocombe, 111-14. Suva: The Institute of Pacific Studies of the University of the South Pacific in Association with the South Pacific Social Sciences Association.

Ison, Barry, ed. 1975. *Tairu*. Papua New Guinea: Sogeri Senior High School.

Jones, Suzi, ed. 1983. *Pacific Basket Makers, A Living Tradition*. Honolulu: Consortium for Pacific Arts and Cultures.

Kaeppler, Adrienne L. 1983. *Polynesian Dances, with a Selection for Contemporary Performance*. Hawaii: Privately printed by Alpha Delta Kappa.

Kauage. 1977. *Catalogue of an Exhibition*. Boroko:National Arts Schools.

———. 1978. *Catalogue of an Exhibition*. Boroko: National Arts Schools.

Kernot, Bernie. 1984. Review of *Kuai Mau ha, 1933-1981*. *Pacific Arts Newsletter*, no. 19, pp. 11-13.

Koch, Gerd. 1965. *Materielle Kultur der Gilbert-Inseln*. Berlin: Museum für Vülkerkunde.

Kundun, Gickmai, and Benny More. n.d. Catalogue to *Garbage, an Exhibition of Metal Sculpture*. Boroko: National Arts Schools.

May, Patricia, and Margaret Tuckson. 1982. *The Traditional Pottery of Papua New Guinea*. Sydney: Bay Books.

McBean, Angus. 1964. *Handicrafts of the South Seas*. Nouméa: South Pacific Commission.

———. 1976. *Handicrafts of the South Seas*. Nouméa: South Pacific Commission.

Mead, Sidney M., and Bernie Kernot, eds. 1983. *Art and Artists of Oceania*. Palmerston North: Dunmore Press.

Michoutouchkine, Nicolai. n.d. *Aloi Pilioko, Artist of the Pacific*. Suva: South Pacific Social Science Association with the Institute of Pacific Studies.

Nalo, Joseph. 1978. *Catalogue of an Exhibition*. Boroko: National Arts Schools.

Okotai, Temu. 1980. Tourism in the Cook Islands In *Pacific Tourism, As Islanders See It*, ed. Freda Rajotte and Ron Crocombe, 49-55. Suva: The Institute of Pacific Studies of the University of the South Pacific in association with the South Pacific Social Sciences Association.

Pacific 2000. 1983. *Kanak Artefacts*. Nouméa: Association for the Fourth Pacific Festival of Arts.

Pule, Robert T. 1983. *Binabina, the Making of a Gela War Canoe*. Honiara: Solomon Islands Extension Centre and the Institute of Pacific Studies, Suva, Fiji.

Salisbury, Kevin. 1984. Tradition and Change in the Music of Pukapuka, Cook Islands. *Pacific Arts Newsletter*, no. 19, pp. 42-55.

Tausie, Vilsoni. 1980. *Art in the New Pacific*. Suva: Institute of Pacific Studies in collaboration with the South Pacific Commission.

van Wengen, G. D. 1980. Educational Museum Work in Relation to Scientific Work in Presentation in Museums. In *From Field-Case to Show-Case*, ed. W. R. van Gulik, H. S. van der Straaten, and G. D. van Wengen, 139-146. Amsterdam: J.C. Gieben.

Wendt, Albert. 1980. Introduction. In *Lali, A Pacific Anthology*, ed. Albert Wendt, 198-209. Auckland: Longman Paul.

———. 1983. Contemporary Arts in Oceania. In *Art and Artists of Oceania*, ed. Sidney M. Mead and Bernie Kernot, 198-209. Palmerston North: Dunmore Press.

Chapter 19

Best, Elsdon. 1975. *The Pa Maori*. Wellington: Government Printer. (First published 1927.)

Mead, Hirini (Sidney) Moko, ed. 1984. *Te Maori: Maori Art from New Zealand Collections*. New York: Harry N. Abrams and the American Federation of Arts.

———, and Onehou Eliza Phillis. 1982. *Te One Matua: The Abundant Earth. The Centennial of Ruataupare at Kokohinau Marae, Te Teko, 1882-1982*. Te Teko: Ngati Pahipoto and Te Komiti Maori o Kokohinau.

Phillipps, W. J., and J. C. Wadmore. (n.d.) *The Great Carved House Mataatua of Whakatane*. Wellington: The Polynesian Society.

Robley, Major General H. G. 1896. *Moko; Or Maori Tattooing*. London: Chapman and Hall.

Chapter 20

Amadio, N., ed. 1986. *Albert Namatjira: The Life and Work of an Aboriginal Painter*. Melbourne: Macmillan Australia.

Bardon, G. 1979. *Aboriginal Art of the Western Desert*. Adelaide: Rigby.

Batty, J. 1963. *Albert Namatjira: Wanderer Between Two Worlds*. Sydney: Hodder and Stoughton.

Bennett, D. H. 1980. Malangi: The Man Who Was Forgotten Before He Was Remembered. *Aboriginal History* 4:43-47.

Brook, D. 1980. A New Theory of Art. *British Journal of Aesthetics* 20:305- 21.

———. 1982. A Transinstitutional Nonvoluntary Modelling Theory of Art. *Leonardo* 15:54-58.

Burn, Ian. 1983. The Australian National Gallery: Populism or a New Cultural Federalism? *Art Network* 8:39-43.

Craig, B. 1984. Non-violent Land Rights Claims from the Centre. *Artlink* 4:19-20.

Dark, P. J. C., ed. 1984. *Development of the Arts in the Pacific*. Occasional Papers of the Pacific Art Association, No. 1. Wellington: National Museum.

Graburn, N. H. H., ed. 1976. *Ethnic and Tourist Arts: Cultural Expressions from the Fourth World*. Berkeley: University of California Press.

Hill, M. 1983. Review of *Aboriginal Arts and Crafts in the Market* (ed. P. Loveday and P. Cooke). *Australian Aboriginal Studies* 2:91-92.

Hoffberg, J. A. 1984. Jamming at the Jelly Factory. *Artlink* 4:4-7.

Keen, I. 1977. Yolngu Sand Sculptures in Context. In *Form in Indigenous Art*, ed. P. J. Ucko, 165-83. Australian Institute of Aboriginal Studies. London: Gerald Duckworth.

Kesteven, S. 1983. Review in *Aboriginal History* 7:196-200.

Marrie, A. 1985. Killing Me Softly: Aboriginal Art and Western Critics. *Art Network* 14:17-21.

Maughan, J., et al. 1986. *Dot and Circle: A Retrospective Survey of the Aboriginal Acrylic Paintings of Central Australia*. Melbourne: Royal Melbourne Institute of Technology.

Mead, S. M. 1984. Change and Control in the Arts of the Pacific. In *Development of the Arts in the Pacific*, ed. P. J. C. Dark, 1-8. Occasional Papers of the Pacific Art Association, No. 1. Wellington: National Museum.

Megaw, J. V. S. 1982. Western Desert Acrylic Painting — Artefact or Art? *Art History* 5:205-18.

———. 1984a. Dot and Circle — Paradox and Politics. *Art Network* 13:55-61.

———. 1984b. Art Groan — Or Will the Real Aboriginal Artist Stand Up? *Artlink* 4:18.

Mollison, J., and L. Murray. 1982. *Australian National Gallery: An Introduction*. Canberra: Australian National Gallery.

Montgomery, J. 1984. Australia — the French Discovery of 1983. *Art and Text* 12/13:3-15.

Morphy, H. 1977. Schematisation to Coventionalization: A Possible Trend in Yirrkala Bark Paintings. In *Form in Indigenous Art*, ed. P. J. Ucko, 198-204. Australian Institute of Aboriginal Studies. London: Gerald Duckworth.

———. 1980. The Impact of the Commercial Development of Art on Traditional Culture. In *Preserving Traditional Cultures: A New Role for Museums*, ed. R. Edwards and J. Stewart, 81-94. Canberra: Australian Government Publishing Service.

Mountford, C. P. 1949. *The Art of Albert Namatjira*. Melbourne: Bread and Cheese Club.

Pearson, C. 1984. Aboriginal History and Kitsch. *Art and Text* 14:41-49.

Rubin, W., ed. 1984. *"Primitivism" in Twentieth Century Art: Affinity of the Tribal and the Modern*. 2 vols. New York: Museum of Modern Art.

Spens, M. 1983. Dream and Reality — A Paris Viewpoint. *Studio International* 196:13-14.

Strehlow, T. G. H. 1956. *Rex Battarbee: Artist and Founder of the Aboriginal Art Movement in Central Australia*. Sydney: The Legend Press.

Taylor, J. 1975. The Art Museum in the United States. In *On Understanding Art Museums*, ed. S. E. Lee, 34-67. Englewood Cliffs, N.J.: Prentice-Hall.

Tuckson, J. A. 1964. Aboriginal Art and the Western World. In *Australian Aboriginal Art*, ed. R. M. Berndt, 60-68. Sydney: Ure Smith.

Williams, N. 1976. Australian Aboriginal Art at Yirrkala: The Introduction and Development of Marketing. In *Ethnic and Tourist Arts*, ed. N. H. H. Graburn, 266-84. Berkeley: University of California Press.